Liskin's dBASE IV® 1.1 Handbook

Liskin's dBASE IV® 1.1 Handbook

Miriam Liskin

Osborne **McGraw-Hill**

Berkeley New York St. Louis San Francisco
Auckland Bogotá Hamburg London Madrid
Mexico City Milan Montreal New Delhi Panama City
Paris São Paulo Singapore Sydney
Tokyo Toronto

Osborne **McGraw-Hill**
2600 Tenth Street
Berkeley, California 94710
U.S.A.

Osborne **McGraw-Hill** offers software for sale. For information on software, translations, or book distributors outside of the U.S.A., please write to Osborne **McGraw-Hill** at the above address.

Liskin's dBASE IV® 1.1 Handbook

34567890 DOC 9987654321

ISBN 0-07-881016-7

CONTENTS AT A GLANCE

TABLE OF CONTENTS

ACKNOWLEDGMENTS

My thanks again to all the people who worked hard to improve the quality of the writing and the accuracy of the content of this book and the earlier edition of this book, *dBASE IV Made Easy*—

Cindy Hudson, former editor-in-chief, for convincing me to write *dBASE IV Made Easy* in the first place

Jill Pisoni, associate editor, for making sure that the edited chapters found me on time, whether I was home in Berkeley or in places like Santee and Lake Elsinore, reachable only through General Delivery

Fran Haselsteiner and Laura Sackerman, project editors, who consistently stood up for good writing and clear layout

Evelyn Spire and Deborah Craig, freelance copy editors, for improving the prose while adhering so closely to my own writing style that I couldn't identify the corrections without a printout

Richard Ozer, official technical reviewer, for doing a thorough and careful job, and for setting up my networks, and Lisa Biow, for her unofficial tech edit of the first version of this book

Kathy Krause, Linda Medoff, Paul Medoff, and Valerie Haynes Perry for finding errors I would have thought would be evident only to another dBASE IV expert

Thanks also to Peter Harrington, tor making my winter migration south more fun, and for backing the world's largest portable computer into some very tight spaces.

INTRODUCTION

dBASE IV, the latest member of the Ashton-Tate family of data base programs, is one of the most powerful and sophisticated data base managers available today. Like its predecessors, dBASE IV has a reputation for being "unfriendly" and intimidating. In part, this reputation was inherited from its ancestor, dBASE II, and to that extent it is undeserved, because with each new version, dBASE has become easier to learn and easier to use at the same time as it has become more powerful and flexible.

Nevertheless, many users find that getting started with dBASE IV—or, indeed, any data base program—is more difficult than learning to use a word processor or spreadsheet. Some of the concepts are less intuitive, and your work with the computerized data base often does not parallel as closely the way you carry out the same tasks by hand. Data base software is frequently used for applications involving calculations, transfers of information, and decision-making processes that would be complicated and difficult even if you did not have to master new concepts at the same time. Finally, as with any high-end software package, you may find the sheer number of commands and functions overwhelming at first.

This book will help you surmount those barriers and begin doing productive work with dBASE IV almost immediately. The first three chapters introduce the essential data base management concepts that will serve as the foundation for all of your work with dBASE IV, and they outline a basic approach to applications design that can be used effectively by a person with no formal training in systems analysis. Chapters 4 through 10 describe in detail the general strategies and specific commands that you can use to build and maintain dBASE IV data bases, and Chapters 11 through 15 explain how to define a variety of custom forms to display or print data.

Chapters 16, 17, and 19 introduce the commands and concepts that you need to understand to work with multiple data base files and to manage the multitude of disk files that an application inevitably generates as it grows and matures. Chapter 18 describes a variety of ways to customize the dBASE IV working environment to suit your personal preferences and the requirements of your applications, and Chapter 20 addresses some of the problems involved in transferring data between dBASE IV and other programs.

Chapter 21 presents a brief introduction to writing simple batch-type programs, at a level geared for people who do not necessarily intend to become advanced programmers, and Chapter 22 describes the applications generator, which a nonprogrammer can use to build a network of menus that link together previously defined components of a data base application. Finally, Chapter 23 provides an overview of networking and security issues.

You do not need any prior experience with dBASE IV or other data base managers to comprehend any of the material in this book. However, a basic familiarity with the use of an IBM PC, PC XT, PC AT, PS/2, or compatible computer is essential. You should be comfortable with the keyboard layout, know the location and usage of special keys (in particular, the cursor movement keys, CTRL, ESC, and the special function keys), and possess some understanding of the MS-DOS or OS/2 operating system and its built-in commands and utility programs.

You can operate dBASE IV in three distinctly different modes:

- Through a system of pull-down menus centered around a main menu called the Control Center
- By typing commands one at a time, next to a command prompt called the dot prompt, much as you do when you execute operating system commands
- By writing programs in the built-in programming language provided with dBASE IV

Unlike the more limited "Assist" menu system in dBASE III and III PLUS, the dBASE IV menus and the dot prompt are two different but for the most part equally viable user interface alternatives, especially for relatively simple data base systems. Beginners will probably feel more comfortable using the menus, because you do not have to memorize command vocabulary and syntax, and for poor typists, the menu system may continue to be a more hospitable working environment for some time to come. If you have used earlier versions of dBASE, you may gravitate instead toward the dot prompt. The command language, which is concise and logical in its structure, is close enough to human languages that typing commands will soon seem natural and intuitive. Once you have mastered the most common command components, working at the dot prompt offers the advantage of flexibility and immediacy—you can execute commands as fast as you can type them, with few preparatory steps.

This book covers both the menu system and the dot prompt, and strives to give equal treatment to the two user interface alternatives. Each new concept is first introduced in general terms applicable to all dBASE IV users. Next, specific methods are described for carrying out the relevant operations through the menu system, followed by the equivalent dot prompt commands. In some cases, the menu system affords more power or convenience; in others, especially when you perform complex calculations or work with multiple related files, the dot prompt excels in power and flexibility. If you wish, you can follow either the menu or the dot prompt "tracks" through the book, ignoring the other working environment, and you may want to bypass one or the other the first time through, and return later to review the commands that you skipped on the first pass. In the long run, however, you will get the most out of dBASE IV if you become familiar enough with both environments to use each in its areas of greatest strength.

dBASE II, III and III PLUS were easy to use for simple applications, and powerful enough to be used by programmers as an applications development language. dBASE IV provides a full complement of tools that fill in the gap between these two levels and enable you to accomplish far more without programming. Like dBASE IV, this book is aimed squarely at the middle level—it addresses the needs of users who, like many of my students and clients, have relatively sophisticated applications and are willing to devote some time and energy to the learning process, but who do not have the time or the inclination to become programmers. This book will help you attain a level of proficiency that enables you to use dBASE IV to solve a wide variety of real-world business and personal data base problems.

This book is both a tutorial for first-time users and a reference guide for your ongoing work with dBASE IV. The tutorial material and the examples are based on a customer and order-tracking data base for an imaginary company called National Widgets, Inc., which is developed and expanded throughout the book. You will benefit enormously by entering the sample data and working through all of the tutorials, and by trying at least some of the examples presented in the body of the text. If you are actively involved in a data base project, you might also want to try carrying out the same commands or procedures on copies of your own files.

While it is intended for beginners and does not assume any prior knowledge of dBASE IV or of data base management concepts, this book does take you far beyond the beginning level. It covers a fairly wide range of commands and command options, and you may find as you go through a chapter for the first time that there is too much new material to absorb at one sitting. In addition, you will tend to focus more closely on certain topics, perhaps because they are directly applicable to your own data base projects. Later, you may want to return to the same chapters to pick up the concepts that seemed too difficult or the examples that appeared esoteric the first time through, but that may be more relevant in the light of your greater experience.

You may also feel that some of the examples, especially in the later chapters, concentrate on minute details of the National Widgets sample system. Try not to lose sight of the forest for the trees—each of the examples was chosen to clarify the purpose of a commonly used command or to illustrate typical combinations of commands used to carry out fundamentally similar operations that are applicable to virtually any data base. Every attempt was made to model the National Widgets system on real-world data processing needs and to make the command sequences as illustrative as possible of typical solutions to real data base management problems.

No matter what your level of experience, the most important assets you can bring to your work with dBASE IV are an assertive attitude and a willingness to experiment. The best way to overcome your initial intimidation is to jump in and begin working right away. Take the time to set up the National Widgets files and enter the sample data so that you can experiment with unfamiliar commands in a safe setting without risking your own data bases. Try as many command options and variations as you can think of. If you think you see a viable alternative to one of the strategies or techniques presented here, try it—there is often more than one good way to accomplish any particular goal, and your choices may be guided as much by personal style as by more objective factors.

Above all, try to relax and enjoy yourself—have some fun with dBASE IV.

TYPOGRAPHICAL CONVENTIONS

New technical terms and common English words that have specialized meanings in the dBASE IV language are italicized the first time they are used. Menu options and the names of dBASE IV menus are **boldfaced**, and the names of specialized screens and modes, such as the Edit screen or Insert mode, are printed with initial capital letters. Small capital letters are used for the names of special keys, such as PGUP and F1. References to function keys used in the context of the dBASE IV menus and layout editors, where these keys have standard meanings, include the dBASE IV key names, for example, F8 (Copy).

Command syntax paradigms are set off from the text and indented. All keywords are printed in UPPERCASE, and all substitution items in *lowercase italics.* Command examples—complete commands that you could use at the dot prompt or in a dBASE IV program to accomplish a particular objective using specific data bases—are printed in Letter Gothic, monospaced, and aligned at the left margin.

CHAPTER ONE

Introduction to Data Base Management

The term *data base management* describes the diverse operations involved in using a computer to store, manipulate, retrieve, and report on information. What kind of information goes into a data base? That depends entirely on you. A nonprofit organization might have a mailing list data base consisting of names, addresses, telephone numbers, and donation totals; a small business might want to set up an inventory data base that tracks part numbers, item descriptions, costs, selling prices, and quantities sold, on hand, and on order; and a lawyer might need to categorize and cross-reference documents and exhibits introduced as evidence in a trial.

None of these information management activities requires a computer; in fact, many individuals and organizations like the ones just mentioned keep track of their data on paper with manual systems. When a data base is small and is used by a few people who are familiar with the information, even a relatively informal manual system may serve the purpose. With greater volumes of data, however, or in larger organizations where different people may want to access the same information in a variety of ways, computerizing can yield enormous gains, both in processing efficiency and in the utility of the information that can be extracted easily from the mass of raw data.

A FUNCTIONAL DEFINITION OF DATA BASE MANAGEMENT

The easiest way to understand data base management concepts and visualize what you can do with a data base management program like dBASE IV is to work from a functional definition that describes what a data base manager *is* in terms of what it *does.* In general, data base management software allows you to carry out the following operations:

- Define the individual items of data to be maintained
- Design screen layouts for entering and displaying data
- Enter data according to a predefined format
- Retrieve specific data to be viewed or printed
- Change or delete data
- Rearrange data into different orders for screen displays or reports
- Select subsets of the data for specific purposes
- Perform calculations and store, view, or print the results
- Produce printed reports that provide meaningful information to people who are not familiar with computers or data base management software

You may recognize in this definition some of the ways you can computerize the operations that you are currently carrying out manually. For example, defining a screen format for entering or displaying data is equivalent to designing a paper form for recording the same information. Retrieving specific information in order to make changes serves the same purpose as taking a particular form out of a file drawer, crossing out an old address, writing in a new one, and returning the form to its proper place in the file. Selecting a subset of the data for a special purpose and rearranging the selected data into a different order is not unlike typing mailing labels in ZIP code order for those people on a mailing list whose memberships are due to expire the following month.

Perhaps you are upgrading from dBASE III PLUS or are graduating to dBASE IV because you have reached the limits of a less capable file manager, such as PFS:FILE, Rapidfile, or the Data Query commands in Lotus 1-2-3. If so, you already have some familiarity with these fundamental data base operations, but even if you have never used any software billed as a file manager or a data base program, you may already have had some indirect experience with data base management. Anyone who has used an accounting program or specialized software for applications such as medical or law office management, client billing, or job costing has been using a data base manager, since these programs perform the functions that make up the operational definition of data base management.

The difference between these "canned" programs and a general-purpose data base manager like dBASE IV is that the packaged programs are customized for specific applications and cannot easily be adapted to the unique needs of individual users. They operate on predetermined types of data and produce only the reports deemed necessary by their designers. With a canned client billing package, if you wanted to add the client name to a report that listed only the account number, print a client list grouped by city and state rather than in alphabetical order, or use a nonstandard method for computing hourly charges, you would be out of luck.

With dBASE IV, you can carry out the same types of operations on any type of information, design your own screen and report formats, define your own calculations, and specify any criteria for selecting and rearranging the data. You can use the same software for all the vastly different data base applications enumerated at the beginning of this chapter as well for as many others.

Freedom and flexibility have their price, however. If you can find a canned program that satisfies most of your requirements and fits within your budget, you will be able to get the system up and running much faster, and with less effort and frustration, than by doing it yourself with dBASE IV. Be aware also that many data base applications are complex enough to require programming, and you may not have the time, aptitude, or desire to become a dBASE IV programmer. dBASE IV includes an application generator that enables non-programmers to tap some of the power of the built-in higher level language, but it cannot write all the programs required by a complex application.

dBASE IV is a powerful and flexible tool well suited for the data base management needs of many individuals, businesses, and nonprofit organizations. If you are willing to devote time to learning dBASE IV and setting up your applications, you can accomplish many sophisticated data base management tasks without programming.

THE BENEFITS OF COMPUTERIZING

As you work through the analysis and planning phase, keep in mind which kinds of operations can benefit most from computerization. You stand to gain the most

- When you can enter information once and then print it in several formats or sorted orders
- When the computer can do calculations that are complex or tedious by hand
- When the computer gives anyone in the office the ability to perform tasks that would otherwise require special expertise
- When the ability to generate reports provides more timely or less expensive access to management information
- When the ability to cross-reference information helps you produce reports that would be too time consuming to prepare manually

Although computers can perform calculations more quickly than humans, not every job can be done faster or better with a computer. This is especially true when a great deal of user input is required, since it usually takes about the same amount of time to enter information into a computerized data base as it does to write or type it on paper. If the computer must then sort the data and print a report, producing that final piece of paper may actually take longer than typing the report. On the other hand, if you can enter information once, perform a complex calculation, and then produce three different reports drawing on the results, you have realized a substantial gain over your manual system.

DEFINITIONS OF SOME COMMON TERMS

For the most part, this book avoids using "computerese" and attempts to explain new concepts in familiar, nontechnical language. However, in any specialized field, a certain amount of jargon is not only inevitable but beneficial, since it conveys some important concepts concisely and unambiguously.

The definitions of data base terminology presented in this section are consistent with the way the terms are used in the dBASE IV manuals and other books on the subject. Be aware that this usage is "standard" only among users of dBASE and other compatible data base programs. Other popular data base programs that you may have used in the past or may encounter in the future assign different meanings to some of these words or use different terms to express the same concepts.

In a dBASE IV data base, each item of information is called a *field,* and the set of fields that describes one logical unit of information is called a *record.* For example, in a mailing list data base, the logical storage unit is one person. In each person's record, you might have fields for the name, street address, city, state, ZIP code, and telephone number. In an inventory data base, the logical unit of information is one stocked item, and an inventory record might contain fields for the part number, a brief description, cost, selling price, and quantity on hand.

A collection of records that share the same format—have the same fields—is called a *file,* or a *data base* (this term is often written as one word, "database"). If there were 250 people on the simple mailing list in the previous example, the mailing list data base, or file, would have 250 records, each of which contained six fields.

These terms may seem natural and intuitive to you because they are often used in almost exactly the same way to talk about manual filing systems. If you maintained customer records on ledger cards stored in a file folder or file box, you might say, "Go to the accounts receivable file and get me Kelley's records." In another setting, where a file drawer or an entire filing cabinet was devoted to storing accounts receivable information, each customer might have a separate folder, and you would be more likely to say, "Get me Kelley's file." This discrepancy between data base terminology and colloquial usage can be confusing when you begin working with dBASE IV, or later on when you attempt to communicate with less experienced users about your data bases.

The ledger card, or file card, analogy represents one good way to visualize a dBASE IV data base: you can imagine one paper form representing a record, with the fields in a more or less vertical arrangement on the page. The entire stack of ledger cards (or other paper forms) constitutes a file. This model is shown in Figure 1-1.

If you have worked with a spreadsheet program that offers some data base management capabilities, such as Lotus 1-2-3, Excel, or Quattro Pro, you may feel more comfortable visualizing a data base as a table much like a spreadsheet. Many data base programs, especially those derived from mainframe

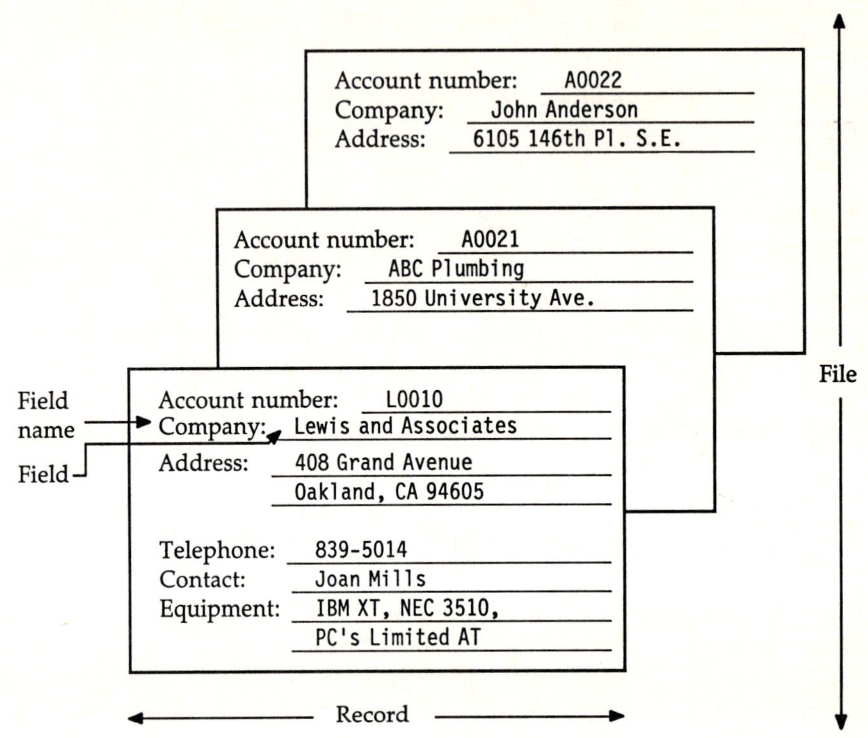

Figure 1-1.

The ledger card model for a data base

software, use the term *table* to describe what is defined here as a data base. (If you use dBASE IV in SQL mode, you will encounter this usage in the *Using dBASE IV SQL* manual supplied with dBASE IV.) In the table model, the fields are lined up in columns, and each record extends horizontally across the page (which might have to be very wide to accommodate all the fields). This model is illustrated in Figure 1-2.

As you will see in Chapter 4, dBASE IV allows you to view a data base on the screen in two standard layouts, one of which closely resembles the ledger card model, while the other approximates the tabular arrangement.

A dBASE IV application may consist of a single data base, or it may require two or more discrete files. For example, many mailing list applications need

Account number	Company	Address	City, State
L0010	Lewis and Associates	408 Grand Avenue	Oakland, CA
A0021	ABC Plumbing	1850 University Ave.	Berkeley, CA
A0022	John Anderson	6105 146th Pl. S.E.	Bellevue, WA
K0010	Carol Klein, M.D.	1849 S.E. 40th Ave.	Portland, OR
M0010	MTK Industries	1400 61st Street	Emeryville, CA

Figure 1-2.

The tabular model for a data base

only a single name and address data base, while a client-billing data base for a professional office might comprise a dozen interrelated files, including one for client names and addresses, one for hourly charges, one for payments, and so on.

dBASE IV allows you to *relate,* or link, two files based on fields that contain information common to both. For example, in an order-tracking system, each customer might be assigned an account number; a field for this code would be included in both the customer file and the order file. By comparing the contents of the account number field in the two files, dBASE IV can associate an order with the matching customer or find all the orders placed by a given customer. Because of its ability to work with multiple related files, dBASE IV is often described as a "relational data base" (this usage does not conform to the more technical definition of the term "relational" as originally developed for mainframe data bases).

Some authors use the term "data base" to describe a set of related files, but the dBASE IV documentation and most books written about dBASE IV use "file" and "data base" more or less interchangeably. One reason for this variation in usage is that some data base management programs store all the information in a set of related data bases in a single disk file, whereas dBASE IV places each data base in a separate disk file (or sometimes in two disk files, as will be explained in Chapter 3).

PLANNING A dBASE IV APPLICATION

Before you can use dBASE IV to set up a data base application, you must define what you want the system to accomplish. The functional definition of data base management presented earlier in this chapter suggests the types of questions you will need to ask yourself in order to clarify your goals:

- What items of information must be maintained?
- How should the data be presented on the screen? Must the data entry and inquiry screens emulate existing paper forms?
- What rules will govern how entered data is formatted and checked for validity?
- What criteria will be used to retrieve records in order to view, change, delete, or print data?
- In what different sequences will data be viewed or printed?
- What subsets of the data (which fields from which records) must be selected for specific purposes?
- What calculations or transformations must be performed on the data?
- What transfers of information (for example, "posting" financial transactions to a customer's cumulative balance) must take place between files or within a file? Must data be archived and then deleted from any files?
- What screen output and printed reports must the system produce?

If your dBASE IV data base will replace or augment an existing manual system, your job will be much easier than if you are trying to computerize a new application or bring operations in-house that are currently being performed by outside contractors or service bureaus. Even if you intend to revamp your present procedures, a careful study of the manual system can provide a valuable framework for analyzing your needs. Without a comparable "paper" system, you have no choice but to proceed directly to a description of the functions that you anticipate you will need. But since your initial study cannot be as complete, be prepared for the eventuality that more extensive revisions will be required as the system grows and evolves.

Undoubtedly, you are already impatient to begin working with dBASE IV, especially if you feel that implementing a new system or improving your old one is long overdue. Yet the process of analyzing your present system and projecting your future needs can be difficult, tedious, and time consuming. It can also be somewhat traumatic, since you will have to rethink all your familiar manual procedures and examine the workings of your organization in greater detail than you have in years—or perhaps ever.

For all these reasons, the temptation will be strong to abbreviate the planning phase or skip it entirely. Try not to yield to this temptation! Regardless of how much or how little prior experience you have with computers or data base management software, any time spent on advance planning will pay big dividends later in time saved, because it will minimize the need for changes and additions to the data bases.

Studying Samples from the Manual System

An excellent way to begin your needs analysis is to gather a complete set of the documents that make up your present manual system. For example, an accounts receivable system might include customer ledger cards, order forms, a price list, invoices, monthly statements, bank deposit slips, a cash receipts journal, an invoice register, an aging report, and a quarterly sales tax summary. Carefully studying these paper forms will help you extract a list of the items of information that must be entered into the system, the many calculations and transfers of information that must be performed, and the printed reports the system must produce. You may also want to use some of the manual forms as models for the system's data entry screens and reports so that the new system presents a somewhat familiar face.

If at all possible, the sample documents should contain matching data. In the accounts receivable example, the invoice you select should match the order form, and the invoice data should appear on the customer ledger card, the statement, the invoice register, the aging report, and the sales tax summary. Similarly, the bank deposit slip and the cash receipts journal should include the payment data for the sample invoice. By matching the samples, you will find it easy to trace the flow of information through the system and reconstruct the calculations and data transfers that must be performed.

Outlining the Work Flow and Schedule

Armed with a set of sample documents (or, for a new application, a description of the required documents), you can proceed to outline the present and projected work flow and processing schedule. If you are emulating or replacing a manual system, you can describe the tasks currently being carried out by hand as well as any new capabilities you would like to add. For a new system, you will necessarily be limited to the proposed new operations. For each task, ask yourself questions like these:

- *What items of information are involved?* Each required item must either be included as a field in one of the data bases or calculated from other fields.
- *How big is each item?* The data base fields must be wide enough to accommodate the required data.
- *Approximately how many of each item are there?* These numbers will help you estimate how large your data bases will be so you can assess your hardware requirements and choose the most efficient ways to manipulate the data.
- *What calculations or transformations are carried out?* Make sure that you know how to carry out all mathematical computations or data transformations that must be performed.
- *What transfers of information are involved?* You will have to design computerized equivalents for such transfers of information as posting transactions or archiving and deleting obsolete data.
- *What prior processing or special preparation is required?* You will have to ensure that any required calculations or transfers of information are carried out before you perform other calculations or print reports that depend on the results.
- *How often is each operation performed?* The frequency of a task influences how important processing speed is and how inconvenient any required special preparations or prior calculations will be.

- *How much time and specialized knowledge are required to carry out the task manually?* This information will provide the perspective from which to gauge which operations can gain the most from computerization and which should be given lower priority.

Your answers to the questions involving sizes and quantities need not be exact. For example, it makes little difference whether you generate 100 invoices per month or 150, but a business that generates 1000 invoices a month might handle posting differently from one with 100. Also, the number of items that are processed is usually more important than the magnitude of the numbers involved. A business with gross annual sales of $1 million that sells $10 items will have a much larger transaction file—which will require more storage space and processing time—than a business with the same annual gross that sells products in the $10,000 range.

If you anticipate that your answers to any of these questions will change significantly during the next year or two, you might make two parallel lists: one that describes your present situation and one with future estimates. For example, if there are currently 2000 names on your mailing list, but you have arranged to purchase another organization's 3000-name list at the end of the year, plan your data base to handle 5000 names comfortably. If the most expensive item in your inventory sells for $49.95, but you expect to add a new product line next year, you might decide to add an extra digit to the price field to accommodate prices over $100.

Try to be realistic, however. It is easy for an organization with 500 donors and a new fund-raising director to make the optimistic prediction that the roster will increase to 5000 in two years. The resulting data base design may turn out to be unnecessarily complicated or cumbersome if the anticipated growth never materializes.

Outlining the Reports

For some people, enumerating the items of information to be maintained in a data base is the most natural approach to the system design process, while others visualize the goals of a system in terms of the printed output it must produce. You can tackle the problem from either perspective, but even if your natural inclination is to begin by specifying the input to the system, it is essential to include in your advance planning a description of the required reports.

In determining exactly which fields are required, the output of the system is often more helpful than the input documents. Any information that appears on a report must either be entered directly into a data base or calculated from other fields. You must include fields for any information you will use, either in selection criteria—to decide which records are included on a given report—or to specify the order in which the records should be printed.

Evaluating the Field List

When you have listed all the data the system must maintain and have outlined the reports it must produce, take a moment to reexamine the field list to make sure that each item is necessary. Studying the present and proposed reports is especially helpful in avoiding a very common pitfall: creating a huge data base with many fields for information that could be maintained just as well by hand or that is already being maintained adequately by hand. There is little point to spending time entering information that already exists on paper if all you ever do is view the data on screen or print it in more or less the same form.

A field belongs in a data base only if it meets at least one of the following tests:

- Do you always need to see the information on screen?
- Must the data be printed on a report?
- Is the information required for a calculation or statistical summary?
- Will the data be used as the basis for selecting which records should be displayed, processed, or printed?
- Will the data be used to specify the order in which records are displayed or printed?

Be especially careful with data bases that appear to require large amounts of text or numerous fields that are not used in calculations. You would not, for example, want to retype a lengthy description of each of your clients' business activities into a data base if this material were already available on paper in the form of handwritten notes. It might, however, be desirable to include several fields for codes identifying each client's type of business and major products or services so that you could quickly extract the ones that matched a given business profile. You could then refer back to the paper files for more detail.

In other cases, deciding what information to include is much less clear-cut. Suppose you were setting up a data base for a doctor who asks all new patients to fill out a four-page medical history questionnaire. Your first inclination might be to enter all the responses into a patient history data base, but depending on how the doctor wanted to use the information, this effort might be unnecessary and inefficient.

For example, the medical history might include questions about allergies. To find out whether a particular patient has hay fever, it would be just as easy to pull the patient's folder from the manual filing system and refer to the original questionnaire as it would be to call up the patient's record in the data base. If, however, the doctor wanted to be able to find out how many patients had allergies, it would be far easier to extract this information from the data base than to thumb through all the patient questionnaires.

Unfortunately, it is easy to weigh the facts, carefully consider your intended use of the data, and still make the wrong decision. The doctor in this example might have decided, based on the foregoing analysis, to omit the allergy data, and most of the other items on the questionnaire, from the patient data base. Six months later, a new drug might appear on the market that effectively treats hay fever symptoms with few undesirable side effects, and the doctor might want to send a pamphlet describing this drug to all patients who have pollen allergies—a contingency that would have been difficult to predict in advance.

The point is that even though you cannot accurately foresee all your future requirements, try to identify at the outset the fields you will need, and at the same time carefully evaluate each item of information to determine whether it belongs in one of your dBASE IV data bases.

Examining Other Software

If commercial packages exist for the application you are computerizing, or for a similar application, taking a look at a few such programs can be valuable, even if you have already decided to "do it yourself" with dBASE IV. These programs may suggest additional fields, calculations, and reports. Think about what you like and dislike about the menus, data entry screens, and printed lists. Evaluating other software can help draw your attention to the factors that go into producing attractive, easy-to-use data entry screens and clear, readable reports.

To some extent, features built into dBASE IV determine the "look and feel" of the applications you design. Other aspects of the user interface—such as screen and report layouts—are largely up to you. Giving these issues some attention early in the design process can ease the transition from manual to computerized operation by helping you design an application that integrates more smoothly into your normal work flow.

AN INTRODUCTION TO THE NATIONAL WIDGETS SYSTEM

The examples in this book are based on a customer- and order-tracking system for an imaginary small business called National Widgets. This firm, located in Berkeley, California, is a mail-order supplier of computer accessories and supplies. National Widgets has been in business for five years and had about $2 million in gross sales last year. The company is managed by the owner and employs four other people full time: a bookkeeper, two clerk-typists who also answer the telephones, and one person who handles shipping and receiving.

National Widgets has about 550 regular customers who account for about one-third of its monthly volume of 1500 orders; the remaining orders come from one-time buyers or people who call so infrequently that their records are dropped between orders. Both the number of customers and the number of orders are expected to double over the next two years.

Eventually, National Widgets hopes to purchase a packaged accounting program or develop one internally, but the bookkeeping is currently manageable on paper. The owner has three overall goals for the initial dBASE IV system:

- To automate and expand the mailing list processing currently being done manually to include more frequent and more selective mailings, and to print letters as well as mailing labels
- To allow the owner and bookkeeper more immediate access to information that is currently difficult and time-consuming to obtain by hand, including customer buying patterns and ordering trends
- To design the system so that it can serve as the core for a more sophisticated accounting system written in dBASE IV

To satisfy these requirements, the system must include information on National Widgets' regular customers, inventory items, and orders. Although it would be desirable to maintain some totals, such as a customer's total purchases, the data bases need not duplicate information required only for accounting purposes, such as invoice totals, payment amounts, or current balances. The information will be maintained in three main data base files:

- A *Customer File,* which stores customer names, addresses, telephone numbers, and year-to-date and overall totals
- An *Order File,* which stores detailed information about each item a customer has ordered, including order date, part number, quantity ordered, selling price, and discount
- An *Inventory File,* which stores information about the company's products, including the part number, description, cost, price, and quantity on hand

The structures of these files are developed more fully in Chapter 3.

CHAPTER TWO

Starting and Running dBASE IV

The dBASE IV user interface—the command structure used to communicate with the software—was designed to allow people who have widely varying levels of experience with computers and data bases to use the program effectively and comfortably. For the most part, dBASE IV allows you to choose the command mode or modes best suited to your expertise and personal preferences without sacrificing functionality. All of the fundamental data base operations can be carried out either by making selections from a menu system or by typing commands directly, although for some more complex operations, one method offers distinct advantages over the other.

dBASE IV offers four distinctly different user interface alternatives:

- *The menu system* In this mode, you execute commands and choose options through a hierarchy of light-bar menus consisting of horizontal menu bars with associated pull-down menus, pop-up pick lists, and dialog or prompt boxes.

- *Command mode* In this mode, also referred to as the *dot prompt,* you type commands directly, in a command language with grammar and syntax that approximates a simplified natural (human) language.
- *SQL (Structured Query Language)* In this mode, which closely resembles command mode, you use ANSI-standard SQL statements to create and update data bases. For data inquiry and reporting, SQL commands may be mixed freely with dBASE IV commands and functions for which there are no SQL counterparts.
- *Programming* In this mode, dBASE IV or SQL commands (including those you can type at the dot prompt and others that are valid only in programs) are combined into *programs* (stored as ordinary text files) for later execution.

The dBASE IV user interface also includes three specialized editing environments, each of which can be invoked from any of the four command modes:

- *Full-screen editors* A comprehensive set of cursor movement, editing, and command keys used to enter and update data base records and text files
- *Layout editors* A group of specialized full-screen editors that allow you to design and edit report and label formats, custom data entry screens, and application menus by typing background text and placing data items on the screen "work surface"
- *Query-by-Example* A menu-driven, graphically oriented screen work surface used to specify selection criteria, define data base update procedures, and create customized views of information stored in one or more data base files

The fact that so many different operational modes can be identified does not mean that the dBASE IV user interface is difficult or complex. The elements that are present in more than one mode, such as the menus, pick lists, and dialog boxes, always look similar and share a common command structure. Some pull-down menus are found, in almost exactly the same form, in the main menu bars of several different editing environments. The layout editors all use the same function key commands to place fields and to copy or move items on the screen, and throughout all the editing modes, a common set of cursor movement and editing command keys is used to move around on the screen and make changes.

The full-screen editors are introduced briefly in this chapter and are discussed in detail in Chapter 4, which describes how to enter and edit data. The layout editors are covered in later chapters on designing labels, reports, custom screens, and application menus. Writing programs, a topic that has filled numerous complete volumes, is touched on briefly in this book, in Chapters 21 and 22. SQL is not covered at all, but if you are already familiar with SQL command syntax, you should have little difficulty with SQL mode once you have mastered command mode (the dot prompt).

This chapter describes the dBASE IV menu system and provides a brief introduction to working at the dot prompt. For most beginners, using the menu system is the best way to begin working with dBASE IV, and if you are a poor typist, you may continue to use the menus, even after you have gained considerable experience. If you have used dBASE II, III, or III PLUS, none of which had a fully functional menu system, you may gravitate instead toward the dot prompt.

The dBASE IV menu system is considerably more complete and capable than its predecessors, the "Assist" menus in dBASE III and III PLUS. The new menu system provides access to nearly all of the program's capabilities, and deciding whether to use the menus or work at the dot prompt is largely a matter of personal preference. This book strives to acquaint you with both interfaces; in general, the method used to carry out a given task through the menus will be presented first, followed by a description of how to accomplish the same objective from the dot prompt. Regardless of your initial preference, experiment with both methods so you can make an informed choice about which command mode (or combination of command modes) to use in your work with dBASE IV.

STARTING UP dBASE IV

The easiest way to run dBASE IV is to log on to the disk drive and subdirectory containing the dBASE IV software before you start the program. For example, if you had installed dBASE IV in a subdirectory on drive C called DBASE4, you could log on to the program subdirectory by typing the following DOS commands:

```
C:
CD \DBASE4
```

If you wish to maintain several separate data base applications, each in its own subdirectory, the most straightforward approach is to add the dBASE IV subdirectory to your DOS search path and then switch to the appropriate application subdirectory before loading dBASE IV. (Chapter 18 describes a method for switching to another directory from within dBASE IV.) To establish a DOS search path that includes three subdirectories called C:\DBASE4, C:\DOS, and C:\UTILITY, you could use the following PATH command:

```
PATH C:\DBASE4;C:\DOS;C:\UTILITY
```

The dBASE IV program subdirectory can be anywhere in the search path, but placing it first, as in the previous example, will result in slightly faster performance. With the dBASE IV subdirectory in the search path, you can run dBASE IV from any subdirectory on any disk drive in your system. For example, to experiment with the sample files supplied with dBASE IV, which the installation program copies to a subdirectory called SAMPLES under the dBASE IV subdirectory, you would use the following DOS commands to switch to this subdirectory before starting up dBASE IV:

```
C:
CD \DBASE4\SAMPLES
```

If you use dBASE IV often, you may want to include the PATH command in your AUTOEXEC.BAT file so that it is executed automatically each time you start up your computer.

To start up dBASE IV, type

```
DBASE
```

dBASE IV will display the Ashton-Tate logo, followed by a sign-on screen that summarizes the terms of the software licensing agreement and includes the name, company, and serial number you entered when you installed the program. On the bottom line of the screen, you will see the prompt "Press ↵ to assent to the License Agreement and begin dBASE IV." You can press ENTER to clear the sign-on display immediately, but if you wait a few seconds, it will disappear on its own. You can suppress the splashy logo and the pause and limit the sign-on display to a simple copyright notice by adding –T or /T to the command you type to start up dBASE IV, as follows:

```
DBASE/T
```

If dBASE IV was installed using the standard procedure described in Appendix A (or the dBASE IV documentation), the main menu, called the *Control Center,* will be displayed automatically. If dBASE IV was installed by someone who preferred to work in command mode, you will see a mostly blank screen, with the prompts "Press the F1 key for HELP" and "Type a dBASE IV command and press the ENTER key (↵)" at the bottom and a dot (the dot prompt) and a blinking cursor in the lower left corner. Depending on the options selected when dBASE IV was installed, there may also be a bar of inverse video (or, on a color monitor, a contrasting color) called the *status bar* just below the dot prompt.

To invoke the menu system from the dot prompt, type

```
ASSIST
```

USING THE MENU SYSTEM

The dBASE IV menu system allows you to execute commands and select options through a system of horizontal light-bar menus with associated pull-down menus and pop-up pick lists and dialog boxes. If you have used Framework III, the appearance and organization of the menus, as well as some of the options, will seem familiar. Users who are upgrading from dBASE III PLUS will recognize some similarity to the old "Assist" menus, although the look of the menus has changed somewhat and there are many new options.

The Control Center, shown in Figure 2-1, is the main menu of the dBASE IV menu system. On the top line of the screen is a horizontal *menu bar* with three options: **Catalog, Tools,** and **Exit**. The time, updated every second, is displayed in the upper right corner of the screen.

Under the menu bar, dBASE IV displays the full path name of the current file catalog. A *catalog* is a list (stored in a standard dBASE IV data base) of all the disk files—data bases and other files—that you intend to use together. When you work in the menu system, dBASE IV automatically creates a catalog called UNTITLED.CAT in each subdirectory from which you load the program, and it updates this catalog whenever you create or delete files. Using the options on the Control Center **Catalog** menu, you can rename a catalog, create a new catalog, switch catalogs, or enter an 80-character description of any file in the catalog. The Control Center display includes only files in the current catalog, so if you use dBASE IV for several applications, you can group the files that belong to each application into separate catalogs. Chapter 19 details how to create, update, and use dBASE IV catalogs.

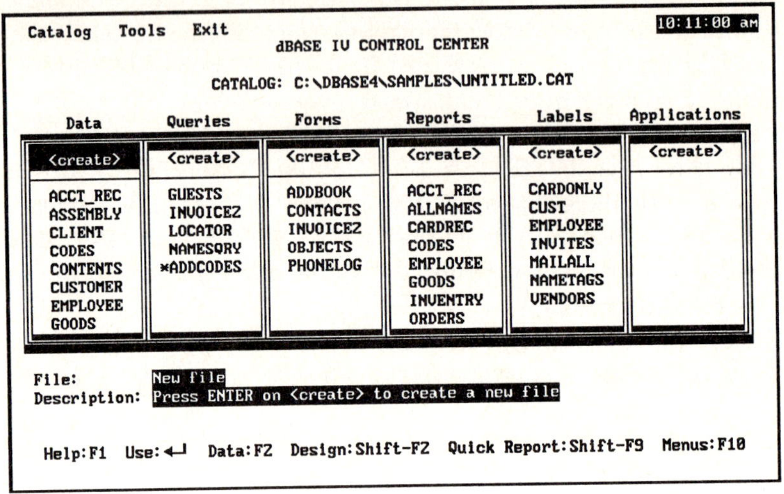

Figure 2-1.

The Control Center

The File Name Panels

Because most of your work with dBASE IV involves defining, editing, and displaying files, the most important portion of the Control Center is not the menu bar, but the six *panels* in the center of the screen containing the names of the disk files used by your application. The names of the panels and the types of files they display are as follows:

Data — Data base files

Queries — Query files, which produce customized views of data and are used for updating data bases

Forms — Format files, which draw custom data entry screens

Reports — Report form files, which produce printed reports

Labels — Label form files, which print mailing labels, envelopes, and Rolodex cards

Applications — Menus produced by the applications generator, and other dBASE IV programs

How to create and use these types of files is detailed in later chapters.

Exactly what file names appear in the panels when you load dBASE IV for the first time depends on how you installed the program, the subdirectory from which you loaded dBASE IV, and the other individuals who have used the program on your computer. If you opted to copy the sample files onto your hard disk when you installed dBASE IV and you loaded the program from the SAMPLES subdirectory, your screen should resemble Figure 2-1. If there are no dBASE IV files in the subdirectory from which you loaded the program, the panels will be empty. If a coworker has used dBASE IV in the same subdirectory, you may see the names of files that he or she created.

You select a file or option in the dBASE IV menu system by "pointing" to it with a cursor that is displayed as a *light bar* of inverse video (or, on a color monitor, as two contrasting colors). The RIGHT ARROW and LEFT ARROW keys move the cursor from one panel to the next, and within a panel, the UP ARROW, DOWN ARROW, PGUP, and PGDN keys move it through the file list.

Under the Control Center file name panels, dBASE IV displays the name of the file highlighted by the cursor and a brief description of its purpose or contents. When you are trying to decide which file to select, this description, an optional entry in the catalog, can prove far more helpful than an eight-character file name.

You can select the **<create>** option from any panel to define a new file of the specified type or choose an existing file by highlighting its name and then pressing ENTER. If you installed dBASE IV using the standard procedure described in Appendix A, a dialog box will pop up to offer additional choices that are appropriate for the type of file you have selected. For example, when you choose a data base, the dialog box, which is shown in Figure 2-2, includes three options: **Use file**, **Modify structure/order**, and **Display data**. For a report format, the choices are **Print report**, **Modify layout**, and **Display data**. When you *open*, or *use*, a data base file (that is, tell dBASE IV that you want to work with the file), its name moves above the horizontal line in the **Data** panel; and related screen forms, reports, and labels shift up in their respective panels, as shown in Figure 2-3.

You can configure dBASE IV to bypass the dialog box and open a file immediately when you highlight the name and press ENTER. If you want to do this, you must use function key shortcuts for the other dialog box options: SHIFT-F2 (Design) for **Modify structure/order**, and F2 (Data) for **Display data**. If someone has set up your copy of dBASE this way, you can restore the dialog boxes for the duration of the current work session, either from the Control Center **Tools** menu or by typing the following command from the dot prompt:

```
SET INSTRUCT ON
```

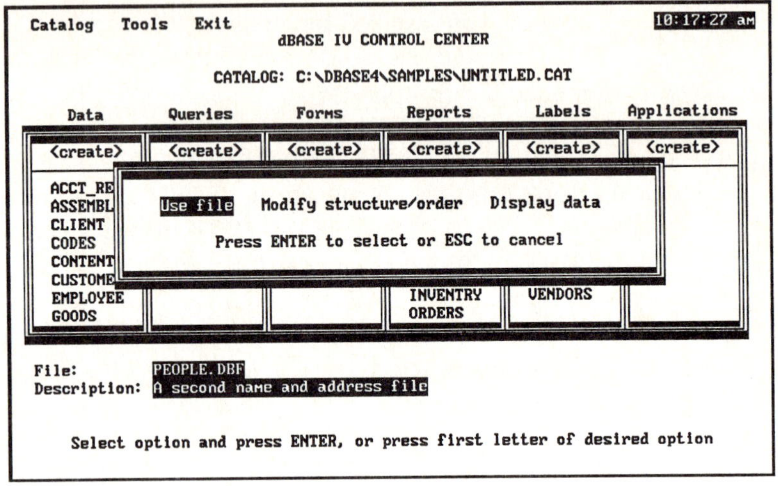

Figure 2-2.

The data base file selection dialog box

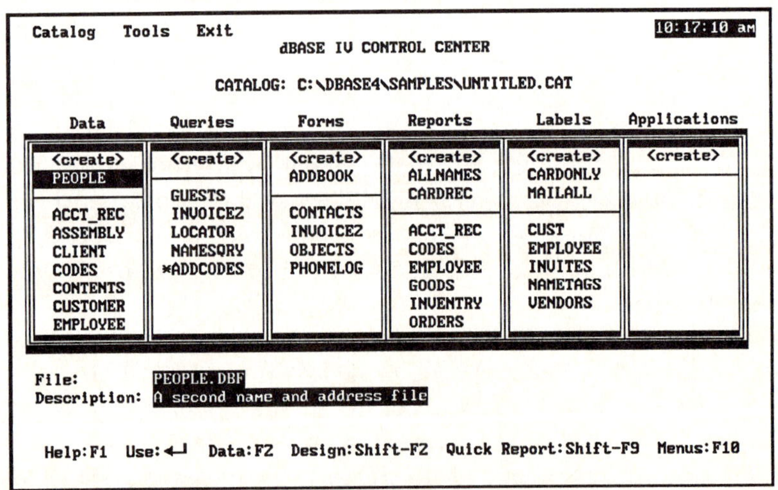

Figure 2-3.

The Control Center display after opening the PEOPLE data base

This and the other configuration options are further explained in Chapter 18.

The Control Center Menu

The Control Center menu bar has three options:

Catalog — This menu contains commands for creating, updating, and selecting file catalogs. The **Catalog** menu commands are described in Chapter 19.

Tools — This menu contains commands for recording and playing back keystroke macros, exchanging data with other programs, using the DOS utilities for disk file management tasks, updating the security (password protection) system, and customizing the working environment. The **Tools** menu options are covered in Chapters 18 and 19.

Exit — This menu contains commands for exiting from the Control Center menu system, either to the dot prompt or to the operating system.

You activate the menu system by pressing F10 (Menu). When a menu is active, the cursor movement keys move the light-bar cursor through the menu options rather than through the file name panels. Despite the linear arrangement on the screen, the menu options behave as if they formed a loop—if you press RIGHT ARROW with the last option on the right selected, the cursor returns to the first option on the left.

Associated with each menu bar option is a menu of additional choices that is automatically *pulled down,* or displayed, when the main menu option is highlighted. On these pull-down menus, options that you can select are displayed in brighter letters than those that are currently unavailable, and menu options that lead to additional submenus, such as the **Import** and **Export** options on the **Tools** menu, are marked with a small triangle. Figure 2-4 illustrates the appearance of the screen with the **Tools** menu pulled down and the **Export** option selected.

You choose menu options the same way that you select file names from the Control Center panels: by using the arrow keys to "point to" (highlight) your choice and then pressing ENTER. As you move up and down through the selections, the cursor skips options that are not currently available. For example, if no file name is highlighted, the **Remove highlighted file from catalog**

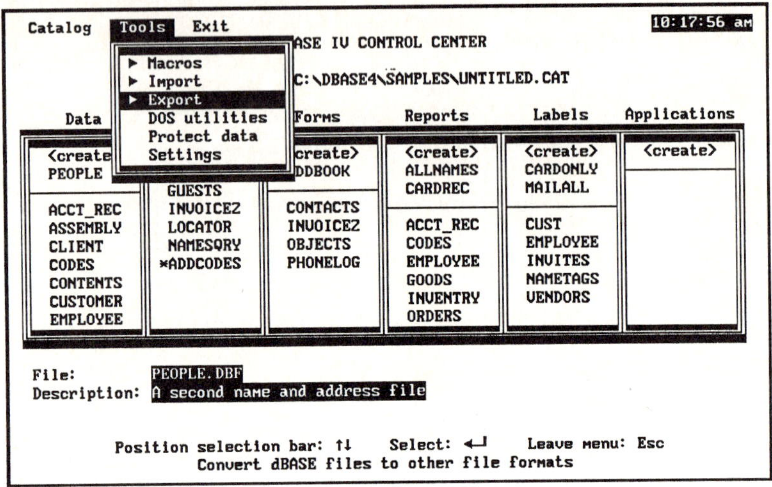

Figure 2-4.

Selecting an option from a pull-down menu

and **Change description of highlighted file** options on the **Catalog** menu are unavailable. From any point in the menu hierarchy, you can back up to the previous level by pressing the ESC key.

In some cases, dBASE IV responds to a command by popping up a dialog box to request further information, present additional choices, or ask for confirmation before carrying out a potentially destructive command. For example, if you exit one of the layout editors without saving your file, dBASE IV presents a dialog box that requests confirmation by asking, "Are you sure you want to abandon operation?" Accepting the default response, **No**, returns you to the editor. When you select a data base file from the **Data** panel, dBASE IV displays the dialog box illustrated in Figure 2-2 to ask what you want to do with the selected file. You can select one of the *buttons*, or options (in this case, **Use file, Modify structure/order**, and **Display data**), either by highlighting it and pressing ENTER or by pressing the key corresponding to the first letter of the description (in this example, U, M, or D).

When a command requires that you enter a file name, field name, or more complex expression, dBASE IV may present a *pick list*—an alphabetical list of available items of the appropriate type. Even when dBASE IV prompts you to type a file name, field name, or expression directly, you can often call up a pick list by pressing SHIFT-F1 (Pick). When a pick list is available, dBASE IV displays a

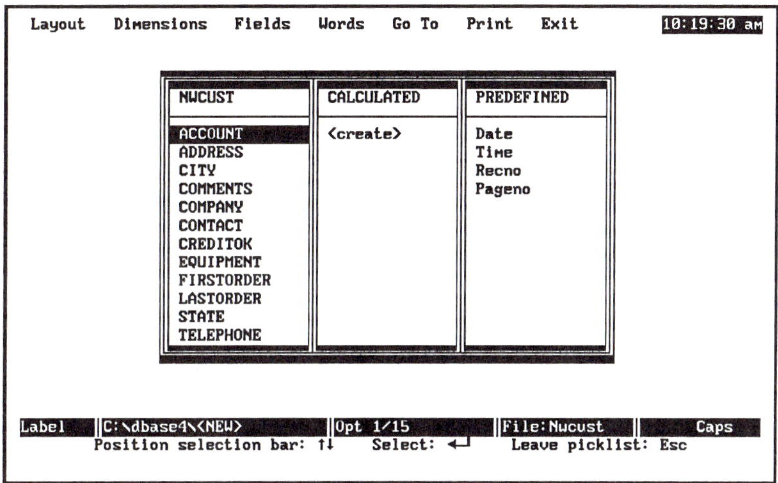

Figure 2-5.

Choosing an item from a pick list

reminder at the bottom of the screen. Figure 2-5 illustrates the pick list displayed during the process of defining a mailing label form based on the National Widgets Customer File. You can choose an item from a pick list by highlighting it and pressing ENTER.

If you prefer to use keyboard commands rather than the cursor movement arrow keys, you can invoke the menu system and at the same time move directly to any main menu option by holding down the ALT key and pressing the first letter of the selection. You can also select an option from any pull-down menu by typing the first letter of the descriptive phrase displayed in the menu box. For example, one way to access the dBASE IV DOS utilities is to press F10 (Menu) to activate the Control Center menu bar, use the LEFT ARROW or RIGHT ARROW key to move the light bar to the **Tools** option, press ENTER, highlight the **DOS Utilities** option on the **Tools** menu, and press ENTER again. Alternatively, you could pull down the **Tools** menu by pressing ALT-T, and then select **DOS Utilities** by pressing D.

You can use a similar technique to select an item from a pick list such as the one shown in Figure 2-5. Pressing any letter key moves the cursor directly to the first item that begins with that letter; you then complete the selection by pressing ENTER. If more than one item on the list begins with the same letter, you can either type a second letter (and additional letters if necessary) to jump to the desired item or use the cursor movement keys to move from the first item highlighted to your desired selection, and then press ENTER to select it.

dBASE IV provides function key shortcuts for the most commonly used commands in each menu and editing environment. For example, you can open a file and move directly to the full-screen editor used to add, view, and update records by highlighting the name of the data base name in the Control Center **Data** panel and pressing F2 (Data). dBASE IV displays the meanings of the most frequently used function keys at the bottom of the screen in the Control Center, as shown in Figure 2-1, and in the layout editors. The precise use of the function keys varies slightly in the different editing environments, but each key is always used for basically the same purpose. The function keys, their names, and their meanings are listed in Table 2-1. A complete list of the cursor movement and function keys used in the menu system appears in Table 2-2.

WORKING AT THE DOT PROMPT

As an alternative to the menu system, dBASE IV offers a command-driven mode. Using this mode is generally referred to as working at *command level,* or at the *dot prompt* (a name derived from the period, or dot, used as the command prompt). In command mode, dBASE IV displays the dot prompt and a blinking cursor in the lower left corner of the screen and, much like the MS-DOS operating system, waits for you to type a command. dBASE IV responds to each command by asking for more information (such as a file name) if necessary, displaying an error message, or, if your command is complete and syntactically correct, carrying out your request. After executing a command, dBASE IV redisplays the dot prompt and waits for you to type another command.

Every dBASE IV command begins with a verb—you are telling the program to do something—and most support additional options that can be combined in various ways to express very sophisticated requests. For example, the command for producing an onscreen listing of all the records in a data base is

```
LIST
```

By adding options to this simple command, you can generate a more specific, selective listing. For example, you could display and print a list of account codes, company names, and telephone numbers for National Widgets' customers in San Francisco with the following command:

```
LIST ACCOUNT, COMPANY, TELEPHONE FOR CITY = "San Francisco" TO PRINT
```

Key	Name	Meaning
F1	Help	Access the online help system
F2	Data	Display the Edit or Browse screen
F3	Previous	Move to the previous item
F4	Next	Move to the next item
F5	Field	Add or remove a field from a work surface
F6	Select	Mark a block of items
F7	Move	Move the selected items
F8	Copy	Copy the selected items
F9	Zoom	Expand or contract data entry or display area
F10	Menu	Activate the menu system
SHIFT-F1	Pick	Display a pick list
SHIFT-F2	Design	Transfer to a design screen or layout editor
SHIFT-F3	Find Previous	Search backward for the same string of characters
SHIFT-F4	Find Next	Search forward for the same string of characters
SHIFT-F5	Find	Search for a string of characters
SHIFT-F6	Replace	Replace one string of characters with another
SHIFT-F7	Size	Change the size of the selected item
SHIFT-F8	Ditto	Copy data into current field from the same field in the previous record
SHIFT-F9	Quick Report	Print a Quick Report based on the current data base or view
SHIFT-F10	Macro	Record a keystroke macro

Table 2-1.

The dBASE IV Menu System Function Keys

From the Control Center, you can switch to command mode by choosing the **Exit to dot prompt** option from the **Exit** menu. You can also exit the Control Center without activating the menu bar by pressing ESC. Because it is easy to press the ESC key accidentally, dBASE IV asks you to confirm your intention to exit by asking, "Are you sure you want to abandon operation?"

Control Key	Command Key	Function
	F10 (Menu)	Activate the menu system
	ALT-*letter*	Activate the menu system and pull down the menu whose description begins with *letter*
	letter	Select the option on the active pull-down menu whose description begins with *letter*
	ENTER	Select the highlighted option or item from the active menu, panel, or pick list
	ESC	Cancel the selected option and back up one level in the menu system
CTRL-D	RIGHT ARROW	Advance to the next menu bar option or panel
CTRL-S	LEFT ARROW	Back up to the previous menu bar option or panel
CTRL-X	DOWN ARROW	Advance to the next pull-down menu or pick list option
CTRL-E	UP ARROW	Back up to the previous pull-down menu or pick list option
	HOME	Move to the first (top) option on the active pull-down menu or panel
	END	Move to the last (bottom) option on the active pull-down menu or panel
CTRL-C	PGDN	Display the next group of items in the active panel
CTRL-R	PGUP	Display the previous group of items in the active panel

Table 2-2.

The dBASE IV Menu System Cursor Movement and Command Keys

Accepting the default response, **No**, returns you to the Control Center; selecting **Yes** transfers you to the dot prompt. From the dot prompt, you can switch to the menu system by pressing F2 (Data) or by typing

```
ASSIST
```

Working at command level can be intimidating at first, because you must know exactly what you want to do, understand which commands to use to accomplish your goal, memorize the command syntax, and remember all the required file and field names. Anyone who does not type or spell well will be at a distinct disadvantage that may not diminish with time. In contrast, the menu system allows you to select commands, options, files, and fields (as well as other dBASE IV language components not yet introduced) from menus and pick lists by using only the cursor movement and function keys.

Although many people find command mode difficult to *learn,* it can be easy to *use* once you have gained some experience. Just about all dBASE IV commands and options are accessible through the menus, but typing commands at the dot prompt is often more direct. In some cases, stepping through several levels of menus and choosing multiple items from a pick list may require more keystrokes or take more time than typing the equivalent command at the dot prompt. Whatever your initial preference, the only way that you can get a feel for the advantages of each is by spending some time working with both interfaces.

FULL-SCREEN EDITING WITH dBASE IV

The terms *full screen* and *full-screen editing* are used to describe all the dBASE IV commands that present data on the screen in a predefined format and offer a variety of cursor movement and editing command keys that you can use to move freely among the fields and enter, change, or delete data.

Figure 2-6 illustrates a typical full-screen display, in this case the screen used to edit a record in the National Widgets Customer File. All full-screen edit modes use the field names as prompts, arranged either vertically or horizontally on the screen, to identify the data to be entered into each field. Once you have worked with a data base for a while, you will appreciate the value of making your field names self-explanatory and arranging them in the most convenient order for entering and updating records.

dBASE IV uses normal text (light characters on a dark background) for the field name prompts and inverse video (dark characters on a light background) for data that you enter. This color scheme clearly separates the data entry areas and makes the field widths evident. If you have a color monitor, you can select any combination of display colors for prompts and data. Chapter 18 describes how to customize the display colors and many other aspects of the data entry environment to suit your preferences. When you fill a field completely, dBASE IV sounds a "bell" (an electronic beeper) and advances the cursor automatically to the next field.

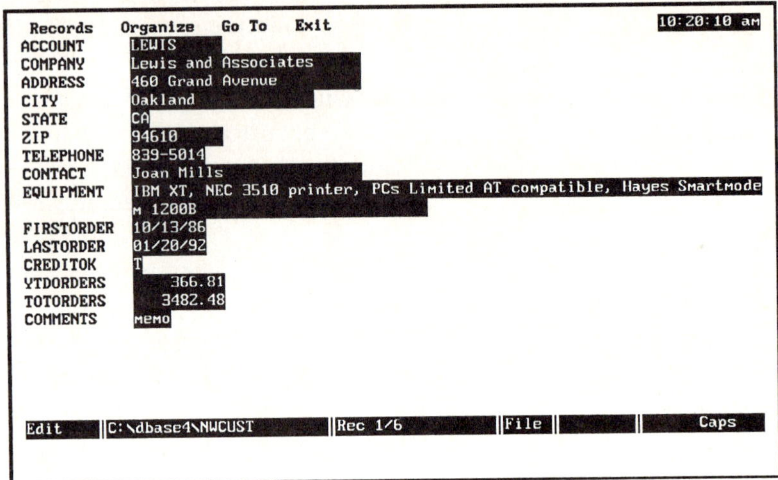

Figure 2-6.

The Edit screen with the status display on

The full-screen editors share a similar set of cursor movement and editing command keys, which are explained in Chapter 4. In most cases, there are both keypad and control key equivalents. For example, to move the cursor right one character, you can press a numeric keypad key—RIGHT ARROW—or use a control key combination—CTRL-D. In some cases, there is only one choice; and occasionally, there are three. dBASE IV does not support a mouse.

To use a control key command, you press the CTRL key and continue to hold it down while you press the other key(s) in the combination. If you are unfamiliar with control key commands, it may help to think of CTRL as working much like the SHIFT key: by itself it does nothing, but pressed in combination with other keys, it alters the functions of those keys and allows you to generate additional characters or commands.

Note also that the NUM LOCK key functions just like the CAPS LOCK key, except that it affects only the numeric keypad. When NUM LOCK is on, the keypad keys produce numbers; when it is off, they generate nonprintable character codes that are used as commands by most programs. If your keyboard does not have an LED (light-emitting diode) that lights when NUM LOCK is on, you can determine the status of this key by looking for the "Num" indicator in the status bar or on the top line of the screen.

If you have used other programs that have similar command structures, you may already have a strong preference for either the control key or keypad commands. WordStar or Sidekick users will feel at home with the control key commands, while Lotus spreadsheet users will probably find their hands reaching instinctively for the numeric keypad or cursor keypad. When there are alternatives, most of the examples in this book cite keypad commands, but you can always substitute an equivalent command listed in the reference tables.

THE STATUS DISPLAY

dBASE IV offers an option to use the bottom three lines on the screen for a *status display* that monitors the current status of the working environment, presents additional information about the currently running command, and provides a brief summary of available commands or instructions for navigating through the current menu.

You can use several methods, which are described in Chapter 18, to turn the status display on or off at the dot prompt and in the full-screen editors. Regardless of your selection, the status display is always present on the layout editor screens, and it is never present when the Control Center menu is displayed. Installing dBASE IV using the standard procedure described in Appendix A turns the status display on, and the examples in this book assume that it is on. If you do not see the status display in the full-screen editors or at the dot prompt, you can turn it on for the current work session by typing the following command at the dot prompt:

```
SET STATUS ON
```

You can see the status display in Figure 2-6, which illustrates the appearance of the screen as you edit a record in the National Widgets Customer File. The topmost line of the three is a status bar that contains specific information about the current screen environment and the file you are editing. The status bar is divided by double vertical lines into six regions, each of which has a specific purpose. Some of these items are applicable only to data base files, and the corresponding regions are blank if no data base is active. From left to right, the six regions display the following information:

- The name of the current screen or working environment. In Figure 2-6, this is Edit; at the dot prompt, it is Command.
- The path name of the active data base or view, C:\DBASE4\NWCUST in Figure 2-6. If the full path name does not fit, dBASE IV displays as

many components of the path name as possible, starting at the lowest level (the file name) and working back toward the root directory. When no file is open, this space is empty.

- The cursor position in the active file. If you are editing a data base, this is the current record number (in Figure 2-6, record 1 of a total of 6). In a screen, label, or report form, the status bar displays the row and column coordinates of the current cursor location.
- The source of the data, either File (as in Figure 2-6) or View (views are introduced in Chapter 6).
- Specialized information relevant to the current screen or working environment—for example, "ReadOnly" when you cannot edit the displayed data, or, on a network, whether or not the current file or record is locked.
- The names of the keyboard toggle keys—INS, NUM LOCK, and CAPS LOCK—that are currently "on." If a data base is open and the current record is marked for deletion, "Del" is also displayed in this region.

Below the status bar is the *navigation line,* which displays a concise summary of the most important available cursor movement and function key commands. This display is *context sensitive*—it changes as you select menu options or execute commands, so it contains only commands relevant to the current editing environment. For example, in the Control Center, the navigation line reads "Help:F1 Use:↵ Data:F2 Design:Shift-F2 Quick Report:Shift-F9 Menus:F10," as shown in Figure 2-3. In the layout editors, the navigation line displays the function keys that are used to place and move items on the screen: "Add field:F5 Select:F6 Move:F7 Copy:F8 Size:Shift-F7." With any menu bar option selected, the navigation line tells you how to select options from the associated pull-down menu or switch to an adjacent menu: "Position selection bar: ↑↓ Select:↵ Leave menu: Esc."

As you can see from these examples, the navigation line is far from self-explanatory if you have never used dBASE IV. These concise messages are not intended to enable you to learn to use dBASE IV without reading the manuals, but to use as a handy reference guide to the commands most commonly used in the current context, so that if you understand a command but have forgotten which key to press to invoke it, you don't have to refer to the printed documentation for help.

Below the navigation line, on the last line of the screen, is the *message line,* which displays a brief description of the currently selected command option or data item. For example, as shown in Figure 2-4, if you select the **Export** option on the **Tools** menu, the message line explains that this option is used to "Convert dBASE files to other file formats." In the label or report layout editor, the message line might display the name, data type, width, and number of decimal places for a data base field or the expression used to compute a calculated field.

GETTING MORE HELP

dBASE IV, like many other programs, uses the F1 key as a general-purpose "Help" key. You can press F1 (Help) at any point—from the Control Center, the dot prompt, or any of the full-screen editors—to obtain a context-sensitive help message that describes the specific command or option you were using when you requested help. From the dot prompt, you can also request help by typing

```
HELP
```

To ask for help with a specific command, include the verb in the HELP command:

HELP *command verb*

The dBASE IV help system consists of a network of screens that are linked by their contents. The help system is divided into five sections—Dot Prompt Commands and Functions, Control Center, SQL Main Topics, Help on Help, and Reference—each of which has its own table of contents and hierarchy of information screens. The help screens describing menu options are organized along the same lines as the menus, but regardless of where you enter the help system, you can move easily to any related or unrelated subject.

The further you have progressed toward completing a command when you press F1 (Help), the more detailed the help message will be. For example, from the Control Center, with no menu active, pressing F1 (Help) calls up a general help screen describing the type of file displayed in the panel that contains the cursor. With any menu option selected, the help system displays a screen describing that command or option. Figure 2-7 illustrates the help screen that is displayed when you press F1 (Help) with the **DOS Utilities** option on the

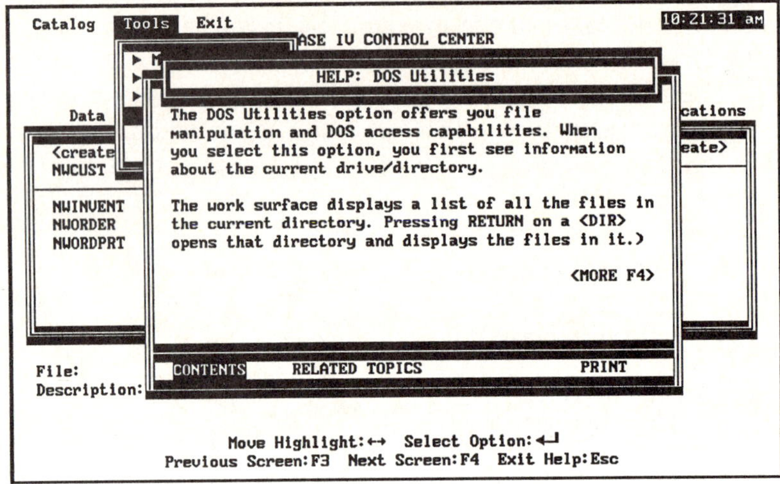

Figure 2-7.

A dBASE IV help screen

Control Center **Tools** menu highlighted. If you press F1 (Help) from the bare dot prompt, dBASE IV cannot guess which screen you need to see, so it presents the table of contents for the Dot Prompt section of the help system. If you ask for help in the middle of typing a command, dBASE IV displays a help screen that summarizes the syntax and function of the command.

The text of the help screen is displayed in a pop-up *help box* with a title at the top that identifies the topic. At the bottom of the help box is a horizontal light-bar menu with buttons that you can select to navigate through the help system. At the bottom of the display screen (not the help box), the navigation line and message line summarize the keys used to select menu options and move through the help system.

You select help box buttons with the same cursor movement and command keys used in the other dBASE IV menus. You can select a button either by using the LEFT ARROW and RIGHT ARROW keys to highlight the desired option and then pressing ENTER, or by pressing the first letter of the button name. At any level of the help system table of contents, the F4 (Next) and F3 (Previous) keys display more specific and more general lists of topics, respectively. Within a topic, these keys advance you to the next screen on the same topic and return you to the previous screen. To exit the help system and return to the point from which you requested help, press ESC. If you invoked the help system from the dot prompt, the help box remains on the screen for reference while you type your next command. The cursor movement and function keys used to navigate through the help system are listed in Table 2-3.

Control Key	Command Key	Function
	F1 (Help)	Access the online help system
	letter	Select the button (option) whose description begins with *letter*
	F4 (Next)	From the table of contents, display a more specific list of topics. From within a topic, advance to the next screen page, if any, on the same topic
	F3 (Previous)	From the table of contents, display a more general list of topics. From within a topic, back up to the next screen page, if any, on the same topic
	ENTER	Select the highlighted button (option) or pick list item
	ESC	Exit from the help system
CTRL-D	RIGHT ARROW or spacebar	Advance to the next button (option)
CTRL-S	LEFT ARROW or BACKSPACE	Back up to the previous button (option)
CTRL-X	DOWN ARROW	Advance to the next pick list option
CTRL-E	UP ARROW	Back up to the previous pick list option
	HOME	Move to the first (top) option on the active pick list
	END	Move to the last (bottom) option on the active pick list
CTRL-C	PGDN	Display the next group of items in the active pick list
CTRL-R	PGUP	Display the previous group of items in the active pick list

Table 2-3.

The dBASE IV Help System Cursor Movement and Command Keys

The help box options are as follows·

CONTENTS	Display the table of contents for the section of the help system corresponding to the environment that was active when you requested help.
RELATED TOPICS	Display a pick list of help topics related to the currently displayed screen. You can select a topic by highlighting the description and pressing ENTER.
BACKUP	Back up to the help screen displayed immediately prior to the current screen (not necessarily the previous screen "page" if a topic has multiple pages). This option allows you to retrace your steps through a series of screens in reverse order.
PRINT	Print the current help screen. dBASE IV strips out the borders of the help box to facilitate using a printer that does not support the extended ASCII graphics characters.

When you work at the dot prompt, dBASE IV responds to incorrect commands by popping up a dialog box with three buttons, or options: **Cancel**, **Edit**, and **Help**. If you select the **Help** button, dBASE IV displays the help screen summarizing the syntax and usage of the command verb, just as if you had pressed F1 (Help) while typing the command.

Although the help system is comprehensive, you cannot learn to use dBASE IV by reading the help screens alone. The online help does serve, however, as a concise guide to the syntax and use of all dBASE IV commands, functions, and editors so you can review a difficult concept or get a quick answer to a question.

EXITING dBASE IV

From the Control Center, you can exit dBASE IV and go to the operating system (MS-DOS or OS/2) by selecting the **Quit to DOS** option from the **Exit** menu. From the dot prompt, you exit by typing

```
QUIT
```

SUMMARY

This chapter introduced two of the dBASE IV working environments—the Control Center menu system and the dot prompt—that will be described more fully in the rest of this book. Even if you already prefer one of these two command modes, it is a good idea to spend some time experimenting with both as you read the next few chapters. The menu system can serve as an easy, unintimidating introduction to dBASE IV, since using the menus does not require that you memorize command syntax. Also, every user must know how to work with the menu system in the full-screen editors and the layout editors used to define reports, labels, custom screens, and application menus. Even if you intend to work primarily at the dot prompt, practicing with the Control Center menus is a good way to familiarize yourself with a command structure that you will use extensively in later work with dBASE IV.

For users who at first feel more comfortable using the menus, some time spent working at command level may pay off later on. Once you surmount the initial learning barrier and gain experience, you may find that your preference for the menu system is not as strong as it was initially. Although some dBASE IV users stick to one mode exclusively, most people incorporate both into their working style—using the menus when they seem more convenient and the dot prompt when typing commands is more direct and expedient. The command-driven mode of operation also provides an easier transition into dBASE IV programming, where you *must* know how to type syntactically correct commands.

CHAPTER THREE

Planning and Designing a Data Base

Chapter 1 described the process of analyzing your requirements and compiling a list of the items of information you want to maintain using dBASE IV. One more preliminary step is required before you can begin entering data: you must translate your list of required items into a dBASE IV *file structure,* which serves as a kind of template, or blank format, for typing in the data.

You might visualize this step as roughly equivalent to designing a preprinted paper form on which the same information could be recorded. The design process includes deciding how much space to provide for each entry and what labels or headings to print on the form to remind you what to enter in each box or blank line.

DEFINING THE FIELDS

A dBASE IV data base can have up to 255 fields, which can total 4000 bytes (characters). Every item of information that you view as a discrete, self-contained entity should be a separate field. It is also a good idea to place in a separate field any item that you intend to use as a basis for selecting or sorting (rearranging) records. Even when it is not strictly necessary, this strategy will greatly simplify the commands and expressions you must use to specify your selection criteria and sorting instructions.

In a mailing list, for example, you might view the city, state, and ZIP code as a single logical unit—the last line of the mailing address—but if you need to send a special mailing to everyone who lives in the state of Texas or produce mailing labels in ZIP code order, it would be better to use three separate fields.

Names can be even more problematical. To print or view records in alphabetical order, you could create two separate fields for a person's first and last names, and combine them for printing reports and labels. But this structure is not flexible enough to accommodate all the variations you might find on your list, such as records having no first name, a company name instead of a person's name, or combined names like "John and Karen Smith" or "John Kelly and Mary Smith." One solution, which will be used in the National Widgets Customer File, is to use one field for the full name, entered exactly as it would be printed in a mailing address, and create another short character field for an account code or ID code, constructed from the last name or company name so that it can be used to determine alphabetical order.

This ID code field serves another important purpose and illustrates a general principle not limited in its applicability to name and address data bases: it can be used as a unique identifier for each person on the list. Many other types of data bases should also contain a field or combination of fields that uniquely identifies each record. Using techniques described in Chapter 9, you can retrieve any record almost instantly, even in a very large file, based on the contents of this field.

The ability to uniquely identify a record is crucial for many commands that operate on multiple data bases. For example, to display an order record together with data from the matching customer record, you must be sure that for each order, dBASE IV can find the right customer. To post transaction data to a customer record (add a transaction amount into a cumulative year-to-date total), dBASE IV must be able to match the transaction with one—and only one—customer record.

Often, it is immediately apparent what the unique field should be. In an inventory data base, it is the part number; in a patient list, it might be a preassigned medical record number; in a name and address list, you can easily construct an account code or ID code if one does not already exist. Keep in mind, when you assign these codes, that since you will use them to search for records, making them easy to remember or reconstruct will greatly facilitate the process of retrieving and editing specified records. An ID code consisting of part of a person's name or company name will be much easier to remember than a numeric account number that bears no relationship to the company it represents.

Not every data base has an obvious candidate for this unique identifier, and sometimes this is because none is required. To continue with the accounts receivable example, the Customer File needs a unique field, because each customer really should have only one record in this file. The related Order File might not have any unique combination of fields; one customer might have many orders, and if each order record represented one line item on an order form or invoice (one stocked item), there would be multiple records for the same customer on the same date, and with the same order number or invoice number.

When you define the data base structure, you must name the data base and provide five items of information to describe each field:

- *Field name* A name used to identify the field in lists displayed by dBASE IV and in commands that you type.
- *Data type* The type of information that may be entered into the field. dBASE IV recognizes six data types: character, numeric (fixed-point), floating-point, logical, date, and memo (the data types are described in detail later in this chapter).
- *Field width* The maximum number of characters you would ever need to enter into the field.
- *Decimals* The number of digits to the right of the decimal point in a numeric or floating-point field.
- *Index* Whether or not you want dBASE IV to automatically build and maintain an index based on the field (indexing is explained in Chapter 9).

All these terms are explained more fully in the following sections of this chapter.

File and Field Names

Before you finalize your data base structures, a few words about file and field names are in order. Developing a consistent scheme for assigning names to files and fields, so that the names clearly suggest the field contents and are easy to type and pronounce, will greatly enhance the "friendliness" and ease of use of a data base application, especially for coworkers not privy to the design process.

Under MS-DOS and OS/2, a file name consists of two parts separated by a period: a name consisting of up to eight characters and an optional three-character extension (the period is not displayed in directory listings). Like many other programs, dBASE IV uses the extension to distinguish the different types of files that it recognizes: DBF for data base, FRM for report format, LBL for label format, and so on. dBASE IV assigns these extensions automatically in most contexts, and for the most part, you need not type file extensions unless you wish to deviate from the defaults. When you define file names, you therefore have up to eight characters to work with.

A dBASE IV data base file name can consist of almost any combination of letters and numbers, except that you cannot use the single letters A through J as file names or begin a file name with a numeric digit. Spaces are not permitted in file names, but dBASE IV allows you to include any punctuation marks permitted by your operating system. (If you are unsure as to which symbols are prohibited, or if you use certain older communications programs, utilities, and disk format conversion programs that allow only letters and digits in file names, it is advisable to avoid using punctuation.)

If your application requires more than a few disk files—and even simple systems usually do—it is convenient to assign file names that help you easily identify the files that make up the system and manipulate them as a group. The dBASE IV file catalog, which is described in Chapter 19, is a powerful tool for organizing disk files, but when you work outside dBASE IV or use the **DOS Utilities** option in the **Tools** menu, the catalog does not help you identify files that belong together.

Including a common prefix in the names of all the files in an application makes it easy to see from a glance at the disk directory which files are part of the system. With only eight characters at your disposal, you will generally want to use no more than two or three for the prefix. The files in this book share the prefix NW for National Widgets. Instead of your company name, you might use a prefix like AR for accounts receivable, INV for an inventory data base, or DON for a donor tracking system.

Using the same prefix in the names of all the files in an application also enables you to take advantage of the ability of DOS, OS/2, and many operating system utility programs to recognize *wildcard* characters in file names and process files in groups. The two wildcard characters are the question mark (?), which stands for any single character, and the asterisk (*), which stands for any group of any number of characters. The common prefix thus enables you to display, copy, or back up with a single command all the files that make up an application. For example, you could display a directory of all the National Widgets files with the following command:

```
DIR NW*.*
```

You could back up only the National Widgets files from a hard disk to floppies, regardless of which other files are present in the same subdirectory, by typing

```
BACKUP C:NW*.* A:
```

When you work with a dBASE IV data base, fields are identified by their names. dBASE IV uses the field names as prompts in the default screens it presents for entering and editing data, and you must choose fields by name when you select from a list presented by one of the dBASE IV menus as well as when you type commands at the dot prompt.

dBASE IV field names can be up to ten characters long. A field name must begin with a letter, but it can otherwise contain any combination of letters and numbers. Strive to make your field names as descriptive and self-explanatory as possible within the ten-character limit. If you use ordinary words and standard abbreviations, your field names will be readable and easy to remember and type—for both you and your coworkers.

No spaces are permitted within a field name, and the only allowable embedded punctuation mark is the underscore (_). Some people feel that using the underscore to substitute for the prohibited blank space—for example, naming a field ZIP_CODE rather than ZIPCODE—greatly improves readability. Others find field names containing underscores too awkward to type. The field names in this book do not contain underscores; whether or not you use them is a matter of personal preference.

dBASE IV Data Types

dBASE IV recognizes six data types. Different kinds of calculations and comparisons are permitted on each, and data entered into the various field types is formatted and validated according to different rules. The six data types are as follows:

- *Character fields* can contain any keyboard characters, including letters, numbers, and punctuation marks.
- *Numeric fields* can contain only digits, a decimal point, and a minus sign. They are treated as fixed-point numbers, which means that only the number of decimal places specified in the structure is used in comparisons (although more digits may be considered significant in calculations).
- *Float fields* contain floating-point numbers, in which up to 15 digits are treated as significant in calculations, even if fewer digits are displayed. Float fields can contain only digits, a decimal point, and a minus sign.
- *Logical fields* can contain only the logical values "True" and "False," which are equivalent to "Yes" and "No." Only the characters T, t, Y, and y (for "True" or "Yes" values) and F, f, N, and n (for "False" or "No" values) can be entered into logical fields.
- *Date fields* contain valid calendar dates, usually displayed in *mm/dd/yy* format (for example, 07/05/92 for July 5, 1992).
- *Memo fields* are variable-length fields that can accommodate an almost unlimited amount of free-form text.

Assigning Field Widths

Specifying the field widths in a dBASE IV data base is analogous to deciding how long a line or how big a box to place on a printed form intended to accommodate the same data. The data base structure is more restrictive than a paper form, however. When you fill out a form, you can write smaller or squeeze an extra line of text between two others if the allotted space proves too small. dBASE IV gives you no such leeway.

With one important exception (memo fields, which are described in the next section, "Choosing the Appropriate Data Type"), dBASE IV stores data in *fixed-length fields*. This means that for each field, dBASE IV always stores the same number of characters—the number you assigned as the field width when you defined the file structure. If you leave a field partially or completely blank, it is filled to its maximum length with blank spaces. For example, if you make a name field 30 characters long and then enter "Susan Lee" into the field, the full 30 characters are stored on disk—the 9 characters you typed plus 21 blank spaces. Typing the number 525 into a numeric field 8 digits wide would result in storing 5 leading spaces, followed by the 3 digits you entered.

Making your fields too long wastes disk space, whereas if you make them too short, you will have to abbreviate in ways that may render the information less useful or less presentable. Although you should certainly give some thought to assigning field widths judiciously, you will probably guess wrong in a few instances. Don't worry about this, because it is easy to lengthen or shorten fields later on, even after you have entered data into the file. Keep in mind, however, that if you lengthen a field that is included in many of the system's data entry screens or reports, you may spend quite a bit of time editing these forms to accommodate the new field length.

You need only specify the widths of character, numeric, and float fields; dates are always 8 characters wide, logical fields take up 1 space, and memo fields require 10. Character fields can range in width from 1 to 254 characters, and numeric (fixed-point) and float fields can have up to 20 digits with up to 15 decimal places; numbers with zero decimal places are integers (whole numbers).

Numeric fields must be wide enough to accommodate the decimal point, if any, and to permit entry of the minus sign in a negative number. For example, if an account balance could range from –$10,000.00 to $10,000.00, the field must be 9 digits wide: 2 for the pennies, 1 for the decimal point, 5 for the dollars, and 1 for the minus sign. (Note that commas and dollar signs are not stored in numeric fields, although you can edit, display, and print numbers in this format.)

Choosing the Appropriate Data Type

Almost any kind of data can be stored in a character field, which can contain any combination of keyboard characters. By making all your fields character fields, however, you would sacrifice the ability to manipulate and validate data in special ways that are possible only with other data types. dBASE IV provides a variety of ways to convert data of one type to another, but it is best to avoid such complexity whenever possible.

Only numeric data can be used in mathematical calculations such as addition, multiplication, computing sums and averages, and compiling report totals and subtotals, so numeric or float fields should be used for data consisting solely of numeric digits that must be used in calculations. For example, in an order record, the selling price and quantity ordered should be numeric so you can multiply them to arrive at the extended price. A customer's year-to-date orders field should also be numeric, because it must accumulate the dollar value of all orders placed during the year, and because you might want to print this field on a report and total the column.

Float fields, because they use more significant digits, yield more accurate calculated results than numeric (fixed-point) fields. However, numeric fields give more predictable results when the results of calculations are compared to constants (arbitrary values), because they are not susceptible to round-off errors. For example, the floating-point number 1.0 might be stored internally as 0.999999999, which is not exactly equal to the constant 1.0, whereas a numeric field containing the value 1.0 is always considered equal to the constant. For this reason, you should use numeric fields for percentages and dollar amounts in business data bases, whereas scientific or engineering applications may require the greater accuracy of floating-point numbers.

If you do not foresee using a number in mathematical calculations, it may be preferable to store it in a character field. For example, because you would never do arithmetic on an area code, there is no advantage to making it a number, even though it consists entirely of numeric digits. Because numeric fields cannot contain embedded punctuation marks (except the decimal point), a telephone number or social security number (both of which contain dashes) should be a character field. And, as you will see later, it is easier to combine character fields for purposes such as building indexes than it is to mix data types.

There are other, subtler distinctions. In true numbers, leading zeros are meaningless (01001 has exactly the same numeric value as 1001); dBASE IV automatically strips leading zeros entered into numeric fields and replaces them with blank spaces. Thus, if you made a ZIP code a numeric field (assuming of course, that you had no foreign postal codes containing letters or ten-digit ZIP codes with embedded dashes), leading zeros would be removed from ZIP codes such as 01001, leaving it unclear to the post office whether you meant 01001, 10010, or something else entirely.

If you need to arrange records in numerical order based on the contents of a field, either the field must be numeric or you must add leading zeros so that all your entries in this field occupy the maximum field width. The reason is that dBASE IV sorts character data just as you would alphabetize. While the numeric digits come out in the right order—0 comes before 1, which comes before 2, and so on—character fields are alphabetized one character at a time, starting from the leftmost character. Just as any name beginning with A will come before any name beginning with B, regardless of the remaining letters, any character field that begins with 1 will come before one that begins with 2. Thus, 10 alphabetizes before 2, but not before 02.

Fields that contain the answers to yes-or-no questions should be assigned the logical data type. Since dBASE IV permits only the characters T, F, Y, N and their lowercase equivalents to be entered into logical fields, using a logical field rather than a character field makes it more difficult to enter a meaningless value inadvertently, such as by accidentally pressing U instead of Y.

Calendar dates should be stored in date fields to allow for the validations and specialized operations that are possible only with true dates. For example, dBASE IV will not permit the entry of erroneous dates such as 13/42/92 or 02/29/91 (1991 is not a leap year) in a date field. You can choose from several display formats for dates, including the popular *mm/dd/yy* ("American") and *mm-dd-yy* ("USA") formats. Regardless of the display format, dBASE IV can always arrange dates in true chronological order or compare two dates to determine which is earlier or later.

If you store a date in a character field, however, attempting to sort or compare dates would be subject to some of the same problems outlined earlier for numeric data. Because character fields are alphabetized from left to right, the two digits representing the month in a date stored in *yy/mm/dd* format are examined before the two digits that represent the year. Any date in the month of January would therefore be "alphabetized" earlier than any date in February, regardless of the year, because 01 comes before 02 in alphabetical order.

dBASE IV also supports date arithmetic. You can add a number to a date to yield a valid calendar date the specified number of days in the future, subtract a number from a date to yield a past date, and subtract two dates to determine the elapsed time in days. All these calculations are impossible without programming if the dates are stored in character or numeric fields.

Memo fields are often the best way to store variable amounts of free-form text. dBASE IV provides a rudimentary word processor for editing memo fields that offers far better editing capabilities, including word wrap and a search-and-replace command, than the commands used to edit character fields. You can view and edit a memo field in a small window on a custom data entry form or "zoom" the field to fill the entire screen, and you can reformat memo fields to conform to any margins for screen or printer output. Furthermore, if you had more than 254 characters of text (the maximum width of a character field), you would need to divide the entry among two or more fields, and this would make it awkward to enter and edit the text.

A data base can have more than one memo field. The text entered into all the memo fields in a data base is stored in a separate file on disk. In the main data base file, a memo field occupies only 10 characters, whether or not you have entered any text. Space in the memo text file is allocated dynamically in fixed-length blocks that are 512 characters long by default.

The average length of the text and the number of records that contain entries in this field determine whether using a character or memo field will result in the most efficient use of storage space. When a relatively small percentage of the records in a file have associated text, using a memo field can result in a considerable savings in disk space, compared to a long character field, which would remain blank for most of the records. If more than half the records will contain text, the choice of data type should be based on ease of editing and the anticipated length of the text. For applications in which most records require more than 254 characters of text, a memo field is easier to enter and edit than two or more long character fields. If few records are likely to require more than 200 characters, however, you would be wasting space by using a memo field, since at least 512 characters will be used to store each entry. (You can specify a larger block size, as described in Chapter 18, to speed up access if the average size of the memos is very large, but you cannot reduce the block size.)

In summary, a field should be evaluated according to the criteria detailed in this section to see if it requires any of the special treatment that is possible with numeric, float, date, logical, and memo fields. If not, it should be a character field.

PLANNING THE DATA BASE STRUCTURES

After you have identified all the information that must go into your data bases, you can begin to lay out the file structures. If your application seems simple and straightforward, it will be tempting to turn on the computer, start up dBASE IV, and begin creating the data bases. But even in a small system that requires only one file, a little advance planning on paper will greatly reduce the amount of time you will spend later making changes. Keep in mind, however, that it is almost impossible to predict all your needs and that you do not have to be permanently committed to your original file structures—you can modify them later without losing data.

The design of the file structures should be guided by the overall goals for any dBASE IV system:

- To carry out all the required operations and produce all the necessary reports
- To use disk space efficiently
- To optimize the performance of the system
- To maximize the accuracy of the information in the data base

In Chapter 1, a data base was described as a group of records that belong together logically and share the same format. Conversely, data that requires substantially different sets of fields should be placed in separate files. For example, the data National Widgets must maintain on its customers requires fields for the account number, name, address, phone number, and year-to-date totals, whereas the order information consists of the order date, part number, price, quantity, and extended price.

With 255 fields available, you might consider putting order data into the Customer File by including multiple sets of identical fields. However, any given customer might have no orders, 1, or 50. If you created five sets of order fields in the Customer File, you would be wasting space if most customers had fewer than five orders, and you would have to create duplicate customer records for those with more. This type of "one-to-many" relationship—one customer might have many orders—generally calls for two files.

Since dBASE IV allows you to work with more than one data base at a time and link them based on a field or fields common to both, you can omit from a file any field that you can "look up" in another. For example, there is no need to include a field for the item description in the Order File, because this information can be retrieved from the Inventory File based on a match on the part number. You can thus eliminate a great deal of redundancy, save disk space, and in some cases save time. You might have several hundred inventory items but thousands of order records. If the description field were 25 characters long, 300 copies of this field would occupy 7500 bytes on disk, compared to 75,000 if this field were included in the Order File.

In general, you need not create fields that can be calculated from other fields in the same or another data base, but sometimes including a few such "unnecessary" fields is worthwhile because it gives you instant access to important information. For example, a customer's total orders could be calculated by adding up all the individual orders, but this can be a time-consuming process,

CUSTOMER FILE

1	Account number or code	ACCOUNT	C	~~8~~ 10
8	Name	CONTACT	C	25
2	Company name	COMPANY	C	25
3	Address	ADDRESS	C	25
	~~City, State, Zip~~	~~CITY~~	~~C~~	~~25~~
7	Phone number	TELEPHONE	C	8
9	Type of computer equipment	EQUIPMENT	C	~~28~~ 100
10	First order date	FIRSTORDER	D	
11	Most recent order date	LASTORDER	D	
13	Year-to-date orders	~~YEARTODATE~~ YTDORDERS	N	10 2
14	Total orders	TOTORDERS	N	10 2
	~~Year-to-date payments~~			
4	City	CITY	C	20
5	State	STATE	C	2
6	ZIP Code	ZIP	~~N~~ C	~~8~~ 10
15	Comments	COMMENTS	M	
12	Is credit OK?	CREDITOK	L	

Figure 3-1.

The Customer File design worksheet

one that is best carried out for the entire file in a batch, rather than while you are waiting impatiently to see the results for a single customer. If you store the order total in the Customer File, it is available instantly for viewing on the screen or printing in a report.

One good way to lay out the data base structures is to start with a blank sheet of paper for each file. Working from your sample documents and lists of required information, and beginning with the file you understand best, write down all the fields you will need. Next, go back and assign field names, types, lengths, and decimal places.

Be sure to give the sequence of the fields some thought. The placement of fields on the default data entry and editing screens is determined by their positions in the file structure; thus fields should be arranged in the order in which you would most frequently want to enter the data. You need not be overly concerned about writing down all the items in exactly the right order, however; once you have accounted for all the required data, you can go back over your lists and number the fields to remind yourself of the correct sequence when you create the file structures. Figures 3-1, 3-2, and 3-3 illustrate the file design worksheets for the National Widgets system.

ORDER FILE

1	Customer account code	ACCOUNT	C	10	
4	Product category	CATEGORY	C	6	
5	Part number	PARTNUMBER	C	6	
~~6~~	~~Description~~	~~DESCRIPTION~~	~~C~~	~~25~~	
6 ~~7~~	Quantity ordered	QUANTITY	N	4	
7 ~~8~~	Unit price	~~UNIT~~PRICE	N	7	2
8 ~~9~~	Subtotal (quantity x price)	SUBTOTAL	N	7	2
9 ~~10~~	Discount	DISCOUNT	N	7	2
10 ~~11~~	Invoice total for item (Subtotal - discount)	INVAMOUNT	N	7	2
2	Invoice number	INVNUMBER	C ~~N~~	5	
3	Invoice date	INVDATE	D		

Figure 3-2.

The Order File design worksheet

INVENTORY FILE

1	Product category	CATEGORY	C	6	
2	Part number	PARTNUMBER	C	6	
3	Description	DESCRIP~~TION~~	C	25	
5	Most recent cost	COST	N	7	2
6	Unit selling price	PRICE	N	7	2
4	Preferred vendor (code)	VENDOR	C	8	

Figure 3-3.

The Inventory File design worksheet

ESTIMATING FILE SIZES

The total record length is an important number: together with the anticipated number of records in the file, it enables you to estimate how much disk space you will need for your application. dBASE IV cannot work with a data base that spans multiple disk files or multiple floppy disks, although you can extend your storage capacity somewhat by keeping some files on your hard disk and some on floppies.

To a limited extent, you can split a large file into several parts and work with the segments in sequence, but this would prevent you from being able to cross-reference information in different sections of the file. Suppose, for example, that you have little room on your hard disk, and you want to maintain a 2-megabyte mailing list data base on 1.2-megabyte floppy disks. If you split the list in half alphabetically, it would be relatively easy to retrieve and edit records, since you would always know on which disk a particular name could be found. However, dividing the data alphabetically would make it impossible to produce a single set of mailing labels in ZIP code order.

If you use floppy disks, you should also realize that because of the way that the operating system (MS-DOS or OS/2) updates the disk directory, switching disks with a data base file open can severely damage the file or the disk directory. In general, it is safest to plan your application so that all the disk files it requires are available to dBASE IV without your having to switch disks.

In the National Widgets system, the Customer File has a record length of 273 bytes, and the company anticipates having 1100 customers in the near future. The eventual size of this file will therefore be 273 * 1100 = 300,300 bytes. Estimating the size of the memo text file is a less precise calculation. If 20 percent of the records contain entries in the COMMENTS field, and most have between 500 and 1000 characters, most entries will require two 512-byte blocks, and the memo text file (NWCUST.DBT) will require approximately 1100 * 0.20 * 1024 = 225,280 bytes.

You should carry out a similar calculation for each data base file in your application. As you will see in later chapters, a dBASE IV application requires many types of disk files besides data base files, some of which may be quite large. Furthermore, you should never fill any disk (floppy or hard) to more than about 70 to 80 percent of its total capacity. In some situations, you may need even more work space. For example, sorting a file requires that you have free disk space equal to the size of the original file. Keep in mind also that the dBASE IV program itself occupies between 2.5 and 5 megabytes of disk space (depending on whether you have the Standard Edition or the Developers Edition and on how many of the optional files you install).

The kind of rough estimate outlined here can help you determine the hardware requirements for your system. For example, if you estimate the combined size of your data base files at over 5 million bytes, you can rule out running the system on a 10-megabyte hard disk or on a hard disk that is already nearly filled to capacity (unless you can temporarily back up and erase other files to provide more work space when necessary).

Naturally, it is preferable to do these calculations before you buy a new computer devoted to managing your data bases. If you discover that you are close to exceeding the limitations of your present hardware, you may want to delete or shorten some fields, or reduce the number of records retained in historical files. National Widgets, for example, might choose to maintain only the current month's orders in the Order File instead of an entire year of detail.

CREATING A DATA BASE STRUCTURE

Once you have settled on your file structures, you can use a specialized layout editor, the data base design work surface, to create the empty data bases.

From the Menus

To access the data base design work surface from the Control Center, you select the <**create**> option from the **Data** panel. The name of the new data base is assigned later, when you save the structure.

From the Dot Prompt

From the dot prompt, you use the CREATE command to access the data base design work surface. You can include the name of the new data base in the command, as follows:

CREATE *data base name*

If you simply type CREATE, dBASE IV displays the message "Enter the name of the new file:" to prompt you for the data base name.

Using the Data Base Design Screen

The data base design work surface presents a table into which you type the file structure specifications. Fields are listed vertically on the screen, with columns for field names, types, widths, decimal places, and index information. When you create a new file, the table is initially blank. Sixteen fields fit on the screen at once, but when you fill up the screen, the display scrolls down to allow you to enter another group of 16 fields, until you reach the limit of 255. As you define fields, dBASE IV displays the number of characters remaining (of the total, 4000) in the upper right corner of the screen. Figure 3-4 illustrates the appearance of the data base design screen after defining the National Widgets Customer File.

If you are new to dBASE IV, the data base design screen will be your first introduction to the dBASE IV layout editors and the full-screen editing commands used to enter and update data base fields and text. As in all the full-screen edit modes, there is a menu bar at the top of the screen; like the other layout editors, the data base design screen always includes the status display at the bottom. All layout editors share some common menus and menu options and use fundamentally similar cursor movement and editing keys, with a few minor differences that depend on context.

As you type your field specifications, you can press ENTER to advance from one item to the next and use the arrow keys to move up, down, left, and right to make changes or correct mistakes. A light-bar cursor indicates how wide each entry can be. If you fill up the allotted space when you are entering the field name or width, the cursor advances automatically to the next item; if not, you must press ENTER or one of the arrow keys. dBASE IV does not require—or allow—you to enter unnecessary information such as the widths of date,

Layout Organize Append Go To Exit 9:41:48 am

Bytes remaining: 3728

Num	Field Name	Field Type	Width	Dec	Index
1	ACCOUNT	Character	10		N
2	COMPANY	Character	25		N
3	ADDRESS	Character	25		N
4	CITY	Character	20		N
5	STATE	Character	2		N
6	ZIP	Character	10		N
7	TELEPHONE	Character	8		N
8	CONTACT	Character	25		N
9	EQUIPMENT	Character	100		N
10	FIRSTORDER	Date	8		N
11	LASTORDER	Date	8		N
12	CREDITOK	Logical	1		N
13	YTDORDERS	Numeric	10	2	N
14	TOTORDERS	Numeric	10	2	N
15	COMMENTS	Memo	10		N

Database C:\dbase4\NWCUST Field 1/15 Caps

Enter the field name. Insert/Delete field:Ctrl-N/Ctrl-U

Field names begin with a letter and may contain letters, digits and underscores

Figure 3-4.

Creating the National Widgets Customer File

logical, and memo fields (which are always 8, 1, and 10 characters, respectively). You can move the cursor into the **Decimals** column only for numeric and float fields, since this entry does not apply to the other data types.

dBASE IV assumes that most fields will be character fields, and when you define a new field, the default data type displayed in the **Field Type** column is "Character." If you in fact want to create a character field, you can simply press ENTER to confirm the default and move on to the **Width** column. There are two ways to change the data type: you can type the first letter, either in uppercase or lowercase; or, if you aren't sure which type you want, you can press the spacebar to cycle through the possible choices and press ENTER to confirm your selection when the type you want is displayed. When you select the data type by typing the first letter, do not press ENTER afterward—dBASE IV expects only a single character of input and advances the cursor automatically to the next column. If you do press ENTER, dBASE IV will interpret this keystroke as your entry in the next column—that is, as an attempt to move past the **Width** column without entering a valid width—and will display the "Illegal field width" error message at the bottom of the screen.

As in all of the full-screen and layout editors, dBASE IV displays additional status information, a concise summary of available commands, and a brief reminder of the purpose or usage of the currently selected option on the status, navigation, and message lines at the bottom of the screen. For example, with the cursor in the **Type** column, the navigation line displays the message "Change field type:Spacebar." As you press the spacebar, the message line displays a description of each field type. For example, with **Numeric** selected, this line reads, "Numeric fields contain signed numbers that may be either integer or decimal."

In a file structure with 15 or 20 fields, the arrow keys generally suffice for moving around on the screen and making changes. For larger structures or more extensive editing, you can use the commands on the **Go To** menu to jump quickly to the top or bottom of the structure (the first or last field) or to any field, specified by number. Table 3-1 lists the cursor movement and editing

Control Key	**Command Key**	**Function**
	F10 (Menu)	Activate the menu system
	ALT-*letter*	Activate the menu system and pull down the menu whose description begins with *letter*
	ENTER	Select the highlighted option or item from the active menu, panel, or pick list
	letter	Select the menu option whose description begins with *letter*
CTRL-W	CTRL-END	Save the structure and exit
CTRL-Q	ESC	Exit without saving the new or modified structure
CTRL-E	UP ARROW	Back up to the previous field in the data base structure table
CTRL-X	DOWN ARROW	Move down to the next field in the data base structure table
CTRL-D	RIGHT ARROW	Move the cursor right one character
CTRL-S	LEFT ARROW	Move the cursor left one character

Table 3-1.

Command Keys Used in the Data Base Design Screen

Control Key	Command Key	Function
CTRL-I	TAB	Advance to the next column
CTRL-A	SHIFT-TAB or CTRL-LEFT ARROW	Back up to the previous column
CTRL-F	CTRL-RIGHT ARROW	Move the cursor to the end of the current entry, then the end of the current column, then the next column, then the next field
CTRL-Z	HOME	Move to the first column
CTRL-B	END	Move to the last column
CTRL-C	PGDN	Display the next group of 16 fields
CTRL-R	PGUP	Display the previous group of 16 fields
CTRL-G	DEL	Delete the character at the cursor position
	BACKSPACE	Delete the character to the left of the cursor
CTRL-T or CTRL-Y		Delete the characters from the cursor to the end of the word
CTRL-U		Delete the selected field from the structure
CTRL-V	INS	Turn Insert mode on (if it is off) or off (if it is on)
CTRL-N		Insert a new field before (above) the selected field

Table 3-1.

Command Keys Used in the Data Base Design Screen (*continued*)

commands used to create a new data base or modify the structure of an existing file.

As in the Control Center, you activate the horizontal light-bar menu at the top of the screen by pressing F10 (Menu) or by using the ALT key in combination with the first letter of one of the menu options to jump directly to the corresponding menu. Note that the menus are available only when a field is highlighted; if you have just pressed ENTER to advance past the last defined field, dBASE IV ignores the command keys that activate menus.

The data base design screen menu bar has five options, not all of which are directly related to creating a new data base structure. Keep in mind that the same work surface is also used to modify the structure of an existing file, add records to a file, and change the "organization" of a file by sorting or indexing. The structure of the menu is diagrammed in Figure 3-5.

If you define 255 fields, dBASE IV assumes that you are finished. With a smaller file structure, you can exit the data base screen and return to the command mode from which you invoked it (either the Control Center or the dot prompt) by choosing the **Save changes and exit** option from the **Exit** menu. If you wish to exit without saving your new or modified structure, you can select **Abandon changes and exit** instead.

There are two other ways to exit the data base design screen. With the cursor positioned below the last defined field, you can press ENTER, or, from anywhere in the structure, you can press either of the two standard "exit and save" keys used throughout dBASE IV: CTRL-END or CTRL-W. (You can think of CTRL-END as meaning "End this editing session and save my changes," and CTRL-W as "Write my changes to disk and exit.") When you exit via the **Exit** menu, dBASE IV asks you to confirm your intention with the prompt "Press ENTER key to confirm. Press any other key to resume." If you press ENTER, dBASE IV asks, "Input data records now? (Y/N)." You can press Y ("Yes") to move immediately to the Edit screen (described in Chapter 4) and begin entering data, or N ("No") if you are not ready to begin entering data.

You can save your structure without exiting from the data base design screen by selecting the **Save this database file structure** option from the **Layout** menu. If you have not already named the data base, dBASE IV prompts you to enter the file name the first time you choose this option. Each time you repeat the command, this name appears as a default, which you can change if you wish.

dBASE IV saves the data base structure in a disk file with the eight-character file name you specified and the extension DBF (for "data base file"). If the structure contains memo fields, dBASE IV also creates a file with the same first name as the DBF file and the extension DBT (for "data base text") to store the text entered into the memo fields. If you entered "Yes" in the **Index** column for any field, dBASE IV also prepares to build the specified indexes. (Indexes are explained in Chapter 9.)

In addition to the file name, you can enter a description of the contents or purpose of the file by selecting the **Edit database description** option from the **Layout** menu. This description, which can be up to 80 characters long, is stored in the file catalog and is displayed, together with the full path name, under the Control Center file name panels whenever the data base name is highlighted.

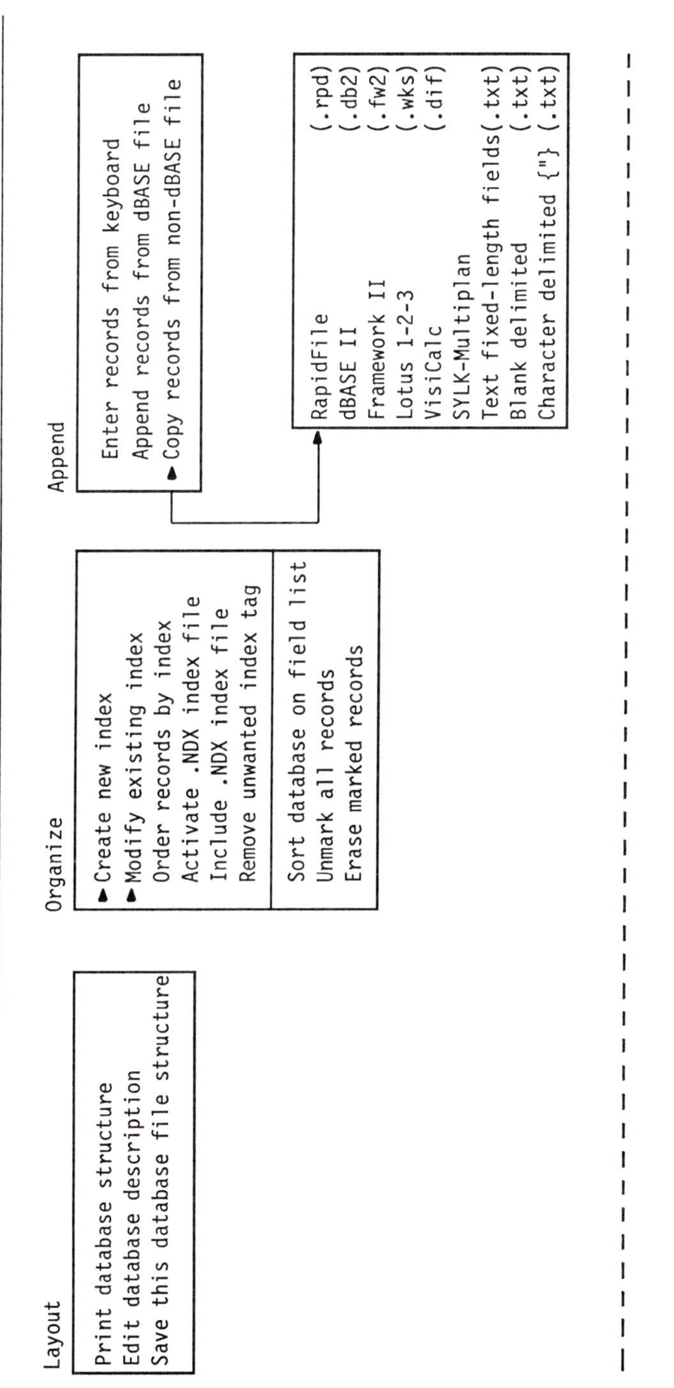

Figure 3-5.

The structure of the data base design screen menus

For example, you might assign the description "Customer name, address, and summary data" for the National Widgets Customer File.

After you create a new data base, dBASE IV leaves the file open, or active. If you are working in the Control Center, the name of the new file is displayed above the horizontal bar in the **Data** panel, and if you entered a longer description, this text is displayed at the bottom of the screen, below the path name. If you are working at the dot prompt with the status display on, the name of the new file appears in the second segment of the status bar.

Printing a File Structure

It is a good idea to print a copy of each of your file structures and keep these listings on hand whenever you are working with the data bases, so you can see at a glance all the relevant information about each of your files. The printout includes, in a tabular form similar to the screen display, the field specifications you have defined as well as a header consisting of the name of the file, the number of records it contains (0 for a new empty file structure), and the date the file was last updated (modified in any way). At the bottom of the field list is the record length, or the number of bytes occupied by one record (obtained by totaling the individual field widths).

From the Menus

From the data base design work surface, you can print a copy of the file structure by selecting the **Print database structure** option from the **Layout** menu.

From the Dot Prompt

From the dot prompt, you can view the structure of the active data base file by typing

```
LIST STRUCTURE
```

or

```
DISPLAY STRUCTURE
```

By including the phrase TO PRINT in the command, you can generate a printed listing at the same time the structure is displayed on the screen.

The difference between LIST STRUCTURE and DISPLAY STRUCTURE is that the DISPLAY command pauses when the screen is full, to allow you to read the display at your leisure, and then it instructs you to "Press any key to continue . . . ." DISPLAY STRUCTURE is best for viewing data base structures that have many fields. LIST STRUCTURE displays the entire structure without pause, which is fine if all the fields fit on a single screen. It is also more suitable for printing the structure, since the printout will not be disrupted by the "Press any key to continue . . ." message. The printout of the structure of the National Widgets Customer File is illustrated in Figure 3-6.

If you examine the structure printout carefully, you will note that the listed record size is one greater than the sum of the field widths (273 instead of 272 in the Customer File). dBASE IV sets aside one extra character in each record to store a deletion marker. As Chapter 4 explains in detail, when you request that a record be deleted, dBASE IV does not instantly erase the record from the disk—it simply marks the record as deleted. If you wish, you can configure

```
Structure for database: C:\DBASE4\NWCUST.DBF
Number of data records:        0
Date of last update   : 09/06/88
Field  Field Name  Type       Width      Dec       Index
    1  ACCOUNT     Character     10                    N
    2  COMPANY     Character     25                    N
    3  ADDRESS     Character     25                    N
    4  CITY        Character     20                    N
    5  STATE       Character      2                    N
    6  ZIP         Character     10                    N
    7  TELEPHONE   Character      8                    N
    8  CONTACT     Character     25                    N
    9  EQUIPMENT   Character    100                    N
   10  FIRSTORDER  Date           8                    N
   11  LASTORDER   Date           8                    N
   12  CREDITOK    Logical        1                    N
   13  YTDORDERS   Numeric       10        2           N
   14  TOTORDERS   Numeric       10        2           N
   15  COMMENTS    Memo          10                    N
** Total **                     273
```

Figure 3-6.

The printed Customer File structure

dBASE IV to ignore "deleted" records, or you can use a separate command to remove them permanently from the data base.

STRATEGIES FOR TESTING WITH SAMPLE DATA

Before you actually begin to add records to a data base, give some thought to your initial testing strategy. No matter how much advance planning you do, it is impossible to anticipate every conceivable variation in the data that must be entered, much less all the ways you will want to select and sort data to extract useful information from your files.

Although dBASE IV allows you to change the structure of a data base without losing information that has already been entered, it is best to make these changes while your files are still small. For example, if you add a field to the structure, you will have to call up each existing record to enter data into the new field; shortening a field may force you to search for entries that were truncated and should be edited to fit more gracefully within the new field width.

Your initial testing should be designed to help you verify the following:

- That you have included all necessary fields and have eliminated extraneous fields that are rarely filled in
- That your field widths are neither too long nor too short
- That you have chosen the most appropriate data type for each field
- That you can carry out all necessary calculations
- That you can establish required linkages and carry out transfers of information between files
- That you can specify your selection and sorting criteria
- That you can produce all the requested screen displays, reports, and printed forms

To carry out this testing, you must enter some sample data—usually between 25 and 100 records—into each data base file in your system. The test data should be drawn from your real application, not from your imagination, to ensure that it is representative of the full range of values that the system will eventually handle. When you invent data for testing purposes, there is a strong tendency to make the data conform to the file structures, rather than presenting the challenges that will enable you to verify that your file structures are correct and complete.

During the testing phase, you will gain valuable insight into some of the non-computer-related problems you may encounter as you convert from manual to computerized procedures. You will uncover any difficulties associated with gleaning the required information from the manual system and interpreting the input documents, and you will be able to estimate how long the initial data entry will take. Any special preparations, such as assigning ID codes or calculating beginning balances, will be brought to your attention, so you can begin to work on these preliminaries early enough to keep the system implementation on schedule.

Entering the test data will help you clarify the data entry sequence. You will be able to outline which fields must be filled in first, so that others may be calculated, and which fields should not be entered at all, because they will be derived from data in other fields or files. Knowing how long data entry will take can also help you realistically evaluate how much historical data or transaction detail to enter into the data base.

SUMMARY

The initial data base design phase is an essential, and often overlooked, part of the system development process. The mechanics of creating the data bases—using the data base design screen to build the file structures—are easy compared to the preliminary planning steps. Before you begin creating the data bases that will make up your application, you must identify the information the system will track, decide how many data base files you need and which items of information belong in each, and choose appropriate field lengths and data types. Before you can begin entering data, you must outline the startup procedures and data entry sequence, and define a strategy for testing the system with a realistic set of sample data.

If you have no prior experience with data base design, the planning process can be difficult and confusing, and it will be further complicated if you have no parallel manual record-keeping system. In order to finalize the data base structures, you may have to scrutinize your business or organization and any existing manual procedures more closely than you ever have before, and this examination can be traumatic for the entire staff.

While the planning, design, and testing phases can be difficult and time-consuming, these steps are crucial to the successful development of a computerized data base system. dBASE IV gives you a great deal of flexibility to change data base structures without losing information that you have already entered, and no matter how careful your advance planning was, you will undoubtedly need to make changes to handle contingencies you could not have predicted in advance. Nevertheless, the time that you spend laying out your file structures and planning the flow of information through the system in advance will pay off later on as the application grows in size and complexity.

CHAPTER FOUR

Entering and Updating Data

Once you have defined the structure for a data base, you can begin to enter data and perform the routine daily maintenance procedures required to keep the information accurate and up to date. You will need to add new records, call up existing records to view the data on screen, page forward or backward through the file to examine a range of records, edit individual fields, and remove records you no longer need.

dBASE IV allows you to carry out these activities by means of a set of full-screen editors, all of which present a template (a data entry form) derived from your file structure and offer a full complement of commands for moving around the screen to add, delete, or edit data. You can switch at will between the two display styles briefly described in Chapter 1: the "ledger card," or "file card," style, which displays the fields in a record vertically on one or more screens, and the "spreadsheet" style, which displays 17 or more records at a time, one per line, with the fields lined up in columns.

OPENING AND CLOSING DATA BASE FILES

Before you can work with a data base—to add, edit, display, or delete records—it must be open, or active. When you *open* a file, a process often referred to as *using* the file, dBASE IV reads the structure from the disk and retains in memory all the essential information recorded there, including the field names, lengths, and data types; the date the file was last updated; and the total number of records—all the information you see when you display or print the file structure. Once a data base is in use, or open, all subsequent commands act on that file, until you *close* it, or make it inactive.

As described in Chapter 2, you open a data base from the Control Center by highlighting the file name in the **Data** panel and pressing ENTER. dBASE IV pops up a dialog box that offers three options: **Use file, Modify structure/order**, and **Display data**. To simply open the file, without displaying or editing records, you can choose the **Use file** option.

Using this command sequence is not the only way to open a data base, but it is the one that most clearly illustrates the distinction between opening a file and viewing or updating data. You can open a data base and immediately begin editing by choosing **Display data** rather than **Use file** from the dialog box described in the previous paragraph. There is also a function key shortcut—you can highlight the file name in the Control Center **Data** panel and press F2 (Data) to open the data base and move directly to one of the full-screen edit modes. Finally, as noted in Chapter 3, after you create a new data base, dBASE IV leaves the file open, on the assumption that you will want to begin adding records right away.

The distinction between opening a file and displaying or editing records will become clearer as you learn to use commands that do not directly display data, such as those for designing and printing reports or calculating statistics. If you try to select a Control Center command that requires an open file but you do not have a data base open, a message box pops up to remind you, "Please put a database file or view into use first." At command level, dBASE IV prompts you for the file name with the message "No database in use. Enter filename:." You can either type in the file name or press SHIFT-F1 (Pick) to invoke a pick list of data base files and select a data base from this list. After you provide the data base name, dBASE IV opens the specified file and proceeds to execute your command. If no data base is open, and you do not want to open one, you can press ESC when dBASE IV prompts you to enter a file name to cancel your command and return to the dot prompt.

There are several easy ways to determine whether a data base is open, or which one is open. In the Control Center, the name of the open data base is displayed above the horizontal line in the **Data** panel. Whenever the status display is on, the full path name of the active file appears in the second segment of the status bar. From the dot prompt, if you prefer to work with the status display off, you can verify which file is open by typing DISPLAY STRUCTURE.

If a data base is already open when you try to open another, dBASE IV closes the open file, and the new data base takes its place as the currently active file. (dBASE IV also permits you to open more than one file at a time, using methods described in Chapter 17.) If you want to close the active file without opening another one, highlight the file name in the Control Center menu and press ENTER. Because the file is already open, there is no **Use file** option in the pop-up dialog box; in its place is a **Close file** option, which closes the selected data base without opening another.

It is important to remember to close a file when you are finished with it, for reasons that are not intuitively obvious. dBASE IV must always know how many records a file currently contains, and normally this number is retained and updated in memory while you work with a file and stored on disk only when you close the data base. If you reboot or turn off the computer after opening a data base and adding records, this vital statistic will not be recorded on disk. The next time you try to work with the data base, you will discover that any new records added during the interrupted work session are inaccessible, because even though records are saved one at a time as they are entered, dBASE IV cannot find any record with a number higher than the record count stored with the file structure.

Chapter 18 describes how to use the AUTOSAVE configuration setting to force dBASE IV to update the record count automatically after each new record is added to a data base, but this added measure of safety will slow down data entry. If you do not yet know how to use the AUTOSAVE setting, or do not want to pay the price in performance, it is safest to close a file as soon as you are finished working with it. You might even want to close and then reopen a file periodically during a long data entry session, just to make sure that a power failure or hardware crash does not leave you with a large number of new records and a mismatched record count. It is also prudent to close a file before you walk away from the computer if you share your office and your computer equipment with coworkers who are not aware of the danger of rebooting in the middle of a work session with dBASE IV.

VIEWING AND EDITING RECORDS

When you move from the Control Center menu into full-screen editing for the first time in a work session, records are displayed in the spreadsheet-style tabular format referred to as the Browse screen. (If the active data base is empty, dBASE IV instead displays the forms-style Edit screen, which is better suited for adding new records.) You can switch at any time from the Browse screen to the Edit screen, or from Edit to Browse, by pressing F2 (Data).

You can leave either full-screen edit mode and return to the Control Center by selecting the **Exit** option from the **Exit** menu (or by using several other methods that will be described shortly). The next time you invoke the full-screen editor, dBASE IV returns to the same data display format (Browse or Edit) that was in force last. When you use F2 (Data) to switch between the Browse and Edit screens, or if you return to the Control Center and then invoke either full-screen editor again, the same record remains selected. You can use the cursor movement and editing command keys listed in Table 4-1 to move around the screen to view, enter, and update data.

In the Browse display, records are laid out horizontally in tabular format. There is one record per line, and the fields are lined up in columns with the field names as column headers. Fields wider than 78 characters occupy the full width of the screen; otherwise, the default column width is the width of the field or the width of the field name, whichever is greater. The appearance of the Browse screen with the National Widgets Customer File displayed is illustrated in Figure 4-1.

The number of *records* you can view at once depends on your video display adapter and on whether the status display is turned on. On a standard 25-line screen, dBASE IV can display 17 records at once if the status display is off or 18 if it is on. In 43-line mode on an EGA or VGA screen, you can view 35 records at a time with the status display off, or 36 records if it is on. Note that although you can view data from 17 or more records, only one at a time is available for editing; the selected field in this record is highlighted and the record's sequential number is displayed in the third section of the status bar.

The number of *fields* that are visible at one time depends on their widths. Unless your data base has only a few short fields, you will be unable to view an entire record within the 80-column screen width. You can visualize the data base as a large chart (or worksheet, if you are familiar with spreadsheet programs) with the information in each record spread across one row and the

Control Key	Command Key	Function
	F10 (Menu)	Activate the menu system
	ALT-*letter*	Activate the menu system and pull down the menu whose description begins with *letter*
	letter	Select the option on the active pull-down menu whose description begins with *letter*
	ENTER	Select the highlighted option or item from the active menu, panel, or pick list
CTRL-W	CTRL-END	Save changes and exit
CTRL-Q	ESC	Exit without saving changes
CTRL-E	UP ARROW	Move up one screen line
CTRL-X	DOWN ARROW	Move down one screen line
CTRL-D	RIGHT ARROW	Move right one character
CTRL-S	LEFT ARROW	Move left one character
CTRL-I	TAB or F4 (Next)	Move to the next field
	SHIFT-TAB or F3 (Previous)	Move to the previous field
CTRL-F	CTRL-RIGHT ARROW	Move right one word
CTRL-A	CTRL-LEFT ARROW	Move left one word
	ENTER	Move to the next field (Edit)
CTRL-Z	HOME	Move to the beginning of the field (Edit) or to the first field (Browse)
CTRL-B	END	Move to the end of the field (Edit) or to the last field (Browse)
CTRL-C	PGDN	Display the next group of fields (Edit) or records (Browse)

Table 4-1.

The Full-Screen Cursor Movement and Command Keys

Control Key	Command Key	Function
CTRL-R	PGUP	Display the previous group of fields (Edit) or records (Browse)
	CTRL-PGDN	Move to the last record in the file
	CTRL-PGUP	Move to the first record in the file
CTRL-G	DEL	Delete the character at the cursor position
	BACKSPACE	Delete the character to the left of the cursor
CTRL-T		Delete the characters from the cursor to the end of the word
CTRL-Y		Delete the characters from the cursor to the end of the field
CTRL-U		Mark the current record for deletion or clear the deletion marker
CTRL-V	INS	Turn Insert mode on (if it is off) or off (if it is on)
	CTRL-HOME or F9 (Zoom)	Invoke memo field editor
	F2 (Data)	Switch between Browse and Edit
	SHIFT-F4 (Find Next)	Search forward for the next occurrence of the same text string
	SHIFT-F3 (Find Previous)	Search backward for the previous occurrence of the same text string
	SHIFT-F7 (Size)	Adjust column display width (Browse)
	SHIFT-F8 (Ditto)	Carry over data from the same field in the previous record

Table 4-1. The Full-Screen Cursor Movement and Command Keys (*continued*)

```
Records   Organize   Fields   Go To   Exit                          10:26:25 am

ACCOUNT    | COMPANY                  | ADDRESS                  | CITY
LEWIS      | Lewis and Associates     | 460 Grand Avenue         | Oakland
ABCPLUMB   | ABC Plumbing             | 1850 University Avenue   | Berkeley
KLEIN      | Carol Klein, M.D.        | 1849 S.E. 40th Avenue    | Portland
MTK        | M.T.K. Industries        | 1400 61st Street         | Emeryville
ANDERSON   |                          | 6105 146th Place S.E.    | Bellevue
RAPIDTYPE  | RapidType Secretarial Svc| 2457 Union Street        | San Francisco
PHOENIX    | Phoenix Construction     | 2125 Providence Street   | Eugene
KELLY      | Kelly and Sons Furniture | 14800 Bancroft Avenue    | San Leandro
GREENTHUMB | Green Thumb Landscaping  | 1240 Hearst              | Berkeley
HOMEMOVIES | Home Movies Video Rentals| 2982 College Avenue      | Berkeley
SHAPEUP    | Shape Up Fitness Center  | 2832 MacDonald Avenue    | Richmond
FLOORPLAN  | Floor Plan Carpet Center | 2020 N.E. Oregon Street  | Portland
JOHNSON    | J. Thomas Johnson, CPA   | 50 California Street     | San Francisco
ELLISMFG   | Ellis Manufacturing      | 832 130th N.E.           | Bellevue
IMAGEMAKER | The Image Makers         | 1900 Powell Street       | Emeryville
WHITNEY    | Financial Planning Svcs. | 1800 Peralta Blvd.       | Fremont
HRINSURANC | H & R Insurance          | 1225 Van Ness Avenue     | San Francisco

Browse  ||C:\dbase4\NWCUST      ||Rec 1/20      ||File ||       ||      Caps
                              View and edit fields
```

Figure 4-1.

Using the Browse screen to view the National Widgets Customer File

fields lined up in columns. You can move up and down one row at a time using the UP ARROW and DOWN ARROW keys, advance to the next field by pressing TAB or F4 (Next), and back up to the previous field with SHIFT-TAB or F3 (Previous). You can move the window up or down one screenful of records with PGUP or PGDN, and "pan" the data "window" all the way to the right or left with HOME or END. In general, dBASE IV treats the display screen like a small window that you can position anywhere above this large data table to view different records and fields. If you "move off the edge" of the screen in any direction, dBASE IV automatically pans the display to reveal the next row (record) or column (field).

Figure 4-2 illustrates the forms-style Edit screen with the first record of the National Widgets Customer File displayed. The field names are listed vertically down the left side of the screen as prompts. If a character field is too wide to fit on the same line as its prompt (an example is the EQUIPMENT field in Figure

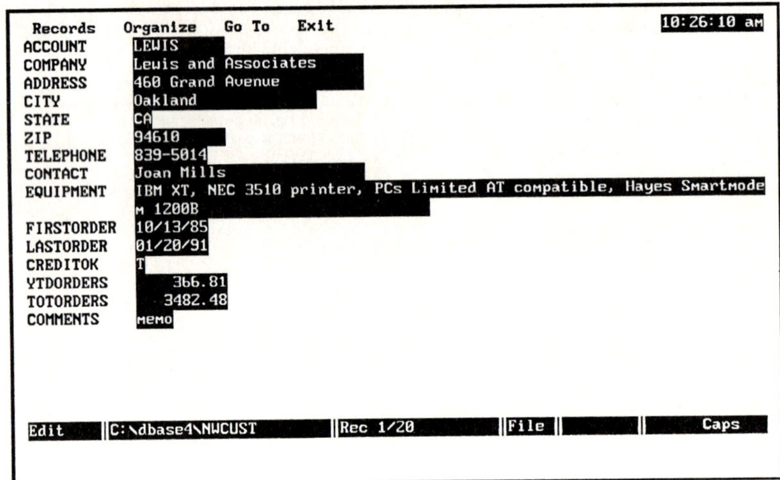

Figure 4-2.

Using the Edit screen to view a customer record

4-2), the data wraps around onto one or more additional lines. However, a character field is always treated as one long string of characters, not as a formatted paragraph of text. Even if a field occupies multiple lines, you cannot use the UP ARROW and DOWN ARROW keys to move through the field; these keys always move the cursor to the previous or next field. Instead, you must use the cursor movement keys that move left and right—among them LEFT ARROW and RIGHT ARROW to move one character at a time and CTRL-LEFT ARROW and CTRL-RIGHT ARROW to move one word at a time (or the CTRL-key equivalents).

Exactly how many fields you can view at once depends on the field widths, your display adapter, and whether the status bar is displayed. With the status bar occupying the last three lines on the screen, a maximum of 17 fields are visible in 25-line mode or 35 in 43-line mode (fewer if some require more than one line); turning off the status display leaves room for 20 or 38 fields. If there are more fields in the structure of the active data base than will fit on the screen at once, you can use the PGUP and PGDN keys to move up and down in the structure by one "page" (screenful) of fields at a time. As in Browse mode, dBASE IV automatically pages the display up or down when you move the cursor up beyond the first field on the screen or down past the last.

On both the Browse and Edit screens, changes are saved on disk one record at a time. When you use any of the cursor movement commands to move to the next or previous record in the file, dBASE IV first saves any changes you made to the current record.

The Browse and Edit Menus

On both the Browse and Edit screens, you can execute commands by choosing options from a horizontal light-bar menu displayed at the top of the screen. These menus are diagrammed in Figure 4-3. If the status display is on, the menu is visible at all times; if the status display is turned off, dBASE IV also suppresses the menu bar. Whether or not it is visible at the top of the screen, you can always activate the menu bar by pressing F10 (Menu) or choose one of the main menu options and pull down the associated submenu by pressing the ALT key in combination with the first letter of the desired option.

The **Records, Organize, Go To,** and **Exit** menus are identical in both Browse and Edit modes; the Browse screen also has a **Fields** menu with options not applicable to Edit mode. The **Organize** menu offers commands that enable you to change the order in which records are displayed; the methods used to effect these selections—sorting and indexing—are covered in Chapters 8 and 9. Some of the other menu options also access more advanced features that are covered in later chapters, but you will find many of the menu commands useful immediately.

The **Go To** menu includes options to move quickly to the **Top record** or **Last record** in the active file. You can jump directly to any record by selecting the **Record number** option and entering the appropriate record number when you are prompted to do so. To move forward or backward more than one record at a time, select the **Skip** option. dBASE IV pops up a dialog box to ask how many records to skip. You can press ENTER to accept the default value of ten or enter any positive number (to skip forward) or negative number (to skip backward).

The **Records** menu contains options for adding and deleting records; these will be described in detail in the next two sections of this chapter. The **Blank record** option blanks out all of the fields in the current record, and the **Undo change to record** option reverses any changes (including blanking out the fields) made to the current record. Be careful to check each record before you move forward or backward in the file (which is easy to do inadvertently in

```
Records
 Undo change to record
 ---------------------------------
 Add new records
 Mark record for deletion
 Blank record
 Lock record
 Follow record to new position

Organize
 ► Create new index
 ► Modify existing index
   Order records by index
   Activate .NDX index file
   Include .NDX index file
   Remove unwanted index tag
 ---------------------------------
   Sort database on field list
   Unmark all records
   Erase marked records

Fields
   Lock fields on left {0}
   Blank field
   Freeze field        {}
 ► Size field
```

```
Go To
 Top record
 Last record
 Record number        {0}
 Skip                 {10}
 ---------------------------------
 Index key search
 Forward search       {}
 Backward search      {}
 Match capitalization YES

Exit
 Exit
 Transfer to Query Design
```

Note: The **Fields** menu is present only in Browse mode

Figure 4-3.

The structure of the Browse and Edit menus

Browse mode) because dBASE IV saves all changes when you leave the current record, and once the original data has been overwritten on disk, you cannot undo the changes.

The **Fields** menu, which is present only in Browse mode, contains options that are not deemed applicable to Edit mode. The **Blank field** option blanks out the highlighted field in the selected record. (You can do the same thing, in either Browse or Edit, by positioning the cursor at the beginning of a field and pressing CTRL-Y). You can use the **Size** option to temporarily change the display width of a column without changing the field width in the data base structure. The function key shortcut for this command is SHIFT-F7 (Size). In either case, you adjust the width of the column with the LEFT ARROW and RIGHT ARROW keys and then press ENTER to fix the width. This option is useful for reducing the space required to display wide character fields, to allow more fields to fit on the screen at once. When you edit a wide field in a narrow column, the contents scroll within the designated width to permit access to all the data. Note that you cannot make a field narrower than its name (which is used as the column heading) and that the new display width remains in effect only until you exit from the full-screen edit mode and return to the Control Center.

The **Lock fields on left** option allows you to designate one or more fields to remain stationary at the left side of the screen as you pan the display to view other fields. For example, in the National Widgets Customer File, you might lock the ACCOUNT field, or perhaps the ACCOUNT and COMPANY fields, as illustrated in Figure 4-4, so that you can still recognize a customer after panning the display to the right to view the order dates and totals. When you choose **Lock**, dBASE IV prompts you for the number of fields to lock: "Enter number of fields to remain stationary:." The fields you lock need not be first in the file structure (like ACCOUNT and COMPANY in the Customer File), but they must be consecutive and positioned at the left edge of the screen when you select the command. To unlock the display, choose **Lock fields on left** again and enter zero for the number of fields to lock.

The **Freeze field** option restricts editing to a single field, which you identify by name. With a field "frozen," you cannot pan the display left or right or move the cursor into any other field. To cancel this setting and return to editing all the fields in the record, select **Freeze field** again, and leave the field name blank when dBASE IV prompts you to "Enter field name:." The columnar Browse screen is especially well suited for updating the contents of a single field in a series of records, and the **Freeze field** option enables you to avoid the inconvenience of moving the cursor left (to return to the column you are editing) as well as down (to advance to the next record) after each entry.

Records Organize Fields Go To Exit 10:27:04 am

ACCOUNT	COMPANY	LASTORDER	CREDITOK	YTDORDERS	TOTORDERS
LEWIS	Lewis and Associates	01/20/91	Y	366.81	3482.48
ABCPLUMB	ABC Plumbing	04/30/91	Y	796.41	5248.90
KLEIN	Carol Klein, M.D.	12/28/90	Y	0.00	1053.89
MTK	M.T.K. Industries	02/03/91	Y	108.59	823.92
ANDERSON		12/01/90	Y	0.00	832.58
RAPIDTYPE	RapidType Secretarial Svc	03/10/91	Y	348.52	348.52
PHOENIX	Phoenix Construction	07/06/87	N	0.00	249.59
KELLY	Kelly and Sons Furniture	01/23/91	N	87.35	87.35
GREENTHUMB	Green Thumb Landscaping	12/19/89	Y	0.00	357.73
HOMEMOVIES	Home Movies Video Rentals	04/18/91	Y	548.15	2047.15
SHAPEUP	Shape Up Fitness Center	11/12/91	Y	435.42	867.38
FLOORPLAN	Floor Plan Carpet Center	11/20/88	Y	0.00	184.18
JOHNSON	J. Thomas Johnson, CPA	12/06/90	Y	0.00	368.42
ELLISMFG	Ellis Manufacturing	02/16/90	N	0.00	669.58
IMAGEMAKER	The Image Makers	11/12/88	Y	0.00	389.50
WHITNEY	Financial Planning Svcs.	02/13/91	Y	201.87	1584.45
HRINSURANC	H & R Insurance	10/26/90	Y	0.00	738.43

Browse | C:\dbase4\NWCUST | Rec 1/20 | File | Caps

Figure 4-4.

The Browse screen with the ACCOUNT and COMPANY fields locked

To save the current record and exit the Edit or Browse screen, you can select the **Exit** option on the **Exit** menu or press CTRL-END or CTRL-W with the cursor positioned in any field. If you want to exit without saving changes made to the current record, press ESC or CTRL-Q instead.

ADDING NEW RECORDS TO A DATA BASE

You add new records to a data base with the same full-screen editors used to view and edit previously entered records. As in Edit and Browse, dBASE IV presents a blank data entry form, with the field names as prompts, which you fill in for each new record. There are several ways to begin adding records to a dBASE IV data base:

- If you move from the Control Center to full-screen editing when the selected data base is empty, dBASE IV displays the Edit screen with a blank data entry form on which you can enter your first new record.

- If you exit from the data base design screen after creating a new data base by pressing ENTER after defining the last field, or by pressing CTRL-W or CTRL-END from anywhere on the screen, dBASE IV asks, "Input data records now? (Y/N)." You can move directly to data entry by pressing Y ("Yes").
- From the data base design screen, you can choose the **Enter records from the keyboard** option from the **Append** menu. This method is the most convenient way to begin entering data after you create a new file or modify a file structure.
- With a data base open, you can type APPEND at the dot prompt.
- In either Browse or Edit mode, if you move past the last record in the file, dBASE IV assumes that you want to add new records and asks you to confirm your intention with the message "Add new records? (Y/N)." If you moved past the end of the file by mistake, you can press N ("No") to return to editing the last record. If you do want to add new records, press Y ("Yes").
- You can select the **Add new records** option from the **Records** menu in either the Browse or Edit screen.

The last two methods are available only if a data base already contains at least one record.

When you add new records to a data base, all the same cursor movement and editing keys used to edit existing records are available to you. In addition, you can use the SHIFT-F8 (Ditto) key to copy data automatically into the selected field in the current record from the same field in the previous record. This command is particularly useful when you enter a small group of new records that have a few fields in common. For example, if you entered several San Francisco customers into the National Widgets Customer File, you could use SHIFT-F8 (Ditto) to avoid having to retype "San Francisco" in the CITY field and "CA" in the STATE field for each new record. If nearly all of the fields in a series of new records are identical, or if a few fields are identical in nearly all the new records, you can use the CARRY option (described in Chapter 18) to automatically carry over some or all fields from the previous record into each new entry.

dBASE IV assumes that you want to add more than one record at a time, possibly many records in a single data entry session. When you press the ENTER or DOWN ARROW key to move past the last field in the structure, dBASE IV saves the completed record and presents a new blank form for the next. When you have finished adding records, you can return to the Control Center by using any of the standard Edit or Browse exit alternatives: press CTRL-END or CTRL-W to save the current record and exit, press ESC or CTRL-Q to exit without saving, or select the **Exit** option on the **Exit** menu.

There is one additional exit option applicable only to adding new records—you can press ENTER with the cursor in the first field of a new blank data entry form. In order to make this exit possible, dBASE IV does not allow you to leave the first field in a new record blank by pressing ENTER to skip over it, as you can with any other field. You can, however, use DOWN ARROW or CTRL-X to bypass the first field.

You may find that after entering several fields, you wish to leave all the remaining fields in the record blank. With the cursor positioned in any field, you can save the current record and advance to the next one by pressing PGDN. If the data base has too many fields to fit on one screen, this command displays the next screenful of fields, so you may have to press PGDN more than once to arrive at a new blank entry form.

You can minimize the number of times you have to press ENTER to pass over individual fields by designing your data base structures so that fields that are frequently left blank, or that will be calculated later based on other fields, are placed close to the end of the structure. This is not always an easy judgment to make in advance, but you can modify the structure without losing data if you decide to rearrange the fields after entering some records.

Figure 4-5 lists the National Widgets Customer File sample data. If you are building the sample system as a tutorial, you may want to enter some or all of this data so that when you try the examples in later chapters, your results will match the illustrations.

ENTERING AND EDITING MEMO FIELDS

A memo field can accommodate up to 64K (approximately 65,000) characters of free-form text, far too much to edit conveniently with the handful of full-screen editing commands that operate on character fields. The Edit and Browse screens do not include the full text of a memo field; instead, dBASE IV displays a *memo marker* in the data entry area to remind you that the field is not a character field. This marker is "memo" if the field is empty, or "MEMO" if the field contains text.

Record 1:

ACCOUNT	LEWIS
COMPANY	Lewis and Associates
ADDRESS	460 Grand Avenue
CITY	Oakland
STATE	CA
ZIP	94610
TELEPHONE	839-5014
CONTACT	Joan Mills
EQUIPMENT	IBM XT, NEC 3510 printer, PCs Limited AT compatible, Hayes Smartmodem 1200B
FIRSTORDER	10/13/85
LASTORDER	01/20/91
CREDITOK	Y
YTDORDERS	366.81
TOTORDERS	3482.48
COMMENTS	

Record 2:

ACCOUNT	ABCPLUMB
COMPANY	ABC Plumbing
ADDRESS	1850 University Avenue
CITY	Berkeley
STATE	CA
ZIP	94703
TELEPHONE	861-4543
CONTACT	Ed Williams
EQUIPMENT	Kaypro 4, Kaypro 10, Kaypro 286 PC, Epson FX-286 printer
FIRSTORDER	12/01/87
LASTORDER	04/30/91
CREDITOK	Y
YTDORDERS	796.41
TOTORDERS	5248.90
COMMENTS	This company has two older Kaypro computers in addition to their AT-compatible. They are still interested in disks, supplies, and accessories for the older machines, and they generally respond to special mailings by calling and placing an order. They are also interested in sources of public domain or inexpensive software for their CP/M-based Kaypros.

Figure 4-5.

The National Widgets Customer File sample data

Record 3:

ACCOUNT	KLEIN
COMPANY	Carol Klein, M.D.
ADDRESS	1849 S.E. 40th Avenue
CITY	Portland
STATE	OR
ZIP	97214
TELEPHONE	232-2842
CONTACT	Judy Barnes
EQUIPMENT	IBM AT, Quietwriter
FIRSTORDER	10/13/86
LASTORDER	12/28/90
CREDITOK	Y
YTDORDERS	0.00
TOTORDERS	1053.89
COMMENTS	Referred by Dr. James Reynolds.

Record 4:

ACCOUNT	MTK
COMPANY	M.T.K. Industries
ADDRESS	1400 61st Street
CITY	Emeryville
STATE	CA
ZIP	94608
TELEPHONE	655-7200
CONTACT	Leslie Cohen
EQUIPMENT	Two XT-compatibles, two AT-compatibles, HP ThinkJet printers, Toshiba P-1350 printers
FIRSTORDER	06/23/87
LASTORDER	02/03/91
CREDITOK	Y
YTDORDERS	108.59
TOTORDERS	823.92
COMMENTS	Interested in receiving additional information on new lines of computer furniture, ergonomic workstations, glare screens, and similar items. Talk to Leslie about orders, but ask for Joe in the Bookkeeping Department for accounts receivable questions.

Figure 4-5.

The National Widgets Customer File sample data (*continued*)

Record 5:

ACCOUNT	ANDERSON
COMPANY	
ADDRESS	6105 146th Place S.E.
CITY	Bellevue
STATE	WA
ZIP	98006
TELEPHONE	747-8201
CONTACT	John Anderson
EQUIPMENT	Apple IIGS, Imagewriter
FIRSTORDER	08/08/87
LASTORDER	12/01/90
CREDITOK	Y
YTDORDERS	0.00
TOTORDERS	832.58
COMMENTS	

Record 6:

ACCOUNT	RAPIDTYPE
COMPANY	RapidType Secretarial Svc
ADDRESS	2457 Union Street
CITY	San Francisco
STATE	CA
ZIP	94123
TELEPHONE	861-4048
CONTACT	Kathy McDonald
EQUIPMENT	IBM AT, Epson Equity III, Epson LQ-2500, HP LaserJet
FIRSTORDER	03/10/91
LASTORDER	03/10/91
CREDITOK	Y
YTDORDERS	348.52
TOTORDERS	348.52
COMMENTS	This company is a word processing and secretarial service. They are looking for one vendor to provide a high volume of supplies. Quick delivery and varied product line are more important than lowest prices, but would like volume discounts.

Figure 4-5.

The National Widgets Customer File sample data (*continued*)

Record 7:

ACCOUNT	PHOENIX
COMPANY	Phoenix Construction
ADDRESS	2125 Providence Street
CITY	Eugene
STATE	OR
ZIP	97401
TELEPHONE	683-8751
CONTACT	
EQUIPMENT	AST Model 140, NEC P2200 printer
FIRSTORDER	04/28/87
LASTORDER	07/06/87
CREDITOK	N
YTDORDERS	0.00
TOTORDERS	249.59
COMMENTS	

Record 8:

ACCOUNT	KELLY
COMPANY	Kelly and Sons Furniture
ADDRESS	14800 Bancroft Avenue
CITY	San Leandro
STATE	CA
ZIP	94578
TELEPHONE	357-7482
CONTACT	Richard Kelly
EQUIPMENT	IBM PS/2 Model 80, two IBM PS/2 Model 30's, IBM Proprinters, HP LaserJet
FIRSTORDER	01/23/91
LASTORDER	01/23/91
CREDITOK	N
YTDORDERS	87.35
TOTORDERS	87.35
COMMENTS	

Figure 4-5.

The National Widgets Customer File sample data (*continued*)

Record 9:

ACCOUNT	GREENTHUMB
COMPANY	Green Thumb Landscaping
ADDRESS	1240 Hearst
CITY	Berkeley
STATE	CA
ZIP	94702
TELEPHONE	549-8901
CONTACT	Celia Lopez
EQUIPMENT	Kaypro 396, Okidata 192
FIRSTORDER	08/16/88
LASTORDER	12/19/89
CREDITOK	Y
YTDORDERS	0.00
TOTORDERS	357.73
COMMENTS	

Record 10:

ACCOUNT	HOMEMOVIES
COMPANY	Home Movies Video Rentals
ADDRESS	2982 College Avenue
CITY	Berkeley
STATE	CA
ZIP	94705
TELEPHONE	843-1148
CONTACT	Mark Vogel
EQUIPMENT	Novell network, Novell file server, Compaq 286 workstations, HP LaserJet II, Epson EX-100 printers
FIRSTORDER	09/13/88
LASTORDER	04/18/91
CREDITOK	Y
YTDORDERS	548.15
TOTORDERS	2047.15
COMMENTS	Owner is a friend of Jim's, so they get a 10% discount on all orders. However, they often take a long time to pay.

Figure 4-5.

The National Widgets Customer File sample data (*continued*)

Record 11:

ACCOUNT	SHAPEUP
COMPANY	Shape Up Fitness Center
ADDRESS	2832 MacDonald Avenue
CITY	Richmond
STATE	CA
ZIP	94804
TELEPHONE	236-7687
CONTACT	Jeanne Lee
EQUIPMENT	Macintosh II, Apple ImageWriter printer
FIRSTORDER	02/15/88
LASTORDER	11/12/91
CREDITOK	Y
YTDORDERS	435.42
TOTORDERS	867.38
COMMENTS	

Record 12:

ACCOUNT	FLOORPLAN
COMPANY	Floor Plan Carpet Center
ADDRESS	2020 N.E. Oregon Street
CITY	Portland
STATE	OR
ZIP	97232
TELEPHONE	232-8430
CONTACT	Louise Robbins
EQUIPMENT	NorthStar Advantage, NorthStar network, HP LaserJet printer
FIRSTORDER	11/20/88
LASTORDER	11/20/88
CREDITOK	Y
YTDORDERS	0.00
TOTORDERS	184.18
COMMENTS	

Figure 4-5.

The National Widgets Customer File sample data (*continued*)

Record 13:

ACCOUNT	JOHNSON
COMPANY	J. Thomas Johnson, CPA
ADDRESS	50 California Street
CITY	San Francisco
STATE	CA
ZIP	94111
TELEPHONE	433-6488
CONTACT	Carolyn Sumner
EQUIPMENT	IBM XT, Epson MX-100, AT-compatible, HP ThinkJet
FIRSTORDER	06/28/88
LASTORDER	12/06/90
CREDITOK	Y
YTDORDERS	0.00
TOTORDERS	368.42
COMMENTS	

Record 14:

ACCOUNT	ELLISMFG
COMPANY	Ellis Manufacturing
ADDRESS	832 130th N.E.
CITY	Bellevue
STATE	WA
ZIP	98005
TELEPHONE	455-1421
CONTACT	Barbara Goddard
EQUIPMENT	IBM PS/2 Model 60, Okidata 193, Macintosh SE, Apple ImageWriter
FIRSTORDER	10/18/88
LASTORDER	02/16/90
CREDITOK	N
YTDORDERS	0.00
TOTORDERS	669.58
COMMENTS	Don't accept any orders unless accompanied by prepayment. These people have always been slow to pay and have been avoiding phone calls regarding seriously past due balance, which is now in collections.

Figure 4-5.

The National Widgets Customer File sample data (*continued*)

Record 15:

ACCOUNT	IMAGEMAKER
COMPANY	The Image Makers
ADDRESS	1900 Powell Street
CITY	Emeryville
STATE	CA
ZIP	94608
TELEPHONE	653-1250
CONTACT	Lisa Burns
EQUIPMENT	IBM PC, NEC 7710
FIRSTORDER	11/12/89
LASTORDER	11/12/88
CREDITOK	Y
YTDORDERS	0.00
TOTORDERS	389.50
COMMENTS	

Record 16:

ACCOUNT	WHITNEY
COMPANY	Financial Planning Svcs.
ADDRESS	1800 Peralta Blvd.
CITY	Fremont
STATE	CA
ZIP	94536
TELEPHONE	791-7474
CONTACT	James Whitney
EQUIPMENT	Compaq Deskpro 286, Zenith laptop, Brother HR-15 printer, Epson EX-800 printer
FIRSTORDER	10/04/86
LASTORDER	03/13/91
CREDITOK	Y
YTDORDERS	201.87
TOTORDERS	1584.45
COMMENTS	This guy likes to talk. Appreciates good advice, but will take up a lot of your time on the phone if you go along with it.

Figure 4-5.

The National Widgets Customer File sample data (*continued*)

Record 17:

ACCOUNT	HRINSURANC
COMPANY	H & R Insurance
ADDRESS	1225 Van Ness Avenue
CITY	San Francisco
STATE	CA
ZIP	94109
TELEPHONE	398-1441
CONTACT	Jill Henley
EQUIPMENT	Epson Equity III, Epson FX-1000, Apple IIGS
FIRSTORDER	07/12/87
LASTORDER	10/26/90
CREDITOK	Y
YTDORDERS	0.00
TOTORDERS	738.43
COMMENTS	

Record 18:

ACCOUNT	DELTADESGN
COMPANY	Delta Design
ADDRESS	N.W. 245 Sunrise Drive
CITY	Pullman
STATE	WA
ZIP	99163
TELEPHONE	332-7373
CONTACT	Andrea Bennett
EQUIPMENT	Macintosh II, Macintosh SE, TOPS network, Imagewriter, Apple LaserWriter Plus
FIRSTORDER	09/14/88
LASTORDER	02/23/91
CREDITOK	Y
YTDORDERS	188.15
TOTORDERS	1235.87
COMMENTS	Referred by Chris Johnson.

Figure 4-5.

The National Widgets Customer File sample data (*continued*)

Record 19:

ACCOUNT	ARONOFF
COMPANY	
ADDRESS	601 First Street
CITY	Benicia
STATE	CA
ZIP	94510
TELEPHONE	745-1813
CONTACT	Gina Aronoff
EQUIPMENT	IBM AT, IBM Quietwriter, Apple IIc, ImageWriter
FIRSTORDER	10/09/87
LASTORDER	12/14/90
CREDITOK	Y
YTDORDERS	0.00
TOTORDERS	1232.50
COMMENTS	

Record 20:

ACCOUNT	YORKPUMP
COMPANY	York Pump, Inc.
ADDRESS	632 Charcot Avenue
CITY	San Jose
STATE	CA
ZIP	95131
TELEPHONE	946-9975
CONTACT	Sharon Fern
EQUIPMENT	Two AT clones, Okidata 193, Epson LQ-2400
FIRSTORDER	10/18/88
LASTORDER	04/10/91
CREDITOK	Y
YTDORDERS	157.38
TOTORDERS	608.42
COMMENTS	Send information on CRT and printer stands when new flyer is ready.

Figure 4-5.

The National Widgets Customer File sample data (*continued*)

To facilitate entering and editing memo field text, dBASE IV provides a rudimentary word processor, or word wrap editor, which has many features in common with the layout editors used to create and modify report, label, and screen formats. (If you prefer, you can substitute another text editor or word processor for the dBASE IV editor, using commands described in Chapter 18.) You invoke the editor from the Browse or Edit screen by positioning the cursor in the memo marker next to the field name and pressing CTRL-HOME or F9 (Zoom). If you move to a memo field from the previous field by pressing F4 (Next) or from the following field by pressing F3 (Previous), these commands also call up the text editor.

The dBASE IV word processor presents a mostly blank screen for typing and editing text. As in the other full-screen and layout editors, there is a menu bar at the top of the screen. Below the menu is a ruler line that displays the current margin and tab settings; by default, the margins are set at columns 1 and 65, and there are tab stops every 8 spaces. As you move around on the screen work surface, the cursor row and column position is displayed in the third segment of the status bar, and a moving indicator in the ruler line mirrors the cursor column position. Figure 4-6 illustrates the appearance of the screen with a memo field from the National Widgets Customer File displayed.

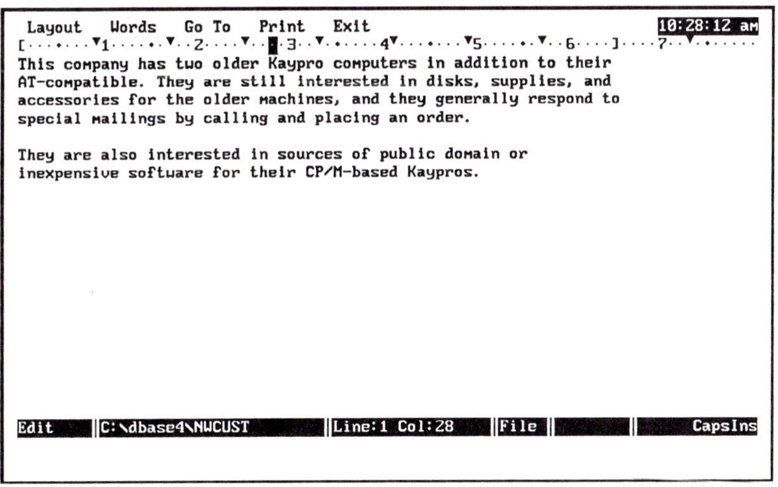

Figure 4-6.

Using the dBASE IV memo field editor

The dBASE IV word processor is called a *word wrap editor* because it automatically wraps text into paragraphs by inserting a *soft return* and beginning a new line whenever you type beyond the right margin. If more space remains on the current line but a carriage return is required—for example, at the end of a paragraph—you must press ENTER to generate a *hard return.* Think of a hard return as immutable—its position never changes, and it always produces a new line in a printout or screen display. In contrast, when you add or delete characters so that a line falls short of the right margin or extends beyond it, the memo editor automatically moves soft returns as necessary to adjust the paragraph to conform to the standard margins.

The cursor movement and editing command keys used in the memo field editor are listed in Table 4-2. The memo field editor supports most of the same

Control Key	Command Key	Function
	F10 (Menu)	Activate the menu system
	ALT-*letter*	Activate the menu system and pull down the menu whose description begins with *letter*
	letter	Select the option on the active pull-down menu whose description begins with *letter*
	ENTER	Select the highlighted option or item from the active menu, panel, or pick list
CTRL-W	CTRL-END or F9 (Zoom)	Save changes and exit
CTRL-Q	ESC	Exit without saving changes
CTRL-E	UP ARROW	Move up one screen line
CTRL-X	DOWN ARROW	Move down one screen line
CTRL-D	RIGHT ARROW	Move right one character
CTRL-S	LEFT ARROW	Move left one character
CTRL-I	TAB	Move to the next tab stop, inserting spaces if Insert mode is on
	SHIFT-TAB	Move to the previous tab stop

Table 4-2.

The Cursor Movement and Command Keys Used in the Memo Field Editor

Control Key	Command Key	Function
CTRL-F	CTRL-RIGHT ARROW	Move right one word
CTRL-A	CTRL-LEFT ARROW	Move left one word
CTRL-Z	HOME	Move to the beginning of the line
CTRL-B	END	Move to the end of the line
CTRL-C	PGDN	Display the next screen "page"
CTRL-R	PGUP	Display the previous screen "page"
	CTRL-PGDN	Move to the end of the memo
	CTRL-PGUP	Move to the top of the memo
CTRL-G	DEL	Delete the character at the cursor position
	BACKSPACE	Delete the character to the left of the cursor
CTRL-T		Delete the characters from the cursor to the end of the word
CTRL-Y		Delete the entire line containing the cursor
CTRL-V	INS	Turn Insert mode on (if it is off) or off (if it is on)
CTRL-N		Insert a hard return before the cursor position
	ENTER	Insert a hard return (if Insert mode is on) or move down one line (if Insert mode is off)
	F7 (Move)	Move selected text block to cursor location
	F8 (Copy)	Copy selected text block to cursor location
	SHIFT-F5 (Find)	Search for a text string
	SHIFT-F6 (Replace)	Search for a text string and replace it with another
	SHIFT-F4 (Find Next)	Search forward for the next occurrence of the same text string
	SHIFT-F3 (Find Previous)	Search backward for the previous occurrence of the same text string

Table 4-2.

The Cursor Movement and Command Keys Used in the Memo Field Editor (*continued*) cursor movement and editing keys as the full-screen Browse and Edit modes, together with others that are not required for editing shorter character fields. In particular, there are commands for moving, copying, and deleting text blocks.

To define a block of text, you position the cursor on the first character, press F6 (Select), move the cursor to the last character in the block, and press ENTER; as you move the cursor, dBASE IV highlights the selected characters so you can confirm your block definition. There are several shortcuts you can use to facilitate the text selection process. Pressing F6 (Select) twice selects the word containing the cursor; pressing F6 (Select) a third time selects the entire paragraph (all the text up to the next hard return).

With a text block defined, you can move the cursor anywhere on the work surface and then press F7 (Move) to move the text block to the cursor location or F8 (Copy) to duplicate the block. You can delete the highlighted block of text by pressing DEL. Once you have marked a text block, the block remains selected until you explicitly cancel the selection by pressing ESC, so you can easily make more than one copy of the same text.

The memo field editor shares the same menu bar options as the report, label, and screen layout editors, but some of the pull-down menus have fewer options (the options that are not applicable to editing memos are omitted). As in the full-screen editors, the menu bar is visible all the time if the status display is on. If the status display is off, the menu bar appears only when you press F10 (Menu) or an ALT-key combination that activates a submenu. The structure of the menus is diagrammed in Figure 4-7.

The **Print** menu, which is present in nearly identical form in all of the dBASE IV layout editors, will be covered in Chapter 13.

The **Words** menu includes options for editing and formatting text. The **Hide ruler** option suppresses the ruler line display. The **Enable automatic indent** option, which is set to **Yes** by default, sets the left margin for each paragraph to the location of the cursor when you begin typing the paragraph rather than to the margin set in the ruler line. You can take advantage of this feature to indent a new paragraph relative to the previous one by pressing TAB (to move the margin to the right) or SHIFT-TAB (to move the margin to the left) one or more times before you begin typing. **Add line** and **Remove line** serve as alternatives to the CTRL-N and CTRL-Y control key commands. **Insert page break** inserts a *hard page break,* which is analogous to a hard return—it causes dBASE IV to begin a

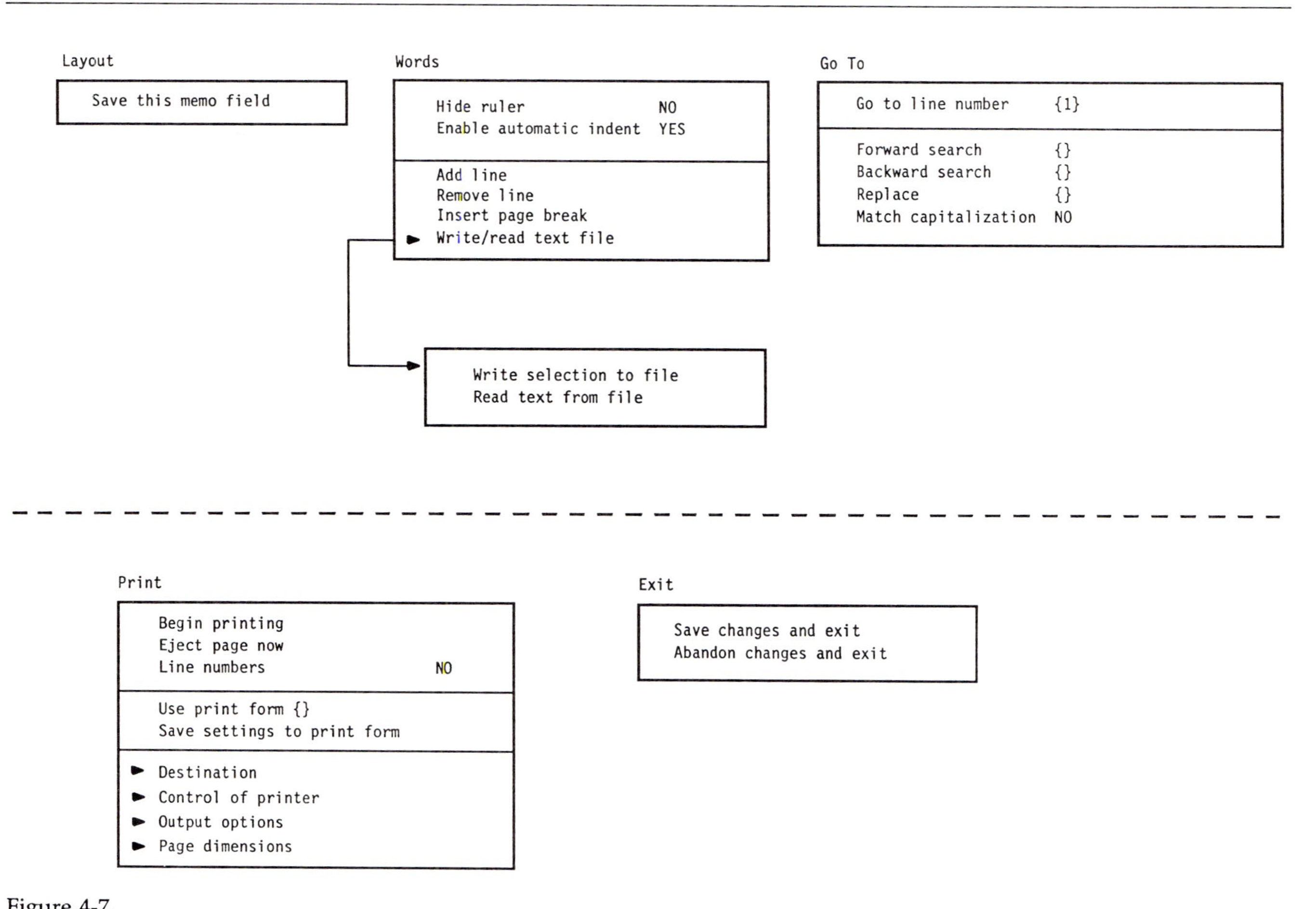

Figure 4-7.

The structure of the memo field editor menus

new page at the specified position when the text is printed, even if there is still space on the current page.

The **Go To** menu includes options for moving to a specific line, identified by number, and for searching either forward or backward from the current cursor position for a word or phrase. You can use the **Match capitalization** option to specify whether or not the search should be *case sensitive,* that is, whether or not uppercase and lowercase letters should be treated as equivalent. After searching once for a character string, you can press SHIFT-F4 (Find Next) to search forward or SHIFT-F3 (Find Previous) to search backward from the cursor position for the same sequence of characters.

The **Replace** option, which is equivalent to the function key command SHIFT-F6 (Replace), enables you to search for one string of characters and replace it with another. When you use the **Replace** command, dBASE IV prompts you for both a search string and a replacement string. It then highlights each occurrence of the search string in turn and displays your options at the bottom of the screen: "Replace/Skip/All/Quit? (R/S/A/Esc)." You can press R (Replace) to replace the highlighted occurrence of the search string and look for the next or S (Skip) to leave the highlighted text unchanged and look for the next occurrence of the search string. If you press A (All), dBASE IV replaces all remaining occurrences without confirmation and then displays a message at the bottom of the screen that informs you how many replacements it carried out. At any point, you can use ESC to discontinue the search and replace operation.

You can save your text and continue editing by selecting the **Save this memo field** option (the only option) on the **Layout** menu. To save your text and exit from the editor, you can select the **Save changes and exit** option on the **Exit** menu or use either of the standard dBASE IV "save and exit" commands—CTRL-END or CTRL-W. If you did not make any changes, you can safely choose **Abandon changes and exit** from the **Exit** menu or press ESC or CTRL-Q. You can also use these options to intentionally discard your changes or new text. If you have in fact altered the memo text, dBASE IV asks you to confirm your intention to abandon the changes by asking, "Are you sure you want to abandon operation?" You can select **Yes** to exit or **No** to return to the memo editor. After any of these exit commands, dBASE IV returns you to the same full-screen mode from which you invoked the memo editor and leaves the cursor positioned in the memo field marker next to the field you were just editing.

DATA FORMATTING AND VALIDATION

In all the full-screen edit modes, dBASE IV automatically formats and validates your entries as follows, based on the data type:

- In a *character* or *memo* field, any keyboard characters are permitted, and since there is no way to guess your intentions, dBASE IV performs no special validations on your entries. In a character field, text is left-justified. In a memo field, text is "word wrapped" into paragraphs.
- In a *numeric* or *float* field, the digits you type appear at the left side of the field until you press DOWN ARROW or ENTER to move to the next field or type a period to indicate that you are ready to enter digits to the right of the decimal point. In either case, dBASE IV right-justifies the number to align with the decimal point (or the right side of the field if no decimal places are defined). Note that if there are decimal places but all the digits to the right of the decimal point will be zeros, you need not type the zeros; they are filled in automatically when you press ENTER.
- In a *logical* field, the only permissible entries are T, t, Y, and y (for "True" or "Yes") and F, f, N, and n (for "False" or "No"). If you try to type any other character, dBASE IV beeps and refuses to advance the cursor to the next field. You can, however, leave a logical field blank, in which case dBASE IV treats it as if you had entered the logical value .F.
- In a *date* field, you need only enter the six digits representing the month, day, and year (or eight digits if you have configured dBASE IV to display 4-digit years). The punctuation marks between the three components of the date—by default, slashes (/)—are supplied automatically, and the cursor jumps over these positions during data entry. You must enter all six (or eight) digits, and you cannot substitute a space for a leading zero if the month or day is less than 10. dBASE IV verifies that the month is between 1 and 12 and that the date is consistent with the number of days in the month. If you enter an impossible date such as 13/12/92, dBASE IV beeps and displays an error message at the bottom of the screen: "Invalid date (press SPACE)." The cursor will not leave the field until you enter a valid date (of course, dBASE IV cannot determine if you have entered the correct date) or blank out the entry by pressing CTRL-Y with the cursor at the beginning of the field.

DELETING AND UNDELETING RECORDS

You can mark a record for deletion from a data base by selecting the **Mark record for deletion** option from the **Records** menu in the Browse or Edit screen. If you prefer keyboard commands, you can press CTRL-U in Edit mode or with the record selected on the Browse screen. When you "delete" a record, it does not disappear from the screen, and it is not removed immediately from the data base—as the wording of the menu option suggests, the record is only marked, or tagged, to identify it as deleted.

You can verify that the selected record is deleted by the "Del" indicator displayed in the far right segment of the status bar or, if you have turned off the status display, on the top line of the screen. You can edit "deleted" records just as you can any other records in a data base. In fact, the act of marking a record deleted is no different from any other change you might make while editing, such as changing an address or correcting the spelling of a name. If you press CTRL-U to mark a record as deleted, the "Del" indicator appears immediately in the status bar, but the deletion marker is not saved on disk until you move to another record or choose one of the "exit and save" options. If you exit from the editor by pressing ESC, the "Del" indicator disappears, and dBASE IV does not save the deletion marker with the record—just as it would not save any other alterations to the data.

The fact that deletions are not carried out instantly gives you an opportunity to change your mind about deleting a record. When a deleted record is displayed on the screen, the **Mark record for deletion** option disappears from the **Records** menu and is replaced by **Clear deletion mark**. To "undelete" a record, you can either select this option or press CTRL-U with the record displayed in any full-screen edit mode. CTRL-U thus acts as a toggle—it switches the status of a record between deleted and undeleted by setting and removing the deletion marker.

Although the ability to recover a deleted record affords a margin of safety, this is not the reason dBASE IV carries out deletions the way it does, but a beneficial side effect. Think about what is involved in physically removing a record from a file. Deleting, say, the third record would leave a gap, which could be filled in by copying Record 4 over it. Record 5 could then be moved up into the space formerly occupied by Record 4, and so on. In a large file, this process can take a long time. Instead, dBASE IV allows you to instantly mark individual records for deletion and defer until later the much slower process that physically erases them from the file. As you will see in Chapters 5 and 18, you can configure dBASE IV to ignore deleted records so that they do not appear on screen displays or reports and are not included in calculations.

To permanently remove from the disk all records that have been marked for deletion, you select the **Erase marked records** option from the **Organize** menu on the Edit, Browse, or data base design screen. You can use the **Unmark all records** option on the same menu to undelete all marked records by removing the deletion marker.

There are no hard and fast rules governing how often to erase deleted records, but two important factors should be considered. The first is whether you might later change your mind and want to clear the deletion marker. Once you have erased deleted records from a data base, there is no way to recover them, because the data has been physically overwritten on the disk. You might never need to recover certain deleted records, such as those that were originally entered in error. However, in the course of your normal processing cycle, you may also delete records, either one at a time or in groups, based on their contents. For example, National Widgets might delete customers who have not placed an order in over a year. Occasionally, you might want to recover a few such deleted records.

The second issue to consider is the number of records marked for deletion and, therefore, how much space they take up. If you have a file of several thousand records and every month you delete two or three, you might erase deleted records only once a year, since the deletions occupy very little space in the file. When the number of deleted records begins to approach 10 to 25 percent of the total, however, you might want to remove the deleted records to reduce the size of the file. By doing so, you will speed up processing and recover disk space.

Before you erase deleted records, make sure that you have at least one printed report that includes the deleted data and that you have backed up the entire data base onto floppy disks. You can use this backup to recover the deleted records if necessary, but even more important, it can help you recover easily from the damage that may occur if a power failure or a hardware crash prevents the operation from completing normally. If this happens, dBASE IV may be unable to determine how many records should be in the file or, in extreme cases, to read the data base at all. Your best guarantee of safety is to have a backup copy of the entire data base so you can begin again.

SUMMARY

The full-screen edit commands explained in this chapter enable you to carry out all the routine file maintenance operations listed in the functional definition of data base management presented in Chapter 1. From either the Edit or Browse screen, you can add new records to a data base, view and edit records on the screen, and mark records for later deletion or clear the deletion marker (make all the changes necessary to keep your data accurate and current). With these tools at your disposal, you can begin to build and maintain your own data bases. Chapter 5 introduces the commands that enable you to invoke the full-screen editors from the dot prompt and carry out the basic file maintenance operations by using keyboard commands rather than by selecting options from the menus.

CHAPTER FIVE

Working at the Dot Prompt

Thus far, all your work with dBASE IV has been through the menu system. Chapters 2 through 4 described how to use the Control Center to execute commands by making selections from the menus, choose options from pick lists, and open and close data base files. Entering and updating data records on the Edit and Browse screens involves using a mixture of menu selections and full-screen editing command keys. The full-screen editors enable you to view data in a clear, easy-to-read format and to move freely among the fields in a record and from one record to the next to enter new data and make changes. These editors are well suited for building new data bases and carrying out the routine maintenance operations required to keep your files accurate and up to date.

This chapter introduces the dot prompt, or command-driven, working environment and presents simple commands that are equivalent to some of the full-screen editors' menu bar commands and options. Note, however, that although the full-screen editors form part of the dBASE IV menu system, they are not inextricably linked to the Control Center. You can also invoke the

Browse, Edit, and data base design screens (as well as the forms editors described in later chapters) from the dot prompt.

When you work at the dot prompt, there is a clearer distinction between *viewing* and *editing* data than there is in the full-screen editors: some dot prompt commands allow you only to view data, while others are used to update or edit records without displaying the data. This chapter emphasizes this important distinction—the difference between selecting a record to be acted on by a subsequent command and viewing or editing the data in the record. It also introduces the concepts of the dBASE IV record pointer and the current record, which are essential for ensuring that your commands operate on the intended records.

If you have worked with dBASE II, III, or III PLUS, the commands and concepts presented in this chapter should be familiar to you. If you are new to dBASE, you may find the dot prompt uninviting or even intimidating, but try to resist the temptation to skip this chapter. If you work through the examples with the sample data, this safe, guided tour of the dot prompt should both help you overcome the initial learning barriers and encourage you to do some of your work at the dot prompt.

WORKING AT COMMAND LEVEL

If you have done most of your work in the menu system, remember that you can switch to the dot prompt from the Control Center by selecting **Exit to dot prompt** from the **Exit** menu or by pressing ESC, and you can return to the Control Center by typing ASSIST or by pressing F2. Chapter 18 describes how to configure dBASE IV to bypass the Control Center and display the dot prompt immediately when you start up the program.

When you work with dBASE IV at command level, you type commands one at a time next to a dot prompt, and dBASE IV responds to each by executing it, requesting additional information if necessary, or displaying an error message. All dBASE IV commands begin with a verb—you are commanding the program to do something—followed by other *keywords* and *clauses*, some of which are required and some of which are optional.

You can type a command line of up to 254 characters at the dot prompt. If you type more than 80 characters, the command line at the bottom of the screen scrolls to accommodate your entry. You can edit a command line using the standard cursor movement and editing commands, and you must press ENTER to execute the completed command.

If you try to type more than 254 characters, dBASE IV displays the message "Command too long, press CTRL-HOME to edit in zoom window" at the bottom of the screen. Pressing CTRL-HOME invokes an editor similar to the memo field editor that supports the same full-screen editing commands. To exit from the editor and execute the command, press CTRL-END or select **Save changes and exit** from the **Exit** menu. You can also invoke the text editor at any point (by pressing CTRL-HOME) while entering a shorter command line.

You can type commands, file names, and field names in any combination of uppercase and lowercase letters. You can abbreviate command words, provided that you type at least the first four letters of each word. For example, you could write the DISPLAY STRUCTURE command (which displays the structure of the active data base) as DISP STRU or DISP STRUCT, but not as DISP STR.

OPENING AND CLOSING DATA BASE FILES

Before using a data base, you must *open* it, or make it active so you can work with it. To open a data base from the dot prompt, you employ the USE command:

USE *data base file name*

Think of this command as meaning "I want to *use* this file now." If another data base is already open, dBASE IV closes it before opening the file specified in the new USE command.

If you forget to open a data base before typing a command that requires an open file, dBASE IV prompts you for the file name with the message "No database in use. Enter file name:." After you type a file name, dBASE IV opens the file and executes your command.

As described in Chapter 4, a file is automatically closed when you leave dBASE IV or open a different file. To close a file without opening another or leaving dBASE, you can type

```
USE
```

Think of this command as the verb USE followed by no file name, which means "Use no file" or "I don't want to use any file at all."

MOVING THE RECORD POINTER

dBASE IV keeps track of its position in the file—the record you most recently accessed or the one affected by your last command—whenever a data base is open. The indicator that marks your file position is called the *record pointer,* and the record it points to is often referred to as the *current record.*

To work effectively at the dot prompt, you must understand the concept of the dBASE IV record pointer and remain aware of its current position in a file. Most of the dBASE IV commands used to display and print data, and many of the commands that carry out calculations or change data, can operate on a single record, a group of records, or an entire data base. When a command acts on one record, the affected record is the one at the current position of the record pointer, unless you explicitly override this default by including another record number in your command. Some of the ways you can specify a group of records to be acted on by a dBASE IV command depend on your ability to position the record pointer at the first record in the group before you execute the command.

If you imagine your data base written on a big wall chart laid out like the Browse screen, you can think of the record pointer as a pointing stick, or spotlight, that moves up and down the chart and enables you to "point out" to dBASE IV which record you want to see or operate on. In all your subsequent work with dBASE IV, it is vital to keep track of the position of the record pointer to ensure that the commands you type act on the right records.

Although you may not realize it, you already have considerable experience in positioning the dBASE IV record pointer where you want it. In the full-screen editors, you position the pointer using keypad or CTRL-key commands. For example, when you press PGDN in Edit or DOWN ARROW in Browse, the record pointer advances to the next record in the file.

Because the full-screen commands were designed to facilitate viewing records and making individual editing changes, you are probably accustomed to thinking of these commands primarily as ways to display different records in the active file. However, each of these commands involves two separate steps: first, dBASE IV moves the record pointer forward or backward, and then it displays the data from the record at the new position of the pointer (in Edit mode) or highlights the record (in Browse) to indicate that you can type changes. When you work with dBASE IV at the dot prompt, it is important to distinguish between these two steps, because often you will want to position the pointer on a particular record and perform some operation on that record or on a group of records beginning with that one without necessarily displaying the data.

Whether or not you are aware of the record pointer, and whether or not you have typed any commands explicitly to move the pointer, dBASE IV always keeps track of its position. It is worth reiterating that *the record pointer is always somewhere in the current data base.* When you first open a data base by typing a USE command, the record pointer is at the "top" of the file. In all the examples presented so far, the record at the top of the file is Record 1, the first record entered. (You will see in Chapter 9 that the record at the "top" of a file is not always Record 1.) Subsequent data editing and display commands may reposition the pointer to any record in the file.

You can always determine the position of the record pointer by looking at the status bar, which displays the current record as well as the total number of records in the file. For example, if you entered all the sample data into the National Widgets Customer File, you would see the following in the third section of the status bar as you edited the fifth record:

```
Rec 5/20
```

The record pointer can also be at the *end-of-file (EOF),* a special location that you can visualize as "just past" the last record in a file. As you will see in Chapter 7, many commands that process an entire data base leave the record pointer at the end-of-file. The record pointer may also wind up at the end-of-file after you use certain commands, such as the SKIP command (described later in this chapter), to attempt to advance beyond the last record. When the record pointer is at the end-of-file, this fact is reflected in the status bar display:

```
Rec EOF/20
```

The end-of-file is not the same as the "bottom" of the file, which in the examples presented so far is the last record entered. You already know how to move to the bottom of a file by selecting the **Last record** option from the **Go To** menu in any of the full-screen editors. When the record pointer is at the end-of-file, it is not positioned at the last record or at any valid record. This distinction is important, because commands that operate on a single record—the current record—will have no effect if the record pointer is at the end-of-file.

When you use any standard exit commands, such as CTRL-END or ESC, to return to the dot prompt or the Control Center from one of the full-screen editors, the record pointer does not move from its current position. If you are editing Record 3, for example, and you press CTRL-END to save your changes and exit, you will return to the dot prompt with the pointer still at Record 3, a fact that you can confirm by looking at the status bar. If you then reenter any of the full-screen editors before executing any command that would move the record pointer, the first record displayed is Record 3, the one at the current position of the pointer.

USING GOTO TO POSITION THE RECORD POINTER

In the full-screen edit modes, you move the record pointer forward or backward using command keys such as PGUP and PGDN on the Edit screen or UP ARROW and DOWN ARROW in Browse mode. You can also jump directly to a particular record by using the **Top record, Last record,** or **Record number** option in the **Go To** menu in any of the full-screen editors. At the dot prompt, you can accomplish the same thing with the GOTO command, which can be abbreviated as GO. To position the record pointer at the top of the file, you can use

```
GOTO TOP
```

or

```
GO TOP
```

You can move to the bottom of the file with

```
GOTO BOTTOM
```

or

```
GO BOTTOM
```

You can also GOTO any record, specified by number, with

GOTO *record number*

or

GO *record number*

Since dBASE IV command verbs never begin with a number, you can omit the verb entirely and type just a number at the dot prompt to move the record pointer to the corresponding record. For example, to move to Record 4, you could type

```
4
```

Unlike the full-screen commands that position the record pointer, GOTO does not display the record, much less present it on the screen in a format suitable for editing. When you first begin to work with dBASE IV, this behavior may be disconcerting, but ultimately the separation of the positioning and display commands adds flexibility to the dBASE IV command language.

When you use GOTO to position the record pointer on a particular record, dBASE IV makes no assumptions about what you want to do with that record. You might want to edit the data, display it without editing, mark it for deletion, remove a previously entered deletion marker, carry out a computation on the data in the fields, or print it on paper. The program therefore does nothing but move the record pointer and then wait for further instructions.

To confirm that the data base is in fact positioned on the requested record, dBASE IV displays the file name and the new position of the record pointer after executing a GOTO command. For example, with the National Widgets Customer File open, dBASE IV would display the following message after a GOTO 4 command:

```
NWCUST: Record No       4
```

If you would like to see the data to confirm that the current record is the one you want, you can use the EDIT command to display the record on the Edit screen (the EDIT command is explained later in this chapter) or use the DISPLAY command (introduced later in this chapter and described in detail in Chapter 6) to display the record without editing the data.

USING SKIP TO POSITION THE RECORD POINTER

From the dot prompt, you can move the record pointer forward or backward a specified number of records by using the SKIP command, as follows:

SKIP *number*

To advance the pointer three records, you would type

```
SKIP 3
```

By default, the SKIP command moves the pointer forward one record, so you can omit the 1 if you want to move to the next record:

```
SKIP
```

You can also move backward by specifying a negative number in the SKIP command. To back up to the previous record, you would type

```
SKIP -1
```

After a SKIP command, dBASE IV displays the new position of the record pointer. For example, if you began with the record pointer positioned at Record 2 in the Customer File and typed SKIP 4, dBASE IV would advance the pointer four records and display the following message:

```
NWCUST: Record No       6
```

The record number display and other messages that dBASE IV uses to respond to your commands and confirm the actions taken are called "talk." This ongoing "conversation" between you and the program is one reason that the dot prompt is also referred to as *interactive mode.*

Just like the GOTO command, the SKIP command does nothing but reposition the dBASE IV record pointer; it does not display or otherwise operate on the record. If you want to see the record to confirm that it is the right one, you can EDIT or DISPLAY it.

UPDATING A DATA BASE

Working from the dot prompt, you can invoke the same full-screen editors that are available from the Control Center to add records to a data base or edit existing records. To add records to the end of a dBASE IV data base (or to an empty data base), you open the file and then type

```
APPEND
```

To invoke the spreadsheet-style Browse display, you type

```
BROWSE
```

To enter the full-screen edit mode, you can use the EDIT or CHANGE command. These two command verbs serve the same purpose, and you can use them interchangeably. (The examples in this book use EDIT rather than CHANGE.) To begin editing records, type

```
EDIT
```

or

```
CHANGE
```

The resulting screens are identical, and they are also identical to the Edit screen invoked from the Control Center. The current record—the one that you most recently accessed—is displayed in the standard full-screen format, with the cursor in the first field. If you have just finished adding records, the EDIT command will display the last record added to the file. If you have just begun a new work session and opened a file with a USE command, dBASE IV displays the first record in the file.

The cursor movement and editing keys function exactly as they do when you enter the full-screen editor from the Control Center. As described in Chapter 4, you can page forward and backward through a file, alternate between adding new records and accessing previously entered records, switch from the Edit screen to the Browse screen, and delete and "undelete" records. The only difference is that when you exit the editor with CTRL-END or ESC or select the **Exit** option from the **Exit** menu, dBASE IV returns you to the dot prompt rather than to the menu system.

All the Browse and Edit menu options also work exactly the same as when you enter the full-screen editor from the Control Center. In addition, dBASE IV offers *command line equivalents*—keywords that you can add to the BROWSE command—that have the same effects as the options on the **Fields** menu. You can use the LOCK keyword to lock one or more fields on the left side of the display, and you can use the FREEZE keyword to restrict editing to one field, as in the following:

```
USE NWCUST
BROWSE LOCK 2 FREEZE EQUIPMENT
```

A variety of additional keywords allow you to customize other aspects of the full-screen editing environment that you cannot change from within the Browse or Edit screen. For example, the WIDTH keyword enables you to specify the maximum column width for all fields on the Browse screen, so that you do not have to individually resize many long character fields. NOAPPEND prevents you from adding new records, NODELETE prevents you from deleting records, and NOMENU disables the menu bar.

If you include the NOCLEAR keyword, dBASE IV does not clear the screen when you exit from Edit or Browse to the dot prompt, so that the data you were last viewing remains visible for reference as you type your next command. NOINIT prevents dBASE IV from reinitializing the Browse or Edit display options, so that you can return to either full-screen editor after typing commands at the dot prompt and find the same options—column widths, locked or frozen fields, and so on—in effect as in the previous editing session.

In any of the full-screen editors, you can delete records or clear a previously set deletion marker by pressing CTRL-U or by selecting the **Mark record for deletion** or **Clear deletion mark** option from the **Records** menu. From the dot prompt, you can do the same thing with the DELETE and RECALL commands. By default, both of these commands operate on one record—the one at the current position of the record pointer.

To mark a record for deletion, you can use any command you know (for example, GOTO or SKIP) to move the pointer to the correct record and type

```
DELETE
```

dBASE IV confirms that it has deleted a record with the message "1 record deleted."

You can recover a record previously marked for deletion by positioning the record pointer on the correct record and typing

```
RECALL
```

In response, dBASE IV displays the message "1 record recalled."

Note again that you do not have to display or edit a record to mark it as deleted or to undelete it. In a real application, you might GOTO several records by number, based on information in a printed list, and delete or recall them rapidly without looking at any data.

As described in Chapter 4, records marked for deletion are not immediately erased from the disk. Instead, dBASE IV enables you to mark records individually, recall deleted records if you change your mind, and later carry out the relatively slow process of compacting the file to remove records marked for deletion. To have dBASE IV ignore deleted records, you can type

```
SET DELETED ON
```

To return to displaying deleted records, you would type

```
SET DELETED OFF
```

After a SET DELETED ON command, records marked for deletion are ignored by most dBASE IV commands—they do not appear in displayed or printed output, they are not included in calculations, and when you page forward or backward in the full-screen editors, they are passed over. If, at any time, you want to be able to process deleted records again, you can SET DELETED OFF. (Chapter 18 explains how to set the DELETED option ON or OFF through the menus.)

To understand this seemingly contradictory terminology, it is helpful to think of the DELETED setting as a kind of *filter*. This term is used by dBASE IV to describe a set of selection criteria applied to a data base, not just for a single command but for an indefinite period of time. Only records that satisfy the criteria are included in subsequent processing, just as if you had poured the file through a specially designed filter, or sieve, that permits only the desired records to pass through. When you SET DELETED ON, you are turning on this filtering process, which excludes deleted records, or selects records that are not marked for deletion. SET DELETED OFF turns off the filter and thereby reveals all the records.

By using the DELETED setting to ignore deleted records selectively, you can enjoy the benefits of instantaneous deletion—the "deleted" records seem to disappear from the data base immediately—and can postpone the slower process of physically removing the "deleted" records from disk.

When DELETED is ON, you can still position the record pointer on a deleted record, but only by using a command that explicitly includes the record number. For example, if Record 3 is marked as deleted, you can access it with

```
GOTO 3
```

Once the record pointer is positioned on the record, you can EDIT, DISPLAY, or RECALL it. However, if you execute a SKIP command with the record pointer on Record 2, it will jump over Record 3 to land on Record 4, just as pressing PGDN with Record 2 displayed on the Edit screen will pass over the deleted Record 3.

You can permanently remove all deleted records from a data base with the PACK command. This is equivalent to using the **Erase marked records** option on the **Organize** menu on the Edit, Browse, or data base design screen. To use this command, you open the data base and type

```
PACK
```

The PACK command performs the process, described in Chapter 4, of recopying a file in place, minus the deletions. Records are "moved up" in the file into the positions formerly occupied by records marked for deletion, and all the records after the first deletion are renumbered. This process can take some time in a large file, but in most applications you need not PACK your files very often.

USING LIST AND DISPLAY TO VIEW RECORDS

The full-screen editors are best suited to viewing and updating records one at a time. Even the Browse screen, which *displays* multiple records, is geared to *editing* records one by one. If you want to view all or selected fields without making changes, you can use the LIST and DISPLAY commands at the dot prompt. LIST and DISPLAY are similar, and, as you will see in Chapters 6 and

7, you can achieve similar results with either command. One difference is that, by default, LIST operates on all the records in a data base, while DISPLAY acts on the current record only—the one at the position of the record pointer. To display all the records in a data base, you would type

```
LIST
```

To view only one record, you could type

```
DISPLAY
```

Both commands require that a data base be open; you cannot display data from a file without opening it first, and there is no single command that opens a file and then displays its contents. If you type either of these commands with no data base open, dBASE IV prompts you for a file name.

Figure 5-1 illustrates how the screen would look if you typed a LIST command after entering the first three records into the National Widgets Customer File and deleting Record 3. By default, LIST displays all the fields from all the records in the file. The sequential record number is included at the beginning of each record. Records are listed in the order in which they were entered into the data base, with each beginning on a new line, and the fields from each record are spread across the screen.

In a small data base with only a few fields, the data will align neatly in columns. If there are too many fields to fit on one line, dBASE IV wraps the data from a record onto as many lines as it requires, which makes the display less readable. In the National Widgets Customer File, a record is 273 bytes long and occupies four lines on the screen.

Recall that when you delete a record, it is not immediately removed from the data base but is marked for later removal. The deletion marker, an asterisk (*), is included in the output produced by the LIST and DISPLAY commands, between the record number and the first data field. In Figure 5-1, you can see this marker next to the account code in Record 3.

By default, dBASE IV displays the field names at the beginning of the output produced by a LIST or DISPLAY command, to serve as "column headings" that identify the data being displayed. The amount of space a field occupies in a LIST or DISPLAY is either the field width or the width of the field name, whichever is greater. Even in a relatively small file like the Customer File, which has only 15 fields (you are permitted a maximum of 255) that add

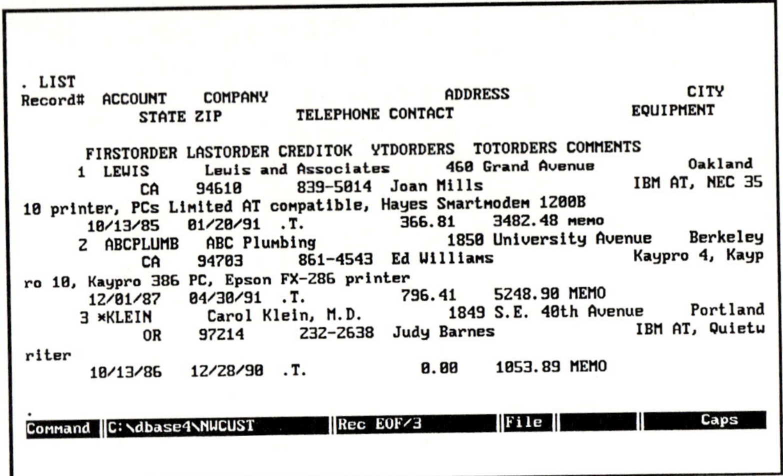

Figure 5-1.

Using the LIST command to display data

up to 273 bytes (the maximum is 4000), the data wraps around onto four lines, and the headings are not particularly helpful. You can turn off the field heading display by typing the following command at the dot prompt:

```
SET HEADING OFF
```

As you will see shortly, the headings are much more useful when you LIST only selected fields. You can turn the heading display back on with

```
SET HEADING ON
```

As you can see from Figure 5-1, LIST and DISPLAY always show logical fields as .T. ("True") or .F. ("False"), even if you entered Y or N. A logical field that was left blank is displayed as .F., which is consistent with the way logical data is evaluated—a logical field can be treated as having a true value only if you have specifically entered .T. or .Y.; otherwise, it is false.

The output of a LIST or DISPLAY command does not include the contents of any memo fields in your data base. As in the Browse and Edit screens, dBASE IV displays "MEMO" if a memo field contains text, or "memo" if it is blank, presumably because you would not want the display cluttered with large amounts of text. There is an easy way to LIST or DISPLAY the contents of a memo field, which is explained in Chapter 6.

If you LIST a file that contains more than a few records, the data may scroll up the screen and disappear too fast for you to read it. Chapter 6 introduces several variations of the LIST and DISPLAY commands that you can use to circumvent this problem, but there are also two keyboard commands that you can use to pause temporarily any display produced by dBASE IV (and DOS as well). CTRL-S acts as a toggle: It stops the display when it is scrolling or resumes scrolling if the display is paused. An alternative command on many keyboards is PAUSE (located above the numeric keypad or cursor keypad), which differs from CTRL-S in that it can only be used to pause the display, not to restart it. In either case, you can resume scrolling by pressing any key on the keyboard except PAUSE. To abort a LIST command—and most other dBASE IV commands—and return to the dot prompt to type a new command, press ESC.

If you allow a LIST command to run to completion, the record pointer will wind up at the end-of-file. Keep this fact in mind when you work with a data base at the dot prompt and use LIST commands to verify the results of your updates. When the record pointer is at the end-of-file, commands that normally act on one record, such as DELETE, RECALL, and DISPLAY, will have no effect. However, if you attempt to execute any of these commands at the end-of-file, dBASE IV does not consider this to be an error and does not display an error message. For example, a DISPLAY command simply does not display any data, and a DELETE command results in the message "No records deleted," with no explanation.

RETRIEVING AND EDITING PREVIOUS COMMANDS

When you type commands at the dot prompt, dBASE IV retains your last few commands in memory. By default, this command *history* consists of the 20 most recently executed commands. At any point, you can retrieve one of these commands so as to repeat a previous command, edit or add to a command and resubmit it in changed form, or obtain a reminder of what you just did. As your commands grow in length and complexity, this feature will become increasingly useful. You can increase or decrease the size of the command history default by using the SET HISTORY command, the syntax of which is given in Appendix D. (General methods for using SET commands to customize the working environment are discussed in Chapter 18.)

You can use the UP ARROW and DOWN ARROW keys to page up and down through the list of commands in history. You might visualize the command history as a list, or stack, of commands that is accessed from the bottom up, as if the commands you typed at the dot prompt were progressing up the screen, with the most recent one on the line just above the command line and earlier commands gradually pushed off the top. Pressing UP ARROW at the dot prompt causes dBASE IV to display your previous command, and as you continue to move up, you will see older (earlier) commands closer to the top of the list. When you type your twenty-first command in a work session, the first one is displaced from the top of the history list and can no longer be retrieved.

To see the entire command history, you can type

```
LIST HISTORY
```

When you use the arrow keys to retrieve a previous command from history, dBASE IV displays the command next to the dot prompt, with the cursor on the first character. To repeat the command in exactly the same form, press ENTER.

You can also use any of the full-screen editing keys to edit the command line. You can use the RIGHT ARROW and LEFT ARROW keys to move through the command one character at a time, or use HOME and END to move one word at a time. You can delete single characters with DEL or BACKSPACE, you can delete an entire word with CTRL-T, and you can delete all characters to the right of the cursor with CTRL-Y. When you are ready to resubmit your modified command, press ENTER with the cursor positioned anywhere within the line. If you change your mind and decide to type a new command at the dot prompt, press ESC to erase the line and start fresh.

Every command executed from the dot prompt is added to the history list, regardless of whether you typed the command from scratch or retrieved and reentered a previous command. Thus, if you type DELETE, press UP ARROW to retrieve the command, and press ENTER to repeat it unchanged, a LIST HISTORY command will reveal that the history list contains two copies of the DELETE command.

RESPONDING TO ERRORS AND REQUESTING HELP

When you work at the dot prompt, dBASE IV responds to erroneous commands with a pop-up dialog box that displays an error message. If the first word in a command is not recognizable as a valid command verb, the error message will be "***Unrecognized command verb." If you make a typographical error or forget how to spell a field name, the error message is usually "Variable not found." This means that dBASE IV looked for a variable—a field—with the specified name but failed to find one in the data base that is currently open.

Figure 5-2 illustrates the error message box that is displayed if you misspell the command verb DISPLAY. The error dialog box offers three options: **Cancel**, **Edit**, and **Help**. If you select **Cancel**, dBASE IV cancels the command and returns you to the dot prompt, where you can try again to construct the command correctly or type an entirely different command. Choosing **Help** calls up the same help screen that would have been displayed had you explicitly requested assistance by pressing F1 (Help).

If you select **Edit**, your erroneous command is redisplayed next to the dot prompt, and you can edit and resubmit it, just as if you had retrieved the command from history. You will probably use this option more often as your knowledge of dBASE IV commands and syntax grows, and the majority of the error messages you receive result not from any true misunderstanding but from typographical errors or because you have forgotten or misspelled field names.

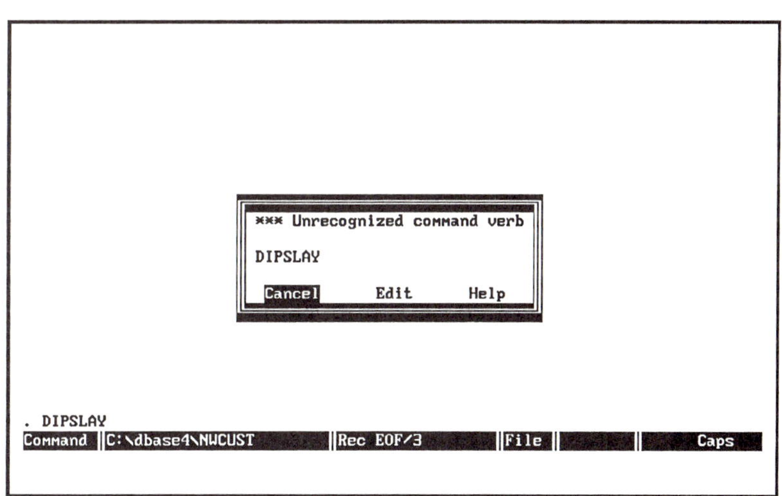

Figure 5-2.

The dBASE IV error response dialog box

SUMMARY

In this chapter, you learned how to carry out many of the same file maintenance operations by typing commands that you can accomplish with the full-screen editors. You also learned the commands that enable you to access the dBASE IV full-screen editors from the dot prompt. Whether you do most of your work at the dot prompt or use the Control Center as your base of operations depends on personal preference. To some extent, your choice of the full-screen commands or their dot prompt equivalents for operations such as deleting and recalling records will also depend on the kind of work you are doing. The full-screen commands are generally better suited for adding and editing data, while the dot prompt commands are more effective for operating on records without looking at all the fields.

For example, when you are working from a printed list that includes record numbers, the fastest way to mark a dozen widely separated records for deletion is to use a series of GOTO commands, each followed by a DELETE command. This method is faster and more direct than using the **Go To** menu in the Edit or Browse screen to find each record and then selecting the **Mark record for deletion** option in the **Records** menu. But if you were adding new records, editing others, and deleting a few at the same time, working entirely in Edit or Browse mode would be more convenient. If you are new to dBASE IV, your goal should be to feel comfortable and confident working in either environment so that you can choose the combination that is right for you.

CHAPTER SIX

Selecting Fields

When your files are small and you are familiar with their contents, the Edit screen is adequate for viewing the data in a few specific records; if you prefer working at the dot prompt, you can employ the DISPLAY command for the same purpose. If you need to search for a record, see at a glance what data has been entered into certain fields in many records, or quickly scan a data base to spot trends, you can display multiple records on the Browse screen or use the simple LIST command introduced in Chapter 5. With files that have more fields or more records, the mass of information displayed by these commands can be visually overwhelming, and you may find it difficult to pick out specific items of interest.

The typical data base user spends a great deal of time conducting various inquiries, or queries—retrieving data in order to view information onscreen or generate printed listings. To make these displays and printouts more selective, and therefore more useful, you will want to specify selection criteria that limit processing to certain records and/or fields, rather than displaying all the information in the data base. dBASE IV provides an array of tools for implementing record and field selection criteria. One of these tools is a layout editor that enables you to define *queries*—files that contain detailed instructions for retrieving specific subsets of the information stored in one or more data bases. If you prefer to work at the dot prompt, you can add options to the basic LIST and DISPLAY commands explained in Chapter 5 to implement the same selection criteria.

This chapter describes a variety of techniques for specifying field selection criteria. (Record selection criteria are covered in Chapter 7.) You can think of these methods as ways to construct a *field list*, which consists of fields from the active data bases and calculated fields that are derived from data base fields. The field list determines which items are displayed or printed. If you prefer the menu-driven environment, you can use a specialized layout editor—the query design screen, which is also known as Query-by-Example—to define the field list. From the dot prompt, you can add a field list to many commands such as LIST, DISPLAY, EDIT, and BROWSE, or you can define a field list with a SET FIELDS command that remains in effect and governs the data displayed by one or more subsequent commands until you explicitly cancel it.

INTRODUCTION TO dBASE IV QUERIES

A dBASE IV query is a set of instructions for displaying or processing data. There are two types of queries, which are defined using the same layout editor but serve different purposes. *View queries* are used to display selected fields and records from one or more data bases. For example, you could define a query that displays just the account code, company name, contact name, and telephone number fields from National Widgets' customers in California. *Update queries* describe procedures for changing or deleting selected records in a single data base. For example, you could use an update query to delete all customers whose last order was placed more than two years ago. (Update queries are explained in Chapters 10 and 16.)

You can think of a view query as a description of how to produce a customized *view* of data contained in one or more data bases. In the dBASE IV documentation, the words "query" and "view" are used almost interchangeably, but you can avoid confusing the two by remembering that "view" refers to the data, while "query" describes the instructions for extracting this data from the full data base files. You can save a query on disk and use it to reconstruct the same view in a later work session without having to repeat the definition steps.

Views are sometimes described as *virtual files,* meaning that *a view behaves as if it were a real data base file,* although in fact, the data in a view is derived from other, preexisting data bases and in many cases is never actually stored on disk. For example, when you open the hypothetical view described earlier in this section, it seems as if you are working with a file that has 4 fields—ACCOUNT, COMPANY, CONTACT, and TELEPHONE—and contains 14 records (National Widgets' customers in California). In fact, dBASE IV is reading the Customer File, and showing you only the information from the specified 4 fields and 14 records. You can define as many different views as you like in order to display or edit various sets of fields and records in the underlying data bases, while saving the time and disk space that would be required to create, store, and update multiple independent copies of the data. Occasionally, you may want to save precisely the fields and records selected by a view in a real data base file, and you can do this using a method that is explained in Chapter 16.

If you have used dBASE III PLUS, note that in dBASE IV the terms "query" and "view" are used differently. A dBASE IV view query is analogous to a dBASE III PLUS "view," although the two programs use different disk file formats to store view specifications. In dBASE III PLUS, the term "query" was used for a file that stores record selection criteria on disk. dBASE IV has no direct counterpart for the dBASE III PLUS query file, nor does it need one, because you can include record selection criteria in a view query.

dBASE IV provides a specialized layout editor, the *query design screen,* for defining, editing, and executing both view and update queries. The dBASE IV query editor is said to have a *Query-by-Example* interface, because you specify selection criteria by typing examples of the data you want to select. You can access the query design screen from the **Queries** panel in the Control Center, from the full-screen Edit and Browse modes, and from the dot prompt.

From the Menus

To facilitate the integration of field and record selection criteria with the commands that display or print data, the query design screen is accessible from many different points in the dBASE IV menu system. From the Control Center, you can create a new query by selecting the **<create>** option from the **Queries** panel. To edit an existing query, you highlight its name in the **Queries** panel, press ENTER, and select the **Modify query** option from the pop-up dialog box shown in Figure 6-1.

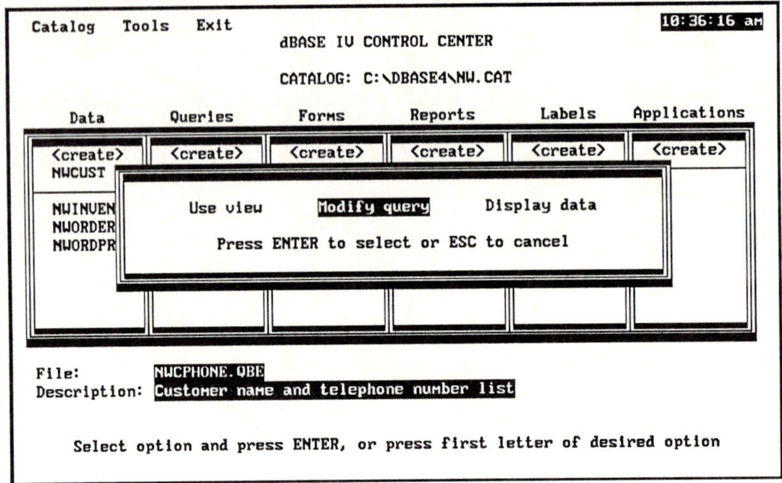

Figure 6-1.

Invoking the query design screen to edit a view query

Both the Edit and Browse screens offer a **Transfer to Query Design** option on their **Exit** menus. You can also use a function key shortcut—SHIFT-F2 (Design)—to move directly to the query design screen from the Control Center, Edit, Browse, or any of the layout editors used to design data bases, screens, reports, and labels. From the Control Center, you must highlight a query name or the **<create>** option in the **Queries** panel before you press SHIFT-F2 (Design). When you enter the query design screen through the menu system to define a new query, you do not assign a name to the file until you save it.

D From the Dot Prompt

From the dot prompt, you invoke the query design screen by typing

CREATE QUERY *query file name*

or

MODIFY QUERY *query file name*

Because the terms "query" and "view" are both commonly used to describe query files, you may also use

CREATE VIEW *query file name*

or

MODIFY VIEW *query file name*

Although the two different verbs imply that you should use a CREATE command to define a new query file and a MODIFY command to edit an existing file, in practice all four command variants are interchangeable. If the query form named in a CREATE QUERY or CREATE VIEW command already exists, dBASE IV pops up a dialog box to warn you, "File already exists." You have two options: **Modify**, which loads the query as if you had typed MODIFY QUERY, and **Cancel**, which returns you to the dot prompt. When you create a new disk file from the dot prompt, you must name the file in advance by including the name in the CREATE QUERY or MODIFY QUERY command; if you omit the file name, dBASE IV prompts you to enter it.

The query design screen presents an initially blank work surface on which you display a graphical representation of the view you are building together with the data base files that will contribute data to the view. A query can draw data from up to eight data bases, but this chapter and Chapter 7 discuss only single file queries (multifile queries are covered in Chapter 17).

The query design screen menu bar has five options, which are used for the following purposes:

Layout	Select the data base files that will contribute data to the view, define the relationships between files, and name and save the query
Fields	Select the fields to be included in the view
Condition	Reveal or hide the optional condition box used to enter record selection critera
Update	Define or execute an update query
Exit	Exit the query design screen

The structure of the query design menu is shown in Figure 6-2.

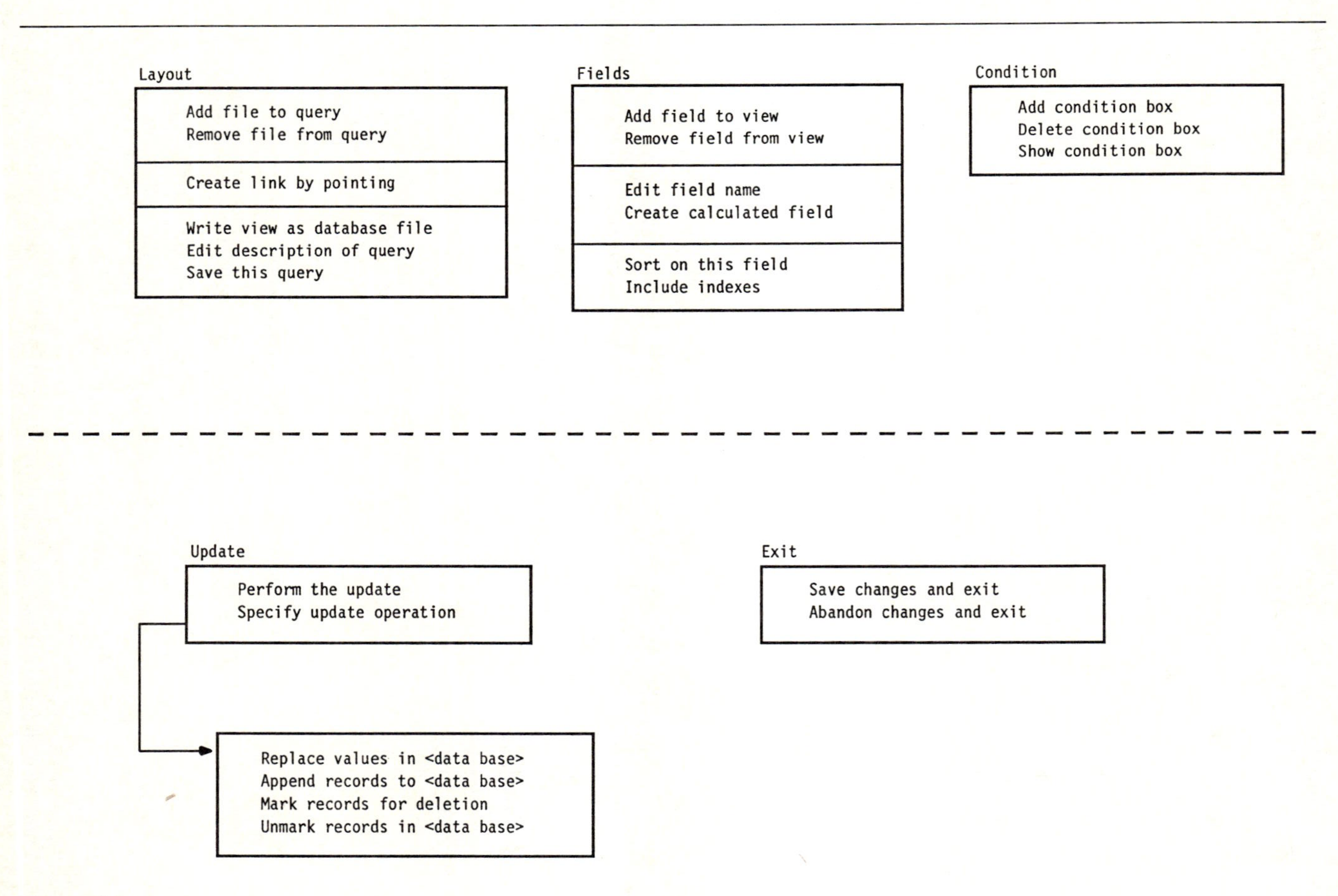

Figure 6-2.

The structure of the query design screen menu

Data bases are represented on the query design work surface as *file skeletons*, a tabular format in which the field names are laid out horizontally, somewhat like the Browse display. As you will see in Chapter 7, record selection criteria are entered in one or more rows of this table below the field names. The representation of the view defined by the query is referred to as the *view skeleton*. The view skeleton is always displayed at the bottom of the screen, just above the status bar (the status bar is always present in the query design screen, even if you have turned off the status display for other work). dBASE IV also displays as many file skeletons as will fit on the screen at once and at your discretion a skeleton containing calculated field definitions. Figure 6-3 illustrates the query design screen with the National Widgets Customer File and a view skeleton displayed.

If a data base is already open when you invoke the query editor, dBASE IV displays a skeleton for this file at the top of the screen, and the view skeleton will include all of its fields. If a data base is not open, dBASE IV automatically pulls down the **Layout** menu, with the **Add file to query** option highlighted to remind you that you must begin by opening at least one file. In the second segment of the status bar, dBASE IV displays the name of the view you are constructing, or <NEW> if you have not yet assigned a name to it.

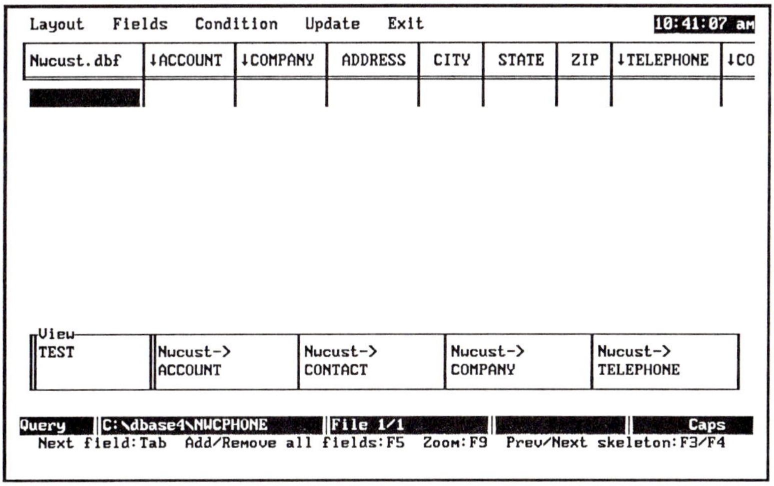

```
Layout   Fields   Condition   Update   Exit                          10:41:07 am

Nwcust.dbf | ↓ACCOUNT | ↓COMPANY | ADDRESS | CITY | STATE | ZIP | ↓TELEPHONE | ↓CO

View
TEST   | Nwcust->  | Nwcust->  | Nwcust->  | Nwcust->
       | ACCOUNT   | CONTACT   | COMPANY   | TELEPHONE

Query  | C:\dbase4\NWCPHONE  | File 1/1 |  |  Caps
  Next field:Tab  Add/Remove all fields:F5  Zoom:F9  Prev/Next skeleton:F3/F4
```

Figure 6-3.

The Query-by-Example work surface

To open a data base and display its skeleton on the work surface, you select the **Add file to query** option from the **Layout** menu and then choose the file name from a pick list that displays the names of available data bases. As you move up and down the list, the file descriptions stored in the catalog are displayed in a pop-up box in the lower left corner of the screen to help you choose the right file. As in any dBASE IV pick list, you select a file by highlighting its name and pressing ENTER.

dBASE IV displays as many fields as possible from each data base file skeleton. Initially, the widths of the columns are derived from the field names, but as you type selection criteria, the columns expand dynamically to accomodate your entries. Regardless of the length of the field names, dBASE IV always displays four fields at a time from the view skeleton. When more than one file skeleton appears on the screen, you can switch to the next by pressing F4 (Next) or go back to the previous skeleton with F3 (Previous). Like menu bar options, skeletons are treated as if they were arranged in a circle; pressing F4 (Next) from the view skeleton (which is always last) returns you to the first file skeleton, and pressing F3 (Previous) from the first file skeleton moves the highlight into the view skeleton.

You can pan the display to the right by pressing TAB or to the left by pressing SHIFT-TAB to reveal additional fields. The HOME key jumps directly to the first field in the skeleton, and END takes you to the last field. In the file skeletons, the frame around the column headings indicates clearly whether there are more fields "off the screen" to the right. At the left side of the file skeleton, and at both sides of the view skeleton (which includes at most four fields), dBASE IV displays a small triangle, or "arrowhead," on the line below the field names if there are additional fields not visible on the screen. The leftmost column, which has the file name instead of a field name as a header, represents the entire data base and remains stationary as you pan the display to the left or right.

Table 6-1 lists all the cursor movement and editing keys used in the query design screen.

Defining Field Selection Criteria

To add a field to the list of fields included in the view you are constructing, you position the highlight under the field name and either select the **Add field to view** option from the **Fields** menu or press F5 (Field). When you select a field,

Control Key	Command Key	Function
	F10 (Menu)	Activate the menu system
	ALT-*letter*	Activate the menu system and pull down the menu whose description begins with *letter*
	letter	Select the option on the active pull-down menu whose description begins with *letter*
	ENTER	Select the highlighted option or item from the active menu, panel, or pick list
CTRL-W	CTRL-END	Save changes and exit
CTRL-Q	ESC	Exit without saving changes
CTRL-E	UP ARROW	Remove the current row and contract file skeleton
CTRL-X	DOWN ARROW or ENTER	Add a row to the file skeleton
CTRL-D	RIGHT ARROW	Move right one character
CTRL-S	LEFT ARROW	Move left one character
CTRL-F	CTRL-RIGHT ARROW	Move right one word
CTRL-A	CTRL-LEFT ARROW	Move left one word
CTRL-I	TAB	Move to the next column
	SHIFT-TAB	Move to the previous column
	F4 (Next)	Move to the next skeleton
	F3 (Previous)	Move to the previous skeleton
	ENTER	Move to the next field (Edit) or to the next record (Browse)
CTRL-Z	HOME	Move to the first column in the current skeleton
CTRL-B	END	Move to the last column in the current skeleton
CTRL-C	PGDN	Display the next group of file skeletons

Table 6-1.

The Cursor Movement and Editing Keys in Query-by-Example

Control Key	Command Key	Function
CTRL-R	PGUP	Display the previous group of file skeletons
	CTRL-PGDN	Move to the last row in the file skeleton
	CTRL-PGUP	Move to the first row in the file skeleton
CTRL-G	DEL	Delete the character at the cursor position
	BACKSPACE	Delete the character to the left of the cursor
CTRL-T		Delete the characters from the cursor to the end of the word
CTRL-U		Delete the current row from the file skeleton
CTRL-Y		Delete the characters from the cursor to the end of the expression
CTRL-V	INS	Turn Insert mode on (if it is off) or off (if it is on)
CTRL-N		Insert a new row into the file skeleton
	F9 (Zoom)	Expand the data entry area to fill the screen
	F2 (Data)	Switch to Browse or Edit to view the data selected by the query (return to QBE with SHIFT-F2 (Design))
	F5 (Field)	Add or delete fields from the work surface
	F6 (Select)	Mark the first in a group of fields (indicate the end of the group by pressing ENTER)
	F7 (Move)	Move the selected group of fields

Table 6-1.

The Cursor Movement and Editing Keys in Query-by-Example (*continued*)

dBASE IV creates a new column in the view skeleton, with the field name at the top, and it places a downward-pointing arrow to the left of the field name in the file skeleton as a reminder that this field is part of the current view. To remove a field from the view skeleton, you highlight the corresponding column in either skeleton and select the **Remove field from view** option from the **Fields** menu or press F5 (Field).

Columns in the view skeleton are arranged in the order in which you selected them (added them to the view), which is not necessarily the order of the fields in the contributing data bases. When you execute the query, dBASE IV displays fields in the order in which they occur in the view skeleton.

You can select all the fields in a data base (or all the remaining fields if you have already added some fields to the view skeleton) by placing the highlight under the file name in the first column of the file skeleton (which represents the entire data base) and issuing either of the "add field" commands. When you create a view that includes many fields, it is often easier to select all the fields in the contributing data bases and then delete the unwanted ones than it is to choose fields one by one. You might also want to select all the fields if you are creating a view only to define record selection criteria or if you are building a view that includes all the fields from one data base together with selected fields from another. (These operations are described in Chapters 7 and 17.) To remove all the fields in a file from the view skeleton, highlight the data base name column (the first column) in the file skeleton, and then issue either "remove field" command.

Note that in different contexts, the same key, F5 (Field), can be used to add a field to the view skeleton, add all the fields in a file, delete a field, or delete all the fields. dBASE IV reminds you about the changing meaning of this function key by displaying the message "Add/Remove all fields:F5" on the navigation line when the data base name column in a file skeleton is highlighted or "Remove from view:F5" when a field name is highlighted in the view skeleton.

You can rename a field in the view skeleton by typing the new name directly above the original field name in the view skeleton, or by selecting the **Edit field name** option from the **Fields** menu and entering the new name in a pop-up dialog box. Renaming a field in the view skeleton does not change the field name in the original data base—it simply allows you to refer to the field by a different name when you use the view to access data. The original field name is displayed in the view skeleton to reflect this fact, with the alternate name above it, as shown in Figure 6-4.

To delete a group of fields, or move a field or group of adjacent fields to a new position in the view skeleton, you use commands that are similar to the text block manipulation commands in the memo field editor to select the fields and indicate the new position. As in the memo field editor, you mark the beginning of the block by pressing F6 (Select), in this case, with the first field in the desired group highlighted. dBASE IV surrounds the field with a shaded box to confirm its inclusion in the marked block. You can expand or contract the block to include more or fewer fields by pressing the standard cursor movement keys; when you have selected the desired fields, press ENTER. To delete the

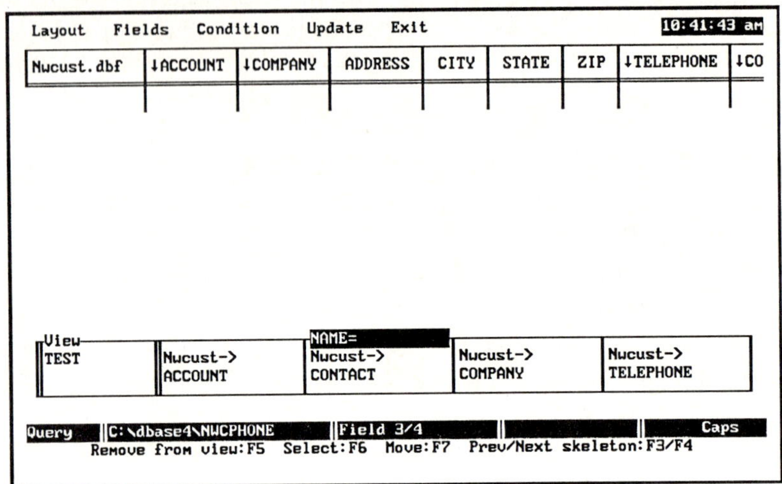

Figure 6-4.

Renaming a field in the view skeleton

marked fields, press F5 (Field). To move the block, press F7 (Move); use LEFT ARROW, RIGHT ARROW, TAB, and SHIFT-TAB to "drag" the selected block through the view skeleton to its new position; and press ENTER to "lock" the fields in place.

The view shown in Figure 6-4, which is called NWCPHONE, includes only the ACCOUNT, CONTACT, COMPANY, and TELEPHONE fields from the Customer File; you might use this view to display or print a customer name and telephone list. Note that the order of the fields differs from their sequence in the Customer File structure and that the CONTACT field is renamed NAME in the view. As you can see in Figure 6-4, the field names in the view skeleton include a reference to the name of the underlying data base, NWCUST–>. This notation is used in many of the dBASE IV form design screens because, for operations that involve multiple files, dBASE IV requires the data base name to identify the source of each field (this is especially important when the same field name occurs in more than one data base). It is explained more fully in Chapter 17.

Defining Calculated Fields

In addition to fields drawn from one or more data bases, a view query can include *calculated fields,* which take on values derived from fields in the view skeleton itself or from the contributing data bases. To define a calculated field, you select the **Create calculated field** option from the **Fields** menu, and then specify the expression that defines the calculated field. Chapter 10 explains in detail the rules for constructing syntactically correct dBASE IV expressions, but a simple example should suffice to illustrate the concept of calculated fields. Figure 6-5 shows the query design screen with a calculated field that computes the ratio of a customer's year-to-date and total orders as YTDORDERS divided by TOTORDERS.

When you add the first calculated field to a view, dBASE IV creates a *calculated field skeleton*, which is displayed on the work surface above the view skeleton. The most direct way to enter the expression that defines a calculation is to type it in the "column heading" area, which is normally used for the field name. If you type an expression that is wider than the space provided, the data entry area in the calculated field skeleton scrolls to accommodate it. When you type a long or complex expression, you can expand the data entry area to fill most of the screen by pressing F9 (Zoom); when you are finished editing, press F9 (Zoom) again to return to the standard query design screen.

You can also enter all or some of the components of an expression by selecting them from a pick list of available fields, operators, and functions

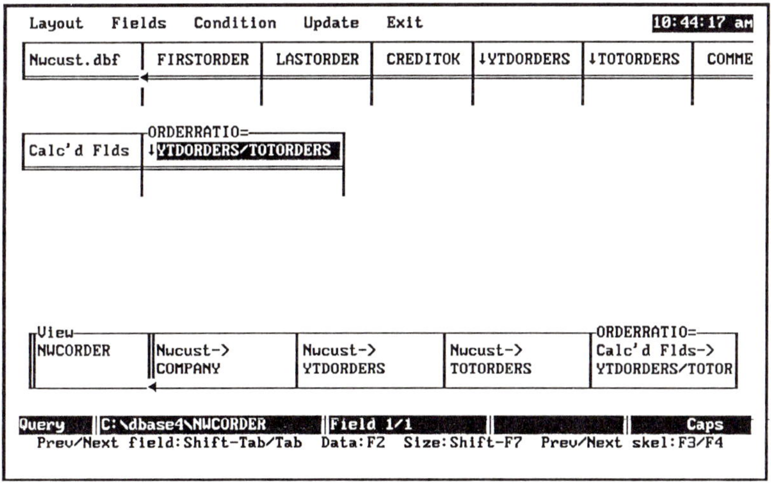

Figure 6-5.

Adding a calculated field to a view

invoked by pressing SHIFT-F1 (Pick), and illustrated in Figure 6-6. For example, to enter the YTDORDERS field into the expression that defines the order ratio, you could press SHIFT-F1 (Pick) to call up the pick list, press PGDN to bring the YTDORDERS field into view and then use the DOWN ARROW key to highlight it, and finally, press ENTER to select this field name from the **Fieldname** panel. You could repeat this process to choose the division operator (/) from the **Operator** panel, and again to select the TOTORDERS field.

Keep in mind that you can use any combination of these two methods for constructing a calculated field expression. Typing the expression directly is usually faster, but the pick list is especially convenient if you have forgotten the exact spelling of a field name or the name of a dBASE IV function.

To name a calculated field, select the **Edit field name** option on the **Fields** menu—the same command that you would use to rename a field in the view skeleton. (You cannot rename a calculated field by typing the field name directly in the calculated field skeleton.) You do not have to name every calculated field you create, and if you plan to use a field solely as the basis for record selection criteria, the name is unnecessary. However, dBASE IV does require that you name every field in the view skeleton, and it pops up a dialog

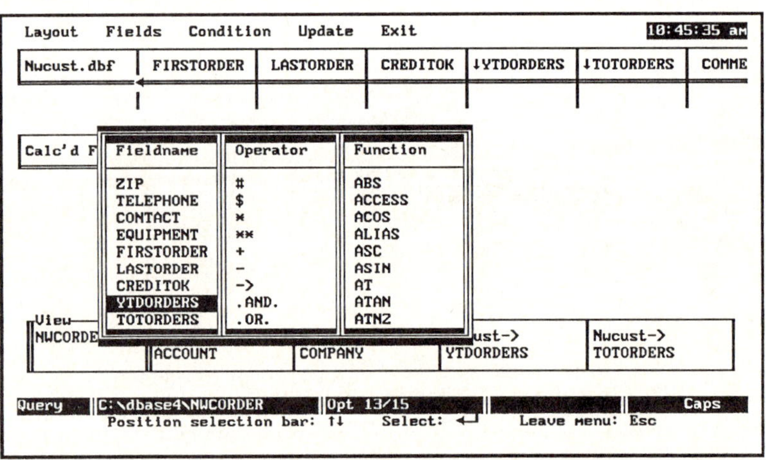

Figure 6-6.

Choosing expression components from the Query-by-Example pick list box prompting you to "Enter field name:" if you attempt to add an unnamed calculated field to the view you are building. In the example shown in Figure 6-5, the calculated field representing the ratio of YTDORDERS to TOTORDERS is called ORDERRATIO.

Saving a Query

Although you do not have to save a query on disk before you can use it to view data, saving the query enables you to repeat the same inquiry in a later work session without having to repeat the definition process.

You can save the current query and continue working by selecting the **Save this query** option from the **Layout** menu. To save your changes and exit the query design screen, select the **Save changes and exit** option from the **Exit** menu. In either case, dBASE IV prompts you to enter the query file name. If you have already assigned a name to the query file—in a prior save command or by invoking Query-by-Example from the dot prompt and including the name in the CREATE QUERY or MODIFY QUERY command—this name will appear as the default, which you can change, or accept by pressing ENTER. You can exit without saving your changes by selecting **Abandon changes and exit**.

In addition to the file name, you can assign a longer description (up to 80 characters) of the query by using the **Edit description of query** option on the **Layout** menu. This description appears under the file name in the Control Center panels whenever the file name is highlighted in the **Queries** panel, just like the corresponding entries for data bases and, as you will see in later chapters, all other types of files. Both in the menu system and at the dot prompt, the description is particularly helpful as a reminder of the purpose or use of a query. As you will learn in Chapter 19, it can also become an important component of the documentation of a dBASE IV application.

Both of the "exit" commands just described return you to the Control Center or the dot prompt, depending on which environment was originally active. If you moved to the query design screen from the screen, label, or report form layout editor, the **Exit** menu will contain an additional option for returning to that screen. Regardless of how you entered Query-by-Example, you can switch to Edit or Browse (whichever was last active) by pressing F2 (Data).

dBASE IV does not automatically save the current query when you exit to one of the full-screen or layout editors. This makes it easy to fine-tune a query—you can verify the effect of the query by viewing the data it selects, and then return to the design work surface to make changes. If you fail to save your work before you exit the full-screen editor, dBASE IV redisplays the query design screen automatically and pops up a dialog box to remind you, "Query design has been changed. Do you want to save it?" You can select **Yes** to save the file or **No** to discard the changes.

The instructions defined on the query design work surface are stored in a file with the extension QBE (for "Query-by-Example"). Figure 6-7 shows the contents of the QBE file that stores the query specifications shown in Figure 6-5. This file includes some information about the query stored in an encoded, proprietary format, followed by the simple dBASE IV commands you could use at the dot prompt or as part of a longer program to create the same customized view of your data.

Even if you do not understand what each command means, a brief look at the contents of a query file should underscore an important concept: *It does not contain data, but instead contains the instructions for retrieving the specified fields and records from real dBASE IV data base files.* After you learn more about dBASE IV command syntax, you might want to examine some other QBE files to see how they work, although some knowledge of programming is required to understand the longer QBE files generated by more complex query specifications.

Using a Query to View Selected Data

When you use a view query to display or edit data, dBASE IV opens the files that contribute to the query and selects the fields and records specified on the query design screen to create a customized view of the information stored in

```
* dBASE IV .QBE file
CLOSE DATABASES
SELECT 1
USE NWCUST.DBF
SET EXACT ON
SET FILTER TO
GO TOP
SET FIELDS TO A->ACCOUNT,A->COMPANY,A->YTDORDERS,A->TOTORDERS,ORDERRATIO;
=(A->YTDORDERS/A->TOTORDERS)
```

Figure 6-7.

The contents of a simple query file

the data bases. Although a view does not contain data—the fields it appears to contain are drawn from one or more true data files—a view query behaves like a data base and can be substituted for a data base in many situations.

In keeping with this similarity, opening a view is in many ways similar to opening a data base. When you exit the query design screen after creating or modifying a query, dBASE IV automatically places it in effect, just as a newly created data base remains open after you exit the data base design screen. You can open a previously defined query file with commands that are similar to those used to open a true data base. You do not have to first open the data bases that contribute to the view, because the query file contains instructions for opening all required files. If a data base is already open, whether or not it is part of the view, dBASE IV closes it when you open a query from the Control Center. Similarly, if a view query is in effect when you open a data base file from the Control Center, dBASE IV first closes the view.

When a view query is open, it seems as if you are working with a data base that contains only the fields selected by the query, arranged in the order in which they were placed in the view skeleton on the query design screen. The Edit and Browse screens include only the specified fields, as does the output of LIST and DISPLAY commands typed at the dot prompt. If the status display is on, the status bar displays the name of the view rather than the name of the true data base supplying the data, and "View" appears in the fourth segment to remind you that you are not working directly with the whole file.

If a view includes calculated fields, dBASE IV displays these fields, but does not allow you to edit them, because they are not actually saved with the data base. When you use the Browse screen to change data base fields that contribute to calculations, dBASE IV instantly updates and redisplays the values of any calculated fields that are affected by the change. In Edit mode, you must use PGUP or PGDN to move to another record and then return before you can see the result of updating the calculation.

If you renamed any fields in the view skeleton, the new names are used in all the full-screen displays, in pick lists, and in the "column headings" produced by LIST and DISPLAY. When you type field names in commands at the dot prompt, you must also use the new names. However, you cannot edit renamed fields because of the way that dBASE IV creates them: renaming a field is equivalent to creating a calculated field with the new name, and assigning it a value based on the original data base field. For this reason, you cannot edit "renamed" fields, just as you cannot edit other calculated fields.

You may add new records to a data base with a query in effect, but because only the fields included in the query are presented on the screen, all others will remain blank in the new records. Normally, you would not want to add more than an occasional new record in this way. For the most part, you will use view queries to edit, display, and print selected fields from the underlying data bases without having to see all the other data at the same time.

From the Menus

To open a query from the Control Center, you highlight its name in the **Queries** panel and press ENTER. dBASE IV pops up a dialog box much like the one that is displayed when you select a data base name from the **Data** panel, with three similar options: **Use view**, **Modify query**, and **Display data**.

The similarity of the options reflects the parallel use of views and data bases. Just as you can open a data base without immediately viewing records, you can choose the **Use view** option to open a view without leaving the Control Center. You might want to do this if you next intend to define a report or custom data entry screen based on the view. If you want to move directly to the Edit or Browse screen to display data, you can choose **Use file** (when opening a data base) or **Use view** (when opening a view). To edit a query, choose **Modify query**, which is analogous to the **Modify structure/order** option for data bases. The function key shortcut used to invoke the Edit or Browse screen is also the same: Press F2 (Data) with the name of the query file highlighted in the **Queries** panel.

When a view query is open, the name of the query file and the names of all screen forms, reports, labels, and applications based on the view move above the horizontal lines in their respective Control Center panels.

From the Dot Prompt

From the dot prompt, you execute a query with the SET VIEW command:

SET VIEW TO *query file name*

This command simply opens the view without displaying data; just as when you type a USE command to open a data base file, dBASE IV does not make any assumptions about what you want to do next. Once the view is open, all subsequent commands—including EDIT, BROWSE, LIST, and DISPLAY—operate on only the fields and records selected by the view.

USING A FIELD LIST TO PROCESS SELECTED FIELDS

As described in the previous section, you can use view queries, either from the menu system or from the dot prompt, to display or edit data selectively. In a query, you construct the list of fields you want to include by placing them in the view skeleton. When you work at the dot prompt, you can add an explicit field list to many commands, including LIST, DISPLAY, EDIT, and BROWSE.

In dBASE IV, a *list* consists of one or more items—such as field names or more complex algebraic expressions—separated by commas (unless there is only one item in the list). If you think of the dBASE IV command language as being similar to English and other natural languages, you can imagine beginning with a simple imperative sentence consisting of a verb—a sentence that commands dBASE IV to do something—and gradually building up a more detailed description of exactly what you want by adding optional "phrases," or "clauses." For example, you could list only the ACCOUNT, CONTACT, COMPANY, and TELEPHONE fields from the National Widgets Customer File by naming these fields in the LIST command, as follows:

```
LIST ACCOUNT, CONTACT, COMPANY, TELEPHONE
```

To view the same fields from a single record, you would use

```
DISPLAY ACCOUNT, CONTACT, COMPANY, TELEPHONE
```

The output produced by these commands, operating on a Customer File that contains only five records, is illustrated in Figure 6-8. Just as the fields in a view are displayed in the order in which they occur in the view skeleton, fields displayed by a LIST or DISPLAY command appear in the order in which they were named in the field list, which need not be the same as the field sequence in the file structure.

You may recall from the examples in Chapter 5 that dBASE IV does not include memo field text in the output of a simple LIST or DISPLAY command, but displays instead the memo marker ("MEMO" if the field contains text or

```
. DISPLAY ACCOUNT, CONTACT, COMPANY, TELEPHONE
Record#  ACCOUNT    CONTACT                        COMPANY                        TELEPHON
E
      1  LEWIS      Joan Mills                     Lewis and Associates           839-5014

. LIST ACCOUNT, CONTACT, COMPANY, TELEPHONE
Record#  ACCOUNT    CONTACT                        COMPANY                        TELEPHON
E
      1  LEWIS      Joan Mills                     Lewis and Associates           839-5014

      2  ABCPLUMB   Ed Williams                    ABC Plumbing                   861-4543

      3  KLEIN      Judy Barnes                    Carol Klein, M.D.              232-2638

      4  MTK        Leslie Cohen                   M.T.K. Industries              655-7200

      5  ANDERSON   John Anderson                                                 747-8201

.
Command ||C:\dbase4\NWCUST          ||Rec EOF/5          ||File ||          ||       Caps
```

Figure 6-8.

Using LIST and DISPLAY to display selected fields

"memo" if it is empty). To view the text, you must name the field explicitly. For example, you could produce the display shown in Figure 6-9 with the following command:

```
DISPLAY ALL ACCOUNT, COMMENTS
```

By default, dBASE IV displays the record number and the deletion marker, if any. You cannot suppress the deletion marker, since failing to make some distinction between deleted and nondeleted records would be potentially misleading, but you can exclude the record number by adding the keyword OFF to a LIST or DISPLAY command, as in the following example:

```
LIST ACCOUNT, CONTACT, COMPANY, TELEPHONE OFF
```

When you type a list of items, such as field names or file names, you need not add a space after each comma, as you would if you were typing a list on a typewriter or using a word processing program. Thus, you could also type the previous command as follows:

```
LIST ACCOUNT,CONTACT,COMPANY,TELEPHONE OFF
```

Because you might want to add fields to a previously defined field list, successive SET FIELDS commands add fields to the list rather than replacing the old field list with a new one. The field list is automatically canceled when you close the data base it refers to. You can cancel a field list explicitly by typing

```
SET FIELDS TO
```

This construction is common to many dBASE IV commands that customize the working environment or open and close files. To cancel the field list, you use the same command that invoked it but omit the list, as if to say "Set the field list to no list at all" or "I don't want to specify a field list." You must use this command to cancel a field list placed in effect through a query before you establish a new field list from the dot prompt.

You can give a different name to a field by specifying the new name in the same form described earlier for the EDIT and BROWSE commands. The following command makes available the same set of fields as the BROWSE and EDIT command examples in the previous section:

```
SET FIELDS TO ACCOUNT, NAME=CONTACT, COMPANY, TELEPHONE
```

You can include calculated fields in the list by assigning the names and defining the calculations in the SET FIELDS command. The following command establishes a field list that includes the same calculated field as the view query explained earlier in this chapter (which expresses the ratio of a customer's year-to-date to total orders):

```
SET FIELDS TO ACCOUNT, COMPANY, ORDERRATIO=YTDORDERS/TOTORDERS
```

Just as when you include calculated fields in a view, you cannot change a renamed or calculated field on the Browse or Edit screen. In Browse mode, dBASE IV automatically updates and redisplays calculated fields to reflect any changes you make to the underlying data base fields; in Edit mode, you must leave the record and return in order to see the change. You can also prohibit editing any true field by adding the /R option after the field name to designate it as read/only. For example, you could display the year-to-date and total order fields but not allow these fields to be changed with the following:

```
SET FIELDS TO ACCOUNT, COMPANY, YTDORDERS/R, TOTORDERS/R
```

With a field list in effect, subsequent commands display and process only the fields specified by SET FIELDS, and fields are presented in the order in which they were listed in the SET FIELDS command(s). When you display or print the structure of the file, the output includes all fields, identified by the names stored in the structure, with the ones selected by SET FIELDS marked with the greater-than symbol (>). Calculated fields, which are not part of the structure, are not included in the structure listing. Any other attempt to access a field that is not on the list, or to refer to a field that was renamed in a SET FIELDS command by its original name, results in a "Variable not found" error message, just as if you were viewing a true data base that contained only the fields specified in the SET FIELDS command.

You can disable the field list temporarily, so you can view all fields in the structure with

```
SET FIELDS OFF
```

and then place the list back in effect with

```
SET FIELDS ON
```

You might want to do this if you need to add new records to the data base during an editing session (to ensure that all the fields are filled in), but then return to viewing or editing only selected fields. By default, dBASE IV assumes that the field list is OFF and that all fields are available. When you use a SET FIELDS command to define a field list, this command also activates the list, as if you had explicitly typed a SET FIELDS ON command.

There is an important difference between SET FIELDS OFF and SET FIELDS TO, although they produce the same apparent result—enabling you to access all the fields in a data base structure. SET FIELDS TO cancels the field list and leaves dBASE IV with no record of the fields that the list previously contained. In contrast, SET FIELDS OFF suspends the field list temporarily; you can return to viewing only the selected fields without retyping the list by using SET FIELDS ON.

GENERATING QUICK REPORTS

The Browse screen and the LIST command are useful for carrying out inquiries and viewing multiple records onscreen. If you need to share data with your colleagues and coworkers, especially those who do not understand dBASE IV, you will probably need to print the same information on paper. Defining and printing formatted reports is covered in detail in Chapters 11 through 14, but several easy techniques for quickly producing simple printed listings of selected fields in a data base may be useful to you immediately.

From the Menus

From the Control Center and the Browse, Edit, and query design screens, you can generate a *Quick Report* by pressing SHIFT-F9 (Quick Report). In the Control Center, you must identify the data base or view query that will provide the data by highlighting the name in the **Data** panel or **Queries** panel before you press the Quick Report function key (you do not have to open the file or view explicitly).

Although the format of a Quick Report is predetermined, dBASE IV offers a menu of print options, so you can select the output device (the screen or any available printer) and edit the page dimensions if necessary. The print menu is illustrated in Figure 6-10. You can use the **View report on screen** option to preview the data on screen or select **Begin printing** to generate a printed copy.

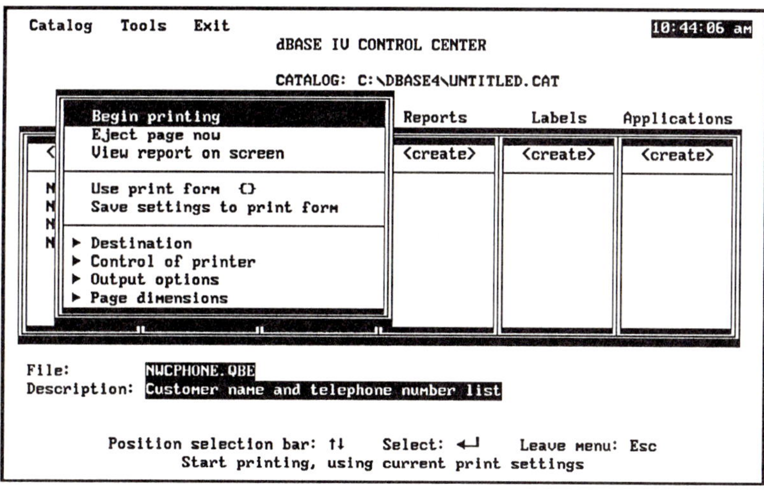

Figure 6-10.

The Quick Report print option menu

Figure 6-11 illustrates the Quick Report generated from the NWCPHONE view query explained earlier in this chapter. As you can see from this example, a Quick Report is a simple columnar listing that uses the field names as column headings. If you include numeric fields, dBASE IV prints column totals below these fields at the end of the report. The system date and a page number are printed in the upper left corner of each page, but there are no other titles or embellishments.

When you view a report on the screen, dBASE IV assumes a "page" width of 80 characters. After each screenful of data, dBASE IV pauses to allow you to read the screen and displays a reminder on the message line at the bottom of the screen that you can press ESC to abort the report or press the spacebar to view the next group of records.

Quick Reports are paginated properly based on a default page length of 66 lines: dBASE IV adds a top and bottom margin to skip over the perforations in

```
Page No.    1
01/16/91

ACCOUNT        NAME               COMPANY                      TELEPHONE

LEWIS          Joan Mills         Lewis and Associates         839-5014
ABCPLUMB       Ed Williams        ABC Plumbing                 861-4543
KLEIN          Judy Barnes        Carol Klein, M.D.            232-2638
MTK            Leslie Cohen       M.T.K. Industries            655-7200
ANDERSON       John Anderson                                   747-8201
RAPIDTYPE      Kathy McDonald     RapidType Secretarial Svc    861-4048
PHOENIX                           Phoenix Construction         683-8751
KELLY          Richard Kelly      Kelly and Sons Furniture     357-7482
GREENTHUMB     Celia Lopez        Green Thumb Landscaping      549-8901
HOMEMOVIES     Mark Vogel         Home Movie Video Rentals     843-1148
SHAPEUP        Jeanne Lee         Shape Up Fitness Center      236-7687
FLOORPLAN      Louise Robbins     Floor Plan Carpet Center     232-8430
JOHNSON        Carolyn Sumner     J. Thomas Johnson, CPA       433-6488
ELLISMFG       Barbara Goddard    Ellis Manufacturing          455-1421
IMAGEMAKER     Lisa Burns         The Image Makers             653-1250
WHITNEY        James Whitney      Financial Planning Svcs.     791-7474
HRINSURANC     Jill Henley        H & R Insurance              398-1441
DELTADESGN     Andrea Bennett     Delta Design                 332-7373
ARONOFF        Gina Aronoff                                    745-1813
YORKPUMP       Sharon Fern        York Pump, Inc.              946-9975
```

Figure 6-11.

A Quick Report

continuous-form paper and prints the date, page number, and column headings at the top of each page. However, no assumptions are made about the width of the report, because dBASE IV cannot determine the physical width of your printer or paper, or the character pitch set. If the selected fields do not fit on one line on the screen or the printer, the data is wrapped onto one or more additional lines. Because this reduces the clarity and readability of the output, Quick Reports are best suited for small data bases or, more commonly, view queries that select only as many fields as will fit within the page width of the selected output device.

D From the Dot Prompt

When you display selected fields with the HEADING setting turned ON so that dBASE IV includes field names as column headings, the LIST command produces output in a format that is clear and readable enough to serve as a useful printed report. You can instruct dBASE IV to route the output of a LIST or DISPLAY command to the printer as well as to the screen by including the phrase TO PRINTER or TO PRINT in the command. To print a list of account codes, company names, and telephone numbers similar to the one displayed on the screen in Figure 6-8, you would type

```
LIST ACCOUNT, NAME=CONTACT, COMPANY, TELEPHONE OFF TO PRINT
```

If your printer is wide enough to accommodate 14-inch paper, or if you can select a "compressed" mode and print more than 80 characters on 8 1/2- by 11-inch paper, you can include more fields in a printout than will fit within a screen line. For example, you could print all the name and address fields in the National Widgets Customer File with the following:

```
LIST ACCOUNT, CONTACT, COMPANY, ADDRESS, CITY, STATE, ZIP OFF TO PRINT
```

Remember that you can type dBASE IV command verbs, file names, and field names in any combination of uppercase and lowercase letters. When dBASE IV displays or prints field headings in a LIST or DISPLAY command, the headings conform to the same combination of uppercase and lowercase letters that you used when you typed the list of field names in the command. To produce a report in which the field name headings are printed with initial capital letters, you could type the LIST command as follows:

```
LIST Account, Contact, Company, Address, City, State, Zip OFF TO PRINT
```

Note that the case used to type the command verb and other command words (LIST, OFF, and TO PRINT) does not affect the display.

The printouts produced by LIST TO PRINT commands are relatively crude. The field name headings are printed only once, at the very beginning, and unlike Quick Reports, the listings are not paginated—dBASE IV prints data over the perforations on continuous-form paper, with no provision for top and bottom margins or page numbers. Since it is so easy to generate a better-looking printout by using the Quick Report feature, you may end up using LIST TO PRINT only for "quick-and-dirty" reports for your own use or for informal presentations.

BUILDING COMPLEX COMMANDS

As you begin to build longer commands, give some thought to the order of the various phrases, clauses, and options. In every dBASE IV command, the verb must be the first word. When you add optional clauses or phrases to the basic verb, the order in which you type these components is usually unimportant. Thus, instead of

```
LIST ACCOUNT, NAME=CONTACT, COMPANY, TELEPHONE OFF TO PRINT
```

you could type

```
LIST OFF ACCOUNT, NAME=CONTACT, COMPANY, TELEPHONE TO PRINT
```

or

```
LIST TO PRINT OFF ACCOUNT, NAME=CONTACT, COMPANY, TELEPHONE
```

The order of the command components in the examples in this book was chosen to make the commands read like normal English imperative sentences.

As you do your own work with dBASE IV, experiment with different variations to see which ones make the most sense to you.

SUMMARY

As you work with larger data base files, especially if the file structures contain more than 10 or 12 fields, you will find it increasingly helpful to use the techniques presented in this chapter to construct a field list that enables you to view and edit selected subsets of fields. Of the three methods described here, working at the dot prompt and adding a field list to commands such as DISPLAY, LIST, and EDIT gives you the most flexibility to view many different groups of fields and thus carry out fast ad hoc inquiries. To operate on the same set of fields with several successive commands, you can use SET FIELDS to make the field list more "permanent," or you can use the query design screen to define an equivalent view query. If you plan to process the same set of fields in the future, creating and saving a query file offers an additional advantage: It enables you to store the field list on disk so that you can retrieve and reuse it in later work sessions rather than having to re-create the field selection criteria from scratch.

CHAPTER SEVEN

Selecting Records

Chapter 6 introduced the concept of processing data selectively to obtain concise, useful, and informative displays and printed listings. That chapter also described several tools—including view queries, the SET FIELDS command, and the use of field lists in commands typed at the dot prompt—for specifying which fields should be affected by subsequent commands. In addition to processing fields selectively, you will often want to limit the range of records that dBASE IV acts on. Once a data base grows beyond a hundred or so records, you will rarely want to see all of them at once, and picking the ones you need out of a lengthy listing can be difficult and tedious.

Chapter 5 presented one specific technique for processing records selectively—the SET DELETED ON command, which causes dBASE IV to ignore deleted records or, viewed another way, to select only nondeleted records. SET DELETED is one of many commands that you can use to select records based on their contents (the deletion marker may be considered part of the data, since it is stored in the record). This chapter covers more general methods for establishing selection criteria based on the information entered into a data base. These techniques can be implemented through view queries or by typing commands at the dot prompt. You will also learn how to search for individual records and how to select records based on their position in the file (the order in which they were entered).

By combining these commands and command options in different ways, you can display or print specific fields from specific records in a data base and thus perform sophisticated inquiries and display meaningful extracts of the mass of data stored in a dBASE IV file. As you read this chapter, keep in mind that many of the techniques illustrated by commands that display data are also applicable to commands (described in later chapters) that perform calculations or update records.

SPECIFYING RECORD SELECTION CRITERIA USING QUERY-BY-EXAMPLE

A view query can include instructions for selecting records, as well as for selecting fields. Chapter 6 compared the format of the file skeletons on the query design work surface to the tabular Browse screen, and, in fact, the file skeletons serve as tables into which you enter record selection criteria. Each column in a file skeleton represents a field, and you can enter selection criteria in the appropriate columns of the skeleton under the field names (you can also use an optional condition box, which is described later in this chapter). *Each row of the file skeleton table represents a separate, complete set of record selection criteria.* Before you enter any conditions, only one row is displayed, but you can add additional rows to expand the table as necessary by pressing DOWN ARROW with the cursor in any field column of the skeleton.

You can use the query design screen to define any combination of field and record selection criteria. These sets of criteria are independent—that is, you do not have to include in the view skeleton any of the fields used as the basis for selecting records. For example, you might want to select customers by city, but although the contents of the CITY field determine which records are displayed, you might want to view or edit only the ACCOUNT, CONTACT, COMPANY, and TELEPHONE fields in each selected record. Nevertheless, when you first begin to experiment with complex selection criteria, it is a good idea to display all the fields named in each condition, at least until you have verified that the right records were selected and have confirmed that you expressed the conditions correctly.

EXPRESSING SIMPLE CONDITIONS

Whether you work at the dot prompt or use Query-by-Example to establish record selection criteria, you must understand how to form the *conditions* and *expressions* that state your criteria in correct dBASE IV syntax. A condition is *any expression that can take on the logical values .T. (True) or .F. (False).* When dBASE IV executes a command that includes a condition, it evaluates the condition separately for each record; the condition is either true or not true for any particular record, and the command acts on only the records for which the condition is true.

The simplest conditions specify an exact, or constant, value for a field. A *constant* is an arbitrary number, such as 10.75; character string, such as "San Francisco"; date, such as 08/15/92; or logical value, such as .T.. dBASE IV cannot change the value of a constant. When you compare a field to a constant, both must be of the same data type—character fields must be compared to character string constants, numeric fields to numbers, and so on. The data type of a field is established when you define the data base structure, and dBASE IV deduces the data type of a constant by the way it is written.

Character strings must be enclosed in any of three permissible delimiters: double quotation marks ("), single quotation marks ('), or square brackets ([]). If a character string contains one of these punctuation marks, you must choose one of the others to surround the entire string. For example, to compare the contents of the EQUIPMENT field to the text *IBM AT "clone" system*, you must use single quotes or brackets around the character string constant: either [IBM AT "clone" system] or 'IBM AT "clone" system'.

Keep in mind that a constant is an arbitrary value that is taken literally by dBASE IV with no further interpretation and that every character must be typed exactly as you want it to be used in comparisons. Uppercase and lowercase letters are not equivalent, the uppercase letter O is not the same as the digit 0, the lowercase letter l differs from the number 1, and spaces and punctuation marks are as significant as any other characters. Thus, "Berkeley" is not the same as "BERKELEY" or "berkeley", and "KayPro" is different from "Kaypro".

When you work at the dot prompt, dBASE IV normally compares two character strings by beginning with the first character in the first string and examining only as many characters as are present in the second; if all these characters are equal, the two strings are deemed equal. If you wish, you can turn the EXACT setting ON to have the program consider two character strings equal only if they are the same length and have the same contents.

Chapter 18 explains in detail how to customize the working environment by changing EXACT and other environment settings, but you may want to experiment with the EXACT setting right away. (The remaining dot prompt command examples in this chapter assume that EXACT is OFF, and you will probably want to set it OFF for much of your own work as well.) You can view or change the status of the EXACT setting by selecting the **Settings** option from the Control Center **Tools** menu. dBASE IV displays the **Settings** menu bar with the **Options** menu pulled down, and you can change the status of any of the listed options by selecting the desired option and pressing ENTER. From the dot prompt, you can type

```
SET EXACT OFF
```

or to reverse this setting

```
SET EXACT ON
```

When you compare a field to a character string constant with the EXACT setting OFF, you need to type only as many characters as are necessary to identify the group of records you want. For example, "Berk" would probably suffice to retrieve customers in Berkeley. But if you compared the CITY field to the constant "San"—intending to select customers in San Francisco—you would also see customers in San Jose, San Leandro, Santa Clara, and any other city having a name that begins with the letters S, a, and n.

Using an abbreviation so short that it selects unwanted records is an easy error to make, but you can also take advantage of the way dBASE IV carries out character string comparisons to retrieve all the records in which the entry in a field begins with a specified character string. For example, you could select all customers who have account codes beginning with B by specifying that the ACCOUNT field must be "equal to" the constant B.

When dBASE IV executes a query, it always turns the EXACT setting ON; when you close the view, it restores the default setting (which is OFF, unless you changed the default using methods described in Chapter 18). If you want to compare partial character strings in Query-by-Example, you must use the **Like** operator, which is described later in this chapter.

When you compare a numeric field to a constant value, you do not have to surround the numeric constant with any special delimiters. Since a dBASE IV field name cannot begin with a numeric digit, a constant consisting of digits (and optionally, a decimal point or a minus sign) could not represent anything but a numeric constant.

Logical values are enclosed within two periods (.). You can regard the period as a special kind of quotation mark that distinguishes the logical values from the single-character constants that they resemble (T, N, y, and so on).

Date constants are surrounded by braces ({ and }, also called curly brackets) to identify them as true dates. For example, January 20, 1992 would be written as {01/20/92}. Without the date delimiters, dBASE IV would attempt to interpret 01/20/92 as a numeric expression involving division (1 divided by 20 divided by 92).

M From the Menus

To define a query that selects records in which a particular field is equal to a specific value, you enter the constant value under the field name in the appropriate file skeleton column. For example, to include in a view only customers in Berkeley, you would type "Berkeley" in the CITY column in the Customer File skeleton, as illustrated in Figure 7-1. Remember that because dBASE IV turns the EXACT setting ON when it executes a query, you cannot abbreviate "Berkeley". You could request only customers who did not place

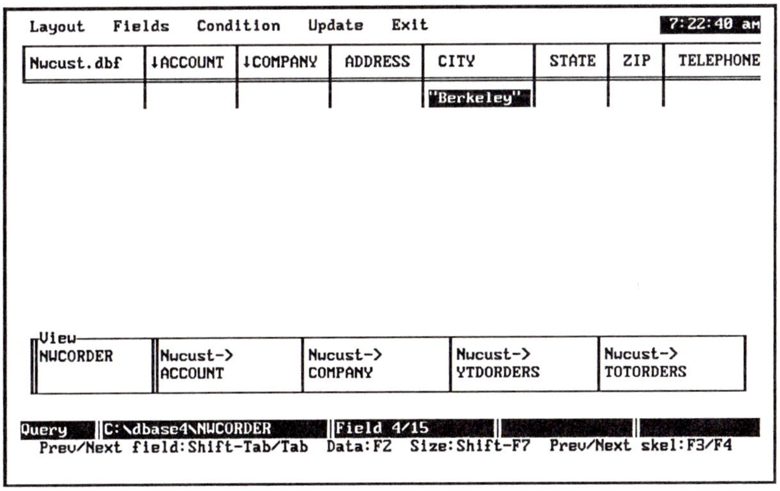

```
Layout  Fields  Condition  Update  Exit                              7:22:40 am

Nwcust.dbf | ↓ACCOUNT | ↓COMPANY | ADDRESS | CITY       | STATE | ZIP | TELEPHONE
           |          |          |         | "Berkeley" |       |     |

View
NWCORDER  | Nwcust->  | Nwcust->  | Nwcust->  | Nwcust->
          | ACCOUNT   | COMPANY   | YTDORDERS | TOTORDERS

Query  | C:\dbase4\NWCORDER  | Field 4/15 |
 Prev/Next field:Shift-Tab/Tab  Data:F2  Size:Shift-F7  Prev/Next skel:F3/F4
```

Figure 7-1.

A query that selects customers in Berkeley

any orders during the current year by entering 0 in the YTDORDERS column. To select customers based on their credit status, you would enter .T. or .Y. under CREDITOK in the Customer File skeleton to select customers with approved credit, or .F. or .N. for those with a bad credit rating.

If your entry is wider than the original width of the column in the file skeleton (the width of the field name), the column expands as you type to accommodate additional text. By pressing F9 (Zoom), you can expand the data entry area to a box that fills most of the screen, so you can see the entire condition at once; pressing F9 (Zoom) again returns you to the standard query design display.

From the Dot Prompt

From the dot prompt, you define record selection criteria by adding a condition, introduced by the keyword FOR, to commands such as LIST and EDIT. Although conditions serve the same purpose whether you work in Query-by-Example or at the dot prompt, you enter them in a slightly different form in each environment. On the query design screen, you type only part of the complete condition that describes the selection criteria—you identify the fields to be tested by the placement of your conditions in the file skeletons, and when you test a field for equality to a constant value, you do not have to type the equal sign, only the value.

When you work at the dot prompt, you must follow the keyword FOR with a complete, syntactically correct condition. The simplest condition, one that compares a field and a constant for equality, consists of a field name, the equals operator, and the constant value. For example, you could list the ACCOUNT, CONTACT, COMPANY, and TELEPHONE fields for National Widgets' customers in Berkeley with the following:

```
LIST ACCOUNT, CONTACT, COMPANY, TELEPHONE FOR CITY = "Berkeley"
```

Within a condition, spaces are optional. You can omit extra spaces to type commands faster or include them to improve readability and make it easier to edit commands (recall that you can use CTRL-RIGHT ARROW and CTRL-LEFT ARROW to move through a command line one "word" at a time). The previous command could also have been written with no spaces before or after the equal sign, as follows:

```
LIST ACCOUNT, CONTACT, COMPANY, TELEPHONE FOR CITY="Berkeley"
```

If you are sure that no other cities begin with the letters "Berk", you could also abbreviate the constant that identifies the city (provided that the EXACT setting is ON), as follows:

```
LIST ACCOUNT, CONTACT, COMPANY, TELEPHONE FOR CITY="Berk"
```

The quotes (remember that you can use double quotes, single quotes, or square brackets) enable dBASE IV to distinguish a character string constant from an intended field name. In the previous example, if the condition were stated as CITY = Berkeley, dBASE IV would interpret both CITY and Berkeley as field names and would assume that you want to display records in which the contents of a field called CITY are the same as the contents of a field called Berkeley. It is legitimate to compare the contents of two fields; for example, you might want to select records in which YTDORDERS = TOTORDERS. However, the condition CITY = Berkeley would generate a "Variable not found" error message because there is no field named BERKELEY in the Customer File.

Note that in the previous example, the CITY field was not displayed, although it was tested in the condition to determine whether a given record should be selected. In general, when you begin experimenting with conditions or when you test a new, complex condition, it is a good idea to display all relevant fields to verify that you have stated the condition correctly and have selected the intended records.

As in the query editor, numeric constants are identified by their initial digit, minus sign, or decimal point, so no special delimiters are required. For example, with the following command you could list all the customers who did not place any orders during the current year:

```
LIST ACCOUNT, COMPANY, TELEPHONE, YTDORDERS FOR YTDORDERS = 0
```

Logical constant values must be enclosed within two periods (.), and dates must be surrounded by braces ({}). When you type conditions involving logical fields, you should also keep in mind that a condition is defined as any expression that has the value .T. (True) or .F. (False). A logical field by itself fits this definition and therefore constitutes a valid condition. You do not have to use an equal sign in a logical comparison, although it is not wrong to do so. For example, to display all the records with .T. in the CREDITOK field, you would use the following command:

```
LIST ACCOUNT, COMPANY, TELEPHONE, CREDITOK FOR CREDITOK
```

This command might be translated as "List the ACCOUNT, CONTACT, COMPANY, TELEPHONE, and CREDITOK fields for all records in which CREDITOK is true." If you name your logical fields carefully, a condition such as the one in the previous example reads almost like an English sentence: "List the account, contact, company name, telephone, and credit status for customers whose credit is OK."

In general, you can read a LIST command containing a FOR clause something like this: "List these fields for every record in which the following is true...." Remember that the condition is evaluated for one record at a time, not in some global manner for the entire data base. When you execute a command, such as LIST, which operates on many records, dBASE IV evaluates the condition for each record and displays only the ones in which the condition is true.

USING COMPARISON OPERATORS

So far, the examples presented in this chapter tested a field and a constant for equality. You can also test a field to see if it is greater than or less than a specified value, not equal to a value, or, for character strings, similar to a value. The symbols used to express these relationships are referred to as *comparison operators,* or *relational operators*—they enable you to make comparisons or express relationships between two values. The comparison operators, the data types to which they apply, and their meanings are listed in Table 7-1.

Most comparisons can be carried out on character, numeric, or date fields. When applied to character fields, the "greater than" and "less than" comparisons refer to alphabetical order. Thus, for the CITY field, the condition > "S" selects all cities that begin with "S" or any letter that occurs after "S" in the alphabet. When applied to date fields, > and < mean later or earlier, in chronological order. There are two symbols for "not equal": the number sign (#), which resembles the ≠ sign used in algebraic formulas, and <>, in which the less-than and greater-than operators are combined to connote "either less than or greater than." If you use <>, be careful not to type a space between the two symbols.

Operator	Data Types (in file skeletons)	Data Types (dot prompt, condition box)	Meaning
=	C, N, D	C, N, D	Equal to
<>	C, N, D	C, N, D	Not equal to
>	C, N, D	C, N, D	Greater than
>=	C, N, D	C, N, D	Greater than or equal to
<	C, N, D	C, N, D	Less than
<=	C, N, D	C, N, D	Less than or equal to
$	C	C, M	Contained within
Like	C	C	Matches pattern
Sounds Like	C	C	Matches Soundex code

Table 7-1.

The dBASE IV Comparison (Relational) Operators

You cannot use any of the operators in Table 7-1 except = with logical fields, and you do not actually need to use the = operator. A logical field can take on only one of two values—true or false—and the only comparison that makes sense is determining whether it has one of these values. Note also that none of the comparison operators can be applied to memo fields in conditions entered into the file skeletons on the query design screen, but some comparisons involving memo fields are permitted at the dot prompt or in the condition box.

The operators reserved for character strings (character and memo fields) deserve special mention. The *substring operator,* symbolized by a dollar sign ($), tests whether one character string is a substring of—appears anywhere within—another. The $ operator is particularly useful for finding records in which a given sequence of characters occurs at varying positions within a field, since you can test for equality only if you know the beginning of the field. For example, you might want to list every customer who owns IBM equipment, but because the characters "IBM" might occur anywhere in the equipment field, you cannot test whether EQUIPMENT equals "IBM". You must use the $ operator to test whether the EQUIPMENT field contains the text "IBM" in any position.

Two character string operators, **Like** and **Sounds Like**, are permitted only in the file skeletons on the query design screen. The **Like** operator tests the contents of a character field against a specified pattern of characters and selects records that match the pattern. The pattern can include the standard DOS wildcard characters: the question mark (?), which stands for any single character; and the asterisk (*), which stands for any sequence of characters. For example, even though Query-by-Example turns the EXACT setting ON, you could select all customers whose account codes begin with B with the condition LIKE "B*". If you don't remember the exact spelling of the word or name you want to select, you can use the **Sounds Like** operator, which conducts a *Soundex* search—a search based on the way a word is pronounced rather than on its spelling. For example, searching for a name using the condition SOUNDS LIKE "Merriam" would retrieve Miriam (as well as Marian, Marion, Mary, and others). Note however, that the first character must be correct in order for a Soundex search to succeed.

From the Menus

To enter conditions involving comparisons on the query design screen, you first type the symbol for the comparison operator and then the value to which you want to compare the field. For example, to select customers with last order dates before January 1, 1992, you would enter < {01/01/92} in the LASTORDER column in the Customer File skeleton. You can think of this notation as an implicit "equation" in which you type the operator and the item on the right side of the equation (the constant) and identify the item on the left side (the field) by the placement of the equation in the file skeleton.

The previous section stated that you can test a field and a constant for equality by typing just the constant in the file skeleton. For consistency, you can enter the equal sign explicitly like any other comparison operator. Thus, to select customers in Berkeley, you could enter either "Berkeley" or = "Berkeley" in the Customer File skeleton. Recall also that in conditions (and all other dBASE IV expressions), spaces are optional before and after the operators.

dBASE IV does not limit you to comparing the value of a field to a constant. You can use any legitimate expression in a condition. Constructing complex expressions is discussed in detail in Chapter 10, but another type of simple condition you may want to use immediately involves comparing two fields in the same record. For example, to select customers whose first and last order dates are not the same, you could enter the expression <> LASTORDER in the FIRSTORDER column of the Customer File skeleton.

You can also construct conditions by selecting items from a pick list of fields, comparison operators, and dBASE IV functions. To use this method to build the comparison described in the previous paragraph, you could move the highlight into the FIRSTORDER column, press SHIFT-F1 (Pick), and select # or <> from the **Operator** panel in the pick list illustrated in Figure 7-2. After you choose each item, the pick list disappears from the screen to allow you to type a constant value. If you want to choose another item, you can press SHIFT-F1 (Pick) to pop up the list again. In this example, you would redisplay the pick list and

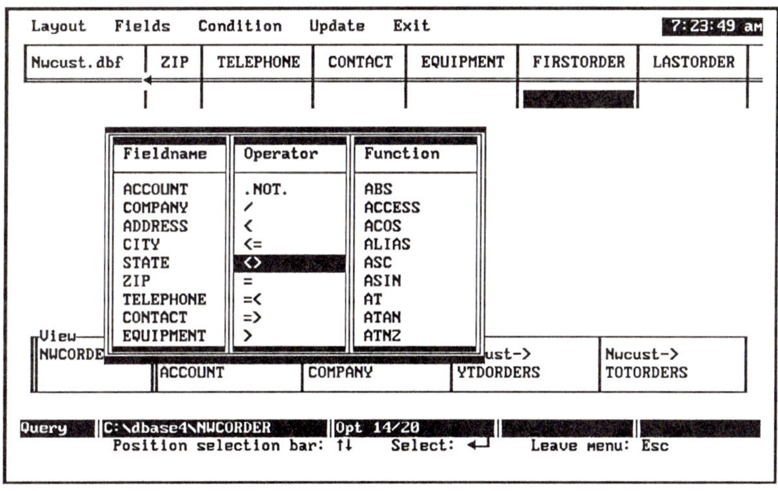

Figure 7-2.

Constructing a condition by selecting items from a pick list select LASTORDER from the **Fieldname** panel, forming the condition <> LASTORDER in the FIRSTORDER column. Note that the **Like** and **Sounds Like** operators do not appear on the pick list; to use one of these operators in a condition, you must type it in the file skeleton.

From the Dot Prompt

You can use most of the comparison operators listed in Table 7-1 in conditions that you type at the dot prompt (**Like** and **Sounds Like** must be expressed using functions, which are described in Chapter 10). For example, you could list customers with $500 or more in orders this year with the following:

```
LIST ACCOUNT, COMPANY, YTDORDERS FOR YTDORDERS >= 500
```

To select customers whose last order date was before January 1, 1992, you could use

```
LIST ACCOUNT, COMPANY, LASTORDER FOR LASTORDER < {01/01/92}
```

The syntax of the substring operator is slightly different at the dot prompt from its usage in the query editor: At the dot prompt, the constant string is placed first, followed by the $ operator and the field. For example, you could list records in which the EQUIPMENT field contains the text "IBM" with the following:

```
LIST ACCOUNT, COMPANY, EQUIPMENT FOR "IBM" $ EQUIPMENT
```

You might read this condition aloud as "IBM is a substring of the EQUIPMENT field" or "IBM is contained in the EQUIPMENT field."

If you include in a LIST command a condition that is not satisfied by any of the records in the open data base, dBASE IV does not display a warning or error message. After reading through the data base without displaying any records, it redisplays the dot prompt, in effect treating your command as a legitimate inquiry that did not yield any output. Such an inquiry does provide meaningful information, however: it informs you that no records matched your selection criteria.

USING COMPLEX CONDITIONS

The simple record selection criteria described thus far apply a single test based on the contents of a single field. You can state more complex and sophisticated selection criteria by linking separate conditions based on the same or different fields.

dBASE IV provides three logical operators for constructing complex conditions: .AND., .OR., and .NOT. When you type these operators, they must be surrounded by the same period delimiters that identify the logical values .T. and .F.. Spaces are not required before or after the logical operators, and like all dBASE IV command words, you can type them in any combination of uppercase and lowercase letters. In Query-by-Example, you generally do not type the logical operators explicitly; they are implied by the placement of your conditions in the file skeletons. At the dot prompt and in the condition box (which is described in the next section) on the query design screen, the logical operators are required to construct syntactically complete complex conditions.

When you combine conditions with .AND., only records that pass all the tests are processed. For example, the following condition selects customers in San Francisco who have not placed any orders this year:

```
CITY = "San Francisco" .AND. YTDORDERS = 0
```

When you combine conditions with .OR., a record is processed if it passes any one of the tests. The following condition selects all customers in San Francisco (regardless of their current year order total), as well as those who have not placed any orders this year (regardless of where they are located):

```
CITY = "San Francisco" .OR. YTDORDERS = 0
```

The logical operator .NOT. negates a condition and thus enables you to select all the records that do not satisfy the specified condition. For example, you could select all customers who do not have approved credit with the following:

```
.NOT. CREDITOK
```

dBASE IV does not limit you to two conditions. You can combine as many conditions as you need to express complicated selection criteria, except that at the dot prompt, you must not exceed the maximum permissible length of a command line—1024 characters.

When you translate selection criteria from colloquial English into dBASE IV conditions, there are several common pitfalls. First, it is easy to choose the wrong logical operator. You might say, for example, "I want to see all the customers in San Francisco and Berkeley." Although you would use the word "and" in this sentence, the two dBASE IV conditions must be linked with .OR., as in the following:

```
CITY = "San Francisco" .OR. CITY = "Berkeley"
```

This condition selects records in which either of the two conditions linked with .OR. is true: Either the city is San Francisco or the city is Berkeley. If you asked for records in which CITY = "San Francisco" .AND. CITY = "Berkeley", no records would be displayed, since the CITY field would never contain both San Francisco and Berkeley.

Also remember that each separate condition linked with .AND. or .OR. must be a complete dBASE IV condition that could stand on its own. You cannot write a condition like CITY = "San Francisco" .OR. "Berkeley" because "Berkeley" by itself is not a valid condition. Although it may seem as if there is a closer relationship between conditions that test the value of the same field than between those that do not, dBASE IV does not make this distinction.

Finally, when you combine conditions with .AND., .OR., and .NOT. at the dot prompt, you must also take into account the order in which the comparisons are evaluated. This subject is covered in greater detail in Chapter 10, but in the meantime, try to avoid mixing different logical operators in the same condition.

From the Menus

In Query-by-Example, there are two ways to define complex conditions. The first uses only the tabular file skeletons: to define conditions based on two or more fields, you make entries in multiple columns, and to combine several separate conditions, you enter them on separate rows. The second method involves typing a condition in a *condition box.* Some conditions can be expressed using either method, while others—such as comparisons involving memo fields, some based on multiple files, or conditions not based on fields—require the use of the condition box.

When you enter conditions in more than one column in one row of a file skeleton, only records that satisfy all the conditions are selected, as if you had linked the conditions with the logical operator .AND. described in the previous section. For example, to select customers who are located in San Francisco, have year-to-date orders totaling more than $500, and have approved credit, you could enter "San Francisco" in the CITY column, > 0 in the YTDORDERS column, and .T. in the CREDITOK column.

To enter more than one condition based on the same field, you enter the conditions, separated by commas, in the appropriate column in the file skeleton. For example, to select customers who have placed between $250 and $500 in orders this year, you would enter the following condition in the YTDORDERS column in the Customer File skeleton:

```
>= 250, <= 500
```

If you expand a file skeleton to encompass multiple rows, the combination of conditions on each row is evaluated separately, and a record is selected only if all the conditions entered on any one of the rows are fulfilled. In effect, the conditions on separate rows are treated as if they were linked with the logical operator .OR. Thus, if you entered "San Francisco" in the CITY column of the first row of the Customer File skeleton and "Berkeley" in the CITY column of the second row, the query would select all records in which the city is San Francisco or Berkeley. Entering "San Francisco" under CITY in one row and > 0 under YTDORDERS in a second row would select all customers in San Francisco as well as all customers whose year-to-date order totals are greater than 0. If you have used the Data Query commands in Lotus 1-2-3, Excel, or Quattro Pro, this strategy for entering selection criteria should seem familiar.

The fact that dBASE IV evaluates each row in a file skeleton separately has a very important, but often overlooked, implication—*each row must specify a complete, self-sufficient condition.* For example, to select all customers located in San Francisco or Berkeley who have placed orders this year, you would enter "San Francisco" in the CITY column in one row and "Berkeley" in the same column in another row. What may not be obvious is that you must also enter the condition > 0 in the YTDORDERS column in both rows, as illustrated in

Figure 7-3. (In this figure, most of the columns in the Customer File skeleton have been resized to make the CITY and YTDORDERS fields visible at the same time.) The reason is that each row must completely describe one possible combination of data that passes the selection tests. The first row selects records in which the city is "San Francisco" and YTDORDERS is greater than 0, and the second row selects those in which the CITY is "Berkeley" and YTDORDERS is greater than 0.

If this is confusing, keep in mind that the conditions in the query are applied separately to each record, not to the data base as a whole. In colloquial English, you might state the condition as, "I want customers in San Francisco and Berkeley who have an order total greater than zero." However, a closer approximation of the way dBASE IV interprets the query is, "I want *each record* in which the city is San Francisco and the order total is greater than 0 *or* in which the city is Berkeley and the order total is greater than 0."

If you define a set of selection criteria that are not satisfied by any records in the open data base, you cannot move from the query design screen to Browse or Edit. If you press F2 (Data), dBASE IV displays the message "No records selected" and refuses to leave the Query-by-Example screen. You can, however,

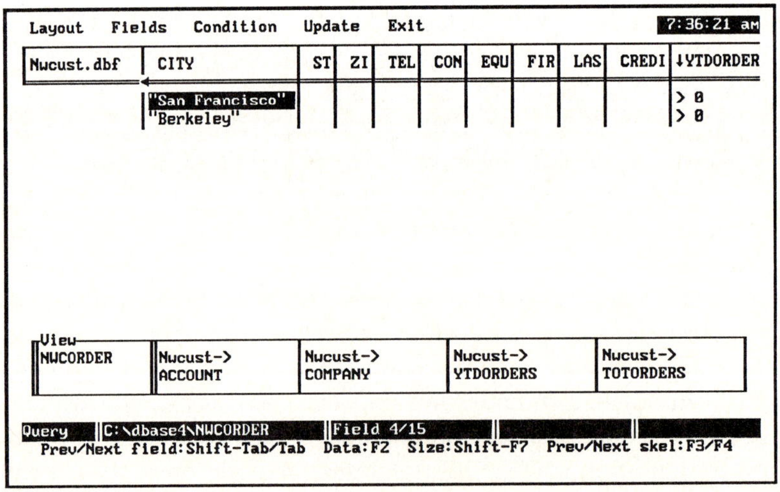

```
Layout  Fields  Condition  Update  Exit                                  7:36:21 am

Nwcust.dbf | CITY             | ST | ZI | TEL | CON | EQU | FIR | LAS | CREDI | ↓YTDORDER
           | "San Francisco"  |    |    |     |     |     |     |     |       | > 0
           | "Berkeley"       |    |    |     |     |     |     |     |       | > 0

View
NWCORDER | Nwcust->  | Nwcust->  | Nwcust->   | Nwcust->
         | ACCOUNT   | COMPANY   | YTDORDERS  | TOTORDERS

Query    C:\dbase4\NWCORDER    Field 4/15
  Prev/Next field:Shift-Tab/Tab  Data:F2  Size:Shift-F7  Prev/Next skel:F3/F4
```

Figure 7-3.

Selecting customers in San Francisco and Berkeley with orders in the current year save a query that does not select any records, either by selecting **Save this query** from the **Layout** menu, or by exiting via the **Save changes and exit** option on the **Exit** menu. At times you may want to do this, especially during the early stages of system development when you have not entered many records into your data bases.

From the Dot Prompt

At the dot prompt, you construct complex conditions by combining conditions with the logical operators .AND., .OR., and .NOT., and you can use them in FOR clauses just as you would simple conditions. For example, you could list customers in San Francisco who have placed an order this year with the following:

```
LIST FOR CITY = "San Francisco" .AND. YTDORDERS > 0
```

To select customers in San Francisco and Berkeley, you would use the following:

```
LIST FOR CITY = "San Francisco" .OR. CITY = "Berkeley"
```

Remember that you can combine more than two conditions, up to the maximum command line length of 1024 characters. Be aware, however, that to construct conditions containing two or more different logical operators, you must understand the order in which dBASE IV evaluates complex expressions, a subject that is discussed in detail in Chapter 10.

Using the Condition Box in Query-by-Example

One way to define complex conditions on the query design screen is to place conditions in multiple columns (to represent the logical .AND. operator) or multiple rows (to represent the logical .OR.) in the file skeletons. If you prefer to type a condition, much as you would in a FOR clause at the dot prompt, you can use the condition box.

Because not every query requires it, dBASE IV initially does not display the condition box on the Query-by-Example screen; you must explicitly request it by selecting the **Add condition box** option from the **Condition** menu. To remove the condition box from the screen and cancel any conditions entered in it, you select the **Delete condition box** option from the **Condition** menu.

dBASE IV displays the condition box at the right side of the screen just above the view skeleton. It is 28 characters wide, but the data entry area within the box scrolls to accommodate a much longer entry as you type your condition. If you need to see the entire condition at once, you can press the F9 (Zoom) key to enlarge the box to fill most of the screen; pressing F9 (Zoom) again shrinks the box back to its original size.

Conditions entered in the condition box must adhere to the same rules of syntax as conditions added to commands typed at the dot prompt. If you have worked with earlier versions of dBASE or you already prefer the dot prompt environment, you may want to use the condition box for complex conditions that would otherwise require entries in many rows and columns of the file skeleton.

You can also use the condition box to express some conditions and enter others in file skeletons. If you use both methods in the same query, the condition in the condition box is superimposed on conditions typed in the file skeletons, as if you had linked them with .AND., so only records that satisfy both sets of conditions are selected. One way to use slightly varying record selection criteria in a series of inquiries without defining dozens of separate queries is to enter the constant conditions—the ones common to all the proposed inquiries—in the condition box, and enter the variable conditions—the ones that you intend to change frequently—in the file skeletons. When you return to the query design screen from Browse or Edit, your current selection criteria will be visible on the screen, and you can easily change the conditions and return to Browse or Edit to view the results. For example, suppose National Widgets wanted to examine customers in different cities who had placed orders during the current year. To do this, you could enter the condition YTDORDERS > 0 in the condition box and choose the cities by making entries in the CITY column of the Customer File skeleton.

As you can see from Table 7-1, you use several comparison operators differently in the condition box and in the file skeletons. If you want to use the $ operator to search for text within a memo field, you must use the condition box, because the $ operator is not permitted with memo fields in the file skeletons. In contrast, **Like** and **Sounds Like** are allowed only in the file skeletons. Conditions that are not directly based on data base fields must also be written in the condition box. For example, as you will see in Chapter 10, many conditions are based on the result of evaluating functions that operate on data base fields, and these conditions cannot be entered in the file skeletons. Chapter 10 also describes a function that you can use to select only deleted records. Because this function measures the status of a record as a whole, rather than operating on a single field, you cannot enter it in one of the field columns in a file skeleton; however, you can use it in the condition box.

USING SCOPE CLAUSES

When you use the full-screen editors, dBASE IV processes records singly and displays them either one at a time (as on the Edit screen) or in groups (as in Browse), and data remains on the screen until you give a command, such as PGDN, to move to another record or screenful of records. Working at the dot prompt, where commands such as LIST might act on too many records to view at once, it is convenient to be able to limit processing to a group of records based on their position in the file. You might, for example, want to list the next five records, or, after interrupting a listing by pressing ESC, resume from the point of interruption to view the rest of the data in the file.

You can limit the range of records acted on by most dBASE IV dot prompt commands by including a *scope clause.* Every command has a default scope, which determines how many records are processed unless you explicitly override it. This default is usually either all the records in the file or a single record—the one at the current position of the record pointer. It is always safe to reiterate a default value; if you forget the default, you can type the scope explicitly. The permissible scopes are as follows:

ALL	All the records in the current data base
RECORD *n*	A single record specified by number
The current record	A single record, the one at the position of the record pointer (available only as a default value)
NEXT *n*	The group of *n* consecutive records, beginning with and including the current record
REST	All the remaining records in the file, beginning with and including the current record

You have already seen one example of the effects of different default scopes. By default, LIST acts on all the records in a data base, whereas DISPLAY affects only the current record. You can override these standard values by including an explicit scope clause in a LIST or DISPLAY command. Thus, to display all the records in a file, you could use either

```
LIST
```

or

```
DISPLAY ALL
```

To display a single record, the current one, you can use either

```
LIST NEXT 1
```

or

```
DISPLAY
```

When used with any other scope, such as REST or NEXT 10, LIST and DISPLAY display the same records.

There is a more important difference between the LIST and DISPLAY commands than the default scope. LIST scrolls data continuously, whereas DISPLAY ALL causes dBASE IV to pause the listing when the screen is full and display the message "Press any key to continue . . ." to give you as much time as you need to read the screen. You can then press ESC to abort the listing and return to the dot prompt, or press any other key to display the next screenful of records. Knowing that you can override the default scopes, you can use LIST and DISPLAY interchangeably based on whether or not you prefer the pause.

The selection of the default scope is generally governed by the destructive potential of a command. For most commands that display or print data, or calculate statistics such as the sum or average of numeric fields, the default scope is ALL (DISPLAY is an exception to this rule), since these commands do not alter or delete data. Commands that do have the potential to change data or delete records have a default scope of one record. For example, the DELETE command acts on the current record only, unless you override this default. Thus, an inadvertent DELETE command that goes unnoticed can remove at most one record from the file.

As you begin to build complex commands, it will become increasingly important to keep track of the position of the record pointer before and after dBASE IV executes a command, and this depends on the scope, according to the following rules:

ALL	dBASE IV positions the record pointer at the top of the file, executes the command, and leaves the pointer at the end-of-file rather than at any valid record.
RECORD *n*	dBASE IV positions the record pointer at the specified record and leaves it there after the command is executed.
The current record	dBASE IV does not move the record pointer before it executes the command and leaves it positioned at the same record afterward.
NEXT *n*	dBASE IV does not move the record pointer before it executes the command, which acts on the current record and enough subsequent records to amount to a total of *n*. After the command completes, the record pointer is positioned at the last record in the group or at the end-of-file if *n* is larger than the number of records remaining.
REST	dBASE does not move the record pointer before it executes the command, which acts on the current record and all the remaining records in the file. After the command completes, the record pointer is positioned at the end-of-file.

If you visualize the location of the record pointer as the top, or beginning, of the current record, the inclusion of the current record in a NEXT *n* or REST scope will make more sense. The relationship between the scope clause and the record pointer is especially important when you type several commands in a row, some of which depend for proper functioning on the position of the pointer. For example, immediately after you execute a LIST command, which leaves the record pointer at the end-of-file, a command with a scope of REST, NEXT *n*, or a single record will have no effect. In this situation, no error or warning message is displayed, and if your command includes a FOR clause, you may jump to the erroneous conclusion that no records fulfilled the specified condition, when in fact none were processed.

Combining a Scope and a Condition

You can include both a scope and a condition in a dBASE IV command. Both clauses are evaluated independently, and only records that satisfy both tests are processed. For example, with the record pointer positioned at any arbitrary record in the Customer File, the following command would test the next five records and display those in which the CITY field contains the value "San Francisco":

```
LIST NEXT 5 ACCOUNT, COMPANY, TELEPHONE, CITY FOR CITY = "San Francisco"
```

Although the scope and FOR clauses may at first appear contradictory, in reality they interact to form a combined condition that must be satisfied for a record to be displayed. The scope clause determines how many records dBASE IV examines, and of those records only those that pass the test in the condition are actually processed. Thus, if you typed the previous command with the record pointer positioned at Record 13 in the National Widgets Customer File, five records, 13 through 17, would be tested, and of those only the two in which the CITY field contained "San Francisco", Records 13 and 17, would be displayed.

CORRECTING ERRORS

As you begin to type longer and more complex conditions, you will inevitably make mistakes. At the dot prompt, dBASE IV responds to errors by displaying a message in a pop-up dialog box like the one illustrated in Figure 7-4. Often, the cause of a "Syntax error," "Variable not found," or "Unrecognized phrase/keyword" error message is immediately apparent. The most common causes for these errors include omitting a required space (say, following the command verb or the word FOR) or a comma, making a spelling or typing error in a field name (such as the YTDORDERS field in Figure 7-3), forgetting to enclose a character field in quotes, omitting a required keyword such as FOR, and combining incomplete conditions with .AND. or .OR.

If you see the cause of the error, you can choose **Edit** to redisplay the command line, just as if you had retrieved it from history, so you can correct it. By selecting the **Help** option, you can call up a help screen to review the correct syntax of the command. If you want to type other unrelated commands

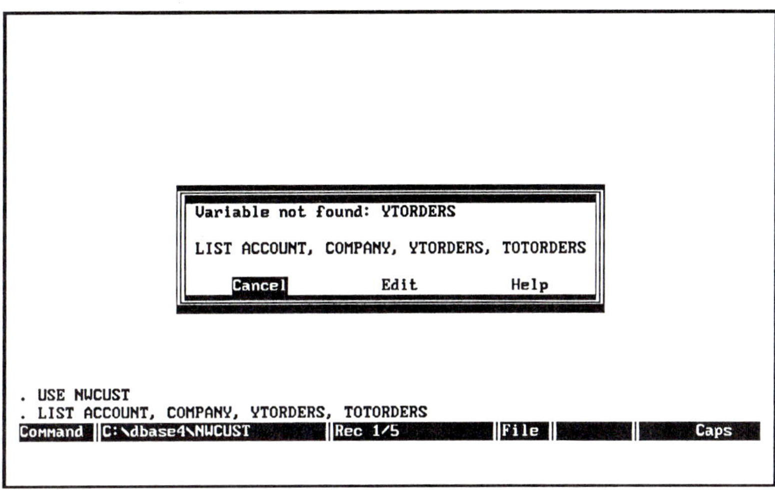

Figure 7-4.

An error message dialog box

to uncover the source of the problem (for example, you might want to use DISPLAY STRUCTURE to verify the spelling of a field name), you can select **Cancel** and later retrieve your previous attempt from history and correct the error.

If you enter an incorrect condition in a file skeleton or in the condition box on the query design screen, dBASE IV can often detect the error immediately, and in these cases, it responds by displaying an error message—usually "Syntax error," "Data type mismatch," or "Unterminated string"—on the message line at the bottom of the screen. You can continue working on the query design screen without correcting the error, but any attempt to use the query to display data will result in the error message "Cannot go to Browse/Edit or return to previous design screen if errors exist." If you save the query and exit without correcting the error, dBASE IV displays the warning "Query not executable. Saved anyway.," but allows you to save the file and exit.

If you make an error that dBASE IV cannot detect without executing the query—for example, forgetting to enclose a character string constant in quotes—the appropriate error message will appear only when you save the query or try to use it to display data. For instance, if you enter the condition

CITY = Berkeley into the condition box, attempting to execute the query by pressing F2 (Data) from the Query-by-Example screen yields the error message "Variable not found: BERKELEY." If you save such a query, a later attempt to execute it results in the "Errors in query definition - cannot be executed" error message.

Don't be lulled into a false sense of security when a command or query does not generate an error message. This means only that your command is syntactically correct; it is no guarantee that the command has produced the intended results. When you begin to experiment with complex conditions, take the time to double-check your results to ensure that the right records were selected. If you always include the field(s) being tested in a view query or in the output of a LIST command, you can examine the output to confirm that only records that satisfy the condition in the FOR clause are selected. It is equally important to verify that no records were overlooked. You can do this by examining the entire data base on the Browse screen, using LIST to display the records, or reading through a printout produced by generating a Quick Report or by using a LIST TO PRINT command that names the relevant fields. Obviously, this testing process will be easier with a small sample file than with a large data base.

SEARCHING FOR INDIVIDUAL RECORDS

The techniques described in this chapter for defining record selection criteria—using view queries and adding FOR clauses to commands such as LIST or DISPLAY—are best suited for displaying or printing *as a group* all the records that satisfy a given condition. These commands are valuable for querying the data base to uncover trends or patterns and for printing lists quickly.

At other times, you will want to search for records one at a time, and, optionally, view and edit each record after it is found. If you plan to use the same selection criteria more than once—such as to find all the customers in Berkeley and edit the COMMENTS field—a query will serve this purpose. With the query in effect, you can browse through the selected records on the Browse or Edit screen and make whatever changes are necessary. For occasional searches based on unique or idiosyncratic conditions, you can specify the search criteria in a query and discard the query without saving it; you can use search commands from Edit or Browse; or you can use the LOCATE command at the dot prompt.

From the Menus

From the Edit or Browse screen, you can use the search options on the **Go To** menu to find records based on the contents of one field. The **Forward search** option starts at the current record and searches forward toward the end-of-file, while the **Backward search** option searches backward from the current position of the record pointer. You can set the **Match capitalization** option to **ON** to request a case-sensitive search or select **OFF** to treat uppercase and lowercase letters as equivalent.

You identify the field you want to search by positioning the cursor within the field before you select **Forward search** or **Backward search** from the **Go To** menu. In either case, dBASE IV pops up a dialog box that prompts you to enter the value you want to find. Despite the wording of the prompt message—"Enter search string:"—you can search date and numeric as well as character fields (but not memos or logical fields).

As in Query-by-Example, you cannot enter a partial field value when you use the **Forward search** or **Backward search** option, regardless of the status of the EXACT setting. Instead, you must specify the search string as a pattern that includes the standard wildcard characters—a question mark (?) to represent a single character, and an asterisk (*) to represent any group of characters—as you do when you use the **Like** operator in a query. For example, you could search for "Berk" in the CITY field by entering the search string as Berk*, and you could retrieve a San Francisco customer by looking for *Francisco. You can also use wildcard characters in date and numeric fields. For example, you could search the LASTORDER field for dates in January 1992, by entering the search string as 01/??/92. Because dBASE IV can determine the data type of the field you are searching (it is stored in the file structure), you need not surround character strings with quotes or use braces to delimit date fields.

If a search initiated from the Edit screen is successful, dBASE IV displays the record it retrieved in the standard Edit format; in Browse mode, it redraws the screen with the selected record at the top. If dBASE IV fails to find a matching record, it leaves the record pointer in its original position and displays the message " ** Not Found ** " in a pop-up dialog box that prompts you to "Press any key to continue...." After one successful search, you can scan forward to find the next matching record by pressing SHIFT-F4 (Find Next) with the cursor in the same field, or backward with SHIFT-F3 (Find Previous).

To search based on more complex criteria, you can use the **Find** operator in Query-by-Example. You enter this operator in the first column of the file skeleton, which represents the entire data base, with conditions in the individual columns (or in the condition box) that specify the search criteria. For example, if the only fact you remember about a customer is that the business is located on Van Ness Avenue in San Francisco, you could enter "San Francisco" in the CITY column and $ "Van Ness" in the ADDRESS column (you must use the $ operator rather than = because "Van" is not the first word in the address—the number comes first). If your sole purpose for creating a query is to search for records, you will probably want to add all the fields in the data base to the view skeleton by pressing F5 (Field) with the cursor in the first column of the file skeleton before you execute the query.

When you execute a query containing the **Find** operator, dBASE IV searches for the first record that satisfies your selection criteria, but it does not limit processing to records that satisfy the specified conditions. The first matching record is displayed on the Edit screen or at the top of the Browse screen (depending on which full-screen mode was last active), but you are free to move through the file and view or edit other records. There is no easy way to find the next record that satisfies the same criteria, comparable to pressing SHIFT-F4 (Find Next) after searching in Edit or Browse, so this method is best suited for finding a single record based on criteria that you are not likely to repeat.

D From the Dot Prompt

From the dot prompt, you can use the LOCATE command to search forward from the current position of the record pointer. LOCATE is far more powerful and flexible than the search options on the Edit and Browse **Go To** menus, because it is not limited to searching a single field. Note, however, that there is no equivalent for the **Backward search** option and that conducting a case-insensitive search is more difficult than setting the **Match capitalization** option **OFF** (it requires using functions that are covered in Chapter 10).

The LOCATE command accepts the same scope and FOR clauses that were explained in the preceding sections for LIST and DISPLAY and thus allows you to express complicated, precise search criteria. The default scope is ALL; if you do not override this default, dBASE IV will begin at the top of the file and search for the first record that matches the specified criteria. For example, to find the first customer in San Francisco who has not placed an order this year, you could use the following:

```
LOCATE FOR CITY = "San Francisco" .AND. YTDORDERS = 0
```

When it finds a record, dBASE IV confirms the success of the search by displaying the record number, as in the following example:

```
Record =        3
```

dBASE IV makes no assumptions about what you might want to do with the record retrieved by a LOCATE command. Thus, it does not, as you might at first expect, display the record or present it for editing on the Edit or Browse screen. This is consistent with the behavior of other commands, such as SKIP and GOTO, which simply position the record pointer and then let you decide what to do next. If you need to view or edit the record, you can type a command such as DISPLAY or EDIT.

After you find the first match with a LOCATE command, you can use the CONTINUE command to keep searching for additional records that satisfy the same criteria, starting from the current position of the record pointer. You can type other commands between LOCATE and CONTINUE, but be careful if you use any commands that reposition the record pointer. CONTINUE always causes dBASE IV to resume its search at the current position of the record pointer; it makes no difference how the pointer arrived at that record. You might want to note the record numbers displayed after each CONTINUE command so that you can return to a given record later if necessary (with GOTO).

When a LOCATE or CONTINUE command fails to find a record that matches your condition within the specified scope, dBASE IV displays the message "End of LOCATE scope." This is not an error message; dBASE IV is informing you that in attempting to search further for a record that satisfies your condition, it reached the last range of records to be included in the search before finding another match. If the scope encompassed all the remaining records in the file, the record pointer will be positioned at the end-of-file; if not, it will point to the last record in the scope.

USING FILTERS TO VIEW SELECTED RECORDS

Typing LIST or DISPLAY commands individually at the dot prompt, with different scope and FOR clauses in each, is a fast and flexible way to carry out varying inquiries into a data base. Building a query is more convenient if you want to work with the same group of records for an extended period of time or use the same selection criteria in many different work sessions. If you prefer working at the dot prompt, you can avoid having to type the same FOR clause repeatedly by using a filter to specify record selection criteria.

A filter is a condition that is placed in effect with a single command and remains active to govern which records are processed by subsequent dBASE IV commands until you close the active data base, exit dBASE IV, or explicitly cancel the filter. You have already used one specialized type of filter, the SET DELETED option, which you can turn ON to limit processing to nondeleted records. You can establish a filter based on any valid condition by using the SET FILTER command as follows:

SET FILTER TO *condition*

In the National Widgets Customer File, for example, you could restrict processing to San Francisco customers with the following command:

```
SET FILTER TO CITY = "San Francisco"
```

With a filter in effect, your data base seems to contain only records that satisfy the condition in the SET FILTER command. The Browse and Edit screens display only the selected records, as do LIST and DISPLAY commands typed at the dot prompt. GOTO TOP moves the record pointer to the first record that satisfies the filter condition, and typing SKIP at the dot prompt or pressing PGDN from the Edit screen positions the pointer at the next record that satisfies the condition. The filter also defines the range of records processed by many other dBASE IV commands that will be covered in later chapters, including commands that print reports and perform calculations.

If you include a FOR clause in a command such as LIST, the condition in the FOR clause is superimposed on the filter as if the two conditions had been stated explicitly and combined with .AND.—only records that satisfy both conditions are processed. Thus, with the filter of the previous example in effect, you could display San Francisco customers who did not place any orders this year with the following command:

```
LIST ACCOUNT, COMPANY, TELEPHONE, YTDORDERS FOR YTDORDERS = 0
```

If you include a scope clause as well, the scope is evaluated relative to the filter, according to the following rules:

ALL	All the records in the current data base that satisfy the filter condition
RECORD *n*	A single record, specified by number, regardless of whether it satisfies the filter condition
The current record	A single record, the one at the current position of the record pointer, regardless of whether it satisfies the filter condition
NEXT *n*	Of the next *n* consecutive records, beginning with and including the current record, the ones that satisfy the filter condition
REST	All the records that satisfy the filter condition, beginning with and including the current record, and continuing to the end of the file

If you have also SET DELETED ON, all scope clauses take both this setting and the filter condition into account—only nondeleted records that satisfy the condition in the SET FILTER command are selected.

You can use the SET FIELDS command introduced in Chapter 6 together with SET FILTER to avoid having to type the same field list repeatedly. For example, to display the ACCOUNT, COMPANY, CITY, and YTDORDERS fields for customers in Berkeley, Oakland, and San Francisco, you could use the following (this command is too long to fit on one line in this book, but when you type long commands, remember not to press ENTER until you get to the end of the command):

```
LIST ACCOUNT, COMPANY, CITY, YTDORDERS FOR CITY = "Berkeley" .OR.
   CITY = "Oakland" .OR. CITY = "San Francisco"
```

With the following field list and filter in effect, a simple LIST command would generate the same output:

```
SET FIELDS TO ACCOUNT, COMPANY, CITY, YTDORDERS
SET FILTER TO CITY = "Berkeley" .OR. CITY = "Oakland" .OR.
   CITY = "San Francisco"
LIST
```

Using a filter and field list is particularly convenient when you want to view the same fields for selection criteria that vary slightly. For example, you might want to look at customers in Berkeley, Oakland, and San Francisco with different year-to-date order totals. By establishing the field list and using a filter that selects only the desired cities, you can use very concise commands to specify additional selection criteria, as in the following example:

```
LIST FOR YTDORDERS > 500
```

To use filters effectively, keep in mind one crucial fact about the way they operate: dBASE IV tests records against a filter condition only when the record pointer is repositioned. The SET FILTER and SET DELETED commands themselves do not reposition the record pointer and therefore do not cause dBASE IV to test the current record. If your subsequent command does not move the record pointer either, the current record will be acted on regardless of whether it passes the filter test. You can force dBASE IV to reposition the record pointer, and thus evaluate the filter condition, by typing a command such as SKIP or GOTO TOP immediately after SET FILTER or SET DELETED.

Like a query, a filter saves you typing time but does not speed up processing—dBASE IV must still read every record within the specified scope and test it against the filter condition. Chapter 9 describes another method, based on indexes, which yields much faster performance when you need to access a small fraction of the records in a large data base. Note also that regardless of the filters currently in effect, you can always access any record by number, either with a GOTO command or by including the record number explicitly in a RECORD *n* scope clause.

You can switch to a different filter at any time by typing a new SET FILTER command. To cancel a filter and return to viewing all records in the data base, you would use

```
SET FILTER TO
```

This construction is another example of a convention used throughout dBASE IV: The command that cancels a setting is the same as the one that invokes it, minus the setting itself (in this case, the condition). Leaving the command line blank beyond the words "SET FILTER TO" implies "Use no filter" or "I don't want to use any filter," just as "USE" means "I don't want to use any data base." One exception to this syntax rule is the DELETED option, which in many ways is equivalent to a filter but must be canceled with SET DELETED OFF.

SUMMARY

The new commands in both this chapter and the last should substantially increase your ability to extract precisely the information you want from your data base files. If you have not already done so, this is a good time to experiment further with the sample data in the National Widgets Customer File or to apply some of the same techniques to your own data bases. You need not be concerned about damaging data during these trials, since all the tools described for establishing selection criteria only display information—they do not change the contents of a data base.

Being able to carry out inquiries based on constantly varying selection criteria is one of dBASE IV's strong points. Working at the dot prompt affords a great deal of power and sophistication coupled with flexibility and convenience. By using Query-by-Example, you can tap into this power without having to memorize as much command syntax but at the expense of having to carry out a few more preliminary steps. Depending on your personal preferences and how often your field and record selection criteria change, you can use any combination of several different methods to create highly customized views of your data. For constantly changing criteria, typing commands individually at the dot prompt is the fastest, most direct method. For conditions that should remain in effect longer, you can use the SET FIELDS and SET FILTER commands at the dot prompt or build a view with the query editor. If you plan to use the same selection criteria in later work sessions, creating and saving a query allows you to reconstruct the same view of the data without having to repeat the original commands.

As you continue to work with dBASE IV, it will become increasingly important to recognize the general concepts illustrated by the examples in this and previous chapters, including the use of field lists, scope clauses, FOR clauses, and filters to narrow the range of data acted on by dBASE IV commands. These command components, illustrated primarily with LIST and DISPLAY, can also be combined in the same ways for use with many other dBASE IV commands, including those that perform calculations, accumulate statistics, and print reports. In particular, the concept of the "condition" will be used extensively throughout your work with dBASE IV.

CHAPTER EIGHT

Sorting a Data Base

In all the work you have done so far with dBASE IV—from the Control Center, at the dot prompt, and in the full-screen edit modes—you accessed records in the order in which you entered them into a data base. If you use any of the methods explained in the last few chapters to specify record selection criteria—defining view queries or using SET FILTER, excluding deleted records with SET DELETED ON, or adding a scope or FOR clause to a command typed at the dot prompt—not every record will be displayed, but the ones that are will appear in record number order.

In most data base applications, the order of entry is rarely the order in which you want to display or print records, since it usually bears little relationship to the information in the file. For example, you would enter records into the National Widgets Customer File in roughly chronological order based on their first order dates. However, you might want to view customers on the screen in alphabetical order by account code; print reports in order by account code, city, or year-to-date sales; and generate mailing labels in ZIP code order.

Displaying records in the order of entry also does not facilitate finding a particular record that you need to view, edit, or delete. When a file is small and you are familiar with the data, this is rarely a problem: You can generally pick out the desired record from the Browse screen and switch to the Edit screen to make the changes. From the dot prompt, you can use a LIST or DISPLAY ALL command to obtain the record number and then use a GOTO command or the **Record number** option on the **Go To** menu in Browse or Edit to move to the record. If you do not immediately spot the record you need, you can search based on the contents of one field by using the **Forward search** or **Backward search** options on the **Go To** menu in Browse or Edit mode, or type a LOCATE command at the dot prompt to search based on any condition.

All these methods break down rapidly as a data base grows larger, however. Scanning through a file in record number order is as frustrating as flipping through a stack of paper ledger cards or a box of index cards, and LOCATE becomes very slow in a data base containing more than a few thousand records. While this is perfectly acceptable for occasional searches based on unusual criteria, it is less than ideal when you are routinely retrieving records to perform daily file maintenance operations.

This chapter describes *sorting*—one of two very different methods for processing records in a dBASE IV data base in a sequence that is different from the order of entry. Sorting physically rearranges the records and rewrites them to a new data base in the specified order. The second method, *indexing,* which is covered in Chapter 9, retains the original record sequence on disk but enables you to display or otherwise process records in a different order. By using one or both techniques, you can display or print data in a sequence determined by the contents of one or more fields in the data base.

SORTING A DATA BASE

Sorting lets you physically rearrange the records in a dBASE IV file, based on the contents of up to ten fields. The field or fields used as the basis for sorting a file are referred to as *sort keys* or *key fields.* When you sort, dBASE IV reads records from the active data base, determines the new sequence based on the specified keys, and copies the records to a new data base in this order while leaving the original data base intact. This concept is illustrated schematically in Figure 8-1 (this figure includes just the account code, company name, and ZIP code; the remaining fields are represented by ellipses).

When you sort based on a numeric key, the records in the new data base are arranged in numerical order. Using a date as the basis for a sort yields chronological order. In either case, you can choose *ascending* order (lowest to highest for numbers and earliest to latest for dates) or *descending* order (highest to lowest or latest to earliest). You cannot sort based on a logical or memo field.

1	LEWIS	Lewis and Associates	...	94610	...
2	ABCPLUMB	ABC Plumbing	...	94703	...
3	KLEIN	Carol Klein, M.D.	...	97214	...
4	MTK	M.T.K. Industries	...	94608	...
5	ANDERSON		...	98006	...
6	RAPIDTYPE	RapidType Secretarial Svc	...	94123	...
7	PHOENIX	Phoenix Construction	...	97401	...
8	KELLY	Kelly and Sons Furniture	...	94578	...
9	GREENTHUMB	Green Thumb Landscaping	...	94702	...
10	HOMEMOVIES	Home Movies Video Rentals	...	94705	...
11	SHAPEUP	Shape Up Fitness Center	...	94804	...
12	FLOORPLAN	Floor Plan Carpet Center	...	97232	...
13	JOHNSON	J. Thomas Johnson, CPA	...	94111	...
14	ELLISMFG	Ellis Manufacturing	...	98005	...
15	IMAGEMAKER	The Image Makers	...	94608	...
16	WHITNEY	Financial Planning Svcs.	...	94536	...
17	HRINSURANC	H & R Insurance	...	94109	...
18	DELTADESGN	Delta Design	...	99163	...
19	ARONOFF		...	94510	...
20	YORKPUMP	York Pump, Inc.	...	95131	...

Sort by account

1	ABCPLUMB	ABC Plumbing	...	94703	...
2	ANDERSON		...	98006	...
3	ARONOFF		...	94510	...
4	DELTADESGN	Delta Design	...	99163	...
5	ELLISMFG	Ellis Manufacturing	...	98005	...
6	FLOORPLAN	Floor Plan Carpet Center	...	97232	...
7	GREENTHUMB	Green Thumb Landscaping	...	94702	...
8	HOMEMOVIES	Home Movies Video Rentals	...	94705	...
9	HRINSURANC	H & R Insurance	...	94109	...
10	IMAGEMAKER	The Image Makers	...	94608	...
11	JOHNSON	J. Thomas Johnson, CPA	...	94111	...
12	KELLY	Kelly and Sons Furniture	...	94578	...
13	KLEIN	Carol Klein, M.D.	...	97214	...
14	LEWIS	Lewis and Associates	...	94610	...
15	MTK	M.T.K. Industries	...	94608	...
16	PHOENIX	Phoenix Construction	...	97401	...
17	RAPIDTYPE	RapidType Secretarial Svc	...	94123	...
18	SHAPEUP	Shape Up Fitness Center	...	94804	...
19	WHITNEY	Financial Planning Svcs.	...	94536	...
20	YORKPUMP	York Pump, Inc.	...	95131	...

Figure 8-1.

Sorting a data base file

When you sort on a character field, an ascending sort places the records in alphabetical order (A to Z) and a descending sort yields reverse alphabetical order (Z to A). You can also choose either *ASCII* or *dictionary* order. The ASCII option causes dBASE IV to sort character strings based on the ASCII codes used internally to represent the characters. If you want to look at these codes, you can find an ASCII table in the dBASE IV *Language Reference* manual or the DOS or BASIC manual that came with your computer. The important point is that the codes for uppercase and lowercase letters are different, and that all uppercase letters come before lowercase letters. The numeric digits 0 through 9 sort before any letters of the alphabet, as do most punctuation marks.

In dictionary order, in contrast, uppercase and lowercase letters are considered equivalent. If a field contains only uppercase or lowercase letters, or a combination such as an initial capital letter followed by lowercase letters, ASCII and dictionary sorts will yield the same results, since character strings are sorted one character at a time starting from the left. However, if data entry was inconsistent, either intentionally or inadvertently, an ASCII sort may not arrange records in the order you would expect. For example, if you sort the National Widgets Customer File by state and some of the California records contain "CA" in the STATE field while others contain "Ca", the California records will not all be grouped together in the sorted file, because "CA" comes before "CO" (Colorado) and "CT" (Connecticut), but "Ca" comes after (followed by "Co" and "Ct"). Requesting a dictionary sort resolves these inconsistencies by ensuring that "CA" and "Ca" are treated as identical.

From the Menus

The SORT command is found on the **Organize** menu in Edit, Browse, and the data base design screen introduced in Chapter 4 (which described how to use this work surface to create a new file structure). Recall that to move to the data base design screen from the Control Center, you highlight a file name in the **Data** panel, press ENTER, and then select the **Modify structure/order** option from the pop-up dialog box. There is also a function key shortcut for this command sequence: press SHIFT-F2 (Design) with the data base name highlighted. If the selected data base is not already open, dBASE IV opens it before displaying the data base design screen.

When you invoke the data base design screen with a file already open, dBASE IV automatically pulls down the **Organize** menu. On the Edit or Browse screen, you can either press F10 (Menu) to activate the menu bar, highlight the **Organize** option, and press ENTER, or you can activate this pull-down menu directly by pressing ALT-O.

To sort the active data base, you select the **Sort database on field list** option and fill out a table of sort instructions in a pop-up dialog box. You can base a sort on up to ten fields, and you can specify ascending or descending order for each. When you sort on a character field, you can also choose ASCII order (all the uppercase letters sort before the lowercase letters) or dictionary order (uppercase and lowercase letters are considered equivalent).

You can type field names directly in the **Field order** column of the sort specifications table, or you can select fields from a pick list invoked by pressing SHIFT-F1 (Pick). The sort table and pick list are illustrated in Figure 8-2. After selecting each field, press ENTER or TAB to move to the **Type of Sort** column and choose the sort order by pressing the spacebar to cycle through the possibilities: **Ascending ASCII, Descending ASCII, Ascending Dictionary,** and **Descending Dictionary**. To sort in ascending ASCII order based on a single field, you enter the field name in the **Field order** column and retain the default entry in the **Type of sort** column. When the table is complete, press ENTER with the highlight in a blank row or press CTRL-END from anywhere in the table. dBASE IV prompts you in a pop-up dialog box to "Enter name of sorted file:" and then begins sorting.

From the Dot Prompt

From the dot prompt, you sort a file by opening it with a USE command and typing a SORT command. To sort in ascending order based on a single field, you specify the key field and the name of the sorted file you want to create:

SORT ON *key field* TO *new file name*

You can request a descending sort by including the abbreviation /D after the name of the key field. To sort the National Widgets Customer File in ascending alphabetical order by account code to create a new file called NWCACCT.DBF, you would use the following command:

```
SORT ON ACCOUNT TO NWCACCT
```

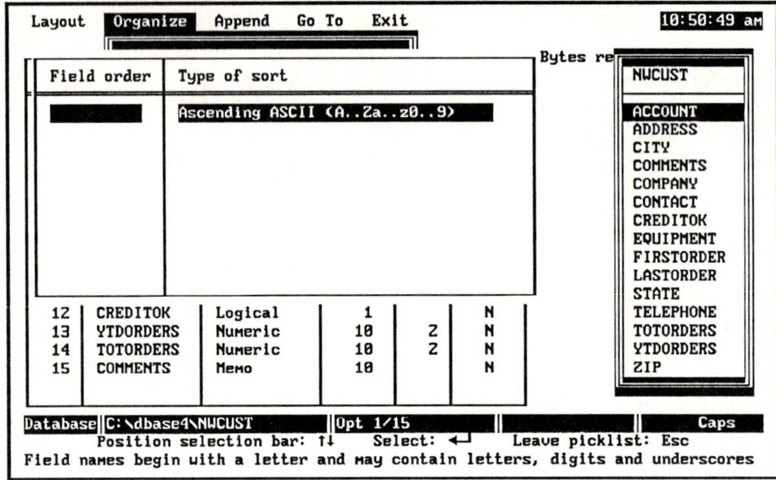

Figure 8-2.

Selecting the sort key fields from a pick list

To sort in descending chronological order by last order date, you could use

```
SORT ON LASTORDER /D TO NWCDATE
```

When you sort on a character field, you can cause dBASE IV to ignore case and sort in dictionary order by including the /C (for "case insensitive") option after the key field name in the SORT command. If you include two options for a field, such as /D and /C, only one slash is required:

```
SORT ON STATE /CD TO NWCSTATE
```

Sorting the File

Sorting always produces a new data base file with the same structure as the original. When you name this file, dBASE IV checks to see whether there is already a file with the same name on the disk, and if so, it displays a pop-up dialog box to warn you, "File already exists," and offers two options: **Overwrite** and **Cancel**. If you are intentionally re-creating a previously sorted file, choose

Overwrite, and dBASE IV will replace the existing file with the new sorted data base. If you used the name of an existing data base inadvertently, choose **Cancel** instead, and then repeat the sort instructions but enter a different file name when you are prompted to do so. Chapter 18 describes how to configure dBASE IV to suppress the warning message and allow you to overwrite existing files without requesting confirmation.

Because it can take some time to sort a large file, dBASE IV displays a percentage indicator of the number of records sorted, so you can monitor the progress of the command. If you are working in the menu system, the status message appears in a pop-up box that also displays the equivalent SORT command that you could use at the dot prompt. If you executed the sort from the dot prompt, the message appears directly below the SORT command. When you sort a small file, the counter jumps from 0% to 100% without displaying any intermediate values.

When dBASE IV sorts a data base that contains memo fields, it must not only generate a new DBF file but also create a matching DBT file that contains the text of the memo fields. This process may also take some time with a large file—often, more time than sorting the data records—so dBASE IV displays another status message, "Copying text file," and a running indicator of the number of records copied. If you initiated the sort from the data base design screen, you can exit from this work surface when the sort is complete by selecting either option on the **Exit** menu: **Save changes and exit** or **Abandon changes and exit** (the **Abandon** option is safe because sorting does not change the structure of the open data base). Depending on how you moved to the data base design screen, dBASE IV returns you either to the Control Center or to the dot prompt.

After completing a sort, dBASE IV leaves the original data base open. If you work in the Control Center, you can see that the original file name is still above the dividing line in the **Data** panel, although the name of the new sorted file also appears. From the dot prompt, or from the Edit or Browse screen, if the status display is ON, you will see the original data base name in the status bar, and the order in which records are displayed on the Browse screen will not change to reflect the sort. *Regardless of how you issued the sort instructions, you must close the original data base and open the sorted copy to view records in the new sequence.*

If you work with multiple sorted copies of a data base, it is your responsibility to remember which copy to open to view records in a given order. Having completed a sort, dBASE IV retains no record of any relationship between the original file and the sorted copies. In the Control Center, all the file names appear in the **Data** panel as independent data bases. You may want to use the

Edit database description option on the **Layout** menu on the data base design screen (or the **Change description of highlighted file** option on the Control Center **Catalog** menu, which is described in Chapter 19) to assign to each sorted file a descriptive title that identifies the original data base and the sort order. For example, you might give the NWCACCT.DBF file described earlier the title "Customer File Sorted by Account Code." Viewing the title underneath the file name at the bottom of the Control Center display will then remind you of the origin and purpose of this data base.

From the dot prompt, you can list all the data base files in the current subdirectory with the DIR (directory) command, which is similar to the DOS DIR command except that by default dBASE IV lists only data base files. Figure 8-3 illustrates the directory listing displayed after sorting the Customer File in the three ways described earlier in this chapter. The directory display includes the number of records, the date of the last update, and the size of each file in bytes—the information displayed at the top of the listing produced by the LIST STRUCTURE command. You can see that the three copies of the Customer File are the same size and have the same number of records, but nothing else would indicate that these files contain the same data.

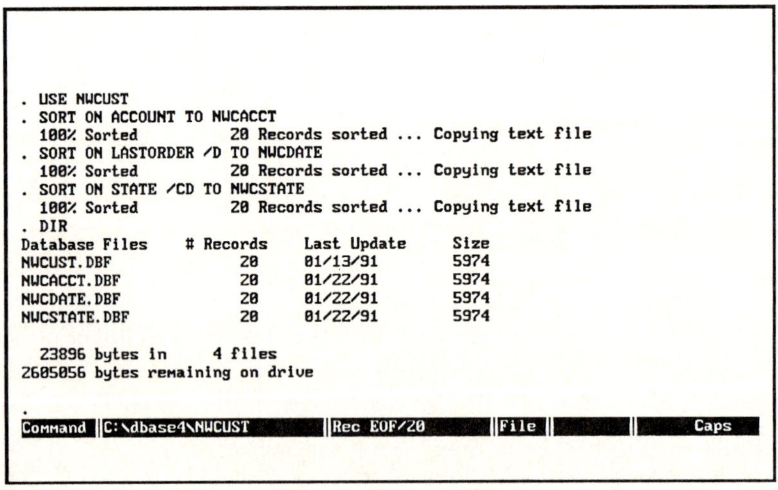

```
. USE NWCUST
. SORT ON ACCOUNT TO NWCACCT
  100% Sorted          20 Records sorted ... Copying text file
. SORT ON LASTORDER /D TO NWCDATE
  100% Sorted          20 Records sorted ... Copying text file
. SORT ON STATE /CD TO NWCSTATE
  100% Sorted          20 Records sorted ... Copying text file
. DIR
Database Files     # Records    Last Update      Size
NWCUST.DBF                20    01/13/91         5974
NWCACCT.DBF               20    01/22/91         5974
NWCDATE.DBF               20    01/22/91         5974
NWCSTATE.DBF              20    01/22/91         5974

  23896 bytes in      4 files
2605056 bytes remaining on drive

.
Command ║C:\dbase4\NWCUST          ║Rec EOF/20       ║File ║        ║      Caps
```

Figure 8-3.

Displaying a list of available data base files from the dot prompt

SORTING ON MULTIPLE FIELDS

As mentioned, dBASE IV allows you to specify up to ten sort key fields. For example, you might want to sort the National Widgets Customer File by state and within each state by city. If there are multiple customers in a city, you may want to arrange them in alphabetical order by account code. Sort keys are always listed in *major-to-minor* order, which means that the field that determines the largest record grouping must be listed first, followed by the field governing the next largest grouping, and so on. In this example, the STATE field is the major sort key, followed by the CITY field, with the ACCOUNT field being the most minor key.

From the Menus

Working from the menus, you can sort on multiple key fields by entering more than one line in the sort specifications table described in the previous section. The sort keys must be listed in major-to-minor order, with the major key on the first line. Figure 8-4 illustrates the sort specifications for ordering the National Widgets Customer File by state, city, and account code using a dictionary sort for the STATE and ACCOUNT fields. You can use all the standard full-screen cursor movement and editing commands to move around in the sort specifications table and edit your entries. When the table is complete, press CTRL-END to initiate the sort.

From the Dot Prompt

From the dot prompt, you can specify multiple sort keys by listing them in major-to-minor order separated by commas (as in any dBASE IV list) in the SORT command. You can request that dBASE IV sort in descending order based on all the key fields by including the keyword DESCENDING in the command, or in ascending order based on all fields (the default) by including the keyword ASCENDING. To request a descending or dictionary sort for an individual key field, you can add /D or /C after the field name. For example, to sort the National Widgets Customer File by state, city, and account code, ignoring the case distinction for the STATE and ACCOUNT fields, you would use

```
SORT ON STATE /C, CITY, ACCOUNT /C TO NWCSTATE
```

To sort in ascending dictionary order based on the STATE and CITY fields, and in descending order by TOTORDERS, you could use the ASCENDING keyword to specify the overall sort order, and add /D after TOTORDERS to override the default for this field only, as follows:

```
SORT ON STATE /C, CITY /C, TOTORDERS /D ASCENDING TO NWCSTATE
```

SORTING SELECTED FIELDS OR RECORDS

Although you will often want to sort an entire data base, sorting can also be a crucial preparatory step in executing an onscreen inquiry or printing a report that includes only selected records or certain fields. When you work through the menu system, you can define sort keys on the query design screen to make the sort instructions part of the view query specifications, so that dBASE IV displays or prints the records selected by the query in sorted order. At the dot

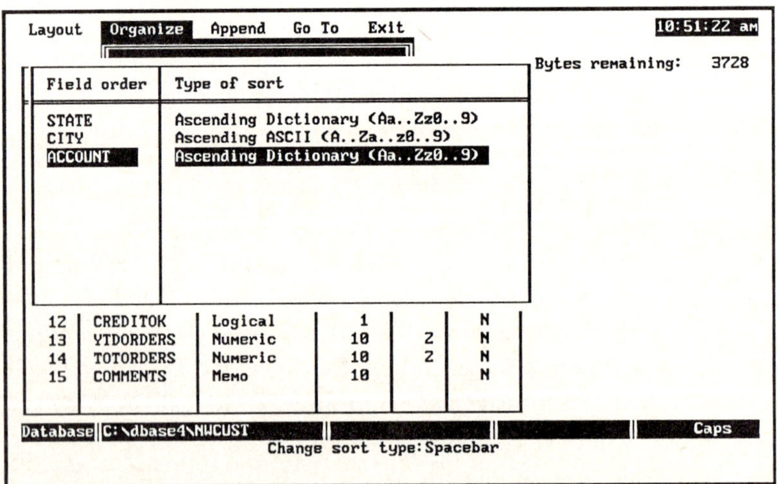

Figure 8-4.

Sorting the Customer File by state, city, and account code

prompt, you can select records using all the techniques illustrated in earlier chapters with the LIST command. In either working environment, dBASE IV includes records that are marked for deletion in the sorted file, unless the DELETED setting is ON.

From the Menus

You can sort the records selected by a view query by entering sorting operators in the appropriate columns of the view skeleton. There are four operators, which correspond to the four types of sorts: **Asc** and **Dsc** for ascending and descending ASCII order, respectively, and **AscDict** and **DscDict** for ascending and descending dictionary order. To sort on multiple fields, you add a number to each operator. The numbers need not be sequential, but they must correspond to the major-to-minor sort order, with a lower number representing a more major sort key. For example, to sort by state, city, and account code, ignoring the case distinction for the STATE and ACCOUNT fields, you could enter "AscDict1" in the STATE column, "Asc2" in the CITY column, and "AscDict3" under ACCOUNT.

One way to enter a sorting operator is to select the **Sort on this field** option from the **Fields** menu with the desired key field highlighted, and then select the type of sort from the resulting pop-up dialog box. dBASE IV enters the corresponding sorting operator into the file skeleton and assigns the numbers, so you must be careful to select fields in major-to-minor order if you use this method. If you prefer, you can type the sorting operators directly in the file skeletons, just as you enter record selection conditions, and you can edit a sorting operator entered by dBASE IV if you later change your mind about the sort order. You can enter both a sorting operator and a condition into the same column in a file skeleton the same way that you combine two conditions based on the same field—by separating the items with commas. For example, to include only California customers in the sorted file described in the previous paragraph, you would enter the following in the STATE column:

```
"CA", AscDict1
```

Keep in mind that *sorting always produces a new file containing data from the original but rearranged into a different order.* When a view query includes sorting operators, the data that is displayed when you execute the query comes from a sorted copy, not the original file. If you edited the data displayed by the view, the changes would not be reflected in the original data base. For this reason, when you use the Edit or Browse screen to view data selected by a query that includes sorting operators, dBASE IV displays "ReadOnly" in the status bar and does not allow you to make any changes.

From the Dot Prompt

When you sort from the dot prompt, you can limit the range of records copied to the new file by using any of the techniques presented in earlier chapters for specifying record selection criteria—you can use a SET FILTER command prior to the sort, and include a scope or a FOR clause in the SORT command. As with any other dBASE IV command, if you combine several options, only records that satisfy all the selection conditions are processed by the SORT command and copied to the sorted file. For example, you could create a subset of the Customer File that contains only California records, sorted by ZIP code, with the following:

```
SORT ON ZIP TO NWCZIP FOR STATE = "CA"
```

MAINTAINING A DATA BASE IN SORTED ORDER

If you intend to access a data base in one particular sequence most of the time, you can periodically sort the file and then delete the original. For example, you could sort the NWCUST.DBF file by ACCOUNT to create the NWCACCT.DBF file, which would then become your working copy of the Customer File. To retain the name NWCUST.DBF for the file you use most often, you must delete the original file, NWCUST.DBF, and then rename NWCACCT.DBF.

Remember that a data base that contains memo fields consists of two files with the same first name and different extensions (DBF and DBT) and that you must erase or rename both. If you are comfortable with the DOS or OS/2 commands for erasing and renaming files, you can use these commands, outside dBASE IV, to erase your original file and rename the sorted copy with the original name:

```
ERASE NWCUST.DBF
ERASE NWCUST.DBT
REN NWCACCT.DBF NWCUST.DBF
REN NWCACCT.DBT NWCUST.DBT
```

You can also erase and rename files, and carry out other disk file maintenance activities, by using commands accessed through the **DOS Utilities** option on the Control Center **Tools** menu. These commands and their dot prompt equivalents are explained in Chapter 19.

Whichever method you choose, never try to erase or rename an open file. If you want to use these commands immediately after performing a sort, you must close the original file by typing USE at the dot prompt or by selecting the file from the **Files** panel in the Control Center, and then choosing the **Close file** option from the pop-up dialog box. Also, when you work with files from a real application, always be sure that you have a backup copy of any file before you erase it.

SUMMARY

Although sorting is easy to understand, it is often not the most efficient way to control the order in which records are displayed or printed, especially if your files are large. Suppose, for example, that you want to view the Customer File onscreen, print reference lists in alphabetical order by account code, and print mailing labels in ZIP code order. You also want to print specialized reports sorted by state, city, and account code, and in descending order by first order date. To accommodate all these requirements, you could create four sorted copies of the file, called perhaps NWCACCT, NWCZIP, NWCSTATE, and NWCFIRST. From the dot prompt, you could create these files with the following commands:

```
USE NWCUST
SORT ON ACCOUNT /C TO NWCACCT
SORT ON ZIP TO NWCZIP
SORT ON STATE /C, CITY, ACCOUNT /C TO NWCSTATE
SORT ON FIRSTORDER /D TO NWCFIRST
```

You could then use these files interchangeably by selecting the one arranged in the order appropriate to the circumstances. To view customers on screen, you could open NWCACCT; to print labels you could use NWCZIP; and so on. Although this approach solves the problem, it has several serious drawbacks.

One problem is that although dBASE IV can sort relatively quickly, sorting a large file can take quite a bit of time, especially if you need to sort four times. A far more serious problem is that maintaining five copies of the same data—the original data base and the four sorted files—can occupy a considerable amount of disk space, perhaps more than you have or more than you are willing to devote to a single data base application. For example, an 80-megabyte hard disk can comfortably accommodate a 10-megabyte data base, but not if you have to maintain five complete copies of the file, together with other data bases and other software.

Furthermore, keeping a set of sorted files up to date can create massive housekeeping headaches. Although you would view the five files in this example as equivalent because you know they contain the same data, dBASE IV treats them as separate, unrelated data bases. If you need to add, delete, or change records, it is up to you to ensure that the changes are reflected in all the relevant files.

When you enter a new record, dBASE IV adds it to the end of the data base in use. If you appended new records to all five copies of the Customer File (an undesirable alternative in itself), none of the sorted copies would be in the correct order. Sorting seems even less attractive when you consider the problems involved in editing the sort key fields in existing records, which essentially involves moving each affected record to a new position in one of the sorted files. For example, if a customer moves to another city, and you change the address fields in all five copies of the file, the record will no longer be in the right sequence in the files sorted by city and ZIP code.

The only safe way to maintain the integrity of the data in a set of sorted files is to add, delete, and change records only in the original data base (or one designated copy) and regenerate the sorted copies of the file when they are needed. However, there is another solution to all these problems that also supports very rapid searches and a faster method than using a filter or query to implement many selection criteria: instead of sorting, you can build indexes, an alternative that is explained in detail in Chapter 9. Nevertheless, sorting does have a place in your dBASE IV command repertoire. If your data rarely changes or your files are small, and you do not need many different sorted orders, the problems just enumerated are often not very serious.

CHAPTER NINE

Indexing a Data Base

Chapter 8 described one method—sorting—for accessing dBASE IV data base records in a sequence other than the order in which they were entered into the file. Sorting is easy to understand, and for small files, it is a practical solution to the problem of introducing order into a data base. When your files are large or you must access data in many different sequences, maintaining multiple sorted copies of the same data can take too much time and disk space. Furthermore, you are forced to assume full responsibility for ensuring that each separate sorted file is complete and up to date.

dBASE IV offers a powerful alternative—indexing—that solves these problems and offers additional advantages. An *index* is an auxiliary file that enables you to view a data base in a sequence that is different from the physical order of the records. Indexing allows you to maintain a single copy of your data but display or otherwise process the records in various orders. The information dBASE IV stores in an index takes up much less space than a sorted copy of the data base, and indexing is usually faster than sorting, although for small files (under a few thousand records), the difference may be insignificant or sorting may actually be faster. Unlike sorted copies of a data base, indexes can be updated automatically to reflect changes and additions to the data base. In a simple application, you may need to enter the indexing specifications only once, after which the indexes are maintained by dBASE IV without further instructions from the operators.

Indexing also enables you to carry out operations that cannot be accomplished through sorting. Using an index, you can retrieve any record, virtually regardless of the size of the data base, almost instantly. You can process a small group of records that are physically scattered throughout the data base but are close in indexed order, without having to read through an entire file. Finally, as you will see in Chapter 17, indexes serve as the basis for linking files and accessing matching records in two related data bases.

USING INDEXES TO ACCESS RECORDS IN DIFFERENT ORDERS

Like sorting, building an index involves specifying a *key expression* that determines the order in which dBASE IV processes records, but unlike sorting, building an index does not create another complete copy of the data base file. *For each record in the data base, an index file contains only the value of the key expression and a reference, often called a pointer, to the record number.* dBASE IV offers more flexibility in constructing an index key than in specifying sort keys, which must be discrete data base fields. An index key can consist of any legitimate dBASE IV expression up to 220 characters long. The key itself—the result of evaluating the expression—may not exceed 100 characters.

The simplest index key consists of a single character, numeric (or float), or date field, and the resulting index accesses records in ascending or descending alphabetical, numerical, or chronological order, respectively. You cannot index on a logical or memo field, but you can use expressions based on these data types in an index key.

In the National Widgets system, you might need three index keys for the Customer File: one to access records in alphabetical order by account code, one chronologically by first order date, and a third in ascending numerical order by ZIP code. Figure 9-1 shows a schematic representation of the relationship between the Customer File and each of these indexes (this is not an exact reproduction of the contents of a dBASE IV index, but it is a good analogy). Note that the data base itself remains in the original order, and each index contains only the key field and a *pointer* to the record number.

Record	ACCOUNT	COMPANY		ZIP		FIRST ORDER
1	LEWIS	Lewis and Associates	...	94610	...	10/13/85
2	ABCPLUMB	ABC Plumbing	...	94703	...	12/01/87
3	KLEIN	Carol Klein, M.D.	...	97214	...	10/13/86
4	MTK	M.T.K. Industries	...	94608	...	06/23/87
5	ANDERSON		...	98006	...	08/08/87
6	RAPIDTYPE	RapidType Secretarial Svc	...	94123	...	03/10/91
7	PHOENIX	Phoenix Construction	...	97401	...	04/28/87
8	KELLY	Kelly and Sons Furniture	...	94578	...	01/23/91
9	GREENTHUMB	Green Thumb Landscaping	...	94702	...	08/16/88
10	HOMEMOVIES	Home Movies Video Rentals	...	94705	...	09/13/88
11	SHAPEUP	Shape Up Fitness Center	...	94804	...	02/15/88
12	FLOORPLAN	Floor Plan Carpet Center	...	97232	...	11/20/88
13	JOHNSON	J. Thomas Johnson, CPA	...	94111	...	06/28/88
14	ELLISMFG	Ellis Manufacturing	...	98005	...	10/18/88
15	IMAGEMAKER	The Image Makers	...	94608	...	11/12/88
16	WHITNEY	Financial Planning Svcs.	...	94536	...	10/04/86
17	HRINSURANC	H & R Insurance	...	94109	...	07/12/87
18	DELTADESGN	Delta Design	...	99163	...	09/14/88
19	ARONOFF		...	94510	...	10/09/87
20	YORKPUMP	York Pump, Inc.	...	95131	...	10/18/88

Index on account

ACCOUNT	RECORD
ABCPLUMB	2
ANDERSON	5
ARONOFF	19
DELTADESGN	18
ELLISMFG	14
FLOORPLAN	12
GREENTHUMB	9
HOMEMOVIES	10
HRINSURANCE	17
IMAGEMAKER	15
JOHNSON	13
KELLY	8
KLEIN	3
LEWIS	1
MTK	4
PHOENIX	7
RAPIDTYPE	6
SHAPEUP	11
WHITNEY	16
YORKPUMP	20

Index on ZIP

ZIP	RECORD
94109	17
94111	13
94123	6
94510	19
94536	16
94578	8
94608	4
94608	15
94610	1
94702	9
94703	2
94705	10
94804	11
95131	20
97214	3
97232	12
97401	7
98005	14
98006	5
99163	18

Index on first order date (descending)

FIRST ORDER	RECORD
03/10/91	6
01/23/91	8
11/20/88	12
11/12/88	15
10/18/88	20
10/18/88	14
09/14/88	18
09/13/88	10
08/16/88	9
06/28/88	13
02/15/88	11
12/01/87	2
10/09/87	19
08/08/87	5
07/12/87	17
06/23/87	4
04/28/87	7
10/13/86	3
10/04/86	16
10/13/85	1

Figure 9-1.

The Customer File and three indexes that access it in different orders

A dBASE IV index is analogous in many ways to a book index, which is also an alphabetical list of keywords and references to locations of more complete data. You can consider an index entry in a book equivalent to the contents of a dBASE IV index entry and the page number reference equivalent to the pointer to the record number. On the numbered page itself, which corresponds to a data base record, is the complete information pointed to by the index entry.

dBASE IV supports two different types of index files, which are commonly referred to by their file name extensions. *MDX index files*, or *multiple index files*, can store indexing information for up to 47 key expressions, which are identified by names that are called *tags*. The first time you ask dBASE IV to build an index for a data base, unless you explicitly request an NDX index (explained in the next paragraph), dBASE IV creates a *production MDX file*—an MDX index file with the same first name as the data base. Thereafter, dBASE IV opens the production MDX file every time you open the data base, updates it to reflect changes made to the data base, and adds new index tags to this file. If you like, you can maintain more than one MDX index for a data base, but only the production MDX file is opened and updated automatically.

An *NDX index file* contains information for indexing a data base on a single key expression (which may, however, include data from more than one field). NDX indexes were supported in dBASE II, III, and III PLUS (although the NDX file format has changed over the years) and dBASE IV can read NDX indexes created by dBASE III and III PLUS. Perhaps because they were retained primarily for compatibility with dBASE III PLUS, NDX indexes can be constructed only from the dot prompt, not from the new dBASE IV menu system. However, compatibility with earlier versions of dBASE is only one of several reasons (others are presented later in this chapter) for using NDX index files. You can build as many NDX indexes as you like, but you can open and update at most ten simultaneously.

Indexing on multiple fields is not as straightforward as sorting on a list of fields, because an index key must be a single expression. To build an index based on more than one field, you must combine them to form the key. This is easiest with character fields, which can be added together, or *concatenated*, with the + operator. For example, to build an index that accesses the National Widgets Customer File in alphabetical order by state, within each state by city, and within each city alphabetically by account code (the same order as the NWCSTATE.DBF file created in Chapter 8 by sorting), you would specify the key expression as follows:

```
STATE + CITY + ACCOUNT
```

In effect, dBASE IV combines the contents of the three separate fields to form a single, longer character string and then builds the index based on this string. Since character fields are alphabetized from left to right, all the index entries with the same first letter in the key will be grouped together. Within this group, they will be arranged according to the second letter, and so on. Thus, when you access the data base through this index, all the records with the same value in the first field in the key will appear to be grouped; within this group, the sequence will be determined by the second field in the key; and so on.

To index on a combination of fields of different data types, you have to convert date and numeric fields to character fields using methods that are explained in Chapter 10.

BUILDING INDEXES

The instructions for building an MDX index tag that accesses a data base in ascending order based on a single field can be stored in the data base structure itself. If you know in advance which fields will serve as index keys, you can enter **Y** (for "Yes") in the **Index** column for these fields when you create the file structure. Figure 9-2 illustrates the appearance of the data base design screen if the ACCOUNT and ZIP tags for the National Widgets Customer File were created in this way. When you save the structure, dBASE IV creates a production MDX index with a tag for each index key field using the field names as tag names.

Despite your best efforts at advance planning, you will inevitably require additional index keys later on, and you can add these to the production MDX file at any point. When you build an index tag, you must specify the tag name, the field or expression on which to base the index, an optional FOR clause, the order (ascending or descending), and how to handle duplicate keys. There is no direct way to index in dictionary order (treat uppercase and lowercase letters as equivalent) but you can do this by indexing on an expression that converts all or part of the key to uppercase or lowercase letters (the specific method for doing this is covered in Chapter 10).

Index tag names must conform to the same rules as data base field names: A tag name can be up to ten characters long and must begin with a letter, but it can otherwise contain any mixture of letters, digits, and underscores. When you index on a single field, the field name is a good choice for the tag name

```
Layout   Organize   Append   Go To   Exit                         1:12:57 pm

                                                     Bytes remaining:   3728
Num  Field Name   Field Type   Width   Dec   Index

 1   ACCOUNT      Character      10            Y
 2   COMPANY      Character      25            N
 3   ADDRESS      Character      25            N
 4   CITY         Character      20            N
 5   STATE        Character       2            N
 6   ZIP          Character      10            Y
 7   TELEPHONE    Character       8            N
 8   CONTACT      Character      25            N
 9   EQUIPMENT    Character     100            N
10   FIRSTORDER   Date            8            N
11   LASTORDER    Date            8            N
12   CREDITOK     Logical         1            N
13   YTDORDERS    Numeric        10      2     N
14   TOTORDERS    Numeric        10      2     N
15   COMMENTS     Memo           10            N

Database C:\dbase4\NWCUST         Field 1/15
        Enter the field name.  Insert/Delete field:Ctrl-N/Ctrl-U
Field names begin with a letter and may contain letters, digits and underscores
```

Figure 9-2.

Storing MDX index tag information in the data base structure

because it is easy to remember; for a complex key, the tag name might be composed of portions of the names of the component fields.

From the Menus

The commands for working with MDX index tags are located on the **Organize** menu, which is present on the data base design screen, the Edit screen, and the Browse screen. Often, the need for a new index will arise as you are viewing or updating a data base on the Edit or Browse screen. If you have not yet opened a data base, you may find it more convenient to access the **Organize** menu from the data base design screen. (If this placement seems strange, keep in mind that the data base design screen is more often used to modify the structure, organization, or data of existing data bases than to create new ones.) Recall that to move from the Control Center to the data base design screen, you highlight the name of the file in the **Data** panel, and then either press SHIFT-F2 (Design) or press ENTER and choose **Modify structure/order** from the pop-up dialog box. Because you are opening an existing data base rather than creating a new one, dBASE IV displays the data base design screen with the **Organize** menu pulled down.

To build a new MDX index tag, you select the **Create new index** option and enter the four required items of information and, optionally, a FOR clause in a pop-up dialog box, which is illustrated in Figure 9-3 with the description of the FIRSTORDER index tag filled in. If you work only in the menu system, you *must* use this method to build all index tags except those based on single fields (the only tags that can be stored with the file structure), and dBASE IV constructs all tags in the production MDX file.

You can type the index key directly, or you can build the key expression by selecting components from a pick list invoked by pressing SHIFT-F1 (Pick). By default, dBASE IV indexes in ascending order, and the **Display first duplicate key only** option is set to **No**; you can change either default by highlighting it, and then pressing ENTER or the spacebar to alternate between the two possibilities. When the four entries are complete, press CTRL-END to begin indexing.

Because it can take some time to index a large file, dBASE IV displays a message box with a percentage indicator of the number of records indexed to monitor the progress of the operation. Figure 9-4 illustrates the message box that is displayed as dBASE IV builds the ACCOUNT tag for the Customer File. Note that dBASE IV also shows you the equivalent command that you could use at the dot prompt to build the same index tag. If the index tag is based on one field, dBASE IV enters **Y** in the **Index** column of the data base structure after building the tag.

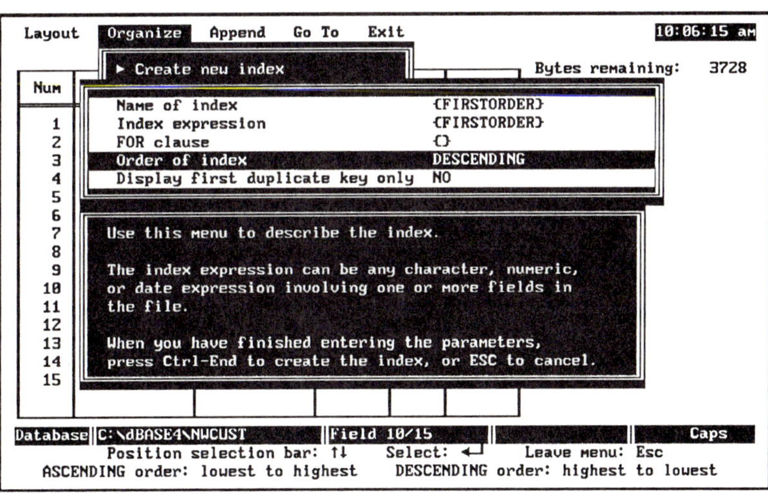

Figure 9-3.

Defining a new MDX index tag

```
Layout  Organize  Append  Go To  Exit                              1:14:18 pm
                                                  Bytes remaining:    3728
 Num  Field Name   Field Type   Width   Dec   Index

  1   ACCOUNT      Character     10             Y
  2   COMPANY      Character     25             N
  3   ADDRESS      Character     25             N
  4   CITY         Character     20             N
  5   STATE        Character      2             N
  6   ZIP          Character     10             Y
  7   TELEPHONE    Character      8             N

  INDEX ON ACCOUNT TAG ACCOUNT

     00% indexed

 14   TOTORDERS    Numeric       10      2      N
 15   COMMENTS     Memo          10             N

Database C:\dbase4\NWCUST        Field 1/15                          Caps
             Enter the field name. Insert/Delete field:Ctrl-N/Ctrl-U
Field names begin with a letter and may contain letters, digits and underscores
```

Figure 9-4.

Building a new MDX index tag

You can change an existing MDX index tag by using the **Modify existing index** option on the **Organize** menu. This option calls up the same dialog box as **Create new index** and allows you to change any of the five items that describe the index tag. You will use this option most often with indexes based on complex keys, to fine-tune the key expression.

From the Dot Prompt

From the dot prompt, you use the INDEX command to build a new tag in an MDX file. Although the resulting file is quite different, the syntax is similar to that of the SORT command:

INDEX ON *key expression* TAG *tag name*

For example, you could build an index tag in the production MDX file for the National Widgets Customer File based on the ACCOUNT field with the following command:

```
INDEX ON ACCOUNT TAG ACCOUNT
```

If no data base is open when you type the INDEX command, dBASE IV prompts you for the name of the file with the message "No database in use. Enter filename:." By default, dBASE IV adds each new tag to the production MDX file, which is created if one does not yet exist. If you want to store the new index tag in a different MDX file, you must specify the name, as follows:

INDEX ON *key expression* TAG *tag name* OF *MDX file name*

You can index in descending order by adding the keyword DESCENDING to the INDEX command. For example, you could build an index tag to access the Customer File in descending order by first order date with the following:

```
INDEX ON FIRSTORDER DESCENDING TAG FIRSTORDER
```

You can use a variation of the INDEX command to build an NDX index file. You *must* construct NDX indexes from the dot prompt; there is no equivalent command or option in the menu system. To build an NDX index, you substitute a file name for a tag name, and use the keyword TO instead of TAG:

INDEX ON *key expression* TO *index file name*

To build an NDX index based on the ZIP code, you could use the following:

```
INDEX ON ZIP TO NWCZIP
```

Note that because index tags are stored in a single disk file, which in most cases has the same name as the associated data base, there is no reason to include the system file name prefix ("NW" for the National Widgets files) in a tag name. An NDX index, however, is stored in a separate disk file and should be given the standard prefix to identify it as part of your application. An index name should also include some reference to both the data base and the key fields insofar as this is feasible within the eight-character file name limit. In the previous example, the name NWCZIP represents "National Widgets" (NW) "Customer File" (C) indexed by ZIP code (ZIP).

As dBASE IV builds either an MDX index tag or an NDX index file, it displays a status message similar to the percentage indicator that monitors the progress of a sort. When the index is complete, this display concludes with the total number of records indexed.

At the dot prompt, no special command is required to change the key expression used to construct an index tag or NDX index: You simply rebuild the index by using another INDEX command that specifies a new key expression and the same tag or file name you used originally. dBASE IV pops up a dialog box to warn you, "Index TAG already exists" or "File already exists." You can select **Overwrite** to replace the original index with the new one if you are intentionally changing the key expression, or **Cancel** to abort the command and return to the dot prompt.

Deleting Indexes

Even if you never run up against the limit of 47 tags per MDX file, you should remove tags that you no longer use from the production MDX file. By doing so, you can speed data entry, for reasons that are explained later in this chapter. Eventually, you can reclaim the disk space occupied by deleted index tags, but dBASE IV does not, as you might expect, immediately begin reusing this space—it compacts the MDX file only when you copy a data base or permanently remove records marked for deletion. (Recall that you can remove deleted records by using the **Erase marked records** on the **Organize** menu or by typing PACK from the dot prompt.)

If you no longer need any indexes for a data base, you can delete all the tags one by one, or you can erase the MDX file from the disk. Note, however, that dBASE IV records the existence of the MDX file in the data base itself; it deletes this reference if all the tags are deleted, but not if you erase the MDX file. Attempting to open a data base for which the production MDX file is missing results in a dialog box that displays the error message "Production MDX file not found" and offers three options: **Cancel**, **Proceed**, and **Help**. If you select **Proceed**, dBASE IV deletes the reference to the MDX file from the data base and allows you to open the file.

From the Menus

You can remove an index tag from the production MDX file by selecting the **Remove unwanted index tag** option from the **Organize** menu on the data base design screen, the Edit screen, or the Browse screen.

From the Dot Prompt

From the dot prompt, you can remove an index tag from the production MDX file with the DELETE TAG command, as follows:

DELETE TAG *tag name*

If the tag is not in the production MDX file, you must name the MDX file in the DELETE TAG command, as follows:

DELETE TAG *tag name* OF MDX *file name*

To delete an NDX index file, use the DOS or dBASE IV ERASE command to erase it from the disk.

WORKING WITH INDEXED DATA BASES

Whenever an index is *open*, or active, *all dBASE IV commands that position the record pointer act relative to the index.* The sequence of records displayed on the Browse screen and in the output of commands such as LIST is determined by the index rather than the true order of the records in the file. *The records themselves are not physically rearranged or renumbered, as they are when you sort.* Figure 9-5 illustrates the result of executing a DISPLAY ALL command with the ACCOUNT index tag active. You can see that each record retains its original number, but the records are displayed in alphabetical order based on the ACCOUNT field.

With an index active, the **Top record** option on the Edit and Browse **Go To** menus, and the equivalent GOTO TOP command at the dot prompt, position the record pointer on the record referenced by the first index entry, not the first physical record. Similarly, **Last record** and GOTO BOTTOM position the record pointer on the record corresponding to the last index entry. The command keys used to move to the next or previous record in the full-screen editors (PGDN and PGUP on the Edit screen and DOWN ARROW and UP ARROW in Browse) move forward or backward to the next or previous record *in indexed order,* as do SKIP and SKIP −1 at the dot prompt.

Figure 9-6 illustrates the appearance of the Browse screen with the STATE-CITY tag, which is based on the combination of state, city, and account code, selected as the master index for the Customer File. (In this figure, the width of

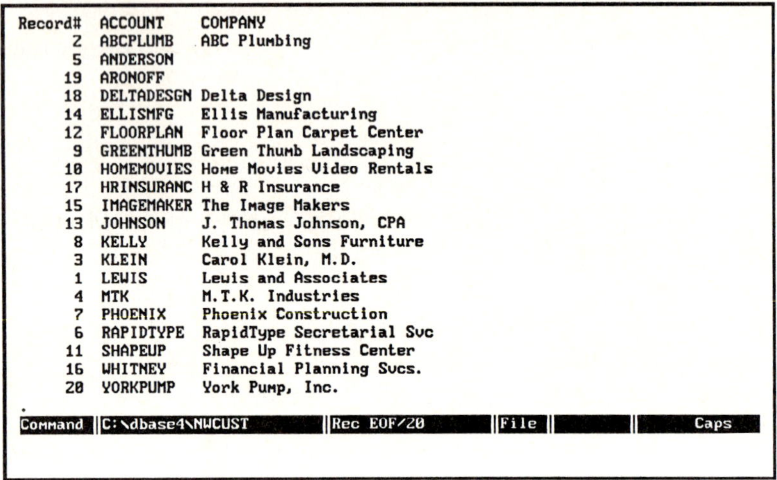

```
Record#  ACCOUNT    COMPANY
      2  ABCPLUMB   ABC Plumbing
      5  ANDERSON
     19  ARONOFF
     18  DELTADESGN Delta Design
     14  ELLISMFG   Ellis Manufacturing
     12  FLOORPLAN  Floor Plan Carpet Center
      9  GREENTHUMB Green Thumb Landscaping
     10  HOMEMOVIES Home Movies Video Rentals
     17  HRINSURANC H & R Insurance
     15  IMAGEMAKER The Image Makers
     13  JOHNSON    J. Thomas Johnson, CPA
      8  KELLY      Kelly and Sons Furniture
      3  KLEIN      Carol Klein, M.D.
      1  LEWIS      Lewis and Associates
      4  MTK        M.T.K. Industries
      7  PHOENIX    Phoenix Construction
      6  RAPIDTYPE  RapidType Secretarial Svc
     11  SHAPEUP    Shape Up Fitness Center
     16  WHITNEY    Financial Planning Svcs.
     20  YORKPUMP   York Pump, Inc.
.
Command ║C:\dbase4\NWCUST ║Rec EOF/20 ║File ║ ║ Caps
```

Figure 9-5.

Displaying records in indexed order

Records Fields Go To Exit 1:21:39 pm

ACCOUNT	COMPANY	ADDRESS	CITY	STATE
ARONOFF		601 First Stre	Benicia	CA
ABCPLUMB	ABC Plumbing	1850 Universit	Berkeley	CA
GREENTHUMB	Green Thumb Landscaping	1240 Hearst	Berkeley	CA
HOMEMOVIES	Home Movies Video Rentals	2982 College A	Berkeley	CA
IMAGEMAKER	The Image Makers	1900 Powell St	Emeryville	CA
MTK	M.T.K. Industries	1400 61st Stre	Emeryville	CA
WHITNEY	Financial Planning Svcs.	1800 Peralta B	Fremont	CA
LEWIS	Lewis and Associates	460 Grand Aven	Oakland	CA
SHAPEUP	Shape Up Fitness Center	2832 MacDonald	Richmond	CA
HRINSURANC	H & R Insurance	1225 Van Ness	San Francisco	CA
JOHNSON	J. Thomas Johnson, CPA	50 California	San Francisco	CA
RAPIDTYPE	RapidType Secretarial Svc	2457 Union Str	San Francisco	CA
YORKPUMP	York Pump, Inc.	632 Charcot Av	San Jose	CA
KELLY	Kelly and Sons Furniture	14800 Bancroft	San Leandro	CA
PHOENIX	Phoenix Construction	2125 Providenc	Eugene	OR
FLOORPLAN	Floor Plan Carpet Center	2020 N.E. Oreg	Portland	OR
KLEIN	Carol Klein, M.D.	1849 S.E. 40th	Portland	OR

Browse ║C:\dbase4\NWCUST ║Rec 19/20 ║File ║ ║ Caps

View and edit fields

Figure 9-6.

Viewing the Customer File through the STATECITY index tag

the **Address** column was adjusted so that the three fields that make up the index key are all visible at the same time.) Note that the customer records appear grouped by state, within each state by city, and within each city in alphabetical order by account code.

To process records in indexed order, dBASE IV constantly reads information from two files: the data base and the index. When you issue a command that requires repositioning the record pointer, dBASE IV first reads the index to determine which record to display or process next and then moves the record pointer to that record.

When an index is open, dBASE IV updates it automatically to reflect the addition of new records to the data base as well as changes made to the key fields. When you append a new record, it is added to the end of the data base and is assigned the next sequential record number. dBASE IV also adds an entry for the new record to each index tag in the production MDX file, inserted in its proper position so that the record can immediately be displayed or processed in correct indexed order. If you edit the contents of an index key field in an existing record, the affected index entries are moved to new positions based on the changed data. Marking a record for deletion does not require any index changes, since the deletion marker is stored in the data base file, not in the indexes.

The production MDX file is always opened whenever you open the data base that it references, so you do not have to do anything special to ensure that all the tags it contains are up to date. If you use NDX indexes, you must explicitly open the ones you want to activate in a particular work session.

In addition to the production MDX file, you can open up to ten other *index files*—either NDX indexes or additional MDX files up to a total of 47 index keys—simultaneously. In practice, however, data entry will slow down if too many indexes are open. The crucial fact to remember is that although dBASE IV can keep track of which data base an index refers to (if you work in the menu system), *only the production MDX file is opened automatically, and only the index files that are open at any given time are updated to reflect changes to the underlying data base.*

An application may require many different indexes, all of which can be open simultaneously, but you can view records on the screen in only one order at a time. The MDX index tag or NDX index that currently governs the sequence in which records are displayed, printed, or otherwise processed is referred to as the *master index.* Immediately after dBASE IV constructs a new MDX index tag or NDX index file, this index becomes the master index. Thus, if you build three index tags for the National Widgets Customer File based on ACCOUNT, FIRSTORDER, and ZIP, and then view the file on the Browse screen, records will be displayed in ZIP code order.

Although dBASE IV automatically opens the production MDX file when you open a data base, it does not select a tag; when you first open a data base, you view records in the order of entry. You can designate a new master index at any time, chosen either from the MDX index tags or the open NDX files, and often you will need to switch master indexes several times during a work session. For example, in working with the National Widgets Customer File, you might use the ACCOUNT tag to find, view, and edit records; switch to the ZIP index to print mailing labels; and then use the FIRSTORDER index for a sales report.

Verifying Which Indexes Are Open

From the dot prompt, you can verify which indexes are open, the key expression for each, and which one is currently the master index by using the DISPLAY STATUS command. Even if you do most of your work in the menu system, you may want to use this command frequently to avoid confusion as you begin to work with more than one or two indexes. DISPLAY STATUS shows you several screens (the actual number depends on how many data base files and indexes are open) that summarize the current status of the working environment. Figure 9-7 shows what the first screen of the status display would look like after opening the National Widgets Customer File with two NDX indexes as well as the production MDX index and designating the ACCOUNT tag as the master index.

Although some of the information in the status display may not mean much to you yet, this command will become more helpful as your understanding of dBASE IV grows. The status display includes the names of the data bases that are currently open—in this case only one—as well as the list of index tags, NDX index files, and index key expressions. The screen identifies the master index and informs you that there is a memo text file associated with the data base. If a filter or query were currently in effect, those facts would also be included on the status screen.

Next, dBASE IV displays some of the current environment default values (such as the default disk drive, path, and left margin for report output), followed by the current status of many of the dBASE IV SET options (none of which are visible in Figure 9-7 because too many lines are occupied by index information), and finally, a listing of the current meanings assigned to the programmable function keys. If you prefer to eliminate the pause between

```
Currently Selected Database:
Select area:  1, Database in Use: C:\DBASE4\NWCUST.DBF    Alias: NWCUST
           Index file:   C:\DBASE4\NWCZIP.NDX  Key: ZIP
           Index file:   C:\DBASE4\NWCSTATE.NDX  Key: STATE+CITY+ACCOUNT
Production   MDX file:   C:\DBASE4\NWCUST.MDX
           Index TAG:      ZIP  Key: ZIP
    Master Index TAG:      ACCOUNT  Key: ACCOUNT
           Index TAG:      FIRSTORDER  Key: FIRSTORDER (Descending)
           Index TAG:      STATECITY  Key: STATE+CITY+ACCOUNT
           Memo file:    C:\DBASE4\NWCUST.DBT

File search path:
Default disk drive: C:
Print destination:  PRN:
Margin =       0
Refresh count =     0
Reprocess count =     0
Number of files open =     8
Current work area =     1

Press any key to continue...
Command  C:\dbase4\NWCUST          Rec 2/20          File              Caps
```

Figure 9-7.

The first screen of output from a DISPLAY STATUS command

screens, you can use LIST STATUS instead of DISPLAY STATUS, and you can add the phrase TO PRINT to produce a hard copy of the output.

From the Menus

As noted earlier, dBASE IV automatically opens the production MDX file whenever you open a data base. From the menus, you cannot create or open other MDX files, and you must explicitly open any NDX files that you want to activate in a work session. Because you can construct NDX indexes only from the dot prompt, these files are not automatically included in the list of files associated with an application. (This list of files is called the catalog, and is described in more detail in Chapter 19.) One additional step is necessary the first time you activate a given NDX index file through the menu system: You must use the **Include .NDX index file** option on the **Organize** menu to add the NDX index to the catalog. This option invokes a pick list of available NDX indexes from which you can make your selection. To include more than one NDX index, select the **Include .NDX index file** option again.

In subsequent work sessions, you can open an NDX index so that it is updated to reflect changes to the data base by using the **Activate .NDX index**

file option on the **Organize** menu. Like **Include .NDX index file,** this option displays a pick list from which you can select one NDX file at a time; to open more than one, you must repeat the process. The **Include .NDX index file** option also activates the selected index, so you do not have to follow this command with **Activate .NDX index file** to make it available in the current work session.

You can choose a new master index at any time by selecting the **Order records by index** option from the **Organize** menu. This command invokes a pick list of available index tags similar to the one illustrated in Figure 9-8. The pick list includes all MDX index tags in the production MDX file, all currently active NDX index files (identified in the pick list by the NDX extension), and a **Natural Order** option, which cancels the current master index (if one is selected) and returns to viewing records in the order of entry. To help you choose an index, a pop-up message box displays the key expression for the highlighted index (FIRSTORDER in Figure 9-8).

When you select a new master index from the **Organize** menu, dBASE IV moves the record pointer to the top of the file and, if you accessed the **Organize** menu from the Browse or Edit screen, redraws the screen. If you canceled the master index by selecting **Natural Order,** the record pointer remains where it was, but dBASE IV redraws the Browse screen so that you can

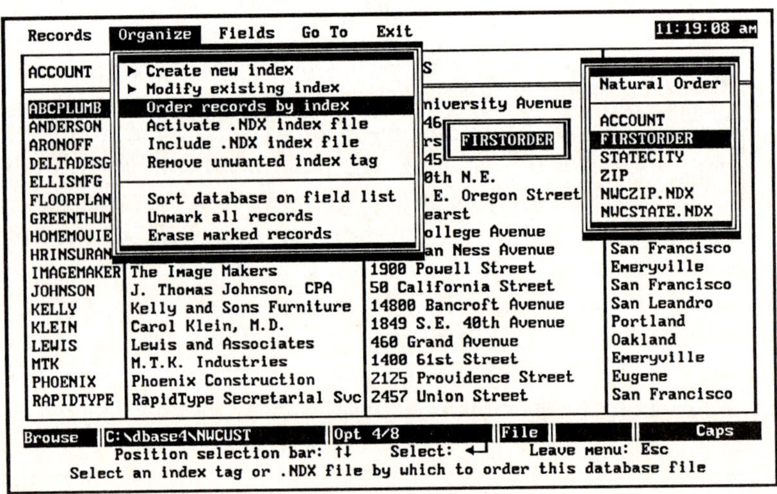

Figure 9-8.

Choosing a new master index

confirm the new record processing sequence. If you moved to the **Organize** menu from the data base design screen, you can return to the Control Center by selecting either **Exit** option (because you have not changed the data base structure, the **Abandon changes and exit** option is as "safe" in this case as **Save changes and exit**).

From the Dot Prompt

When you open a data base with a USE command, dBASE IV automatically opens the production MDX file if one exists. You can open, or activate, one or more NDX indexes at the same time as well as additional MDX files by listing them in the USE command, as follows:

USE *data base name* INDEX *MDX/NDX index file list*

The keyword INDEX is atypical in that it can function as two different "parts of speech" in the dBASE IV command vocabulary. In the INDEX command, which instructs dBASE IV to build an index tag or NDX index file, "INDEX" is a verb. In the USE command, it might be called a preposition—it introduces the clause that identifies which NDX index (or indexes) should be opened with the data base. Remember that *naming an index in a USE command does not construct the index*; if dBASE IV cannot find the designated NDX file on disk, it displays the "File does not exist" error message.

If a data base is already open, you can activate NDX indexes with the SET INDEX command:

SET INDEX TO *index file list*

To open two NDX indexes, NWCZIP and NWCSTATE, with the National Widgets Customer File, you could use either of the following:

```
USE NWCUST INDEX NWCZIP, NWCSTATE
```

or

```
USE NWCUST
SET INDEX TO NWCZIP, NWCSTATE
```

In either case, the first index named in the USE or SET INDEX command, NWCZIP in these examples, becomes the master index. You can select a new master index at any time from among all active (open) indexes—all tags in the production MDX file and any other open MDX index, and all open NDX indexes—with the SET ORDER command, as follows:

SET ORDER TO TAG *index tag name*

or

SET ORDER TO *NDX file name*

This command does not activate an index; it designates one of the active indexes as the master index. The keyword TAG in the SET ORDER command is optional, which should not be surprising in light of the functional similarity between index tags and NDX indexes. For example, with the National Widgets Customer File open as described in the previous example, you might first select the ACCOUNT tag as the master index with the following:

```
SET ORDER TO ACCOUNT
```

dBASE IV confirms your index tag selection by echoing the tag name: "Master index: ACCOUNT." To print labels, you could designate the NDX index based on ZIP code as the new master index, as follows:

```
SET ORDER TO NWCZIP
```

From the dot prompt, you can open a data base and select an MDX index tag at the same time by adding an ORDER clause to the USE command:

USE *data base name* ORDER *index tag name*

The USE command can also name one or more NDX files to open with the data base. The ORDER clause, if present, takes precedence over the NDX file list in determining which becomes the master index. Thus, you could open the Customer File and the NWCZIP and NWCSTATE NDX indexes, and choose the ACCOUNT tag in the production MDX file to control the apparent order of the records with the following:

```
USE NWCUST INDEX NWCZIP, NWCSTATE ORDER ACCOUNT
```

You can ignore all indexes and view records in the order of entry with

```
SET ORDER TO
```

dBASE IV responds with the message "Database is in natural order." Note that the SET ORDER TO command does not close (inactivate) any indexes. Although dBASE IV returns to processing the data base in record number order, all open indexes remain open and are still updated to reflect changes and additions.

Because you can open a new set of NDX indexes with the SET INDEX command, you can also use this command to switch master indexes, but unless you also want to close some of the indexes or open others, SET ORDER is preferable. SET INDEX reopens all the specified indexes from scratch, which involves rereading a portion of each one from the disk, and is therefore slower than SET ORDER, which selects a different master index from among the ones that are already open. If you no longer need to have any active NDX indexes, you can close them but still leave open the data base and the production MDX file by typing

```
SET INDEX TO
```

This usage is consistent with the USE command, which closes an open data base, and SET FILTER TO, which cancels the current FILTER condition. You can think of it as "Set indexes to no indexes" or "I don't want to use any indexes."

USING INDEXES WITH QUERY-BY-EXAMPLE

Chapter 8 described how to sort the records in a view by using the **Sort on this field** option on the query design screen **Fields** menu. You can also use MDX tags (but not NDX indexes) to determine the order in which the records selected by a view query are displayed. You use the same command to use an index tag based on a single field as you do to sort based on the field: With the index key field highlighted, choose the **Sort on this field** option from the **Fields** menu. In fact, to order the records selected by a view query based on one field, you do not even need to know whether an index tag based on this field exists.

If an index tag exists, dBASE IV will activate it; if not, it will sort the file or build the required index tag.

If you need to be reminded about which MDX index tags are available, you can set the **Include indexes** option on the **Fields** menu to **Yes**. When you include indexes in the file skeletons, dBASE IV displays a number sign (#) next to the name of each index key field and creates a new column for each complex index tag (a tag based on any expression other than a single field). Figure 9-9 illustrates the column added to the Customer File skeleton to represent the NWCSTATE index tag, which is based on state, city, and account code. You can choose a complex index to control the order of the records in the view, just like any other tag, by selecting the **Sort on this field** option with the appropriate column highlighted (STATE + CITY + ACCOUNT in this example).

When you sort the records in a view, dBASE IV does not allow you to edit the data, because you are viewing a sorted copy, not the original data base. If you use an index, you can edit data through the query, because query presents the original records (but in a different order determined by the index). Note, however, that if you choose an index key field but request dictionary order, dBASE IV cannot use the index tag, so it sorts the file. In cases like these, the "ReadOnly" indicator in the status bar reminds you that you cannot edit the

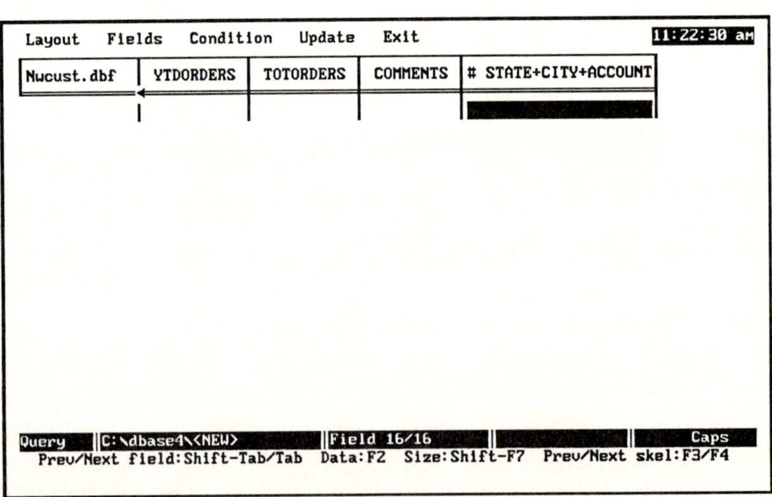

Figure 9-9.

Column added to the Customer File skeleton to represent NWCSTATE data displayed by the query. You can work around this problem by indexing on an expression (explained in Chapter 10) that achieves the same effect as sorting in dictionary order.

USING INDEX KEY SEARCHES FOR RAPID RETRIEVAL

In addition to allowing you to view data in a sequence other than the order of entry, indexes enable you to conduct very fast searches based on the index key. You have already seen how to search for records based on the contents of any field by using the **Forward search** and **Backward search** options on the **Go To** menus in Browse and Edit modes, and how to use the **Find** operator in Query-By-Example and the LOCATE command from the dot prompt to find records based on any search criteria. These commands work by testing records one by one until a record is found that satisfies the specified conditions, and in a large file this process can take a long time. Index key searches are carried out using an entirely different, and much faster, search strategy: *dBASE IV first finds the entry in the master index that matches the specified key value* and then positions the record pointer on the corresponding record in the data base.

To understand how the index key search works, consider again the book index analogy. Suppose you wanted to find the section in this book that covers sorting. One strategy, which is analogous to using the **Forward search** or LOCATE command, involves starting on page 1 and skimming each page until you find the one you want. By using the index, however, you can conduct a more efficient search and find any subject much faster. To look up "SORT" in the index, you would open the index somewhere close to the middle, perhaps at the M section. Knowing that M comes before S, you would move forward in the index, approximately halfway between M and Z, which might leave you in the T section. Realizing that you had gone too far, you would back up a page or two, and continue this process until you found the "SORT" entry. Once you knew the correct page number, you could quickly flip to the page that contains the full information on the desired topic.

Despite this lengthy and cumbersome description, looking up a word in an alphabetical list is fast, as is a dBASE IV index key search. Both the index of a book and a dBASE IV index are lists of keywords, presorted in alphabetical order, with references to the locations of more complete information. In both cases, fast search techniques are based on a knowledge of alphabetical order and an effective scheme for deciding how far to move forward or backward on each pass through the index.

An index key search can retrieve any record in a file, almost regardless of how many records it contains, in at most a few seconds. *By making sure that every data base has an index tag (or less commonly, a stand-alone NDX index file) based on the field or combination of fields that forms a unique (or nearly unique) identifier for each record, you can ensure that you will be able to retrieve any record quickly to view, edit, or delete it.*

You can customize two aspects of the index key search: whether you must specify the full key value to retrieve a record and what happens when dBASE IV fails to find a record that exactly matches your search specifications. The EXACT setting, explained in Chapter 7, determines whether dBASE IV can retrieve a record based on a partial key. As you may recall from Chapter 7, you can change this setting either from the Control Center **Tools** menu or by typing SET EXACT ON or SET EXACT OFF at the dot prompt. By default, dBASE IV assumes that EXACT is OFF, and you will probably want to leave it OFF for much of your own work.

When EXACT is ON, you must enter the full contents of the key field(s) to retrieve a record; when it is OFF, you can specify a partial key value, but the portion you enter must start at the beginning of the key. For example, based on the ACCOUNT index tag for the Customer File, you could retrieve the record for ABC Plumbing by searching for "ABCPLUMB", "ABCPL", or "ABC".

If you specify a partial key that is not unique, an index key search finds the *first* matching record in the index. Thus, if there were a company called ABC Electrical Services with the account code ABCELECT, dBASE IV would retrieve this record rather than ABCPLUMB if you searched for "ABC". Since the index is arranged in alphabetical order, all records in which the account code begins with "ABC" are adjacent in the index; you could find the one you wanted by pressing PGDN in Browse or Edit, or by using the SKIP command at the dot prompt to move forward through the file. If a data base contains more than one record with exactly the same key value, an index key search will retrieve the one entered first—the one with the lowest record number.

When you search based on an index key made up of multiple fields, you must be careful to specify the key expression starting from the beginning. For example, using the STATECITY index tag, which accesses the Customer File in order by city, state, and account number, you could search for the first customer in a California city with a name that begins with B by searching for "CAB". You could not, however, find the first Berkeley customer without knowing that Berkeley is in California. Also, remember that you cannot search for a partial key value in an index based on a date or numeric field.

The NEAR setting determines where dBASE IV positions the record pointer after an unsuccessful search. By default, this setting is OFF, and when an index key search fails to find a record, the record pointer either remains where it was when you initiated the search (if you are working in the menu system) or it is positioned at the end-of-file (if you search from the dot prompt). When NEAR is ON, dBASE IV displays the usual error message but positions the pointer at the first record with a key value *after* the value you searched for. Thus, if you tried to find "LOUIS" in the Customer File, based on the ACCOUNT index, the record pointer would land on Record 4, which has the account code MTK.

You cannot change the NEAR setting from the Control Center **Tools** menu. From the dot prompt, you can type

```
SET NEAR ON
```

or

```
SET NEAR OFF
```

From the Menus

To carry out an index key search from the menu system, you select the **Index key search** option from the **Go To** menu of the Browse or Edit screen. This option is available only when an index tag or NDX index is active, and the search is carried out based on the master index, even if there are other tags in the production MDX file. If no index key is active, or if the wrong one is active, you must select a new master index using the **Order records by index** option on the **Organize** menu.

When you choose the **Index key search** option, dBASE IV displays a dialog box to prompt you for the key value you want to find. The prompt message, which is illustrated in Figure 9-10, displays the index key expression to remind you which index is currently the master index; in this example, the key consists of just the ACCOUNT field. If the search is successful, dBASE IV displays the record it finds on the Edit screen or redraws the Browse screen with the record at the top (depending on which full-screen edit mode was active when you initiated the search). If dBASE IV cannot find a matching record, it displays a

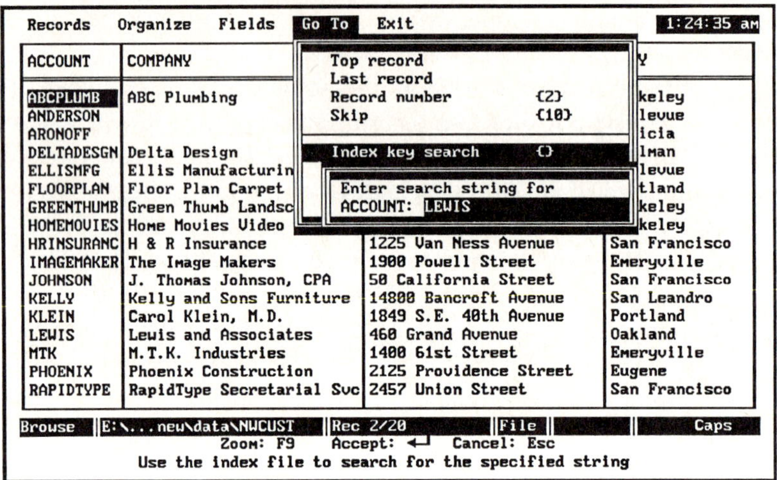

Figure 9-10.

Using an index key search to find a customer record by ACCOUNT code

pop-up box with the error message "** Not Found **" and prompts you to "Press any key to continue . . . ." The record pointer remains where it was when you initiated the search.

From the Dot Prompt

From the dot prompt, you use the SEEK command to carry out an index key search:

SEEK *index key value*

The *index key value* can be any legitimate dBASE IV expression, but when you work at the dot prompt, it is usually a constant value (a number, a character string, or a date). Remember that you must enclose character strings in quotation marks to distinguish them from field names. To find the customer with account code ABCPLUMB, you could use the following:

```
SEEK "ABCPLUMB"
```

Like many other dBASE IV commands, SEEK positions the record pointer without displaying data or making any other assumptions about what you might want to do with the record you have found. Unlike LOCATE, it does not even display the record number, perhaps because once you begin to use indexes to access records based solely on their contents, you may no longer care much about the record numbers. You can always confirm the position of the record pointer after a successful SEEK by looking at the status bar, and you can use a DISPLAY or EDIT command to view the data.

If a SEEK command fails to find a matching key value in the index, dBASE IV displays the error message "Find not successful." (This message derives from the verb "FIND", a dot prompt command that is similar to SEEK and was retained in dBASE IV primarily for compatibility with earlier versions of dBASE.) When you conduct an index key search through the menus, dBASE IV tells you which is the master index when it prompts you for the key value to find; at the dot prompt, you are responsible for ensuring that your search is based on the current master index. If, for example, you search for "KELLEY" in the National Widgets Customer File when the master index is the ZIP tag, dBASE IV does not deduce that your command is unreasonable—it searches for the character string "KELLEY" in the index and then simply informs you that it cannot find a matching record.

Also unlike an index key search executed through the menus, an unsuccessful SEEK command normally leaves the record pointer positioned at the end-of-file, as if dBASE IV had searched each record in turn and reached the last one without finding a match (although this is *not* how SEEK works). If you prefer, you can use SET NEAR ON to configure dBASE IV to position the record pointer on the nearest match instead. Figure 9-11 illustrates the appearance of the screen after you open the National Widgets Customer File, activate the ACCOUNT code tag in the production MDX file, execute two SEEK commands, the second of which is successful, and display the record for M.T.K. Industries.

REBUILDING INDEXES

One of the advantages of using MDX indexes is that dBASE IV automatically opens the production MDX file and updates it to reflect changes to the data every time you open the data base. If you use NDX indexes, you must remember to open them each time you make changes that affect the key fields. If you

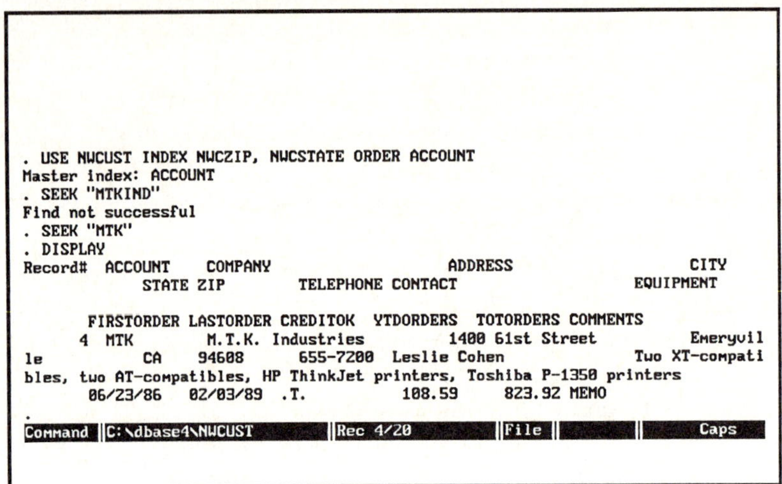

```
. USE NWCUST INDEX NWCZIP, NWCSTATE ORDER ACCOUNT
Master index: ACCOUNT
. SEEK "MTKIND"
Find not successful
. SEEK "MTK"
. DISPLAY
Record#  ACCOUNT    COMPANY                          ADDRESS                    CITY
              STATE ZIP         TELEPHONE CONTACT                          EQUIPMENT

       FIRSTORDER LASTORDER CREDITOK  YTDORDERS  TOTORDERS COMMENTS
      4  MTK          M.T.K. Industries            1400 61st Street           Emeryvil
le             CA     94608       655-7200  Leslie Cohen                 Two XT-compati
bles, two AT-compatibles, HP ThinkJet printers, Toshiba P-1350 printers
       06/23/86   02/03/89  .T.           108.59      823.92 MEMO
.
Command  C:\dbase4\NWCUST          Rec 4/20          File                    Caps
```

Figure 9-11.

Using the SEEK command to find a customer record by account code

ever add records, edit an index key field, or erase records marked for deletion, any indexes that were not open will no longer match the data base. New records added to the data base will have no corresponding entries in the index. After you erase deleted records, the index will contain too many entries, some of which point to the wrong records or ones that no longer exist in the file. If you edit the key field in a record, the index entry for that record will still contain the obsolete value, and you will be unable to find the record with a SEEK command based on its new contents.

Often, a mismatch between a data base and one of its indexes generates an error message the next time you open the index, but sometimes the problem can go unnoticed, and records that should be processed by a command may be passed over while others that should not be are included. Certain danger signals suggest a potential problem with an index:

- An index key search fails to retrieve a record, but you can see the record on the Browse screen or in the output of a LIST command, or find it using a method that does not depend on the index, such as the **Forward search** option on the **Go To** menu in Edit or Browse, or the LOCATE command at the dot prompt.

- A command results in a "Record is not in index" error message.
- A command results in a "Record is out of range" error message.

Fortunately, it is easy (if sometimes time-consuming) to rectify these problems, since an index consists entirely of information derived from a data base, and it can always be reconstructed if necessary. The easiest way to do this is to use the REINDEX command from the dot prompt. REINDEX rebuilds all open indexes, including MDX tags and NDX indexes, based on the original key expressions. Just as when you build an index in the first place, dBASE IV displays status messages to allow you to monitor the progress of this potentially lengthy operation. Note also that after executing a PACK command, which permanently removes deleted records, dBASE IV automatically rebuilds all open indexes.

There is no menu equivalent for the REINDEX command, presumably because when you work in the menu system, all index tags are placed in the production MDX file, and under ideal conditions you would never need to rebuild the production MDX file. Nevertheless, MDX indexes are not immune to damage; if you turn off the computer or reboot while entering or editing records, the indexes may no longer match the data bases, and a hardware or software failure might render the MDX file unreadable. There is a somewhat indirect method for rebuilding MDX index tags through the menus if you want to avoid the dot prompt entirely: the **Erase marked records** option on the **Organize** menu, like the equivalent PACK command, causes dBASE IV to rebuild all MDX tags after removing deleted records.

The REINDEX command is convenient because it does not require that you remember the index key expressions, and it allows you to reconstruct several indexes with a single command. However, REINDEX depends on the fact that the index key expressions are stored in the MDX and NDX files, and for precisely this reason, using REINDEX is not always the best way to regenerate the indexes associated with a data base. If an index file is damaged due to a hardware or software failure and dBASE IV cannot read the key expressions, you will not be able to use this command.

You can always rebuild an index in exactly the same way that you constructed it—by using the **Create new index** command on the **Organize** menu from Browse, Edit, or the data base design screen, or by using an INDEX command from the dot prompt. Note that if an index is damaged, you will not be able to open it for any purpose, so you cannot use DISPLAY STATUS to determine the key expressions. Be sure to generate a printed copy of the index keys before any problems arise, by printing the file structure (which stores single-field index keys) and then opening all the indexes and typing

```
LIST STATUS TO PRINT
```

USING INDEXES TO SELECT RECORDS

When you impose record selection criteria on a data base by defining a query, by adding a FOR clause to a command typed at the dot prompt, or by using a filter, dBASE IV must read every record to determine whether it satisfies the specified condition. Regardless of how many or how few records are selected, the time required to execute the command is dependent on the total number of records in the file.

If you need to select records based on a range of values in an index key, you can use an alternative strategy to speed the search. Suppose, for example, that you wanted to select customers in a region of California defined by the ZIP code range 94700 through 94899. If you designate the ZIP code index tag as the master index, dBASE IV processes the Customer File in ZIP code order, and the desired records will be grouped in any display or printout. *To select just these records, you could position the record pointer on the first record in the group and then read records until you find one that is outside the group.*

This method works with both MDX index tags and NDX indexes, and you can use any command you wish to position the record pointer on the first record in the desired group. For example, if you knew the record number, you could use the **Record number** option on the **Go To** menu of any full-screen editor or type a GOTO command from the dot prompt. It is the second step—processing only records that fall within the desired group—that depends on the index. In most cases, however, you will use an index key search to position the record pointer initially—an index key search based on the contents of a key field is generally the most efficient way to find a record, especially as your files grow and you find it more difficult to remember record numbers.

More often than not, you will want to specify a partial key value in the initial index key search command. For example, you might not know the lowest ZIP code between 94700 and 94899 that is actually represented in the Customer File. Rather than trying ZIP codes one by one, beginning with 94701 (94700 is not a legitimate ZIP code), you could search for "947". (At the dot prompt, you could also SET NEAR ON and search for "94700".) Similarly, to list records alphabetically, starting with the first customer whose account code begins with K, you could search for "K". With the record pointer positioned on the first record in the group, you can use several commands to find the rest of the matching records.

From the Menus

To use the technique outlined in the previous section in Browse or Edit mode, you could find the first record by using the **Index key search** option on the **Go To** menu. You could then use PGDN in the normal way to page through the file and stop when you see that you have reached the end of the group.

From the Dot Prompt

From the dot prompt, you can use indexes to access selected records by using a SEEK command to position the record pointer on the first record in the group you want to view, and then adding a condition to your next command that defines the end of the group, introduced by the keyword WHILE rather than FOR. For example, to list only customers with ZIP codes between 94700 and 94899, you could use the following commands to find the first record:

```
SET ORDER TO ZIP
SEEK "947"
```

To find the first customer in Berkeley, you could use

```
SET ORDER TO STATECITY
SEEK "CABerkeley"
```

If you did not remember the correct spelling of the city name, you could search based on a partial key, as follows:

```
SEEK "CAB"
```

Once the record pointer is positioned on the first record in the group, you can use a WHILE clause in the next command to process the remaining records in the group. Unlike FOR, *WHILE does not cause dBASE IV to reposition the record pointer before executing your command, and it causes dBASE IV to stop reading records as soon as one is encountered that does not satisfy the condition.* Thus, after the SEEK "947" command in the previous example, you could use the following to list only customers with ZIP codes between 94700 and 94899:

```
LIST ACCOUNT, COMPANY, TELEPHONE, ZIP WHILE ZIP <= "94899"
```

After this command completes, the record pointer is positioned on the first record that does not satisfy the condition in the WHILE clause—in this example, the first record with a ZIP code of 94900 or higher. Note that the WHILE clause behaves much like a scope: it selects records based on their position in the display sequence. The difference is that the display sequence is based on the index (which is determined by the data in the records), not on the order in which the records were entered into the data base. If the condition in the WHILE clause is not true for the record at the position of the record pointer when the command is executed, no records will be displayed, just as if you had typed LIST REST or LIST NEXT 5 with the record pointer already at the end-of-file.

You can include both a FOR and a WHILE clause in a command to specify two separate conditions. When you do this, dBASE IV reads records in the group determined by the WHILE clause, and of those records, processes only the ones that satisfy the condition in the FOR clause. For example, you could use the following commands to list all customers with ZIP codes between 94700 and 94899 who did not place any orders this year:

```
SEEK "947"
LIST ACCOUNT, COMPANY, TELEPHONE, ZIP WHILE ZIP <= "94899" FOR YTDORDERS = 0
```

You can also add a scope, in which case the more restrictive of the scope and WHILE clauses determine which records are processed. You can use a view query or filter to establish additional selection criteria, which are superimposed on conditions specified with FOR. In other words, *only records that satisfy all the conditions specified in a command—through queries, filters, scope, FOR, and WHILE clauses—are processed by dBASE IV.*

Using Conditional Indexes to Select Records

You cannot always build an index that supports a direct index key search command to find any given record. For example, National Widgets might want to select customers who own IBM equipment for a special mailing. Because the characters "IBM" might not occur at the beginning of the EQUIPMENT field, you cannot use an index to access the file in alphabetical order by equipment vendor. As noted in Chapter 6, you can define a query that describes these selection criteria, or, at the dot prompt, use a FOR clause or a filter based on a condition such as the following:

```
"IBM" $ EQUIPMENT
```

A faster way to select the same group of records is to build a *conditional index,* which includes pointers to only those records in a data base that satisfy a given condition. Note that the index key—the expression on which the index tag is based—and the field or fields referenced in the FOR clause are entirely independent: The key expression determines the order of the index entries, while the FOR clause determines which records are included in the index. Only records that satisfy the condition in the FOR clause—in this case, records in which the EQUIPMENT field contains the text "IBM"—are represented. When you add a new record to the data base, dBASE IV adds a corresponding entry to a conditional tag only if the new record satisfies the FOR clause, and if you edit the field or fields referred to in the FOR clause, dBASE IV adds, deletes, or adjusts the index entry accordingly.

In order to build a conditional index for an existing data base, dBASE IV must read every record in the file. Thereafter, when the tag is selected as the master index, dBASE IV can process the subset of records it references very fast, because it can move the record pointer directly from one record represented in the index to the next. In contrast, adding the same FOR clause to a LIST command or establishing the same selection criteria by using a view query or a SET FILTER command would result in much slower processing, because dBASE IV would continue to read every record in the file whenever the filter was in effect. If you examine the QBE files used to store view query specifications, you will see that dBASE IV uses SET FILTER to implement your records selection criteria.

If you take into account the time required to build the tag, using a conditional index will result in greater time savings with larger data bases, especially when you will use the index repeatedly to access the same group of records. Thus, if National Widgets frequently sends mailings only to customers that own IBM equipment, using the conditional index in the previous example is preferable. For a one-time mailing to customers who still own CP/M computers, a FOR clause in the command that prints the labels might be nearly as fast as creating and then deleting another tag if the Customer File is small. If your files are large, however, using a conditional index is usually faster—including the time it takes to construct the index—than the other methods for implementing record selection criteria, even if you need to use a tag only once.

Conditional indexes are not ideal when you need to select multiple values of a particular field. For example, to select customers in California, you could build a conditional index based on the STATE field. However, if National Widgets selected records for mailings by state, but did not mail to any one state more than the others, it would be preferable to build a standard index tag that accesses all the customer records. You could then use a SEEK command, followed by a command that includes a WHILE clause, to select customers in any given state.

M From the Menus

To build a conditional index from the menu system, select the **Create new index** option on the **Organize** menu of the Edit, Browse, or data base design screen, and then fill in the **FOR clause** option. For example, to build an index tag for the Customer File that accesses the file in ZIP code order and selects only customers that own IBM equipment, you would enter the following index tag specifications:

Name of index	IBMZIP
Index expression	ZIP
FOR clause	"IBM" $ EQUIPMENT
Order of index	ASCENDING
Display first duplicate key only	NO

From the Dot Prompt

From the dot prompt, you can add the appropriate FOR clause to the INDEX command that constructs the tag. You cannot specify a condition when you build a stand-alone NDX index. For example, to build an index tag for the Customer File that accesses the file in ZIP code order and selects only customers that own IBM equipment, you could use the following command:

```
INDEX ON ZIP TAG IBMZIP FOR "IBM" $ Equipment
```

ADVANTAGES OF MDX AND NDX INDEXES

Because the production MDX index file is updated automatically, and because it can accommodate up to 47 index tags, which is more than sufficient for most applications, you might conclude that there is no reason to use NDX indexes. MDX files are, in fact, ideal for indexes that are used frequently and that should therefore always be kept up to date. Included in this category are indexes used to retrieve individual records with index key searches, to control the order in which records are often viewed on screen, and for reports that are printed once a week or more often.

Some applications, particularly those that generate many different reports, require so many index keys that keeping them up to date can slow data entry significantly. For each new record added to a data base, dBASE IV must update every open index tag, and when you edit fields that contribute to any index key, the corresponding tags must also be adjusted. If your files are large and your index keys are long or numerous, the lag after each new entry or change can become annoying, especially if the delay approaches the amount of time it takes a fast typist to enter the data.

One solution to this problem is to use the **Remove unwanted index tag** option to delete a tag from the production MDX file when you know it will not be used again for some time. If, for example, you use an index once every few months to print a report, you need not keep it up to date all the time. You can remove the tag after printing the report and re-create it right before the next print run. However, as noted earlier, dBASE IV does not immediately reclaim the disk space occupied by the deleted tag (it does so only when you remove deleted records or copy the data base). If you frequently build and then delete tags, the MDX file will grow larger and larger, and index updates will become progressively slower.

Another solution is to use NDX files for indexes that are used infrequently. You can erase them from the disk after each use and rebuild them when you need them again. If you prefer to use only MDX indexes, you can build all temporary tags in a nonproduction MDX file, and periodically erase this file from the disk. If you want to build conditional indexes, you *must* use MDX indexes, because NDX indexes do not support the optional FOR clause. In either case, you need not open the temporary index files when you carry out daily maintenance operations on your data base, provided that you remember to rebuild the relevant MDX index tags or NDX indexes before you use them to view data, print reports or, carry out calculations.

SUMMARY

This chapter introduced some unfamiliar and difficult concepts. If you do not thoroughly understand indexes at this point, be sure to reread this chapter. Indexes will be used throughout this book—and in most of your work with dBASE IV—to display and process records in orders that are more meaningful than the sequence in which they were entered into the file and to carry out fast searches based on the contents of the index key.

If you are working at the dot prompt, you have already learned most of the major elements of the dBASE IV command syntax. Think of a dBASE IV command as consisting of discrete, independent components: the verb, and optionally a field list, a scope, a FOR clause, a WHILE clause, and other keywords such as OFF or TO PRINT. In the following chapters, these components are used in many other dBASE IV commands, in ways that are analogous to those illustrated thus far primarily with LIST and DISPLAY. For example, the same FOR and WHILE clauses used in the LIST examples in this chapter could also be used to select records when you print reports and labels. Make sure that you understand the purpose and use of common command components before you go on. In the rest of this book, you will combine these clauses into increasingly complex dBASE IV commands just as you would begin to form longer and longer sentences as you learn a foreign language.

CHAPTER TEN

Performing Calculations

You have already had a brief introduction to performing calculations in dBASE IV. Chapter 6 explained how to include calculated fields in a field list established through Query-by-Example or typed explicitly in a command at the dot prompt. Chapter 7 introduced the concept of dBASE IV expressions with a discussion of how to combine data base fields, constants, and comparison operators into conditions that express record selection criteria. (By definition, a condition is a logical expression that evaluates to either true or false.) In Chapter 9, you saw an example of a character string expression, when three character fields—STATE, CITY, and ACCOUNT—were concatenated, or added together, to form an index key.

As you continue to work with dBASE IV, you will need to construct a wide variety of expressions that operate on all types of data, not only for establishing more detailed selection criteria, but also for building indexes and performing calculations. This chapter presents the remaining components of the dBASE IV command language and further describes the rules that govern how these components can be combined to form more complex expressions. This chapter demonstrates ways to use these increasingly sophisticated expressions to perform calculations and display or print the results and to permanently change the values of fields in a data base.

WORKING WITH COMPLEX EXPRESSIONS AND CONDITIONS

An *expression* is a combination of data base fields, memory variables, constants, functions, and operators (these terms are described in detail later in this chapter). An expression can incorporate elements of more than one data type as long as they are combined according to the rules of dBASE IV syntax, but it always evaluates to a single quantity of a particular data type: character, numeric, float, date, or logical (you cannot construct memo type expressions, although you can use memo fields in expressions).

Because an expression evaluates to a single quantity, *you can almost always substitute an expression for a data base field or a constant of the same data type.* You can regard the result of evaluating an expression as a kind of calculated field. As you read about constructing expressions, bear in mind that in most of the commands presented in earlier chapters, expressions could substitute for the field names used in the examples. In fact, the concept of the field list introduced in Chapter 5 can be generalized—most dBASE IV commands accept an *expression list.* You can display the result of evaluating any expression with LIST and DISPLAY, just as you can display calculated fields on the Browse and Edit screens. For example, the following command lists the ACCOUNT, COMPANY, YTDORDERS, and TOTORDERS fields from the Customer File and the ratio of year-to-date to total orders (computed using the same expression that defined the calculated field ORDERRATIO used in several commands in Chapter 6):

```
LIST ACCOUNT, COMPANY, YTDORDERS, TOTORDERS, YTDORDERS/TOTORDERS
```

For a single record, you could view the same items with DISPLAY:

```
DISPLAY ACCOUNT, COMPANY, YTDORDERS, TOTORDERS, YTDORDERS/TOTORDERS
```

In these commands, the expression YTDORDERS/TOTORDERS evaluates to a single quantity, in this case a number, which is equivalent in every way to the other four quantities displayed (ACCOUNT, COMPANY, YTDORDERS, and TOTORDERS).

As with dBASE IV commands, you can type expressions in any combination of uppercase and lowercase letters. You can add spaces freely to an expression to improve readability (as you will see in the examples in this chapter), but spaces are not required within an expression.

USING THE ? COMMAND TO DISPLAY INFORMATION

When you begin to experiment with complex expressions, it is helpful to have a convenient way to display the result of evaluating any expression instantly. This kind of experimentation is best done from the dot prompt, even if you generally prefer to use the menu system, and even if you are testing expressions that you will later use through the menus. You can use the DISPLAY command for this purpose; for example, you could have dBASE IV add 2 and 4 and show you the result with the following command:

```
DISPLAY 2 + 4
```

Because the DISPLAY command was intended to operate primarily on data base fields, its output normally includes the current record number from the data base in use and the headings that identify the items the command displays, even if they are meaningless or irrelevant. For example, with any data base open and positioned on the first record, the previous command would produce the following output:

```
Record#       2 + 4
      1           6
```

If you attempt to execute a DISPLAY command with no data base open, dBASE IV reminds you that this command requires an open file and prompts you for the name in a pop-up dialog box: "No data base in use. Enter file name:."

The ? command is more general—it can display the result of evaluating any expressions, which may or may not include data base fields. For example, to display the result of adding 2 and 4, you could use

```
? 2 + 4
```

dBASE IV responds with

```
        6
```

To display the values of several expressions, you list them in the ? command, separated by commas (as in any dBASE IV list). The specified items are displayed with a single space between each pair. For example, with the Customer File open, the following would display the same data as the DISPLAY command described earlier:

```
? ACCOUNT, COMPANY, YTDORDERS, TOTORDERS, YTDORDERS/TOTORDERS
```

If you are familiar with the National Widgets system, you can see that this particular ? command requires an open data base to obtain the values of the ACCOUNT, COMPANY, TOTORDERS, LASTORDER, and FIRSTORDER fields. However, dBASE IV does not assume that these items are field names; they might also refer to memory variables (defined in the next section). Thus, if you execute this command with no data base open, dBASE IV displays "Variable not found" instead of "No data base in use."

The ? command is especially useful for testing a complex expression at the dot prompt before you incorporate it into a report or include it in a lengthy LIST command. Even if it takes you several tries to get the results you want, these attempts will take less time than repeatedly modifying a report form or editing a long LIST command. As you read this chapter, use the ? command to experiment on your own and test your understanding of the operators, functions, and expressions illustrated in the examples.

USING dBASE IV OPERATORS

Chapter 7 briefly introduced the concept of operators and explained the comparison or relational operators used to test the relationship between two values of the same data type. As noted earlier, you can use these operators with character strings, numbers, or dates; depending on the data type, "greater than" and "less than" refer to alphabetical, numerical, or chronological order. An expression that makes use of one of these operators to compare the values of two other expressions always evaluates to the logical value .T. (True) or .F. (False). Chapter 7 also introduced the logical operators .AND., .OR., and .NOT., which link two logical expressions to yield another logical value.

dBASE IV recognizes the four standard arithmetic operators; + (addition), – (subtraction), * (multiplication), and / (division); as well as exponentiation (raising a number to a power), which is expressed as ^ or **. If you are not familiar with algebra, note that the symbols used to represent these operators differ from the way the same operations are commonly written on paper. You cannot use an "X" to represent multiplication, because it could easily be confused with a field or memory variable named X, and the standard division symbol (÷) is missing from the IBM keyboard (although it can be displayed on the screen). The superscript notation generally used for exponentiation is inconvenient for most display screens and printers.

You can apply mathematical operators to numerical data in the standard ways. You can also use the addition and subtraction symbols, with slightly different meanings, to operate on dates. You can subtract one date from another to yield the number of days elapsed between the two, and you can add a number (assumed to represent days) to a date or subtract a number from a date to obtain a calendar date that is the specified number of days in the future or past.

As described in Chapter 9, where several character fields were combined to form an index key, you can add, or concatenate, character strings with +, which places the beginning of the second string at the end of the first. If you use the – operator instead, dBASE IV moves all the trailing blanks in both strings to the end of the combined string, a process that was colorfully described in the original dBASE II manual as "string concatenation with blank squash."

Table 10-1 summarizes the dBASE IV operators and their effects on data of different types. Note that although many of the operators can be used with more than one type of data, not every combination is possible. For example, you can apply the + operator to character strings, numbers, and dates, but you cannot use it to add a number to a character string or to add two dates together. Attempting to combine data of different types in a way not permitted in the dBASE IV language will result in the "Data type mismatch" error message.

Relational Operators

Operator	Data Types (QBE Skeleton)	Data Types (Dot Prompt, Condition Box)	Meaning
=	C, N, F, D	C, N, F, D	Equal to
< > or #	C, N, F, D	C, N, F, D	Not equal to
>	C, N, F, D	C, N, F, D	Greater than
> =	C, N, F, D	C, N, F, D	Greater than or equal to
<	C, N, F, D	C, N, F, D	Less than
< =	C, N, F, D	C, N, F, D	Less than or equal to
$	C	C, M	Contained within
Like	C		Matches skeleton
Sounds Like	C		Matches Soundex code

Logical Operators

Operator	Data Types	Value of Resulting Expression
.AND.	L	.T. if both expressions linked are .T.
.OR.	L	.T. if either expression linked is .T.
.NOT.	L	.T. if following expression is .F.

Mathematical Operators

Operator	Data Types	Meaning
+	N, F	Addition
	C	Concatenation
	D + N	Adds specified number of days to date
−	N, F	Subtraction
	C	Concatenation, embedded blanks combined at end
	D − N	Subtracts specified number of days from date
	D − D	Elapsed time in days between dates
*	N, F	Multiplication
/	N, F	Division
^ or **	N, F	Exponentiation

Table 10-1.

The dBASE IV Operators

USING MEMORY VARIABLES

The expressions in all the command examples presented so far are composed of data base fields and constants, which are combined and related by using the arithmetic, logical, and comparison operators. dBASE IV also allows you to define *memory variables* to store constant values or the results of performing calculations. A memory variable is a temporary quantity retained in memory during a work session with dBASE IV. Unless you save memory variables on disk, their values are lost when you turn off the computer or exit dBASE IV.

By default, dBASE IV allows you to define up to 500 memory variables at a time (you can increase this default, but unless you write programs, it is unlikely that you will ever need to). Imagine that dBASE IV has provided you with a pad of 500 small Post-it notes, each of which has room for a single quantity and a name that identifies what the value represents.

Typically, memory variables store separate, unrelated quantities that do not necessarily belong to any one data base file and that do not share a common structure that would merit creating a data base. You can store constants in memory variables so that you do not have to retype the values repeatedly to include them in conditions, calculations, queries, reports, and labels. You can also use memory variables to store the results of performing time-consuming calculations, such as the total of a numeric field in a large data base, so that you can use these values later without having to repeat the original calculations. Although you can use memory variables in commands accessed through the menu system, you have to type at the dot prompt most of the commands provided specifically for creating, displaying, and manipulating groups of memory variables.

Memory variables can take on five of the six data types allowed for data base fields: character, numeric, float, logical, and date. Like field names, memory variable names can be up to 10 characters long and can contain an embedded underscore (_). If you name your memory variables strategically, you should be able to remember their names and what the values represent. Beginning all memory variable names with the letter M clearly distinguishes them from data base fields. When there is a relationship between a memory variable and a field, giving the memory variable a name consisting of the letter M followed by the field name will remind you of the correspondence. For example, if you compute the sum of the YTDORDERS field in the National Widgets Customer File (using the SUM or CALCULATE commands covered later in this chapter), you might assign the name MYTDORDERS to the variable used to store the sum.

Some of the commands that are explained later in this chapter, such as SUM and CALCULATE, can create memory variables automatically; you simply provide the names. You can also create a memory variable by explicitly *initializing* it—naming it and assigning it a value.

You initialize memory variables with the STORE command or the assignment (=) operator. For example, to create a memory variable called MX and assign it an initial value of 1, you could use either

```
STORE 1 TO MX
```

or

```
MX = 1
```

Do not confuse this use of the equal sign with its meaning in a condition that tests whether the values of two expressions are equal. The command line MX = 1 does not test whether the variable MX currently equals 1; it *creates* a memory variable called MX and *assigns* to it the value 1.

Although the = variation is more concise, there is an advantage to the STORE syntax: you can use it to assign the same value to several variables simultaneously. For example, you could create three variables—MA, MB, and MC—and give them all the value 100.00 with the following command:

```
STORE 100.00 TO MA, MB, MC
```

If you assign a new value to an existing memory variable by reusing the name of a previously created variable in a new STORE command, the variable is essentially re-created from scratch and the old value and data type are lost.

As you might have guessed from the previous examples, dBASE IV determines the data type of a memory variable by the data type of the initial value. Data consisting of only numeric digits is assumed to be a number, text enclosed in any of the standard character string delimiters is assumed to be a character string, single letters delimited by two periods are interpreted as logical values, and values within braces are treated as dates. Note that the value assigned to a memory variable need not be a constant; it can be the result of evaluating any legitimate dBASE IV expression made up of constants, data base fields, functions (defined shortly), and other memory variables. For example, you could create a numeric variable called MORDRATIO that stores the ratio of a customer's year-to-date to total orders with the following:

```
MORDRATIO = YTDORDERS/TOTORDERS
```

If you do not include any decimal places in the initial value, dBASE IV displays numeric memory variables as integers (whole numbers) that are 10 digits long. If a number does include a fractional portion, dBASE IV by default displays two decimal places (you can configure dBASE IV to display more or fewer decimal places by using methods described in Chapter 19). However, up to 19 significant digits are stored in memory and are used in calculations. If the initial value is a constant, dBASE IV creates a fixed-point numeric field. You can create float type numeric variables by assigning an initial value based on a float field, an expression that mixes fixed and floating-point numbers, or certain mathematical and trigonometric functions.

Like character fields, character memory variables can be up to 254 characters long, and dBASE IV derives the length from the initial value. Thus, the following command creates a character variable called MCITY, which is 8 characters long and has the initial value "Berkeley":

```
STORE "Berkeley" TO MCITY
```

Remember that an arbitrary, or constant, character string such as "Berkeley" must be enclosed in quotation marks to prevent dBASE IV from interpreting it as a reference to a data base field or another memory variable and displaying a "Variable not found" error message.

Logical memory variables are initialized by assigning them the logical values .T. (True), .F. (False), or the equivalents, .Y. (Yes) or .N. (No):

```
MCREDIT = .T.
```

Here, the data type is established by the period delimiters, which distinguish the logical values from the single characters T, F, Y, and N.

To create a date variable, you specify a constant date as the initial value. For example, you could assign the date January 10, 1992 to the variable MDATE with the following:

```
MDATE = {01/10/92}
```

Again note that the delimiters, in this case { and }, identify 01/10/92 as a constant date, rather than the numeric expression 1 divided by 10 divided by 92.

Using memory variables gives you the freedom to type commands that are independent of the precise values on which they operate. For example, suppose that National Widgets wanted to compare its year-to-date orders for customers in each state to an arbitrary sales goal. First, you could store the goal and the state in memory variables as follows:

```
MYTDORDERS = 200.00
MSTATE = "CA"
```

You could use the memory variable MYTDORDERS in Query-by-Example or at the dot prompt in an expression that computes the percent of the goal represented by each customer's orders. The expression—which divides the data base field YTDORDERS by MYTDORDERS and multiplies by 100 to convert the result to a percent rather than a fraction—looks like this:

```
YTDORDERS / MYTDORDERS * 100
```

In Query-by-Example, this expression could define a calculated field, and you could enter the variable MSTATE in the STATE column of the Customer File skeleton, just as you would a constant value such as "CA", to specify record selection criteria based on the STATE field. Figure 10-1 illustrates such a query. Note that the memory variables MYTDORDERS and MSTATE must exist when you define the query and each time you try to execute it. The advantage of using a memory variable rather than the constant "CA" is that you need not edit the query file every time you need to change the sales goal or the record selection criteria—you can just assign new values to MGOAL and MSTATE.

At the dot prompt, you could use the variables in a LIST command just as you would the equivalent constants, for example:

```
LIST ACCOUNT, YTDORDERS, TOTORDERS, YTDORDERS / MYTDORDERS * 100
   FOR CITY = MCITY
```

You could easily vary the city or the goal by assigning new values to either or both memory variables and retrieving the LIST command from history to repeat it unchanged. The resulting display is illustrated in Figure 10-2.

You can display the names, types, and values of all currently existing memory variables with

```
DISPLAY MEMORY
```

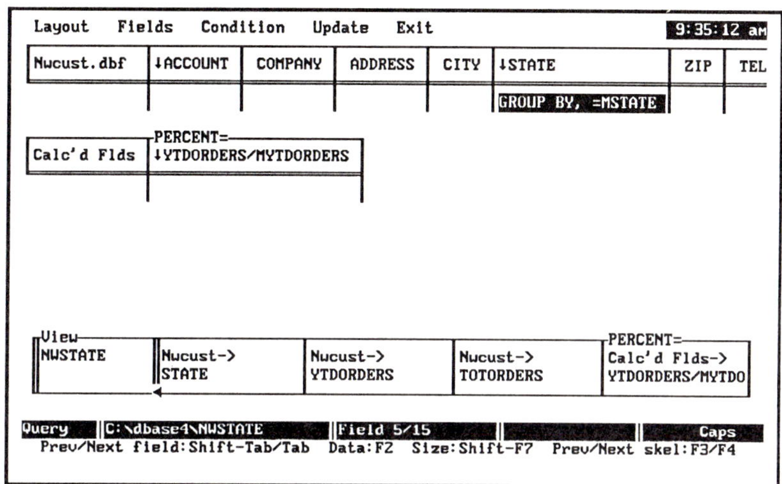

Figure 10-1.

Using memory variables in Query-by-Example

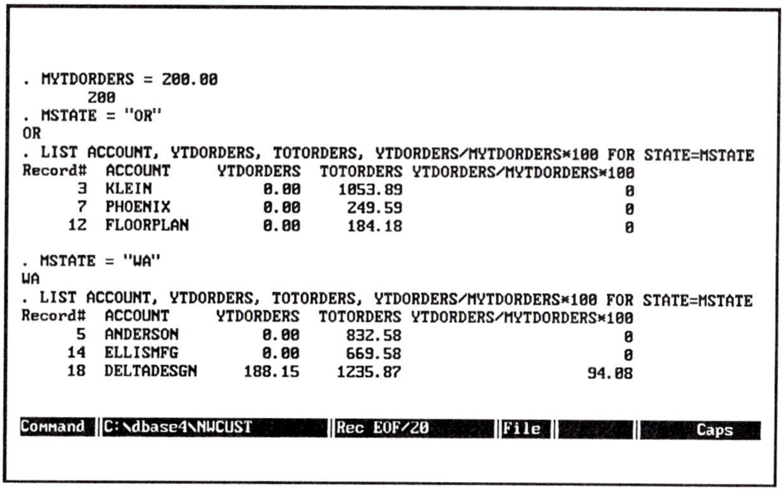

```
. MYTDORDERS = 200.00
       200
. MSTATE = "OR"
OR
. LIST ACCOUNT, YTDORDERS, TOTORDERS, YTDORDERS/MYTDORDERS*100 FOR STATE=MSTATE
Record#  ACCOUNT       YTDORDERS  TOTORDERS YTDORDERS/MYTDORDERS*100
      3  KLEIN              0.00    1053.89                        0
      7  PHOENIX            0.00     249.59                        0
     12  FLOORPLAN          0.00     184.18                        0

. MSTATE = "WA"
WA
. LIST ACCOUNT, YTDORDERS, TOTORDERS, YTDORDERS/MYTDORDERS*100 FOR STATE=MSTATE
Record#  ACCOUNT       YTDORDERS  TOTORDERS YTDORDERS/MYTDORDERS*100
      5  ANDERSON           0.00     832.58                        0
     14  ELLISMFG           0.00     669.58                        0
     18  DELTADESGN       188.15    1235.87                    94.08

Command  C:\dbase4\NWCUST         Rec EOF/20         File            Caps
```

Figure 10-2.

Using memory variables at the dot prompt

or

```
LIST MEMORY
```

You can add the phrase TO PRINT to get a hard copy of the display. As with any DISPLAY or LIST command, the DISPLAY variant pauses when the screen is full to give you time to read the display, whereas LIST scrolls data continuously. In addition to the variables that you have created, these commands display memory variables created automatically by dBASE IV to store information about your printer as well as menus, windows, and pop-ups that you define using the applications generator. These variables are of interest to dBASE IV programmers and application designers; you can disregard this portion of the display produced by LIST MEMORY. If you use DISPLAY MEMORY, you can press ESC when dBASE IV prompts you to "Press any key to continue..." as soon as it has displayed or printed all the memory variables you created. Figure 10-3 illustrates the output of a DISPLAY MEMORY command executed after defining the memory variables in the illustrations presented thus far in this chapter.

```
          User Memory Variables

MDATE       pub   D  01/10/92
MCREDIT     pub   L  .T.
MCITY       pub   C  "Berkeley "
MORDRATIO   pub   N            0.11  (0.105330109577083000)
MC          pub   N          100  (100.0000000000000000)
MB          pub   N          100  (100.0000000000000000)
MA          pub   N          100  (100.0000000000000000)
MX          pub   N            1  (1.000000000000000000)
MSTATE      pub   C  "CA"
MYTDORDERS  pub   N          200  (200.0000000000000000)

   10 out of 500 memvars defined (and 0 array elements)


          User MEMVAR/RTSYM Memory Usage

   2800 bytes used for 1 memvar blocks (max=10)
    850 bytes used for 1 rtsym blocks (max=10)
      0 bytes used for 0 array element memvars
Press any key to continue...
Command  C:\dbase4\NWCUST          Rec 1/20       File                  Ins
```

Figure 10-3.

Displaying the values of memory variables

You can preserve the values of memory variables for use in a later work session by storing them in a disk file with the SAVE command. To save all the variables currently in memory, you would use

SAVE TO *memory file name*

This command creates a file with the extension MEM, which identifies it as a memory variable file. You can save variables selectively, based on a similarity among their names, by specifying a *skeleton,* a pattern made up of text characters and wildcard symbols that describes the variable names that you want to select. The wildcard characters are the same as those used by DOS and dBASE IV to represent file names: a question mark (?) to symbolize any single character and an asterisk (*) for any group of characters. Thus, you could save all the variables that have names beginning with MX with the following:

```
SAVE ALL LIKE MX* TO MEMFILE1
```

You can save all variables with names that do not match a certain pattern by using the keyword EXCEPT instead of LIKE. For example, you could save all variables in which the second two letters of the name are not AB with the command

```
SAVE ALL EXCEPT ?AB* TO MEMFILE2
```

The skeleton ?AB* stands for file names in which the first position contains any character, the second must be A, the third must be B, and the rest of the name can be any combination of characters.

You can read the values stored in a memory file back into memory by using the RESTORE command as follows:

RESTORE FROM *memory file name*

When you use this form of the command, any variables currently in memory are lost. If you prefer, you can add the set of variables in the file to any that currently exist by including the keyword ADDITIVE in the RESTORE command:

RESTORE FROM *memory file name* ADDITIVE

You can erase the values of variables from memory with the RELEASE command to make room for more variables if you are nearing the limit of 500, or more likely, so that the output of DISPLAY MEMORY commands is not cluttered by values that you no longer need to see. Like the SAVE command, RELEASE allows you to specify a group of variable names in a LIKE or EXCEPT clause, or you can list the variables individually.

USING dBASE IV FUNCTIONS

A function is a specialized operator that adds to the dBASE IV language the ability to perform calculations not possible using the operators listed in Table 10-1. A function takes a certain kind of input and processes it in a specific way to yield a particular type of output. You can think of a function as a kind of "black box" or machine that, when given the right raw materials (the input), can predictably crank out a particular product (the output).

For example, the SQRT (square root) function takes as its input a number (or numeric expression) and returns as output a floating-point number that when multiplied by itself yields the original number. To use this function, you do not have to know how to calculate a square root (although you may once have learned a method for doing so), and you do not need to know how dBASE IV does it.

To include a dBASE IV function in an expression, you write the name of the function followed by a pair of parentheses that enclose the inputs. For example, to display the square root of 25, you could use

```
? SQRT(25)
```

If a function requires more than one item as input, the inputs must be listed (separated by commas, as in any other dBASE IV list) in the correct order within the parentheses. For example, the PAYMENT function, which calculates the payment amount on a loan, takes three inputs: loan amount, interest rate, and number of installments. You can use this function to calculate the monthly payment on a $5000 loan amortized over three years (36 months) at an annual interest rate of 12 percent (1 percent, or 0.01 per month) as follows:

```
? PAYMENT(5000, 0.01, 36)
```

Not all functions require that you provide input. For example, the expression DATE( ) evaluates to the system date, and the expression DELETED( ) evaluates to the logical value .T. if you have marked the current record in an open data base for deletion. Note however, that *every function reference must include a pair of parentheses,* in order to identify it as a function so that dBASE IV does not mistake it for a data base field or memory variable with the same name. Strictly speaking, DATE, DELETED, and other such functions do have input, although you do not explicitly supply the input. DATE takes its input from DOS, which obtains the date from a hardware clock or from the date you entered when you first booted your computer. DELETED looks for the deletion marker in the record at the position of the record pointer.

These two functions may be used, like any others, in an expression or a condition. For example, you could list only deleted records with the following command:

```
LIST FOR DELETED()
```

Although dBASE IV offers a number of mathematical functions, performing numerical calculations is not its strong point, and most business applications do not require complex math. Some of the most useful functions are those provided for manipulating character strings and converting data of one type to another. The UPPER function converts a character string to all uppercase letters, and the corresponding LOWER function converts to lowercase letters. Recall that when you use the search options on the **Go To** menus in Edit and Browse modes, you can set the **Match capitalization** option to **No** to carry out a case-independent search, and you can specify dictionary order to ignore case distinctions when you sort. You can use the UPPER and LOWER functions for situations in which an explicit option for ignoring case is not provided. For example, if the STATE field had been entered with an inconsistent mixture of uppercase and lowercase letters, you could convert this field to all uppercase letters in the index tag based on state, city, and account code by specifying the key as follows:

```
UPPER(STATE) + CITY + ACCOUNT
```

As stated earlier, certain operators and functions work with particular data types. To overcome some of these limitations, dBASE IV provides a number of functions that convert data from one type to another. For example, although you can sort on up to ten fields of any combination of data types, an index key must be a single expression. You can index on a single character, numeric, or date field to yield an index that accesses a data base in alphabetical, numerical, or chronological order, but to index on multiple fields of different data types, you must convert all the key fields to character strings and then concatenate them to form the key expression.

The DTOS (date-to-string) function converts a date to a character string in year/month/day order. For example, if the FIRSTORDER field in a customer record contained the date 10/13/85, DTOS(FIRSTORDER) would evaluate to the character string "19851013". You can combine the string produced by the DTOS function with another character field in an index key to yield correct chronological order. In contrast, if dates in the standard *mm/dd/yy* format were converted to character strings and "alphabetized," all the records with the same month would be indexed in a group, within which they would be grouped by day and finally by year. Thus, any record in which the month is January would index before any record in February, regardless of the year. To index the Customer File on the combination of state, city, and last order date, you would index on the following expression:

```
UPPER(STATE) + CITY + DTOS(LASTORDER)
```

The STR function converts a number to a character string. This function has three inputs: the numeric expression to be converted, the length of the resulting string, and the number of decimal places to include. If you omit the length, the output string is 10 characters long; if you omit the number of decimal places, it is assumed to be zero. You could use this function in an index key expression that accesses the Customer File by total orders within state as follows:

```
UPPER(STATE) + STR(TOTORDERS, 10, 2)
```

To index in descending order by total orders, you could subtract TOTORDERS from an arbitrarily large number and convert the result to a character string, as in the following index key expression:

```
UPPER(STATE) + STR(9999999.99-TOTORDERS, 10, 2)
```

This expression yields the desired result because subtracting a larger number from 9999999.99 (the largest value that fits in the TOTORDERS field) yields a smaller result—which indexes earlier—than subtracting a smaller number. A simpler example may help to clarify this strategy: subtracting a larger number such as 80 from 100 yields a smaller number (20) than subtracting a smaller number such as 60 from 100 (which yields 40).

You can use a similar technique to index in descending order by date. To get reverse chronological order, you subtract the date from an arbitrary date some time in the future, such as 12/31/99. A later date is closer to the reference date than an earlier date, so the subtraction will yield a smaller result and the later date will occur earlier in the index. The number that results from the subtraction (which represents the elapsed time in days) must be converted to a character string using the STR function if you need to combine it with a character field to form the index key. The following index key expression groups records by state, and within each state, in descending order based on the first order date:

```
UPPER(STATE) + STR({12/31/99}-FIRSTORDER, 6, 0)
```

To build an index key based on a logical field (which you cannot do directly) or on the combination of a character and logical field, you must transform the logical field to a character string. dBASE IV does not have a function for exactly this purpose, but you can use the IIF function. IIF, which resembles the @IF function used in Lotus 1-2-3 and other spreadsheets, requires three inputs: a condition to be tested, the value to use if the condition is true, and the value to use if the condition is false. The IIF function therefore evaluates to one of two different values—one if the condition it tests evaluates to .T., and the other if the condition evaluates to .F.. A logical field itself satisfies the definition of a condition and can therefore serve as the first input to the IIF function. Thus, the following expression evaluates to Y if CREDITOK is true or to N if it is false:

```
IIF(CREDITOK, "Y", "N")
```

You could index the Customer File by state, and group the records within each state by credit status, with the following command:

```
INDEX ON UPPER(STATE) + IIF(CREDITOK, "Y", "N") TAG STATECRED
```

If you construct the STATECRED index tag as shown in this example, customers with bad credit (for whom the IIF function evaluates to N) will be grouped before customers with good credit (for whom the IIF function evaluates to Y), because N precedes Y in alphabetical order. If you prefer the opposite order, you can substitute "A" and "B" or 1 and "2" for "Y" and "N" as inputs to the IIF function. The actual characters, which are never displayed or printed, are immaterial, as long as the character used for the group that must index first comes earlier in alphabetical order.

You can use the index built in the previous example to expedite any operation carried out on customers in a particular state with a given credit status. For example, to list customers in California who have good credit, you could use an index key search to find the first record in which the state is "CA" and the result of evaluating the IIF function in the index key expression is Y (CREDITOK is true), and then use a WHILE clause to process only the records in the desired group, as follows:

```
SEEK "CAY"
LIST ACCOUNT, COMPANY, YTDORDERS, TOTORDERS WHILE STATE = "CA" .AND. CREDITOK
```

Note that the condition in the WHILE clause does not follow the form of the index key, but it does express exactly the same condition. dBASE IV cannot check whether a WHILE clause is reasonable, or whether it expresses a condition that makes sense in combination with any previous or subsequent commands. It is up to you to ensure that the condition takes into account the active index, the contents of the data base, and the position of the record pointer when you execute the command.

In addition to the type conversion functions, dBASE IV offers a full complement of other functions for operating on dates. The DOW (day-of-week) function takes a date as input and returns a number corresponding to the day of the week (1 for Sunday, 2 for Monday, and so on). The DAY, MONTH, and YEAR functions extract the individual components of the date as numbers, and a parallel set of functions returns the names of the days and months. The CDOW (character-day-of-week) function yields a character string that spells out the name of the day (for example, "Sunday" or "Monday"); CMONTH evaluates to the name of the month ("January", "February", and so on); and MDY yields a complete date in the form "January 10, 92".

Remember that the expression consisting of a function name, the obligatory pair of parentheses, and its inputs (if any) is synonymous with the output of the function and can be used anywhere that an expression of that data type is permitted—in a LIST command at the dot prompt, on a report, to initialize a memory variable, in an index key expression, in a query, and in many other contexts. Among other things, this means that one function may serve as the input to another function. For example, the CDOW function takes a date as input and returns a character string as output. If the DATE function—which evaluates to a true calendar date, the DOS system date—serves as the input to the CDOW function, the result is the current day of the week. For example, on July 5, 1992, the expression CDOW(DATE( )) would yield the character string "Sunday".

You can use functions in conditions that define record selection criteria in queries as well as in conditions typed at the dot prompt. In most cases, you have to enter conditions that include function references in the condition box, rather than in a file skeleton. For example, to define a query that selects only deleted records, you could enter the condition DELETED( ) in the condition box. This condition does not refer to any single field in the file structure, but rather to the entire record, so you cannot enter it in the file skeleton.

When a condition tests the result of operating on a field with a function rather than testing the field itself, you must also use the condition box, because there is no way to express this relationship in the file skeleton. Thus, you must also enter conditions such as YEAR(FIRSTORDER) = 1990 or "COMPAQ" $ UPPER(EQUIPMENT) in the condition box. However, you can use the file skeleton for conditions that compare a field to the result of evaluating an expression that includes a function. For example, to select customer records in which the account code is found within the company name, you could enter $ UPPER(COMPANY) in the ACCOUNT column in the Customer File skeleton.

The dBASE IV language offers a wealth of functions for performing mathematical calculations, manipulating character strings and dates, transforming one data type to another, obtaining information about the data base in use in the selected work area, and determining what hardware and operating system software are present. Some of these functions are of interest only to programmers, while others can be useful almost immediately. The remaining chapters of this book present additional functions as they are needed. You will find a complete list of dBASE IV functions in Appendix E.

Precedence of Evaluation

When dBASE IV evaluates a complex expression, it does not simply proceed from left to right. Within an expression, dBASE IV performs the indicated operations in the following order:

- Evaluation of functions
- Exponentiation
- Multiplication and division, from left to right

- Numeric addition and subtraction, from left to right
- Character string concatenation
- Evaluation of relational operators, from left to right
- Evaluation of logical operators, in the following order: .NOT., .AND., .OR.

dBASE IV scans a complex expression as many times as necessary to adhere to this precedence of operators. For example, consider a simple expression intended to calculate a customer's orders from prior years as a percent of the total orders. To perform this computation on a hand-held calculator, you would subtract the YTDORDERS field from the TOTORDERS field, divide the result by TOTORDERS, and multiply by 100 to convert the result to a percent. If YTDORDERS were 100.00 and TOTORDERS were 400.00, the result would be 75 percent. Your first inclination might be to write the dBASE IV expression as follows:

```
TOTORDERS - YTDORDERS / TOTORDERS * 100
```

Because all multiplication and division operations are carried out before any subtraction, dBASE IV evaluates this expression by dividing YTDORDERS by TOTORDERS, multiplying this number by 100, and subtracting the result from TOTORDERS. Using the numbers cited in the previous paragraph, you would obtain the value 375.

You can override the default order in which expressions are evaluated by using parentheses. dBASE IV evaluates any expression that contains parentheses by starting within the innermost set of parentheses and working outward. To force dBASE IV to perform the order calculation correctly, you must add parentheses as follows:

```
(TOTORDERS - YTDORDERS) / TOTORDERS * 100
```

To calculate the length of time in years that National Widgets has been doing business with a customer, you could subtract the first order date from the last order date (to yield the elapsed time in days) and then divide the result by 365, as follows:

```
(LASTORDER - FIRSTORDER) / 365
```

If you omitted the parentheses in this expression, dBASE IV would attempt to carry out the division before the subtraction, and would display the "Data type mismatch" error message, because dividing a date by a number is not permitted.

Equally important is the fact that dBASE IV does not evaluate the logical operators .AND., .OR., and .NOT. from left to right. Consider a condition that you might use to select all customers whose invoices total more than $500 and who own either IBM or Compaq equipment:

```
("IBM" $ UPPER(EQUIPMENT) .OR. "COMPAQ" $ UPPER(EQUIPMENT))
   .AND. TOTORDERS > 500
```

If you omitted the parentheses from this expression, the precedence of .AND. over .OR. would cause dBASE IV to group the conditions "COMPAQ" $ UPPER(EQUIPMENT) and TOTORDERS > 500 together and link the result to the condition "IBM" $ UPPER(EQUIPMENT). Thus, the condition would select all customers who own IBM equipment, regardless of their total orders, together with those who own Compaq equipment and have more than $500 in invoices.

In Query-by-Example, you can often avoid these complexities by entering conditions in multiple rows and columns of the file skeletons rather than typing them explicitly in the condition box. When you use the condition box or work at the dot prompt, understanding precedence is crucial to obtaining accurate results. Errors caused by misunderstanding the rules of precedence are often difficult to detect, because the conditions you write may be syntactically correct and may select approximately the number of records you anticipated—but they may not be the right records. As you use more complex expressions to specify selection criteria, it becomes increasingly important to check the displays or lists produced by a query or LIST command to ensure that you have obtained the results you expected.

COMPILING STATISTICS

dBASE IV offers several methods for compiling statistics based on all or selected records in a data base. Using Query-by-Example, you can compute sums and averages, find the maximum and minimum values, and count records. If the query includes record selection criteria, entered either in the file skeleton or in the condition box, these statistics are based on the records that satisfy the selection criteria. You can also group records based on one or more fields and calculate statistics for each group. From the dot prompt, you can calculate the same statistics, as well as the standard deviation and variance, for all the records in a data base or for a subset of the records—those that meet the record selection criteria specified by any combination of a filter, scope, FOR clause, and WHILE clause.

From the Menus

Using Query-by-Example, you can define a view query that calculates statistics based on all or selected records in a data base. For example, National Widgets might want to compute the average year-to-date and total orders placed by its customers in San Francisco. You identify the type of computation and the field or expression that will supply the data by placing one of five *summary* or *aggregate* operators in the appropriate columns of the file skeleton or calculated field skeleton. The summary operators and the types of data on which they operate are listed in Table 10-2. These operators are not included in the pick list of fields, operators, and functions invoked by pressing SHIFT-F1 (Pick); you must type them explicitly in the file skeleton.

Figure 10-4 illustrates a query created to calculate the average year-to-date and total orders for customers in San Francisco. The CITY column contains the condition ="San Francisco", and the averages on the YTDORDERS and TOTORDERS fields are requested by entering AVG in the respective columns

Operator	Data Types	Meaning
Sum	N, F	Sum (Total)
Avg or **Average**	N, F	Average
Cnt or **Count**	All	Count
Min	C, N, F, D	Minimum
Max	C, N, F, D	Maximum

Table 10-2.

The Query-by-Example Summary Operators

in the Customer File skeleton (in Figure 10-4, most of the columns were narrowed drastically so that the CITY, YTDORDERS, and TOTORDERS fields are all visible at the same time). These summary fields make up the view skeleton. The data calculated by this query is shown in Figure 10-5 as it appears on the Edit screen. When you use the **Count** summary operator, you can place the operator in any column of the file skeleton, because dBASE IV always counts whole records, not single fields. When you compute averages or counts, you may want to include a condition that excludes zero values, in this case <> 0 in the TOTORDERS field column. Note that this condition also applies to each record as a whole. You cannot specify different selection criteria for different fields in the view skeleton; if you do, dBASE IV uses the condition entered for the first summary field and does not warn you that the other conditions have no effect on the output of the query.

There is a fundamental difference between queries that include summary operators and the queries described in Chapters 6 and 7, although this may not be evident on the Edit or Browse screen, since the output can be displayed in the same format. The view queries described earlier may not display all the records in a data base and they may not include all the fields in each record that they do display, but each row in the Browse display represents a separate

```
Layout  Fields  Condition  Update  Exit                                  9:48:28 am

Nwcust.dbf | CITY              | ST | ZI | TE | CO | EQ | FI | LA | CR |↓YTDORD |↓TOTORDER
           |="San Francisco"   |    |    |    |    |    |    |    |    |AVG     |>= 0, AVG

View
NWAVGORD   | Nwcust->   | Nwcust->
           | YTDORDERS  | TOTORDERS

Query  |C:\dbase4\NWAVGORD   |Field 4/15  |  |  Ins
 Prev/Next field:Shift-Tab/Tab  Data:F2  Size:Shift-F7  Prev/Next skel:F3/F4
```

Figure 10-4.

Using aggregate operators in Query-by-Example

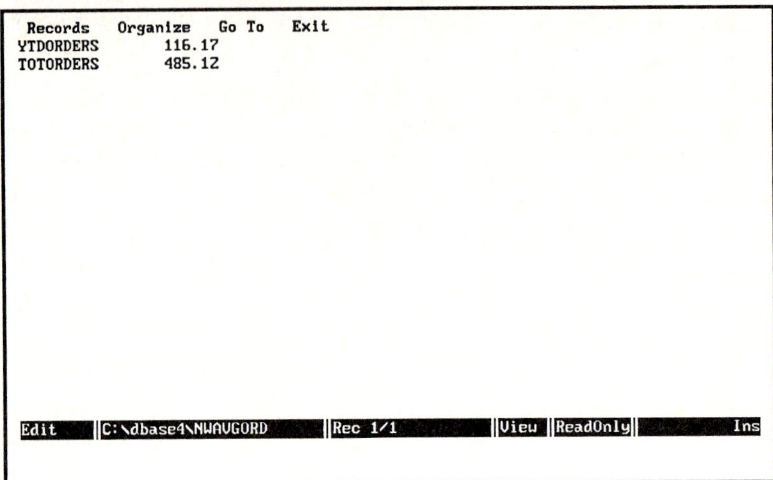

Figure 10-5.

Displaying data calculated using summary operators

record in the underlying data base. When you compute summary statistics, each row on the Browse screen represents statistics derived from many records in the original data base.

Because each row may draw data from more than one record, it makes little sense to edit the data displayed by a query that computes summary statistics. As you can see in Figure 10-5, dBASE IV displays the "ReadOnly" indicator in the status bar when you work with such a view. For the same reason, you would not normally include in the view skeleton fields that could vary within the group of selected records, such as the ACCOUNT or COMPANY field. If you do include such fields in the view skeleton, they appear blank in the resulting view.

At times you will need to calculate statistics, not just for one value of a field, but for all the different values that occur in the file. For example, you might want to see the order sums for not only San Francisco but each city in which National Widgets has customers. To do this, you enter the **Group By** operator in the file skeleton under the name of the field that determines the record groupings, in this case CITY. Like the summary operators, **Group By** does not appear in the pick list invoked by pressing SHIFT-F1 (Pick); you must type it in the file skeleton.

Figure 10-6 illustrates the result of executing the query described in the previous example and displaying the data in the view on the Browse screen. This view includes one row for each unique value of the CITY field in the Customer File, and the statistics in the computed columns are drawn from the records that make up each city grouping. A view that summarizes data from one group of records should include only the fields on which the statistics are based—the record selection criteria specified in the query tell you what the records in the group have in common. When you use the **Group By** operator, you must identify the groups by including in the view the field used as the basis for grouping records. Thus, the CITY field is included in the query illustrated in Figure 10-6.

It might also make sense to include other fields that you know do not vary within the group, such as the STATE field shown in Figure 10-6. However, because dBASE IV cannot determine that the values of these fields are constant in each group, it leaves them blank in the view. Similarly, when you combine the **Group By** operator with **Max** or **Min** to find the maximum or minimum value in a field, the query will select only one record in each group, and you might want to see other fields from this record—the one that contains the

---

Records Fields Go To Exit 1:34:32 pm

CITY	STATE	YTDORDERS	TOTORDERS
Bellevue		0.00	1502.16
Benicia		0.00	1232.50
Berkeley		1344.56	7653.78
Emeryville		108.59	1213.42
Eugene		0.00	249.59
Fremont		201.87	1584.45
Oakland		366.81	3482.48
Portland		0.00	1238.07
Pullman		188.15	1235.87
Richmond		435.42	867.38
San Francisco		348.52	1455.37
San Jose		157.38	608.42
San Leandro		87.35	87.35

Browse C:\dbase4\NWCCITY Rec 1/13 View ReadOnly Caps

View and edit fields

Figure 10-6.

Displaying data calculated using the Group By operator

maximum or minimum values. However, as you can see from Figure 10-7, which illustrates the output of a view query that groups records by CITY and requests the maximum value in the TOTORDERS field, dBASE IV displays only the field that defines the groups (CITY) and the field that supplies the statistics (TOTORDERS).

To compute summary statistics, all the records that contribute data to each group must be processed together. If an index tag based on the field used to define the groups already exists, dBASE IV uses it; if not, dBASE IV either builds an index or sorts the file. If you prefer to display the output of the view in a different order, you can add a sorting operator to the appropriate column in the file skeleton on the query design screen. After computing the statistics (in most cases, using an index to determine the record processing sequence) dBASE IV sorts the "records" in the view into the order specified by your sorting operator.

There are some important limitations to the way that you can combine summary operators in dBASE IV queries. dBASE IV does not allow you to compute statistics based on calculated fields, and you cannot calculate more than one statistic—for example, the sum and the average—of a single field by entering both summary operators in the same column of the file skeleton (you must place two skeletons for the file on the work surface, as described in Chapter 17).

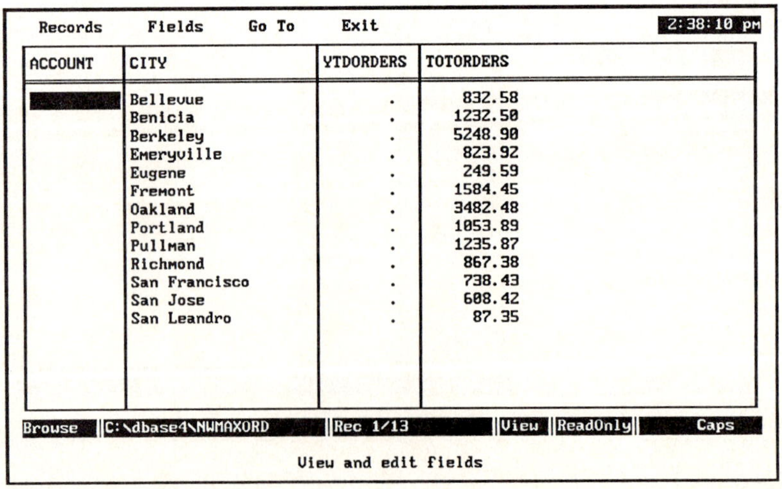

```
Records     Fields     Go To     Exit                                2:38:10 pm

ACCOUNT   CITY                 YTDORDERS  TOTORDERS

          Bellevue                 .          832.58
          Benicia                  .         1232.50
          Berkeley                 .         5248.90
          Emeryville               .          823.92
          Eugene                   .          249.59
          Fremont                  .         1584.45
          Oakland                  .         3482.48
          Portland                 .         1053.89
          Pullman                  .         1235.87
          Richmond                 .          867.38
          San Francisco            .          738.43
          San Jose                 .          608.42
          San Leandro              .           87.35

Browse  C:\dbase4\NWMAXORD     Rec 1/13     View  ReadOnly      Caps
                         View and edit fields
```

Figure 10-7.

Finding the maximum value of a field in each group

D From the Dot Prompt

At the dot prompt, you can use the SUM, AVERAGE, COUNT, and CALCULATE commands to compile statistics similar to those computed by using summary operators in Query-by-Example for the range of records selected by a filter, scope, FOR clause, and WHILE clause. These commands are more flexible than their menu-driven equivalents, however—they can operate on the results of evaluating expressions (analogous to calculated fields in Query-by-Example). SUM and AVERAGE operate on numeric fields or expressions, and you can count records with the COUNT command. You can accumulate the same statistics—as well as minimum, maximum, standard deviation, variance, and net present value—by using the more versatile CALCULATE command.

SUM, AVERAGE, and COUNT are convenient when you need to perform only one type of calculation, especially if you need to carry out the same calculation on many fields. For example, you could compute the sum of all the numeric fields in the National Widgets Customer File for customers in San Francisco with

```
SUM FOR CITY = "San Francisco"
```

To summarize only certain fields, or to compute statistics based on the result of evaluating expressions, you can add an expression list to a SUM or AVERAGE command. SUM and AVERAGE can operate on any expression that evaluates to a number. Thus, although you cannot calculate an "average date," you can determine the average elapsed time between two dates, which is a true numeric value (a number of days). For example, National Widgets could calculate the average length of time it has done business with its San Francisco customers, together with the average year-to-date and total orders, with the following:

```
AVERAGE YTDORDERS, TOTORDERS, DATE() - FIRSTORDER FOR CITY = "San Francisco"
```

The output produced by this command is illustrated in Figure 10-8.

Because the scope, FOR, and WHILE clauses always determine which records a command acts on, you cannot apply different selection criteria to separate calculations executed with a single SUM or AVERAGE command.

The COUNT command returns the number of records that satisfy the record selection criteria specified in the command. For example, you could determine how many customers in San Francisco have placed an order during the current year with the following:

```
COUNT FOR CITY = "San Francisco" .AND. YTDORDERS > 0
```

Remember that when dBASE IV executes any command that can process an entire data base, it reads all the records defined by the scope and WHILE clauses, even if a filter or FOR clause narrows the range of records that are actually affected by the command. Thus, counting how many records contributed to the averages computed by the previous example would require two passes through the data base (once for the AVERAGE command and once for the COUNT command), which in a large file could be very time-consuming. If you need to accumulate more than one type of statistic for the same set of records, you can use the CALCULATE command.

CALCULATE can compute eight types of statistics, identified by the eight functions listed in Table 10-3, for a group of records defined by any combination of a filter, scope, FOR clause, and WHILE clause. The SUM, AVG, STD, and VAR functions take a single input, which must be a numeric expression. When applied to dates, MIN and MAX yield the oldest and most recent dates, respectively; with character fields, they find the first and last in alphabetical order. These rules are consistent with the way date and character fields are treated in conditions containing the < and > comparison operators, and with

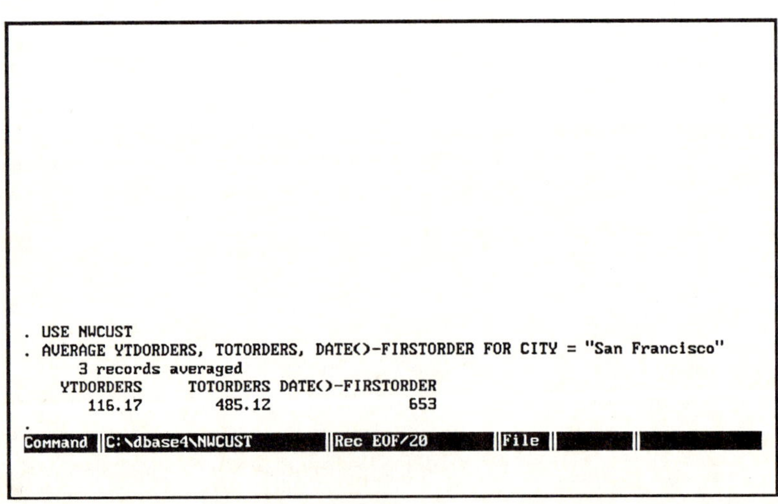

Figure 10-8.

Using the AVERAGE command at the dot prompt

the way these fields are sorted and indexed. The CNT function does not require any input, because you cannot count fields or expressions separately—CNT always counts the number of records processed by a CALCULATE command. The NPV (net present value) function requires three numeric expressions as input, representing the discount rate, cash flows, and initial investment.

You can combine these functions to calculate all the statistics produced by the previous three SUM, AVERAGE, and COUNT examples for National Widgets' San Francisco customers, together with the maximum and minimum year-to-date order total, with the following:

```
CALCULATE CNT(), SUM(YTDORDERS), SUM(TOTORDERS), AVG(YTDORDERS),
   AVG(TOTORDERS), AVG(DATE() - FIRSTORDER), MAX(YTDORDERS), MIN(YTDORDERS)
   FOR CITY = "San Francisco"
```

The appearance of the screen after executing this CALCULATE command is illustrated in Figure 10-9. The COUNT, SUM, AVERAGE, and CALCULATE commands read through the selected records, compile the specified statistics, and display the results without storing them in any form. Although the calculated quantities are identified by the usual "headings," the display is difficult to read because the data wraps onto two lines. Also, you may want to take another look at the computed values later on, after they have scrolled off the top of the screen or in a later work session.

Function	Data Types	Meaning
CNT		Counts records
SUM	N, F	Sum
AVG	N, F	Average
MAX	C, N, F, D	Maximum
MIN	C, N, F, D	Minimum
STD	N, F	Standard deviation
VAR	N, F	Variance
NPV	N, F	Net present value

Table 10-3.

The CALCULATE Functions

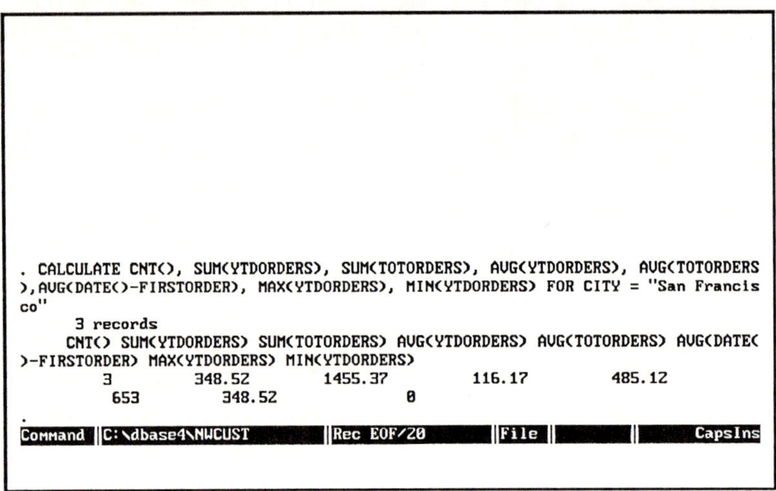

Figure 10-9.

Using the CALCULATE command to compute statistics

You can solve these problems and also make the statistics available for use in further calculations by saving them in memory variables. To do this, you include a list of memory variable names in the SUM, AVERAGE, COUNT, or CALCULATE command, as in the following two examples:

```
COUNT TO MSF FOR CITY = "San Francisco" .AND. YTDORDERS > 0

CALCULATE CNT(), SUM(YTDORDERS), SUM(TOTORDERS), AVG(YTDORDERS),
   AVG(TOTORDERS), AVG(DATE() - FIRSTORDER), MAX(YTDORDERS),
   MIN(YTDORDERS) TO MCOUNTSF, MYTDSUMSF, MTOTSUMSF, MYTDAVGSF,
   MTOTAVGSF, MAVGTIMESF, MYTDMAXSF, MYTDMINSF FOR CITY = "San Francisco"
```

Be sure to supply a memory variable name for each value computed by the CALCULATE command; if there are too many or too few variable names, dBASE IV displays the "Syntax error" message. To view the calculated results later in the work session, you could type DISPLAY MEMORY or LIST MEMORY (and optionally add the phrase TO PRINT to get a hard copy). If you need to retain the statistics for use in a subsequent work session, you can store them on disk in a memory variable file by using the SAVE command described earlier in this chapter.

The CALCULATE command is limited to compiling statistics based on a single group of records. From the dot prompt, you cannot group records based on the contents of a field and compute statistics for each group of records in a single pass through a data base, as you can by using the **Group By** operator in Query-by-Example. As you will see in Chapter 12, you can define a report that performs these calculations, but you might prefer to use Query-by-Example to summarize data in ways that are impossible from the dot prompt.

CHANGING THE CONTENTS OF DATA BASE FIELDS

The commands and techniques explained so far in this chapter perform calculations, display the results, and in some cases store the computed results in memory variables, all without making any changes in the file that provides the data. You also know how to change, delete, and recall records in a data base individually by using the full-screen editors or at the dot prompt, but often you will want to update so many records that typing in the new data one field at a time is out of the question.

For example, at the end of each year, National Widgets must zero out the YTDORDERS field in the Customer File to prepare to accumulate the year-to-date total for the new year. Periodically, you might delete all customers who have not placed an order since an arbitrary cutoff date or recall records erroneously marked for deletion. There is also little point to entering data that dBASE IV could calculate, either unconditionally—such as the SUBTOTAL and INVAMOUNT fields in the Order File—or for records that satisfy specific selection criteria—like the DISCOUNT.

Working in the menu system, you can add new records, mark records for deletion or remove the deletion marker, or change the values of selected fields by defining update queries. At the dot prompt, you can carry out the same operations with the APPEND, DELETE, RECALL, and REPLACE commands. This section discusses techniques for changing data in one or more records in a data base. Adding, deleting, and recalling records is covered in Chapter 16.

From the Menus

You can change the contents of fields in a single data base file by defining an update query. You can create and edit update queries with the same familiar query design screen that you have been using to create view queries, but while view queries display data without changing it, update queries change data without displaying the records. What they have in common is the techniques used to identify the fields and records affected by the query and, as you will see in Chapter 17, the methods used to link multiple files.

Although an update query can draw on data from more than one data base, only one, the *target file,* can be changed in the process. You identify the target file and the type of update to perform by entering an update operator in the first column of the appropriate file skeleton under the file name. You can either type the operator directly or select the **Specify update operation** from the **Update** menu with the highlight in any column of the file skeleton, and choose an operator from a list such as the one illustrated in Figure 10-10. Note that the name of the target file is included in the menu selections to remind you that only one data base can be affected by an update query. After you specify the update operator, "Target" appears above the file name in the first column of the file skeleton to clearly identify which file will be updated. There are four update operators, which have the following meanings:

Replace	Replace fields with new values
Append	Add new records from another data base
Mark	Mark records for deletion
Unmark	Remove the deletion marker

Because an update query does not display data, the view skeleton is irrelevant; if a view skeleton is present on the query design screen when you select an update operator, dBASE IV pops up a dialog box to warn you, "Changing this view query to an update query will delete the View skeleton," and offers two options, **Cancel** and **Proceed**. The view skeleton might be present because you inadvertently invoked Query-by-Example with a data base already open, but at times you might intentionally change a view query into an update query. One way to predict the effects of a potentially destructive update query is to create a view query that displays the fields and records that would be affected by the update. For example, if you wanted to delete all customers who had not placed an order in two years, you could create a view query that selects these customers, spot-check the list to be sure the right records were selected, and then convert the view query to an update query while preserving the same record selection criteria.

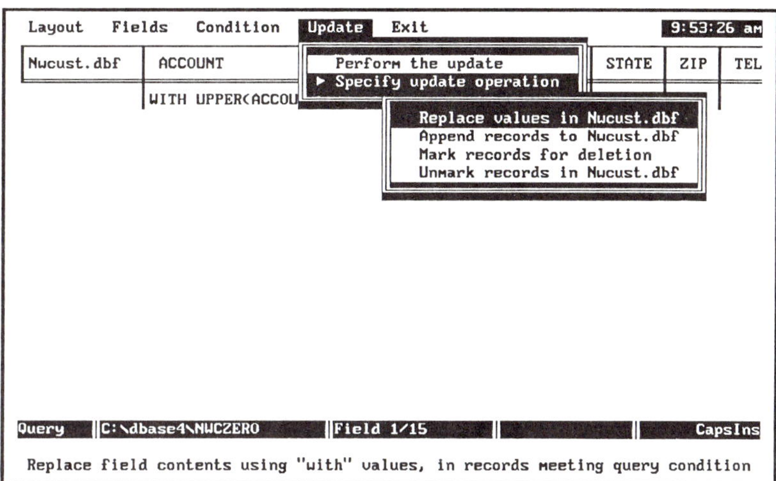

Figure 10-10.

Choosing an update operator in Query-by-Example

An update query that changes data may replace the values of one or more fields with the results of evaluating any legitimate dBASE IV expressions of the same data types. Each expression is entered, introduced by the **With** operator, under the appropriate field name in the file skeleton. For example, in the National Widgets Customer File, you could create an update query to zero out the YTDORDERS field at the end of each year by entering WITH 0 in the YTDORDERS column.

You specify record selection criteria in exactly the same way as you do in a view query, by entering conditions in either the file skeleton or the condition box. For example, to zero out the year-to-date orders field for customers in California, you could enter = "CA" in the STATE column and WITH 0 in the YTDORDERS column. If you want to select records based on the original contents of the field you are updating, enter both the selection condition and the expression that specifies the new value for the field, separated by commas, or place the condition and the expression on separate rows in the file skeleton. For example, to fill in the current date as the first order date for all "new" customer records—those with blank first order dates—you would enter the following in the FIRSTORDER column:

```
= { }, WITH DATE()
```

The first expression, = { }, selects records in which the first order date is blank, and the second, WITH DATE( ), specifies a replacement value for the FIRST-ORDER field in the selected records.

You save an update query in exactly the same way that you save a view query. You can save the query and continue working on the query design screen by selecting the **Save this query** option from the **Layout** menu, or you can choose **Save changes and exit** from the **Exit** menu. dBASE IV assigns the extension UPD rather than QBE. It is always a good idea to save a query on disk before you exit Query-by-Example or execute the update.

You can execute an update query from the query design screen by selecting **Perform the update** from the **Update** menu. In the Control Center **Queries** panel, an asterisk precedes the names of update queries to distinguish them from view queries. To execute an update query from the Control Center, you highlight the name of the query, press ENTER, and select **Run update** from the pop-up dialog box. Because update queries can cause irreversible and potentially destructive changes, dBASE IV prompts you to confirm your intentions with the warning "Do you REALLY want to run this update query?" You can select **No** to cancel the command or **Yes** to proceed with the update. In a large data base, an update can take some time, so dBASE IV displays a pop-up box that monitors the progress of the operation by counting records as they are processed. When the update is complete, dBASE IV pops up another dialog box to remind you that you can press F2 (Data) to view the new data.

Update queries provide the means for quickly and easily making large-scale changes in the contents of selected fields in selected records in a data base, but they also have the potential to do a great deal of damage. Once dBASE IV has performed an update, you cannot recover the original field contents, which are physically overwritten on disk by the new values. Until you are confident about your ability to specify the record selection criteria correctly as well as the expressions that define the calculations, make a backup copy of a data base before carrying out an update query.

From the Dot Prompt

From the dot prompt, you can change data in more than one record at a time, without viewing the affected records, with the REPLACE command. The basic form of this command is

REPLACE *field* WITH *expression*

You can use any combination of scope, FOR, and WHILE clauses to specify the range of records to be processed. The expression may be any legitimate dBASE IV expression of the same data type as the field. For example, in the National Widgets Customer File, you could zero out the YTDORDERS field at the end of each year to prepare to accumulate the new year-to-date total with the following:

```
REPLACE ALL YTDORDERS WITH 0
```

If you had any doubt about whether the state abbreviations had all been entered consistently in uppercase letters, you could convert them to uppercase with:

```
REPLACE ALL STATE WITH UPPER(STATE)
```

Notice that in this command the expression that specifies the new value for the STATE field includes a reference to the field itself. If this seems "circular" to you, consider the way that dBASE IV executes the command: first it evaluates the expression following the keyword WITH (which can be any legitimate dBASE IV expression), and then it enters the result into the named field and overwrites the previous value.

If you need to change more than one field, you can speed the process by replacing more than one field on each pass through the data base. The only restriction is the limit on the length of any dBASE IV command—1024 characters. The fields you replace need not be of the same data type, and the new values can be the same or different, but you must name each field and type its replacement value explicitly, even if some are the same, and you cannot apply different selection criteria to separate fields in the REPLACE command. For example, you could zero the year-to-date and total orders fields and convert the ACCOUNT and STATE fields to uppercase letters for all customers in California with the following:

```
REPLACE YTDORDERS WITH 0, TOTORDERS WITH 0, ACCOUNT WITH UPPER(ACCOUNT),
   STATE WITH UPPER(STATE) FOR STATE = "CA"
```

You can sometimes speed the operation of the REPLACE command with a strategic use of indexes. As mentioned in Chapter 9, the most efficient way to limit processing to a set of records grouped in indexed order is to use a SEEK command to position the record pointer on the first record in the group and then use a WHILE clause to express the selection criteria so that dBASE IV stops reading records as soon as the pointer advances beyond the last record in the group. For example, using an index based on state, city, and account code, you could zero out the year-to-date orders for California customers with the following:

```
SEEK "CA"
REPLACE YTDORDERS WITH 0 WHILE STATE = "CA"
```

If your selection criteria *do not* depend on an index key and the scope of a command is ALL, processing is faster with no index active. When dBASE IV reads through a file in indexed order, it must alternately read data from two files: the data base and the index. Because consecutive index entries may refer to records that are widely separated on the disk, finding the "next" record can involve moving the disk drive head much farther than the physical distance between the two records. You can deactivate the master index and return to viewing records in the order of entry by typing

```
SET ORDER TO
```

You can also gain speed by processing a file in natural (sequential) order when the selection criteria are based on the position of the records in the data base. For example, the fastest way to replace the first order date with the current date in "new" customer records is to position the record pointer on the first new record and include the REST scope in the REPLACE command:

```
REPLACE REST FIRSTORDER WITH DATE()
```

This command works correctly only if all new entries are grouped at the end of the file. If you are not sure where the new records begin, you can position the record pointer anywhere prior to the first new entry and combine the REST scope with a FOR clause that selects the desired records. In this example, you would test for a blank first order date, as follows:

```
REPLACE REST FIRSTORDER WITH DATE() FOR FIRSTORDER = { }
```

There is one potential problem with this strategy: if some longstanding customers had first order dates that were never recorded, the FOR clause would select too many records. This detailed example illustrates an important point about working with potentially destructive commands. *Whenever possible, verify that your expressions are correct and that your scope, FOR, and WHILE clauses select the right group of records by using LIST commands before you carry out a more dangerous REPLACE or DELETE that affects many records.* For example, you could use the following command to display the present values of the fields that would be affected by the REPLACE command in the previous example:

```
LIST REST ACCOUNT, COMPANY, FIRSTORDER, LASTORDER FOR FIRSTORDER = { }
```

From the resulting list, you might see that some of the records with a blank FIRSTORDER field have very low record numbers (indicating that they were not entered recently) or have a later date in the LASTORDER field. You might then enter a very early date into the FIRSTORDER field—a date that you can easily distinguish from the real first order dates in the other customer records but that prevents these records from passing the test for a blank FIRSTORDER field.

In the examples presented thus far in this section, you pay a penalty in performance if you process records in indexed order, but the commands will execute correctly. You *must* process a file in sequential order if a REPLACE command operates on an index key field. Suppose, for example, that you wanted to change all state abbreviations for California customers to uppercase letters. You could do this with the following commands:

```
SEEK "CA"
REPLACE STATE WITH "CA" WHILE STATE = "Ca"
```

If dBASE IV processed the data base in indexed order, the command would fail, because whenever you change an index key field (by REPLACE, EDIT, or any other command), the entry for that record moves immediately to its new position in the index. With an index open, dBASE IV interprets the "next" record as the one corresponding to the next index entry. When the STATE field is changed from "Ca" to "CA", the index entry moves to join the other "CA" records, and the "next" record does not have "Ca" in the STATE field. Thus, processing would stop after dBASE IV had replaced only one record. To avoid this potentially serious problem, dBASE IV temporarily disables the index update process when you issue a REPLACE command that changes the contents of the master index key field in multiple records. Afterwards, it rebuilds the index tag from scratch and leaves the tag active. If you prefer, you can process the file in natural order and rebuild the tag explicitly, as in the following example:

```
USE NWCUST
REPLACE STATE WITH "CA" FOR STATE = "Ca"
INDEX ON STATE + CITY + ACCOUNT TAG STATECITY
```

SUMMARY

The commands in this chapter illustrate one of the strong points of dBASE IV: the power and flexibility it offers for carrying out ad hoc queries, using Query-by-Example, commands typed at the dot prompt, or a combination. The query process is fast and immediate because it requires minimal preparation, especially at the dot prompt. Query files are convenient for repeated inquiries, because they enable you to store specifications for a view or update so you can repeat the process without retyping all the component commands and conditions.

By now you have seen all the elements of dBASE IV syntax— including the major command keywords and clauses, various types of operators and functions, memory variables, and constants—and you understand the rules by which these elements can be combined into commands, complex expressions, and conditions. Although some useful and general applications of these concepts are illustrated in the examples, the commands presented here barely scratch the surface. As you work with dBASE IV, try to review these command components periodically, particularly the list of available functions in Appendix E, to make sure that you do not overlook useful features.

CHAPTER ELEVEN

Defining and Printing Labels

You have already seen several methods for producing printed listings of the data stored in a dBASE IV data base. From the dot prompt, you can print the output of a LIST or DISPLAY command by including the phrase TO PRINT in the command. From several points in the menu system, you can press SHIFT-F9 (Quick Report) to produce a simple columnar report with page numbers and column headings. These commands give you a fast way to produce a clear, readable printout of the contents of selected fields from selected records in a data base. Because they require little or no preparation and yield output immediately, these commands are appropriate for constantly changing ad hoc inquiries and calculations in which the contents of the display are more important than its appearance.

dBASE IV also provides specialized layout editors for designing and printing mailing labels, columnar reports, full-page forms such as insurance forms, and "mailmerge" forms such as personalized letters. The report specifications, including the content (text, data base fields, and calculated fields), page dimensions and layout, print enhancements, and printer control commands are stored on disk in a label or report form file so you can reprint the labels or report for the same or different data without having to repeat the definition steps.

You can use the same form to print data from different data bases that have similar structures or for different sets of records drawn from the same data base. Just as when you view data on screen, you can specify the selection criteria by a view query or, from the dot prompt, any combination of a filter, scope, FOR clause, and WHILE clause. By sorting or indexing the data base, you can print records in different orders and define additional selection criteria based on WHILE clauses. Report and label forms are useful for producing attractively formatted printouts in standard layouts that are easily interpreted by people who are unfamiliar with dBASE IV or even unfamiliar with computers.

This chapter describes how to use the label design screen to define label forms and print labels. Chapters 12 and 14 cover reports, and Chapter 13 covers the print formatting and printing commands that are common to reports and labels. Even if you do not have an immediate need for mailing labels in your application, you should at least skim this chapter. The layout editors used to create report forms and data entry forms have similar menus and use virtually identical cursor movement, editing, and command keys to navigate around the work surface, position text and fields, customize data display formats, and copy and move items.

Despite the use of the term "label" to describe the specialized forms covered in this chapter, the label design screen can be used to produce many types of printouts besides name and address labels. You can design label forms to print inventory labels, file folder labels, name tags, prescription labels, and name and address lists in many other formats not generally viewed as "labels" at all, including envelopes, Rolodex cards, and one-, two-, or three-column reference lists on plain paper.

CREATING AND EDITING LABEL FORMS

To define a label format, you use a specialized layout editor that allows you to build the form by typing text and placing fields, including calculated fields, directly on the screen work surface. Because labels usually include data base fields, you must open a data base or view before you invoke the label form editor to create a new form. If you access the label layout editor from the Control Center, dBASE IV records the name of the data base or view in the catalog entry for the label form (Chapter 19 covers the dBASE IV file catalog). When you modify the form or use it to display or print labels, dBASE IV assumes that you want to open the same data base or view, but you can override the default and use the same label format with different data bases, or with other views based on the same data base, provided that the field names match those specified in the label form. If you want to print labels from the Control Center using a label form that was created at the dot prompt, you must first open any compatible data base or view.

From the Menus

You display and access label formats through the **Labels** panel in the Control Center. To edit an existing label format, you highlight its name, press ENTER, and select **Modify layout** from the pop-up dialog box. To create a new label form, you select the **<create>** option. You can also use the standard function key shortcut in all the Control Center panels to open a file—in this case a label form file—and move directly to the appropriate design work surface: highlight the label form name or **<create>** and press SHIFT-F2 (Design).

If you attempt to invoke the label design screen without first opening a data base, dBASE IV pops up a message box to remind you, "Please put a database file or view into use first." When you create a new label form, you need not supply a name until you save the file.

D From the Dot Prompt

From the dot prompt, you invoke the label editor by typing

CREATE LABEL *label form name*

or

MODIFY LABEL *label form name*

You can use the CREATE and MODIFY variations interchangeably, regardless of whether you are defining a new format or editing an existing one. Of course, if you want to edit an existing format, you must identify it by name. From the dot prompt, you must also name a new file before you enter the layout editor to create it, and if you do not include a label form name in the CREATE LABEL or MODIFY LABEL command, dBASE IV prompts you to enter it. If a data base is not currently open, dBASE IV pops up a dialog box to remind you that you must open one and asks for the file name: "No database in use. Enter filename:." If you cannot remember the name of the data base or view you want to use, you can press SHIFT-F1 (Pick) to display a pick list of available files.

USING THE LABEL DESIGN WORK SURFACE

All your work on the label design work surface is done within a shaded, bordered area that is the same width and height as one label. In most cases, this region is smaller than the screen, but you can define a label up to 255 characters wide and 255 lines high; when you move the cursor "off the edge" of the screen in any direction, dBASE IV scrolls the display to give you access to more of the work surface. Above the upper boundary of the box that encloses the label is a ruler line that indicates the current margins and tab stops. Figure 11-1 illustrates the work surface with a typical mailing label form displayed.

dBASE IV measures the size of a mailing label in characters (horizontally) and lines (vertically). Both lines and columns are numbered starting with 0, not 1, and when you enter the label layout editor, the cursor is in the upper left corner of the label at line 0, column 0. The status bar displays the current command (Label); the name of the label form, or <NEW> if you have not yet named the form; the current cursor position on the label; and the name of the active data base or view query.

You define the contents of a label by typing text and placing fields—including data base fields and calculated fields—directly on the work surface. You can place items on the label in any order, and you can edit, move, copy, and format any item using a combination of cursor movement keys, editing and command keys, and menu commands. The label design screen menu bar contains seven options, which are used for the following purposes:

Layout	Select a data base or view, enter a description of the form, and save the label form
Dimensions	Specify the label size, shape, and overall layout

Fields	Add, remove, or modify fields on the work surface
Words	Add print enhancements, select type styles or fonts, position text relative to the margins, add or delete lines, and edit or hide the ruler line
Go To	Move quickly to a specified line by number or search for a line based on its contents
Print	Customize printer options and display or print labels
Exit	Exit to the Control Center or the dot prompt

The structure of the label layout editor menu is diagrammed in Figure 11-2, and the cursor movement and command keys are listed in Table 11-1.

Defining the Label Dimensions

In most cases, the first step in defining a label form is to specify the size, shape, and page layout, although you can later alter this and all other aspects of the design. A label is defined by its width and height, the indentation from the left

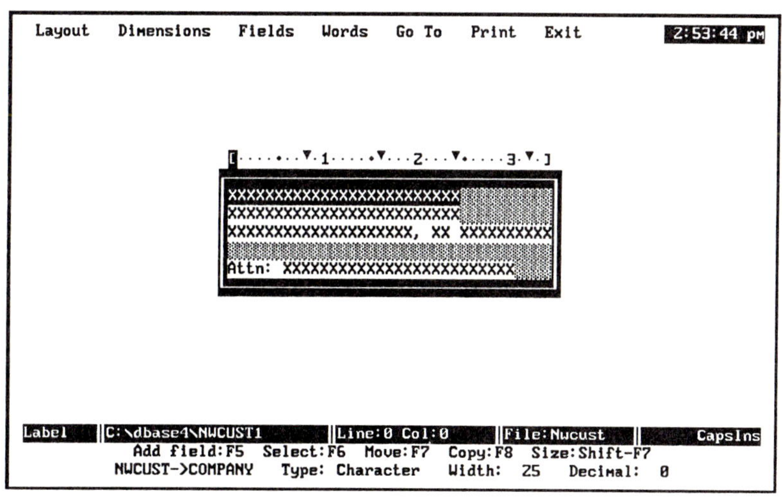

Figure 11-1.

The label design work surface

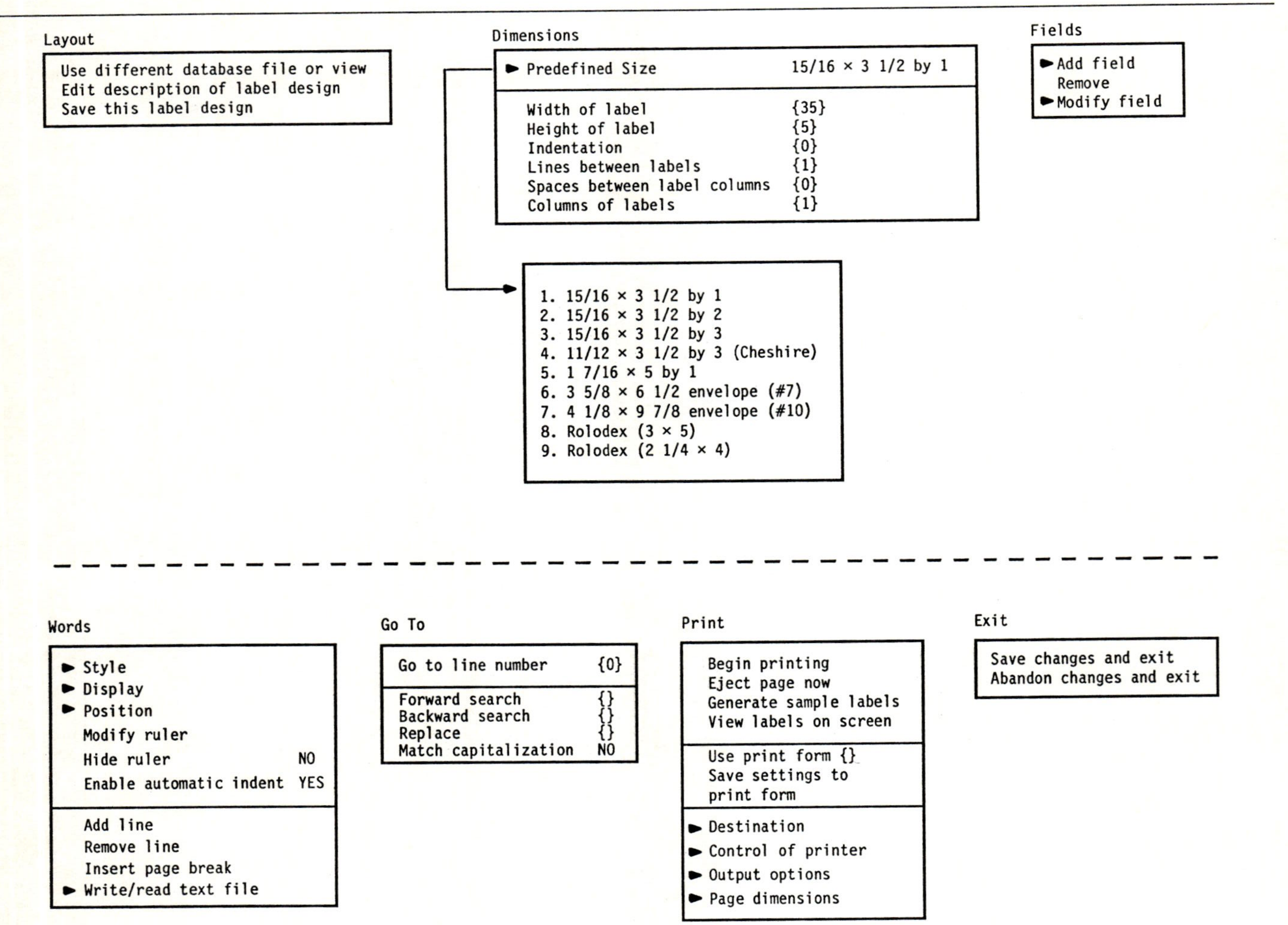

Figure 11-2.

The structure of the label layout editor menus

Control Key	Command Key	Function
	F10 (Menu)	Activate the menu system
	ALT-*letter*	Activate the menu system and pull down the menu whose description begins with *letter*
	letter	Select the option on the active pull-down menu whose description begins with *letter*
	ENTER	Select the highlighted option or item from the active menu, panel, or pick list
CTRL-W	CTRL-END	Save changes and exit
CTRL-Q	ESC	Exit without saving changes
CTRL-E	UP ARROW	Move up one line
CTRL-X	DOWN ARROW or ENTER (Typeover mode)	Move down one line
CTRL-D	RIGHT ARROW	Move right one character
CTRL-S	LEFT ARROW	Move left one character
CTRL-I	TAB	Move to the next tab stop
	SHIFT-TAB	Move to the previous tab stop
CTRL-F	CTRL-RIGHT ARROW or F4 (Next)	Move to the next field
CTRL-A	CTRL-LEFT ARROW or F3 (Previous)	Move to the previous field
CTRL-Z	HOME	Move to the beginning of the line
CTRL-B	END	Move to the end of the line
CTRL-C	PGDN	Display the next group of lines
CTRL-R	PGUP	Display the previous group of lines
	CTRL-PGDN	Move to the last line on the label
	CTRL-PGUP	Move to the first line on the label

Table 11-1.

The Cursor Movement and Editing Keys Used in the Label Layout Editor

Control Key	Command Key	Function
CTRL-G	DEL	Delete the character at the cursor position
	BACKSPACE	Delete the character or field to the left of the cursor
CTRL-T		Delete the characters from the cursor to the end of the expression
CTRL-Y		Delete the line containing the cursor
CTRL-V	INS	Turn Insert mode on (if it is off) or off (if it is on)
CTRL-N	ENTER (Insert mode)	Insert a new line
	CTRL-HOME	Modify the current field
	F9 (Zoom)	Expand the data entry area to an entire line
	F2 (Data)	Switch to Browse or Edit to view data
	F5 (Field)	Add a field or modify the field at the cursor location
	F6 (Select)	Mark one corner of a rectangular region on the work surface (indicate the opposite corner by pressing ENTER)
	F7 (Move)	Move the selected items
	F8 (Copy)	Copy the selected items
	SHIFT-F7 (Size)	Resize the label design work surface

Table 11-1.

The Cursor Movement and Editing Keys Used in the Label Layout Editor (*continued*)

edge of the paper (left margin), the number of lines printed (vertically) between consecutive rows of labels, the number of labels across the page, and the number of spaces printed (horizontally) between adjacent columns of labels (if you print two or more across). Figure 11-3 illustrates the relationship between these parameters and a typical set of printed labels.

dBASE IV offers nine predefined label sizes, each of which is identified by a

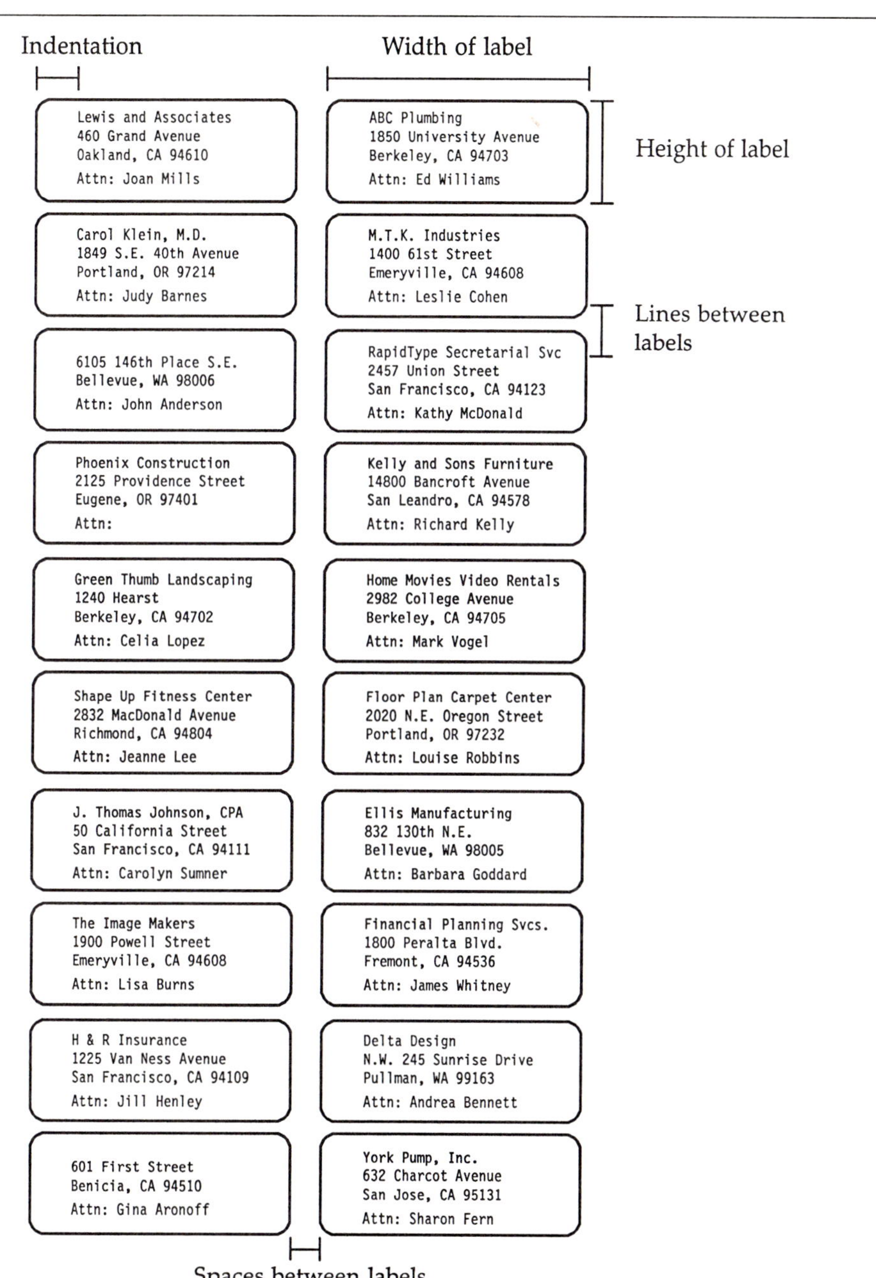

Figure 11-3.

The label page layout parameters

number and is discussed in terms of the width and height of one label, in inches, and the number of labels printed across the page. The predefined sizes and the corresponding label dimensions are listed in Table 11-2 along with the range of permissible values for each setting. If none of the predefined sizes suits your purpose, you can start with the one that comes closest and change any or all of the individual parameters to conform to the spacing of your own labels.

By default, dBASE IV selects the first predefined label size, 15/16 x 3 1/2 by 1, and displays the label design work surface with a bordered region 35 characters wide and 6 lines high in the center. To change the label dimensions, you select the **Predefined Size** option from the **Dimensions** menu and then pick one of the nine choices: either by typing its number or by highlighting it and pressing ENTER. dBASE IV immediately adjusts the label image on the work surface to

	Width	Height	Indent	Lines	Spaces	Across
1. 15/16 x 3 1/2 by 1	35	5	0	1	0	1
2. 15/16 x 3 1/2 by 2	35	5	0	1	2	2
3. 15/16 x 3 1/2 by 3	35	5	0	1	2	3
4. 11/12 x 3 1/2 by 3 (Cheshire)	35	5	0	1	2	3
5. 1 7/16 x 5 by 1	50	8	0	1	0	1
6. 3 5/8 x 6 1/2 envelope (N7)	65	14	0	8	0	1
7. 4 1/8 x 9 7/8 envelope (N10)	78	17	0	8	0	1
8. Rolodex (3 x 5)	50	14	0	4	0	1
9. Rolodex (2 1/4 x 4)	40	10	0	1	0	1
Permissible range	1-255	1-255	0-250	0-16	0-120	*

* Depends on width and spaces between

Table 11-2.

The dBASE IV Predefined Label Sizes

match your selection. If you need to change any page layout parameters, you can pull down the **Dimensions** menu again, highlight the option, press ENTER, and replace the existing value with a new one. You can either type in the new value directly or use the UP ARROW and DOWN ARROW keys to increase or decrease the displayed numeric value one unit at a time.

The most important fact to understand about the label layout parameters is that except in the brief descriptions that identify the predefined formats, *all label dimensions are defined in units of printer movement, not inches.* The horizontal measures—label width, indentation, and number of spaces between labels—are specified in *characters,* and the vertical measures—the number of lines per label and lines between labels—are in *lines.* Dimensions expressed as inches in the predefined size descriptions are converted to characters and lines based on the assumption that you will print labels at 10 characters per inch (cpi) horizontally and 6 lines per inch (lpi) vertically (the default settings on most printers).

It is up to you to match the values you enter for the label size parameters to the character pitch and line spacing you actually use to print the labels. For example, if your labels measure 3 1/2 inches wide and 1 inch deep, the first predefined label size, 35 characters wide and 6 lines high, will work perfectly at 10 cpi and 6 lpi. If you decided to use "compressed" print (say, 16 cpi and 8 lpi) to fit longer addresses onto the same labels, you must reset the label width to 56 (3 1/2 inches at 16 cpi) and the height to 8 (1 inch at 8 lpi). Also note that the height of a label is defined as the number of lines between the top of one label and the top of the next. Because there is always some unusable space between labels, the number of lines on which you can print data is actually one fewer than the nominal height.

Figure 11-4 illustrates a label form that prints a two-column reference list based on the National Widgets Customer File on plain paper at 12 characters per inch. The easiest way to construct this form is to use Predefined Size 8, which is intended to print 3 x 5 Rolodex cards, as a point of departure, and change two of the dimensions: in order to print a two-column list, you must set the **Columns of labels** option to 2 and the **Spaces between label columns** option to 5 (the form is printed at 12 cpi rather than the default 10 cpi). Figure 11-5 illustrates part of the first page of labels produced by this form. Note that when you print labels two or more across, dBASE IV moves from left to right across the page between successive records, *not* down one column of records and then back up to the top of the next.

dBASE IV assumes that labels are fixed in size and continuous (the label stock has no top or bottom margin). When you design label forms such as the one in Figure 11-4 for use on plain paper, you must ensure that the number of

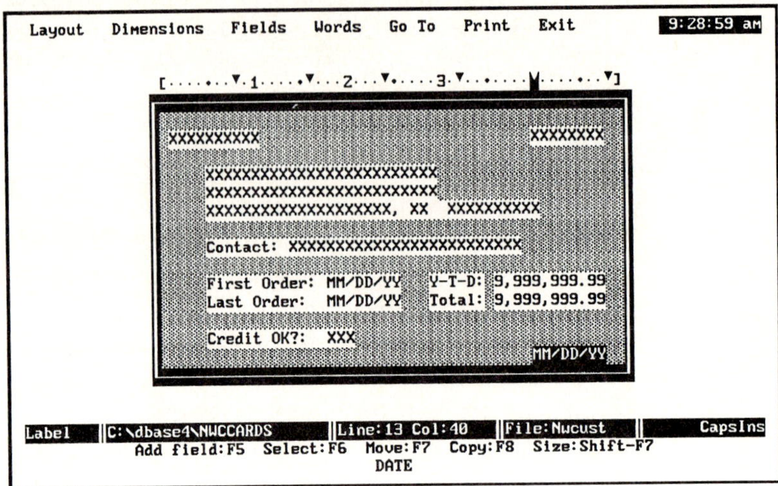

Figure 11-4.

A label form that prints 3 x 5 Rolodex cards

lines available on the physical page is evenly divisible by the number of lines occupied by one "label" (that is, the number of lines between the top of one label and the top of the next—the sum of the **Height of label** and **Lines between labels** settings). With laser printers, which cannot print within 1/4 inch of the top or bottom of the page, there is another potential problem: although you can buy laser label stock on which the unusable areas are blank, you must either choose a printer driver that automatically sets the correct top margin and line spacing, or you must send the equivalent commands to the printer directly. These special considerations are described in more detail in Chapter 13.

Entering Text and Fields on the Label

To enter text onto a label form, move the cursor anywhere within the bounded region on the work surface and begin typing. For example, National Widgets might print the text "Happy Holidays" on the last line of a label form used for its annual Christmas card mailing. You might even define a label that contains

```
LEWIS                      839-5014   ABCPLUMB                   861-4543
 Lewis and Associates                  ABC Plumbing
 460 Grand Avenue                      1850 University Avenue
 Oakland, CA 94610                     Berkeley, CA 94703
 Contact: Joan Mills                   Contact: Ed Williams
 First Order: 10/13/85 Y-T-D:   366.81 First Order: 12/01/87 Y-T-D:   796.41
 Last Order:  01/20/91 Total: 3,482.48 Last Order:  04/30/91 Total: 5,248.90
 Credit OK?:  Yes                      Credit OK?:  Yes
                           05/03/91                              05/03/91

KLEIN                      232-2638   MTK                        655-7200
 Carol Klein, M.D.                     M.T.K. Industries
 1849 S.E. 40th Avenue                 1400 61st Street
 Portland, OR 97214                    Emeryville, CA 94608
 Contact: Judy Barnes                  Contact: Leslie Cohen
 First Order: 10/13/86 Y-T-D:     0.00 First Order: 06/23/87 Y-T-D:   108.59
 Last Order:  12-28-90 Total: 1,053.89 Last Order:  02/03/91 Total:   823.92
 Credit OK?:  Yes                      Credit OK?:  Yes
                           05/03/91                              05/03/91
```

Figure 11-5.

The Customer File Rolodex cards

only text, such as a return address label, although a data base must be open when you define or print the labels.

A label form can also include data base fields, four *predefined items* (described shortly), and calculated fields, which can be defined by any legitimate dBASE IV expression. To place an item on the work surface, you position the cursor surface where you want the item to begin and then either press F5 (Field) or pull down the **Fields** menu and select **Add field**. In response, dBASE IV pops up a pick list similar to the one shown in Figure 11-6, which illustrates the pick list displayed when the National Widgets Customer File is open. The first panel lists the fields in the active data base or view. The second displays the calculated fields, if any, that you have defined for this label form; when you create a new label form, the **Calculated** panel is initially empty. The third panel, **Predefined**, lists four items whose values are always known to dBASE IV and that can be included in any report or label form. These items are as follows:

Date	The current date, derived from the operating system
Time	The current time, derived from the operating system
Recno	The record number of the record being printed
Pageno	The sequential number of the page being printed

You can select any item from the pick list by highlighting it, pressing ENTER, and then filling in the description of the item in a pop-up dialog box such as

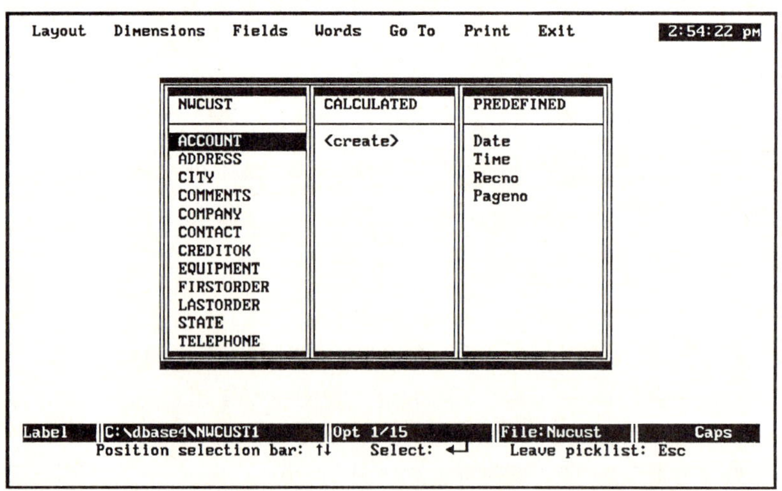

Figure 11-6.

Selecting a label item from a pick list

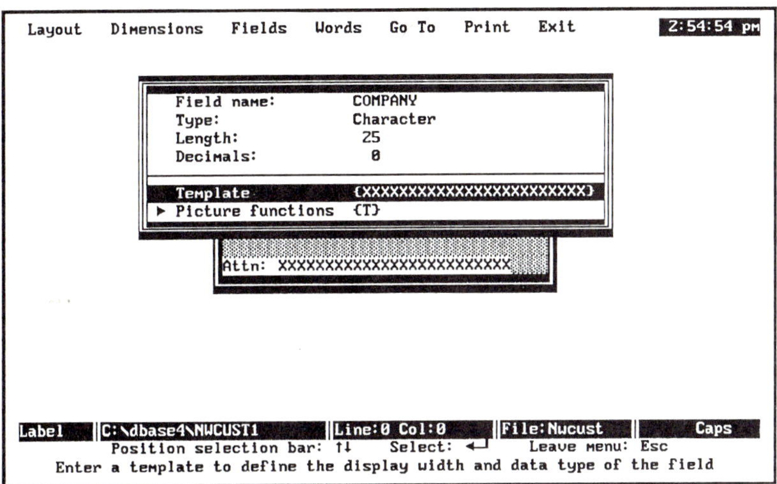

Figure 11-7.

The label item dialog box

the one shown in Figure 11-7. For a data base field, dBASE IV displays the data type, length, and number of decimal places defined in the file structure. When you select a predefined item, the dialog box displays the name. For a calculated field, you must enter the expression that defines the calculation as well as an optional name and a description. The lower half of the dialog box includes options for customizing the display format of a data base field or calculated field with templates and picture functions, which are defined in the next section. For simple label forms, you can usually leave the defaults unchanged and press CTRL-END immediately to confirm your selection and place the item on the work surface at the cursor position.

Text typed on the label design work surface is displayed exactly as you entered it. A data base field, calculated field, or predefined item is represented by a row of symbols that define the width of the item. The symbol itself depends on both the data type and the display format: dBASE IV uses X for character and memo fields, 9 or # for numeric and float fields, L or Y for logical fields, and a symbolic representation of the display format for dates (such as MM/DD/YY for the default month/day/year format).

When you move the cursor into a field, the message line at the bottom of the screen displays the name (including a reference to the data base to help you identify the source of the field if the label form draws data from more than one file), data type, width, and number of decimal places. In Figure 11-1, you can see the description of the COMPANY field on the message line. For calculated fields, dBASE IV displays the name and the expression that defines the calculation; for the predefined items, dBASE IV displays only the name.

When you print labels, dBASE IV automatically suppresses blank lines that would result from empty fields (or expressions that evaluate to strings of blank spaces). For example, if you print the CONTACT, COMPANY, and ADDRESS fields from the National Widgets Customer File on lines 1, 2, and 3 of a label, dBASE IV does not skip a line if the COMPANY field is blank. Instead, it moves the CONTACT field down one line so that CONTACT and ADDRESS print on consecutive lines. As a result, if you are printing labels two or more across, corresponding lines on adjacent labels can contain different fields, but there will never be unsightly blank lines within the address block on one label. However, lines that you leave empty deliberately are preserved; you can identify these lines because the patterned work surface background is visible when you edit the label form. Thus, you can print the COMPANY, ADDRESS, and CITY/STATE/ZIP lines as a block, skip a line, and then print the CONTACT field preceded by "Attn: ".

Formatting Data with Picture Functions and Templates

You can alter the format of data base fields, calculated fields, and some of the predefined items (without, in the case of data base fields, affecting the way the data is stored on disk) by using *picture functions* and *templates.* Picture functions format a field as a whole, while templates offer more precise control by specifying the display format character by character. These formatting devices are also used in reports and custom data entry screens; in screen forms, as you will see in Chapter 15, you can also use them to format and validate data entered through the custom screen.

The formatting options are available through the **Template** and **Picture functions** options in the dialog box that pops up when you add a field to the label design work surface or modify an existing field. When you select **Picture functions,** dBASE IV displays a pick list of functions similar to the one pictured in Figure 11-8 and allows you to choose one or more from the list. When you choose **Template,** dBASE IV displays a help screen of available symbols and allows you to type a template of any length. Note that all the dBASE IV layout editors display the same lists of picture functions and template symbols, even though not all the symbols are relevant to all three types of forms. In all cases, dBASE IV displays available menu and pick list items in brighter text and does not allow you to select options that are not supported in the current context.

A picture function consists of one or more characters that symbolize the overall display format or data entry rules for a field. In the label forms, you can use all the functions that affect the display format of existing data and none that apply only to entered data. The picture functions applicable to label forms are listed in Table 11-3 (Chapter 12 includes a more complete list).

A template is a set of symbols, one for each character position in the field, that define the width of the field and specify the display format (and, in a data entry screen, the characters that can be entered), character by character. For example, each exclamation point (!) in a character field template causes dBASE IV to display the character in the corresponding position in uppercase (characters other than letters are not affected by this template symbol). You can insert commas into a number by using a template such as 9,999,999.99 (a comma is displayed only if there are digits on both sides of it). The template symbols applicable to label forms are listed in Table 11-4.

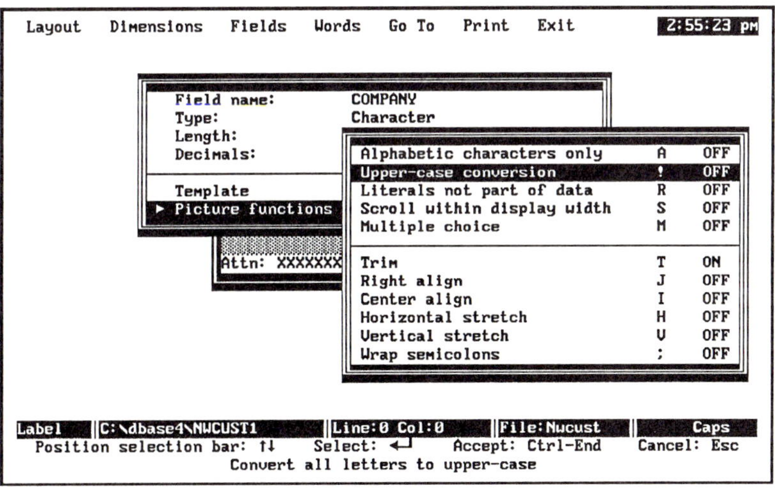

Figure 11-8.

Selecting a picture function from a pick list

Symbol	Data Types	Meaning
C	N, F	Display CR (credit) after a positive number
X	N, F	Display DB (debit) after a negative number
(	N, F	Display a negative number in parentheses
L	N, F	Add leading zeros to fill display width
Z	N, F	Display a zero value as a blank space
$	N, F	Display the currency symbol before the number
#	N, F	Display in exponential format
!	C	Display data in uppercase letters
T	C, N, F	Remove leading and trailing blank spaces
B	N, F	Left-justify within display width
J	C, M	Right-justify within display width
I	C, M, N, F	Center within display width
R	C, M	Insert extra characters in template into data, rather than replacing data characters

Table 11-3.

The Picture Function Symbols Used in Labels

You specify the print width of a field by the number of symbols in the template. By default, dBASE IV matches the template for a data base field to the width defined in the file structure. If you shorten the template for a character field, dBASE IV truncates the data that does not fit, and you can use the B, I, and J picture functions to left-justify, center, or right-justify the data within the designated width. Calculated numeric fields are 10 digits wide (7 digits, the decimal point, and 2 decimal places), and calculated character fields are 25 spaces wide.

The T function, which is assigned by default to all character and numeric fields, *trims,* or removes, all leading and trailing blank spaces so you can print two fields next to each other with no extra blank spaces, even if the entries in the fields vary a great deal in length. For example, when you print an address

Symbol	Data Types	Meaning
A	C, M	Display character unchanged
X	C, M	Display character unchanged
N	C, M	Display character unchanged
!	C, M	Display data in uppercase
9	C, M, N, F	Display character unchanged
#	C, M, N, F	Display character unchanged
.	N, F	Decimal point position
,	N, F	Insert a comma if a digit is present on both sides
*	N, F	Display a digit if present or an asterisk instead of a leading blank space
$	N, F	Display a digit if present or a dollar sign instead of a leading blank space
L	C, M, L	Display value unchanged
Y	C, M, L	Display true as Y and false as N
Other	C, M	Display symbol in place of data character. When combined with R function, insert symbol into data
	N, F	Insert symbol into data

Table 11-4.

The Template Symbols Used in Labels

on a mailing label, you would probably want to combine the city, state, and ZIP code in the standard format: with a comma after the city, and exactly two spaces between the state and the ZIP. To do this, you would place the CITY field on the label and make sure that the T function is **ON**; type a comma and a space immediately following the CITY; place the STATE field; type two spaces; and finally, place the ZIP code. This method was used to create the city/state/ZIP line in the label form illustrated in Figure 11-1.

dBASE IV determines which items belong together on a report or label form by the method used to create the spaces between them. dBASE IV treats items that are separated by space characters—spaces generated by pressing the spacebar—as a unit. The CITY, STATE, and ZIP fields in Figure 11-1 are good examples. In contrast, if you place a field, move the cursor with the arrow keys to a new location on the work surface, and place another field, the two items are handled independently. You could print another item, such as the credit status field, to the right of the city/state/ZIP combination on the same line by using the RIGHT ARROW key rather than the spacebar to advance the cursor to the starting position of the CREDITOK field. You can always identify spaces created with the spacebar, because they are displayed in the background color used for data base fields. When you use the arrow keys to move the cursor, you are not inserting any characters on the work surface (you can confirm this by observing that the patterned background of the work surface remains intact).

You can use both a picture function and a template to format a field, and you can combine the individual function symbols in any reasonable manner. For example, assigning both C and X to a numeric field causes dBASE IV to display CR after the field value if it is positive and DB if it is negative; you might combine these functions with a template that includes inserted commas. For character fields, you might use a template to define the maximum display width and two picture functions: ! to convert the data to uppercase letters and J to right-justify the field within the allotted display width.

The **Words** menu contains additional options for changing the display format of data or text when you add print enhancements such as boldfacing or switch type styles or fonts. Because these options are equally applicable to reports, they are covered in detail in Chapter 13, which follows the chapter about printing columnar reports.

Using Calculated Fields

You have already seen how to create calculated fields in Query-by-Example and in the full-screen Browse and Edit modes. Label and report forms can also include calculated fields, defined by any legitimate dBASE IV expression. The expression can be as simple as a single memory variable or as complex as you can fit within the maximum permissible length of 1024 characters. You can type it directly or construct it by choosing items from a pick list.

To create a new calculated field, you position the cursor where you want to print the field, press F5 (Add field) or select **Add field** from the **Fields** menu, and then choose the **<create>** option from the **Calculated** panel of the label item pick list. dBASE IV pops up a dialog box in which you define the new field by entering a name of up to ten characters, the expression that defines the calculation, and, optionally, a description of the purpose or use of the field. When you enter the calculated field expression, the input line scrolls to accommodate an entry that is wider than the dialog box. If you prefer to see more of your expression at once, you can press F9 (Zoom) while entering the expression to expand the input line to the full width of the screen. You format calculated fields exactly as you would a data base field: by assigning any picture functions or templates appropriate to the data type of the value that results from performing the calculation.

You can combine text, fields, and calculated fields any way you see fit. For example, you could direct a piece of mail to the attention of the contact person at National Widgets by creating a line in this format:

```
Attn: Joan Mills
```

To do this, you would first type "Attn:", press the spacebar to insert a space after the colon, and then place the CONTACT field on the work surface beginning in the next column.

In this example, if the CONTACT field is blank, the word "Attn: " still prints, because you entered it as ordinary text on the label form. To solve this problem, you must enter "Attn: " so as to make printing conditional on a nonblank CONTACT field. One way to print text or fields conditionally is to create a calculated field using the IIF ("immediate if") function introduced in Chapter 10. To print the "Attention" line only if the contact name is not blank, you might define a calculated field (perhaps called ATTENTION) as follows:

```
IIF(CONTACT <> " ", "Attn: " + CONTACT, " ")
```

This expression tests the value of the CONTACT field by comparing it to a blank space. If the CONTACT field is not blank, the condition is true, and the IIF function evaluates to the character string "Attn: " + CONTACT. If the condition is false (the CONTACT field is blank), the IIF function evaluates to a single blank space, which is invisible on printed labels.

You can sometimes use a calculated field to squeeze onto a single label line a combination of fields that would otherwise not fit. For example, in the

National Widgets Customer File, if the CITY and ZIP fields are filled to their maximum lengths, printing the full city, state, and ZIP code in the standard form ("San Francisco, CA 94101-0123") requires 36 spaces—20 for the city, 2 for the comma and space following the city, 2 for the state abbreviation, 2 for the 2 spaces following the state, and 10 for the ZIP code. In order to fit these fields on one line in the NWCUST1.LBL label form shown in Figure 11-1, only 1 space was placed between the STATE and ZIP fields, but if your mailing labels were only 30 characters wide, this method would fail.

One solution is to shorten the template for the CITY field, the ZIP field, or both, so that the combined length of the fields is only 30 characters, but this strategy is less than ideal. If you make the ZIP template 5 characters wide, *all* the ZIP codes in the file will be truncated to this width, even when the city name is short enough that the full combination would fit on the line. Similarly, if you narrowed the CITY field template, long city names would be truncated even in records in which 5 characters would suffice for the ZIP code.

You can solve this problem by printing the entire city/state/ZIP code combination as a single calculated field, and adjusting the template width for this field to the maximum number of characters that fit on a label line. The expression that defines the calculated field looks like this:

```
TRIM(CITY) + ", " + STATE + "  " + ZIP
```

This expression consists of five separate character strings, concatenated (added together) with the + operator. The TRIM function removes trailing blank spaces from the CITY field before the next component—a character string consisting of a comma and a blank space—is added on. Then the STATE field, which is always 2 characters long, a character string consisting of 2 blank spaces, and the ZIP field, are appended to the expression. By specifying the template width for this field as 30 characters, you ensure that the *first* 30 characters of the combination are always printed on the label.

Modifying a Label Form

You can edit a label form by using any of the standard full-screen cursor movement and editing keys to move around the work surface and make changes. dBASE IV offers both function key and menu command alternatives for many common editing operations. For example, the **Go To** menu has options for moving quickly to a particular line on a label or searching for text, although using the cursor movement keys is faster and easier for all but very large label forms.

You can insert a blank line before (above) an existing label line by placing the cursor at the beginning of the line and either pressing CTRL-N or selecting the **Add line** option from the **Words** menu. You can delete a line with either CTRL-Y or the **Remove line** option on the **Words** menu, and you can delete a field either by pressing DEL with the cursor in the field, by backspacing over the last character in the field, or by selecting the **Remove field** option from the **Fields** menu.

To modify the display format of a field, you position the cursor anywhere within the field and press F5 (Field) or select the **Modify field** option from the **Fields** menu. dBASE IV pops up the same dialog box that is displayed when you first place a field on the work surface, and you can change the picture function and/or template. For a calculated field, you can also change the description and the expression that defines the calculation. You cannot edit the name, type, or length of a data base field, which are stored in the file structure. Thus, you cannot substitute one field for another by entering a new field name; instead, you must delete the unwanted field and add the new field to the work surface in its place.

The commands that move or copy a block of fields or text are similar to those used in the memo field editor, which was explained in Chapter 4. A block can encompass any rectangular region of the work surface and can include text, fields, and the blank space between them. To begin the move or copy sequence, you mark the beginning of the block by pressing F6 (Select) with the cursor positioned in one corner of the block (or one end if the block lies within a single row), and then you move the cursor to the opposite corner (or end) of the selection and press ENTER. dBASE IV highlights the selected text and fields so you can clearly identify the marked block. Because dBASE IV treats a field as a single entity, not a string of separate characters, selecting a single field is even easier: move the cursor into the field (dBASE IV automatically positions the cursor on the first character), press F6 (Select), and then press ENTER.

To move or copy a marked block, press F7 (Move) or F8 (Copy) and then use the arrow keys to move the cursor to the new position of the block. As you move the cursor, it "drags" a shaded box the size and shape of the selected block behind it on the label design work surface to help you visualize the block in its new location. If you prefer, you can move the cursor to the new position of the block before pressing F7 (Move) or F8 (Copy); the shaded box will appear at the cursor location when you press the command key. To complete the move or copy operation, press ENTER to lock the block into position. If the block would overlap existing fields or text in its new position, dBASE IV asks you to confirm your intention to overwrite these items with "Delete covered text and fields? (Y/N)." In most cases, this warning results from moving an item slightly so that its new position overlaps the old location, and you can press Y (for "Yes") to place the block. If you press N ("No"), dBASE IV "unlocks" the block and allows you to continue moving it around the work surface to find a new location.

After you move or copy a block, it remains selected, and you can move or copy the same block again without repeating the selection steps. You must, however, press the F7 (Move) or F8 (Copy) key to specify which operation to carry out on the marked block. To make multiple copies of a block of text, for example, you would select the text, press F8 (Copy), move the cursor to the location of the first copy, press ENTER, press F8 (Copy) again, move the cursor to the location of the next copy, press ENTER again, and so on. When you are finished with a marked block, you can cancel the selection by pressing ESC, or you can leave the block selected until you need to mark a new block, which automatically cancels the previous selection.

Saving a Label Form

You can save a label form on disk and continue working on the label design screen by selecting the **Save this label design** option from the **Layout** menu, or you can save the form and exit to the Control Center or the dot prompt by selecting the **Save changes and exit** option from the **Exit** menu. If you choose **Abandon changes and exit**, dBASE IV returns you to the Control Center without saving the new or modified form.

You can exit the label layout editor without saving the form but without losing it. For example, you can press F2 (Data) to view data on the Browse or Edit screen and then move to the query design screen by pressing SHIFT-F2 (Design) or selecting **Transfer to Query Design** from the **Exit** menu. You can move freely between Edit or Browse and Query-by-Example, and then return to the label editor by choosing the **Return to Label Design** option on the **Exit** menu (this option appears on the **Exit** menu of all screens reached directly or indirectly through the label layout editor). If you attempt to exit from any screen to the Control Center or the dot prompt by pressing ESC, dBASE IV redisplays the label design screen and pops up a dialog box to remind you,

"Your label has not been saved. Do you want to save it now?" Whether you select **Yes** or **No**, dBASE IV returns you to the Control Center or the dot prompt.

Note that you can also use a label form to view or print labels without saving the form, using the options on the **Print** menu on the label design screen. You might be tempted to postpone saving the form until you have verified that your layout is correct by viewing or printing the labels, but even if you intend to further refine the specifications, it is a good idea to save the label form before you print. With certain printers (especially those that have a serial interface), a communication problem between the computer and the printer may cause the system to hang up and force you to reboot or turn off the computer, and if you have not yet saved the form on disk, it will be lost.

Each time you save the label form, dBASE IV prompts you for a file name; if you have already named the form, the name is displayed as the default, which you can accept by pressing ENTER, or change to save the file under a different name. You can take advantage of this flexibility to create new forms that are similar to existing ones without starting from scratch. To do this, you edit an existing label form, make the desired changes, and save the modified form under a new name.

dBASE IV stores a label form on disk in two different types of files. The design specifications are stored in a file with the first name you assigned and the extension LBL. This file stores the layout in the form required by the label layout editor so that you can later modify the form. From the specifications in the LBL file, dBASE IV generates a *program*, which is compiled and executed to print the labels. This program, which you can edit and modify if you understand the dBASE IV programming language, is given the same first name as the LBL file and the extension LBG (a combination of LBL and PRG, the standard extension for dBASE IV programs). Most of the disk activity you see when you save a label form results from the construction of this program; the LBL file is created and saved very quickly.

DISPLAYING AND PRINTING LABELS

You can display or print labels from the **Print** menu on the label form layout editor, from the Control Center, or from the dot prompt. In all cases, you can control the sequence in which records are printed by sorting the file or by activating an index, and you can use any means you know to establish record selection criteria. If you work primarily in the menu system, you will usually implement selection criteria by defining a view query and opening this query rather than the underlying data base file. From the dot prompt, you can add a filter, scope, FOR clause, and WHILE clause to the command that initiates printing.

From the Menus

You can print labels directly from the label design screen by using the options on the **Print** menu. From the Control Center, you can select the name of a label form from the **Labels** panel and then choose **Print label** from the dialog box that pops up. Because dBASE IV stores a reference to the data base or view that was active when you created the labels, you can issue the print command from the Control Center without having a data base open.

If you like, you can use a label form defined for one data base or view with a different file or view, as long as the fields printed on the label have the same names. This flexibility is convenient if several files have similar structures. For example, National Widgets might have a mailing list in which the name and address fields have the same names as the corresponding fields in the Customer File, and you could use the same label forms with both files. You might also want to define several view queries that specify different selection criteria or sort sequences and use the same label forms to print the entire data base or just the records selected by any of these views.

If you attempt to print labels based on a file or view other than the one for which the label form was created, dBASE IV displays a dialog box that notes the name of the original file and reminds you, "You may choose to use either the current database file or view, or the database file or view usually associated with the file you just selected." You can either switch to the original file by selecting its name, or choose **Current view** to print using the data base or view that is currently open.

Issuing the print command from the Control Center invokes a pop-up menu that is identical to the **Print** menu on the label design screen. You may recognize this menu (illustrated in Figure 11-9) as the same menu displayed when you request a Quick Report. The **Print** menu contains options for selecting the output device—the screen, a disk file, or any available printer—and for customizing various aspects of the page layout, page dimensions, and print quality. Chapter 13 covers the customization options, since they apply to reports as well as labels. This section covers only the commands that are essential for displaying and printing labels.

The **View labels on screen** option enables you to view the labels and check your page layout to verify that you have selected the correct records. If you are printing on forms that are wider than the screen, the data will wrap around onto two or more screen lines, and the display may not be very readable. You may want to change the **Columns of labels** setting on the **Dimensions** menu to 1 temporarily so that dBASE IV prints labels one-across in order to perfect the label layout without wasting paper or monopolizing a shared printer.

The **Eject page now** option advances the paper to the top of the next page based on the page length set using the **Page dimensions** option (explained in Chapter 13). When the printhead is positioned at the top of a page of labels, select **Begin printing**. To check the alignment of the label stock in the printer, use the **Generate sample labels** option. The sample label consists of a full row of X's for each line in the label form. After printing each sample, dBASE IV pauses and asks, "Do you want more samples? (Y/N)." You can adjust the

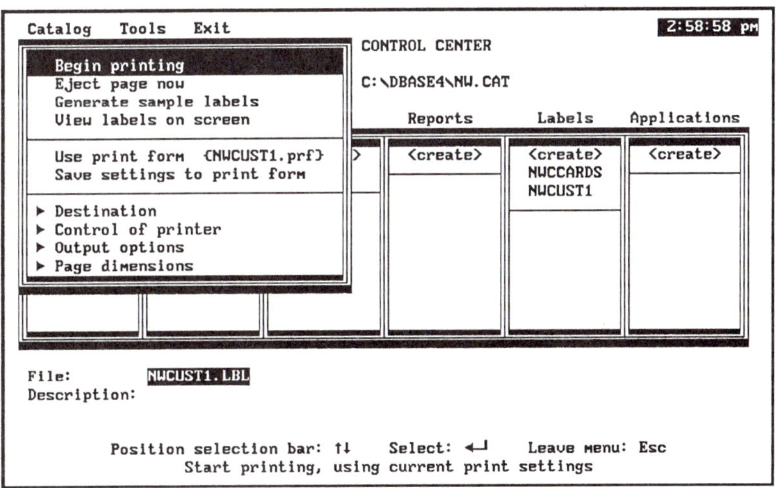

Figure 11-9.

The Print menu

paper and then select **Y** to generate another sample label, or select **N** to begin printing using your data.

As dBASE IV begins to print labels, a status box, which is pictured in Figure 11-10, informs you that you can request a temporary pause at any time by pressing CTRL-S and then resume printing by pressing any key on the keyboard, or cancel the print job entirely by pressing ESC. The pause and cancel commands cause dBASE IV to stop sending data to the printer immediately, but if your printer has an internal buffer (built-in memory for data storage), it will continue to print until the buffer is empty. If the buffer is large, this process might take a long time. If you do not want to wait, you can turn the printer off. Note that when you cancel a print job, you should always press ESC first to instruct dBASE IV to stop sending data to the printer. Then, if necessary, you can press your printer's reset switch or turn the printer off to clear the buffer. If you turn the printer off first, dBASE IV will display a "Printer not ready" error message.

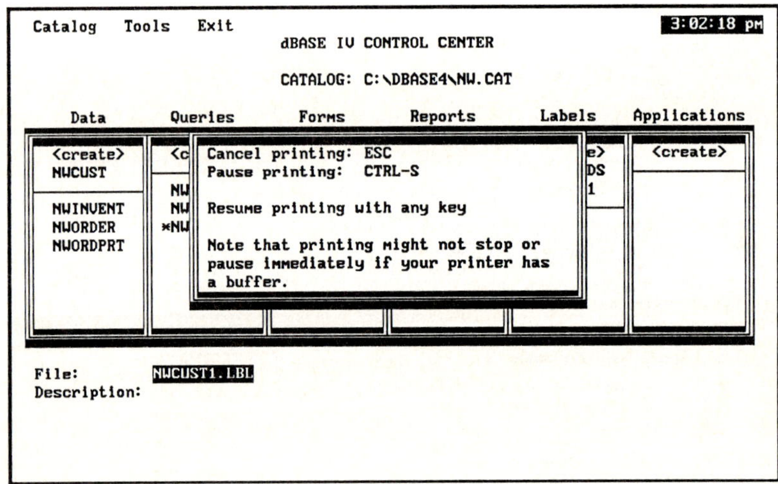

Figure 11-10.

Printing mailing labels

From the Dot Prompt

From the dot prompt, you use the LABEL FORM command to print mailing labels. First, you must open a data base file or view (it does not have to be the one that was active when you defined the label form), and, if you want to, you can activate an index tag or NDX index to control the order in which labels are printed. The syntax of the LABEL FORM command is as follows:

LABEL FORM *label form name*

If you do not specify the name of the label form, dBASE IV pops up a pick list that displays available label forms from which you can make a selection. If you do not have a data base or view open, dBASE IV displays a dialog box to prompt you for the file name.

By default, dBASE IV displays labels on the screen. As described in the previous section, viewing the data on the screen is a handy way to check your page layout and verify that you have selected the correct records before you print on paper. You can route the label output to the printer by adding the phrase TO PRINT to the LABEL FORM command, or to a disk file by adding the phrase TO FILE, followed by the name of the text file you want to create. When you print labels or send the output to a disk file, the data is also displayed on the screen. If you need to check the alignment of the labels in the printer, you can include the SAMPLE option in the LABEL FORM command. This keyword has the same effect as the **Generate sample labels** option on the **Print** menu, which was covered in the previous section.

You can use any of the command clauses and techniques described in earlier chapters to select the records that are included in a label run. For example, you could use the following sequence of commands to print labels in ZIP code order for customers in the ZIP code region 94700 through 94899 who have not yet placed an order this year:

```
USE NWCUST ORDER ZIP
SEEK "947"
LABEL FORM NWCUST1 TO PRINT WHILE ZIP <= "94899" FOR YTDORDERS = 0
```

SUMMARY

This chapter introduced the first of the dBASE IV layout editors used to design custom forms for displaying and entering data. Using the label editor, you can easily create mailing labels and other printed forms that present data in a clear, attractive format. Keep in mind that the layout editors used to create reports and data entry screens employ many of the same command keys and menu options as the label form editor, and much of the material presented in this chapter is applicable to these forms as well. Also remember that you can use "labels" to produce a much wider variety of printed forms than the name implies. In Chapter 13, you will learn how to further improve the appearance of labels and other printed forms by adding print enhancements, and how to exercise more precise control over your printer and paper forms.

CHAPTER TWELVE

Printing Columnar Reports

Chapter 11 explained how to design label forms with a specialized layout editor. You can create and edit dBASE IV reports with a similar layout editor that also allows you to type text and place fields on a screen work surface and move, copy, and format these items. Although designing a report on the layout editor work surface is straightforward, reports can be considerably more diverse and complex than labels in both format and content. To support this variety, the report layout editor offers more commands and menu options, and designing a complex report, especially one with calculations and summary statistics, requires some understanding of how dBASE IV processes a data base when it prints the report.

A dBASE IV report can include text, data base fields, calculated fields, and the same kinds of summary statistics that you already know how to compute at the dot prompt or in a query—counts, sums, averages, standard deviations, variances, and maximum and minimum values. You can define page headers and footers, column titles, an introduction, and a conclusion. Using techniques described in Chapter 13, you can dress up a report with print enhancements such as boldfacing and underlining, and you can access most of the type styles, fonts, and sizes supported by your printer.

dBASE IV classifies reports into three standard categories: column, form, and mailmerge layouts. In a *column* layout, the fields from each record are lined up in columns with headings at the top, much like the Browse display or the output of a LIST command. Typical applications for columnar reports include name and telephone lists and most accounting reports, such as invoice registers and accounts receivable or cash receipts journals.

A *form* layout bears a closer resemblance to the Edit display, with fields arranged vertically, like the standard Edit screen, or spread out across the page like the layout created by a screen form file. Often, each field has its own prompt, and each page of the report contains only one or a few records. You might use a form layout to print all the information on file about a customer, to print an invoice or statement based on data in two or more data base files, or to fill out preprinted forms such as insurance claim forms or medical records. In a *mailmerge* layout, the body of the report consists of free-form text, such as a personalized letter, together with selected fields from the active data base, typically the name and address.

These three standard layouts satisfy such a broad range of reporting requirements that dBASE IV provides a shortcut—a *Quick Layout*—for building a simple report of each type. The three generic layouts also serve as a convenient framework for describing the capabilities of the dBASE IV report layout editor, in this chapter and in Chapter 14. However, the report layout editor does not force you to classify each of the reports you create as one of the three basic types. A given report may combine elements that are characteristic of more than one basic layout, and you should not feel constrained by these definitions, or by the examples in this and the next two chapters, when you design your own report forms.

Designing and printing a report is similar to the label creation process described in Chapter 11. dBASE IV saves your report form specifications on disk so that you can reprint the same report in a later work session, based on any data base or view with a compatible structure. To establish record selection criteria, you can use a view query, or, from the dot prompt, you can use any combination of a scope, filter, FOR clause, and WHILE clause. You can sort, or more commonly, use an index to govern the order in which records are printed, and to define additional selection criteria based on a WHILE clause.

This chapter describes how to design and print columnar reports based on information in one data base file. Form layouts and mailmerge layouts are described in Chapter 14, and special considerations for multifile reports are covered in Chapter 17. The structure of the report layout editor menu is diagrammed in Figure 12-1. Because there are so many options—and so many ways to combine these options to achieve a pleasing, easy-to-read report format—you may want to refer back to this figure frequently as you read this chapter and design your own reports. It should help you find the options you need in order to accomplish a particular task.

CREATING AND EDITING COLUMN LAYOUTS

In a column layout, fields from the active data base or view and calculated fields derived from this data base are lined up across the page in columns. Typically, there is very little fixed text in the body of the report; instead, the data in each column is identified by a heading at the top.

dBASE IV allows you to *group* records on a report. The simplest way to define the groups is to specify an arbitrary number of records. For example, in order to match an existing manual system, an accounting application might require subtotals every 25 or 50 records in transaction listings such as cash receipts or disbursement journals. More often, you will want to group records based on the contents of a field or the result of evaluating an expression, and to print summary statistics such as counts and sums for each group. For example, National Widgets might want to analyze sales patterns geographically or evaluate the performance of its regional salespeople by printing a report that groups customers by state, and within each state by city, and prints the sum and average of the year-to-date and total orders for each city and each state.

Like labels, reports nearly always include data base fields, and you must open a data base file or view before you invoke the report form editor. If you access the report layout editor from the Control Center, dBASE IV records the name of the active data base or view in the catalog entry for the report form (catalogs are described in Chapter 19). When you modify the form or use it to print a report, dBASE IV automatically opens this file or view. However, you can override the default and use the same report form with different data bases, or with other views based on the same data base, provided that the field names in the view or data base match those specified in the report form. If you print from the dot prompt or create a report from the dot prompt, and later use it to print from the Control Center, you must first open a compatible data base or view.

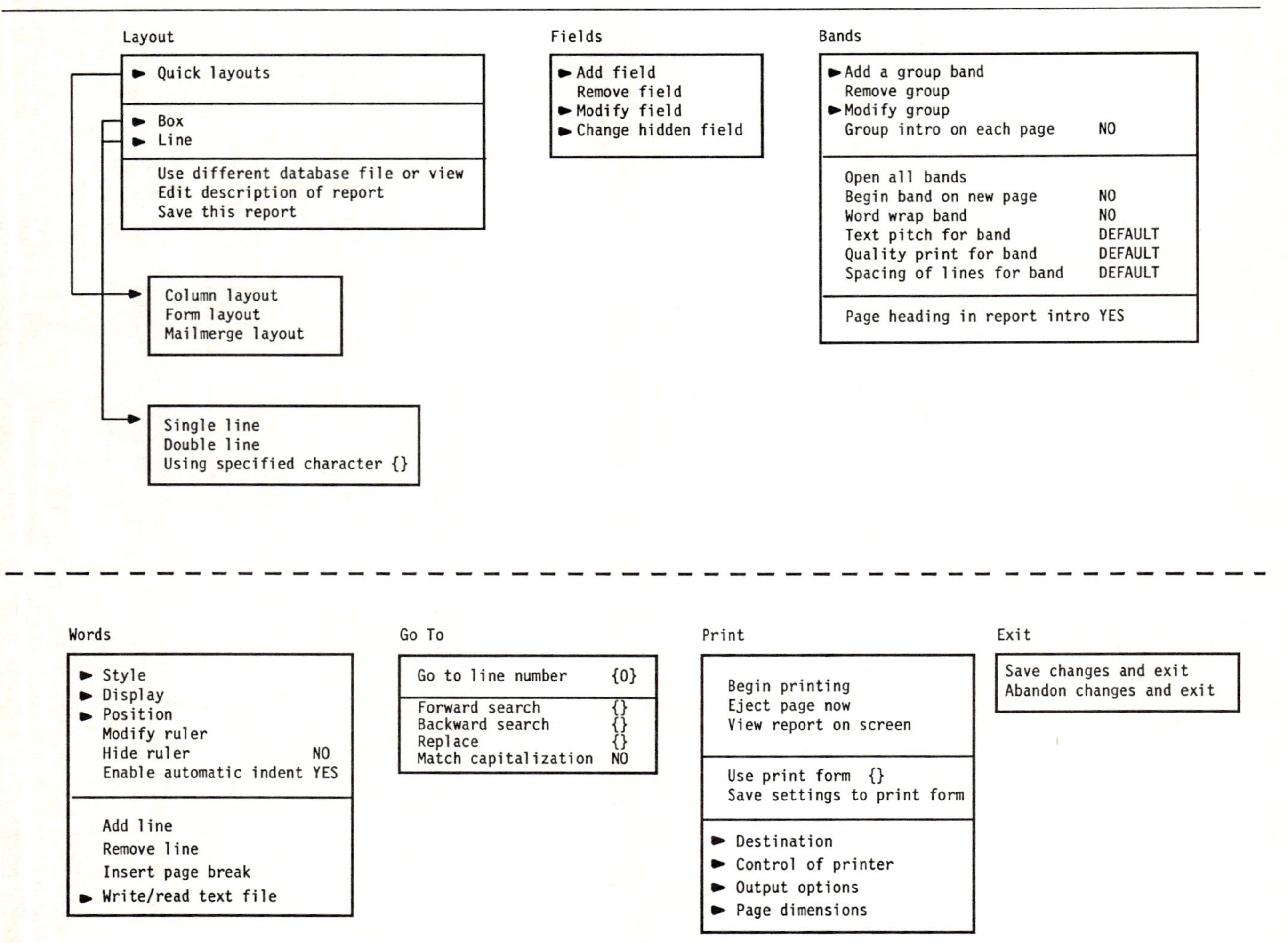

Figure 12-1.

The structure of the report layout editor menu

From the Menu System

You display and access report forms through the **Reports** panel in the Control Center. To edit an existing report form, you highlight its name, press ENTER, and select **Modify layout** from the pop-up dialog box. To create a new report form, you select the **<create>** option. You can also use the standard function key shortcut for opening a file and moving to the appropriate design work surface—simply highlight a report form name or **<create>** and press SHIFT-F2 (Design).

If you attempt to invoke the report layout editor without first opening a data base, dBASE IV pops up a message box to remind you: "Please put a database file or view into use first." As with labels, you need not name a new form until you save it. Thus, you can create a report form, print the report, and exit to the Control Center without ever saving the form, but except for rare instances in which you are sure you will never need to reprint the same or a similar report, it is best to save each report form you create.

From the Dot Prompt

From the dot prompt, you invoke the report editor by typing

CREATE REPORT *report form name*

or

MODIFY REPORT *report form name*

You can use the CREATE and MODIFY variations interchangeably, regardless of whether you are defining a new format or editing an existing one. As always when you work at the dot prompt, you must name a new report form file before you enter the report layout editor to create it. If you do not include a report form name in the CREATE REPORT or MODIFY REPORT command, dBASE IV prompts you to enter it, and if no data base is active, dBASE IV pops up another dialog box to prompt you for the file name.

USING THE REPORT DESIGN WORK SURFACE

The dBASE IV report layout editor enables you to design a wide variety of printed forms which, despite their diversity, share a common structure. All dBASE IV reports are comprised of a series of *bands,* or regions, that extend horizontally across the page and encompass one or more printed lines. There are seven types of bands, each of which is used for information printed in a specific sequence on the report. A report need not include a band of each type, and you may elect not to print a band that you have defined, but *any text or data you wish to print on a report must be entered into a report band.* The seven types of bands are used as follows:

Page header	Information printed at the top of each page, such as the date, page number, page title, and column headings
Report intro	Information printed once at the beginning of the report, such as an extra title, a cover page, or several pages of introductory narrative text
Group intro	Information printed at the beginning of each group, which usually includes the field or expression that defines the group
Detail	Information printed once for each record, including data base fields, calculated fields, and fixed text
Group summary	Information printed at the end of each group, for example, group counts, subtotals, or other statistics, perhaps with some explanatory text
Report summary	Information printed once at the end of the report, such as a concluding statement or grand totals and other summary statistics
Page footer	Information printed at the bottom of each page, such as the date or page number

Figure 12-2 illustrates a typical columnar report, in this case an order summary report based on the National Widgets Customer File, with the location of the seven types of bands indicated on the printout. Figures 12-3 and 12-4 illustrate the specifications for this report as they were entered on the report design screen (two screens are required because the report layout is more than 19 lines long). The report bands are arranged on the screen in the same order in which they are printed, but when you create a report, you need

```
National Widgets, Inc

Customer Order Summary by State


Prepared by Miriam Liskin

10/19/91
```

Report intro

Figure 12-2.

A typical columnar report that illustrates the seven types of report bands

```
            Printed: 10/19/91                                                      Page    1

                                          National Widgets, Inc.
Page                                  Customer Order Summary by State
header

            Account      Company Name                  Y-T-D Orders    Total Orders    Years
            ----------   -------------------------     ------------    ------------    -----
Group       Customers in CA:
intro       ----------------
            ARONOFF                                            0.00        1,232.50      4.0
Detail      ABCPLUMB     ABC Plumbing                        796.41        5,248.90      3.9
            GREENTHUMB   Green Thumb Landscaping               0.00          357.73      3.2
            HOMEMOVIES   Home Movies Video Rentals           548.15        2,047.15      3.1
            IMAGEMAKER   The Image Makers                      0.00          389.50      2.9
            MTK          M.T.K. Industries                   108.59          823.92      4.3
            WHITNEY      Financial Planning Svcs.            201.87        1,584.45      5.0
            LEWIS        Lewis and Associates                366.81        3,482.48      6.0
            SHAPEUP      Shape Up Fitness Center             435.42          867.38      3.7
            HRINSURANC   H & R Insurance                       0.00          738.43      4.3
            JOHNSON      J. Thomas Johnson, CPA                0.00          368.42      3.3
            RAPIDTYPE    RapidType Secretarial Svc           348.52          348.52      0.6
            YORKPUMP     York Pump, Inc.                     157.38          608.42      3.0
            KELLY        Kelly and Sons Furniture             87.35           87.35      0.7
                                                       ------------    ------------
Group          Totals for 14 customers:                    3,050.50       18,185.15
summary
               Average time since first order:                                         3.4

            Customers in OR:
            ----------------
            PHOENIX      Phoenix Construction                  0.00          249.59      4.3
            FLOORPLAN    Floor Plan Carpet Center              0.00          184.18      2.9
            KLEIN        Carol Klein, M.D.                     0.00        1,053.89      5.0
                                                       ------------    ------------
               Totals for 3 customers:                         0.00        1,487.66

               Average time since first order:                                         4.1

            Customers in WA:
            ----------------
            ANDERSON                                           0.00          832.58      4.2
            ELLISMFG     Ellis Manufacturing                   0.00          669.58      3.0
            DELTADESGN   Delta Design                        188.15        1,235.87      3.1
                                                       ------------    ------------
               Totals for 3 customers:                       188.15        2,738.03

               Average time since first order:                                         3.4

                                                       ============    ============
Report      GRAND TOTALS FOR 20 CUSTOMERS:                 3,238.65       22,410.84
summary
            AVERAGE TIME SINCE FIRST ORDER:                                            3.5

Page        Prepared by: M. Liskin
footer
```

Figure 12-2.

A typical columnar report that illustrates the seven types of report bands (*continued*)

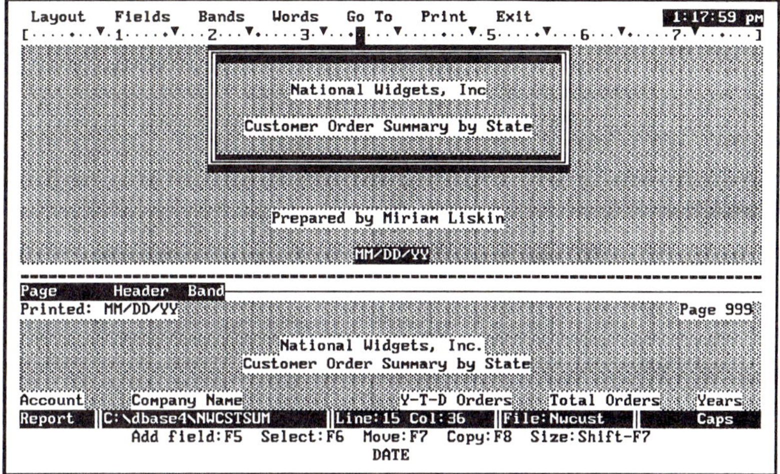

Figure 12-3.

The first screen of specifications for the report in Figure 12-2

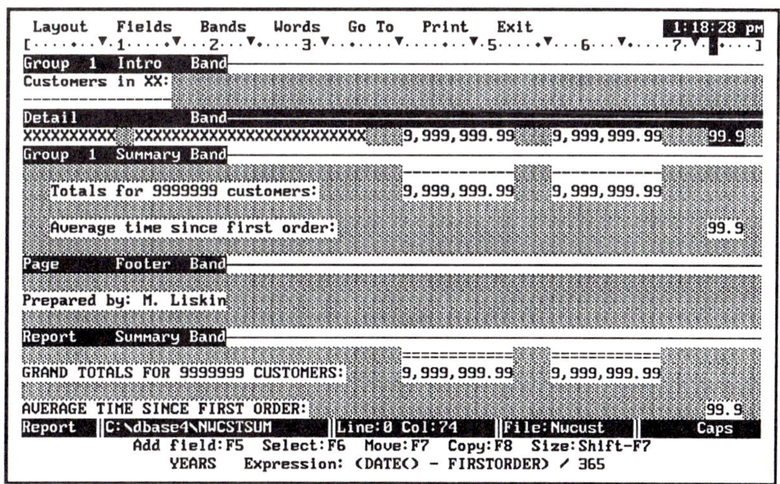

Figure 12-4.

The second screen of specifications for the report in Figure 12-2

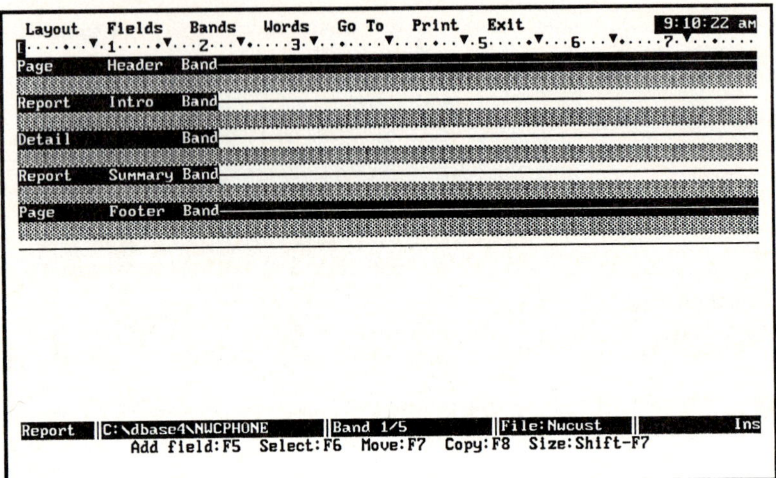

Figure 12-5.

The blank report design work surface

not begin by defining the report intro band and proceeding in sequence through the report summary band. In fact, the best way to lay out a complex report is to first construct the detail band, which contains most of the data. After adjusting the items in this band to fit the required data within the report width and create a clear and readable layout (perhaps aided by several test runs), you can add the header, footer, intro, and summary bands.

When you create a new report from scratch, all bands are initially empty, and the report layout work surface looks like Figure 12-5. No group intro or summary bands are displayed, because unlike the other report bands, you cannot add group bands to a report by typing text or placing fields on the work surface. Instead, you must use a command on the **Bands** menu (described later in this chapter) to add the group band and specify the field or expression that determines the record groupings (in the report in Figure 12-2, this is the STATE field).

As you move around the work surface, dBASE IV highlights the line that identifies the band containing the cursor and, for all except the detail band, the line that identifies the matching band. For example, with the cursor in the page header band, the page footer band is also highlighted. You can expand any report band, including the detail band, to occupy the number of lines required by its contents. To add a new blank line before (above) the line containing the cursor, you can press CTRL-N or press ENTER with the cursor at the beginning of a line with Insert mode turned on. If you select the **Add line** option from the **Words** menu or press ENTER with the cursor at the end of a line, a new blank line is added below. (Pressing ENTER in Typeover mode simply moves the cursor down to the beginning of the next line on the work surface without adding a new line.) You can use blank lines to fine-tune the vertical spacing on a report. For example, you can add blank lines to the page header and footer bands to adjust the top and bottom margins or the spacing between the detail items and the column headings.

At the heart of every columnar report is the detail band, which contains the items that are printed once for each record in the active data base or view that contributes data to the report. The detail band usually contains data base fields, calculated fields, and perhaps some text. A calculated field may be defined by any legitimate dBASE IV expression based on fields in the current record, other calculated fields, active memory variables, constants, and functions. Keep in mind that column layouts are not restricted to printing just one line of data per record. For example, in a customer listing for National Widgets, you might want to include the complete name and address, printed in a block much like a mailing label, with columns for other fields as well. By including several blank lines in the detail band, you can add extra space between records to improve readability or leave room for handwritten notes.

dBASE IV allows you to place any report component in any band—it is entirely up to you to ensure that your report design makes sense, and often this requires some understanding of how dBASE IV processes the active data base when it prints a report. dBASE IV reads one record from the data base, prints the items defined in the detail band, and then goes on to read the next record. The values of all report items printed in the detail band are derived from the current record or the current environment. Thus, if you included the predefined item **Pageno** in the detail band, its value would be the same for all the records printed on one page; on a columnar report, this item makes more sense in the bands that are printed once per page—the report header or report footer. You might, however, use the predefined item **Recno** to print record numbers on the report, or use **Date** in a calculated field that represents elapsed time based on the current date (for example, the age of an invoice, or how much time has passed since a customer's last order). The same principles govern when it is appropriate to include summary items in the detail band, as you will see later in this chapter.

Using the Quick Layouts

In Chapter 6, you learned how to use the SHIFT-F9 (Quick Report) key to produce a quick columnar printout based on the active data base or view. When you print a Quick Report, dBASE IV calculates the page layout and prints or displays the data without saving the report specifications permanently on disk.

If you later need to reprint the same report, dBASE IV repeats the same steps and regenerates the printout from scratch. You can also access the Quick Column Layout (and simple default formats for form and mailmerge layouts, which are explained in Chapter 14) through the **Quick layouts** option on the report design screen **Layout** menu. Using this option, you may want to create a Quick Layout in order to save the report design on disk and expedite reprinting the report, but more often you will use a Quick Layout as a starting point for creating a more complex page layout.

When you invoke the report layout editor from the Control Center to create a new form, dBASE IV displays the report design work surface with the **Layout** menu pulled down and the **Quick layouts** option highlighted if a data base is open (if no data base is open, **Use different database or view** is highlighted). When you select the **Quick layouts** option, dBASE IV displays a pick list with three choices: **Column layout, Form layout**, and **Mailmerge layout**.

The Quick Column Layout produces specifications for a report that is identical to the Quick Report generated when you press SHIFT-F9 (Quick Report) with the same data base or view open. The detail band consists of as many fields as will fit within the maximum report width of 247 characters, arranged in the same order as the fields in the data base structure or view skeleton. Memo fields and character fields longer than 30 characters are assigned a width of 30, and given the V (Vertical stretch) attribute. Otherwise, dBASE IV derives the width of a column from the width of the field it contains or the width of the field name—whichever is greater. Adjacent columns are separated by two spaces to improve readability. dBASE IV constructs a page header band that contains the page number, current system date, and column headings derived from the field names. If the report has numeric fields, the report summary band includes summary fields for calculating and printing column totals.

If the active data base or view has more fields than can fit on one report line, dBASE IV truncates the extra data. In most cases, this means that it is impractical to use the Quick Column Layout to design reports based on files with many wide fields or a total record length of more than about 200 to 250 characters. When you construct a report from scratch, you can choose any fields, arrange them in any order, and print long fields on multiple lines or in narrow columns to fit more data on the report. The Quick Column Layout is most useful for small data base structures or when the source of the report data is a view that includes only selected fields from the original file.

Adding Text and Fields to the Work Surface

If you do not want to use a Quick Layout as the basis for a new report, you can press ESC to close the **Layout** menu and construct the report form by typing text or placing fields directly on the work surface. You can use the vertical pattern on the work surface background to help you line up fields and column headings. Just as in the label layout editor, you add a field to the work surface by pressing F5 (Field) or by using the **Add field** option on the **Fields** menu.

When you use either of the commands just described to add a field to the work surface, dBASE IV displays a pick list of available items such as the one shown in Figure 12-6, which illustrates the list displayed with the National Widgets Customer File open. The report item pick list has four panels, three of which should be familiar from the label layout editor. The first panel lists the fields in the active data base, the **Calculated** panel displays the names of any calculated fields that you have defined for this report form, and the **Predefined** panel lists the same four predefined items that are available for use in label forms: **Date**, **Time**, **Recno**, and **Pageno**.

The **Summary** panel lists the seven types of summary statistics that you can include in a report summary band: **Average**, **Count**, **Max** (maximum), **Min** (minimum), **Sum**, **Std** (standard deviation), and **Var** (variance). These summary fields compile the same statistics as the aggregate operators in Query-by-Example, and they are used in much the same way—to compute statistics based on all the records in a data base or for each in a series of groups of records. (The summary items are explained in detail later in this chapter under "Grouping Data in Reports.")

When you select an item from the pick list, dBASE IV displays a pop-up dialog box like the one illustrated in Figure 12-7, which should also be familiar from the label layout editor. The **Suppress repeated values** option, which is applicable only to reports, is described later in this chapter under "Grouping Data in Reports." You can use the same template characters and picture functions that were explained in Chapter 11 to format report items as well as several additional picture functions not applicable to labels. Table 12-1 lists all available picture functions and their meanings.

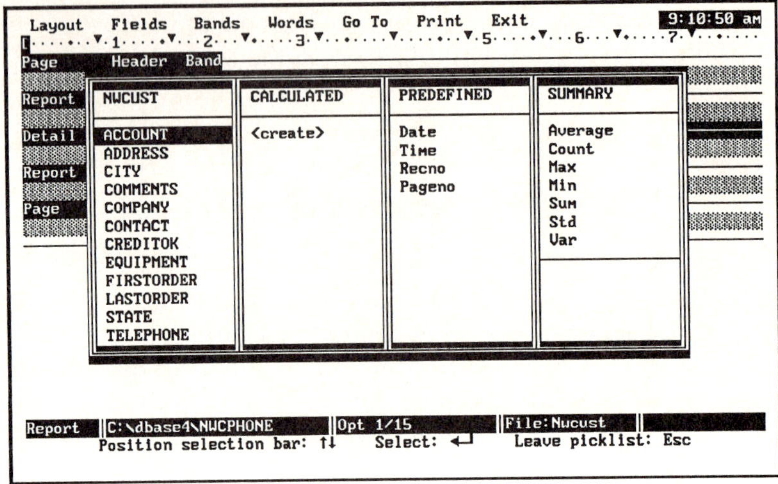

Figure 12-6.

Selecting a report item from a pick list

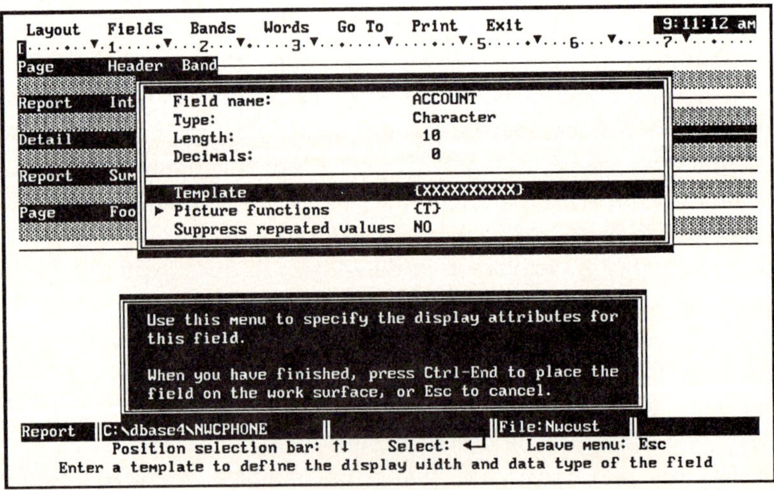

Figure 12-7.

Defining a report item

Symbol	Data Types	Meaning
C	N, F	Display CR (credit) after a positive number
X	N, F	Display DB (debit) after a negative number
(	N, F	Display a negative number in parentheses
L	N, F	Add leading zeros to fill display width
Z	N, F	Display a zero value as a blank space
$	N, F	Display the currency symbol before the number, and trim leading blanks.
#	N, F	Display in exponential format
!	C	Display data in uppercase letters
T	C, N, F	Remove leading and trailing blank spaces
B	N, F	Left-justify within display width
J	C, M	Right-justify within display width
I	C, M, N, F	Center within display width
H	C, M, N, F	Allow field to stretch horizontally
V	C, M	Allow field to stretch vertically to span multiple lines
;	C, M	Insert a hard return when a semicolon is encountered in text
R	C, M	Insert extra characters in template into data rather than replacing data characters

Table 12-1.

Picture Function Symbols Used in Reports

The template defines the print width of a report item. By default, the template for a data base field is the same width as the field itself; numeric calculated fields are 10 digits wide, and calculated character fields are 25 characters wide. dBASE IV also assigns the T (Trim) picture function, which removes leading and trailing blank spaces, and if the template is wider than the data, it left-justifies character, memo, and date fields within the column width and right-justifies numeric and float fields. You can change the print width by lengthening or shortening the template, and you can use the L, I, and J picture functions to left-justify, center, or right-justify the data within the designated width.

As in a label form, fields and text placed next to each other (separated only by spaces that you create by pressing the spacebar) are combined into one unit, whereas fields placed separately—so that the textured background of the work surface is visible in between—are treated independently. If you positioned the CITY field, which is 20 characters wide, at column 10, pressed the spacebar, and then added the STATE field to the work surface at column 31, dBASE IV would always print the CITY and STATE fields one space apart, regardless of the width of the city name. If, however, you placed the CITY field at column 10 and used the RIGHT ARROW key to move the cursor to column 31 to place the STATE field, the STATE field would always be printed at column 31, even when the city name was less than 20 characters long.

Most of the picture functions that are unique to reports apply to formatting long character and memo fields. Unlike items printed on labels, which are fixed in size, report fields can expand vertically, almost without limit, since a report can occupy up to 32,767 pages (a number that you are unlikely to exceed). You can control the formatting of long character and memo fields by combining a template, which sets the column width, with the T (Trim), H (Horizontal stretch), and V (Vertical stretch) picture functions, which determine how dBASE IV treats fields too long to fit within the designated width.

The H (Horizontal stretch) picture function causes dBASE IV to reformat a character or memo field to conform to the current left and right margin settings. The V (Vertical stretch) picture function causes dBASE IV to wrap a character or memo field within the template width, using as many lines as necessary. For example, in the report illustrated in Figure 12-8, the width of the memo field COMMENTS was set to 40 characters. If the field contained 100 characters of text, it would occupy 3 lines on the report; if the field contained 1000 characters of text, it would take up at least 25 lines (even more if the text contained extra hard returns or blank lines). The H function is allowed only in word wrap bands, and the V function is allowed only in layout bands (word wrap bands are introduced in the next section and are described in more detail in Chapter 14). If you set both the H and V picture functions to **OFF**, the template determines the width of the field; memo fields expand vertically (as if you had assigned the V function), while character fields are truncated to fit on one line.

```
Printed: 10/19/91                                                Page   1

Account ID  Company Name                Comments / Notes
--------------------------------------------------------------------------

ABCPLUMB    ABC Plumbing                This company has two older Kaypro
                                        computers in addition to their
                                        AT-compatible. They are still interested
                                        in disks, supplies, and accessories for
                                        the older machines, and they generally
                                        respond to special mailings by calling
                                        and placing an order.

                                        They are also interested in sources of
                                        public domain or inexpensive software for
                                        their CP/M-based Kaypros.



ANDERSON

ARONOFF

DELTADESGN  Delta Design                Referred by Chris Johnson.


ELLISMFG    Ellis Manufacturing         Don't accept any orders unless
                                        accompanied by prepayment.  These people
                                        have always been slow to pay, and have
                                        been avoiding phone calls regarding
                                        seriously past due balance which is now
                                        in collections.


FLOORPLAN   Floor Plan Carpet Center

GREENTHUMB  Green Thumb Landscaping

HOMEMOVIES  Home Movies Video Rentals   Owner is a friend of Jim's, so they get
                                        a 10% discount on all orders.  However,
                                        they often take a long time to pay.
```

Figure 12-8.

Printing a long field in a narrow column

dBASE IV automatically assigns the V picture function to memo fields, but you can also use it for long character fields. Once you have specified the V picture function for a field, you cannot change the display width by editing the template. Instead, you must use the SHIFT-F7 (Size) key: press SHIFT-F7 (Size) with the cursor within the field, use the LEFT ARROW and RIGHT ARROW keys to adjust the field width, and then press ENTER. You can apply the vertical stretch attribute to more than one field in a columnar report. For example, you could add another column after the COMMENTS column in the report in Figure 12-8 to print the EQUIPMENT field, also formatted with the V picture function. It is also safe to place additional columns to the right of vertically stretched fields; thus, you could add columns to the report in Figure 12-8 for the CONTACT and TELEPHONE fields. However, you cannot "stack up" two or more fields in a single column to the right of a vertically stretched field. If you placed CONTACT and TELEPHONE one below the other in a column to the right of the COMMENTS column, dBASE IV would print the first field (CONTACT) next to the first line of the COMMENTS field, but not print the second field (TELEPHONE) until after the last line of the COMMENTS field contents.

The ; (Wrap data at semicolons) picture function causes dBASE IV to break a line wherever it encounters a semicolon in the text of a character or memo field. This picture function was intended for printing text entered with earlier versions of dBASE, which interpreted a semicolon as a request for a line break. You can also use it to control where line breaks are inserted into a long calculated field made up of several shorter fields of varying lengths. This technique is described in more detail in Chapter 14.

Word Wrap Bands

dBASE IV recognizes two fundamentally different editing modes in report forms: layout and word wrap. In a *layout* band, each text or field item is an independent entity that prints exactly where you place it on the work surface (except that adjacent items assigned the T picture function are treated as a unit). In a *word wrap* band, as in the memo field editor, text is word wrapped at the right margin to form paragraphs. Word wrap mode is convenient for entering and editing long text passages, such as the body of a letter in a mailmerge layout (mailmerge forms are covered in Chapter 14) or a report intro band that prints a cover letter or narrative introduction.

By default, all the bands in a columnar report are assumed to be layout bands, because this mode is best for placing fixed-length fields and small amounts of background text, such as field name prompts, on the work surface. To select word wrap mode, set the **Word wrap band** option on the **Bands** menu to **Yes**. To distinguish word wrap bands from layout bands, dBASE IV uses a solid color for the background in a word wrap band instead of the pattern used in layout bands (perhaps because you do not need the pattern to help you line up items in a word wrap band). You can easily change a layout band to a word wrap band, and in a complex report you may want to place most of your fields in layout mode and then switch to word wrap mode to enter a paragraph or more of text. Turning a word wrap band into a layout band is more problematical: dBASE IV converts each paragraph of text into a series of lines, each of which ends with a hard return, and preserves the hard returns, even if you return to word wrap mode, so you can no longer edit the paragraph as a unit.

Word wrap mode is covered in greater detail in Chapter 14, which describes mailmerge layouts.

Editing a Report Layout

Using the standard full-screen cursor movement and editing keys, you can navigate around the work surface, move freely between bands, and add or edit items in any order. Table 12-2 lists the cursor movement and editing commands used in the report layout editor. Just as in the label layout editor, you can add or delete lines by using menu options or control key shortcuts. For example, to add a line above the line containing the cursor, you can either press CTRL-N or select the **Add line** option from the **Words** menu. To delete a line, you can press CTRL-Y or use the **Remove line** option, which is also on the **Words** menu. You can delete a field by pressing DEL with the cursor anywhere within the field, by backspacing over the last character in the field, or by selecting the **Remove field** option from the **Fields** menu.

You can add a *hard page break*, which causes dBASE IV to eject the paper to the top of the next sheet, even if additional space remains on the page, by using the **Insert page break** option on the **Words** menu. You can use this option much as you would use hard page breaks in a word processor—to begin a new page at a specific point without having to add extra blank lines to force a page break.

Control Key	Command Key	Function Key
	F10 (Menu)	Activate the menu system
	ALT-*letter*	Activate the menu system and pull down the menu whose description begins with *letter*
	letter	Select the option on the active pull-down menu whose description begins with *letter*
	ENTER	Select the highlighted option or item from the active menu, panel, or pick list
CTRL-W	CTRL-END	Save changes and exit
CTRL-Q	ESC	Exit without saving changes
CTRL-E	UP ARROW	Move up one line
CTRL-X	DOWN ARROW or ENTER (Typeover mode)	Move down one line
CTRL-D	RIGHT ARROW	Move right one character
CTRL-S	LEFT ARROW	Move left one character
CTRL-I	TAB	Move to the next tab stop
	SHIFT-TAB	Move to the previous tab stop
CTRL-F	CTRL-RIGHT ARROW or F4 (Next)	Move to the next field
CTRL-A	CTRL-LEFT ARROW or F3 (Previous)	Move to the previous field
CTRL-Z	HOME	Move to the beginning of the line
CTRL-B	END	Move to the end of the line
CTRL-C	PGDN	Display the next group of lines
CTRL-R	PGUP	Display the previous group of lines
	CTRL-PGDN	Move to the last line in the band
	CTRL-PGUP	Move to the first line in the band
CTRL-G	DEL	Delete the character at the cursor position
	BACKSPACE	Delete the character or field to the left of the cursor
CTRL-T		Delete the characters from the cursor to the end of the expression
CTRL-Y		Delete the line containing the cursor
CTRL-V	INS	Turn Insert mode on (if it is off) or off (if it is on)
CTRL-N	ENTER (Insert mode)	Insert a new line
	CTRL-HOME	Modify the current field
	F9 (Zoom)	Expand the data entry area to an entire line

Table 12-2.

The Cursor Movement and Command Keys Used in the Report Layout Editor

Control Key	Command Key	Function Key
	F2 (Data)	Switch to Browse or Edit to view data
	F5 (Field)	Add a field or modify the field at the cursor location
	F6 (Select)	Mark one corner of a rectangular region on the work surface (indicate the opposite corner by pressing ENTER)
	F7 (Move)	Move the selected items
	F8 (Copy)	Copy the selected items
	SHIFT-F7 (Size)	Resize the field containing the cursor

Table 12-2.

The Cursor Movement and Command Keys Used in the Report Layout Editor (*continued*)

Many report editing commands can operate on any rectangular region within a band, selected exactly as you mark a text block in the memo field editor. First, position the cursor on one corner of the block, press F6 (Select), move the cursor to the diagonally opposite corner, and press ENTER. If you move "off the edge" of the screen in any direction while defining the selection, dBASE IV scrolls the display to follow the cursor, but the marked block must lie entirely within one band. In a layout band, pressing F6 (Select) twice selects the entire line containing the cursor, and pressing F6 (Select) a third time selects the entire band. In a word wrap band, pressing F6 (Select) the second time selects the word or field containing the cursor; the third time, the entire paragraph (all the text up to the next hard return) is selected; and the fourth time, the entire band is selected. (Remember to press ENTER to confirm your selection after using any of these shortcuts.)

You can delete a selected block of items by pressing DEL. When you delete text from a word wrap band, dBASE IV moves the following text over to fill in the gap. In a layout band, because each item is treated as an independent entity, deletions do not affect other text or fields on the work surface. To remove a column and shift the remaining columns to the left, you must first delete the desired field or text and then move the other items to the left to fill in the space.

You can move or copy a selected block by pressing F7 (Move) or F8 (Copy) and using the cursor movement keys to "drag" the selected items to a new position on the work surface. When you press F7 (Move) or F8 (Copy), dBASE IV immediately displays the image of the block with the upper left corner at the cursor position. You may find it easiest, especially if you are only moving the block a few spaces, to move the cursor to the new position of the block before you press F7 (Move) or F8 (Copy). Alternatively, you can highlight the block by indicating the lower right corner first and end in the upper left corner, so that when you press F7 (Move) or F8 (Copy), the "ghost" image of the block superimposes exactly on the original block.

When you move or copy items in a word wrap band, dBASE IV inserts the selected material into the existing text at the cursor position. In a layout band, it adds the items to the work surface at the indicated location. If the move or copy operation would displace existing text or fields, dBASE IV warns you by asking if you want to "Delete covered text and fields?" You can answer **Yes** to confirm the new position of the selected items or **No** to return to moving the marked block around the work surface.

Because you cannot select a region that spans more than one band, you cannot use a single move command to move a field in the detail band together with its column heading (which might be in the page header or group intro band). Instead, you must move the field to its new position in the detail band, and then use a second move command to realign the header text. Similarly, if you move a group of fields to make room for another or to close up the gap left after deleting a field, you must adjust the column headings separately.

You may find it convenient to enter the entire set of column headings in a page header (or group intro) band as one long string of text rather than as a series of separate items (that is, press the spacebar to advance from one heading to the next rather than using the LEFT ARROW and RIGHT ARROW keys). This strategy enables you to edit the column headings as a unit and facilitates moving a portion of the band to the right or left by adding or deleting spaces. Note, however, that you can avoid many problems by fine-tuning the detail band (which may involve printing the report several times to test the field placement) before you add the page header and group intro bands.

Hiding Fields and Bands

At times, you may want to perform a calculation without printing the result. For example, in the report shown in Figure 12-2, the last column contains a calculated field called YEARS, which represents the number of years the customer has done business with National Widgets. This field is computed by subtracting the first order date from the current date and then dividing the result by 365 using the following expression:

```
(DATE() - FIRSTORDER) / 365
```

Using the DATE function to express the current date, rather than typing an explicit date such as {06/30/92}, enables you to use the report at any time without editing the form to enter a new current date. Note also that the parentheses are required in order to override the default precedence of division over subtraction and force dBASE IV to subtract the first order date from the current date before dividing by 365.

Instead of printing the calculated YEARS field for every customer record, you might want to print just the average in the report summary band. To do this, you could designate the field as **Hidden** in the dialog box in which you define the calculation. Although hidden fields do not print, they are available for use in further calculations. You can hide calculated and summary fields; there is no need to hide data base fields because you can base a calculation or summary field on a data base field without printing the field itself.

Because dBASE IV does not display hidden fields on the work surface, you cannot modify a hidden field by positioning the cursor in the field and pressing F5 (Field) or selecting **Modify field** from the **Fields** menu. Instead, you have to choose the **Change hidden field** option from the **Fields** menu and then select the field name from a pick list. You can delete a hidden field by choosing the **Remove field** option from the **Fields** menu with the cursor positioned anywhere on the work surface *except* within a field (if the cursor is in a field, dBASE IV deletes this field when you choose this menu option), and then selecting the name from a pick list.

You can close, or hide, a report band or reopen a band that you previously closed by pressing ENTER with the cursor anywhere within the highlighted line that identifies the band. Closing a band temporarily removes the contents of the band from the work surface, leaving only the band identifier line. When you edit a complex report, you may want to close bands that occupy a great deal of space to compress the display and reduce the number of keystrokes required to navigate among the bands you are currently editing. You can later reopen bands one by one, or open all bands at once by selecting the **Open all bands** option on the **Bands** menu.

dBASE IV does not print closed bands, so you must remember to reopen bands that you closed to facilitate editing before you save the report or print it from the **Print** menu within the report editor. You can also use this fact to your advantage to print different versions of a report or reprint specific sections. For example, you might close the report intro band on a draft copy of a report that contains a lengthy introduction, or close the detail band on a report with two or three levels of group bands to obtain a concise printout of summary data derived from a large data base. Figure 12-9 illustrates the order summary report from Figure 12-2 printed with the detail band closed. As you can see from this printout, the rows of dashes used to underline the columns of numbers look awkward with the detail band missing. If you plan to print a summary report in this way, you should take this fact into account when you design the group intro and group summary bands.

Other Band Options

Report options that apply only to specific bands or are frequently specified for a band as a whole are located on the **Bands** menu. Three of these options—**Spacing of lines for band**, **Text pitch**, and **Quality print for band**—control aspects of print formatting that are explained in Chapter 13.

The **Page heading in report intro** option determines whether the page header band is printed above (before) the text of the report intro band. If the report intro band contains only a few extra heading lines, you would probably want to print the page header (which typically contains the date, page number, and column headings) above the text. In contrast, if you use the report intro band to print a separate cover page or report introduction, you may want to suppress the page header on this page. If you select **No** for the **Page heading in report intro** option, dBASE IV moves the report intro band above the page header band on the work surface to conform to the new printing sequence—the page header band will be printed for the first time only after the report intro has been printed.

You can use the **Begin band on new page** option to force dBASE IV to eject the paper to the top of the next page before printing a band, even if space remains on the previous page. For example, you might set this option to **Yes** in a page header band if the report intro band that precedes it does not exactly fill a page, or in a group header band to ensure that each group begins on a new page if you intend to divide the report into sections by group and distribute these sections to different people. The **Group intro on each page** option causes dBASE IV to repeat the group intro band at the top of each page if the records in the group span multiple pages. If each group occupies more than a page or two, setting this option to **Yes** makes it clear from a glance at any page of the printout which group of records you are looking at. The default setting for both of these options is **No**.

```
Printed: 10/19/91                                                  Page    1

                         National Widgets, Inc.
                      Customer Order Summary by State


Account     Company Name                  Y-T-D Orders   Total Orders   Years
----------  -------------------------     ------------   ------------   -----

Customers in CA:
----------------
                                          ------------   ------------
   Totals for 14 customers:                   3,050.50      18,185.15

   Average time since first order:                                        3.4

Customers in OR:
----------------
                                          ------------   ------------
   Totals for 3 customers:                        0.00       1,487.66

   Average time since first order:                                        4.1

Customers in WA:
----------------
                                          ------------   ------------
   Totals for 3 customers:                      188.15       2,738.03

   Average time since first order:                                        3.4


                                          ============   ============
GRAND TOTALS FOR 20 CUSTOMERS:                3,238.65      22,410.84

AVERAGE TIME SINCE FIRST ORDER:                                           3.5




Prepared by: M. Liskin
```

Figure 12-9.

A columnar report printed with the detail band closed

GROUPING DATA IN REPORTS

Often, you will want to group data in reports based on the contents of one or more fields in the data base. In the simplest case, you may only be concerned with the printing sequence. For example, National Widgets might print a customer address and phone list grouped by state and within each state by city, with each state group beginning on a new page. More often, you will need to print summary statistics such as counts and sums for the groups. The common principle is that when dBASE IV prints a report with group bands, it prints the group intro band before the first detail record in the group, and it checks after printing each record to see if the requisite number of records have been printed or the value of the field or expression that defines the group has changed. If so, it prints the group summary band, followed by the group intro band for the next group, and so on.

If you have used other data base programs or earlier versions of dBASE, you may have encountered slightly different terminology for the same basic concepts. For example, the term *subtotal group* is often used instead of the more general *group,* even if you are not printing subtotals or are printing other statistics as well. The field that defines the groups is commonly referred to as a *break field,* and the special processing (printing extra text and statistics, accumulating grand totals, and resetting subtotals to 0) that is carried out when the value of the break field changes is called *break processing.*

Figure 12-10 illustrates a simple listing of National Widgets' customers grouped by state and city. As you can see from this report, the state and city fields in the detail band are redundant, because the values do not change within each group. One easy way to improve the appearance of a report such as this one is to select the **Suppress repeated values** option from the dialog box that is invoked when you place the CITY and STATE fields on the work surface. This option causes dBASE IV to print the specified field for only the first in a series of consecutive records that share the same field value. Figure 12-11 illustrates the result of setting **Suppress repeated values** to **Yes** for the CITY and STATE fields in the customer list shown in Figure 12-10.

If you need to print a more elaborate introduction or conclusion to each report group or calculate summary statistics for the records in the group, you must define one or more group bands. To create a group band, select **Add a group band** from the **Bands** menu. dBASE IV automatically creates a group header band and a matching group summary band. The cursor must be in a band that lies above the detail band, and the new group header band is always inserted between the band containing the cursor and the band immediately below it on the work surface. Because dBASE IV always adds new bands to the

Printed: 10/19/91 Page 1

National Widgets, Inc
Customer Telephone List

State	City	Account ID	Company Name	Phone
CA	Benicia	ARONOFF		745-1813
CA	Berkeley	ABCPLUMB	ABC Plumbing	861-4543
CA	Berkeley	GREENTHUMB	Green Thumb Landscaping	549-8901
CA	Berkeley	HOMEMOVIES	Home Movies Video Rentals	843-1148
CA	Emeryville	IMAGEMAKER	The Image Makers	653-1250
CA	Emeryville	MTK	M.T.K. Industries	655-7200
CA	Fremont	WHITNEY	Financial Planning Svcs.	791-7474
CA	Oakland	LEWIS	Lewis and Associates	839-5014
CA	Richmond	SHAPEUP	Shape Up Fitness Center	236-7687
CA	San Francisco	HRINSURANC	H & R Insurance	398-1441
CA	San Francisco	JOHNSON	J. Thomas Johnson, CPA	433-6488
CA	San Francisco	RAPIDTYPE	RapidType Secretarial Svc	861-4048
CA	San Jose	YORKPUMP	York Pump, Inc.	946-9975
CA	San Leandro	KELLY	Kelly and Sons Furniture	357-7482
OR	Eugene	PHOENIX	Phoenix Construction	683-8751
OR	Portland	FLOORPLAN	Floor Plan Carpet Center	232-8430
OR	Portland	KLEIN	Carol Klein, M.D.	232-2638
WA	Bellevue	ANDERSON		747-8201
WA	Bellevue	ELLISMFG	Ellis Manufacturing	455-1421
WA	Pullman	DELTADESGN	Delta Design	332-7373

Figure 12-10.

A report with records grouped by state and city

work surface nested within existing pairs of bands, you cannot add a group band from inside the detail band, which is not paired with any other band. For example, to add the first group band to a report, position the cursor in the band above the detail band (which might be the page header band or the report intro band). To remove a group (both intro and summary bands), press DEL with the cursor in either of the highlighted lines that identify the bands, or select **Remove group** from the **Bands** menu with the cursor anywhere in the group intro or group summary band.

```
Printed: 10/19/91                                                    Page    1

                                  National Widgets, Inc
                                 Customer Telephone List

State  City                Account ID  Company Name                  Phone


 CA    Benicia             ARONOFF                                   745-1813
       Berkeley            ABCPLUMB    ABC Plumbing                  861-4543
                           GREENTHUMB  Green Thumb Landscaping       549-8901
                           HOMEMOVIES  Home Movies Video Rentals     843-1148
       Emeryville          IMAGEMAKER  The Image Makers              653-1250
                           MTK         M.T.K. Industries             655-7200
       Fremont             WHITNEY     Financial Planning Svcs.      791-7474
       Oakland             LEWIS       Lewis and Associates          839-5014
       Richmond            SHAPEUP     Shape Up Fitness Center       236-7687
       San Francisco       HRINSURANC  H & R Insurance               398-1441
                           JOHNSON     J. Thomas Johnson, CPA        433-6488
                           RAPIDTYPE   RapidType Secretarial Svc     861-4048
       San Jose            YORKPUMP    York Pump, Inc.               946-9975
       San Leandro         KELLY       Kelly and Sons Furniture      357-7482
 OR    Eugene              PHOENIX     Phoenix Construction          683-8751
       Portland            FLOORPLAN   Floor Plan Carpet Center      232-8430
                           KLEIN       Carol Klein, M.D.             232-2638
 WA    Bellevue            ANDERSON                                  747-8201
                           ELLISMFG    Ellis Manufacturing           455-1421
       Pullman             DELTADESGN  Delta Design                  332-7373
```

Figure 12-11.

Suppressing repeated values of the STATE and CITY fields

When you add a group band to a report, dBASE IV displays a dialog box in which you can enter the number of records in the group or the field or expression that defines the group. Once you have created the group band, you can enter text and fields just as you would in any other band. In most cases, the group intro band includes the field or expression that defines the group as well as variable amounts of explanatory text. A typical group intro band is shown in Figure 12-2. In most cases, you do not have to repeat the field or fields that define the group in the detail band; for example, the detail band in the report in Figure 12-2 does not include the STATE field.

The group summary band is often used to print summary statistics based on the records in the group. In the report shown in Figure 12-2, the group summary band includes the sums of the year-to-date and total orders as well as the number of records in each group. Note that a field need not be printed in the detail band to contribute to summary statistics in the group summary or report summary band. For example, you could print the customer order totals by state in a report that lists only the company name and address fields in the detail band.

To define a summary item, press F5 (Field) with the cursor in the group summary or report summary band, and select the desired summary field from the **Summary** panel on the report item pick list. dBASE IV displays a dialog box much like the one used to define calculated fields; Figure 12-12 illustrates this dialog box with the specifications for the year-to-date order total summary field filled in. As with calculated fields, the name and description are optional. dBASE IV automatically fills in the **Operation**, in this case **Sum**, based on your selection from the pick list.

You must specify which field supplies the data for the summary field and how often to reset this field to zero. dBASE IV cannot deduce these relationships from the sequence in which records are printed or the location of the

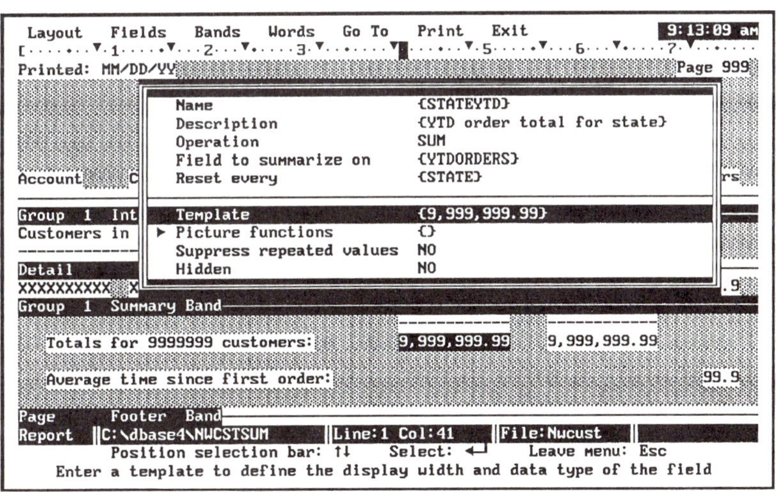

Figure 12-12.

Defining a summary field

summary items on the report design work surface, although the reason may not be obvious when you examine reports such as the one shown in Figure 12-2. In this report the sums are printed below the columns from which they are derived, but in other cases, you may not want to place the summary fields in such close proximity to the corresponding detail items, or you may not even need to print the contributing fields in the detail band. The **Field to summarize on** option, which is required for all the summary statistics except **Count,** specifies the field on which to base the sum, average, maximum, minimum, standard deviation, or variance. When you create a **Count** field, this entry is not required, since it makes no sense to count fields—dBASE IV can only count whole records. Note that you must enter a *field,* not an expression, as the basis for the summary statistics. You can, however, create a calculated field defined by any legitimate dBASE IV expression, hide this field if you do not want it to appear in the detail band, and base the summary statistics on the calculated field.

For all the summary field types, you must specify how often to reset the summary field value to zero by using the **Reset every** option. This option invokes a pick list that always includes two standard choices: **< REPORT >** and **< PAGE >**. If the summary field is in a group band defined by the contents of a field, the pick list also includes the names of all such fields, and you will generally want to reset the summary fields when the value of the field that defines the band changes. For example, in a report that counts National Widgets' customers in each state, you would reset the counter every time the STATE field changes to begin accumulating the count for the next state. You would choose the **< PAGE >** option to reset counts and totals printed in a page footer band, and **< REPORT >** to reset the statistics only once, after printing the entire report. Resetting the statistics at the end of a report run, which may not at first seem necessary, is essential when you print multiple copies of a report, as described in Chapter 13.

The examples presented so far are guidelines that illustrate typical ways to use group bands and summary fields. Keep in mind, however, that you can print any type of data—fields, calculated fields, and summary items—in any report band, and you can reset summary items whenever you wish. For example, on an accounting report, you might define a summary field that computes the sum of a numeric field and is reset to zero only once for the entire report. You could then include the summary field in the detail band to arrive at a running total printed with each transaction.

To achieve the intended results with group bands, you must ensure that the file providing the data is either sorted or indexed by the fields that define the groups. When dBASE IV prints a report, it reads records in sequence starting from the top of the file (or index). Each time the record pointer advances to the next record, dBASE IV checks whether the values of any of the expressions that define the groups have changed. If so, it prints the group summary bands for all groups that are complete and the group intro bands for the next groups and resets the corresponding summary fields in preparation for accumulating a new set of statistics.

Unless dBASE IV processes records in a sequence that matches the groups defined in the report, more than one set of records will have the same value for the expression that defines at least one of the groups, possibly printed far apart in the report. Figure 12-13 illustrates the beginning of the output that results from printing the customer order summary by state without activating any index for the Customer File. As specified in the report form, dBASE IV prints the group summary band whenever the value of the STATE field changes, but because the records are not processed in a sequence that depends on the STATE field, there is more than one group for each state.

Understanding how dBASE IV processes a data base while printing a report should clarify why you cannot print certain types of statistics. For example, National Widgets might want to print the percentage each customer's order total represents of the total for the state or the ratio of the state total to the grand total. This is impossible because when dBASE IV prints the detail record, it has not yet finished accumulating the subtotal for the group; when the state totals are printed, the grand totals are not yet known.

Saving a Report Form

You can save a report form on disk and continue working on the report design screen by selecting the **Save this report design** option from the **Layout** menu, or you can save the form and exit to the Control Center or the dot prompt by selecting the **Save changes and exit** option from the **Exit** menu. As with labels, you can print a report from the **Print** menu without exiting the report layout editor and without saving the report form, but it is always wise to save a form before you attempt to print in case a communication problem between the computer and the printer causes the system to hang up and forces you to reboot.

Each time you save a report form, dBASE IV prompts you for a file name; if you have already named the form, the name is displayed as the default, which

```
Printed: 10/19/91                                                    Page   1

                           National Widgets, Inc.
                       Customer Order Summary by State

Account     Company Name                  Y-T-D Orders   Total Orders   Years
----------  -------------------------     ------------   ------------   -----

Customers in CA:
----------------
LEWIS       Lewis and Associates                366.81       3,482.48     6.0
ABCPLUMB    ABC Plumbing                        796.41       5,248.90     3.9
                                          ------------   ------------
   Totals for 2 customers:                    1,163.22       8,731.38

   Average time since first order:                                        5.0

Customers in OR:
----------------
KLEIN       Carol Klein, M.D.                     0.00       1,053.89     5.0
                                          ------------   ------------
   Totals for 1 customers:                        0.00       1,053.89

   Average time since first order:                                        5.0

Customers in CA:
----------------
MTK         M.T.K. Industries                   108.59         823.92     4.3
                                          ------------   ------------
   Totals for 1 customers:                      108.59         823.92

   Average time since first order:                                        4.3

Customers in WA:
----------------
ANDERSON                                          0.00         832.58     4.2
                                          ------------   ------------
   Totals for 1 customers:                        0.00         832.58

   Average time since first order:                                        4.2

Customers in CA:
----------------
RAPIDTYPE   RapidType Secretarial Svc           348.52         348.52     0.6
                                          ------------   ------------
   Totals for 1 customers:                      348.52         348.52

   Average time since first order:                                        0.6

Customers in OR:
----------------
PHOENIX     Phoenix Construction                  0.00         249.59     4.3
                                          ------------   ------------
   Totals for 1 customers:                        0.00         249.59

   Average time since first order:                                        4.3
```

Figure 12-13.

Printing a report with group bands without activating the right index you can either accept by pressing ENTER or change to save the file under another name. Like label forms, report forms are stored on disk in two different types of files. The design specifications are stored in a file with the first name you assigned and the extension FRM. This file stores the report layout in the form required by the report layout editor so you can later modify the form. From the specifications in the FRM file, dBASE IV generates a program with the same first name as the FRM file and the extension FRG (a combination of FRM and PRG), which is executed to print the report.

PRINTING REPORTS

You can display or print reports from within the report layout editor, from the Control Center, or from the dot prompt. As with labels, you can control the sequence in which records are printed by sorting or indexing, and you can establish record selection criteria by defining a view query or by using a filter, scope, FOR clause, or WHILE clause.

From the Menus

You can print a report directly from the **Print** menu on the report design screen. To print from the Control Center, you select the name of the report form from the **Reports** panel and then choose **Print report** from the pop-up dialog box. Because dBASE IV stores in the catalog a reference to the data base or view that was active when you created the report, you need not open a data base before you issue the print command unless you want to use a different data base file or view. If you do open a new file, dBASE IV displays the name of the default data base or view in a dialog box and allows you to confirm your intentions to print using the current view or switch back to the default.

When you print from the Control Center, dBASE IV displays the same **Print** menu that you can access directly from the report layout editor. This menu allows you to customize many print attributes for an individual print run (these are detailed in Chapter 13) before you choose **View report on screen** or **Begin printing**. Because it is easier to align paper than label stock, there is no option analogous to **Generate sample labels** on the report **Print** menu; dBASE IV assumes that the printhead is positioned at the upper left corner of the first sheet of paper when you issue the **Begin printing** command.

If you choose to view a report on screen, dBASE IV pauses after each screenful of data and displays the message "Cancel viewing: ESC, Continue viewing: SPACEBAR" on the message line at the bottom of the screen to remind you how to display the next screen or abort the report. When you print on paper, dBASE IV displays a message box to remind you that you can "Press ESC to cancel, CTRL-S to pause and then any key to resume printing." (If you are also viewing the report on screen, this reminder is displayed on the message line.) The message box also explains that although dBASE IV stops sending data to the printer when you press ESC or CTRL-S, a printer with an internal buffer may not stop printing immediately. When you cancel a print job, remember to stop the computer first by pressing ESC. After dBASE IV has stopped transmitting data, press the printer's reset switch or turn the printer off to clear the buffer.

From the Dot Prompt

From the dot prompt, you use the REPORT FORM command to print a previously defined report. You must open a data base file or view before you issue the REPORT FORM command, but this need not be the same one that was active when you defined the report form (of course, it must have a compatible structure). You may also want to activate an index tag or NDX index to control the order in which records are printed on the report. The syntax of the REPORT FORM command is as follows:

REPORT FORM *report form name*

If you do not specify the name of the report form, dBASE IV prompts you to "Enter report filename." By default, reports are displayed on screen, but you can route the output to the printer as well by adding the phrase TO PRINT to the REPORT FORM command, or to a disk file by adding the phrase TO FILE followed by a name for the output file you want to create. You can use any combination of methods you know to establish record selection criteria. For example, you could print the report shown in Figure 12-11 using a report form called NWCPHONE for customers in California whose credit is good by using the following sequence of commands:

```
USE NWCUST ORDER STATECITY
SEEK "CA"
REPORT FORM NWCPHONE TO PRINT WHILE STATE = "CA" FOR CREDITOK
```

From the dot prompt, you can access some of the features available through the **Print** menu by adding special keywords to the REPORT FORM command. Although most of these options are explained in Chapter 13, which details all the **Print** menu choices, three options that are applicable only when you work at the dot prompt deserve mention here. The PLAIN option causes dBASE IV to suppress the date and page number (if the report header includes these items) on all pages and to print the page header only on the very first page and the page footer only on the last page of the report. This option is useful when you print a report to a disk file (using methods covered in Chapter 13) for later inclusion in a word processing document; in this situation, it is preferable to let the word processor paginate the listing.

When you print a report with group bands, you can suppress the detail band and print only the group header and summary bands by adding the keyword SUMMARY to the report form command. This option enables you to use the same report form to print either full detail or summary statistics, without having to edit the report form and open or close the detail band. For example, you could print only the state totals on the National Widgets order summary by state with the following:

```
USE NWCUST ORDER STATECITY
REPORT FORM NWCORD1 TO PRINT SUMMARY
```

The output is identical to the printout shown in Figure 12-9, which was obtained by closing the detail band before printing the report.

You can also include an additional line of header text in the REPORT FORM command, introduced by the HEADING keyword. dBASE IV prints this text centered on one or more lines at the very top of the page header band. The report layout editor does not have an equivalent menu option, one in which you could type the text in the page header band and delete or change it later. The HEADING clause is intended to enable you to include an "extra" line of text describing a particular print job without having to edit the report form again. You might use this extra header line to print the values of memory variables used in calculations or to reiterate the criteria used to select records for the report, as in the following:

```
REPORT FORM NWCORD1 TO PRINT FOR CREDITOK
   HEADING "Customers with Approved Credit Only"
```

SUMMARY

This chapter introduced the dBASE IV report layout editor and described how to design and print the most common type of report—columnar layouts, in which selected fields are lined up in columns, usually with headings at the top and summary statistics at the bottom. The dBASE IV report editor is a powerful and flexible tool that enables you to define a wide variety of reports. While it may take just a few minutes to set up a simple report, you may spend considerable time laying out and fine-tuning a complex report that requires calculated fields, subtotal groups, and summary statistics.

When you set up a new data base system, you may find that most of your attention during the early stages of development is focused on entering and editing data, but ultimately, the printed reports produced are the most important component of the application. Report and label output is the primary vehicle for sharing your data and the results of the calculations and manipulations your application performs on the raw data with other people, many of whom may know nothing about dBASE IV. Producing attractive, easy-to-read printouts that clearly convey the necessary information to the reader requires not only a technical understanding of how to use the report editor, but also some attention to the esthetic aspects of the layout.

If you are new to dBASE IV, you may want to try constructing the reports used as examples in this chapter, and printing these reports for various subsets of the sample data bases. If you are developing your own application, you might begin with the columnar reports that you already know you need. In either case, make sure that you know how to establish selection criteria for a print job, and that you understand the relationship between the report band structure and the order in which dBASE IV processes the file that supplies the data, to ensure that reports with group bands and summary statistics are complete and accurate.

CHAPTER THIRTEEN

Customizing Label and Report Forms

Chapters 11 and 12 introduced the layout editors used to create and edit label and report forms, and explained how to print labels and reports from the menus and from the dot prompt. Although these chapters emphasized the content rather than the form of these printouts, dBASE IV offers a variety of commands that enable you to customize and enhance the appearance of reports and labels.

If your printer is supported by dBASE IV and you selected the right printer driver when you installed the software, you do not have to understand the intricacies of printer control codes to access special print features—you can select the character pitch, line spacing, and type font, and use enhancements such as boldfacing and underlining. For example, you could fit a wide report onto 8 1/2-inch-wide paper by printing in "compressed" print (approximately 16 to 20 characters per inch, depending on the printer), print a page title in a larger font to make it stand out, switch from draft quality to near letter quality or correspondence quality print mode on a dot-matrix printer to print the final copy of a report, and boldface or underline text or fields for emphasis.

If you understand your printer's command language, you can access additional special features. This chapter describes how to turn on special fonts by sending control codes directly to the printer, and Chapter 18 explains how to define up to five custom fonts for each printer so that these additional fonts appear in the **Print** menu along with the standard choices.

The dBASE IV **Print** menu offers a variety of options for choosing the output device and customizing other aspects of a particular print run. You can route the report output to a printer, the screen, or a text file and specify the page dimensions, line spacing, print quality, and pagination. Although you must be aware of how the numerous options interact, the purposes of all the print settings are easy to understand, and they are useful even to a novice.

The commands and options explained in this chapter apply to both reports and labels, and this chapter assumes that you are familiar with the report and label form design work surfaces and menus. The commands and menu options in this chapter are organized according to their purpose and use rather than their positions in the menu tree. You may want to refer to the menu diagrams in Figures 12-1 and 13-1 or to Appendix B to find the features you need as you begin to design and print reports.

ACCESSING SPECIAL PRINTER FEATURES

In order to produce standard print enhancements such as boldfacing and underlining, which are supported by virtually all printers, as well as additional fonts and features that are unique to certain printers, dBASE IV uses *printer drivers*. A printer driver is a file that contains the commands or instructions used to control the printer (these commands are different for each printer). Chapter 18 describes how to configure dBASE IV to use up to four different printer drivers (in addition to two "generic" drivers that are always available), how to access up to five special fonts on each, and how to choose which driver should be used as the default destination for printed output. This chapter assumes that you or someone else in your organization has already carried out this configuration step; if you have not, you may want to refer to Chapter 18 now, or review this chapter after you have read Chapter 18.

When you print reports with dBASE IV, you can control the appearance of text by using commands and options that affect the entire report, a single band, or any arbitrary section of a band. The overall settings are located on the **Print** menu, which is diagrammed in Figure 13-1. The options that act on one band

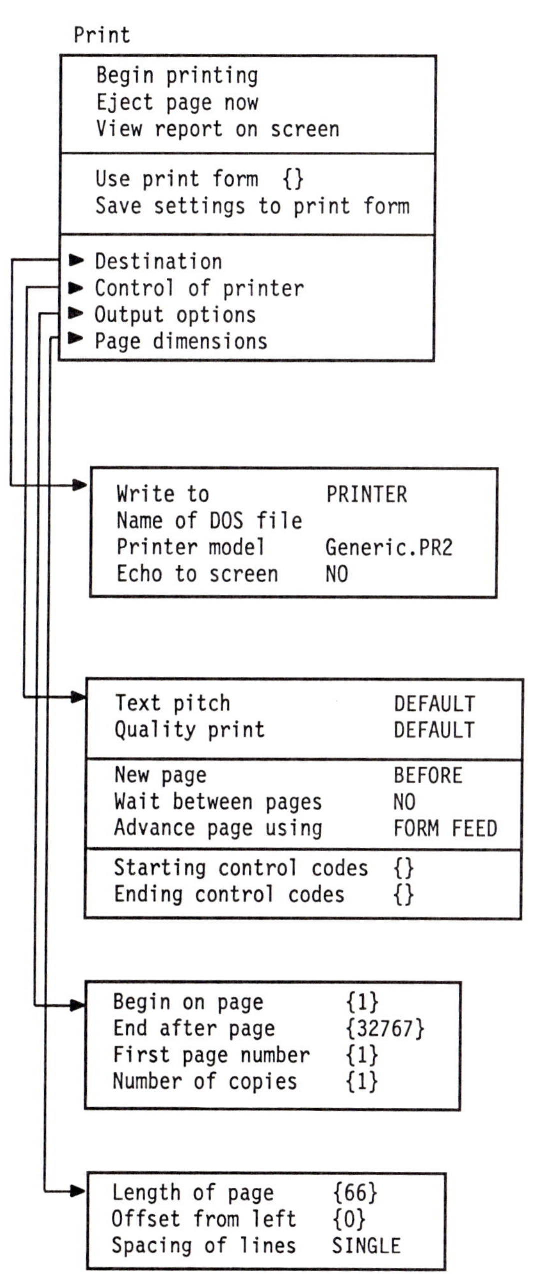

Figure 13-1.

The structure of the Print menu

are on the **Bands** menu (these options apply only to reports, not to labels), and the commands that format portions of a band are on the **Words** menu. The availability of so many options, which can be combined in different ways as you see fit, affords a great deal of flexibility for customizing the appearance of the reports and labels that you generate with dBASE IV.

Establishing the Overall Report Format

You access the options that establish the overall report format through a dialog box invoked by selecting the **Control of printer** option from the **Print** menu. Because the **Print** menu is displayed whenever you print labels or a report through the menu system, you can set these options for a particular print run without editing the label or report form or saving the settings. As you will see later in this chapter, you can also store personalized combinations of the **Print** menu settings on disk so that you can print any report or label form using the same combination of options or print the same report using different settings.

The **Text pitch** option allows you to set the default pitch (horizontal spacing) to **PICA** (10 cpi), **ELITE** (12 cpi), or **CONDENSED** (16 to 20 cpi depending on the printer). If you have a dot-matrix printer with a "near letter quality" print mode, you can choose this mode instead of the faster draft mode by setting the **Quality print** option to **Yes**. If you set either option to **DEFAULT** (the default setting), dBASE IV does not send control commands affecting the setting to the printer and leaves the current printer status unchanged. You should retain the **DEFAULT** setting if you prefer to select the pitch or print mode by using switches on the printer or by entering commands on the printer's control panel.

As with many other dBASE IV menu options that offer a finite number of choices, you select the **Text pitch** and **Quality print** by pressing the spacebar or the ENTER key to cycle through the possibilities and then close the dialog box by pressing ESC, CTRL-END, or one of the arrow keys. If the printer driver that is in effect when you try to print the report or labels does not support your choice for **Text pitch** or **Quality print**, dBASE IV displays the error message "Current printer driver does not support quality."

Keep in mind that regardless of the method used to select the pitch, it is your responsibility to ensure that it is appropriate for the report layout and the paper on which you are printing. If you design a report that is 130 characters wide, intending to print either on wide paper or in condensed print on 8 1/2- by 11-inch paper, you must either set the correct pitch using the **Text pitch** option or you must select the right pitch or font on the printer's control panel before you begin printing. If a report line does not fit within the page width, dBASE IV either wraps the data onto two or more lines (on most dot-matrix printers) or truncates it (on many laser printers).

If you understand your printer's command language, you can use the **Starting control codes** and **Ending control codes** options on the **Control of printer** menu to define two command sequences, which dBASE IV sends to the printer at the beginning and end of the report, respectively. Like the "setup string" used by Lotus 1-2-3 and other spreadsheets, you can use these options to access print features that are not supported directly by dBASE IV. For example, you might enter the command to switch to a special font on a laser printer as the **Starting control codes** entry and the command to return to the built-in Courier font under **Ending control codes**. If you are unsure about the ending codes, you can restore any printer to its default start-up condition by turning it off briefly and then turning it back on. (Turning off the printer is not a good idea if you share a printer with other users on a network, since part of another user's print job may already be in the printer's buffer.)

For the uninitiated, a short course in printer control commands is in order. Most printers (including dot-matrix, daisy wheel, laser, and inkjet) are controlled by two types of commands: single *control characters* and longer *escape sequences* (command sequences that begin with ESC, the character generated by pressing the ESC key). For example, on most Epson printers, CTRL-O turns on compressed print, and ESC-G initiates double-strike printing.

Your printer manual should have a complete list of the commands used to access its special features. Because there is no one standard notation for describing printer control codes, you may find the codes identified by key names (such as CTRL-O or ESC), or by the ASCII codes used internally to represent the characters. To make matters more confusing, ASCII codes may be listed as decimal (base 10) or hexadecimal (base 16) numbers. If you need to look up codes or convert hexadecimal to decimal, refer to the ASCII table in Appendix G of the dBASE IV *Language Reference* manual.

When you choose the **Starting control codes** or **Ending control codes** option, dBASE IV prompts you to "Enter a string," but you cannot enter a command sequence such as ESC-G by pressing the ESC key followed by the G key. ESC has its own meaning in dBASE IV: to cancel the command or operation in progress and return to the previous menu or prompt. Pressing the ESC key returns you to the **Control of printer** dialog box rather than entering an ESC character into the printer control string. To circumvent this problem, you must express the characters that have special meanings to dBASE IV via their decimal (base 10) ASCII codes or by using special key names enclosed in braces (curly brackets). For example, you can express the ESC character as {27}, {ESC}, or {ESCAPE}. Using this notation, you could enter the command to initiate compressed print on the Epson as {CTRL-O} or {15}; ESC-G could be expressed as {ESC}G or {27}G. All the special key names and the corresponding ASCII codes are listed in Table 13-1.

Formatting Report Bands

The methods explained in the previous section specify print attributes that apply to an entire report or label run. You can also set the text pitch, print quality, and line spacing for one report band by using options on the **Bands** menu. Unlike the **Print** menu settings, the **Bands** options are accessible only from the report design screen, and dBASE IV saves your selections with the report form. If you want to change one of these settings for a single print run, you can edit the report form, print the report from within the report layout editor, and exit without saving the changed form.

It is convenient to be able to set some of the print options one band at a time, because frequently the report bands are used for different types of information that demand different visual presentations. For example, if you use the report intro band to print a cover sheet, cover letter, or narrative report introduction, you might want to print this band double-spaced at 12 characters per inch using near letter quality print mode; for the tabular data in the body of the report, draft quality might be adequate; and condensed print might be required to accommodate a wide report.

To set the vertical spacing for a band, you use the **Spacing of lines for band** option, which allows you to select **SINGLE**, **DOUBLE**, or **TRIPLE** spacing. The **Text pitch for band** and **Quality print for band** options offer the same choices that were explained in the previous section: You can select **PICA**, **ELITE**, or **CONDENSED** for the pitch and set the **Quality print for band** option to **Yes** to select near letter quality print mode on a dot-matrix printer. Like the corresponding options on the **Print** menu, these three options offer a **DEFAULT** setting (which is the default), but selecting **DEFAULT** on the **Bands** menu has a slightly different effect: it instructs dBASE IV to print the band using the settings established overall for the report on the **Print** menu (which may or may not match the printer's control panel settings).

Key Name	ASCII Code
{CTRL-@} or {NULL}	0
{CTRL-A}	1
{CTRL-B}	2
{CTRL-C}	3
{CTRL-D}	4
{CTRL-E}	5
{CTRL-F}	6
{CTRL-G} or {BELL}	7
{CTRL-H} or {BACKSPACE}	8
{CTRL-I} or {TAB}	9
{CTRL-J} or {LINEFEED}	10
{CTRL-K}	11
{CTRL-L}	12
{CTRL-M} or {RETURN}	13
{CTRL-N}	14
{CTRL-O}	15
{CTRL-P}	16
{CTRL-Q}	17
{CTRL-R}	18
{CTRL-S}	19
{CTRL-T}	20
{CTRL-U}	21
{CTRL-V}	22
{CTRL-W}	23
{CTRL-X}	24
{CTRL-Y}	25
{CTRL-Z}	26
{CTRL-[} or {ESC} or {ESCAPE}	27
{CTRL-\}	28
{CTRL-]}	29
{CTRL-^}	30
{CTRL-_}	31
{DEL} or {DELETE}	127

Table 13-1.

The Special Key Names

Formatting Within a Report Band

You can access five standard print styles—boldfacing, underlining, italics, superscript, and subscript—for any arbitrary section of a label form or report band through the **Style** option on the **Words** menu. Because you might want to apply these styles to portions of a report ranging from a single word or field to an entire band, you must use the same method employed by many word processors to format existing text: First, select the items you want to format, and then choose the style. You can use the F6 (Select) key to select any rectangular area *within one report band;* with the desired text and fields selected, choose the **Style** option from the **Words** menu, and set the desired print features **ON**.

You can combine styles in any reasonable manner. For example, you can turn on **Bold** and **Underline** at the same time. If you request a feature that your printer does not support, dBASE IV substitutes underlining when it prints the report. You can also configure dBASE IV to access up to five special fonts on each printer specified when you installed the software, using methods that are explained in Chapter 18. If you have installed any special fonts, they are listed in the bottom half of the **Style** pick list. You can use these styles alone or in any combination with the five standard choices.

Because you can install a variety of print styles and fonts, many of which could be simulated onscreen only by using high-resolution graphics, dBASE IV does not attempt to represent fonts or special attributes on the screen exactly as they will print. Boldfaced text is displayed using bright characters, and all other styles are represented by inverse video or a contrasting set of colors on a color monitor so that you can verify that the text is enhanced. If you need to identify the actual enhancement, you can redisplay the **Styles** menu with the cursor positioned anywhere in the text, and check which print styles are set **ON**.

Regardless of the pitch or type size, all characters occupy an equal amount of space on the screen, so the alignment of the various report elements may not match the final appearance of the printed page. This will present problems only if you use different type sizes for adjacent sections of a report that must be aligned precisely. For example, if you print column headings in the page header band in a larger, wider font than the data printed in the columns below, you may need to print the report several times to adjust the spacing so that the data is positioned directly below the headings. If you define a special font, dBASE IV does not "know" its pitch or size; it only knows the control codes required to turn the font on and off. Some experimentation may be required to fine-tune the placement of text and fields printed in any of the five custom styles.

Drawing Lines and Boxes

You can draw lines and boxes composed of single or double lines or any other character by using the **Box** and **Line** options on the **Layout** menu. If your printer supports graphics characters, these lines are printed using the same continuous-line characters that are displayed onscreen; otherwise, dBASE IV substitutes dashes, colons, and plus signs. To draw a box, select **Box** from the **Layout** menu, and choose the line-drawing character from the pop-up dialog box. You can choose **Single line**, **Double line**, or **Using specified character**.

If you select **Using specified character**, dBASE IV displays a pick list that includes all the printable characters in the standard IBM extended ASCII character set. Although the pick list includes the decimal and hexadecimal ASCII codes for reference, you will usually find the character you want by searching visually, and then select it from the pick list by highlighting it and pressing ENTER. In most cases, you should not choose a control character (a character that has an ASCII code below 32) as your box- or line-drawing character. As explained earlier in this chapter, control characters are widely used as printer control commands, so most printers cannot reproduce the onscreen graphics representations of these characters; instead, the printer attempts to interpret them as commands and gives you results that you may not have anticipated.

After you select the box-drawing character, dBASE IV prompts you with the following message at the bottom of the screen: "Position upper left of box with cursor keys, complete with ENTER." The box-drawing character is displayed within the cursor as you move around the work surface. After you set the upper left corner, dBASE IV instructs you to "Stretch box with cursor keys, complete with ENTER." As you move the cursor to the position of the lower right corner, the box expands to surround the indicated portion of the work surface. When you select a graphics character other than the standard single or double line for the box border, dBASE IV fills in the corners with matching characters to create a smooth, continuous box. Drawing a horizontal or vertical line is similar; using the same command sequence you use to draw a box, you define the line by indicating the two endpoints.

More often than not, boxes and lines are used to enclose text or to separate regions on a page, but dBASE IV treats boxes and lines as independent entities separate from any text and fields on the work surface, including text that falls within a box or coincides with a line or box border. You can move or copy the text inside a box without affecting the box itself, and you can move or copy only the box. You select a line or box by placing the cursor anywhere on the line or box border and pressing F6 (Select) and then ENTER. You can select just the text within a box, but not the box border, by pressing F6 (Select) twice with the cursor anywhere within the box. To select both a box and its contents, place the cursor on the box border and press F6 (Select) three times.

THE PRINT MENU

When you print labels or reports from any point in the menu system, dBASE IV displays essentially the same **Print** menu, which you can use to control many aspects of the print job. You can specify where to direct the output of the report, eject the paper, define the page dimensions and range of pages to print, and customize some of the overall report format parameters. The structure of the **Print** menu is diagrammed in Figure 13-1.

The **Print** menu settings are arranged in three groups that are separated visually by horizontal lines in the menu frame. The options in the first group cause actions to take place immediately; these are used to eject the paper and initiate a print job. The two options in the middle group enable you to save the current print settings in a print form file on disk for future use or retrieve a previously stored form to establish the settings for the current print job. The third group of options allows you to select an output device, describe your paper forms, and format the report output. Each option in this group invokes a dialog box in which you make additional selections, either by entering information when requested or by pressing the spacebar or ENTER to display the available choices.

Choosing the Output Device

The output of a report or label run can be viewed onscreen, printed on any available printer, or sent to a text file on disk and later printed with the DOS PRINT command, edited and printed using a word processor, or incorporated into a larger word-processed document.

Chapters 11 and 12 explained how to view a report or label run on the screen: you select the **View report on screen** or **View labels on screen** options from the **Print** menu. These commands are equivalent to the **Begin printing** option: They initiate the print job immediately using the current print settings. If you need to customize any aspects of the print job using other **Print** menu options, you must do so before you choose the appropriate **View** option.

To select a printer or to route report or label output to a text file, you use the **Destination** option on the **Print** menu. First, select the **Write to** option to choose between a printer and a text file. If you select **DOS FILE**, you can accept the default file name, which has the same first name as the report form file and the extension PRT or TXT (if you use the ASCII Text printer driver described later in this section), or select the **Name of DOS file** option to assign a new name for the text file. The text file created by this command contains an exact image of the printed report, including all text, fields, blank lines, page breaks, and in most cases, printer control and formatting codes. Each line contains as many characters as dBASE IV would print on one line, and each line ends with a hard return.

In some cases, you might choose to send report or label output to a text file so that you can print it later, when a shared printer is less busy, or you might send the output of a long report to a disk file overnight and then print the file during the day, when you are available to refill the paper tray on a laser printer or attend to a paper jam. You might also want to incorporate all or part of a dBASE IV report in a larger document created with a word processing program. Although you can include quite a bit of text in a dBASE IV report and enhance the output with different print styles and fonts, the dBASE IV report layout editor does not match the capabilities of most word processors, to say nothing of desktop publishing software, in its editing or formatting capabilities. You will probably find the report design screen adequate for typing a simple report intro band consisting of several pages of text, but you might not want to use it for longer documents. You might also need to make use of print features such as proportional spacing, access more than five fonts in a report, or incorporate several short dBASE IV reports into a single long document with text passages in between. In all these cases, you can "print" the required dBASE IV reports to disk and read the output files into a document constructed with your word processor.

When you print either to a printer or a text file, you can use the **Echo to screen option** to determine whether or not dBASE IV also displays the report or labels on the screen. Note that dBASE IV cannot reproduce the appearance of most fonts and special print features on the screen, so the output echoed to the screen will not look exactly like the printout. On a wide report, long lines will wrap onto multiple screen lines. Viewing the report on the screen is useful for monitoring the progress of a print job when you route the output to a text file or when your printer is physically distant from the computer and you cannot easily see how many pages have printed.

The **Printer model** option enables you to choose a printer driver from among those that you selected when you first installed dBASE IV. The installation procedure also allows you to specify the default driver; if you did not choose a default driver, dBASE IV uses GENERIC.PR2 (which will work with virtually any printer) as the default. If you have more than one printer, if you have installed multiple drivers to control a single printer (for example, to achieve different line spacing or print in landscape orientation on a laser printer), or if you have requested print enhancements in your label or report form other than boldfacing or underlining, be sure to choose the right driver so that dBASE IV sends the correct control commands to the printer.

When you route report output to a text file, dBASE IV normally includes in this file the printer codes required to produce any enhancements specified in the report so that you can later print the report using software that lacks formatting capabilities. If you plan to incorporate the text file into a word processing document, the printer codes may cause problems; it is best to eliminate them entirely and format the document using the word processor's commands. You can create a text file that does not contain printer codes, even if the report or label form includes special print enhancements, by choosing **ASCII TEXT** as your **Printer model**. (The term "ASCII text file" is generally used to denote a text file containing only the normal printable characters you can generate from the keyboard: letters, numbers, and punctuation marks.) When you choose this driver, dBASE IV uses TXT rather than PRT as the default extension for the disk file that receives the output.

If you plan to incorporate a dBASE IV report into a word-processed document, you may want to suppress the page header and footer bands, and perhaps the report intro, and allow the word processor to paginate the listing. The dBASE IV data can then begin or end in the middle of another page that contains text, and you can number the pages consecutively in a single sequence. You cannot suppress report bands through the **Print** menu—you must edit the report form and close any bands that you do not want to print. As described in Chapter 12, when you print from the dot prompt, you can use command line options such as PLAIN (to suppress the headers and footers) or SUMMARY (to suppress the detail band).

Specifying Page Dimensions and Paper Type

You can define the size and shape of the paper forms used for a report with the **Output options, Page dimensions,** and **Control of printer** options on the **Print** menu. The page layout specifications are illustrated in Figure 13-2, superimposed on a typical report page.

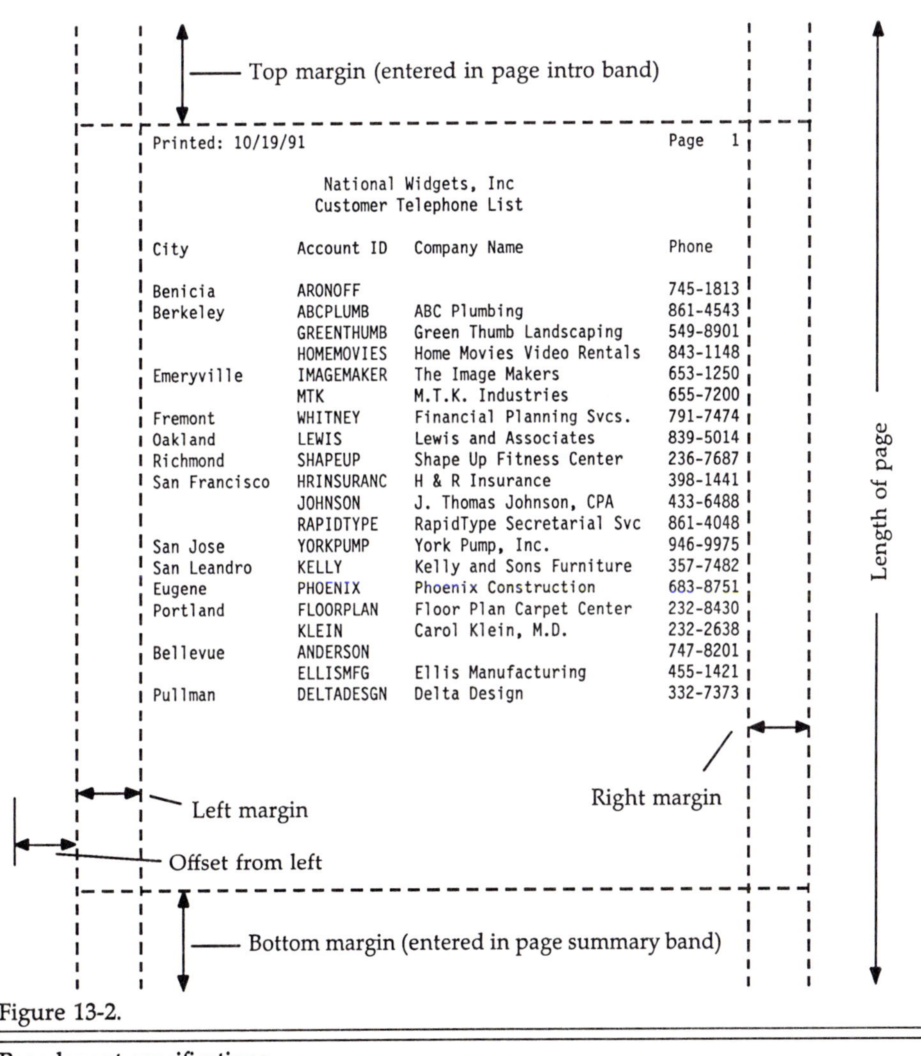

Figure 13-2.

Page layout specifications

The **Page dimensions** dialog box contains three selections. The **Length of page** setting specifies the physical length of the printed page in lines. The default is 66 lines, which is correct for printing on standard 11-inch continuous paper at 6 lines per inch (the default vertical line spacing set on most printers). Because the page length is defined in terms of lines rather than inches, you must change this setting if you print using a different vertical line spacing. For example, if you print at 8 lines per inch (a setting that works well with condensed print), a standard 11-inch page contains 88 lines. You must also change the page length to print on larger or smaller forms (such as continuous index card stock or envelopes), on single sheets of letterhead (most impact printers can use only about 10 inches of a hand-fed 11-inch sheet of paper), or on most laser printers, which cannot print on the top 1/4 inch or the bottom 1/4 inch of the page.

When you use forms of differing length, you must take into account the relationship between the form length you establish via the **Print** menu and the printer's internal form length setting. For example, most impact printers are set to print 66 lines per page, and when you issue a "form feed" command, either by pressing the form-feed button on the printer's control panel or by sending the "form-feed" character (decimal ASCII code 12, which is recognized by virtually all printers) through software, it advances the paper *based on this setting.* When you change the **Length of page** setting on the **Print** menu, *dBASE IV does not send a command to the printer to change its internal form length setting.* The **Length of page** setting only determines how many lines dBASE IV prints before sending the command to advance the paper to the top of the next sheet.

If the page length setting in your report does not match the printer's internal form length setting, the printer will advance the paper the wrong number of lines. For example, many laser printers are configured at the factory to print 58 lines per page. If you print a report on such a printer using the default page length setting of 66 lines per page, dBASE IV sends a form feed command to the printer every 66 lines. However, the printer automatically ejects the paper after receiving 58 lines of output, and the result is two sheets of paper for each report "page": the first with 58 lines and the second with the last 8.

Conversely, if the page length established through the **Print** menu is shorter than the printer's setting, the form feed command sent by dBASE IV will eject the paper too far. For example, if you are printing continuous-form invoices that are 8 inches long (48 lines at 6 lines per inch), dBASE IV will send a form feed command after printing 48 lines, and this command will advance the paper to a point 66 lines from the top of the first form, which will be somewhere in the middle of the second invoice. In most cases, it is easier to solve these problems by changing the *method* that dBASE IV uses to advance the paper than it is to reset the printer's internal form length setting.

You can control how dBASE IV advances the paper with the **Advance paper using** option. With **FORM FEED** (the default setting) selected, dBASE IV advances the paper by sending a "form feed" command to the printer. This method is appropriate only if the report page length matches the printer's internal form length setting. If you change the **Advance paper using** setting to **LINE FEEDS**, dBASE IV moves the paper by sending enough "line feed" commands (this is equivalent to printing blank lines) to reach the top of the next page, *based on the number of lines defined in the form.*

As mentioned in Chapter 11, laser printers present several special problems, especially when you print labels. First of all, most cannot print on the top or bottom 1/4 inch of a sheet of paper. You can buy sheets of gummed labels designed for laser printers, in which the first row of labels begins 1/2 inch down from the top of each sheet and the last ends 1/2 inch from the bottom. However, the dBASE IV label layout editor makes no provision for defining a top or bottom margin (in a report, you can create margins by adding blank lines to the page header and page footer bands). Also, the standard HP LaserJet printer drivers set the printer to print 66 lines per page by changing the vertical spacing to approximately 6.5 lines per inch. The difference is barely noticeable, and this solution is perfectly acceptable for printing reports, but if you print labels at 6.5 lines per inch, the data will not line up with the labels.

You can solve the vertical spacing problem, so that your data lines up properly on the labels, by choosing the right printer driver. The portrait mode drivers that print at 6 lines per inch print 60 lines per page, and the corresponding landscape drivers print 45 lines per page, so you must be sure to set your page length to match. (You should consult the dBASE IV documentation, in particular the *Release Notes* or *Change Summary* packaged with the version 1.1 upgrade, for information on the latest printer drivers.)

dBASE IV provides an additional mechanism for controlling pagination when you print labels: the DOS environment variable DTL_LBLOPT. If you assign this variable the value "ON", dBASE IV displays a menu of additional page layout options whenever you save a label form. Through this menu, which is pictured in Figure 13-3, you can set the top and bottom page margins, specify the method dBASE IV should use to advance the page (form feed or line feeds), and enable or disable widow checking. When widow checking is on, dBASE IV will not split a label across a page boundary. If the number of lines per page is evenly divisible by the number of lines occupied by each label, widow checking is unnecessary, but it does no harm to enable this feature. As

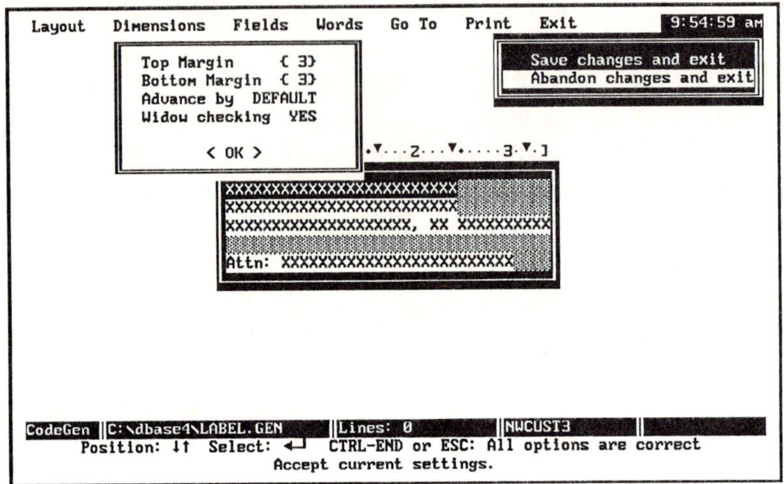

Figure 13-3.

The menu of page layout options triggered by the DTL_LBLOPT environment variable

always, it is your responsibility to ensure that the page length set through the **Print** menu matches the number of lines your printer can access on the label stock.

To set the DTL_LBLOPT variable, you type the following command at the DOS prompt (not the dBASE IV dot prompt):

```
SET DTL_LBLOPT=ON
```

You may want to put this command in your AUTOEXEC.BAT file if you frequently design dBASE IV labels for use on a laser printer or on single sheets of paper in an impact printer (in which case, you also cannot print on the first few or last few lines of each page).

If you have a laser printer for which Ashton-Tate does not supply an appropriate driver, you must establish the page margins and vertical spacing by sending commands to the printer. The easiest way to do this is by entering the appropriate printer commands as the **Starting control codes**. For example, the following command sets the top margin to 3 lines, the page length to 60 lines, and the vertical spacing to 6 lines per inch on the HP LaserJet II:

```
"{ESC}&l3e60f6D"
```

The remaining **Page dimensions** settings are much more straightforward than the **Length of page** option. The **Offset from left** option adds the specified number of spaces to the left margin defined in the report itself. You can use the page offset to compensate for differences in the width of the perforated strip on various types of continuous paper so that you do not have to adjust the tractors each time you switch forms. You might also want to use this setting to establish a wide left margin (to allow room for punching holes or binding a report) without wasting space on the screen when you define and edit the report form.

The **Spacing of lines** option sets the default line spacing for the report as a whole to **SINGLE**, **DOUBLE**, or **TRIPLE** spacing. As described earlier in this chapter, you can override the default for individual report bands by using the **Spacing of lines for band** option on the **Bands** menu.

The **Output options** selection on the **Print** menu allows you to control page numbering and specify how many complete copies of a report or sets of labels to print. You can use these options to reprint one section of a report or resume printing a report or label run from the point of interruption after a paper jam or if a lengthy print job is aborted in the middle to free the printer for a more important task. You specify the starting and ending page with the **Begin on page** and **End after page** options, respectively; by default, they are set to 1 and 32767 (the maximum permissible page number) so that dBASE IV prints the entire report. When you specify a range of page numbers, dBASE IV reads records starting from the top of the file (or index, if one is open), counts pages, and accumulates summary statistics as if it were printing the complete report; however, it does not begin sending output to the printer until it reaches the specified starting page, and it stops printing after the ending page is complete. Thus, if you restart a lengthy report in the middle, the grand totals printed at the end will be accurate, and you can combine the two sets of pages into one report.

The **First page number** option sets the number that dBASE IV prints on the first page of the report. You might want to adjust the starting page number to arrive at a single continuous numbering sequence when you combine several separate reports into a single package. If you print only part of a report that begins with a page number other than 1, be careful to specify the starting and ending page numbers (using the **Begin on page** and **End after page** options) relative to the first page number. For example, if you print page number 15 on the first physical page of a report, you must instruct dBASE IV to set the **Begin on page** option to 16 and the **End after page** option to 18 to reprint the second through fourth pages of the report.

You can print more than one copy of a report or set of labels by using the **Number of copies** option. In each copy, the pages are numbered consecutively starting with the number set using the **First page number** option. When you print multiple copies of a report or label set, *dBASE IV prints each copy from start to finish the specified number of times.* For example, if you request three copies of a set of labels, dBASE IV does not print three copies of the first label, three copies of the second, and so on—it prints one set of labels, starts again at the top of the file, prints the second set, and repeats the process a third time. In a report with summary statistics, you must remember to set the **Reset every** option to **< REPORT >** when you define the summary items printed in the report summary band (this is the default setting), in order to ensure that dBASE IV resets them to zero before beginning each new copy of the report.

Several options accessed through the **Control of printer** option on the **Print** menu allow you to control the way dBASE IV paginates a report. If you are printing on hand-fed forms, such as individual sheets of letterhead or envelopes, set the **Wait between pages** option to **Yes**. This setting causes dBASE IV to pause before printing each page to give you time to insert and adjust the paper; a modified version of the print status message box reminds you during the pause that you can continue printing by pressing the spacebar "after loading paper."

The **New page option** determines when dBASE IV sends a command to the printer to advance the paper to the top of the next form. This option enables you to avoid having to advance the paper manually by pressing the printer's form-feed button; it is especially convenient if the printer is far from your computer. You can select **BEFORE, AFTER, BOTH,** or **NONE.**

You would need a page eject *before* printing a report if you had just used another program or other dBASE IV print command (for example, LIST TO PRINT or LIST STRUCTURE TO PRINT) that does not paginate the output or eject the paper automatically when the printout is complete, or if you share a printer with other users and are not sure whether someone else's print job may have left the printer in the middle of a page. If you are printing only dBASE IV reports or label forms, you can eject the paper either before or after each print run. **NONE** is useful when you print several related reports in sequence to form a single set of pages. If you occasionally need to eject the paper without changing the overall report defaults, you can use the **Eject page now** option on the **Print** menu, which causes an immediate page eject, as if you had pressed the form-feed button on the printer.

If you use the same report or label form to print several reports in succession, dBASE IV retains the settings for options that you are likely to reuse, including the **Destination** options, the **Control of printer** options, the first page number, page length, left offset, and line spacing. Printer settings that are temporary or unique to a particular print run—the starting and ending page numbers and number of copies—revert to the default settings after each report or label run.

USING PRINT FORMS

If you frequently use certain combinations of **Print** menu options, you can save the settings in print form files on disk to avoid having to reenter them. You can create as many print forms as you like and use any print form with any report or label form. In some cases, you may want to use several print forms to produce different versions of the same report. For example, you might print a preliminary copy of a report on 14-inch paper using draft quality on a dot-matrix printer and produce the finished version on a laser printer in landscape mode in a small font. You might also define several standard print forms, each of which can be used with many different report or label forms. If you have more than one printer, or if you frequently print reports to disk, using print forms is a convenient way to reset all the relevant print parameters before each report or label run.

If you edit a report or label form and change any print settings, except the ones considered transitory that automatically revert to the defaults after every report run, dBASE IV offers to save the current settings in a print form when you save the edited report or label form. If you select **Yes** in answer to the question "Print form settings are new or changed. Do you want to save them?" dBASE IV prompts you to enter a name for the print form file. The default form name has the same first name as the current report or label form and the extension PRF. It is advisable to retain the default name for print forms that are used with only one report or label form. If you intend to use the same print form with many different report or label forms, you may want to make the name very general or more descriptive of the settings established through the print form. For example, you might use the name DRAFT.EPS for a form that you use to print rough drafts on an Epson printer, and name the form that describes the high-quality final copy QUALITY.EPS.

You can save the current print settings at any time by selecting the **Save settings to print form** option on the **Print** menu and entering a name for the print form file. To use a previously saved print form with the current report or label form, you select **Use print form** from the **Print** menu and then choose from a pick list of available print forms. If a print form is active when you save a report or label form, dBASE IV stores the name of this form in the report or label form. Every time you edit the report form or print the report, the settings stored in this print form are used as defaults. Of course, you can override any of these settings by using the individual options on the **Print** menu, and you can specify a new form as the default by editing the report form, loading a new print form with the **Use print form** option, and saving the report form again.

PRINTING FROM THE DOT PROMPT

When you print labels or a report from the dot prompt, dBASE IV does not display the **Print** menu, and you must use different methods to control the print job. You can specify some of the options available throught the **Print** menu, as well as several that are applicable only when you print from the dot prompt, by adding keywords to the REPORT FORM or LABEL FORM command. Chapter 12 described the SUMMARY keyword, which suppresses the detail band in a report with group bands; the PLAIN keyword, which suppresses the page number and date and causes dBASE IV to print the page header and footer bands only once, at the very beginning and end of the report, respectively; and the HEADING clause, which allows you to specify an extra line of heading text that is added to the report intro band.

You can use the NOEJECT keyword to prevent dBASE IV from sending a form feed command to the printer before it starts to print the report, as if you had set the **New page** option on the **Print** menu to **AFTER**. You can direct the report to a disk file by adding the phrase TO FILE, followed by a file name, instead of specifying the report destination by using the **Print** menu **Destination** option. For example, you could print the customer order summary to a disk file with the same name as the report form with the following:

```
USE NWCUST ORDER STATECITY
REPORT FORM NWCORDER TO FILE NWCORDER
```

The best way to customize a group of **Print** menu settings for use when you print from the dot prompt is to store them in a print form, which includes nearly all the **Print** menu settings. Note, however, that *when you print from the dot prompt, dBASE IV does not automatically use the printer driver or print form stored with the report or label form.* You must identify these files before you print by assigning their names to two *system memory variables* named _PDRIVER and _PFORM. For example, you could select the Epson printer driver and the QUALITY.EPS print form with the following commands:

```
_PFORM = "QUALITY.EPS"
_PDRIVER = "FX85_1"
```

The print form includes the name of the printer driver, so if you are sure that the form specifies the right driver, you need not assign a value to _PDRIVER. If you are not sure, or if you want to select a printer driver other than the one stored in the print form, make sure that you assign the driver name to _PDRIVER *after* you assign the print form name to _PFORM, so that the new driver overrides the one stored in the print form.

If you understand your printer's command language, you can send commands directly to the printer from the dot prompt by using the ??? command. Just as when you enter starting and ending control codes through the **Control of printer** option on the **Print** menu, you can enter control codes using the key names listed in Table 13-1. The ??? command is a variation of the ? command introduced in Chapter 10; it sends characters directly to the printer without advancing the printhead so that the alignment of subsequent output is not disrupted. You must enclose printer commands in quotes, and you can express them as any combination of ASCII codes, special key names, and ordinary text characters. For example, you could send the ESC-G command, which initiates double-strike mode on an Epson printer, with any of the following commands:

```
??? "{ESC}G"
```

or

```
??? "{27}G"
```

or

```
??? "{27}{71}"
```

SUMMARY

The dBASE IV **Print** menu offers a wide variety of options for controlling the printing process and customizing the appearance of the output produced by a report or label form. If you have used previous versions of dBASE, most of these features will be entirely new. If you are just beginning to learn dBASE IV, you may find the sheer number of choices overwhelming, and the interaction between the various settings can be even more confusing. As you design increasingly complex reports, you may want to return to this chapter to review the individual settings that you need to accomplish a particular goal.

For the most part, it is easier to learn and experiment with the various print settings from within the menu system, where you can navigate through the **Print** menu and its submenus to find the options you need. In particular, you may want to print from within the report or label layout editor during the design stages, because you can fine-tune the print settings and adjust your form specifications at the same time. Printing from within the forms editors is far less time-consuming than repeatedly editing a form, saving it, and then printing it from the dot prompt or the Control Center.

Note also that dBASE IV offers more flexible mechanisms for exerting precise control over the printing process when you generate reports and labels through the menu system. Even if you work primarily at the dot prompt, you may prefer to execute print commands from the report design screen or from the Control Center, so that you can change settings on the **Print** menu if you need to change settings for different print runs based on the same report or label form. If you repeatedly use several different standard sets of printer settings, it is more efficient to save these settings in print forms so that you do not have to choose all of the required options individually before a print run.

CHAPTER FOURTEEN

Printing Form and Mailmerge Reports

Chapter 12 described how to design and print columnar reports, in which the fields in a record are lined up in columns, often with subtotals or other summary statistics at the bottoms of the columns. In many cases, a record in a column layout occupies only one line, although dBASE IV does not place any restrictions on the depth of the detail band in this or any other type of report. The introduction to Chapter 12 mentioned the other two basic report styles that dBASE IV supports: form and mailmerge layouts. This chapter covers these layouts in greater detail and suggests some typical applications.

If you are reading this book in sequence and have followed the examples, you should already be familiar with the label and report layout editors, and you should feel reasonably comfortable using the commands provided for moving around the work surface and constructing a report layout. In Chapter 13, you learned how to enhance the appearance of text and fields on a dBASE IV report and how to use the **Print** menu options to select a printer, describe your basic page layout and page dimensions, and customize other aspects of individual print jobs. This chapter does not repeat material covered earlier; it concentrates on the features that distinguish form and mailmerge layouts and on strategies for designing and using these types of reports effectively.

Keep in mind that despite the three Quick Layouts on the report editor **Layout** menu—column, form, and mailmerge—and the organization of the report chapters in this book, dBASE IV does not limit you to these three basic report styles when you create your own forms. Although the classification is useful as a framework for discussion, and it accurately describes several general, frequently used types of reports, many of the reports that you create will be "hybrids" that combine some of the features of two or all three of the basic layouts. You have already seen that you can print more than one line of data per record in a column layout. Similarly, a form layout can include features that you may normally associate with columnar reports, such as group bands with summary statistics, but the statistics are generally not printed in such close proximity to the fields from which they are derived.

Although word wrap bands are the hallmark of mailmerge layouts, any report can contain a word wrap band, for example, to print a report introduction or a closing statement. You can also add bands to a mailmerge layout that are typically associated with column or form layouts, such as report header and footer bands. As you will see in Chapter 17, reports that combine information from two or more data base files often use features of more than one report layout. For example, an invoice or statement consists of a "header" portion containing the customer's name and address, followed by a "detail" or "line item" section that closely resembles the basic columnar layout.

DESIGNING FORM LAYOUTS

In a form layout, sometimes referred to as a full-page form or page-oriented report (in contrast to the line-oriented columnar layout), the fields from a record are laid out vertically, or spread out across the printed page. As the name suggests, form layouts can be used to "fill in the blanks" on preprinted forms such as insurance claim forms, medical records, and personnel forms, or, if your printer supports the required fonts and type sizes, to reproduce a form in its entirety, including both data and background text. In reports like these, one record usually occupies a whole page or more than one page. Other form layouts, such as a customer list or a membership referral directory, may require only a few lines for each record. The distinguishing feature of the form layout is that no distinct columns appear in the printout: fields and text can be placed independently anywhere on the page.

Form layouts are also well suited for a class of report that might be called a "complete reference list"—a listing of all or most of the information in a data base (or several related data bases), printed for all or selected records. These reference lists, which function as the computerized analogs of paper forms such as ledger cards and personnel records, serve several purposes. You can distribute a printed list to colleagues and coworkers who do not or should not have access to the information online. Even for the everyday users of a data base, finding information on a report is often easier and faster than looking it up on-screen. This is especially true if the need for the information arises while the computer is running a different application or is occupied carrying out another time-consuming dBASE IV procedure. Finally, a reference list, if it is printed often enough, can provide an extra measure of protection against the loss of data. If your data base is damaged by a hardware or software "crash," the printout can help you verify the accuracy of the data after you recover the data bases from a backup, or, as a last resort, can allow you to reenter the data if the backup proves faulty.

Keep in mind when you design form layouts based on preprinted forms that dBASE IV defines report coordinates in terms of printer positions, not in an absolute measure such as inches or centimeters. If you position a field at column 12, the field will print 1 inch from the left side of the page if you print the report in elite type (12 characters per inch), whereas in pica type (10 cpi), it will be almost 1 1/4 inches from the left side. If you are attempting to superimpose data on a preprinted form, a transparent overlay with a grid that matches the report spacing can be very helpful. Such overlays are available through stationery and office suppliers.

Be particularly careful if you mix fonts and type sizes within a line. As noted in Chapter 13, if you defined special fonts for your printer when you installed dBASE IV (the procedure for doing this is covered in Chapter 18), the program can send the required commands to the printer, but it "knows" nothing about a font except how to turn it on and off, and it cannot take into account the size of the characters or change the horizontal spacing to match the font size. Some experimentation may be necessary to align all the report items properly on the printed form.

Using the Quick Form Layout

Recall from Chapter 12 that you can use the **Quick layouts** option on the report design screen **Layout** menu to choose one of three Quick Layouts. To create a Quick Form Layout, choose **Form layout** from the pick list that pops up when you select the **Quick layouts** option. Figure 14-1 illustrates the detail band from the Quick Form Layout generated for the National Widgets Customer File. The Quick Form Layout looks much like the Edit screen—it includes all the fields in the data base, arranged vertically in the detail band, with the field names as prompts. To improve clarity and readability, dBASE IV places each field at column 12 so that the fields line up regardless of the lengths of the prompts.

In most cases, the template that dBASE IV assigns to set the width of a field on the Quick Form Layout matches the field width defined in the data base structure. If a character field is too long to fit in the allotted space (the maximum report width of 254 characters, minus the 12 spaces reserved at the left side of each line for the prompt), the template is truncated to 242 characters. The template for a memo field matches the standard screen display width, which is 50 characters unless you have altered this setting with the MEMOWIDTH configuration option (using methods explained in Chapter 18).

By default, character fields are left-justified within the template, and numeric and float fields are right-justified if the data does not completely fill the

```
Layout   Fields   Bands   Words   Go To   Print   Exit                11:59:24 am
Page No. 999
MM/DD/YY
Report   Intro   Band
Detail           Band

ACCOUNT     XXXXXXXXXX
COMPANY     XXXXXXXXXXXXXXXXXXXXXXXXX
ADDRESS     XXXXXXXXXXXXXXXXXXXXXXXXX
CITY        XXXXXXXXXXXXXXXXXXXX
STATE       XX
ZIP         XXXXXXXXXX
TELEPHONE   XXXXXXXX
CONTACT     XXXXXXXXXXXXXXXXXXXXXXXXX
EQUIPMENT   XXXXXXXXXXXXXXXXXXXXXXXXXXXXXXXXXXXXXXXXXXXXXXXXXXXXXXXXXXXXXXXXXXXX
FIRSTORDER  MM/DD/YY
LASTORDER   MM/DD/YY
CREDITOK    Y
YTDORDERS   9999999.99
TOTORDERS   9999999.99
COMMENTS    VVVVVVVVVVVVVVVVVVVVVVVVVVVVVVVVVVVVVVVVVVVVVVVVVV
Report  C:\dbase4\<NEW>   Line:15 Col:0   File:Nwcust              Ins
           Add field:F5   Select:F6   Move:F7   Copy:F8   Size:Shift-F7
```

Figure 14-1.

The Quick Form Layout for the National Widgets Customer File maximum width. Character, numeric, float, date, and logical fields occupy one line in the Quick Form Layout. dBASE IV automatically assigns the V (Vertical stretch) picture functions to memo fields so that the text can expand vertically to occupy as many lines as required.

The page header band is exactly the same as in the Quick Column Layout. The page number is printed in the form "Page No. 999" (using the predefined item PAGENO) in the upper left corner, and right below it on line two is the date (specified as the predefined item DATE). The report intro band is closed at first, and the report summary and page footer bands are open but empty. Keep in mind that these aspects of the layout are initial, default assumptions; you can change any of them to conform to the demands of a particular report.

Designing and Editing Form Layouts

You can often use the Quick Layout as is to print a "quick and dirty" reference list of all the information in a data base. More commonly, this layout serves as the starting point for designing a somewhat better-looking report. The Quick Layout is appropriate when a data base has many character fields that are long enough to make a columnar format awkward but short enough to fit within the page width, or when a data base has many memo fields, which become less readable when they are squeezed into narrow columns.

Figure 14-2 illustrates what the detail band looks like after you have made a few modifications to the Quick Form Layout generated for the Customer File, and the first page of the resulting printout is shown in Figure 14-3. Once you are proficient at using the report layout editor, you can design reports such as this one in a half-hour or less. This report was derived from the Quick Form Layout by combining the city, state, and ZIP code into one line, erasing the prompts for the address fields, and adding blank lines to separate groups of related fields and make the report less dense and cluttered. A horizontal line was added to separate records (this line is not visible in Figure 14-2, but you can see it in the output pictured in Figure 14-3). The placement and format of the date and page number were changed, and a centered title was added to the page header band.

To print the report in Figure 14-3 on 8 1/2- by 11-inch paper, the width of the template for the EQUIPMENT field was reduced from 100 (the same as the field width) to 60 characters, and the V picture function was assigned to allow it to expand vertically onto a second line if necessary. The template for the

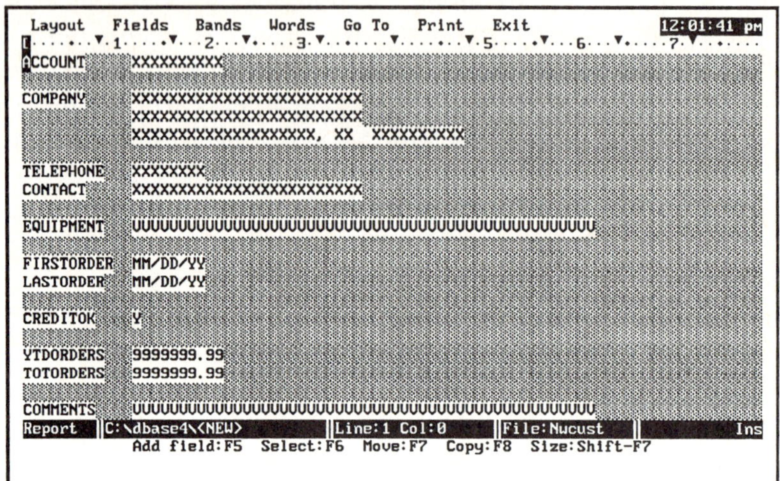

Figure 14-2.

Modifying the Quick Form Layout

memo field COMMENTS was also lengthened to 60 characters to match. Recall that you can edit the specifications for a field by positioning the cursor in the field and either pressing F5 (Field) or selecting the **Modify field** option from the **Fields** menu.

In a form layout, you can often use the V picture function to overcome a limitation of the report layout editor: In reports, unlike labels, dBASE IV does not automatically suppress blank lines that result from empty fields. For example, you might want to include both the CONTACT and COMPANY fields, either of which might be blank, in an address block, without leaving a blank line if the second field is empty. In order to do this, you can create a calculated field defined by the expression CONTACT + COMPANY (or COMPANY + CONTACT if you prefer to print the company name first) and print this field using a template 25 characters wide (the width of both fields). If you also assign the V and T picture functions, the calculated field will expand to fill two lines only if both fields are filled in.

When you work with long character and memo fields, it is especially important to understand the interactions among the picture functions used to format these fields. In the last two examples, if you did not retain the T (Trim) picture function (assigned by default to all character fields) to remove trailing

```
Printed: 11/17/91                                                 Page   1

                          National Widgets, Inc
                         Customer Reference List

ACCOUNT      LEWIS

COMPANY      Lewis and Associates
             460 Grand Avenue
             Oakland, CA  94610

TELEPHONE    839-5014
CONTACT      Joan Mills

EQUIPMENT    IBM XT, NEC 3510 printer, PCs Limited AT compatible, Hayes
             Smartmodem 1200B

FIRSTORDER   10/13/85
LASTORDER    01/20/91

CREDITOK     Y

YTDORDERS        366.81
TOTORDERS       3482.48

COMMENTS
- - - - - - - - - - - - - - - - - - - - - - - - - - - - - - - - - - - - -
ACCOUNT      ABCPLUMB

COMPANY      ABC Plumbing
             1850 University Avenue
             Berkeley, CA  94703

TELEPHONE    861-4543
CONTACT      Ed Williams

EQUIPMENT    Kaypro 4, Kaypro 10, Kaypro 286 PC, Epson FX-286 printer


FIRSTORDER   12/01/87
LASTORDER    04/30/91

CREDITOK     Y

YTDORDERS        796.41
TOTORDERS       5248.90

COMMENTS     This company has two older Kaypro computers in addition to
             their AT-compatible. They are still interested in disks,
             supplies, and accessories for the older machines, and they
             generally respond to special mailings by calling and placing
             an order.

             They are also interested in sources of public domain or
             inexpensive software for their CP/M-based Kaypros.
- - - - - - - - - - - - - - - - - - - - - - - - - - - - - - - - - - - - -
Prepared by: M. Liskin
```

Figure 14-3.

The report produced by modifying the Quick Form Layout slightly blanks from the EQUIPMENT field or the calculated field that prints the CONTACT and COMPANY combination, these items would always occupy two lines, because the V (Vertical stretch) function allows a field to expand vertically to accommodate its full width (that is, the field width defined in the file structure, not the width of the data actually entered).

Note also that when **Vertical stretch** is **ON**, dBASE IV disables the **Template** option in the dialog box used to describe the field. One way to reset the template width is to set **Vertical stretch** to **OFF** temporarily, edit the template, and then turn **Vertical stretch** back **ON**. For short fields in which you can easily count template symbols, this is often the easiest method.

Another way to resize any field, which is particularly useful for vertically stretched fields, is to position the cursor inside the field on the work surface and press the SHIFT-F7 (Size) key. You can use the LEFT ARROW and RIGHT ARROW keys to adjust the width of the field and then press ENTER to confirm the new width. dBASE IV automatically adjusts the template to conform to the size specified on the work surface. This method is easier than editing the template directly for long fields, especially if you can use other items on the work surface to help you visually determine the appropriate field width.

Depending on the structure of your data base and the intended purpose of the report, you may want to further refine the layout and appearance of a printout based on the Quick Form Layout. If most of the fields in the data base are short, you may want to place several fields on each line so that a record occupies fewer lines and more records can fit on a page. Often, the field names are unnecessarily obscure to anyone unfamiliar with your data base, and more descriptive prompts are in order, while other fields do not require prompts at all. For example, the company name and address fields in the report in Figure 14-3 do not need labels, whereas the order dates and dollar amounts would benefit from less cryptic identifiers than the field names.

Figure 14-4 illustrates the detail band in a form layout for the Customer File that prints a complete reference list in a more compact format than the one derived from the Quick Layout. This report bears little resemblance to the original Quick Layout, and you can more easily construct a report like this by starting from scratch with a blank work surface and placing text and fields individually than you can by editing the Quick Form Layout.

It is easy to forget that despite the three Quick Layouts, dBASE IV does not force you to define a report as a column, form, or mailmerge layout: You are free to combine elements of the three basic designs. For example, because you often need to print sums, counts, and averages below columns of numbers, it is natural to think of the report summary band, group bands, and summary

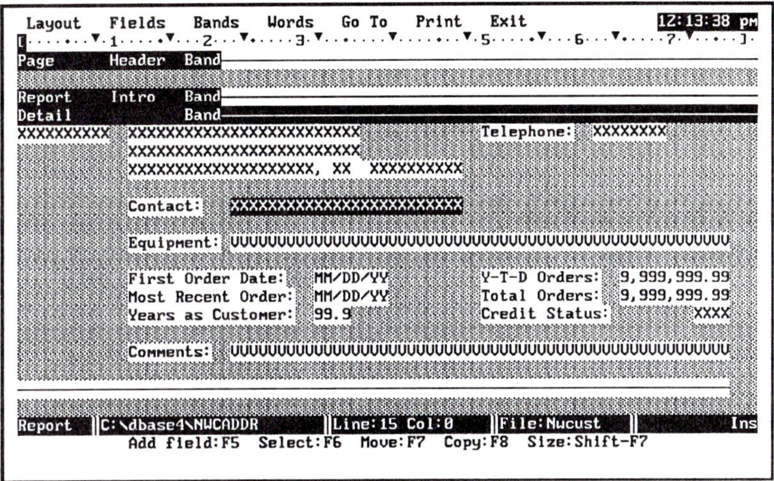

Figure 14-4.

A more compact reference list for the National Widgets Customer File

statistics as properties of columnar reports. However, the way that dBASE IV processes a data base when it prints a report is exactly the same regardless of the layout and appearance of the printout. Even if a report looks more like a form layout, you can accummulate overall summary statistics and print them in the report summary band, and if the data base is indexed or sorted, you can define group bands and print the same group summary statistics as you would in a columnar report. The only difference is that the summary statistics are generally not printed in as close proximity to the fields from which they are derived as they are in a column layout.

Figure 14-5 illustrates the group band added to the report in Figure 14-4 to print customers grouped by state and calculate order statistics for each state. The group intro band (not visible in Figure 14-5) is empty, and the group summary band prints the sum, average, maximum and minimum year-to-date and total orders, and the total number of customers in the state. The **Begin band on new page** option on the **Bands** menu was set to **Yes** for this band so that each set of summary statistics begins on a new sheet of paper. A page break after the summary statistics, added with the **Insert page break** command on the **Words** menu, ensures that the next group of customers also starts on a

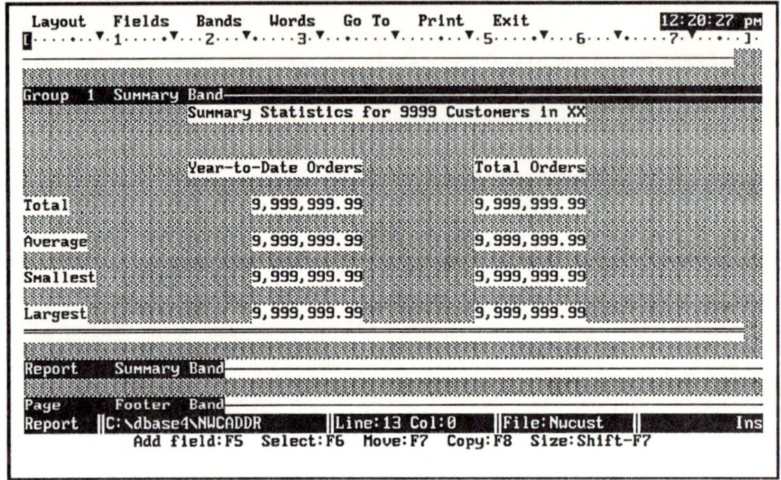

Figure 14-5.

Adding a group summary band to a form layout

new page rather than immediately following the statistics. You can achieve the same result by placing two page breaks in the group summary band—one at the top and one at the bottom.

DESIGNING MAILMERGE LAYOUTS

Mailmerge layouts are frequently used to produce documents, such as personalized letters, in which individual fields from a data based are *merged*, or integrated, with free-form text. You can also use mailmerge layouts to print any report that combines fixed, word-wrapped text with data base fields and calculated fields.

To facilitate entering the constant, or fixed, text and formatting the report to accommodate the inserted data base fields, dBASE IV assumes that the detail band in a mailmerge layout is a word wrap band rather than a layout band, and the distinguishing features of mailmerge layouts are derived from the basic characteristics of the dBASE IV word wrap editor. Working in a word wrap band on the report design work surface resembles entering and editing memo field text more than it does placing individual items in a layout band on a columnar or form report. If you have some experience with data bases that contain memo fields, the word wrap environment should seem familiar.

The Quick Mailmerge Layout

dBASE IV cannot predict the contents or placement of the text and fields in a mailmerge report, and when you select the Quick Mailmerge Layout, it does not place any data on the work surface. It simply sets up the band structure and band options as they are most often used in mailmerge reports: The **Word wrap band** option is set **ON** for the detail band, and all other bands are initially closed. The **Begin band on new page** option is set to **Yes** for the detail band, a setting that is appropriate for printing personalized letters. When you design a form that prints two or more pages per record, you can use the **Insert page break** option on the **Words** menu to begin a new page at any arbitrary point, or you can allow dBASE IV to calculate the locations of the page breaks based on the page length set on the **Print** menu. Figure 14-6 illustrates the appearance of the work surface after you have selected the Quick Mailmerge Layout and pulled down the **Bands** menu to reveal the settings.

To create forms such as personalized letters, you type the text as if you were using a word processor or the memo field editor. You can place fields in specific locations on the work surface, just as you would in a layout band. For example, in the letter shown in Figure 14-7, the inside address block is made up of the COMPANY, ADDRESS, CITY, STATE, and ZIP fields in exactly the same arrangement as in the customer reference list described earlier in this chapter. You can also embed data base fields or calculated fields within the word-wrapped text, and dBASE IV adjusts the surrounding text to conform to the length of the inserted item. The first paragraph of the letter in Figure 14-7 includes the COMPANY field and a calculated field called THISYEAR; this calculated field also appears in the last paragraph with a related item called NEXTYEAR. THISYEAR is defined by an expression that uses the YEAR function to extract the year from the current date: YEAR(DATE()). NEXTYEAR is computed by adding 1 to the current year, using the expression YEAR(DATE()) + 1.

If the inside address block might include blank lines, it requires special treatment. As noted earlier in this chapter, dBASE IV does not suppress blank

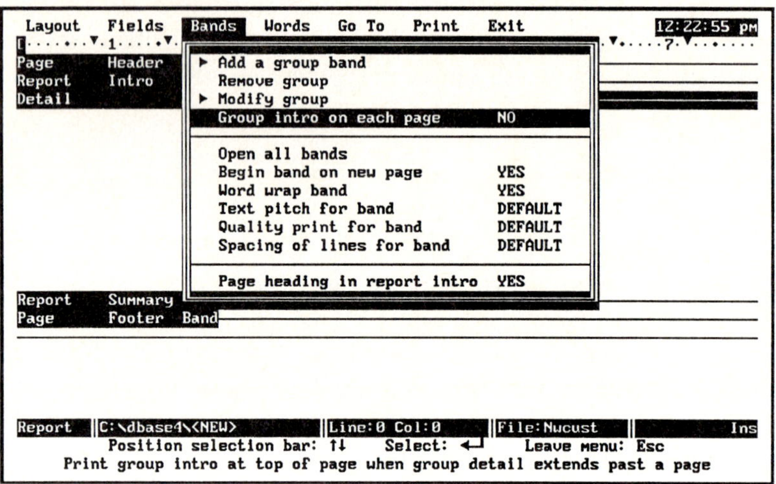

Figure 14-6.

The Quick Mailmerge Layout

lines in reports that result from empty fields, but you may not be able to solve the problem by using the technique described in the previous section—combining several fields into one calculated field and assigning this field the V (Vertical stretch) picture function. First of all, dBASE IV disables the V picture function in word wrap bands. In some cases, you can work around this limitation by substituting a layout band. For example, in a one-page letter, you could print the inside address in the page header band rather than as part of the detail band, and make the page header band a layout band. This strategy will not work for letters longer than one page, because dBASE IV prints the page header band at the top of each page, and it will not help you print an address block within the detail band.

Furthermore, in the method described earlier, the two fields combined into one calculated field were the same length; when this is the case, you can match the template width to the field length, and the combined field always breaks at the right spot if data is present in both fields. If the fields are not the same length, you must use a technique based on the ; (Semicolon) picture function, which causes dBASE IV to recognize an embedded semicolon as a request for a line break. (This picture function was retained for compatibility with earlier

```
December 1, 1991


Lewis and Associates
460 Grand Avenue
Oakland, CA 94610

Dear Valued Customer:

     We are writing to let you know about our special year-end sale on
all computer supplies and accessory products. National Widgets had a
really good year in 1991, thanks to valued customers like Lewis and
Associates, and we want to celebrate the holiday season by passing
along some terrific values to you.

     Floppy disks from all manufacturers are on sale at 15% off our
normally low prices, and all TrueData products, including disks and
magnetic tape cartridges, are 20% off. Other special sale items that
make ideal gifts for the computer owners among your friends and
business associates include

     *    Dust covers for all Macintosh computers, and for most
          keyboards and monitors
     *    Glare screens for monochrome and color monitors
     *    Cleaning kits for 5 1/4 and 3 1/2 inch floppy drives,
          Bernoulli Box drives, and tape backup subsystems
     *    Printer stands, ergonomically designed monitor stands, and
          keyboard stands

     Here's hoping that 1991 has been as good a year for you as it has
been for us, and that 1992 will bring even greater prosperity and
personal happiness.

Sincerely,


All the Folks at National Widgets, Inc.
```

Figure 14-7.

A personalized letter printed as a mailmerge report

versions of dBASE, which *always* broke output lines at a semicolon.) Suppose, for example, that the inside address consisted of a contact name, company name, and two address lines, stored in fields called CONTACT, COMPANY, ADDRESS1, and ADDRESS2 (the National Widgets Customer File has only one address line). If these fields were not all the same length, and any but the

ADDRESS1 field might be blank, you could combine them into a calculated field defined by the following expression:

```
CONTACT + ";" + TRIM(COMPANY) + IIF(COMPANY <> " ", ";", "") + ADDRESS1 + ";" +
   TRIM(ADDRESS2) + IIF(ADDRESS2 <> " ", ";", "")
```

In this expression, the CONTACT and ADDRESS1 fields are added unconditionally into the calculated field, each followed by a semicolon to force a line break (ADDRESS1 is never blank, and an extra line at the top of the inside address block that would result from a blank CONTACT field would not be noticed). For each field that would cause problems if it were blank—COMPANY and ADDRESS2 in this example—you must remove trailing spaces with the TRIM function, and follow the field with an expression based on the IIF function. This expression tests the value of the relevant field, and evaluates to a semicolon (to add a line break) if the field is not blank, or to a *null string* if it is (a null string is an empty character string *of length zero,* specified by placing two quotation marks next to each other with no intervening spaces). The template for this calculated field must be wide enough to accommodate the longest of the component fields, and you must assign both the V and ; picture functions.

If you intend to print on single sheets of letterhead, you can set the **Wait between pages** option to **Yes**; you access this setting through the **Control of printer** option on the **Print** menu. The easiest way to print the envelope is to make it the last "page" of the letter to facilitate matching each letter with the corresponding envelope. To set up the form in this way, insert a page break after the last line of the letter, copy the inside address fields as a block onto the new page that follows the page break symbol, and reset the left margin for this page (as described in the next section) so that the address is printed in the middle of the envelope rather than at the left edge.

If the address block might include empty fields, you cannot use the technique just described to suppress these lines, because the V picture function is prohibited in word wrap bands. If blank lines would present a serious problem, you might prefer to print the envelopes by using a separate label form (you may recall from Chapter 11 that two of the predefined label sizes are designed to print addresses on envelopes).

Working in a Word Wrap Band

As described in Chapter 12, which introduced the concept of layout and word wrap bands, dBASE IV formats text in a word wrap band to form paragraphs that conform to the current margins, whereas dBASE IV treats items in a layout band as independent entities and prints them exactly where you placed them on the work surface. Entering and editing text in a word wrap band is similar to entering memo field text. You can use all the familiar cursor movement and editing keys to move around the screen and add, change, insert, and delete text. To incorporate a data base field or calculated field into the text in a word wrap band, you place the field on the work surface just as you would in a layout band. By default, dBASE IV assigns the T (Trim) picture function to all fields, and reformats the surrounding text to accommodate the substitution, regardless of the length of the data.

You can select a block of text with the F6 (Select) key and then move or copy the block by using F7 (Move) and F8 (Copy). Just as in a layout band, you can add print enhancements to existing text by selecting the text and then choosing the desired enhancements from the dialog box invoked by pulling down the **Words** menu and choosing the **Style** option. You can also use a method similar to the one employed by most word processors: pull down the **Words** menu, select one or more **Style** options, type some text (which acquires the designated styles), and then pull down the **Words** menu again to cancel any or all of the style settings. Note that while you can apply any print style to a field as a whole, you cannot use print styles to format a portion of a long character or memo field, because the report layout editor treats each field as a single entity.

You cannot draw boxes or lines in a word wrap band (although you can substitute underlining or a row of dashes or equal signs for horizontal lines). This limitation makes sense when you consider that dBASE IV positions boxes and vertical lines independently of other items on the work surface that normally have fixed positions. In a word wrap band, the placement of all text is determined dynamically, so dBASE IV cannot accurately predict the relationship between a box and its intended contents. The only way to draw a box or a vertical line in a word wrap band is to change the band to a layout band by setting the **Word wrap band** option on the **Bands** menu to **No**. However, you may not want to convert a word wrap band that contains variable-length data items such as a name or company name field into a layout band, even if you no longer need to edit the text. When you turn off word wrap mode, dBASE IV inserts a hard return at the end of each line of text in the band. Because text cannot then flow onto the next line, the lines that contain embedded fields may differ in length.

dBASE IV formats text in a word wrap band based on the margins set for the current paragraph. Initially, the margins are at columns 0 and 254 (the maximum report width), the paragraph indentation (the position of the first line in a paragraph) is set at column 0, and there are tab stops at every eight spaces. You can change all these settings for the current paragraph by using the **Modify ruler** option on the **Words** menu. When you select this option, the cursor moves up into the ruler line at the top of the screen. You can navigate within the ruler line by pressing HOME, END, LEFT ARROW, and RIGHT ARROW, and edit the ruler by pressing the following keys:

[	Set left margin
]	Set right margin
#	Set paragraph indentation
0	Set left margin and paragraph indentation to column 0
!	Set tab
DEL	Clear tab or paragraph indentation
=*n*	Set tabs every *n* spaces

It makes sense to define only one left margin, right margin, and paragraph indentation setting, so pressing [,], or # cancels the old setting and moves the corresponding symbol in the ruler line to a new position. The ruler line can contain as many tab stops as you need. You can set a single tab by pressing ! with the cursor at the desired location, or clear the tab at the cursor location by pressing DEL. To set tab stops at regular intervals, press = with the cursor anywhere within the ruler line; dBASE IV pops up a dialog box to prompt you for the interval.

The paragraph indentation is the starting position of the first line in a paragraph; the indentation can coincide with the left margin in a "blocked" format (the initial default), or it can be to the right or to the left. For example, in the letter shown in Figure 14-7, the paragraph indentation for the first, second, and last paragraphs is set five spaces to the right of the left margin. If you set the paragraph indentation to the left of the left margin, a "hanging paragraph" or "outdent" results, as in the bulleted list shown in Figure 14-7. As you can see from Figure 14-8, which illustrates the appearance of a portion of the detail band on the report design screen, dBASE IV represents the space between the left margin and the paragraph indentation by a series of dashes on the ruler line. When you change the left margin, dBASE IV moves the paragraph indentation so as to maintain the same relationship between these two settings. If you want to move both settings *and* change their relative positions, you must first move the left margin and then the paragraph indentation.

As you move around the work surface, the ruler line always displays the margins, indentation, and tabs set for the current paragraph. In most cases, this display is helpful, but if you wish you can suppress the ruler line—and gain an additional line to view your report layout—by setting the **Hide ruler option** on the **Words** menu to **Yes**. You can reverse this setting at any time to bring the ruler line back into view.

When you type in Insert mode, each paragraph inherits the margin, indentation, and tab settings of the previous paragraph. In Typeover mode, the ruler line reverts to the default settings (margins at 0 and 254, no paragraph indentation, and tabs at every 8 spaces) for each new paragraph. If you modify the ruler line, dBASE IV immediately reformats the current paragraph to conform to the new settings; if you then begin a new paragraph, it will inherit these settings. However, if you change the margins for an existing paragraph between two other paragraphs, the new format applies only to the paragraph containing the cursor. There is no way to change the ruler line settings for a block of text larger than a paragraph.

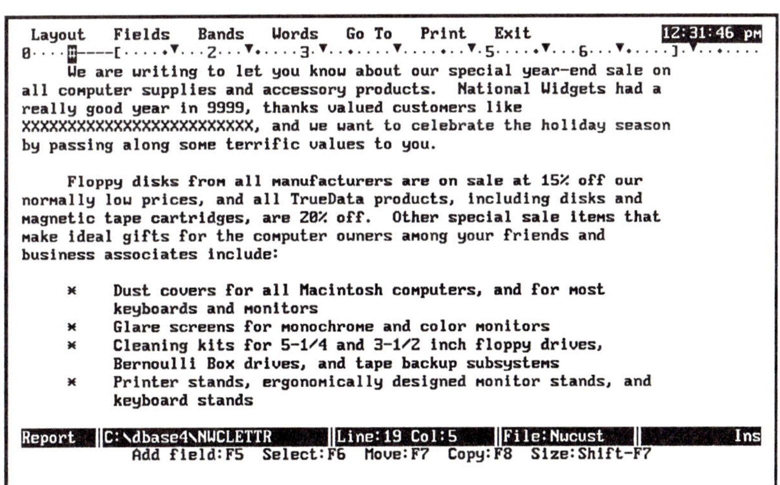

Figure 14-8.

Creating the mailmerge layout to print personalized letters

The **Enable automatic indent** option on the **Words** menu allows you to set the left margin "on the fly." When this option is set to **Yes,** dBASE IV dynamically adjusts the left margin to the position of the cursor when you begin each new paragraph, instead of adhering to the ruler line settings. With **Enable automatic indent** in effect, you can shift the left margin and paragraph indentation to the right one tab stop (while the relative positions of these settings remain fixed) by pressing TAB or to the left by pressing SHIFT-TAB. This feature is especially convenient for constructing forms, such as outlines, in which there are frequent margin changes.

Although word wrap mode is often used in mailmerge forms that print letters, you can design many other types of mailmerge reports. The report shown in Figure 14-9 is an example; it includes each customer's name and address, printed in a block much like the inside address on a letter, followed by a short narrative passage that details the company's history with National Widgets. Like a column or form layout, the report includes a page header and footer band, and prints more than one record per page. Figure 14-10 illustrates the detail band on the report design work surface as this report was created.

The margins were set to columns 12 and 70 for the text paragraph. What may not be so obvious from the printout is that you must modify the ruler line again after this paragraph to reset the left margin to column 0 so that the account code for the next customer begins at the left edge of the page.

Embedded in the narrative passage are two data base fields, TOTORDERS and YTDORDERS, both assigned the $ (Financial) picture function to supply the leading dollar sign, together with a template that inserts a comma at every 3 digits. The date fields FIRSTORDER and LASTORDER are not printed directly, but via two calculated fields, FIRST and LAST, in order to make use of the MDY function to transform the dates into character strings. MDY takes one input, a date, and returns a character string representation of the date in month/day/year order with the month spelled out. Thus, for ABC Plumbing, MDY(LASTORDER) evaluates to "April 30, 91" (to print a 4-digit year, you must turn the CENTURY setting ON, using methods explained in Chapter 18).

Another calculated field, NAME, based on the IIF function, prints the CONTACT field if the COMPANY name is blank. This field, printed in both the address block and the text paragraph, is defined by the following expression:

```
IIF(COMPANY = " ", CONTACT, COMPANY)
```

The condition in this expression compares the COMPANY field to a blank space. If COMPANY is blank, the condition COMPANY = " " has the value .T.,

```
Printed: 10/31/91                                          Page    1

                         National Widgets, Inc
                    Narrative Customer Reference List

ABCPLUMB     ABC Plumbing
             1850 University Avenue
             Berkeley, CA  94703

             ABC Plumbing has been a customer since December 01, 87.
             During that time, the company has placed $5,248.90 in
             orders, of which $796.41 was in the current year. Their
             most recent order was placed on April 30, 91.

ANDERSON     John Anderson
             6105 146th Place S.E.
             Bellevue, WA  98006

             John Anderson has been a customer since August 08, 87.
             During that time, the company has placed $832.58 in orders,
             of which $0.00 was in the current year. Their most recent
             order was placed on December 01, 90.

ARONOFF      Gina Aronoff
             601 First Street
             Benicia, CA  94510

             Gina Aronoff has been a customer since October 09, 87.
             During that time, the company has placed $1,232.50 in
             orders, of which $0.00 was in the current year. Their most
             recent order was placed on December 14, 90.

DELTADESGN   Delta Design
             N.W. 245 Sunrise Drive
             Pullman, WA  99163

             Delta Design has been a customer since September 14, 88.
             During that time, the company has placed $1,235.87 in
             orders, of which $188.15 was in the current year. Their
             most recent order was placed on February 23, 91.

ELLISMFG     Ellis Manufacturing
             832 130th N.E.
             Bellevue, WA  98005

             Ellis Manufacturing has been a customer since October 18,
             88. During that time, the company has placed $669.58 in
             orders, of which $0.00 was in the current year. Their
             most recent order was placed on February 16, 90.
```

Figure 14-9.

A mailmerge report that describes National Widgets' customers

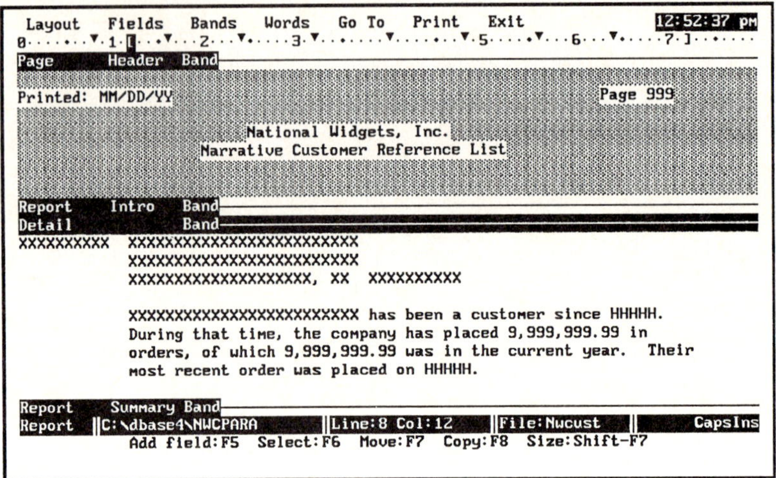

Figure 14-10.

Creating the mailmerge layout for the Customer File

and the IIF function evaluates to the contents of the CONTACT field; otherwise, it evaluates to the value of COMPANY.

Using Your Word Processor

You can read the contents of a text file created by an external editor or word processor into a dBASE IV report band by selecting the **Write/read text file** option from the **Words** menu and then choosing **Read text from file**. dBASE IV prompts you for the file name and then inserts the entire file into the current band at the cursor location. If a report includes more than a page or two of free-form text, you might prefer to use your word processor, because it is faster, more powerful, or more familiar than the dBASE IV word wrap editor. The ability to import external files also allows you to avoid retyping text that already exists in a word processing document.

The file that you import should be an *ASCII text file*—it should contain only the letters, numbers, and punctuation marks that you can generate from the keyboard. There must be no header, document summary, formatting commands, or hidden codes, since these would be meaningless to dBASE IV. Commands for changing horizontal or vertical spacing, selecting a type font, and adding print enhancements, such as boldfacing and underlining, must be entered in the dBASE IV report layout editor after you import the text.

With most word processors, you must select a special editing mode or use a different "save" command to produce a plain text file with no embedded document header or formatting codes. For example, with WordPerfect, you should use the Text In/Out options invoked by pressing CTRL-F5 instead of the standard "Save" key, F10. You can save the document as a "DOS Text File"—in which each line ends with a hard return—or in "Generic Word Processor" format to produce a file that has hard returns only at the ends of each paragraph. The Generic format is preferable if you later want to edit the text in a word wrap band.

If you have Microsoft Word, select the Save As command rather than Save from the Files menu, and select either Text Only w/Breaks format, in which each line ends with a hard return, or Text Only, which produces a file with hard returns only at the end of each paragraph. To generate an ASCII text file with no special codes with WordStar, you must edit the text in "Non-document" mode with word wrap off. (The unavailability of word wrap makes it somewhat less convenient to substitute this particular word processor for the dBASE IV word wrap editor.)

You may need to experiment a bit with your word processor to determine whether it can create a plain text file, and if so, how to do so. As a last resort, you might try configuring the software for the least capable printer it supports—sometimes described as a teletype, a generic printer, or a DOS text printer—and "printing" the text file to disk instead of to the printer. You can use the DOS TYPE command to display the contents of the resulting file to verify that it does not contain any commands or printer codes, which usually appear as graphics characters on the screen. You can also import the file into your dBASE IV report and examine the text in the word wrap editor.

SUMMARY

The examples in this chapter were intended to illustrate typical report styles and components, and suggest ways to combine these elements to create a wide variety of custom formats. However, the examples barely scratch the surface.

Readers who are upgrading from earlier versions of dBASE may want to study the more advanced report concepts in detail, since the dBASE IV report writer offers considerably more power and versatility than its predecessors. If you are following along with the National Widgets case study system, you may want to try creating some of the report forms in this chapter and modifying these forms to further explore the capabilities of the report editor. If you are working on your own application, you might instead apply these concepts to some of the reports you will need in your own system.

CHAPTER FIFTEEN

Creating Custom Data Entry Forms

So far, you have used the standard dBASE IV Edit screen to add, display, and update one record at a time and the Browse screen to view and edit multiple records (and occasionally add records). On the Edit screen, the field names are arranged vertically down the left side of the screen as prompts, and the data entry areas are aligned in another column immediately to the right of the prompts. By default, dBASE IV displays the field names in light characters on a dark background, and the data in inverse video (dark characters on a light background). If the default data entry screen does not satisfy your sense of aesthetics or the needs of your application, you can design a custom screen form that substitutes for the standard Edit screen when you view and update a data base.

The fact that dBASE IV provides a standard data entry form also enables you to begin working with a new file immediately, without having to spend time designing a screen layout, and as long as you choose meaningful and descriptive field names, the Edit screen is more than adequate for many applications. Even if you intend from the start to define a custom screen, it is often best to wait until you have entered some sample data and have completed your initial testing. If the testing phase reveals, as it usually does, that modifications to the file structure are necessary, you will not have to redesign the data entry screen.

When you design custom screens, you can lay out the fields in an attractive and logical manner, group related fields together, and draw lines and boxes to separate the groups. Longer, more descriptive prompts can replace the field names used on the Edit screen, and you can define an informative message that is displayed at the bottom of the screen to describe the purpose, use, or contents of each field. You can collect a long character field in a space narrower than the field width and place several short fields on one line to fit more data on the screen at once. You can display and edit a memo field in a window of any arbitrary size and specify whether a memo should be displayed initially as a memo marker (as it is on the Edit screen) or in a window.

dBASE IV places no limit on the number of custom screens that you can design for a data base. You can create multiple screens for different tasks or different users. You can lay out a screen so that it resembles an existing printed form, in order to reassure less knowledgeable users and speed data entry when you are working from the printed form. If some operations do not require access to all the fields or you want to hide certain data from some users, you can exclude specific fields from a screen form. To prevent anyone from inadvertently or intentionally altering sensitive data or fields whose values should be calculated rather than entered directly, you can display fields but not allow the user to edit the contents.

Even if you find the appearance of the Edit screen acceptable for updating a data base, there are other good reasons to design custom screen forms. Custom screens support an extensive set of data formatting and validation options that help guard against the entry of "impossible" field values and reduce the likelihood that inconsistent data entry will cause problems later in sorting, indexing, or search operations. Using the same basic tools provided to format data on labels and reports—picture functions and templates—you can do such things as convert character fields to all uppercase letters, insert the punctuation in a telephone number or social security number, and prevent the entry of inappropriate characters, such as letters in a telephone number or digits in a state abbreviation.

dBASE IV offers a variety of options for making data entry easier and improving the accuracy of the information in a data base. You can specify a default value for a field, and you can selectively carry over the entries in certain fields from one new record to the next, as if dBASE IV had automatically pressed F8 (Ditto) every time you edited the field. You can test numeric, date, and character fields to ensure that an entry falls within a specified range of values. You can define any arbitrary condition that must be satisfied before dBASE IV permits you to edit a field and another condition that must be fulfilled before the field is accepted and dBASE IV allows you to move the cursor out of the field.

By combining these options, you can design sophisticated data entry screens that are customized for the demands of a particular data base, user, or task. These screens can be more attractive and "helpful" than the standard Edit display, and they can greatly improve the speed and accuracy of data entry. This chapter describes how to create screen forms for updating a data base or a view based on a single data base. Special considerations for multifile data entry screens are discussed in Chapter 17.

CREATING AND EDITING FORMS

To define a custom screen form, you use a specialized layout editor that is very similar to the editors used to design label and report forms. Although screen forms generally include data base fields, this is not an absolute requirement (you could, for example, create a custom screen for entering the values of memory variables that are required for printing a report), so you can invoke the screen form editor without first opening a data base file or view. When you work in the menu system, if you do open a data base or view, a reference to this file is stored in the catalog entry for the screen form; thereafter, the data base or view is automatically opened when you edit the form or use it for data entry.

As with labels and reports, you can override the default and use a form to update other data bases or views with matching field names. If you invoke the screen layout editor to revise a form that refers to fields not present in the active data base, or if you use the **Use different database file or view** option on the **Layout** menu to open an incompatible file, dBASE IV notifies you of the potential problem by listing the names of the missing fields in a pop-up message box. After reading the warning, you can proceed to edit the form. This flexibility allows you to use one predefined screen form as the starting point for designing another similar form for a data base or view with a slightly different structure: you can edit the original screen form, delete the references to missing fields, modify the form in any other way that you see fit, and save it under a new name.

From the Menus

You display and access screen forms through the **Forms** panel in the Control Center. Note that the word "form" is also used to describe the specifications for printing labels and reports, as in the terms "label form" and "report form." To avoid confusion, this book uses the parallel term, "screen form," to distinguish forms used to view and update a data base on the screen from those used to print data.

You can create a new screen form by selecting the **<create>** option from the **Forms** panel or edit an existing screen form by highlighting its name, pressing ENTER, and selecting **Modify layout** from the pop-up dialog box. You can also use the standard function key shortcut for opening a file and moving to the appropriate design work surface: highlight a screen form name or **<create>** and press SHIFT-F2 (Design). As with labels and reports, you need not name a new screen form until you save it. When you edit an existing screen form, dBASE IV automatically opens the data base or view that was open when the form was created or last modified.

From the Dot Prompt

From the dot prompt, you can invoke the screen editor by typing

CREATE SCREEN *screen form name*

or

MODIFY SCREEN *screen form name*

You can use the CREATE and MODIFY variations interchangeably, regardless of whether you are defining a new screen form or editing an existing one.

If the screen form named in a CREATE SCREEN command already exists, dBASE IV warns you in a pop-up dialog box and offers two options: **Modify**, which loads the form into the screen layout editor as if you had typed MODIFY SCREEN, and **Cancel**, which returns you to the dot prompt so you can retype the command with a new screen form name.

As always, when you work at the dot prompt, you must name new files as well as existing ones before you enter the screen layout editor. If you do not include a screen form name in the CREATE SCREEN or MODIFY SCREEN command, dBASE IV prompts you to enter it. If no data base is currently open, dBASE IV warns you in a pop-up message box—"No database in use. Form contains the following fields:"—and displays a list of all the fields defined in the form. You can press ESC to terminate the list and go on to edit the form. You must open a data base with the **Use different data base or view** option on the **Layout** menu before you can place any fields on the work surface.

Saving a Screen Form

You can save a screen form on disk and continue working in the screen layout editor by selecting the **Save this form** option from the **Layout** menu, or you can save the form and exit to the Control Center or the dot prompt by selecting the **Save changes and exit** option from the **Exit** menu. You can move directly from the screen design work surface to viewing and entering data by pressing F2 (Data), and return by pressing SHIFT-F2 (Design) or by choosing **Return to Form Design** from the **Exit** menu. The facility with which you can switch between the screen design work surface and the Edit screen drawn by the form makes it easier to fine-tune a screen layout. dBASE IV does not require that you save the form before you use it to display and enter data, but if you have made extensive changes to the form, it is advisable to do so.

Each time you save a screen form, dBASE IV prompts you for a file name; if you have already named the form, it displays your previous entry as a default, which you can accept by pressing ENTER, or change to save the file under a different name. Like label and report forms, screens are stored on disk in two different kinds of files. The design specifications are first stored in a file with the name you assigned as the first name and the extension SCR; this file is used by the screen layout editor when you edit the form. From the specifications in the SCR file, dBASE IV generates a *format file*, a dBASE IV program containing commands to customize the working environment and display and collect data. The format file has the same first name as the SCR file and the extension FMT; this file is compiled to yield a file with the extension FMO, which is executed to draw the custom screen.

USING THE SCREEN FORM DESIGN WORK SURFACE

The dBASE IV screen layout editor has much in common with the label and report layout editors covered in Chapters 11 through 14, with a few minor differences that reflect the distinguishing features of screen forms. You can use the same cursor movement and editing commands to move around the work surface and add, delete, move, and modify background text, data base fields, and calculated fields. If you don't yet feel comfortable navigating around the work surface, you may want to review the basic concepts in Chapters 11 and 12. The screen layout editor menu bar, which is diagrammed in Figure 15-1, is also similar to the **Report** menu.

Unlike a report, a data entry form cannot be wider than the 80-character screen, and dBASE IV does not allow you to move the cursor beyond column 79 (the 80th column) on the work surface. However, a form can be *longer* than the number of lines that are visible on the screen at once. When you use a long form to update a data base, dBASE IV scrolls the display to follow you if you press PGDN or use the DOWN ARROW key to move the cursor past the last visible line on the screen. There is no need to define separate screen "pages" or identify the location of "page breaks" in the form; in fact, the **Insert page break** option on the **Words** menu is dimmed and unavailable in the screen layout editor. The only way to control the positions of the page breaks in a screen form is to insert enough blank lines to fill the screen and force the next item onto the next "page." However, if you do this and later switch to a different combination of video adapter and monitor—for example, use a form designed for a 25-line screen in 43-line EGA mode—you will have to edit the form to adjust the locations of the "page breaks."

Just as in report and label forms, you can use picture functions and templates to customize the display format for fields displayed on the screen. However, screen forms are used to *edit* data as well as *display* it, and some of

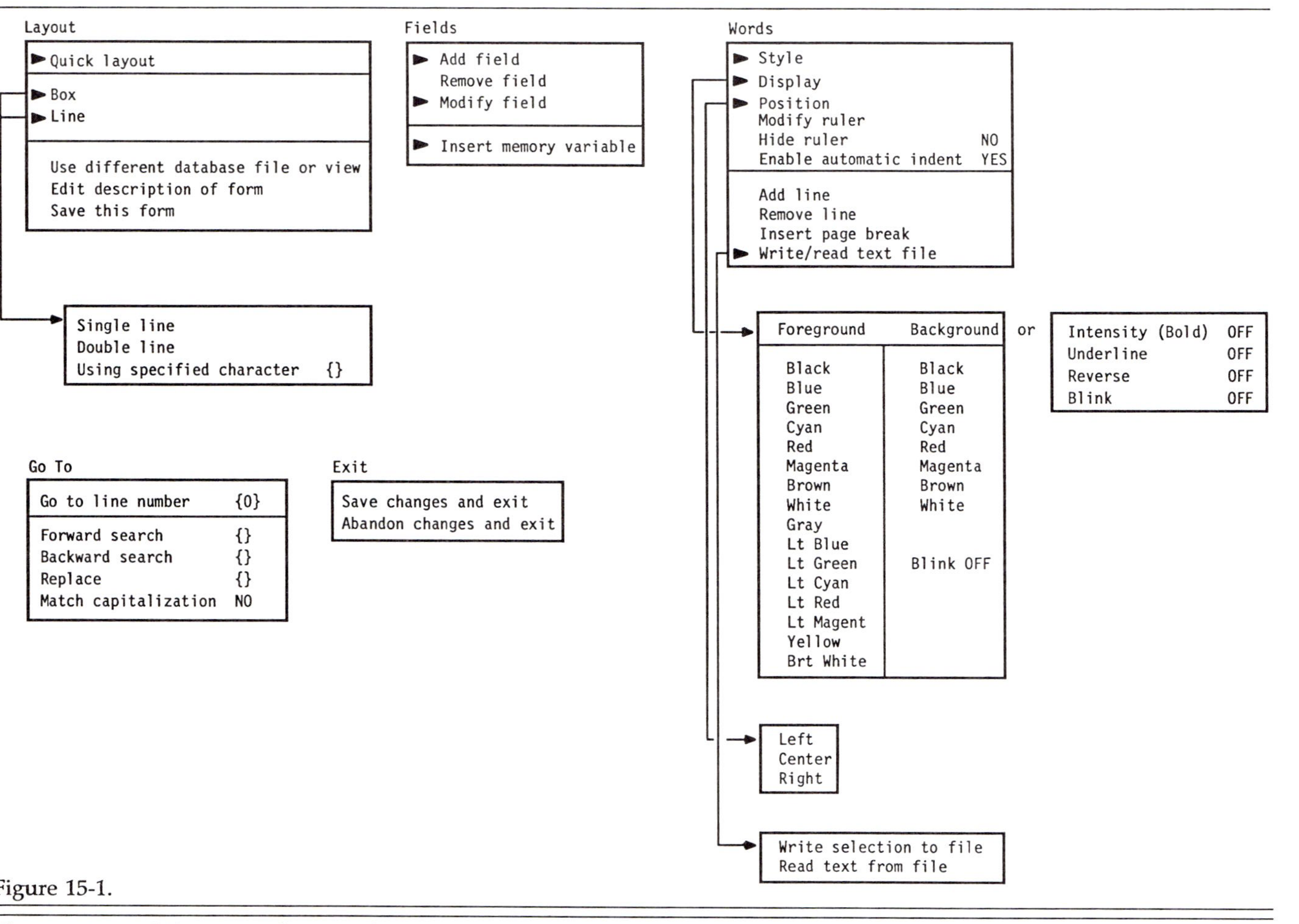

Figure 15-1.

The structure of the screen layout editor menu

the picture functions and template symbols have different meanings for displayed and entered data. dBASE IV also provides picture functions and template symbols that are not applicable to printed forms, as well as a wide variety of validation options and commands for customizing the data entry process for individual fields.

By default, dBASE IV uses different visual attributes to distinguish fields that the user can update from "background" items such as fixed text, borders, calculated fields, and data base fields that cannot be edited. On a monochrome monitor, dBASE IV uses light characters on a dark background for background items and inverse video (dark characters on a light background) for entered data. On a color display, it uses contrasting colors. As you will see later in this chapter, you can override the default display attributes by using the **Display** option on the **Words** menu.

Using the Quick Screen Layout

The screen form editor **Layout** menu offers a **Quick layout** option, which generates a screen form that closely resembles the default Edit screen (and the Quick Layout form for reports, which was explained in Chapter 14). You may want to use this layout as a starting point for creating a more complex form. The vertical orientation is especially well suited to data bases containing many wide character fields that each require a separate line on the screen. The Quick Layout is also useful if you are content with the layout of the Edit screen but want to take advantage of data formatting and validation capabilities that are available only through custom screen forms.

When you invoke the screen layout editor from the Control Center to create a new form, dBASE IV displays the screen design work surface with the **Layout** menu pulled down. If a data base is already open, the **Quick layout** option is highlighted; otherwise, **Use different database file or view** is highlighted to remind you that you must open a data base or view before you can place fields on the work surface.

The Quick Screen Layout generated for the National Widgets Customer File is illustrated in Figure 15-2. The fields are lined up vertically down the left side of the screen, starting with row 1 and occupying as many rows as there are fields (when it constructs the Quick Layout, dBASE IV leaves row 0 blank for status messages, and you should follow the same practice in the screen forms you design). The field names are used as prompts, and the adjacent data entry areas begin at column 12 to guarantee two spaces between the longest field name prompt and the field itself.

The Quick Screen Layout displays memo fields initially as *memo markers*, exactly as in Edit and Browse, but it also includes a large window in the center of the screen in which you can edit the text. The templates for numeric, float, date, and logical fields—and for short character fields—match the field widths defined in the data base structure. One difference from the standard Edit screen is that dBASE IV does not wrap long character fields onto multiple lines; it truncates the templates to 68 characters (the maximum number that can fit on an 80-character screen after subtracting the 12 spaces reserved for the field name prompt and the 2 spaces added between the prompt and the data). If any templates were truncated, dBASE IV displays the following message at the bottom of the screen immediately after generating the Quick Layout: "Data beyond the maximum character limit has been truncated." Be sure to watch for this message, which disappears when you press any key and could easily go unnoticed.

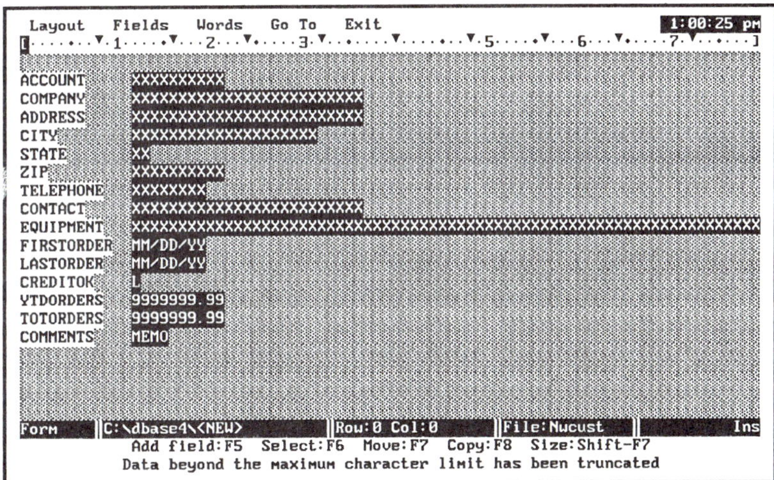

Figure 15-2.

The quick screen layout for the National Widgets Customer File

Adding Text and Fields to the Work Surface

If you do not want to use the Quick Screen Layout as the basis for a new screen, you can press ESC to close the **Layout** menu if it is open and construct the screen form by typing text, drawing lines and boxes, and placing fields directly on the work surface. Figure 15-3 illustrates a screen form for the National Widgets Customer File. Just as in the other dBASE IV layout editors, you add a field to the work surface by pressing F5 (Field) or by selecting the **Add field** option on the **Fields** menu. In either case, dBASE IV displays a pick list of available items similar to the one shown in Figure 15-4, which illustrates the pick list of fields in the Customer File.

The screen item pick list has two panels, which list the fields in the active data base or view and the names of any calculated fields that you have defined for this screen form. When you select a data base field, dBASE IV displays a pop-up dialog box like the one shown in Figure 15-5. Just as in the report and label layout editors, the field name, data type, length, and number of decimal places are displayed for your information only—you cannot change them. You can use many of the same template characters and picture functions as well as

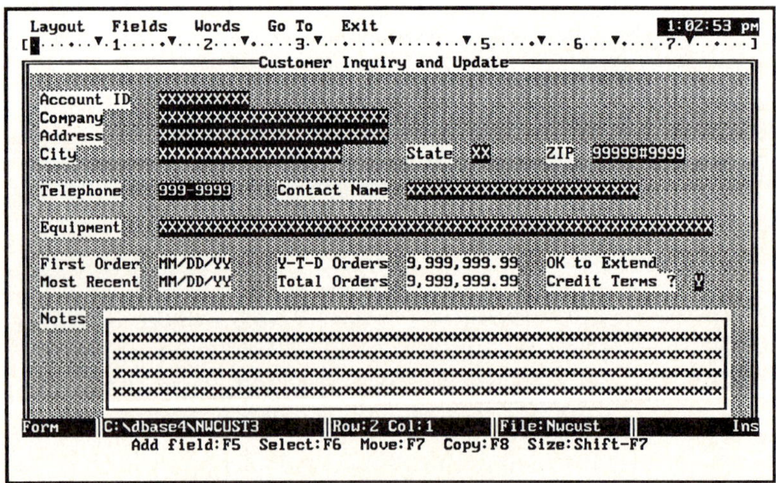

Figure 15-3.

A custom screen form for updating the Customer File

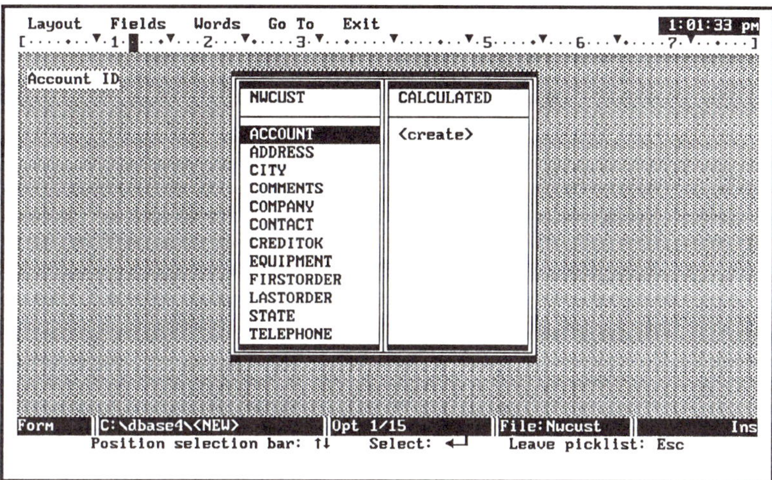

Figure 15-4.

The screen form item pick list

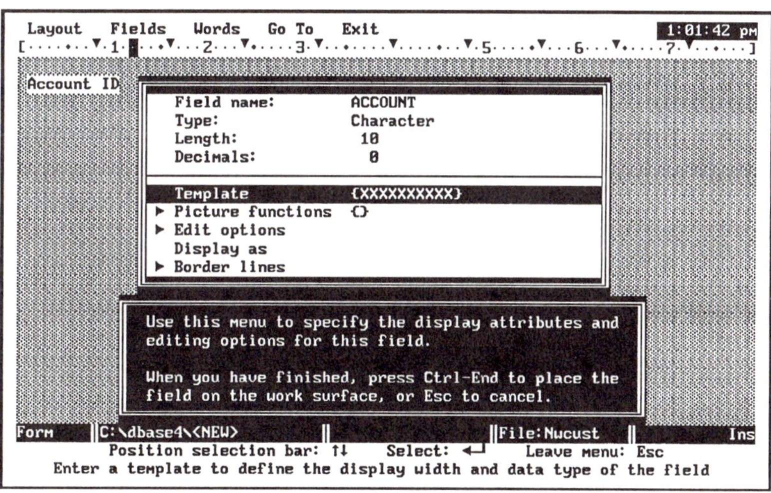

Figure 15-5.

Placing a field on the work surface

several others that are not available for report and label forms. (As noted earlier, some of the picture functions and template symbols have different effects on displayed and entered data.)

The **Edit options**, which are unique to screen forms, allow you to establish default values, prohibit editing to create display-only fields, and specify a variety of validation conditions. These options are explained later in this chapter. The **Display as** option, which is enabled only for memo fields, allows you to select the initial display mode for the field, which can appear either as a memo marker or in a window of any size; the **Border lines** option enables you to choose the character used to draw the border of the memo field window.

You can create a calculated field by selecting the **<create>** option from the **Calculated** panel in the screen item pick list. You define calculated fields just as you do in reports or labels: you must enter the expression used to compute the field value, and optionally, a name and description to identify the field and describe its purpose or use. Because they are derived entirely from other fields in a data base and are not stored on disk, dBASE IV does not allow you to edit calculated fields. Accordingly, only the template symbols and picture functions that are applicable to display-only data base fields are available. Unlike the report editor, the screen layout editor does not permit you to refer to a calculated field in the expression that defines another calculated field; you must incorporate the same expression used to define the first field into the definition of the second.

You can add memory variables to a screen layout, but the names of active memory variables do not appear on the pick list invoked by pressing F5 (Field) or selecting the **Add field** option from the **Fields** menu. You must use the **Insert memory variable** option, also located on the **Fields** menu, which invokes a dialog box similar to the one used to describe data base fields. You must enter the name of the variable and select the data type; you can specify picture functions, templates, and edit options just as you would for a data base field. dBASE IV does not warn you if the named memory variable does not exist; however, it will display the "Variable not found" error message if the variable is undefined when you use the form to edit data.

When you design a screen form, keep in mind that you cannot specify the order in which fields are collected: dBASE IV moves the cursor through the fields in the order in which they appear on the screen, starting in the upper left corner and moving across each line before moving down to the next. Thus, it is impractical to design forms in which groups of related items are arranged in multiple vertical columns, because there is no way (except by modifying the generated format file) to force dBASE IV to move down one column and then up to the top of the next during data entry.

Displaying and Editing Memo Fields

On the standard dBASE IV Edit screen, memo fields are displayed as *memo markers.* The marker for a memo field is displayed in uppercase letters—"MEMO"—if the field contains text, or in lowercase letters—"memo"—if it does not. To view or edit the field, you position the cursor in the marker and press CTRL-HOME or F9 (Zoom) to expand the field to fill the screen and invoke the memo text editor.

Although the marker is the default display mode for memo fields in custom screen forms, you can define a window of any size, positioned anywhere on the screen, to edit a memo field. If you want to, you can display this window initially instead of the memo marker. When you edit the field, you can "zoom" the window to fill the screen, just as in the standard Edit mode. If you have several memo fields in a data base, or if you typically enter massive amounts of text, it may not be practical to make the display windows large enough to view the full contents of each memo field; nevertheless, it is often convenient to be able to see at least some of the text without having to move the cursor into each memo field and press the F9 (Zoom) key.

You select the initial display mode—Marker or Window—with the **Display as** option in the dialog box that is invoked when you add a memo field to the work surface or modify a previously placed field. When you press CTRL-END to place the field on the work surface, dBASE IV initiates the standard box-drawing command sequence and invites you to "Position upper left of memo window with cursor keys, complete with ENTER" and then "Stretch memo window with cursor keys, complete with ENTER." dBASE IV will allow you to overlay other text and fields with the memo display window. For example, you might define the same size window, located in the center of the screen, to edit several different memo fields, as dBASE IV does in the Quick Screen Layout. In most cases, it makes sense to do this only if the memo fields are initially displayed as markers so that the memo text covers other items on the screen only while you are actually editing the contents.

You can select the border character for a memo window (single or double continuous lines or any other character) with the **Border lines** option on the field placement dialog box. By default, dBASE IV draws a continuous single-line box. If you chose the Marker display mode, you must also indicate the position of the marker on the work surface by moving a four-character "shadow" to the desired location. You can resize a memo window by using the SHIFT-F7 (Size) key, just as you would a box drawn on the work surface. If the memo field is displayed as a marker, you must first position the cursor in the marker and press CTRL-HOME to expand the marker to a window and then resize the window.

If the initial display mode is Window, dBASE IV displays as much text as will fit within the window when you use the screen form to edit records. However, it does not reformat the memo text to conform to the window boundaries—it simply superimposes the window on the text. If viewing only part of each line would diminish the usefulness of the display, you must make memo windows wide enough to accommodate the longest possible line of text (65 characters if you use the dBASE IV memo editor, which word wraps text at column 65, to enter memo text).

dBASE IV uses the initial window *only to display text*—it does not allow you to edit the field directly in this window. To edit the text of a memo field, you position the cursor in the memo marker or in the initial display window and press CTRL-HOME or F9 (Zoom). If the text was initially displayed as a marker, dBASE IV expands the data entry area to fill the window that you defined when you placed the field on the work surface. If the window was already displayed, this command enables you to edit the text inside it. In either case, it does not reformat the text to conform to the width of the window, but it does scroll the window to enable you to view and edit all of the text. Pressing F9 (Zoom) with the editing window active expands the window to fill the screen. By pressing this key repeatedly, you can alternate between the smaller editing window and the full-screen display. When you save the memo text and exit, dBASE IV returns the field to its initial display mode.

Using Templates and Picture Functions

As in a report or label form, you establish the display width of a field by editing the template. By default, dBASE IV left-justifies character, memo, and date fields within the template width and right-justifies numeric and float fields. You can override these defaults by using the L, I, and J picture functions to left-justify, center, or right-justify data within the designated display width.

The H (Horizontal stretch) and V (Vertical stretch) picture functions are not available for use in screen forms, and you can assign the T (Trim) function only to fields that are displayed but cannot be edited. When you display a field, dBASE IV truncates data that does not fit on one line, whereas fields that are entered must accommodate as many characters as the field width defined in the file structure. If you need to collect a long character field in a space narrower than the field width, you can use the S (Scroll within display width) picture function to scroll the data through a data entry region of any width. For example, in the screen form illustrated in Figure 15-3, the S function displays and collects the EQUIPMENT field in a space 60 characters wide. dBASE IV automatically assigns this function to any fields in a Quick Screen Layout that it truncated to 68 characters to fit within the screen width.

Even in the standard full-screen Edit and Browse modes, dBASE IV validates and formats your entries to a certain extent: You can enter only numbers, a decimal point, and a minus sign into numeric and float fields; only valid calendar dates are accepted in date fields; and only .T. (T, t, Y, or y) and .F. (F, f, N, or n) are permitted in logical fields. On a custom screen, you can specify a wider variety of validation and formatting rules for these data types and for character fields as well by using picture functions, templates, and the Edit options.

You can use templates and picture functions to format items that are only displayed (calculated fields and data base fields for which editing is prohibited), just as you do in labels and report forms. When you add a field to the work surface, dBASE IV automatically assigns a picture function and/or template that mimics the way the field is displayed and collected on the standard Edit screen. Tables 15-1 and 15-2 list the applicable picture functions and template symbols, the data types they apply to, and their meanings for both displayed and entered data.

When you use picture functions and templates to collect data, they can do more than just alter the display format; in many cases, they transform the data before it is stored in the data base. For example, the ! picture function converts a *displayed* field to uppercase letters and leaves the contents of the field in the data base exactly as it was originally entered. When you apply this function to a field that is *entered* through a screen form, dBASE IV *converts* the characters that you type to uppercase, displays them in uppercase, and stores them in uppercase in the data base.

Several picture functions enable you to restrict the type of data that dBASE IV accepts into a field, just as it prohibits the entry of alphabetic characters in a numeric or float field. For example, the A picture function permits you to enter

Symbol	Data Types	Meaning—Displayed Data	Meaning—Entered Data
C	N, F	Display CR (credit) after positive number	None
X	N, F	Display DB (debit) after a negative number	None
(	N, F	Display a negative number in parentheses	None
L	N, F	Add leading zeros to fill display width	Add leading zeros to fill display width
Z	N, F	Display a zero value as a blank space	Display a zero value as a blank space (data is stored as 0)
$	N, F	Display the currency symbol before the number	Display the currency symbol before the number
^	N, F	Display in exponential format	Display in exponential format
!	C	Display data in uppercase	Convert alphabetic characters to uppercase
A	C	None	Permit only alphabetic characters
R	C	Insert extra characters in the template into data rather than replacing characters	Use extra characters in the template for display only and do not store them with the data
S*n*	C	Display the first *n* characters of the data	Scroll the data through a space of the specified width
M	C	None	Multiple choice—accept only the listed values
T	C	Remove leading and trailing blank spaces	None
B	N, F	Left-justify within template width	Left-justify within template width
J	C	Right-justify within template width	None
I	C, N, F	Center within template width	Center within template width

Table 15-1.

The Picture Function Symbols Used in Screen Forms

Symbol	Data Types	Meaning—Displayed Data	Meaning—Entered Data
A	C	Display character unchanged	Permit only alphabetic character
X	C	Display character unchanged	Permit entry of any character (defines template width)
N	C	Display character unchanged	Permit alphabetic character, digit, or underscore
!	C	Display data in uppercase	Convert alphabetic character to uppercase
9	C, N, F	Display character unchanged	Permit only digit or sign
#	C, N, F	Display character unchanged	Permit digit, sign, space, or decimal point
.	N, F	Decimal point position	Decimal point position
,	N, F	Insert a comma if a digit is present on both sides	Insert a comma if a digit is present on both sides
*	N, F	Display a digit, if present, or an asterisk in place of a leading blank space	Display a digit, if present, or an asterisk in place of a leading blank space
$	N, F	Display a digit, if present, or a dollar sign in place of a leading blank space	Display a digit, if present, or a dollar sign in place of a leading blank space
L	C, L	Display value unchanged	Permit only T, t, Y, y, F, f, N, n
Y	C, L	Display true as Y and false as N	Permit only Y, y, N, n
OTHER	C	Display symbol in place of data character. When combined with R function, insert symbol into data	Insert symbol into data. With R function, only display symbol
	N, F	Insert symbol into data	Display symbol but do not store with data

Table 15-2.

The Template Symbols Used in Screen Forms

only letters of the alphabet (not numbers or punctuation marks) into a character field, and the Y function limits entries in a logical field to Y and N (for "Yes" and "No"). As in reports and labels, you can combine picture functions in any reasonable way. For example, assigning both A and ! to a character field causes dBASE IV to accept only letters of the alphabet and converts the entry to uppercase. You might use this combination in the National Widgets system to ensure that the customer account code contains only alphabetic characters and is always entered in uppercase letters for consistency.

The M (Multiple choice) picture function allows you to specify a finite list of permissible values for a character field. When you choose this option, dBASE IV pops up a dialog box to ask you to "Enter multiple choices." You enter the list of valid choices, separated by commas, as illustrated in Figure 15-6, which lists the two-letter postal abbreviations that constitute acceptable entries in the STATE field. Although you can enter as many choices as you want, the length of the list cannot exceed 254 characters. If you want to see more of the list at once, you can press F9 (Zoom) to expand the data entry region to the full width of the screen and then press F9 (Zoom) again when the list is complete.

When you use a screen form that contains a multiple choice field, dBASE IV displays the existing field contents or the first choice in the list if the field is blank. You can cycle through the choices by pressing the spacebar, much as

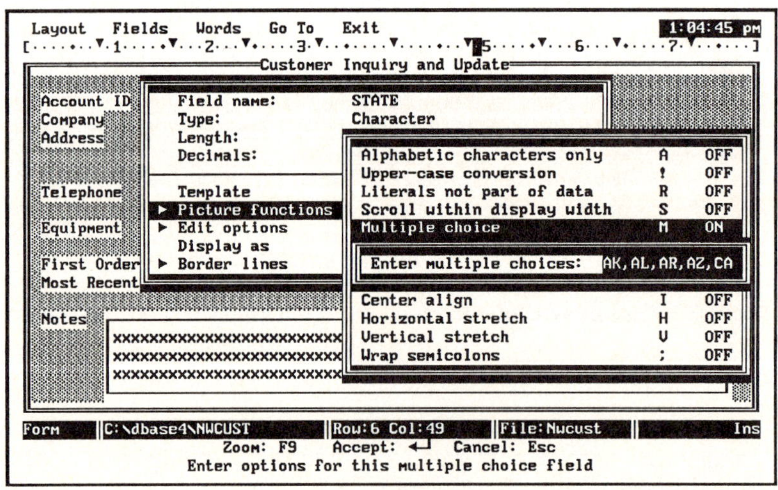

Figure 15-6.

Using the M (Multiple choice) picture function to list permissible entries in a field you do when you make selections from dBASE IV menus such as the **Print** menu. When you move the cursor out of the field, the displayed value is entered into the data base. dBASE IV does not allow you to explicitly type an entry in a multiple choice field, but you can press any key to move directly to the first choice that begins with the specified letter. If this is not the one you want, you must press the spacebar to move forward through the list to find the right one. Thus, this picture function may actually inconvenience you if too many choices are available, especially if many of them begin with the same letter. Note also that because you cannot type an explicit entry that is not in the multiple choice list, there is no need to assign any other picture functions or template symbols to format the data.

You can use templates to format and validate entered data one character at a time, as well as to determine the display width. For example, each exclamation point (!) in a template converts the character displayed or entered in the corresponding position to uppercase; an A allows only an alphabetic character to be entered, and a 9 permits only a digit or a minus sign. If the part numbers in an inventory data base consisted of 3 letters followed by 3 digits, you could collect this field with the template AAA999.

If a template contains any symbols other than the standard template characters, dBASE IV inserts them automatically into the data in the specified positions; during data entry, the cursor passes over these character positions. For example, you could use the template 999-9999 to format the TELEPHONE field in the Customer File as 3 digits, a dash (supplied automatically by dBASE IV), and 4 more digits. If the TELEPHONE field were long enough to accommodate an area code, you could use a template such as (999) 999-9999 or 999/999-9999 to format the field.

"Extra" symbols inserted into character fields normally become a permanent part of the data stored on disk. If you prefer to use these symbols for display purposes only, you can assign the R (Raw) picture function. Thus, a TELEPHONE field collected with the template 999-9999 consists of 8 characters—the 7 digits typed by the user and the dash added automatically by dBASE IV—unless you also specify the R function, in which case only 7 digits are stored in the data base. Unless you can save a great deal of disk space by eliminating extra symbols, allowing dBASE IV to store these "punctuation marks" in the data base makes it easier to build report, label, and screen forms, and makes the fields more readable on the standard Edit and Browse screens, and in the output of LIST and DISPLAY commands typed at the dot prompt.

It is not always appropriate to insert punctuation marks automatically. For example, assigning the template 99999-9999 to the ZIP field in the Customer File would cause dBASE IV to add the dash to *every* ZIP code, and it would appear at the end of 5-digit ZIP codes. You could correct this problem by using the R picture function, but if you did this, the dash entered into 10-digit ZIP codes would *not* be stored with the data, and you would have to add it in whenever you printed or displayed the field. Instead, you might use the template 99999#9999 to collect 10-digit ZIP codes. To permit the entry of the dash, the sixth character of the template must be a # rather than a 9 (in a character field, the 9 symbol permits only a digit or a minus sign, while # accepts a digit, space, minus sign, or decimal point). Of course, you cannot use either 9 or # symbols in the template if you anticipate Canadian or European postal codes, which are different lengths and can contain letters as well as numbers.

When you use picture functions or a template to format a numeric or float field, extra symbols such as commas in the template or a leading dollar sign produced by the $ (Financial) picture function are not stored on disk. If you later use the standard Edit or Browse screen to view the data, you will see that the field contains only digits, perhaps a minus sign, and, if decimal places were specified in the structure, a decimal point. However, extra symbols added for display purposes do occupy space in the template. To display a field that is 10 digits wide (including a decimal point and 2 digits after the decimal) with the $ picture function, you must make the template 11 characters wide.

You can assign any reasonable combination of picture functions and a template. For example, the $ picture function causes dBASE IV to display a currency symbol (by default in the United States, a dollar sign) in front of a numeric field. Often, you may want to combine this function with a template that includes inserted commas and a decimal point. Do not confuse the $ picture function with the $ template symbol, which replaces leading blank spaces with dollar signs. If you assigned the $ picture function and a template such as 9,999,999.99, dBASE IV would display the number 1242.07 as $1,242.07. The template $,$$$,$$$.$$ would result in the display of the form $$$$1,242.07 (this display format is often used to prevent someone from altering a number by adding leading digits, as when you print the dollar amount on a check).

In some cases, you can achieve the same result with either a picture function or a template. For example, to allow only letters in the STATE field, you could use the A picture function or the template AA. In this case, there is no clear advantage to either alternative, but it is usually better to use a picture function if one is available, because the function is independent of the field length. If you later lengthened the field, you would not have to edit the template in the screen form.

To specify more than one attribute for each character in a field, you must use picture functions, or combine a function and a template. For example, to ensure that the first three letters in the inventory part number described earlier are not only letters, but uppercase letters, you could use the ! picture function together with the AAA999 template. To restrict entries in the STATE field to uppercase letters, you could use the A picture function and the template !!, the ! picture function with the template AA, or the ! and A picture functions. (You cannot accomplish this validation using only a template, because a template can contain only one symbol for each character position.) In general, it is best to use picture functions for their intended purpose—to establish the overall format for a field—and use a template to format a field character by character.

Using the Edit Options

The commands described so far in this chapter enable you to control the appearance and format of the data that is displayed and collected on a custom screen form. The Edit options, accessed through the dialog box that is invoked when you add a field to the screen design work surface or modify an existing field, allow you to exercise equally precise control over its content. You can define default values and specify detailed validation tests that determine whether you can edit a field and what conditions must be satisfied before your entry is accepted. The edit options dialog box, with the specifications for the LASTORDER field displayed, is illustrated in Figure 15-7.

The **Editing allowed** option determines whether dBASE IV permits you to edit the field. If you set this option to **No**, dBASE IV displays the field on the screen but does not allow you to edit it, and the other options in the dialog box, all of which control aspects of the data editing environment, become unavailable. You might want to prohibit editing for fields such as the order dates and totals in the National Widgets Customer File, which should be updated only by entering and posting orders, to prevent other users from inadvertently or intentionally changing data without a proper audit trail or in a way that would throw the accounting system out of balance.

The **Message** option defines a message, up to 80 characters long, that is displayed on the message line at the bottom of the screen when the cursor is inside the field. You can use this option to define a brief message that provides more information about the purpose, content, or format of a field than you

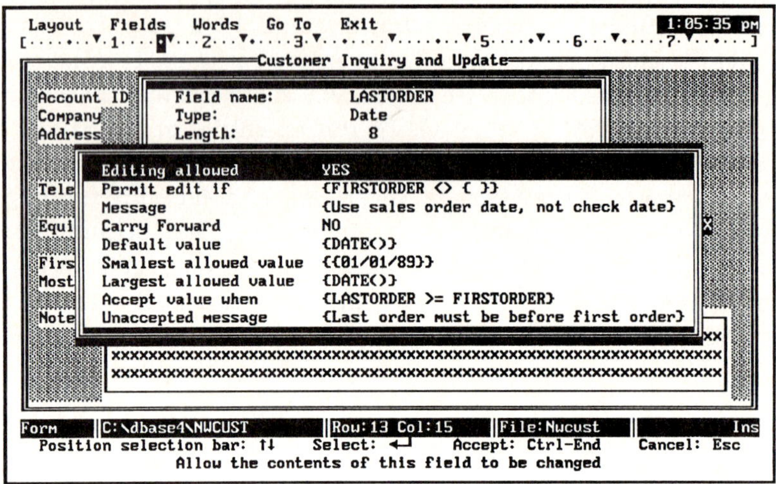

Figure 15-7.

The edit options dialog box

could easily fit on the screen. For example, the message for the CREDITOK field might read, "Enter Y only if credit terms have been approved by the accountant." If any special validation rules are in effect, you might want to summarize them briefly, and if you are using the M (Multiple choice) picture function to collect the field, the message might be a reminder of how multiple choice fields work, such as "Press <SPACEBAR> to display choices, then press <ENTER> to select one."

The **Default value** option establishes a standard value for a field, which dBASE IV fills in automatically when you add new records to the data base. For example, National Widgets does most of its business in California, so you might assign the default value "CA" for the STATE field. Establishing a default value, especially for a field longer than the two-letter STATE, can save time during data entry, and it can improve the accuracy of the data by reducing the potential for typographical errors and inconsistent entries. You can always override the default during data entry by simply typing over it. Note also that the default value has no effect on existing records, even those in which the field is blank.

If you use a constant for the default value, your entry in the edit options dialog box must conform to the usual rules for entering constants: character strings (such as "CA") must be enclosed in quotes, dates must be enclosed in braces (curly brackets), and the logical values .T. and .F. must include the periods. However, the default need not be a constant—you can specify any legitimate expression. For example, you might use the expression DATE() (the result of evaluating the function that yields the current date) as the default value in an order date field, or an expression such as DATE() + 30 (which evaluates to the date 30 days in the future) as the default value for an invoice due date.

The **Carry Forward** option allows you to specify another kind of default value. When this option is set to **Yes**, dBASE IV "carries forward" the data in the previous record entered during the current work session into the corresponding field in each new record to serve as the default value, just as if you had pressed F8 (Ditto). This option is particularly useful when the input documents are grouped so that many consecutive entries have the same value in one or more fields, but there is enough variation that a single default value would be inappropriate.

For example, if you were entering records into a mailing list data base from a printout or a set of labels in ZIP code order, you might set **Carry forward** to **Yes** for the CITY and STATE fields, and if the list were large enough, perhaps for the ZIP as well. Each new record in the mailing list would then inherit the values entered into the CITY, STATE, and ZIP fields in the previous record. Each time one of these fields changed, you could type over the default to enter a new value, which would become the new default for the next record.

The **Smallest allowed value** and **Largest allowed value** options impose a lower and upper limit on the entries in a numeric, date, or character field. For example, to restrict entries in a sales tax rate field to numbers between 0 and 10, you could define the smallest allowed value as 0 and the largest allowed value as 10. To restrict entries in the LASTORDER date field in the Customer File to dates in the current year that are no later than the current date, you would enter {01/01/92} as the smallest allowed value (in 1992) and DATE() (the result of evaluating the current date function) as the largest.

When you use the form to update a data base, entering a value outside the permissible range causes dBASE IV to display an error message such as "Range is 0.00 to 10.00 (press SPACE)" on the message line at the bottom of the screen. Pressing the spacebar clears the error message, but the cursor will not advance to the next field until you enter an acceptable value. By default, dBASE IV applies the range test only to new or changed data. Thus, with a range that limits entries in the LASTORDER field to dates in the current year, you could not enter a date outside this range into a new record or change a date in a previously entered record to one outside the range. However, dBASE IV would allow earlier dates in existing records to stand as entered.

The **Permit edit if** option specifies a *pre-edit condition*: a condition that must be fulfilled *before* you can edit a field. The **Accept value when** option specifies a *post-edit condition:* a condition that must be fulfilled before dBASE IV accepts your entry and allows the cursor to advance to the next field. For each of these options, you can enter any legitimate dBASE IV condition (any expression that evaluates to the logical value .T. or .F.). In most cases, the pre-edit condition is based on other fields in the record, and the post-edit condition is based on the value entered into the field itself.

You can use a pre-edit condition to make a field available only if another field is already filled in. For example, if you added a COUNTRY field to the Customer File to accommodate foreign addresses, you might want to collect this field only if the STATE field was blank, by specifying the **Permit edit if** condition as follows:

```
STATE = " "
```

Post-edit conditions enable you to express more complex validation tests than you could carry out using picture functions, templates, and ranges of permissible entries. For example, you could use a condition such as the following to exclude blank values in the ADDRESS field:

```
ADDRESS <> " "
```

You might test the length of the ZIP code field to ensure that it is exactly 5 digits or exactly 10 digits long with the following **Accept value when** condition:

```
LEN(TRIM(ZIP)) = 5 .OR. LEN(TRIM(ZIP)) = 10
```

In this expression, the TRIM function removes trailing blank spaces from the ZIP field (this function works much like the T picture function). The LEN function takes a character string expression as input and yields as output the length of the string. In this case, the character string that results from trimming trailing blank spaces from the ZIP field serves as input to the LEN function. You must trim the ZIP field before measuring its length, because by default dBASE IV measures the length of a data base field as the field width defined in the structure, even if the data entered does not fill the field.

You may also want to test the relationship between two fields. For example, if you permitted editing for the first and last order dates, you might test LASTORDER to ensure that it is not before FIRSTORDER and not later than the current date with a condition such as the following:

```
LASTORDER >= FIRSTORDER .AND. LASTORDER <= DATE()
```

You can also use a post-edit condition to validate a field by testing it against a list of acceptable values. For example, you might not want to make the STATE field a multiple choice field because there are too many choices, but it would be advantageous to ensure that the entry is one of the legitimate postal abbreviations. To carry out this type of validation, you could enter a post-edit condition that tests whether the field is contained in a longer character string that lists all the legitimate entries, as follows:

```
STATE $ "AK,AL,AR,AZ,CA,DE,OR,WA"
```

Although this example does not include all 50 state abbreviations, it illustrates the general principle. Note that dBASE IV does not recognize this condition as a specialized validation test. As with any other entry for the **Accept value when** condition, it simply evaluates the specified condition (in this case by testing whether the two characters entered into the STATE field occur anywhere within the arbitrary character string enclosed in quotes) and accepts the entry only if the condition evaluates to .T.. In this example, the commas (or other punctuation) are required so that dBASE IV does not interpret erroneous combinations such as "KA" as valid entries. You should also use a picture function, a template, or a combination of the two to ensure that only letters of the alphabet are accepted into the state field to prohibit entries such as "K,", which would pass the validation test. If you want to allow the STATE field to remain blank, you must include two blank spaces somewhere in the test string, as follows:

```
STATE $ "  ,AK,AL,AR,AZ,CA,DE,OR,WA"
```

The **Unaccepted message** option allows you to customize the message that is displayed on the message line, along with the instruction "(press SPACE)" if the entry in a field does not satisfy the **Accept value when** condition. For the

LASTORDER field, you might use a message such as "Most recent order must be after first order and before today." If you fill in a post-edit condition but do not enter a message, dBASE IV uses the generic message "Editing condition not satisfied (press SPACE)."

ENHANCING THE APPEARANCE OF A FORM

When you use a screen form to edit data, dBASE displays data fields and background items such as text, boxes, and display-only fields in the same colors or monochrome attributes that are used in the standard Edit screen. You can change the display colors and otherwise enhance the appearance of your custom data entry screens with options that are similar to those used to dress up printed forms. The **Box** and **Line** options on the **Layout** menu function exactly like their counterparts in the report layout editor: you can draw lines and boxes made up of continuous single or double lines, or any other character selected from a pop-up ASCII table.

Just as in the report layout editor, you use the options on the **Words** menu to enhance the appearance of any region on the screen selected with the F6 (Select) key. Remember that you can select a field, a box, or a line by pressing F6 (Select) and then ENTER. You can use the **Position** option on the **Words** menu to left-justify, center, or right-justify items within the current margins, which are set by default at columns 0 and 79. For example, to create a border with a superimposed title, such as the one in Figure 15-3, you would first use the **Box** option on the **Layout** menu to draw the border. Next, you could type the title for the screen, "Customer Inquiry and Update", anywhere on the top border of the box, select the text with the F6 (Select) key, and center the title by selecting **Position** from the **Words** menu and choosing **Center** from the pick list. Changing the margins later (using the **Modify ruler** option) does not affect items that were left-justified, right-justified, or centered based on the previous margin settings.

The selections accessed through the **Style** option on the **Words** menu apply only to printed forms, and the **Style** option is not available in the screen layout editor. Instead, you use the **Display** options (which are not applicable to printed forms) to alter the appearance of selected items on a custom screen. When you select the **Display** option, dBASE IV displays either the pick list of available colors shown in Figure 15-8 (in black and white) or the list of monochrome attributes illustrated in Figure 15-9, depending on your monitor.

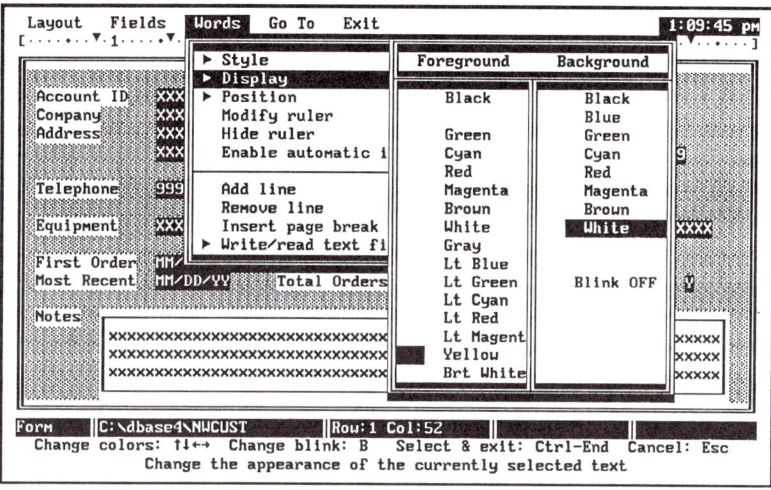

Figure 15-8.

The display colors pick list

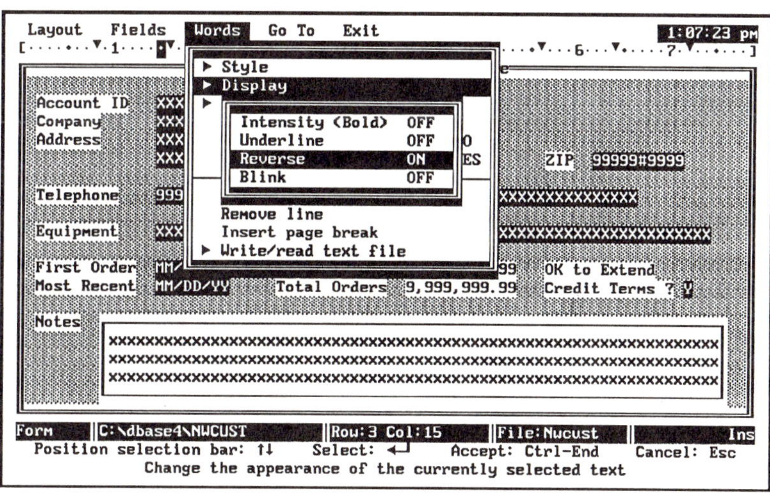

Figure 15-9.

The monochrome attributes pick list

On a monochrome screen, there are four display attributes—**Intensity (Bold)**, **Underline**, **Reverse**, and **Blink**—which you can combine in any way that you see fit.

If you have a color monitor, you can set the foreground and background colors independently for the selected items. As you move among the color names with the arrow keys, you can observe the effects of your current selections in the pick list. The name of the foreground color is always displayed in that color against the currently selected background color, and the background colors appear in the pick list as bars of color with the names superimposed in the currently selected foreground color. The display of the **Blink** option also reflects the current combination of foreground and background colors. You can use the **Blink** option to cause the selected text to blink, or flash (this attribute should be used sparingly, if at all, to call attention to important warning messages).

When you choose a color combination or monochrome attribute, dBASE IV applies this attribute only to the selected items, but it remains in effect until further notice to govern the display format of new items added to the work surface. Thus, the best way to change the display colors or monochrome attribute assigned to a few individual items is to construct your entire screen form using the default colors or attributes and then change the colors for the desired items. If you want to change the colors for *all* prompts or *all* data base fields, it is easier to modify the standard colors used by dBASE IV for these items, using commands covered in Chapter 18.

USING A SCREEN FORM TO VIEW AND UPDATE DATA

The format file created by the screen layout editor draws a custom screen that substitutes for the standard Edit display. Only the appearance and layout of the screen are different. You can use the usual cursor movement and editing command keys to move around the screen and enter and edit data. dBASE IV displays the standard Edit menu bar at the top of the screen and allows you to select all the same options, including the commands for adding and deleting records. If you add new records to a data base using a screen form that does not allow access to all the fields, the fields that are not displayed or that cannot be edited remain blank.

If you specified a pre-edit condition for a field using the **Permit edit if** option, dBASE IV does not allow you to move the cursor into the field unless the condition is satisfied. Similarly, if the entry in a field does not satisfy the post-edit condition specified with the **Accept data when** option, or if it does not fall within the range defined by the **Smallest allowed value** and **Largest allowed value**, dBASE IV displays the usual error message on the message line below the status bar, and does not allow you to move the cursor out of the field until you correct the problem.

Custom screen forms control the layout of the screen only in Edit mode; when you switch to the Browse screen, dBASE IV displays records in the familiar tabular arrangement. However, the data formatting and validation specifications defined using picture functions, templates, and Edit options do apply to data collected on the Browse screen.

This behavior can cause a potentially serious problem: fields that cannot be edited do not even appear in the Browse display. You can solve this problem by using the pre-edit condition .F. to prohibit editing rather than setting the **Editing allowed** option to **No**. Recall that .F., the logical constant "False," by itself constitutes a valid condition (an expression that evaluates to a logical value). Because this condition is never true, using it as the **Permit edit if** condition prevents you from ever editing the field, but because **Editing allowed** is set to **Yes**, dBASE IV displays the field on the Browse screen. If you use this method to prohibit editing, note that dBASE IV displays the field on the edit screen in the colors used for entered data (as it would if you used any other pre-edit condition); if you prefer to use the colors assigned to displayed text, you must set the colors explicitly, using the **Display** option on the **Words** menu.

When you exit the screen layout editor, dBASE IV automatically opens the form that you just created or edited and uses it to draw the screen when you next edit or add records. You can open a previously created screen form in a later work session either from the menu system or from the dot prompt. When you close a data base or view, dBASE IV automatically closes any open form file, since a form file, like an index, can be open only in conjunction with a data base.

From the Menus

To open a screen form from the Control Center, you highlight its name in the **Forms** panel, press ENTER, and select **Display data** from the resulting pop-up dialog box. You can also use the standard function key shortcut for displaying data: press F2 (Data) with the desired screen form name highlighted. As with report and label forms, dBASE IV records the name of the data base that was open when you created the screen form or edited it last, so you need not open a data base before selecting a form.

If you want to use a screen form file to update a different data base or view, you must open the data base or view before you choose the form file from the **Forms** panel. dBASE IV asks you to confirm your intentions with the message "You may choose to use either the current database file or view, or the database file or view usually associated with the file you just selected." Choose **Current view** to use the open data base or view, or the default name to return to the original file or view. If a form refers to fields not present in the active data base, a "Variable not found" error will result when you attempt to edit or append records. The only possible response to this error message is to choose **Cancel** from the pop-up dialog box; dBASE IV then returns you to the Control Center.

From the Dot Prompt

From the dot prompt, you open a screen form with the SET FORMAT command, which is derived from the term "format file," the name used for screen forms in earlier versions of dBASE IV. The syntax is as follows:

SET FORMAT TO *screen form name*

When you open a screen form file from the dot prompt, any data base may be open or none. If no file or view is open, the SET FORMAT command does not generate an error message, so you can type this command before or after the USE command that opens the data base you wish to update. However, if no data base is open when you type APPEND or EDIT, dBASE IV displays the usual "No database in use. Enter filename:" dialog box. From the dot prompt, you can open a screen form with any compatible data base or view—not just the file that was open when you created the form—without any warning from dBASE IV.

When you close a data base or view, dBASE IV automatically closes any open screen form file. After an editing session, dBASE IV leaves both the data base and the form file open when you return to the dot prompt; you can exit the Edit screen, type other commands, and return to editing records without reopening the form file. If you type a new SET FORMAT command, dBASE IV closes any screen form file that was active before opening the new one. You can also close a screen form explicitly without opening another and without closing the active data base by typing

```
SET FORMAT TO
```

or

```
CLOSE FORMAT
```

SUMMARY

Designing custom screen forms that substitute for the standard dBASE IV Edit screen represents a giant step toward customizing the working environment to conform to the needs of an application and its users. A custom screen can be more attractively laid out and include better prompts and more informative messages to help the user during data entry. More importantly, screen forms enable you to format and validate fields, and thus improve the accuracy and consistency of the data entered using the form. This is especially important when many people in an organization update the same data base and when later operations—such as indexing, sorting, or multifile update procedures—depend on this consistency. Even if you do not deviate much from the field arrangement of the Quick Screen Layout, you will find that the time spent creating a form that uses templates, picture functions, and edit options will pay off many times over as you work with the data base.

CHAPTER SIXTEEN

Reorganizing Data Bases

All the commands and procedures described so far in this book have acted on a single data base (at times, opened together with related auxiliary files such as indexes, query files, and label, report, or screen form files) that remained relatively static in structure and content. As a dBASE IV application grows and matures, you will usually find that you need to reorganize the data bases in various ways.

No matter how scrupulous your advance planning was, the initial data entry and testing phase usually reveals the need for some modifications to the file structures. You may have made some fields too long or too short, assigned inappropriate data types, overlooked some required fields, and optimistically added fields to the structure that were never filled in. If you do not use custom data entry screens, you may want to rearrange the order of the fields so that the Edit and Browse screens are more convenient for entering and editing records. You may also need to rename fields. Combining data bases is easiest if the corresponding fields have the same names, and if you work with several similar data bases, assigning matching fields the same names, lengths, and data types allows you to use the same screen, label, and report forms with all the files.

In most applications, you will occasionally need to create new files derived from data stored in existing data bases, or to combine several similar data bases into one. After you have been using an application for a year or two, you may want to summarize and condense data, either to produce analytical reports or to save disk space. You can also reclaim disk space and improve performance by periodically purging a file of "obsolete" records. The definition of "obsolete" depends on the application and the context, however. For example, National Widgets might empty the Order File at the end of each year but retain customers for two or three years after the date of their last order. When you delete records en masse, you may want to transfer them to a summary or archive file before you permanently erase them from your active data base.

This chapter covers the dBASE IV commands and menu options that you can use to restructure and otherwise reorganize your data base files, and it suggests some typical strategies for combining these techniques. Understanding these commands enables you to take a broader view of a dBASE IV application and to add the "housekeeping," or file maintenance, procedures that are necessary in an ongoing application, especially one that makes use of large files.

EXTRACTING A PORTION OF A DATA BASE

You have already had considerable experience in viewing selected information stored in one or more data base files. By using a variety of techniques presented in earlier chapters, you can specify field lists and record selection criteria to view, print, or perform calculations based on specific data subsets. At times, you will need to make these selections permanent and create a new data base that contains selected data extracted from an existing file. For example, National Widgets might want to give away or sell a mailing list of its customers but include on the list only the name and address fields, not the order dates and totals.

You may find after working with a large file for a while that certain records are almost always handled as a group, separate from the rest of the file. By copying these records to a new data base and deleting them from the original, you can make your files smaller and speed up processing. Even when you cannot or prefer not to divide a file permanently, you may be able to expedite certain operations by splitting off a subset of the records and then performing your inquiries or printing reports based on the smaller file. For example, you might be able to work with the smaller data subset on another computer while your main machine is occupied with normal daily processing, or you may want to give the file to a colleague for further analysis.

From the Menus

When you work in the menu system, you use view queries to define both field lists and record selection criteria. As described in Chapter 6, a view query is a virtual file—it behaves as if it were a real data base consisting of the specific fields and records from the original data bases described by the query. You can create a true data base file that contains the information specified by a view query by using the **Write view as database file** option on the **Layout** menu on the query design screen. When you choose **Write view as database file**, dBASE IV prompts you to enter a name for the new file; if you have already assigned a name to the view, this name appears as the default name for the new data base (which is given the standard DBF extension).

The **Write view as database file** option provides one way to make an exact copy of an existing data base. If you invoke Query-by-Example with the original data base open, the view skeleton includes all the fields, and if you do not specify record selection criteria, dBASE IV will copy all the records to the new file. In most cases, there is no need to save the query itself, since it is easy enough to re-create if you ever need to copy the same file again.

Although this method works and is easy to understand, it is not the best way to create an exact duplicate of a data base. The DOS COPY command and the dBASE IV COPY FILE command accessed through the **DOS Utilities** option on the Control Center **Tools** menu (which is described further in Chapter 19) both do the job faster, because these commands copy *any disk file* as a whole, rather than transferring records one by one to a new data base. The real utility of Query-by-Example derives from the flexibility and control it offers over the structure and contents of the new file, which are described by the view skeleton and the selection criteria.

When you use the **Write view as database file** option to create a new data base, the structure includes all the fields in the view skeleton in the order in which they appear on the query design screen. Fields in the view skeleton that you renamed assume the new names rather than the field names in the original data base. If you entered record selection criteria in the file skeleton or the condition box, dBASE IV copies only the selected records to the new data base, and if you specified sorting operators, they determine the record sequence. Records that are marked for deletion are copied, along with the deletion marker, to the new file, unless the DELETED setting is ON to exclude deleted records.

Figure 16-1 illustrates the NWCPHONE query created in Chapter 6 to display a list of the names and telephone numbers of National Widgets' customers, modified slightly to generate a new data base that contains only California customers. The selection criteria were specified by entering the condition = "CA" in the STATE column, and the sorting operator **Asc1** in the ACCOUNT column instructs dBASE IV to sort the output file in ASCII order based on the ACCOUNT field.

Figure 16-2 illustrates the data base created by using the **Write view as database file** option to write the selected fields and records to a data base called NWCALIST (for "National Widgets California List"). The Browse screen in this figure displays the same data as the NWCPHONE view query, but you can see from the "File" indicator in the status bar that the data is drawn from a true data base rather than a view. As is often the case, the data base created by writing the output of a view query to a true data base does not include the field on which the selection criteria were based (the STATE field in this case). If

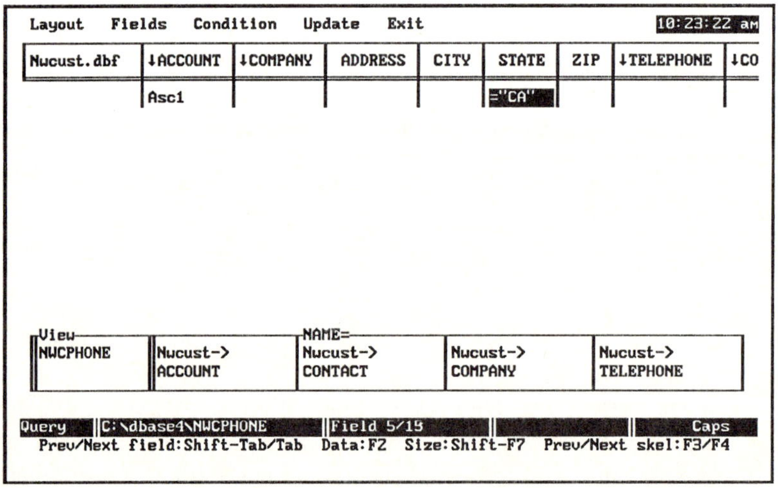

```
Layout   Fields   Condition   Update   Exit                          10:23:22 am

Nwcust.dbf | ↓ACCOUNT | ↓COMPANY | ADDRESS | CITY | STATE | ZIP | ↓TELEPHONE | ↓CO
           | Asc1     |          |         |      | ="CA" |     |            |

View         NAME=
NWCPHONE   | Nwcust->  | Nwcust->  | Nwcust->  | Nwcust->
           | ACCOUNT   | CONTACT   | COMPANY   | TELEPHONE

Query  |C:\dbase4\NWCPHONE   |Field 5/15  |          |   Caps
 Prev/Next field:Shift-Tab/Tab  Data:F2  Size:Shift-F7  Prev/Next skel:F3/F4
```

Figure 16-1.

Defining a view query to extract records to a new data base

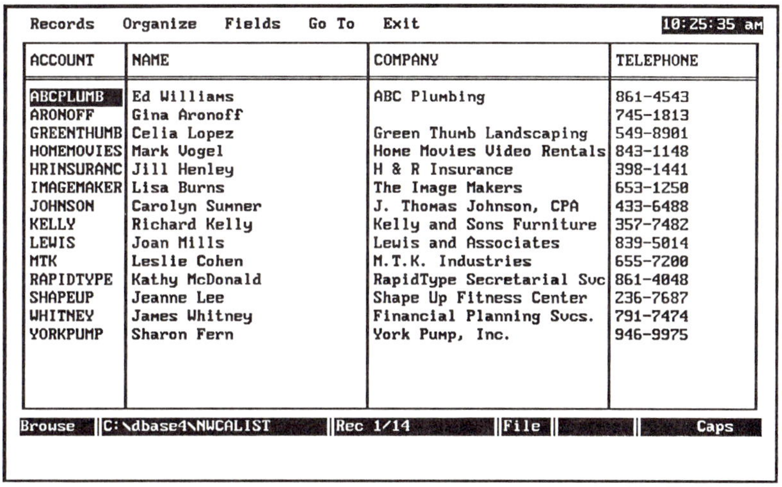

Records Organize Fields Go To Exit 10:25:35 am

ACCOUNT	NAME	COMPANY	TELEPHONE
ABCPLUMB	Ed Williams	ABC Plumbing	861-4543
ARONOFF	Gina Aronoff		745-1813
GREENTHUMB	Celia Lopez	Green Thumb Landscaping	549-8901
HOMEMOVIES	Mark Vogel	Home Movies Video Rentals	843-1148
HRINSURANC	Jill Henley	H & R Insurance	398-1441
IMAGEMAKER	Lisa Burns	The Image Makers	653-1250
JOHNSON	Carolyn Sumner	J. Thomas Johnson, CPA	433-6488
KELLY	Richard Kelly	Kelly and Sons Furniture	357-7482
LEWIS	Joan Mills	Lewis and Associates	839-5014
MTK	Leslie Cohen	M.T.K. Industries	655-7200
RAPIDTYPE	Kathy McDonald	RapidType Secretarial Svc	861-4048
SHAPEUP	Jeanne Lee	Shape Up Fitness Center	236-7687
WHITNEY	James Whitney	Financial Planning Svcs.	791-7474
YORKPUMP	Sharon Fern	York Pump, Inc.	946-9975

Browse | C:\dbase4\NWCALIST | Rec 1/14 | File | | Caps

Figure 16-2.

The NWCALIST data base extracted from the Customer File

you try this example yourself, you may want to include the STATE field in the view skeleton, or compare the resulting data base to the original Customer File to verify that the right records were selected.

D From the Dot Prompt

When you work at the dot prompt, you can use the COPY command to create a new data base that contains selected fields from selected records in the active data base. In its simplest form, COPY makes an exact copy of the original data base:

COPY TO *new data base file*

For example, you could use the following sequence of commands to copy the data in the National Widgets Customer File to a new file called CUSTOMER:

```
USE NWCUST
COPY TO CUSTOMER
```

If the target file (CUSTOMER.DBF in this example) already exists, dBASE IV warns you "File already exists" in a pop-up box and offers two options: **Overwrite** and **Cancel**. If you inadvertently used the name of an existing file, you can select **Cancel**, press UP ARROW to retrieve the COPY command from history, edit the file name, and resubmit the command. The COPY command first creates a new, empty data base file with the specified name and then adds records to this file one at a time. Records marked for deletion are copied, along with the deletion marker, to the new file, unless you have set the DELETED option ON to exclude deleted records.

As noted in the previous section, the DOS COPY command or the dBASE IV equivalent, COPY FILE (these commands are explained in Chapter 19), are faster than the dBASE IV COPY command if you want to create an exact duplicate of an existing data base, since these commands copy a file as a whole. In contrast, the slower dBASE COPY command allows you to specify the fields in the new file structure with a FIELDS clause, determine the record sequence by indexing or sorting the original file, and select which records should be transferred by using a filter, a scope, a FOR clause, and a WHILE clause. For example, the following command sequence copies the name and telephone fields from National Widgets' California customers to a new data base, NWCALIST, which is in alphabetical order by account code:

```
USE NWCUST ORDER ACCOUNT
COPY TO NWCALIST FIELDS ACCOUNT, CONTACT, COMPANY, TELEPHONE FOR STATE = "CA"
```

If you want to rename fields in the new file, you must specify the field list with a SET FIELDS command rather than by including a FIELDS clause in the COPY command. For example, to change the name of the CONTACT field to NAME, you could use the following command sequence:

```
USE NWCUST ORDER ACCOUNT
SET FIELDS TO ACCOUNT, NAME=CONTACT, COMPANY, TELEPHONE
COPY TO NWCALIST FOR STATE = "CA"
```

Copying a Data Base Structure

At times, you may want to copy just the structure of a data base file to create a new, empty data base. For example, you might have several different mailing list files that require exactly the same fields. To begin a new list, you could copy the structure of any existing list rather than creating an identical data base from scratch. You might also want to copy a file structure in order to create a new data base that is similar to an existing file without having to type in all the field specifications. After copying the structure, you could open the new file and modify the structure by adding, deleting, or changing fields (modifying the structure of a data base is explained later in this chapter). It is much easier and more direct to carry out this operation from the dot prompt than from the menu system; even if you prefer to do most of your work in the menus, you may want to use the dot prompt to copy a file structure.

From the Menus

Working in the menu system, there is no direct way to copy just the structure of a data base file, but you can create a query that copies a data base using selection criteria that select no records. For example, to create a copy of the Customer File structure, you could move to Query-by-Example with the Customer File open, so that the view skeleton automatically includes all the Customer File fields. You could then enter any condition in the Customer File skeleton that is not true for any record, such as = "ZZ" in the STATE column, and select **Write view as database file** from the **Layout** menu. Note that dBASE IV must read every record in the Customer File to determine that no records fulfill the selection criteria, and this process may take some time if the file you are copying is large. In most cases, you can exit from the query design screen by selecting **Abandon changes and exit** from the **Exit** menu; even if you need to repeat the process, it is easy enough to re-create the query.

When you use this method to copy a file structure, dBASE IV does not create a production MDX file (or any other indexes) for the new data base. After copying the structure, you must open the new file and build any index tags you need; if you wish, you can do this before you begin entering data into the new file.

From the Dot Prompt

From the dot prompt, you can copy just the structure of an existing data base to create a new empty file by opening the file and using a COPY command that includes the keyword STRUCTURE, as follows:

COPY STRUCTURE TO *new file name* FIELDS *field list*

By default, dBASE IV does not create a production MDX file (or any other indexes) for a data base that you create with a COPY command, and you must open the new file with a USE command and build any index tags or NDX indexes you need. If you want many of the same index tags for the new file that you had in the production MDX file for the original, you can instruct dBASE IV to create a production MDX file by adding the phrase WITH PRODUCTION to a COPY or COPY STRUCTURE command, as follows:

COPY STRUCTURE TO *new file name* FIELDS *field list* WITH PRODUCTION

In early versions of dBASE IV 1.1, it is advisable to carry out the COPY command with no master index tag active if you use the WITH PRODUCTION option, to ensure that the indexes correctly reference the data base. If you want to copy records in indexed order, you can open the new data base after the copy operation completes and use a REINDEX command to rebuild all the tags in the production MDX file that dBASE IV creates.

COMBINING DATA BASES

At times, you may also need to combine data bases, perhaps to assimilate a file created by a colleague or an associate, or to produce combined reports, labels, or statistics from data stored in different files. dBASE IV offers several methods for combining files, and all but one identify matching fields in the *source* file (the file that provides the data) and the *target* file (the file that receives the new records) by name. Corresponding fields need not be the same length, they need not be arranged in the same order, and either file can have additional fields not present in the other. Matching fields can even be of different data types, provided that the data in the source field is a plausible entry in the corresponding field in the target file. For example, you can read a date field into a character field that is at least eight characters long, and the result is a character string that "looks like" a date. Similarly, you can exchange data between numeric, float, or logical fields and character fields.

When the source field is shorter than the target field, dBASE IV pads the data with blank spaces to fill the field width. It truncates a character field that is too long to fit in the target field, but if a numeric value is too long, it fills the target field with asterisks to indicate a *numeric overflow*—a number too long for

the field width or display format—because truncating a number would render the data meaningless. Extra fields in the target file remain blank, and data is lost from fields in the source file that have no counterparts in the target file. These relationships are diagrammed in Figure 16-3, which illustrates schematically the way dBASE IV would add records to a hypothetical mailing list file called MAILLIST.DBF from the National Widgets Customer File.

dBASE IV transfers records to the target file that are marked for deletion in the source file, unless you have turned the DELETED setting ON. However, it drops the deletion marker, on the assumption that if you had wanted to delete the records, you would have used the DELETED setting to exclude them from the target file.

With strategic use of the techniques presented in this and the preceding section, you can maintain several files with similar structures but different data and either combine them or extract groups of records for specific purposes. For example, you might have several mailing list files with the same name and address fields but other structural differences. If you rarely need to include all the names on the lists in a single mailing, keeping the files separate maximizes processing speed in each file. For the occasional combined mailing, you can append all the data into one file and delete the "extra" records later. If you frequently mail to the entire list, however, it is more convenient to store all the names in one file and copy specific subsets of the list to separate files for certain queries or reports.

When you design your data bases, you may not be able to predict all the ways in which you will later want to reorganize them, but it is always prudent to use the same names for fields that have similar purposes to facilitate future data transfers. This may mean that a field name is not always entirely descriptive of its contents. For example, you might end up calling a mailing list field CONTACT instead of NAME to match a customer file or use generic field names such as FIRSTDATE rather than FIRSTMAIL or FIRSTORDER. You can partially compensate for these inconveniences by assigning new names to the fields in view queries or when you invoke the Edit or Browse screen from the dot prompt (if you do not need to edit the fields).

If you frequently combine data bases temporarily and update records in the combined file, adding an extra field that records the original source of the data makes it easy to split up the list afterwards into its component data bases. For example, in a mailing list application, this field could contain a short code (one character is usually sufficient) that identifies which list permanently stores each record. When you extract records from the combined file to split up the list, you can base your selection criteria on this field.

```
Structure for database: C:\DBASE4\NWCUST.DBF
Number of data records:       20
Date of last update   : 11/15/88
Field  Field Name  Type       Width   Dec   Index
    1  ACCOUNT     Character     10             Y
    2  COMPANY     Character     25             N
    3  ADDRESS     Character     25             N
    4  CITY        Character     20             N
    5  STATE       Character      2             N
    6  ZIP         Character     10             Y
    7  TELEPHONE   Character      8             N
    8  CONTACT     Character     25             N
    9  EQUIPMENT   Character    100             N
   10  FIRSTORDER  Date           8             N
   11  LASTORDER   Date           8             N
   12  CREDITOK    Logical        1             N
   13  YTDORDERS   Numeric       10     2       N
   14  TOTORDERS   Numeric       10     2       N
   15  COMMENTS    Memo          10             N
** Total **                     273
```

10 spaces added
10 spaces added
5 spaces lost
5 spaces lost
10 spaces added

```
Structure for database: C:\DBASE4\MAILLIST.DBF
Number of data records:       82
Date of last update   : 11/15/88
Field  Field Name  Type       Width   Dec   Index
    1  CONTACT     Character     35             N
    2  COMPANY     Character     35             N
    3  ADDRESS     Character     35             N
    4  CITY        Character     15             N
    5  STATE       Character      2             N
    6  ZIP         Character      5             N
    7  COUNTRY     Character     15             N
    8  SOURCELIST  Character      5             N
    9  LASTMAIL    Date           8             N
   10  NOTES       Memo          10             N
** Total **                     166
```

Fields 1, 7, 9, 10, 11, 12, 13, 14, 15 not transferred

Fields 7, 8, 9, 10 remain blank

Figure 16-3.

Appending records into a mailing list data base from the Customer File

From the Menus

To add records to the active data base from another dBASE IV data base, you select the **Append records from dBASE file** option on the **Append** menu on the data base design screen and choose the name of the source file from a pick list. The other options on the **Append** menu allow you to append records one by one from the keyboard (as described in Chapter 4) and to "copy" (actually, append) data from files created by other programs (exchanging data with other software is explained in Chapter 20).

You cannot append data from a view query, because view queries do not contain data; they contain only the instructions for extracting the data from a true data base. To append records selectively, you must complete two steps. First, you must design a view query that specifies the record selection criteria, and use the **Write view as database file** option on the query design screen **Layout** menu to copy the selected records to a true data base. The view query can contain all or some of the fields in the source file, and you can rename the fields if you want to. Second, you must append the newly created data base into the target file, and erase the temporary file to reclaim the space it occupied on your hard disk.

From the Dot Prompt

From the dot prompt, you can use the APPEND FROM command to combine two files. (Recall that APPEND by itself invokes the Edit screen to allow you to add records to a data base one at a time.) APPEND FROM reads records into the currently open data base (the target file) from another (the source file). The syntax is as follows:

APPEND FROM *data base name*

You can add a FOR clause to the APPEND FROM command to append records selectively, provided that any fields included in the specified condition are common to both files. Any reference to a field not present in the target file will result in a "Variable not found" error message. You can work around this limitation by opening the source file and using a COPY command to extract the desired records into a temporary file, which you can then APPEND into the target data base.

Combining Files with Dissimilar Structures

The techniques presented in the previous section for combining data bases—the **Append records from dBASE file** option on the data base design screen **Append** menu and the APPEND FROM command at the dot prompt—depend on using the field names to identify matching fields in the source and target files. These procedures also assume that each field in the target file is derived from a single field in the source file. If you need to combine two data bases with dissimilar structures, the easiest way is to use an update query. From the dot prompt, you can copy records to a temporary file, modify the structure or contents of the file, and then append it into the ultimate target file.

From the Menus

You can use Query-by-Example to define an update query that combines records from two files with dissimilar structures. When you define the query, you must place skeletons for both files on the work surface. Because an update query has no view skeleton, it is easiest to invoke the query design screen without having a data base open and then use the **Add file to query** option on the **Layout** menu to add the two file skeletons. Figure 16-4 illustrates an update query that appends records from the Customer File into the hypothetical mailing list file shown in Figure 16-5.

To identify the target file, use F4 (Next) or F3 (Previous) to position the highlight anywhere in the appropriate file skeleton, select **Specify update operation** from the **Update** menu, and choose **Append records** from this menu. You can confirm that the right data base is selected by checking the wording of the update operation menu option descriptions, which should include the target file name. When you select the **Append records** option, dBASE IV displays "Target" above the name of the selected file in the first column of the file skeleton. If you prefer, you can specify the update operation and identify the target file at the same time by typing "Append" under the file name in the target file skeleton.

You identify the correspondence between the fields in the two files by entering *example variables* in the file skeletons. Example variables are symbols used in Query-by-Example to identify matching fields; if you enter the same example variable in two fields, dBASE IV treats the fields as equivalent, even if the names or data types are different. For example, in an update query,

```
Layout   Fields   Condition   Update   Exit                          10:33:29 am
┌Target─
│Maillist.dbf│ ORG     │ STREET  │ CITYSTATE               │ ZIP │ TELEPHONE │ NAME
│Append      │COMPANY  │ADDRESS  │TRIM(CITY)+", "+STATE    │ZIP  │TELEPHONE  │CONTACT

│Nwcust.dbf  │ ACCOUNT │ COMPANY │ ADDRESS │ CITY │ STATE        │ ZIP │ TELEPHON
│            │         │COMPANY  │ADDRESS  │CITY  │STATE, ="CA"  │ZIP  │TELEPHONE

Query  │C:\dbase4\NWMAIL          │File 1/2    │              │        Caps
  Next field:Tab  Add/Remove all fields:F5  Zoom:F9  Prev/Next skeleton:F3/F4
```

Figure 16-4.

An update query that combines files of dissimilar structures

entering the same example variables in two fields indicates that data should be transferred from the field in the source file into the field in the target file. As you will see in Chapter 17, example variables are also used to link files based

```
Structure for database: C:\DBASE4\MAILLIST.DBF
Number of data records:       0
Date of last update   : 02/12/91
Field  Field Name  Type       Width    Dec    Index
    1  ORG         Character     25               N
    2  STREET      Character     25               N
    3  CITYSTATE   Character     25               N
    4  ZIP         Character     10               N
    5  TELEPHONE   Character      8               N
    6  NAME        Character     25               N
    7  MAIL        Logical        1               N
** Total **                     120
```

Figure 16-5.

The structure of the mailing list data base

on the contents of a field in each. The relationship between the fields in the two files is the same as that of the example variables that define the relationship: the actual example variables and field contents are immaterial, but they must be the same in the two related files.

Example variable names must conform to the same rules that govern field and memory variable names: they must start with a letter and can be up to ten characters long. The example variables need not bear any resemblance to the field names or the data in the fields—you can use variables such as X, Y, and Z—but using the field names or abbreviations of the field names makes it easier to decipher the purpose of the query.

To transfer data from the COMPANY field in NWCUST.DBF to the ORG ("Organization") field in MAILLIST.DBF, you enter the same example variable (in Figure 16-4, COMPANY) in both file skeletons. The query in Figure 16-4 transfers the contents of the ADDRESS field in the Customer File to the STREET field in MAILLIST.DBF. ZIP and TELEPHONE have the same names, but you must still enter example variables to establish the correspondence and indicate that data in these fields in the Customer File should in fact be transferred to the mailing list file. In the MAILLIST file, the city and state are combined into one field, which must be filled in with the result of evaluating an expression that combines the CITY and STATE fields from the Customer File:

```
TRIM(CITY) + ", " + STATE
```

This expression applies the TRIM function to the CITY field to remove trailing spaces, adds a character string consisting of a comma and a space, and then adds the contents of the STATE field. Note that the variable names CITY and STATE are meaningful to dBASE IV only because they were entered as example variables in the Customer File skeleton, not because they happen to be the field names. If you entered the example variable "C" under CITY and "S" under STATE, you would have to define the CITYSTATE field in MAILLIST.DBF as follows:

```
TRIM(C) + ", " + S
```

You can append records selectively by entering record selection criteria in the source file skeleton or in the condition box. If you use the condition box, you can identify fields by name or use the example variables entered in the source file skeleton. In Figure 16-4, the condition = "CA" in the STATE column selects only customers in California.

You can save an update query and continue working on the query design screen by selecting the **Save this query** option from the **Layout** menu, or you can save the query and exit Query-by-Example by choosing **Save changes and exit** from the **Exit** menu.

To execute the update from the query design screen, you select **Perform the update** from the **Update** menu. You can also execute an update query from the Control Center by highlighting the name in the **Queries** panel, pressing ENTER, and then selecting **Run update** from the dialog box. Because it can take a long time to execute an update query, and because the query has the potential to change data in many records (possibly with destructive effects), dBASE IV asks you to confirm your intentions by asking, "Do you REALLY want to run this update query?" You can select **No** to return to the Control Center or **Yes** to proceed with the update. From the dot prompt, you can execute an update query by typing

DO *query file name*

As you will see in Chapter 21, the DO command was designed to execute dBASE IV programs, which by default have the extension PRG. You can also use a DO command to run an update query, which is a type of dBASE IV program, but you must include the UPD extension to override the default, as in the following:

```
DO NWMAIL.UPD
```

As dBASE IV executes an upate query, it displays status messages that indicate the number of records updated or added to the target file. The content of these messages may not be entirely clear if you are not familiar with the dBASE IV programming language, but the display is useful because it allows you to monitor the progress of the operation and judge how long it will take to complete. If you run the update from the query design screen, dBASE IV reminds you after it completes the update that you can "Press F2 on Query Design Screen to see changes." You can press F2 (Data) to display the target file on the Browse screen and verify the effects of the update.

DELETING AND UNDELETING RECORDS

You already know how to delete and undelete records individually by setting or clearing a deletion marker that is stored with the record. From the Browse or Edit screen, you can press CTRL-U to delete a record or undelete a previously deleted record, or you can use the equivalent **Mark record for deletion** and **Clear deletion mark** options on the **Records** menu. From the dot prompt, you can use the DELETE and RECALL commands.

If you need to delete or undelete many records at once based on their contents, these methods are impractical. You might want to delete records in a group to carry out housekeeping operations such as purging obsolete records or removing records from a data base that you have copied to a separate file. For example, to conserve disk space and speed processing, National Widgets could delete all customers who have not placed an order in two years or remove all order records that are more than six months old (preferably, after copying the obsolete data to archive files).

From the Menus

You can mark groups of records for deletion or clear the deletion mark by using an update query. You specify record selection criteria as in any other query, by entering conditions in the file skeleton or in the condition box. You identify which update operation to perform by selecting **Specify update operation** from the **Update** menu and then choosing either **Mark records for deletion** or **Unmark records**. You can also type the update operator—**Mark** or **Unmark**—directly in the first column of the file skeleton.

If you do not specify any record selection criteria, dBASE IV deletes or undeletes all the records in the file. Another way to clear the deletion marker from all records in a file is to choose the **Unmark all records** option from the **Organize** menu on the Browse, Edit, or data base design screen. Remember that marking records for deletion does not erase them from the file. When you are sure you have marked the right records, you can remove them permanently by using the **Erase marked records** option on the **Organize** menu. Even if you work primarily from the menus, you can empty a data base much faster using the ZAP command from the dot prompt (which is explained in the next section) than you can by marking all the records for deletion with an update query and then choosing **Erase marked records**.

From the Dot Prompt

From the dot prompt, you can delete or undelete records in groups based on their contents by using the same DELETE and RECALL commands used to delete records individually. You can identify the records you want to delete or undelete by using a filter to specify the selection criteria or by adding a scope or FOR clause (or, if the data base is sorted or indexed, a WHILE clause) to a DELETE or RECALL command. For example, you could mark for deletion all of National Widgets' customers who have not placed an order in two years with the following command:

```
USE NWCUST
DELETE FOR DATE() - LASTORDER > 730
```

The condition in the FOR clause subtracts the customer's last order date from the current date, expressed as the DATE() function, and compares the difference to 730 days (two years). If the difference is greater than two years, dBASE IV will delete the record. Remember that to remove the marked records permanently, you must use the PACK command, which recopies the file, minus the deletions, and then rebuilds all MDX index tags and open NDX indexes.

One way to empty a data base completely is to delete all the records and then PACK the file, as follows:

```
DELETE ALL
PACK
```

However, the ZAP command accomplishes the same operation much faster. The syntax is simple: you open a data base and type

```
ZAP
```

ZAP is very fast because, unlike DELETE ALL and PACK, it does not cause dBASE IV to read every record in the data base. When dBASE IV executes the ZAP command, it marks the file as empty by entering an *end-of-file mark* in the DBF file immediately following the header that stores the file structure (the header is explained in the next section) before the first data record. The end-of-file mark signals to dBASE IV and to the operating system that there is no more data in a file. dBASE IV also reinitializes the production MDX file and any open NDX indexes so you do not have to reindex after you ZAP. Be sure to think twice (and back up your data base) before issuing a ZAP command, because it does its work in a matter of seconds, and there is no easy way (within dBASE IV) to recover the data if you change your mind afterward.

MODIFYING A DATA BASE STRUCTURE

You can modify the structure of an existing data base on the same data base design screen that you used to create the file structure. You can add or delete fields, move fields to new positions in the structure, lengthen or shorten fields, and change data types (provided that the new data type is consistent with the contents of the field), all without losing data. You can also change field names, but this is not quite as simple, because of the mechanism dBASE IV uses to effect the changes.

When you modify the structure of a data base, dBASE IV creates a temporary copy of the file structure to which all your changes are applied. When you choose **Save changes and exit** to leave the data base design screen, it appends records from the original file into the new structure. This process works exactly like the **Append records from dBASE file** option and the equivalent dot prompt command, APPEND FROM. dBASE IV matches fields by name, and if you have changed field lengths, the data is padded with blanks or truncated to fit in the new structure. You can change a date, numeric, float, or logical field to a character field, or vice versa, provided that the contents of the field are appropriate for the new data type. Deleted records are retained and remain marked as deleted, even if you have used the DELETED setting to exclude records marked for deletion.

Because dBASE IV modifies the structure of a data base by essentially recopying all the records, this process can take some time if the file is large, and a status message monitors the progress of the operation. Make sure that there is enough free space on your hard disk for both the old and new copies of the data base. In most cases, this is approximately the combined size of the original DBF and DBT files, assuming that you have not dramatically lengthened or shortened the record.

To understand why dBASE IV must use this seemingly cumbersome method to modify a file structure, you must know a little about how data is stored in the DBF file. The structure of the file—the names, data types, and lengths of the fields—is stored only once, at the beginning of the file, followed by the data, in a series of fixed-length records with no special punctuation to indicate the end of each field or record. Each field occupies exactly the number of spaces defined in the structure, and fields are identifed by their position in the record. Because fixed-length fields add up to a fixed-length record, it is easy to find any record in the file. (Remember that memo fields, which are variable in length, are stored in a separate disk file, the DBT file.)

Because the data portion of the file contains no structural information, just one long, continuous string of characters, you cannot simply edit the structure at the top of the file. If you do, it will no longer match the existing data. Adding a field requires that dBASE IV insert enough blank spaces in each record to accommodate the data to be entered into the field. If you remove a field, the data entered in that field must be deleted from the file and the space it occupied removed from each record. To take a simple example, if you deleted the ACCOUNT field from the Customer File so that COMPANY appeared to be the first field, dBASE IV would read the first 25 characters in the first record as the COMPANY field, whereas in fact the data would consist of the data you entered into the ACCOUNT field plus the first 15 characters of the original COMPANY field. Similarly, when you change the length of an existing field, each record in the data base must be lengthened or shortened to match the length specified in the new structure.

When you save the new structure, dBASE IV reminds you about the importance of field names by displaying the message "Database records will be APPENDED from backup fields of the same name only!!!" After appending records, dBASE IV renames the original DBF file (with the old structure), changing the extension to DBK (for "data base backup"). If there are memo fields in the data base, it gives the original memo text file the extension TBK (for "text backup"), and if there was a production MDX file, this file assumes the extension MBK. For example, after you modify the structure of the National Widgets Customer File, the original data is in three files, NWCUST.DBK, NWCUST.TBK, and NWCUST.MBK, and the three disk files that make up the revised copy of the file will retain their original names, NWCUST.DBF, NWCUST.DBT, and NWCUST.MDX.

Despite the method used to transfer data between the old and new structures, dBASE IV does allow you to change field names without losing data, but you cannot make any other alterations to the file structure at the same time. If you want to make other changes, you must modify the structure in two passes. On the first pass, make all changes except renaming fields, and then modify the structure again and edit the field names. If you have not made any other changes, dBASE IV displays a different message when you choose **Save changes and exit**: "Should data be COPIED from backup for all fields? (Y/N)."

If you answer **Yes,** dBASE IV matches fields on the basis of position rather than name. The data in the first field in the original structure is transferred to the first field in the new structure, regardless of name; the second field in the original structure is transferred to the second new field; and so on. This distinction is important because dBASE IV cannot differentiate between renaming a field, and deleting one field and inserting another field with a different name in the same place in the structure. In the latter case, you would not want to transfer the data from the original field into the new one.

As mentioned, you can change a character field to a date, numeric, float, or logical field, or vice versa, without losing data, but you cannot change a character field to a memo field or a memo field to a character field. To change a memo to a character field, you must add a new character field to the structure, replace the contents of this field with the original memo text, and then modify the structure again to remove the memo field. You can carry out the replacement either by defining an update query or by using a REPLACE command at the dot prompt. For example, to turn the memo field (COMMENTS) in the Customer File into a character field, you would begin by adding a character field, called perhaps NOTES, to the structure. From the dot prompt, you could fill in this field with the text of the memo by using a REPLACE command:

```
REPLACE ALL NOTES WITH COMMENTS
```

Next, you would modify the structure of the file again and delete the COMMENTS field. If necessary, you would modify the structure a third time to change the field name from NOTES back to the original COMMENTS. The maximum length for a character field is 254 characters, and if you use this method to turn a memo field into a character field, dBASE IV truncates the memo text to fit in the defined length of the character field. You may need to edit the character field to remove soft returns entered by the word wrap editor that you used to type the memo text and hard returns created when you pressed the ENTER key; dBASE IV displays these hard and soft returns as graphics characters. When you convert a character field to a memo field, dBASE IV automatically reformats the text to conform to the standard margins.

From the Menus

To move to the data base design screen from the Control Center, you can either highlight the name of a data base in the **Data** panel and press SHIFT-F2 (Design), or press ENTER and select **Modify structure/order** from the resulting pop-up dialog box.

From the Dot Prompt

From the dot prompt, you can invoke the data base design screen by opening a data base and then typing

```
MODIFY STRUCTURE
```

CONDENSING AND SUMMARIZING DATA

You already know several ways to calculate summary statistics based on data in a dBASE IV data base file. You can define a view query that includes summary operators or print a report with summary statistics (if you want to see only the summary statistics, not the detail records, you can close the detail band or include the SUMMARY keyword in a REPORT FORM command typed at the dot prompt). At the dot prompt, you can use the SUM, AVERAGE, COUNT, and CALCULATE commands.

dBASE IV also provides several methods for accumulating summary statistics and saving the results in another data base. One reason for storing statistics in a summary file rather than just printing a report is to maintain an ongoing record of the summarized and condensed data. To illustrate this application, consider the National Widgets Order File, NWORDER.DBF, which contains one record for each item ordered by a customer. The structure of the Order File is illustrated in Figure 16-6, and the sample data is listed in Figure 16-7. The examples in this and the next chapter draw extensively on the order data; if you are following the examples as a tutorial, you may want to take a few minutes to create the file and add some or all of the sample records. The file requires three index tags, ACCOUNT (based on the ACCOUNT field), INVNUMBER (based on the INVNUMBER field), and CATPART (based on CATEGORY + PARTNUMBER).

At the end of each year, National Widgets might summarize the order data by customer and save the totals in a historical file that contains one record per customer per year. The Order File could then be emptied in preparation for entering the following year's orders.

From the Menus

From the menu system, you can use the **Write view as database** option to create a data base to store the statistics calculated by a view query that includes

```
Structure for database: C:\DBASE4\NWORDER.DBF
Number of data records:      33
Date of last update   : 02/12/91
Field  Field Name  Type       Width    Dec    Index
    1  ACCOUNT     Character     10               Y
    2  INVNUMBER   Character      5               Y
    3  INVDATE     Date           8               N
    4  CATEGORY    Character      6               N
    5  PARTNUMBER  Character      6               N
    6  QUANTITY    Numeric        4               N
    7  PRICE       Numeric        7      2        N
    8  SUBTOTAL    Numeric        7      2        N
    9  DISCOUNT    Numeric        7      2        N
   10  INVAMOUNT   Numeric        7      2        N
** Total **                      68
```

Figure 16-6.

The structure of the National Widgets Order File

aggregate operators, just as you would save any other view query. If the query includes a **Group By** operator, the new file will contain one record for each distinct value of the field by which you are grouping; if you are computing overall statistics for the entire data base, dBASE IV generates a data base with only one record.

dBASE IV determines the structure of the new data base from the view skeleton, and it fills in the contents of the summary fields and the field that serves as the basis for defining the groups. If the view skeleton has additional fields, they remain blank in the output file. Essentially, the data base contains the same data that is displayed by dBASE IV on the Browse or Edit screen when you execute the query. Figure 16-8 illustrates a query that you could use to create a summary file based on the Order File. The records are grouped by ACCOUNT (not visible in Figure 16-8), and the query calculates the sum of the SUBTOTAL, DISCOUNT, and INVAMOUNT fields.

D From the Dot Prompt

From the dot prompt, you can create a summary file that contains the sums of numeric fields in a data base, but you cannot generate the other summary

Record#	ACCOUNT	INVNUMBER	INVDATE	CATEGORY	PARTNUMBER	QUANTITY	PRICE	SUBTOTAL	DISCOUNT	INVAMOUNT
1	ABCPLUMB	07302	02/08/92	DISK	101-40	2	19.95	39.90	0.00	39.90
2	ABCPLUMB	07302	02/08/92	FORMS	803-20	1	45.25	45.25	0.00	45.25
3	ABCPLUMB	07302	02/08/92	RIBBON	240-51	2	14.95	29.90	0.00	29.90
4	ELLISMFG	07881	02/16/92	FORMS	820-20	1	21.95	21.95	0.00	21.95
5	ELLISMFG	07881	02/16/92	DISK	101-42	1	19.95	19.95	0.00	19.95
6	ELLISMFG	07881	02/16/92	STOR	481-21	1	16.95	16.95	0.00	16.95
7	WHITNY	06792	01/18/92	ACCESS	541-15	1	92.50	92.50	0.00	83.25
8	WHITNY	06792	01/18/92	FORMS	803-31	1	37.50	37.50	0.00	37.50
9	WHITNY	06792	01/18/92	DISK	101-31	1	0.00	0.00	0.00	0.00
10	WHITNY	06792	01/18/92	COVER	540-13	1	29.95	29.95	0.00	29.95
11	HOMEMOVIES	08563	03/21/92	ACCESS	533-12	1	39.95	39.95	0.00	39.95
12	HOMEMOVIES	08563	03/21/92	FORMS	803-21	2	42.50	85.00	8.50	76.50
13	HOMEMOVIES	08563	03/21/92	STOR	481-20	1	19.95	19.95	0.00	19.95
14	HOMEMOVIES	08563	03/21/92	RIBBON	240-52	3	5.95	17.85	0.00	17.85
15	LEWIS	06942	01/20/92	DISK	101-41	2	32.50	65.00	6.50	58.50
16	LEWIS	06942	01/20/92	STOR	481-10	2	2.75	5.50	0.00	5.50
17	JOHNSON	05173	12/06/91	ACCESS	541-15	1	92.50	92.50	0.00	83.25
18	KLEIN	05720	12/28/91	FORMS	803-31	1	37.50	37.50	0.00	37.50
19	KLEIN	05720	12/28/91	FORMS	820-20	1	21.95	21.95	0.00	21.95
20	KLEIN	05720	12/28/91	COVER	540-13	1	29.95	29.95	0.00	29.95
21	KLEIN	05720	12/28/91	ACCESS	508-13	1	24.95	24.95	0.00	24.95
22	YORKPUMP	07238	02/05/92	DISK	101-41	2	32.50	65.00	6.50	58.50
23	ABCPLUMB	09625	04/30/92	FORMS	820-24	1	64.95	64.95	0.00	58.45
24	DELTADESGN	08044	02/23/92	FORMS	803-31	1	37.50	37.50	0.00	37.50
25	DELTADESGN	08044	02/23/92	STOR	481-11	3	2.50	7.50	0.00	7.50
26	WHITNEY	07792	02/13/92	FORMS	803-31	1	37.50	37.50	0.00	37.50
27	WHITNEY	07792	02/13/92	RIBBON	240-55	2	0.00	0.00	0.00	0.00
28	HOMEMOVIES	09238	04/18/92	FORMS	803-20	2	45.25	90.50	9.05	81.45
29	HOMEMOVIES	09238	04/18/92	RIBBON	260-20	5	5.95	29.75	0.00	29.75
30	MTK	07184	02/03/92	STOR	481-10	12	2.75	33.00	0.00	33.00
31	MTK	07184	02/03/92	FORMS	820-20	1	21.95	21.95	0.00	21.95
32	MTK	07184	02/03/92	FORMS	820-24	1	64.95	64.95	0.00	58.45
33	MTK	07184	02/03/92	COVER	540-13	3	29.95	89.85	8.99	80.86

Figure 16-7.

Order File sample data

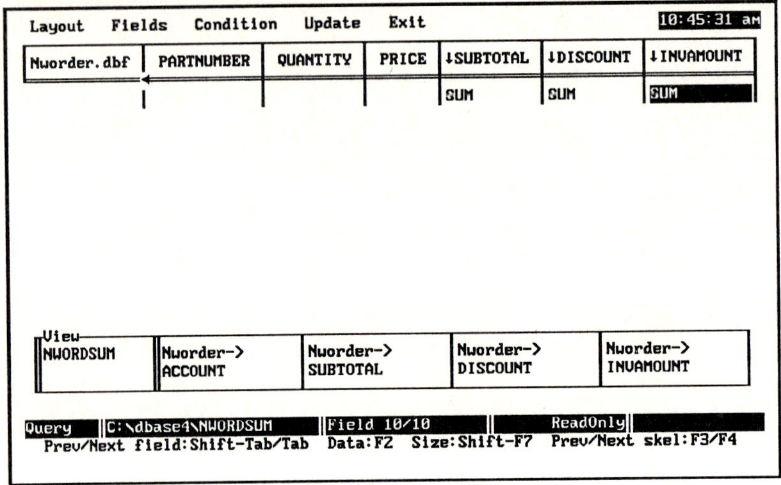

Figure 16-8.

A query created to generate an order summary file

statistics that are available through view queries, such as counts, averages, and maximum or minimum values. To accumulate sums based on the numeric fields in one data base and store them in another data base, you use the TOTAL command, as follows:

TOTAL ON *key expression* TO *new file name*

This command reads records from the active data base and creates a new file with exactly the same structure to contain the totals. dBASE IV always re-creates the new file from scratch—you cannot add records to an ongoing summary file with consecutive TOTAL commands. The operation of the TOTAL command is diagrammed schematically in Figure 16-9.

Just as when you print a report with subtotals, the data base that generates the totals must be sorted or indexed on the key expression—the field or fields that define the subtotal groups—so that dBASE IV processes all the records that contribute to a subtotal in sequence. The file created by the TOTAL command contains one record for each subtotal group in the original data base. By default, TOTAL acts on all numeric fields, but you may include a FIELDS clause to restrict processing to only selected fields. If a total is too large to fit in its

Record#	ACCOUNT	INVNUMBER	INVDATE	CATEGORY	PARTNUMBER	QUANTITY	PRICE	SUBTOTAL	DISCOUNT	INVAMOUNT
1	ABCPLUMB	07302	02/08/92	DISK	101-40	2	19.95	39.90	0.00	39.90
2	ABCPLUMB	07302	02/08/92	FORMS	803-20	1	45.25	45.25	0.00	45.25
3	ABCPLUMB	07302	02/08/92	RIBBON	240-51	2	14.95	29.90	0.00	29.90
23	ABCPLUMB	09625	04/30/92	FORMS	820-24	1	64.95	64.95	0.00	58.45
24	DELTADESGN	08044	02/23/92	FORMS	803-31	1	37.50	37.50	0.00	37.50
25	DELTADESGN	08044	02/23/92	STOR	481-11	3	2.50	7.50	0.00	7.50
4	ELLISMFG	07881	02/16/92	FORMS	820-20	1	21.95	21.95	0.00	21.95
5	ELLISMFG	07881	02/16/92	DISK	101-42	1	19.95	19.95	0.00	19.95
6	ELLISMFG	07881	02/16/92	STOR	481-21	1	16.95	16.95	0.00	16.95
11	HOMEMOVIES	08563	03/21/92	ACCESS	533-12	1	39.95	39.95	0.00	39.95
12	HOMEMOVIES	08563	03/21/92	FORMS	803-21	2	42.50	85.00	8.50	76.50
13	HOMEMOVIES	08563	03/21/92	STOR	481-20	1	19.95	19.95	0.00	19.95
14	HOMEMOVIES	08563	03/21/92	RIBBON	240-52	3	5.95	17.85	0.00	17.85
28	HOMEMOVIES	09238	04/18/92	FORMS	803-20	2	45.25	90.50	9.05	81.45
29	HOMEMOVIES	09238	04/18/92	RIBBON	260-20	5	5.95	29.75	0.00	29.75
17	JOHNSON	05173	12/06/91	ACCESS	541-15	1	92.50	92.50	0.00	83.25
18	KLEIN	05720	12/28/91	FORMS	803-31	1	37.50	37.50	0.00	37.50
19	KLEIN	05720	12/28/91	FORMS	820-20	1	21.95	21.95	0.00	21.95
20	KLEIN	05720	12/28/91	COVER	540-13	1	29.95	29.95	0.00	29.95
21	KLEIN	05720	12/28/91	ACCESS	508-13	1	24.95	24.95	0.00	24.95
15	LEWIS	06942	01/20/92	DISK	101-41	2	32.50	65.00	6.50	58.50
16	LEWIS	06942	01/20/92	STOR	481-10	2	2.75	5.50	0.00	5.50
30	MTK	07184	02/03/92	STOR	481-10	12	2.75	33.00	0.00	33.00
31	MTK	07184	02/03/92	FORMS	820-20	1	21.95	21.95	0.00	21.95
32	MTK	07184	02/03/92	FORMS	820-24	1	64.95	64.95	0.00	58.45
33	MTK	07184	02/03/92	COVER	540-13	3	29.95	89.85	8.99	80.86
26	WHITNEY	07792	02/13/92	FORMS	803-31	1	37.50	37.50	0.00	37.50
27	WHITNEY	07792	02/13/92	RIBBON	240-55	2	0.00	0.00	0.00	0.00
7	WHITNY	06792	01/18/92	ACCESS	541-15	1	92.50	92.50	0.00	83.25
8	WHITNY	06792	01/18/92	FORMS	803-31	1	37.50	37.50	0.00	37.50
9	WHITNY	06792	01/18/92	DISK	101-31	1	0.00	0.00	0.00	0.00
10	WHITNY	06792	01/18/92	COVER	540-13	1	29.95	29.95	0.00	29.95
22	YORKPUMP	07238	02/05/92	DISK	101-41	2	32.50	65.00	6.50	58.50

Record#	ACCOUNT	INVNUMBER	INVDATE	CATEGORY	PARTNUMBER	QUANTITY	PRICE	SUBTOTAL	DISCOUNT	INVAMOUNT
1	ABCPLUMB	07302	02/08/92	DISK	101-40	6	145.10	180.00	0.00	173.50
2	DELTADESGN	08044	02/23/92	FORMS	803-31	4	40.00	45.00	0.00	45.00
3	ELLISMFG	07881	02/16/92	FORMS	820-20	3	58.85	58.85	0.00	58.85
4	HOMEMOVIES	08563	03/21/92	ACCESS	533-12	14	159.55	283.00	17.55	265.45
5	JOHNSON	05173	12/06/91	ACCESS	541-15	1	92.50	92.50	0.00	83.25
6	KLEIN	05720	12/28/91	FORMS	803-31	4	114.35	114.35	0.00	114.35
7	LEWIS	06942	01/20/92	DISK	101-41	4	35.25	70.50	6.50	64.00
8	MTK	07184	02/03/92	STOR	481-10	17	119.60	209.75	8.99	194.26
9	WHITNEY	07792	02/13/92	FORMS	803-31	3	37.50	37.50	0.00	37.50
10	WHITNY	06792	01/18/92	ACCESS	541-15	4	159.95	159.95	0.00	150.70
11	YORKPUMP	07238	02/05/92	DISK	101-41	2	32.50	65.00	6.50	58.50

Figure 16-9.

Operation of the TOTAL command

field, dBASE IV fills the field with asterisks to identify a numeric overflow. You can control the range of records that contribute to the totals by using any combination of filter, scope, FOR clause, and WHILE clause.

To create an order summary file by customer, you would open the Order File, activate the ACCOUNT tag, and use a TOTAL command to generate the summary records:

```
USE NWORDER ORDER ACCOUNT
TOTAL ON ACCOUNT TO NWORDACC
```

The summary file, NWORDACC.DBF, which contains one record for each customer represented in NWORDER.DBF, is listed in Figure 16-10. Because the TOTAL command did not include a field list, dBASE IV totaled all numeric fields, but not all the sums represent meaningful quantities. For example, it makes little sense to total a field such as QUANTITY, because the entries in this field might represent different units for different items.

Note also that non-numeric fields take their values from the first record in each subtotal group. The content of the ACCOUNT field is important, because it identifies the subtotal group, but the other non-numeric "totals" are essentially meaningless—you cannot compute the sum of a character or date field, and the records that contribute to each subtotal may contain widely varying values in these fields. For example, a customer may order many items drawn from several categories.

Because dBASE IV does not give you direct control over the structure of the summary file generated by the TOTAL command, you must either ignore the unwanted fields when you work with the file or eliminate them from the structure. You can delete unwanted fields by using the MODIFY STRUCTURE command, which was explained earlier in this chapter. Another method for maintaining a summary file with a specific structure is detailed in the next section.

Maintaining an Ongoing Summary File

Both of the methods described in the previous section enable you to create a new summary file but not to add records to an existing summary file. In order to maintain an ongoing summary file with a specific structure, you must create a new data base that contains only the required fields, and then add summary

Record#	ACCOUNT	INVNUMBER	INVDATE	CATEGORY	PARTNUMBER	QUANTITY	PRICE	SUBTOTAL	DISCOUNT	INVAMOUNT
1	ABCPLUMB	07302	02/08/92	DISK	101-40	6	145.10	180.00	0.00	173.50
2	DELTADESGN	08044	02/23/92	FORMS	803-31	4	40.00	45.00	0.00	45.00
3	ELLISMFG	07881	02/16/92	FORMS	820-20	3	58.85	58.85	0.00	58.85
4	HOMEMOVIES	08563	03/21/92	ACCESS	533-12	14	159.55	283.00	17.55	265.45
5	JOHNSON	05173	12/06/91	ACCESS	541-15	1	92.50	92.50	0.00	83.25
6	KLEIN	05720	12/28/91	FORMS	803-31	4	114.35	114.35	0.00	114.35
7	LEWIS	06942	01/20/92	DISK	101-41	4	35.25	70.50	6.50	64.00
8	MTK	07184	02/03/92	STOR	481-10	17	119.60	209.75	8.99	194.26
9	WHITNEY	07792	02/13/92	FORMS	803-31	3	37.50	37.50	0.00	37.50
10	WHITNY	06792	01/18/92	ACCESS	541-15	4	159.95	159.95	0.00	150.70
11	YORKPUMP	07238	02/05/92	DISK	101-41	2	32.50	65.00	6.50	58.50

Figure 16-10.

Order data totaled by customer

records to this file. From the menu system, you can use an update query to append records into the ongoing summary file from the files generated by using the **Write view as database option** to capture the data described by a view query. From the dot prompt, you can use APPEND FROM to read in summary records created by using a TOTAL command.

The structure of NWORDHST.DBF, a hypothetical customer order history file for the National Widgets system, is illustrated in Figure 16-11. Because this file is used to store annual customer totals, it contains a field for the year, which you can fill in by defining an update query such as the one shown in Figure 16-12 or by using a REPLACE command at the dot prompt after dBASE IV appends each group of new total records. Be careful to fill in this field only for records in which it is blank—those just added from the latest summary file. If you use an update query to fill in the year, you can do this by entering the condition = 0 in the YEAR column in the file skeleton, along with the new value, specified as WITH 1992 (in the year 1992) or as WITH YEAR(DATE())—the year portion of the current date, expressed via the DATE() function.

From the dot prompt, you must include a condition in the REPLACE command that ensures that the YEAR field is filled in only for new records, when it is blank. The complete command sequence is as follows:

```
USE NWORDER ORDER ACCOUNT
TOTAL ON ACCOUNT TO NWORDTOT
USE NWORDHST
APPEND FROM NWORDTOT
REPLACE YEAR WITH 1992 FOR YEAR = 0
```

```
Structure for database: C:\DBASE4\NWORDHST.DBF
Number of data records:       11
Date of last update   : 02/12/91
Field  Field Name  Type        Width    Dec    Index
    1  ACCOUNT     Character      10               N
    2  YEAR        Numeric         4               N
    3  SUBTOTAL    Numeric         7      2        N
    4  DISCOUNT    Numeric         7      2        N
    5  INVAMOUNT   Numeric         7      2        N
** Total **                       36
```

Figure 16-11.

The structure of the order summary file

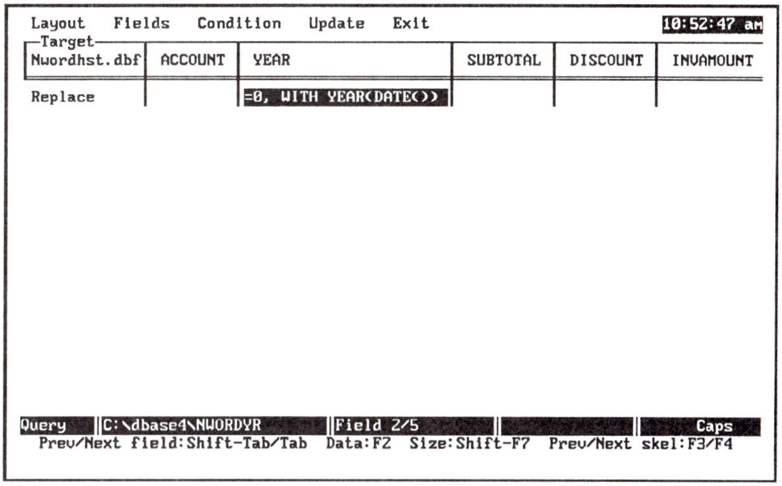

```
Layout   Fields   Condition   Update   Exit                                   10:52:47 am
-Target-
Nwordhst.dbf | ACCOUNT | YEAR                       | SUBTOTAL | DISCOUNT | INVAMOUNT
Replace      |         | =0, WITH YEAR(DATE())      |          |          |

Query | C:\dbase4\NWORDYR | Field 2/5 |  | Caps
 Prev/Next field:Shift-Tab/Tab  Data:F2  Size:Shift-F7  Prev/Next skel:F3/F4
```

Figure 16-12.

An update query that creates a summary file

To analyze sales trends, National Widgets might want to view the records in NWORDHST in various orders, such as by CATEGORY, PARTNUMBER, and YEAR, or in descending order by SUBTOTAL. In Chapter 10, you learned that to build an index based on a combination of character and numeric fields, you must convert the numeric field (YEAR in this example) to a character string with the STR function and that to index in descending numerical or chronological order, you can subtract the numeric or date field from a larger constant value. To create an index tag called CATPRTYR, which indexes the Order History File by category, part number, and year, you could index on the following expression:

```
CATEGORY + PARTNUMBER + STR(YEAR,4)
```

To create a tag called CATSUB, which accesses the file by product category, and within the category in descending order by SUBTOTAL, you could use the following expression:

```
CATEGORY + STR(9999.99 - SUBTOTAL, 4)
```

If you build the indexes from the **Organize** menu, note that although the CATSUB tag accesses the file in descending order by SUBTOTAL, you cannot achieve this order by setting the **Order of index** option to **Descending,** because this option selects ascending or descending order *based on the result of evaluating the full key expression,* not just one component.

SUMMARY

This chapter described several methods for reorganizing data bases and outlined some typical strategies for combining these techniques to split and combine data bases, extract data, archive and delete records, and create ongoing summary files. You will find more uses for these methods as your dBASE IV application grows and matures, and they will become especially important if you need to share data with other dBASE IV users.

Although all the operations described in this chapter can be carried out through the menu system, the dot prompt commands are in many cases far more direct and straightforward. Using Query-by-Example requires more preparation, although once you have defined all the required update queries, performing the updates is easy. If you are accustomed to the dot prompt, the methods that use Query-by-Example may seem convoluted and confusing, and even if you work primarily in the menu system, you may want to try the dot prompt methods as well and think carefully about whether the added convenience and flexibility might make it worthwhile to learn the requisite command syntax.

CHAPTER SEVENTEEN

Working with Multiple Data Bases

Chapter 16 introduced the concept of working with multiple data bases with a discussion of some techniques for splitting and combining files and creating new data bases that contain summarized and condensed data from existing files. Although these operations transferred data between files, in no case did you actually view data from more than one data base at a time. dBASE IV also allows you to open two or more data bases simultaneously, establish linkages between pairs of files based on common fields, and view data from related records in all open files. This chapter introduces the last of the three main data bases that make up the National Widgets system—the Inventory File—and uses the Customer, Order, and Inventory data bases to illustrate a variety of practical techniques for displaying and printing data and performing calculations based on multiple files as well as updating one file based on information contained in another.

Although dBASE IV provides several powerful tools for establishing the logical relationships between files, it is primarily your responsibility to ensure that records are matched properly and updated correctly. You must design the file structures so that they support the required linkages, remember to enter identical values into the key fields so that dBASE IV can find the matching records, and make sure that the integrity of the data is preserved as you add, edit, and delete records. It is also essential to develop strategies for verifying that related files are linked correctly and that data is transferred as intended, since in most cases, dBASE IV does not warn you about potential problems such as records in one file that lack matches in another.

When you work with multiple related files, the differences between the menu system and the dot prompt are more evident than when you are updating a single data base. Query-by-Example is much easier for the beginner, since using this tool does not require that you understand how dBASE IV links files or extracts the matching records, and it provides a fast and convenient way for dBASE IV users at all levels to display or print information from two or more related files. However, if you need to link files based on unusual criteria, transfer data between files, or update records in one file while viewing matching data from another, the dot prompt provides a far more efficient, powerful, and flexible working environment. If you have been working primarily in the menu system, you may want to study the dot prompt techniques in this chapter as well as the methods that involve only menu commands.

Figure 17-1 illustrates the structure of the Inventory File and Figure 17-2 lists the sample data. If you want to try the examples in this chapter, you should create this file, enter the sample data, and build the two required index tags: PARTNUMBER, which is based on the PARTNUMBER field, and CAT-PART, which is based on the combination of CATEGORY and PARTNUMBER (the expression CATEGORY + PARTNUMBER).

OPENING MORE THAN ONE DATA BASE

dBASE IV allows you to work with up to ten data bases simultaneously, each in a separate *work area.* When you work entirely in the menu system, the only way to open more than one file at a time is through Query-by-Example. You can define a query that opens up to eight data bases, link them based on the contents of common fields, and display selected fields from any or all files. Like a single-file query, a query that draws data from more than one data base creates a specialized view of the data, which in most cases is customized for a particular purpose, such as viewing or printing specific information, performing a calculation, or transfering data between files.

```
Structure for database: C:\DBASE4\NWINVENT.DBF
Number of data records:       40
Date of last update   : 11/15/88
Field  Field Name  Type       Width    Dec    Index
    1  CATEGORY    Character      6              N
    2  PARTNUMBER  Character      6              Y
    3  DESCRIP     Character     25              N
    4  VENDOR      Character      6              N
    5  COST        Numeric        7      2       N
    6  PRICE       Numeric        7      2       N
** Total **                      58
```

Figure 17-1.

The structure of the National Widgets Inventory File

From the dot prompt, you can open up to ten data bases, maintain them open—linked or not—throughout a work session, and move freely among work areas to view different fields and records. Because the files are kept open, switching among them is faster than remaining in one work area and opening and closing files sequentially, and at times you may want to open two or three files at once, without linking them, just to take advantage of this convenience. However, the ability to open several files simultaneously is more useful for working with multiple related files and viewing or updating matching records.

Multifile queries are ideal for viewing or printing data drawn from more than one data base. It is easy to open the files, link pairs of files based on the contents of a common field or fields, and select the fields of interest from each data base, all without understanding exactly how dBASE IV executes the query. However, there are some significant limitations to the ways that you can work with the data selected by a query. In particular, all multifile queries are read/only. Even if no sorting is required and there are no calculated fields—all the fields in the view are drawn directly from the contributing data bases—dBASE IV does not allow you to edit data through a multifile query.

When you work at the dot prompt, you have considerably more flexibility to move among the work areas and update files, but it is your responsibility to build the indexes required to support the relationships between files and to ensure that the files are linked correctly. When you link files at the dot prompt, dBASE IV allows you to edit data, but you must be careful not to make changes that would compromise the integrity of the data bases by disrupting the linkages between matching records in separate files.

Record#	CATEGORY	PARTNUMBER	DESCRIP	VENDOR	COST	PRICE
1	RIBBON	270-11	NEC 7700 Multistrike	NEC	3.20	5.45
2	RIBBON	270-10	NEC 7700 Cloth	NEC	3.20	5.45
3	RIBBON	270-13	NEC 3500 Cloth	NEC	5.50	9.95
4	RIBBON	270-12	NEC 3500 Multistrike	NEC	5.50	9.95
5	RIBBON	240-51	Epson FX-285, 286	EPSON	9.75	14.95
6	RIBBON	250-30	Okidata 80, 81, 82, 83	OKIDAT	1.50	2.95
7	RIBBON	250-31	Okidata 84, 94	OKIDAT	3.00	4.95
8	RIBBON	240-50	Epson MX-80, 85, FX-80,85	EPSON	7.09	12.50
9	RIBBON	240-52	Epson EX-80, 100, Black	EPSON	3.60	5.95
10	RIBBON	240-53	Epson EX-80, 100, Color	EPSON	6.50	10.95
11	RIBBON	260-20	Apple ImageWriter II	APPLE	3.00	5.95
12	FORMS	803-20	14-1/2 X 11" Green bar	MOORE	28.50	45.25
13	FORMS	803-21	14-1/2 X 11" White	MOORE	24.00	42.50
14	FORMS	803-31	9-1/2 X 11" White	MOORE	24.50	37.50
15	FORMS	803-30	9-1/2 X 11" Green bar	MOORE	25.00	37.50
16	FORMS	820-20	3-1/2 x 1" Labels, 1-up	AVERY	14.50	21.95
17	FORMS	820-24	3-1/2 x 4" Labels, 4-up	AVERY	39.50	64.95
18	COVER	540-10	Dust cover, Apple IIGS	COMCOV	16.50	24.95
19	COVER	540-11	Dust cover, Mac Plus	COMCOV	18.50	29.95
20	COVER	540-12	Dust cover, Macintosh SE	COMCOV	17.00	26.50
21	COVER	540-13	Dust cover, AT-compatible	COMCOV	18.50	29.95
22	ACCESS	533-12	Plexiglas Printer Stand	INMAC	24.50	39.95
23	ACCESS	541-15	Terminal Swivel Mount	INMAC	68.00	92.50
24	ACCESS	508-13	Glare screen, monochrome	TERMCO	16.30	24.95
25	ACCESS	508-14	Glare screen, 12" color	TERMCO	14.40	21.95
26	ACCESS	508-15	Glare screen, 13" color	TERMCO	15.40	24.95
27	STOR	481-10	5-1/4" Plastic disk case	INMAC	1.15	2.75
28	STOR	481-11	3-1/2" Plastic disk case	INMAC	0.95	2.50
29	STOR	481-20	Locking 5-1/4" Disk Tray	INMAC	12.50	19.95
30	STOR	481-21	Locking 3-1/2" Disk Tray	INMAC	10.50	16.95
31	DISK	101-40	5-1/4" DSDD, 48 tpi	DYSAN	12.35	19.95
32	DISK	101-41	5-1/4" High dens., 96 tpi	DYSAN	20.45	32.50
33	DISK	101-42	3-1/2" DSDD	DYSAN	12.35	19.95
34	DISK	102-20	Iomega 10M cartridge	IOMEGA	45.00	62.50
35	DISK	102-21	Iomega 20M cartridge	IOMEGA	50.00	69.50
36	PRINT	321-11	NEC Courier 10	NEC	8.45	12.50
37	PRINT	321-15	NEC Prestige Elite 12	NEC	8.45	12.50
38	PRINT	340-20	HP LaserJet A	HP	110.00	169.00
39	PRINT	340-21	HP LaserJet B	HP	110.00	169.00
40	PRINT	340-22	HP LaserJet C	HP	110.00	169.00

Figure 17-2.

The Inventory File sample data

Because the two working environments differ in their capabilities for manipulating multiple files, you may want to read all the material in this chapter carefully, even if you already have a preference for the menu system or the dot prompt. If this is your first experience working with multiple related data base files, you may find it easiest to use Query-by-Example to view data or print reports. Once you understand the mechanisms used to link files, you will find that carrying out many operations that transfer data between files is more straightforward at the dot prompt than from the menu system.

From the Menus

Working through the menu system, you must use Query-by-Example to open more than one data base at a time. To open multiple files, you use the **Add file to query** option to place more than one file skeleton on the query design work surface. Figure 17-3 illustrates the query design screen with all three National Widgets files open. You can move among the file skeletons by pressing F4 (Next) and F3 (Previous); when the highlight is in the last skeleton, pressing F4 (Next) moves it back to the first.

```
Layout  Fields  Condition  Update  Exit                         10:56:35 am

Nworder.dbf | ACCOUNT | INVNUMBER | INVDATE | CATEGORY | PARTNUMBER | QUANTITY

Nwcust.dbf  | ACCOUNT | COMPANY | ADDRESS | CITY | STATE | ZIP | TELEPHONE | CO

Nwinvent.dbf| CATEGORY | PARTNUMBER | DESCRIP | VENDOR | COST | PRICE

Query  |C:\dbase4\NWTHREE  |File 3/3  |  |  Caps
 Next field:Tab  Add/Remove all fields:F5  Zoom:F9  Prev/Next skeleton:F3/F4
```

Figure 17-3.

Opening three files in Query-by-Example

If there are too many file skeletons to fit on the screen at once, dBASE IV scrolls the display to reveal the next skeleton when you press F4 (Next) or F3 (Previous); you can also use PGUP and PGDN to display the previous or next "page" of the display. Because the view skeleton remains stationary at the bottom of the work surface, you can always see the customized picture of your data that is described by the query. You can add fields from any open file to the view skeleton, but constructing a multifile view that displays meaningful information depends on linking files based on the contents of common fields so that related or matching records from multiple files contribute to the view. The mechanism for linking files is explained in the next section.

From the Dot Prompt

When you work at the dot prompt, you must explicitly open data base files and specify the work area in which each data base should be opened. When you first load dBASE IV, work area 1 is active, and it remains active until you use the SELECT command to switch to another work area. You can use one of three methods to identify the desired work area. You can refer to work areas by number (1 through 10) or by the equivalent letter (A through J). For example, you could select work area 2 with

```
SELECT 2
```

or

```
SELECT B
```

You can open a data base in a specific work area by selecting the work area before you type the USE command that opens the file, or you can include the work area in the USE command, as follows:

```
USE NWCUST IN 2
```

or

```
USE NWCUST IN B
```

This form of the USE command does not select the designated work area; it is most useful when you want to open two or more data bases with a series of USE commands, without immediately viewing data from each one.

Once a data base is open in a work area, you can select the work area by the file's *alias*. An alias is an alternate name for a data base that you designate in the USE command that opens the file; the alias can be up to ten characters long. If you do not specify an alias, dBASE IV assigns the file name as the alias. For example, you could open the National Widgets Customer File in work area 2, activate the ACCOUNT index tag, and assign to it the alias CUSTOMER with the following command:

```
USE NWCUST IN 2 ORDER ACCOUNT ALIAS CUSTOMER
```

For the remainder of your work session, you could use the following SELECT command to move to work area 2:

```
SELECT CUSTOMER
```

If you did not assign a new alias, you could use the default alias, NWCUST for the Customer File, in a SELECT command, as follows:

```
SELECT NWCUST
```

You can use an alias to refer to a file by a name that is shorter or more intuitively obvious than the DBF file name, to open any of several similar files (such as separate mailing lists with the same structures) in the same context and refer to them by a consistent name, or to call the same file by a different name when you open it in a different context. dBASE IV retains no record of the alias after you close a file; you can open the same file with a different alias or use the alias for a different file in a subsequent work session.

You do not have to use the ten work areas in sequence, opening your first file in work area 1 (A), the second in area 2 (B), and so on. When you work frequently with the same set of related files, you may prefer to associate each data base with a particular work area. In a given situation, you might end up opening files in areas 2, 4, and 7. In general, however, it is easier to remember a file's alias than the number of the work area containing the file, and if you refer to files by their aliases, it makes no difference which work area is used for which file.

dBASE IV maintains a separate record pointer in each work area that does not move when you switch to another area. This allows you to access data from the current record in any open file, regardless of which work area is selected. Fields in all files except the one in the current work area are referred to by a combination of the file alias and field name—for example, CUSTOMER ->CONTACT for the CONTACT field in the NWCUST.DBF file opened with the alias CUSTOMER. This expression might be read aloud as "customer contact" or "customer file contact field." If you prefer, you can use the work area letter as a more concise alias. For example, with the Customer File open in work area 2, you could refer to the CONTACT field as B->CONTACT, but this notation forces you to keep track of which file is open in which work area.

Although dBASE IV allows you to open up to ten data bases at once, your operating system may impose tighter restrictions. Under versions of MS-DOS earlier than 3.3, an application program can open only 15 disk files at once. This limit includes data base files, indexes, screen form files, report and label form files, memory variable files, and if a data base contains memo fields, the DBT file used to store the memo text. If you opened the Customer File, activated two NDX indexes, and invoked the NWCUST screen form file to edit the file, a total of six files would be open: NWCUST.DBF, NWCUST.DBT, the production MDX file, the two NDX indexes, and the screen form file. In practice, since almost every data base has at least one index file—the production MDX file—you can open three to five data bases, which should be sufficient for most purposes. If you need to open more files, you must upgrade to a later version of DOS.

You can close one data base by selecting the appropriate work area and typing USE, as follows:

```
SELECT 2
USE
```

You can also specify the work area in the USE command, just as you do to open the file:

```
USE IN 2
```

You can close all open data bases and return to work area 1 with

```
CLOSE DATABASES
```

Like USE, several other commands, including GOTO and SKIP, allow you to specify the work area in which the action should take place. For example, from work area 1, you could go to the top of the file that is open in work area 2 with the following:

```
GOTO TOP IN 2
```

LINKING FILES BASED ON COMMON FIELDS

The primary motivation for opening multiple data bases simultaneously is to access related records from two or more files. Although the methods you use to establish the relationships vary, they always depend on the fact that matching records are identified by the contents of one or more fields common to the two files. For example, to find the customer record that matches a particular order record, you would search for the customer with the same contents in the ACCOUNT field. To find the matching inventory item, you would search in the Inventory File for a record with the same value in the PARTNUMBER field. In most cases, dBASE IV does not require that the corresponding fields have the same names, but it will be easier for you to keep track of the relationships if they do.

The operational philosophy behind Query-by-Example is that you should not have to understand how dBASE IV executes the query. You place two or more files on the work surface, identify the common fields that link pairs of files, and indicate which fields should be included in the view skeleton. dBASE IV then determines the best way to extract the specified data. However, a little knowledge of the underlying mechanisms will help you plan your data base structures so that they support the required linkages, build indexes that can speed query execution, and ease the transition to working at the dot prompt, where a good understanding of these concepts is essential for conducting multifile inquiries.

When you work with multiple related files at the dot prompt, dBASE IV reads through the data base in the selected work area and "looks up" additional information in matching records in other open files. In most cases, you can display the data you need from any work area, but often you will view one file as the "main" file and select the work area in which that file is open. For example, to display a chronological list of orders that included the customer's full company name, you would read through the Order File in sequence using an index tag based on INVDATE (the invoice date field) and look up the company name in the Customer File based on a matching entry in the ACCOUNT field. If you wanted to print an alphabetical customer list with order dates and totals, however, you would read the Customer File through the ACCOUNT tag and look up the required order information in the Order File.

When you use Query-by-Example, you need not designate which file to process or which work area to select. As long as two files have a common field, dBASE IV can find all the matching records and display the data in the order in which you request it. If there is no existing index tag to support a file linkage, dBASE IV builds one and adds it to the production MDX file. When you execute the query again, dBASE IV rebuilds the tag only if it is no longer present (you may have deleted the tag to conserve space or speed up other operations). If your files are large, the initial indexing will slow execution of the query the first time you use it, so you may want to test and refine a complex query with smaller sample files. A query will execute fastest if dBASE IV can also use an index to control the display order of the data in the view. However, dBASE IV may select a work area that forces it to sort the records in the view rather than building or activating an index tag for one of the component data bases, and query execution will slow considerably if your files are large.

At the dot prompt, you must open all the files explicitly, build any required index tags in advance, remember to activate the tags that will allow you to establish the file linkages correctly, and select the right work area. However, you can almost always avoid sorting and maximize execution speed, a factor that becomes increasingly important as your files grow larger.

From the Menus

You link files in Query-by-Example by entering the same example variable in the common field in each file skeleton. It is easiest to do this with the **Create link by pointing** option on the **Layout** menu. With the highlight in the appropriate column in either of the file skeletons, select **Create link by pointing** from the **Layout** menu. dBASE IV enters the default example variable—LINK1 for the first linkage, LINK2 for the second, and so on—into the file skeleton and prompts you on the message line with "Cursor to another file & press Enter." You can press F4 (Next) or F3 (Previous) to move to another file skeleton, use the cursor movement keys to highlight the matching field (it does not have to have the same name), and press ENTER to place the same example variable in this column. If you prefer, you can type in the example variables. Although you do not have to use variable names such as LINK1 and LINK2, these names clarify the purposes of the example variables when you edit the query.

Figure 17-4 illustrates the addition of file linkage specifications to the three-file query shown in Figure 17-3. Two sets of example variables, LINK1 and LINK2, link the Order File to the Customer File by ACCOUNT and to the Inventory File by PARTNUMBER. You can also link two files based on a complex index, provided that the index tag already exists for both files. Before you can enter the example variables, you must select the **Include indexes** option on the **Fields** menu for both file skeletons so that the complex index key expressions appear in both skeletons. Both files must be preindexed on the same complex key expression because you can enter only one linking variable for each pair of files on the query design screen. You could not, for example, link the Order File to the Inventory File based on the separate fields CATEGORY and PARTNUMBER, although you can link the files based on CATEGORY + PARTNUMBER if *both* files are indexed on this expression. At the dot prompt, you could establish the linkage if *either* file were indexed on CATEGORY + PARTNUMBER.

```
Layout  Fields  Condition  Update  Exit                              10:57:03 am

Nworder.dbf | ACCOUNT | INVNUMBER | INVDATE | CATEGORY | PARTNUMBER | QUANTITY
            | LINK1   |           |         |          | LINK2      |

Nwcust.dbf  | ACCOUNT | COMPANY | ADDRESS | CITY | STATE | ZIP | TELEPHONE | CO
            | LINK1   |         |         |      |       |     |           |

Nwinvent.dbf| CATEGORY | PARTNUMBER | DESCRIP | VENDOR | COST | PRICE
            |          | LINK2      |         |        |      |

Query  ||C:\dbase4\NWTHREE2  ||Field 2/6  ||  ||  Caps
  Prev/Next field:Shift-Tab/Tab  Data:F2  Size:Shift-F7  Prev/Next skel:F3/F4
```

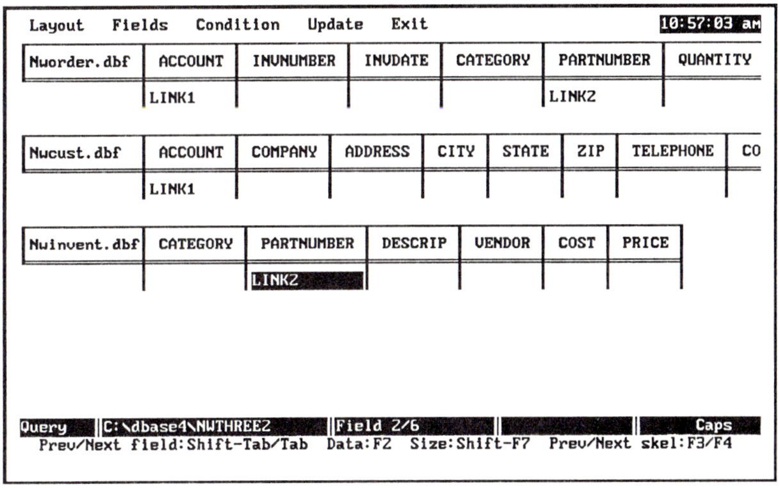

Figure 17-4.

Linking two pairs of files in Query-by-Example

By default, dBASE IV establishes the linkages between files so that the resulting view includes *all possible matches between linked files and no records for which there are no matches.* For example, a query based on the Customer File and Order File, linked by ACCOUNT, would include data from each order record for which dBASE IV could find a customer record with the same account code. The query in Figure 17-4 would display only orders for which both a matching inventory record and a matching customer record could be found. In many cases, this is exactly what you want. At times, however, you may want to view all the records in one file, regardless of whether there is a matching record in the linked file. (In fact, one very important application of this technique is identifying mismatches that arise from data entry errors.)

To display all the records in a file, you must precede the example variable that links this file to another with the **Every** operator. If there is no matching record in the linked file, the fields derived from this file will appear blank in the view. If you type the example variables in the file skeletons yourself, you can simply include "Every" in the linking variable in the appropriate skeleton. If you use the **Create link by pointing** menu option, you can return to the appropriate skeleton after linking the files and add the word "Every" in front of the example variable entered by dBASE IV.

The query illustrated in Figure 17-5 displays every record in the order file; if there is no matching customer record, the COMPANY field is blank. To create a query that displays all customers, regardless of whether there are matching order records, you would place the **Every** operator in the Customer File skeleton, as illustrated in Figure 17-6. The resulting view would display every customer in the Customer File; for each customer who did place orders, each order would be represented separately in the view. Note that although you can display all orders *or* all customers, you cannot create a single query that displays all order records, all customer records, and all possible matches between the two files. Because dBASE IV cannot execute such a query, it does not allow you to create one—a query can include more than one **Every** operator but only one for each pair of linked files.

When more than one record in one file matches each record in another, dBASE IV displays all the matches. To request just one pair of records from each file, you place the **First** operator before the linking example variable in the appropriate file skeleton. For example, you could create a query that displays every customer record as well as data from the first matching order by adding the **First** operator to the linking variable in the Order File skeleton. If you wanted customers who do not have any current orders to appear on the listing, you could also include the **Every** operator with the example variable in the

```
Layout   Fields   Condition   Update   Exit                         10:58:51 am
Nworder.dbf | ACCOUNT      | ↓INVNUMBER | ↓INVDATE | CATEGORY | PARTNUMBER | QUANTI
            | Every LINK1  |            |          |          |            |

Nwcust.dbf  | ↓ACCOUNT | ↓COMPANY | ADDRESS | CITY | STATE | ZIP | TELEPHONE | CO
            | LINK1    |          |         |      |       |     |           |

View
NWORDCST | Nwcust->  | Nwcust-> | Nworder-> | Nworder->
         | ACCOUNT   | COMPANY  | INVNUMBER | INVDATE

Query  ||C:\dbase4\NWORDCST  ||Field 1/10  ||  ||  Ins
 Prev/Next field:Shift-Tab/Tab  Data:F2  Size:Shift-F7  Prev/Next skel:F3/F4
```

Figure 17-5.

A query that displays every order record, whether or not there is a matching customer

```
Layout   Fields   Condition   Update   Exit                         10:58:21 am
Nworder.dbf | ACCOUNT | ↓INVNUMBER | ↓INVDATE | CATEGORY | PARTNUMBER | QUANTITY
            | LINK1   |            |          |          |            |

Nwcust.dbf  | ↓ACCOUNT     | ↓COMPANY | ADDRESS | CITY | STATE | ZIP | TELEPHONE
            | Every LINK1  |          |         |      |       |     |

View
NWORDCST | Nwcust->  | Nwcust-> | Nworder-> | Nworder->
         | ACCOUNT   | COMPANY  | INVNUMBER | INVDATE

Query  ||C:\dbase4\NWORDCST  ||Field 1/15  ||  ||  Caps
 Prev/Next field:Shift-Tab/Tab  Data:F2  Size:Shift-F7  Prev/Next skel:F3/F4
```

Figure 17-6.

A query that displays every customer record, with matching order records if they exist

Customer File skeleton, as illustrated in Figure 17-7. Note that the "first" record is the same one that dBASE IV would retrieve with an index key search—the first one in indexed order. Retrieving the "last" record (in this example, the customer's most recent order) is not easy in Query-by-Example; at the dot prompt, you can build an index that permits you to do this.

dBASE IV allows you to place two or more copies of the same file skeleton on the work surface, and when it executes the query, it opens the same file in more than one work area. As noted in Chapter 10, you can place only one aggregate operator in a file skeleton column, but by adding two or more copies of the same file to the work surface, you can compute more than one summary statistic based on the same field.

Figure 17-8 illustrates a query that uses two copies of the Customer File skeleton to compute both the sums and averages of the YTDORDERS and TOTORDERS fields. When you work with two copies of the same file, you must link them just as you would separate, independent data bases, in this case based on the ACCOUNT field. Because every file must have a different alias, dBASE IV displays the work area designator—the letters B, C, and so on—above each file name to inform you that these will serve as the aliases for all

```
Layout   Fields   Condition   Update   Exit                          10:59:20 am

Nworder.dbf | ACCOUNT     | ↓INVNUMBER | ↓INVDATE | CATEGORY | PARTNUMBER | QUANTI
            | First LINK1 |            |          |          |            |

Nwcust.dbf  | ↓ACCOUNT    | ↓COMPANY | ADDRESS | CITY | STATE | ZIP | TELEPHONE
            | Every LINK1 |          |         |      |       |     |

View
NWORDCST | Nwcust->  | Nwcust->  | Nworder->  | Nworder->
         | ACCOUNT   | COMPANY   | INVNUMBER  | INVDATE

Query  |C:\dbase4\NWORDCST  |Field 1/15  |  |                              Ins
 Prev/Next field:Shift-Tab/Tab  Data:F2  Size:Shift-F7  Prev/Next skel:F3/F4
```

Figure 17-7.

A query that displays every customer record, with the first matching order record for each

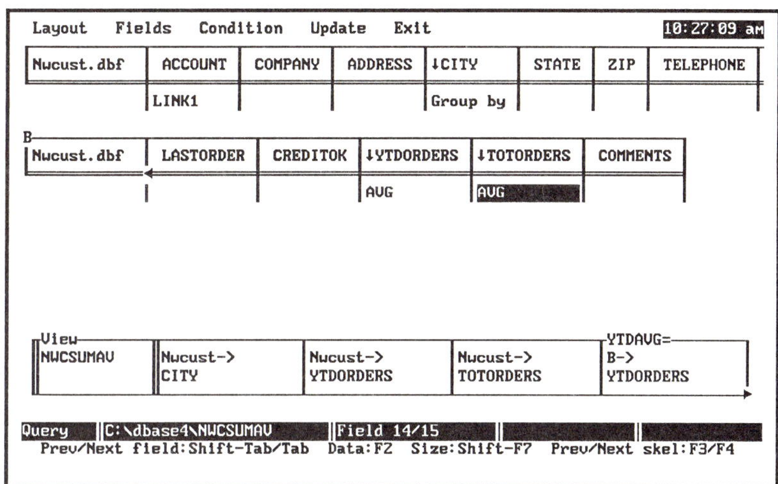

Figure 17-8.

Placing more than one copy of a file on the work surface

but the first copy of a given file. When you add corresponding fields to the view skeleton, dBASE IV requests a new name for each duplicate field.

As in any other query, you can include a **Group By** operator to calculate summary statistics for more than one group of records. The query in Figure 17-8 includes a **Group By** operator in the CITY column of the first Customer File skeleton. The summary operators that compute the sums are entered in the first copy of the Customer File skeleton (these columns are not visible in Figure 17-8), and the averages (one of which is off the screen in the view skeleton in Figure 17-8) are derived from the second copy. The output of the query is illustrated in Figure 17-9.

From the Dot Prompt

When you work with multiple files at the dot prompt, you can use a variety of methods to link files and find matching records in two or more files. Not all these methods depend on establishing any formal relationships between files. For example, you might open the National Widgets Customer File and Order File in work areas 1 and 2 with the following commands:

```
USE NWCUST IN 1 ORDER ACCOUNT ALIAS CUSTOMER
USE NWORDER IN 2 ORDER ACCOUNT ALIAS ORDER
```

You could then search for a particular customer and display the customer record as well as all the matching order records with the following command sequence:

```
SELECT CUSTOMER
SEEK "ABCPLUMB"
DISPLAY
SELECT ORDER
LIST FOR ACCOUNT = "ABCPLUMB"
```

One way to improve this search strategy is to state the condition in the FOR clause more generally so that it applies to any customer, as follows:

```
LIST FOR ACCOUNT = CUSTOMER->ACCOUNT
```

Records   Organize   Fields   Go To   Exit   11:01:29 am

CITY	YTDORDERS	TOTORDERS	YTDAVG	TOTAVG
Bellevue	0.00	1502.16	0.00	751.08
Benicia	0.00	1232.50	0.00	1232.50
Berkeley	1344.56	7653.78	448.19	2551.26
Emeryville	108.59	1213.42	54.30	606.71
Eugene	0.00	249.59	0.00	249.59
Fremont	201.87	1584.45	201.87	1584.45
Oakland	366.81	3482.48	366.81	3482.48
Portland	0.00	1238.07	0.00	619.04
Pullman	188.15	1235.87	188.15	1235.87
Richmond	435.42	867.38	435.42	867.38
San Francisco	348.52	1455.37	116.17	485.12
San Jose	157.38	608.42	157.38	608.42
San Leandro	87.35	87.35	87.35	87.35

Browse | C:\dbase4\NWCSUMAV | Rec 1/13 | View | ReadOnly | Ins

Figure 17-9.

The data displayed by a view that includes two copies of the Customer File skeleton

The condition ACCOUNT = CUSTOMER– >ACCOUNT selects records in which the contents of the ACCOUNT field in the currently selected file (the Order File) matches the ACCOUNT field in the file whose alias is CUSTOMER. Since dBASE IV does not move the record pointer in the Customer File when you switch to the Order File work area, this condition always selects Order File records that match the "current" Customer File record (which you can find with a SEEK command, a GOTO command, or any other method).

After searching for another customer record, you could return to the Order File, retrieve this command from history, and repeat it unchanged to view the new customer's orders. If you plan to use this command sequence more than a few times in a row, you can use a filter to establish the Order File record selection criteria, as follows:

```
SET FILTER TO ACCOUNT = CUSTOMER->ACCOUNT
```

The filter is convenient, but if the Order File is large, finding the matching records will be slow, because dBASE IV executes a filter exactly as if you had included a FOR clause in the LIST command—by reading every order record and testing each against the specified condition. You can speed up processing by using a more efficient search strategy based on the fact that the Order File is indexed by ACCOUNT: Use a SEEK command to find the first matching order record, and then use a WHILE clause to define the group of order records that match the current customer. The command sequence is as follows:

```
SELECT ORDER
SEEK "ABCPLUMB"
LIST WHILE ACCOUNT = "ABCPLUMB"
```

The SEEK command positions the record pointer on the first order record in which the ACCOUNT field contains "ABCPLUMB", and the WHILE clause causes dBASE IV to cease reading records at the end of the group defined by the contents of the ACCOUNT field. You could express the account code more generally, in both the SEEK and LIST commands, so that the same commands work with any customer:

```
SELECT ORDER
SEEK CUSTOMER->ACCOUNT
LIST WHILE ACCOUNT = CUSTOMER->ACCOUNT
```

Linking Data Bases with SET RELATION

The method described in the previous section for accessing related records in two files depends solely on your ability to state selection criteria that define the matching sets of records. If the relationship between two files is based on a common field or fields, and if there is an MDX index tag or an NDX index based on this common key, you can use the SET RELATION command to establish a more formal linkage based on the key expression. The two files must be open, in any two work areas, and the work area that contains the "main" file—the one you intend to process—must be selected. The syntax is as follows:

SET RELATION TO *key expression* INTO *file alias*

The field(s) that make up the key expression must be present in both files, but they need not have the same names. The file accessed through the relation—the one whose alias is named in the SET RELATION command, and which is sometimes referred to as the *related file*—must be indexed on the key expression. The selected file can be indexed on any expression or not at all. You cancel the linkage between two files with

```
SET RELATION TO
```

When two files are linked with SET RELATION, *any command that moves the record pointer in the selected file causes dBASE IV to automatically position the related file to the matching record based on the common key expression.* If there is no match, the record pointer in the related file is positioned at the end-of-file, and all fields in the "current record" in this file appear to be blank. If there is more than one matching record, dBASE IV finds the first one—the same one that a SEEK command would retrieve.

For example, you could open the Customer and Order files, and link them by the common field ACCOUNT, with the following command sequence:

```
USE NWORDER IN 1 ALIAS ORDER
USE NWCUST IN 2 ORDER ACCOUNT ALIAS CUSTOMER
SELECT ORDER
SET RELATION TO ACCOUNT INTO CUSTOMER
```

With the files linked in this way, dBASE IV always positions the Customer File to the record in which the ACCOUNT field matches the ACCOUNT field in the current Order File record, and you have access to any fields from the matching pair of records in the two files. For example, you could use a GOTO command to access a particular order record (chosen at random in this example) and display the customer company name along with (or instead of) the account code and other selected fields from the order record:

```
SELECT ORDER
GOTO 5
DISPLAY ACCOUNT, CUSTOMER->COMPANY, CATEGORY, PARTNUMBER, QUANTITY
```

If the operation of the SET RELATION command seems mysterious, remember that you can obtain the same results—for a single pair of records—by using a SEEK command to carry out the index key search that finds the matching record. For example, with the Customer and Order files both open and the ACCOUNT tag selected as the master index for the Customer File, you could display the same fields as in the previous example with the following command sequence:

```
SELECT ORDER
GOTO 5
SELECT CUSTOMER
SEEK ORDER->ACCOUNT
SELECT ORDER
DISPLAY ACCOUNT, CUSTOMER->COMPANY, CATEGORY, PARTNUMBER, QUANTITY
```

You can set up to ten relations at a time, and you can set more than one relation to or from any work area. To establish more than one linkage from the same file, you list the key expressions and file aliases in one SET RELATION command. For example, you might want to open all three National Widgets files and link the Order File to the Customer File by account code and to the Inventory File based on the part number. For any record in the Order File, you could then display the company name from the Customer File and the item description from the Inventory File. The command sequence is as follows:

```
USE NWORDER IN 1 ALIAS ORDER
USE NWCUST IN 2 ORDER ACCOUNT ALIAS CUSTOMER
USE NWINVENT IN 3 ORDER PARTNUMBER ALIAS INVENTORY
SELECT ORDER
SET RELATION TO ACCOUNT INTO CUSTOMER, PARTNUMBER INTO INVENTORY
SEEK "ELLISMFG"
DISPLAY ACCOUNT, CUSTOMER->COMPANY, CATEGORY, PARTNUMBER, INVENTORY->DESCRIP
```

When you use Query-by-Example to link files based on a complex key expression (rather than a single field), both files must be indexed on the same expression. At the dot prompt, only the file accessed through the relation must be indexed on the expression used to link the files; the main file that you process can be indexed on some other key expression or not at all. It makes no difference how the record pointer arrives at a given record in the main file, so you can read this file in any order. The index is required only to enable dBASE IV to carry out the internal SEEK command that finds the matching record in the related file for each record in the main file.

For example, you might want to display Order File records in order by account code, together with the item descriptions from the matching Inventory File records. If both CATEGORY and PARTNUMBER were required to uniquely identify each inventory item, you would need an index for the Inventory File based on this combination of fields. You could build the index tag as follows:

```
INDEX ON CATEGORY + PARTNUMBER TAG CATPART
```

You could then open the Order File, activate the ACCOUNT tag to read records in alphabetical order by customer account code, and link the two files based on the expression CATEGORY + PARTNUMBER, as follows:

```
USE NWORDER IN 1 ORDER ACCOUNT ALIAS ORDER
USE NWINVENT IN 2 ORDER CATPART ALIAS INVENTORY
SELECT ORDER
SET RELATION TO CATEGORY + PARTNUMBER INTO INVENTORY
SEEK "ELLISMFG"
DISPLAY ACCOUNT, CATEGORY, PARTNUMBER, INVENTORY->DESCRIP
```

When you use SET RELATION to access one record at a time, its only advantage is convenience: it reduces the number of commands you must type to display several consecutive sets of matching Order, Customer, and Inventory File records. The real benefit of SET RELATION is that it offers access to the matching records in related files *for every record in the selected file* processed by commands such as LIST, DISPLAY, REPORT, LABEL, and REPLACE. As dBASE IV moves the record pointer in the selected file while executing any of these commands, it also does the equivalent of a SEEK command "behind the scenes" in the related files. For example, with the Order, Customer, and Inventory files linked, as in the examples presented earlier in this section, you could display the matching customer name and inventory item description with *every* order record:

```
DISPLAY ALL ACCOUNT, CUSTOMER->COMPANY, CATEGORY, PARTNUMBER, INVENTORY->DESCRIP
```

The first screen of output produced by this command is illustrated in Figure 17-10.

Keep in mind that the ability to access data from the current record in the Customer File or Inventory File depends only on those files being open. Using this facility to produce a meaningful display of information in matching records in three files depends on the linkage established with SET RELATION. If you neglected to type a SET RELATION command to link the Order File to the Customer File, for example, the previous LIST command would not produce an error message. However, the record pointer in the Customer File would not move as the pointer advanced through the Order File, and dBASE IV would display the same COMPANY field for every order record—the one from the customer record that was "current" the last time the customer work area was selected.

If you are confused or lose track of which files are open in which work areas, or if commands that you think should work yield unpredictable results,

```
. DISPLAY ALL ACCOUNT,CUSTOMER->COMPANY,CATEGORY,PARTNUMBER,INVENTORY->DESCRIP
Record#  ACCOUNT    CUSTOMER->COMPANY        CATEGORY PARTNUMBER INVENTORY->DES
CRIP
      1  ABCPLUMB   ABC Plumbing             DISK      101-40     5-1/4" DSDD, 4
8 tpi
      2  ABCPLUMB   ABC Plumbing             FORMS     803-20     14-1/2 X 11" G
reen bar
      3  ABCPLUMB   ABC Plumbing             RIBBON    240-51     Epson FX-285,
286
      4  ELLISMFG   Ellis Manufacturing      FORMS     820-20     3-1/2 x 1" Lab
els, 1-up
      5  ELLISMFG   Ellis Manufacturing      DISK      101-42     3-1/2" DSDD

      6  ELLISMFG   Ellis Manufacturing      STOR      481-21     Locking 3-1/2"
 Disk Tray
      7  WHITNY                              ACCESS    541-15     Terminal Swive
l Mount
      8  WHITNY                              FORMS     803-31     9-1/2 X 11" Wh
ite
      9  WHITNY                              DISK      101-31

Press any key to continue...
Command ║C:\dbase4\NWORDER       ║Rec 1/33        ║File ║       ║      Caps
```

Figure 17-10.

Displaying data from three linked files from the dot prompt

the best strategy is to verify that the right files are in fact open and are linked correctly by using DISPLAY STATUS to show you the current status of the working environment. Figure 17-11 illustrates the first two screens of output produced by this command with the National Widgets files open as described in the previous example. The status display includes all open files, all index tags and open NDX indexes, file aliases if you have assigned them, any active filter conditions, and the currently selected work area.

Establishing One-to-Many Relationships

The examples in the preceding section assume that for each record in the file in the selected work area (the Order File in the previous examples), there is one and only one record in each related file (the Customer and Inventory files). If there is more than one matching record, dBASE IV finds the first, just as it would if you had typed a SEEK command. If there is no matching record, the related file is positioned at the end-of-file, and all the fields in this file appear blank.

SET RELATION is also useful when there is more than one record in the related file that matches each record in the selected file. Considered from the point of view of the Order File, its relationship with the Customer File is one-to-one: for each order there is one customer. From the point of view of the Customer File, the relationship is one-to-many: for each customer there may be many orders. If you anticipate more than one matching record in the related file, you can access the entire set by using the SET SKIP command. For example, you could read through the Customer File and display all orders for each customer with the following command sequence:

```
USE NWORDER IN 1 ORDER ACCOUNT ALIAS ORDER
USE NWCUST IN 2 ORDER ACCOUNT ALIAS CUSTOMER
SELECT CUSTOMER
SET RELATION TO ACCOUNT INTO ORDER
SET SKIP TO ORDER
DISPLAY ALL ACCOUNT, COMPANY, ORDER->CATEGORY, ORDER->PARTNUMBER
```

For each record in the Customer File, dBASE IV skips through all the matching order records before it moves to the next customer record when it executes a command such as LIST or prints a report. Note that although the

```
Currently Selected Database:
Select area:  1, Database in Use: C:\DBASE4\NWORDER.DBF   Alias: ORDER
Production   MDX file:  C:\DBASE4\NWORDER.MDX
           Index TAG:     ACCOUNT  Key: ACCOUNT
           Index TAG:     INVNUMBER  Key: INVNUMBER
           Index TAG:     CATPART  Key: CATEGORY+PARTNUMBER
    Related into: CUSTOMER
    Relation: ACCOUNT
    Related into: INVENTORY
    Relation: CATEGORY+PARTNUMBER

Select area:  2, Database in Use: C:\DBASE4\NWCUST.DBF   Alias: CUSTOMER
Production   MDX file:  C:\DBASE4\NWCUST.MDX
    Master Index TAG:     ACCOUNT  Key: ACCOUNT
           Index TAG:     ZIP  Key: ZIP
           Index TAG:     FIRSTORDER  Key: FIRSTORDER (Descending)
           Memo file:   C:\DBASE4\NWCUST.DBT

Select area:  3, Database in Use: C:\DBASE4\NWINVENT.DBF   Alias: INVENTORY
Production   MDX file:  C:\DBASE4\NWINVENT.MDX
           Index TAG:     PARTNUMBER  Key: PARTNUMBER
    Master Index TAG:     CATPART  Key: CATEGORY+PARTNUMBER

File search path:
Default disk drive: C:
Print destination:  PRN:
Margin =      0
Refresh count =     0
Reprocess count =     0
Number of files open =    11
Current work area =     1
```

Figure 17-11.

Using DISPLAY STATUS to verify which files are open

master indexes for the Customer and Order files in the previous example happened to be based on the same field, the SET RELATION and SET SKIP commands depend only on the master index for the related file (the Order File). Note also that a third file, such as the Inventory File, could also be open (this file was omitted from this discussion for simplicity). The first screenful of output from the previous DISPLAY ALL command is illustrated in Figure 17-12.

```
Record#  ACCOUNT     COMPANY                       ORDER->CATEGORY ORDER->PARTNUMBER
      2  ABCPLUMB    ABC Plumbing                  DISK            101-40
      2  ABCPLUMB    ABC Plumbing                  FORMS           803-20
      2  ABCPLUMB    ABC Plumbing                  RIBBON          240-51
      2  ABCPLUMB    ABC Plumbing                  FORMS           820-24
      5  ANDERSON
     19  ARONOFF
     18  DELTADESGN  Delta Design                  FORMS           803-31
     18  DELTADESGN  Delta Design                  STOR            481-11
     14  ELLISMFG    Ellis Manufacturing           FORMS           820-20
     14  ELLISMFG    Ellis Manufacturing           DISK            101-42
     14  ELLISMFG    Ellis Manufacturing           STOR            481-21
     12  FLOORPLAN   Floor Plan Carpet Center
      9  GREENTHUMB  Green Thumb Landscaping
     10  HOMEMOVIES  Home Movies Video Rentals     ACCESS          533-12
     10  HOMEMOVIES  Home Movies Video Rentals     FORMS           803-21
     10  HOMEMOVIES  Home Movies Video Rentals     STOR            481-20
     10  HOMEMOVIES  Home Movies Video Rentals     RIBBON          240-52
     10  HOMEMOVIES  Home Movies Video Rentals     FORMS           803-20
     10  HOMEMOVIES  Home Movies Video Rentals     RIBBON          260-20
     10  HOMEMOVIES  Home Movies Video rentals     RIBBON          260-20
Press any key to continue...
Command  C:\dbase4\NWCUST          Rec 10/20       File                 Caps
```

Figure 17-12.

Displaying data from multiple matching records in two files

The SET SKIP command allows you to open two files, link them based on a common key expression, and display the same data from either work area. Often, this equivalence allows you to choose whichever work area seems more natural based on the operation you are performing or whichever one forces you to type the fewest file aliases in your field lists. Thus, the following command sequence produces the same output as the previous example:

```
USE NWORDER IN 1 ORDER ACCOUNT ALIAS ORDER
USE NWCUST IN 2 ORDER ACCOUNT ALIAS CUSTOMER
SELECT ORDER
SET RELATION TO ACCOUNT INTO CUSTOMER
DISPLAY ALL ACCOUNT, CUSTOMER->COMPANY, CATEGORY, PARTNUMBER
```

In some cases, the choice of work areas is dictated unequivocally by the selection criteria. In the previous example, if you wanted to include all customers, including those with no orders, you would have to select the Customer File work area, and look up the matching records (if any) in the Order File, rather than selecting the Order File work area and looking up the matching Customer File information.

TRANSFERRING DATA BETWEEN FILES

The examples presented so far demonstrate ways to *display* data from matching records in two or more files, but you can also use data from the related records in calculations, and you can change the values of fields in one file based on information in another. For example, for each record in the Order File, there should be only one matching inventory record, based on the contents of the common PARTNUMBER fields, and you could link the files so as to fill in the standard price for each item ordered from the Inventory File instead of typing the prices individually. You can also read through one file, such as the Order File, and "post" data to another. For example, you might want to add the invoice amount (stored in the INVAMOUNT field in the Order File) into the customer's year-to-date and total orders (the YTDORDERS and TOTORDERS fields in the Customer File), and update the customer's last order date (the LASTORDER field in the Customer File) based on the invoice date (the INV-DATE field in the Order File).

From the Menus

From the menu system, you can transfer data between files by using update queries. Figure 17-13 illustrates an update query that copies the PRICE field from the Inventory File into the corresponding field in the Order File and then computes the SUBTOTAL by multiplying PRICE by QUANTITY. The Order File is the target file—the one that is updated by the query—and the files are linked based on PARTNUMBER. As in the query described in Chapter 16 for appending records from a file with a dissimilar structure, you indicate how dBASE IV should transfer data between fields by entering expressions, preceded by the **With** operator, in the file skeleton columns that represent the fields that you want to update. In Figure 17-13, the PRICE field in the Order File is defined as NWINVENT– >PRICE (the value of the PRICE field from the NWINVENT file), and the SUBTOTAL field is calculated as PRICE * QUANTITY. Instead of using the full file alias and field name for the Inventory File PRICE field, you can enter an example variable, such as PRICE, PR, or X in the Inventory File skeleton, and use the same example variable name in the expression in the Order File skeleton PRICE column.

If you want to be able to enter some prices manually and then read in the rest from the Inventory File, you can enter the condition = 0 in the PRICE column in the Order File skeleton along with the replacement value so that the

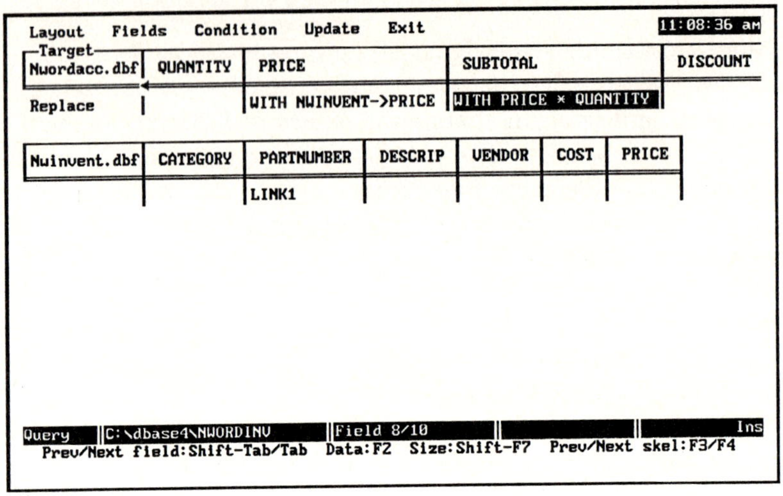

```
Layout   Fields   Condition   Update   Exit                              11:08:36 am
-Target-
Nwordacc.dbf | QUANTITY | PRICE                 | SUBTOTAL                | DISCOUNT
Replace      |          | WITH NWINVENT->PRICE  | WITH PRICE * QUANTITY   |

Nwinvent.dbf | CATEGORY | PARTNUMBER | DESCRIP | VENDOR | COST | PRICE
             |          | LINK1      |         |        |      |

Query  ||C:\dbase4\NWORDINV  ||Field 8/10  ||  ||  Ins
 Prev/Next field:Shift-Tab/Tab  Data:F2  Size:Shift-F7  Prev/Next skel:F3/F4
```

Figure 17-13.

An update query that transfers data between two files

query processes only records in which the PRICE field is blank (zero). If you do this, you must calculate the SUBTOTAL in a second step, using another update query, because this computation should be carried out for all records, not just those in which PRICE is at first 0, and the conditions you enter in a query apply to *all* the calculations defined in the query.

In some cases, you can use an expression based on the IIF function to carry out a conditional calculation and avoid having to define two separate queries. For example, National Widgets gives a 10 percent discount on an order line item if the subtotal is $50 or more and the customer ordered more than one unit of the product. To compute the discount, you could enter the following expression in the DISCOUNT column in the Order File skeleton:

```
WITH IIF(SUBTOTAL >= 50 .AND. QUANTITY > 1, SUBTOTAL * .1, 0)
```

When dBASE IV executes an update, it reads through the target file, NWORDER.DBF in the example illustrated in Figure 17-13, and performs the indicated field replacements for every record that has a match in the Inventory

File. Like a view query, an update query by default processes every pair of matching records in the contributing data bases. Thus, you can use an update query to transfer data between files that have a one-to-many relationship, like the Customer and Order Files. For example, you could "post" the invoice totals in the INVAMOUNT field in the Order File to the YTDORDERS and TOTORDERS fields in the Customer File. You would define the new contents of the YTDORDERS and TOTORDERS fields by the following expressions:

```
WITH YTDORDERS + NWORDER->INVAMOUNT
```

and

```
WITH TOTORDERS + NWORDER->INVAMOUNT
```

One implication of the way that dBASE IV matches up records when it executes an update query is that it skips over any record in the target file for which there is no matching record in the linked data base, and it does not display a warning or error message. In the query in Figure 17-13, if an order record is passed over because there is no matching Inventory File record, the previous entry in the PRICE field remains unchanged. If the original contents of the PRICE field were not 0, the problem could easily go unnoticed even if you examine the Order File after you perform the update.

You can force dBASE IV to process every order record by including the **Every** operator in the PARTNUMBER column in the Order File skeleton. When the Order File is positioned at a record for which there is no match in the Inventory File, the record pointer in the Inventory File is positioned at the end-of-file, where all fields appear blank, and the PRICE field in the Order File acquires the value 0. This makes it easier to identify records that were not updated, but it would be preferable to find the problem records *before* you run the update. *It is up to you to detect and correct possible mismatches before you execute an update query.* Techniques for doing this are presented later in this chapter.

Carrying out a series of calculations similar to the examples in this section (updating all the numeric fields in the Order File) often requires two or more update queries, especially if some fields may be calculated or entered manually. If you cannot use the IIF function to express some or all of the selection criteria, any step that requires unique record selection criteria will require a separate query. In these cases, executing the queries can be time-consuming if the files are large, because each update query requires that dBASE IV read through the entire data base.

From the Dot Prompt

From the dot prompt, you can transfer data between files with the REPLACE command, which was introduced in Chapter 10, and the UPDATE command, which is explained in this section. The REPLACE command can replace a field with the result of evaluating any legitimate dBASE IV expression, which may or may not include fields from more than one file, whereas UPDATE was specifically designed for "posting" data to a record in one file from multiple matching records in another. Both methods read through the file in the selected work area and rely on indexes to find the matching records quickly in another open file.

You could use a REPLACE command to transfer the contents of the PRICE field in the Inventory File into the corresponding field in the Order File. The two files must be open in any two work areas, and they must be linked with SET RELATION before you execute the REPLACE command. The command sequence is as follows:

```
USE NWORDER IN 1 ALIAS ORDER
USE NWINVENT IN 2 ORDER PARTNUMBER ALIAS INVENTORY
SELECT ORDER
SET RELATION TO PARTNUMBER INTO INVENTORY
REPLACE ALL PRICE WITH INVENTORY->PRICE
```

Keep in mind that this example does not illustrate a special form of the REPLACE command. Just as when it executes any other REPLACE command, dBASE IV substitutes the present value of a field with the result of evaluating an expression of the same data type, in this case a field from a file that is open in another work area. As always, you can use any combination of a filter, scope, FOR, and WHILE clause to process order records selectively. For example, to fill in the standard price in new records only—those in which the PRICE field is blank (zero)—you could use the following:

```
REPLACE PRICE WITH INVENTORY->PRICE FOR PRICE = 0
```

If dBASE IV must read every record in the file that you are updating (the Order File in this example), opening the file without assigning a master index will speed processing. Remember that the SET RELATION command does not depend on the sequence in which dBASE IV reads the selected file. For each record in the selected file (the Order File in this example), no matter how the record pointer arrived there, dBASE IV positions the related file (in this case, the Inventory File) record pointer on the matching record. Since dBASE IV does this with the equivalent of a SEEK command, the related file (the Inventory File in this example) must be indexed on the common key expression.

When you execute the REPLACE command in the previous example, if there is no matching record for a particular order record, dBASE IV positions the Inventory File at the end-of-file, where the PRICE field (and every other field) takes on a blank, or 0, value. dBASE IV does not regard this as an error condition; it transfers the 0 value to the PRICE field in the Order File without issuing any warning.

If a REPLACE command does not draw on data from another file, it will execute faster if the file in which you perform the calculation is not linked to another data base. When two files are linked with SET RELATION, dBASE IV must constantly position the record pointer in both files, even if no data from the related file is displayed or otherwise processed.

Even when you use these techniques to maximize processing speed, updating several fields can be time-consuming if the file is large. Often, two or more separate REPLACE commands—two passes through the file—are required. In the Order File example, there are several conditional calculations that depend on different record selection criteria, and the most straightforward way to carry out these steps is to use separate REPLACE commands. The first fills in the PRICE field, the next calculates the discount (if this field is computed rather than entered manually), and yet another fills in the invoice amount. Like the PRICE and DISCOUNT fields, you might compute the INVAMOUNT field conditionally—the sales tax should be 0 for out-of-state customers. For example, this sequence of commands calculates a 10 percent discount for orders of $50 or more, and adds 7 percent sales tax into the invoice total for California customers only:

```
USE NWORDER IN 1 ALIAS ORDER
USE NWCUST IN 2 ORDER ACCOUNT ALIAS CUSTOMER
USE NWINVENT IN 3 ORDER PARTNUMBER ALIAS INVENTORY
SELECT ORDER
SET RELATION TO ACCOUNT INTO CUSTOMER, PARTNUMBER INTO INVENTORY
REPLACE PRICE WITH INVENTORY->PRICE FOR PRICE = 0
REPLACE SUBTOTAL WITH PRICE * QUANTITY
REPLACE DISCOUNT WITH SUBTOTAL * .10 FOR SUBTOTAL >= 50 .AND. QUANTITY > 1
REPLACE INVAMOUNT WITH SUBTOTAL - DISCOUNT FOR CUSTOMER->STATE <> "CA"
REPLACE INVAMOUNT WITH SUBTOTAL - DISCOUNT + .07 * (SUBTOTAL - DISCOUNT)
   FOR CUSTOMER->STATE = "CA"
```

Note that the condition in a FOR clause can refer to fields in any open data base. You must include the file alias for fields in unselected work areas, such as the Customer File STATE field in the previous example.

As noted in the previous section, you can sometimes use an IIF function to carry out conditional calculations that require different selection criteria. For example, you could calculate the price, discount, and sales tax with the following commands:

```
REPLACE PRICE WITH IIF(PRICE = 0, INVENTORY->PRICE, PRICE)
REPLACE DISCOUNT WITH IIF(SUBTOTAL >= 50 .AND. QUANTITY > 1, SUBTOTAL * .10, 0)
REPLACE INVAMOUNT WITH SUBTOTAL - DISCOUNT +
   IIF(CUSTOMER->STATE = "CA", .07 * (SUBTOTAL - DISCOUNT), 0)
```

Because the record selection criteria are expressed by the conditions supplied as input to the IIF functions, you do not need a FOR clause in any of the REPLACE commands, and you can combine all the steps into one, as follows:

```
REPLACE PRICE WITH IIF(PRICE = 0, INVENTORY->PRICE, PRICE),
   SUBTOTAL WITH PRICE * QUANTITY,
   DISCOUNT WITH IIF(SUBTOTAL >= 50 .AND. QUANTITY > 1, SUBTOTAL * .10, 0),
   INVAMOUNT WITH SUBTOTAL - DISCOUNT +
   IIF(CUSTOMER->STATE = "CA", .07 * (SUBTOTAL - DISCOUNT), 0)
```

If the relationship between two files is one-to-many, you must use a SET SKIP command to ensure that dBASE IV transfers data into each record in the selected data base from every one of the matching records in the related file. For example, to add the order total into the YTDORDERS and TOTORDERS fields in the Customer File, you could use the following command sequence:

```
USE NWCUST IN 1 ALIAS CUSTOMER
USE NWORDER IN 2 ORDER ACCOUNT ALIAS ORDER
SELECT CUSTOMER
SET RELATION TO ACCOUNT INTO ORDER
SET SKIP TO ORDER
REPLACE ALL LASTORDER WITH ORDER->INVDATE,
   YTDORDERS WITH YTDORDERS + ORDER->INVAMOUNT,
   TOTORDERS WITH TOTORDERS + ORDER->INVAMOUNT
```

You can accomplish the same transfer of information by reading through the Order File and using SET RELATION to find the matching customer record for each order. You can use a REPLACE command to update the value of a field in an unselected work area, provided that you include the file alias in the field name reference. The command sequence is

```
USE NWORDER IN 1 ALIAS ORDER
USE NWCUST IN 2 ORDER ACCOUNT ALIAS CUSTOMER
SELECT ORDER
SET RELATION TO ACCOUNT INTO CUSTOMER
REPLACE ALL CUSTOMER->LASTORDER WITH INVDATE,
   CUSTOMER->YTDORDERS WITH CUSTOMER->YTDORDERS + INVAMOUNT,
   CUSTOMER->TOTORDERS WITH CUSTOMER->TOTORDERS + INVAMOUNT
```

Both procedures assume that the Order File records are arranged in chronological order so that the most recent order for each customer is processed last, and the LASTORDER field in the Customer File always contains the date of the customer's newest order. If there is any doubt, you can build an index for the Order File that accesses the file by account code and invoice date:

```
USE NWORDER
INDEX ON ACCOUNT + DTOS(INVDATE) TAG ACCTDATE
```

You could then assign this tag as the master index when you open the Order File to carry out either of the command sequences that update the Customer File. As long as the EXACT setting is OFF, a SET RELATION command that links the Customer and Order files based on the ACCOUNT field will find matching records in an index based on the combination of ACCOUNT and INVDATE.

You can also use the UPDATE command to update records in one file based on multiple records in another. The file to be updated and the file that provides the data must be open, in any two work areas, and the file that you want to update must be selected. The two files *must share a common field,* and the most efficient of several ways to use UPDATE is to index the file you want to update on the common field and to read the file that provides the data in record number order. Because this is not the only way to use UPDATE, you must include the keyword RANDOM to indicate that the file that provides the data is in random order with respect to the common field. The syntax for the UPDATE command is as follows:

UPDATE ON *common field* FROM *file alias* RANDOM
REPLACE *field* WITH *expression*

You can update more than one field in the selected file, subject only to the limitation that the UPDATE command may not exceed the 1024-character limit. The UPDATE command replaces the listed fields in the selected file based on records in the file named in the UPDATE command; these records are in random order with respect to the key expression. Because the UPDATE command was specifically designed for this type of "posting" operation, you do not have to link the two files with SET RELATION, although dBASE IV uses exactly the same mechanism, an index key search, to find the matching records. When it finds a match, it replaces each field listed after the REPLACE keyword with the result of evaluating the specified expression. For example, the following command sequence has exactly the same effect as the previous example, which used REPLACE:

```
USE NWCUST IN 1 ORDER ACCOUNT ALIAS CUSTOMER
USE NWORDER IN 2 ALIAS ORDER
SELECT CUSTOMER
UPDATE ON ACCOUNT FROM ORDER RANDOM REPLACE LASTORDER WITH ORDER->INVDATE,
   YTDORDERS WITH YTDORDERS + ORDER->INVAMOUNT,
   TOTORDERS WITH TOTORDERS + ORDER->INVAMOUNT
```

In this example, the Customer File is opened and the ACCOUNT tag is designated as the master index; this is the common field that determines which customer record to update for each order record. The UPDATE command instructs dBASE IV to update the LASTORDER, YTDORDERS, and TOTORDERS fields in the Customer File (the file in the selected work area) based on records in the Order File, which is in random order with respect to the ACCOUNT field.

Note that unlike most dBASE IV commands, including REPLACE, UPDATE does not accept a FOR clause—you must use a filter or a conditional index to perform selective updates. For example, you might want to transfer data to the Customer File only from "new" (previously unposted) Order File records, which you could identify by invoice number or invoice date. To post only orders with invoice dates after March 1, 1992, you could add a FOR clause to a REPLACE command, as follows:

```
USE NWCUST IN 1 ALIAS CUSTOMER
USE NWORDER IN 2 ORDER ACCOUNT ALIAS ORDER
SELECT CUSTOMER
SET RELATION TO ACCOUNT INTO ORDER
SET SKIP TO ORDER
```

```
REPLACE LASTORDER WITH ORDER->INVDATE,
   YTDORDERS WITH YTDORDERS + ORDER->INVAMOUNT,
   TOTORDERS WITH TOTORDERS + ORDER->INVAMOUNT
   FOR ORDER->INVDATE >= {03/01/92}
```

If you use UPDATE, you can specify the condition by using a filter, as in the following:

```
USE NWCUST IN 1 ORDER ACCOUNT ALIAS CUSTOMER
USE NWORDER IN 2 ALIAS ORDER
SELECT ORDER
SET FILTER TO INVDATE >= {03/01/92}
SELECT CUSTOMER
UPDATE ON ACCOUNT FROM ORDER RANDOM REPLACE LASTORDER WITH ORDER->INVDATE,
   YTDORDERS WITH YTDORDERS + ORDER->INVAMOUNT,
   TOTORDERS WITH TOTORDERS + ORDER->INVAMOUNT
```

In many situations, neither UPDATE nor REPLACE offers clear advantages. To use the REPLACE command, you must build an index for the file that provides the data (the Order File in these examples) based on the common field (although you can process the file you are updating in any order). Often, the index you need is available anyway, but if it is not, and you do not plan to repeat the procedure frequently, you may prefer to use the UPDATE command. If you need to process the records that provide the data in a specific order (in these examples, you should read the Order File chronologically) rather than in random order, the REPLACE command sequence, which allows you to use an index to control the processing order, is preferable.

Testing for Mismatches

Whenever you work with linked files, always think about the consequences of mismatches. For example, if you used the REPLACE command explained in the previous section to update the Customer File based on data in the Order File, dBASE IV would replace the LASTORDER date field in the Customer File with a blank date if there were no matching orders (because SET RELATION positions the Order File to the end-of-file). This problem is easy to solve: add a FOR clause that tests the value of any field in the Order File to see if it is blank (all fields are considered to be blank at the end-of-file), as in the following example:

```
REPLACE LASTORDER WITH ORDER->INVDATE,
   YTDORDERS WITH YTDORDERS + ORDER->INVAMOUNT,
   TOTORDERS WITH TOTORDERS + ORDER->INVAMOUNT
   FOR ORDER->ACCOUNT <> " "
```

An order with no matching customer presents a more serious problem, because dBASE IV passes over the record without warning you. If your files are large or you are unfamiliar with the data, you might not notice that some order records were not posted, and significant sums of money could be "lost" from your accounting system.

You can detect mismatches *before* you carry out an update procedure by using the same tools you employ to perform the update.

From the Menus

Working in Query-by-Example, you can define a view query that displays the data that you will later transfer between files by using an update query. Figure 17-14 illustrates such a query, which includes only the ACCOUNT fields from the Order and Customer files. The files are linked by ACCOUNT, and the **Every** operator in the Order File skeleton ensures that the view includes all order records. The result of executing this query with the sample data files is illustrated in Figure 17-15. When the Order File is positioned at a record for which there is no matching customer, such as the orders in which the account code WHITNEY is misspelled WHITNY, the Customer File is positioned at the end-of-file, and the ACCOUNT field appears blank. A query such as this one allows you to find mismatched records and fix the problem (either by entering a new record in the Customer File or by correcting the ACCOUNT field in the Order File) before you execute an update query. In the National Widgets system, you might also want to add the Inventory File to the query in Figure 17-14, linked to the Order File by PARTNUMBER, to verify that every part number entered into an order record has a match in the Inventory File.

If the Order File is large, scanning the output of a view query such as this one can be tedious. You can define a query that displays *only* mismatches by entering the condition = " ", which tests a field to determine whether it is blank, in any column of the Customer File skeleton (at the end-of-file, all fields appear to be blank). Be sure to choose a field, such as the ACCOUNT field, that cannot legitimately be left blank.

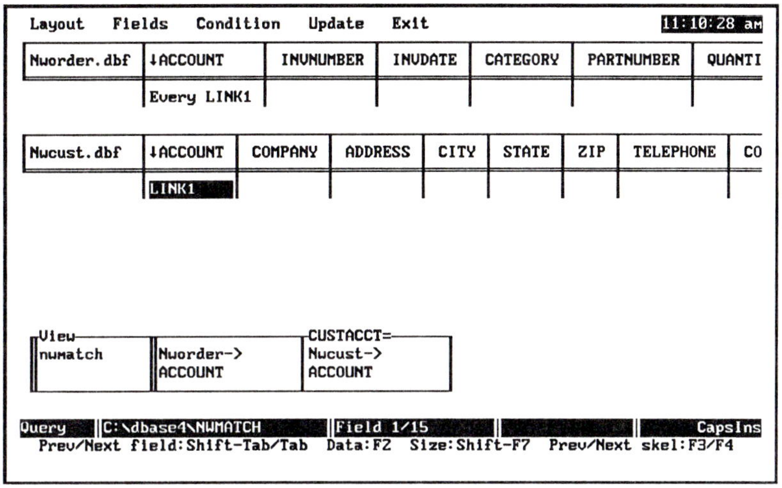

```
Layout   Fields   Condition   Update   Exit                          11:10:28 am

Nworder.dbf | ↓ACCOUNT    | INVNUMBER | INVDATE | CATEGORY | PARTNUMBER | QUANTI
            | Every LINK1 |           |         |          |            |

Nwcust.dbf  | ↓ACCOUNT | COMPANY | ADDRESS | CITY | STATE | ZIP | TELEPHONE | CO
            | LINK1    |         |         |      |       |     |           |

View        Nworder->        CUSTACCT=
nwmatch     ACCOUNT          Nwcust->
                             ACCOUNT

Query  C:\dbase4\NWMATCH     Field 1/15                              CapsIns
 Prev/Next field:Shift-Tab/Tab  Data:F2  Size:Shift-F7  Prev/Next skel:F3/F4
```

Figure 17-14.

A query designed to detect mismatches between two files

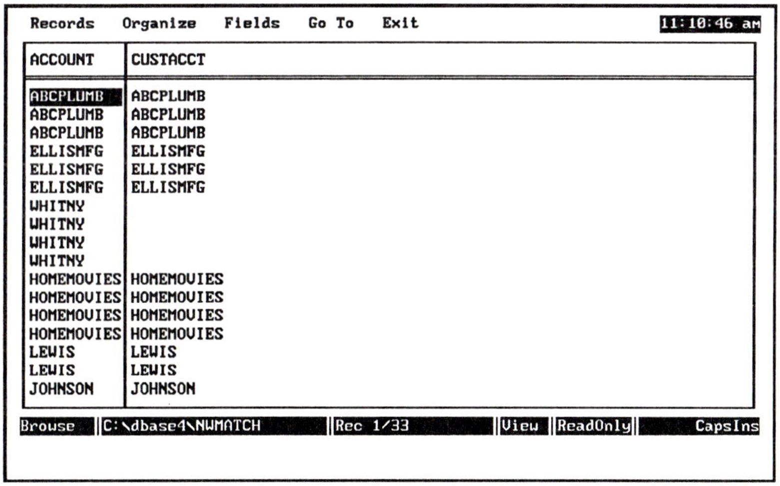

```
Records   Organize   Fields   Go To   Exit                           11:10:46 am

ACCOUNT    | CUSTACCT
ABCPLUMB   | ABCPLUMB
ABCPLUMB   | ABCPLUMB
ABCPLUMB   | ABCPLUMB
ELLISMFG   | ELLISMFG
ELLISMFG   | ELLISMFG
ELLISMFG   | ELLISMFG
WHITNY     |
WHITNY     |
WHITNY     |
WHITNY     |
HOMEMOVIES | HOMEMOVIES
HOMEMOVIES | HOMEMOVIES
HOMEMOVIES | HOMEMOVIES
HOMEMOVIES | HOMEMOVIES
LEWIS      | LEWIS
LEWIS      | LEWIS
JOHNSON    | JOHNSON

Browse  C:\dbase4\NWMATCH    Rec 1/33        View  ReadOnly          CapsIns
```

Figure 17-15.

Finding the order records that have no matches in the Customer File

From the Dot Prompt

At the dot prompt, you can detect records that have no match in another file by linking the data bases exactly as you would to perform an update and displaying corresponding fields from matching records. For example, to detect order records for which there are no matching customers, you could use a command sequence like the following:

```
USE NWORDER IN 1 ALIAS ORDER
USE NWCUST IN 2 ORDER ACCOUNT ALIAS CUSTOMER
SELECT ORDER
SET RELATION TO ACCOUNT INTO CUSTOMER
LIST ACCOUNT, CUSTOMER->ACCOUNT
```

If the output of this LIST command included any records in which the customer file ACCOUNT field were blank or in which the two ACCOUNT fields were not identical, you could correct these problems before executing a REPLACE or UPDATE command. A blank value might result from a missing customer record or an incorrectly entered account code in either file, while different values would occur if you failed to link the files with SET RELATION or if the Customer File ACCOUNT index were damaged.

It is easier to spot mismatches if you display only those records in which the ACCOUNT fields in the Customer and Order files differ, together with the fields in the Order File that would allow you to retrieve each problem record easily to examine, delete, or correct it. In this case, you might display the ACCOUNT and INVNUMBER fields, as in the following:

```
LIST ACCOUNT, CUSTOMER->ACCOUNT, INVNUMBER FOR ACCOUNT <> CUSTOMER->ACCOUNT
```

These techniques are readily adaptable to most operations involving multiple data bases. The important point is that although dBASE IV provides the tools for detecting mismatches between linked files, it is your responsibility to use these tools and correct the problems you uncover before you carry out a potentially destructive command such as REPLACE or UPDATE.

PRINTING MULTIFILE REPORTS

The strategies described earlier in this chapter for accessing matching records in multiple files are equally applicable to printing reports and labels. For example, you could include the customer company name field and the inventory item description on an order summary report such as the one shown in Figure 17-16, provided that all three files are open and linked correctly when you create and print the report.

The order listing is a standard columnar report that differs very little in structure and appearance from a report based on a single data base. In other situations, the necessity to read data from two or more files has a greater impact on the report design. Figure 17-17 illustrates a customer reference list that includes transactions, and Figure 17-18 shows the report on the report layout editor work surface. The format of this report resembles a hybrid of two of the three basic layouts. The detail band, which occupies two lines per order record so as to fit the report on an 8 1/2- by 11-inch page, is a column layout that consists primarily of fields from the Order File, together with the DESCRIP field from the matching Inventory File record. The **Suppress repeated values option** was set to **Yes** for the invoice number and date fields so that these fields are printed only once for each group of order records that make up an invoice.

The group header band for the group band based on the ACCOUNT field is constructed much like a form layout, with the fields from the Customer File laid out as in the customer reference list described in Chapter 14. The customer data is printed as part of the ACCOUNT group intro band because this band is printed before each group of order records that share the same ACCOUNT field contents. If you wanted each customer to begin on a new page, you could set the **Begin band on new page option** to **Yes**. As in most columnar reports, the column headings for the detail band are included in the group intro band. The group summary band consists of three summary fields: the sums of the SUBTOTAL, DISCOUNT, and INVAMOUNT fields.

dBASE IV also allows you to base report selection criteria on fields in any open data bases, whether or not these fields appear in the printout. For example, you might want to print mailing labels for all customers who have ordered products in a certain category. Although the labels include only Customer File fields, the selection criteria refer to fields in the Order File.

Printed: 04/30/92 Page 1

National Widgets, Inc.
Order Summary List

ACCOUNT	COMPANY NAME	INVOICE	DATE	CATEGORY	ITEM	DESCRIPTION	QUANT	PRICE	DISCOUNT	TOTAL
ABCPLUMB	ABC Plumbing	07302	02/08/92	DISK	101-40	5-1/4" DSDD, 48 tpi	2	19.95	0.00	39.90
				FORMS	803-20	14-1/2 X 11" Green bar	1	45.25	0.00	45.25
				RIBBON	240-51	Epson FX-285, 286	2	14.95	0.00	29.90
		09625	04/30/92	FORMS	820-24	3-1/2 x 4" Labels, 4-up	1	64.95	0.00	64.95
DELTADESGN	Delta Design	08044	02/23/92	FORMS	803-31	9-1/2 X 11" White	1	37.50	0.00	37.50
				STOR	481-11	3-1/2" Plastic disk case	3	2.50	0.00	7.50
ELLISMFG	Ellis Manufacturing	07881	02/16/92	FORMS	820-20	3-1/2 x 1" Labels, 1-up	1	21.95	0.00	21.95
				DISK	101-42	3-1/2" DSDD	1	19.95	0.00	19.95
				STOR	481-21	Locking 3-1/2" Disk Tray	1	16.95	0.00	16.95
HOMEMOVIES	Home Movies Video Rentals	08563	03/21/92	ACCESS	533-12	Plexiglas Printer Stand	1	39.95	0.00	39.95
				FORMS	803-21	14-1/2 X 11" White	2	42.50	8.50	76.50
				STOR	481-20	Locking 5-1/4" Disk Tray	1	19.95	0.00	19.95
				RIBBON	240-52	Epson EX-80, 100, Black	3	5.95	0.00	17.85
		09238	04/18/92	FORMS	803-20	14-1/2 X 11" Green bar	2	45.25	9.05	81.45
				RIBBON	260-20	Apple ImageWriter II	5	5.95	0.00	29.75
JOHNSON	J. Thomas Johnson, CPA	05173	12/06/91	ACCESS	541-15	Terminal Swivel Mount	1	92.50	0.00	92.50
KLEIN	Carol Klein, M.D.	05720	12/28/91	FORMS	803-31	9-1/2 X 11" White	1	37.50	0.00	37.50
				FORMS	820-20	3-1/2 x 1" Labels, 1-up	1	21.95	0.00	21.95
				COVER	540-13	Dust cover, AT-compatible	1	29.95	0.00	29.95
				ACCESS	508-13	Glare screen, monochrome	1	24.95	0.00	24.95
LEWIS	Lewis and Associates	06942	01/20/92	DISK	101-41	5-1/4" High dens., 96 tpi	2	32.50	6.50	58.50
				STOR	481-10	5-1/4" Plastic disk case	2	2.75	0.00	5.50
MTK	M.T.K. Industries	07184	02/03/92	STOR	481-10	5-1/4" Plastic disk case	12	2.75	0.00	33.00
				FORMS	820-20	3-1/2 x 1" Labels, 1-up	1	21.95	0.00	21.95
				FORMS	820-24	3-1/2 x 4" Labels, 4-up	1	64.95	0.00	64.95
				COVER	540-13	Dust cover, AT-compatible	3	29.95	8.99	80.86
WHITNEY	Financial Planning Svcs.	07792	02/13/92	FORMS	803-31	9-1/2 X 11" White	1	37.50	0.00	37.50
				RIBBON	240-53	Epson EX-80, 100, Color	2	10.95	0.00	21.90
		06792	01/18/92	ACCESS	541-15	Terminal Swivel Mount	1	92.50	0.00	92.50
				FORMS	803-31	9-1/2 X 11" White	1	37.50	0.00	37.50
				DISK	101-41	5-1/4" High dens., 96 tpi	1	32.50	0.00	32.50
				COVER	540-13	Dust cover, AT-compatible	1	29.95	0.00	29.95
YORKPUMP	York Pump, Inc.	07238	02/05/92	DISK	101-41	5-1/4" High dens., 96 tpi	2	32.50	6.50	58.50

Figure 17-16.

An order listing that includes fields from the Customer and Inventory files

```
Printed: 04/30/92                    National Widgets, Inc.                              Page  1
                                Customer and Order Reference List


ABCPLUMB     ABC Plumbing                      Contact:    Ed Williams             First Order:     12/01/87
             1850 University Avenue            Telephone: 861-4543                 Most Recent:     04/30/92
             Berkeley, CA  94703               Credit:     Good
                                                                                   Y-T-D Orders:      796.41
             Equipment: Kaypro 4, Kaypro 10, Kaypro 286 PC, Epson FX-286 printer   Total Orders:    5,248.90


             INVOICE   DATE    CATEGORY    ITEM   DESCRIPTION          QUANT    PRICE  SUBTOTAL   DISCOUNT    TOTAL

             07302   02/08/92  DISK       101-40  5-1/4" DSDD, 48 tpi     2     19.95    39.90       0.00     39.90
                               FORMS      803-20  14-1/2 X 11" Green bar  1     45.25    45.25       0.00     45.25
                               RIBBON     240-51  Epson FX-285, 286       2     14.95    29.90       0.00     29.90
             09625   04/30/92  FORMS      820-24  3-1/2 x 4" Labels, 4-up 1     64.95    64.95       0.00     64.95

             ORDER TOTALS:                                                              180.00       0.00    180.00

---------------------------------------------------------------------------------------------------------------------

DELTADESGN   Delta Design                      Contact:    Andrea Bennett          First Order:     09/14/88
             N.W. 245 Sunrise Drive            Telephone: 332-7373                 Most Recent:     02/23/92
             Pullman, WA  99163                Credit:     Good
                                                                                   Y-T-D Orders:      188.15
             Equipment: Macintosh II, Macintosh SE, TOPS network, Imagewriter, Apple  Total Orders: 1,235.87
                        LaserWriter Plus


             INVOICE   DATE    CATEGORY    ITEM   DESCRIPTION             QUANT    PRICE  SUBTOTAL   DISCOUNT    TOTAL

             08044   02/23/92  FORMS      803-31  9-1/2 X 11" White          1     37.50    37.50       0.00     37.50
                               STOR       481-11  3-1/2" Plastic disk case   3      2.50     7.50       0.00      7.50

             ORDER TOTALS:                                                                  45.00       0.00     45.00

---------------------------------------------------------------------------------------------------------------------

ELLISMFG     Ellis Manufacturing               Contact:    Barbara Goddard         First Order:     10/18/88
             832 130th N.E.                    Telephone: 455-1421                 Most Recent:     02/16/92
             Bellevue, WA  98005               Credit:     Bad
                                                                                   Y-T-D Orders:        0.00
             Equipment: IBM PS/2 Model 60, Okidata 193, Macintosh SE, Apple ImageWriter  Total Orders:  669.58


             INVOICE    DATE  CATEGORY    ITEM    DESCRIPTION             QUANT    PRICE  SUBTOTAL  DISCOUNT     TOTAL

             07881   02/16/92 FORMS      820-20   3-1/2 x 1" Labels, 1-up   1     21.95    21.95      0.00      21.95
                              DISK       101-42   3-1/2 x 1" DSDD           1     21.95    19.95      0.00      19.95
                              STOR       481-21   Locking 3-1/2" Disk Tray  1     16.95    16.95      0.00      16.95

             ORDER TOTALS:                                                                 58.85      0.00      58.85
```

Figure 17-17.

A customer reference list that includes orders

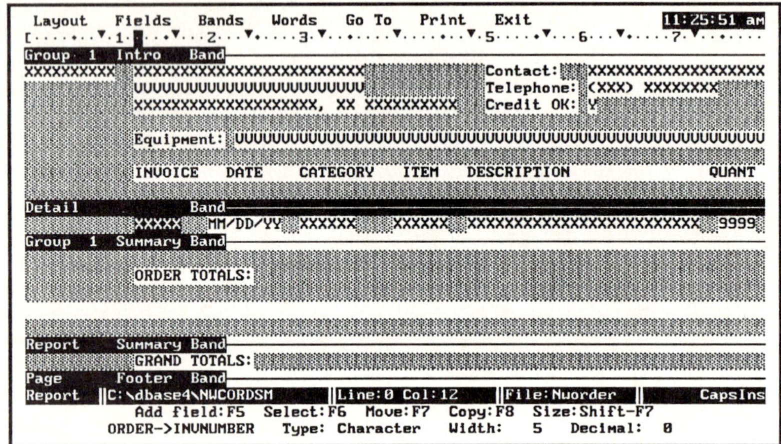

Figure 17-18.

Defining the customer reference list with orders

From the Menus

If you work in the menu system, you must open the required files and establish the linkages by defining a view query, and then open this view instead of a data base file whenever you edit the report or label form or print the report. The view skeleton must include all the fields you want to print, so if you want to be able to use the same query for several reports, you must include in the view all the fields required by each report. When you open a view rather than a data base, the field pick list that is displayed when you add a field to the report or label design work surface includes all the fields in the view and only those fields. This is consistent with the functional equivalence of a view query to a true data base that contains the same data.

When you open files by using a view query, you need not be concerned with how dBASE IV extracts the specified data from the component data bases, but you must be careful to use the appropriate query operators to ensure that all the right records, and no others, are printed. For example, when you print a report such as the customer reference list shown in Figure 17-17, you must enter the **Every** operator in the ACCOUNT column in the Customer File skeleton (the Customer and Order files are linked by ACCOUNT) if you want the report to include customers who do not have any current orders. When you print forms such as invoices, however, you would want to skip over customers with no matching records in the Order File.

To base report selection criteria on any open data base, you enter conditions in the corresponding file skeletons. For example, to include only California customers on the order summary report, you would add the condition = "CA" to the STATE column in the Customer File skeleton in the query defined to print the report illustrated in Figure 17-16.

Defining selection criteria is less straightforward when the relationship between two files is not one-to-one. For example, National Widgets might want to print labels in ZIP code order for a mailing that announces a sale on floppy disks. The selection criteria must be based on the Order File—only customers who have ordered products in the DISK category should receive the mailing. You could describe the selection criteria by entering the condition = "DISK" in the Order File skeleton CATEGORY column, but customers who have purchased DISK products more than once will appear in the view once *for each disk order,* and the resulting printout will include more than one label for each such customer.

To print each customer only once, you can enter the **Unique** operator in the file name column of the Order File skeleton. Because dBASE IV cannot guess which field or combination of fields determines "uniqueness," it executes this query by building an NDX index file based on a key expression formed by concatenating *all the fields in the view skeleton,* and assigns this index the UNIQUE attribute so that each customer appears only once. This method for implementing the query slows execution dramatically, especially if your files are large. Furthermore, you cannot use this type of query if the fields in the view skeleton total more than 100 characters, the maximum length for an index key; if you try, dBASE IV displays the error message "Total size of fields in view too large for UNIQUE query." In most cases, the name and address fields on a mailing label add up to more than 100 characters (in the National Widgets Customer File, for example, the COMPANY, CONTACT, ADDRESS, CITY, STATE, and ZIP fields total 107 bytes). In general, complex selection criteria such as these are much easier to implement from the dot prompt, using methods described in the next section.

From the Dot Prompt

When you work at the dot prompt, you can open the required files in any work areas and link them with SET RELATION, as explained earlier in this chapter. Unless you use a SET FIELDS command to define the list of fields that must be available for the report, the report item pick list includes all the fields in the data base open in the selected work area, and no others. You can, however, access fields from unselected work areas as calculated fields. For example, to design the order listing in Figure 17-16, which includes the COMPANY field from the Customer File and the DESCRIP field from the Inventory File, you could use a calculated field defined by the expression NWCUST –>COMPANY to print the COMPANY field, and another, NWINVENT –>DESCRIP, to print the DESCRIP field (these expressions assume that you did not assign a different alias to the Customer File or Inventory File).

If you use a SET FIELDS command to establish the field list, only the specified fields appear in the pick list, just as when you use a query. If you are printing primarily fields from one file and several others from unselected work areas, you can easily establish the field list with the SET FIELDS TO ALL command, which selects all the fields in one data base, followed by additional SET FIELDS commands that add the remaining fields to the list. For example, you could open and link the files required for the order report and establish the field list with the following commands:

```
USE NWORDER IN 1 ORDER ACCOUNT ALIAS ORDER
USE NWCUST IN 2 ORDER ACCOUNT ALIAS CUSTOMER
USE NWINVENT IN 3 ORDER PARTNUMBER ALIAS INVENTORY
SELECT ORDER
SET RELATION TO ACCOUNT INTO CUSTOMER, PARTNUMBER INTO INVENTORY
SET FIELDS TO ALL
SET FIELDS TO CUSTOMER->COMPANY, INVENTORY->DESCRIP
```

When you work at the dot prompt, you must decide which of several open work areas to select when you print a report that draws data from multiple files. Sometimes you can produce exactly the same results from more than one work area, but, as noted earlier in this chapter, the record selection criteria often govern the choice of work area. For example, when you print the customer reference list shown in Figure 17-17, you must select the Customer File work area if you want the report to include customers who do not have any current orders. To print invoices, which contain essentially the same information but laid out differently on the page, it is easier to read through the Order File and look up the required Customer File fields so that customers who are not represented in the Order File *do not* print.

Figure 17-19 illustates a typical invoice form, and Figure 17-20 shows the invoice. The report is designed to print from the Order File work area, and the Order File fields are printed in the detail band. The report includes a group band based on the INVNUMBER field, and the **Begin band on new page** option was set to **Yes** for this band so that each invoice begins on a new page. The Customer File fields are printed in the page header band as calculated fields (CUSTOMER– >COMPANY, CUSTOMER– >ADDRESS, and so on), and the inventory item description is printed as a calculated field (INVENTORY – >DESCRIP) in the detail band. The invoice total is printed as a summary item that sums the INVAMOUNT field. In this report form, the total is placed in the page footer band so that it always prints at the bottom of the page, regardless of the number of line items on the invoice; if you prefer to print the total directly below the last line item, you could place the summary item in the group footer band instead.

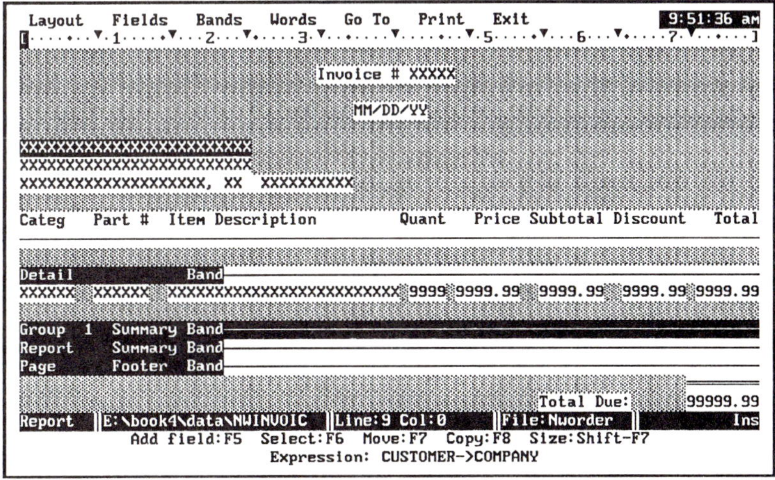

Figure 17-19.

Defining an invoice form

```
                         National Widgets, Inc.
                          943 Parker Street
                          Berkley, CA  94710

                           Invoice # 07302

                              02/08/92

ABC Plumbing
1850 University Avenue
Berkeley, CA  94703

Categ   Part #  Item Description          Quant   Price Subtotal Discount   Total
---------------------------------------------------------------------------------

DISK    101-40  5-1/4" DSDD, 48 tpi           2   19.95    39.90     0.00   39.90

FORMS   803-20  14-1/2 X 11" Green bar        1   45.25    45.25     0.00   45.25

RIBBON  240-51  Epson FX-285, 286             2   14.95    29.90     0.00   29.90




                                                                        ========
                                                 Total Due:               115.05
```

Figure 17-20.

An invoice printed using the NWINVOIC form

Recall that you can use a FOR clause or a filter to establish selection criteria based on fields in any open data base and that you must include the file alias whenever you refer to fields in unselected work areas, as in the following:

```
SET FILTER TO NWCUST->CITY = "San Francisco"
```

or

```
REPORT FORM NWCORDSM TO PRINT FOR NWCUST->CITY = "San Francisco"
```

When you are selecting a small group of records from a large file, you can use a conditional index to speed up processing. For example, to print the customer reference list for just San Francisco customers, you could build a conditional index for the Customer File that includes the appropriate selection criteria, as follows:

```
USE NWCUST
INDEX ON ACCOUNT TAG ACCTCITY OF NWCTEMP FOR NWCUST->CITY = "San Francisco"
```

To print the report, you would work from the Customer File work area, and use SET RELATION and SET SKIP to access the set of order records that match each customer. If you want the report to include only customers who have current orders, you must add a condition to the REPORT FORM command that selects only customers for whom at least one order record exists. The following command sequence takes advantage of the fact that when the internal SEEK triggered by SET RELATION fails to find a record, dBASE IV positions the record pointer in the related file to the end-of-file, where all fields appear to be blank:

```
SELECT 1
USE NWCUST ORDER ACCTCITY OF NWCTEMP ALIAS CUSTOMER
USE NWORDER IN 2 ORDER ACCOUNT ALIAS ORDER
USE NWINVENT IN 3 ORDER PARTNUMBER ALIAS INVENTORY
SELECT ORDER
SET RELATION TO PARTNUMBER INTO INVENTORY
SELECT CUSTOMER
SET RELATION TO ACCOUNT INTO ORDER
SET SKIP TO ORDER
REPORT FORM NWCORDSM TO PRINT FOR ORDER->ACCOUNT <> " "
```

When there is a one-to-many relationship between two files, but you want to select only one of each group of record pairs, it is often easier to open and link the files at the dot prompt than to use Query-by-Example. For example, to print mailing labels for customers who have ordered disk products (as described in the previous section), you can build an index tag for the Order File based on the ACCOUNT and CATEGORY fields (perhaps called ACCTCAT), and use a SET RELATION command that selects only the desired records, as follows:

```
USE NWCUST IN 1 ORDER ZIP ALIAS CUSTOMER
USE NWORDER IN 2 ALIAS ORDER
```

```
SELECT ORDER
INDEX ON ACCOUNT + CATEGORY TAG ACCTCAT
SELECT CUSTOMER
SET RELATION TO ACCOUNT + "DISK  " INTO ORDER
LABEL FORM NWCUST1 TO PRINT FOR ORDER->ACCOUNT <> " "
```

As in the examples in Chapter 11, the label form is based only on fields in the Customer File. The SET RELATION command links the Customer File to the Order File based on the combination of the ACCOUNT field and the product category, to match the expression used to build the ACCTCAT index tag. In this case, the expression in the SET RELATION command includes a constant, "DISK " (including two spaces to fill out the key expression to its full length so that it matches the contents of the Order File key expression exactly). If this seems strange, remember that dBASE IV links files based on the result of evaluating two expressions: the one specified in the SET RELATION command and the index key expression in the related file (the Order File in this example). The only requirement is that *these two expressions must evaluate to the same character string*—they need not use the same field names or even, as in this example, be based only on corresponding data base fields.

UPDATING MULTIPLE FILES

The examples in this chapter illustrate various techniques that you can use to display or print data from two or more related files, and to update one file based on data contained in another. By defining a view query or by linking files at the dot prompt with SET RELATION, you can treat fields from separate records in several different files as if they formed one larger record. For example, when you print the order listing that includes the company name and inventory item description, it appears that these fields are part of each order record, even though they are stored in the Customer File and the Inventory File.

Although you can transfer data en masse between linked files, by defining an update query or by using the REPLACE and UPDATE commands at the dot prompt, updating *individual records* in linked files is more problematical. dBASE IV cannot treat the group of related records in all open files as a set and change all the records in the set in parallel. If you deleted a customer record, dBASE IV would neither delete all the related order records automatically nor warn you that orders exist and caution you to reconsider whether you want to delete the customer. If you change a customer account code, there is no way to enter the same account code automatically into all existing order records; unless you change all the order records yourself, they will no longer be associated with the customer. To guard against such potential disasters, dBASE IV makes all multi-file queries read/only and does not allow you to edit any of the displayed fields, even those that could safely be changed. There is nothing, however, to prevent you from opening a file by itself and making the same potentially destructive changes.

At the dot prompt, you have considerably more flexibility, and within certain limitations you can safely update individual records in any of a set of linked files. For example, you could open the three National Widgets files as illustrated in the status display shown in Figure 17-11 and establish a field list consisting of all the fields in the Order File as well as the COMPANY and EQUIPMENT fields from the Customer File and the DESCRIP field from the Inventory File. When you edit order records, the inventory description helps you verify that the part number was entered correctly, and the EQUIPMENT field enables you to judge whether an order is reasonable, given the customer's computer equipment. Figure 17-21 illustrates the Edit screen with this information displayed for one order record. It is up to you to ensure that you do not make any changes that would disrupt the linkages between files, in this case editing the ACCOUNT and PARTNUMBER fields. As an additional safeguard against this possibility, you can make these fields read/only by specifying the /R option in the SET FIELDS command, as follows:

```
SELECT ORDER
SET FIELDS TO ACCOUNT/R, INVNUMBER, INVDATE, CATEGORY, PARTNUMBER/R,
   QUANTITY, PRICE, SUBTOTAL, DISCOUNT, INVAMOUNT, CUSTOMER->COMPANY,
   INVENTORY->EQUIPMENT, INVENTORY->DESCRIP
```

Although this setup is ideal for *editing* order records, the customer and order data is not available when you add new records to the Order File because dBASE IV does not, as you might expect, automatically display the Customer and Inventory File fields when you enter the ACCOUNT, CATEGORY, and PARTNUMBER into a new order record. This limitation is due to the way that dBASE IV executes the SET RELATION command to find the matching records in the related files, and it affects custom screens that you define using the screen form layout editor as well as the Edit and Browse screens.

When two files are linked with SET RELATION, dBASE IV positions the record pointer to the matching record in the related file at the instant that the

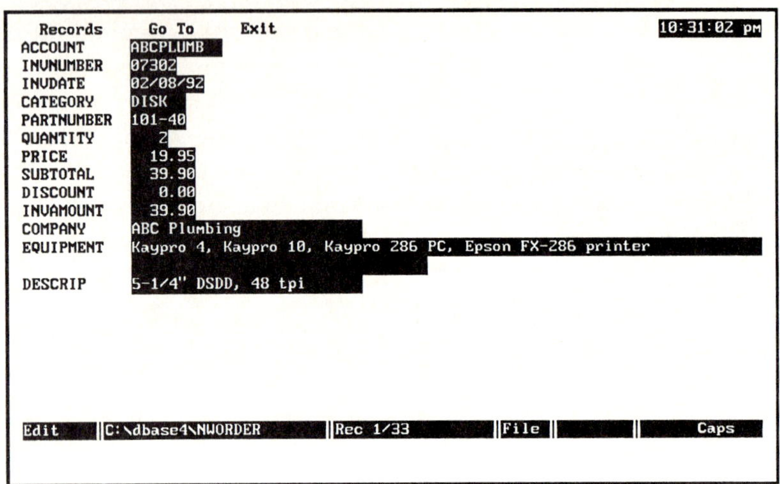

Figure 17-21.

Displaying fields from three files on the Edit screen

pointer moves in the selected work area. As soon as you position the record pointer on an order record, dBASE IV immediately finds the matching customer and inventory records and does not move the record pointers again in these work areas until the record pointer moves in the Order File. When you append a new record to the Order File, the record pointer moves to the new blank record, and immediately afterward, dBASE IV searches for matching records in the two related files. At that instant, all fields in the Order File are blank, so dBASE IV fails to find a matching record in the Customer and Inventory files, and it positions the record pointer at the end-of-file in both related data bases. Filling in the Order File fields does not cause dBASE IV to move the record pointer in the Order File; thus, it does not move the record pointer in the related files, and the COMPANY, EQUIPMENT, and DESCRIP fields remain blank. If you press PGUP to leave the new record and then PGDN to return to it (or vice versa), you will see the data from the COMPANY, EQUIPMENT, and DESCRIP fields filled in.

If you enter data through a custom screen, you can partially overcome this limitation—you can *validate* fields in one file by searching for a matching record in another. Figure 17-22 illustrates a simple data entry screen for viewing and entering the same fields displayed on the Edit screen in Figure 17-21. With the three National Widgets files open and linked as described in the previous example (with the aliases ORDER, CUSTOMER, and INVENTORY), you can

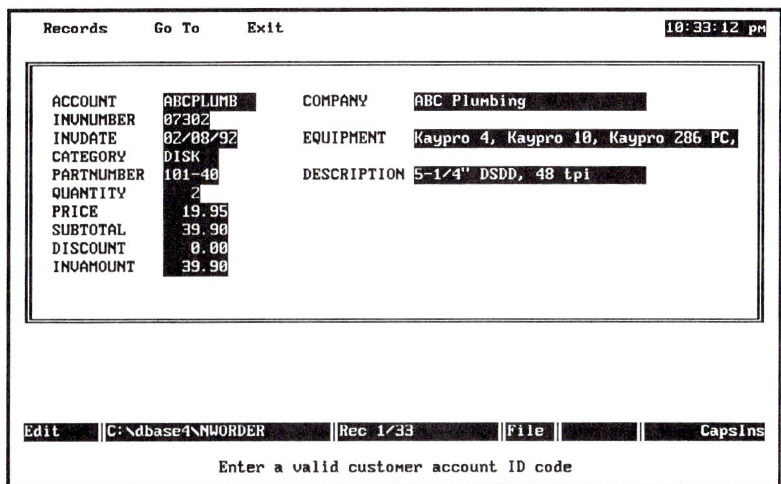

Figure 17-22.

A data entry screen that displays data from three files

validate the ACCOUNT field in the Order File by searching for a match in the Customer File with the SEEK function. This function, which works much like the SEEK command, takes two inputs: the value of the index key expression you want to find, and the alias or work area number of the file in which to perform the SEEK. The SEEK function evaluates to the logical value .T. if the index key search is successful or .F. if it is not.

Figure 17-23 illustrates the Edit options used to carry out this validation and display the appropriate messages. The **Accept value when** condition—SEEK(ACCOUNT, "CUSTOMER")—causes dBASE IV to search the master index tag in the Customer File (in this case, the ACCOUNT tag) for a value that matches the entry in the Order File ACCOUNT field. If dBASE IV finds a record, the SEEK function evaluates to .T. and the validation condition is satisfied; if not, it displays the message defined through the **Unaccepted message** option—"Account ID code not found in Customer File"—and does not allow you to move the cursor out of the field until you correct the entry. You could use a similar expression—SEEK(PARTNUMBER, "INVENTORY")—to validate the PARTNUMBER field by looking for a match in the Inventory File. Note also that although you can validate the ACCOUNT field the instant it is entered, you cannot force dBASE IV to *display* the COMPANY and EQUIPMENT fields from the same Customer File record used for the validation.

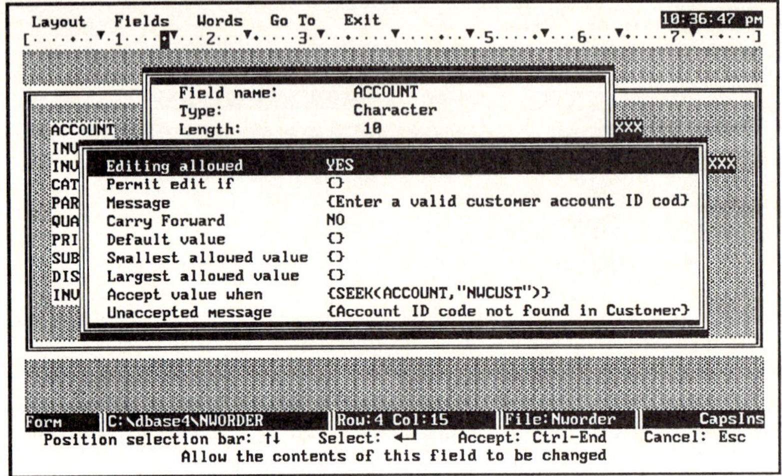

Figure 17-23.

Using the SEEK function to validate entered data

SUMMARY

This chapter presented a variety of methods for working with multiple related data bases. dBASE IV provides a few basic tools for linking files and finding matching records, notably, the ability to link files on the query design screen, and the SEEK, SET RELATION, and SET SKIP commands at the dot prompt. More imporant than understanding the tools themselves is the ability to plan and implement effective strategies for combining these tools to maintain and update your own data bases.

Using dBASE IV successfully to maintain a set of related data bases depends on a number of interacting factors, and to a great extent, it is your responsibility to use the techniques covered in this chapter to maintain a set of related data bases safely and effectively. The initial data base design is important, because dBASE IV identifies the matching records in related files based on the contents of common fields, and index tags based on these fields are required to implement the linkages. You must ensure that identical values are entered into corresponding fields in related files, that a field intended as a unique record identifier never takes on the same value in two different records, and that matching records are added to related pairs of files where necessary. If you change the contents of the index key field in one of several related files, you must make sure to change the contents of the same field in all records in the other related files. In most cases, you should also delete all the matching records from a set of related files as a group. Working with multiple files requires scrupulous attention to detail and error detection strategies that find potential problems before you carry out file update procedures that depend on the accuracy of the data in the files.

Although you can carry out most required operations from either the menu system or the dot prompt, the dot prompt methods are often faster, more direct, and more flexible. If you have been working exclusively in the menu system, you may want to return to this chapter later to try the dot prompt commands. Keep in mind, however, that just because a procedure requires three different update queries does not mean that it is cumbersome or inefficient. Once you have defined and tested the queries, executing them is easy.

CHAPTER EIGHTEEN

Customizing the Working Environment

One of the best features of dBASE IV is the flexibility it offers in customizing the working environment to suit your preferences as well as the demands of your application. You can get started right away using the built-in default settings; later, as you gain experience, you can modify these settings to create a highly personalized data entry environment.

Several configuration options were introduced in earlier chapters, including the DELETED setting, which enables you to ignore records marked for deletion; the EXACT setting, which determines whether two character strings must be the same length to be considered equal; and the NEAR setting, which governs where dBASE IV positions the record pointer if an index key search is unsuccessful. This chapter presents three ways that you can change these settings, as well as numerous others, for the duration of the current work session, and introduces the CONFIG.DB file, a configuration file that stores the settings on disk to serve as the defaults for future work sessions.

This chapter also covers two ways to define typing shortcuts. The first method, which you can employ either in the menu system or at the dot prompt, involves storing keystrokes—including text, menu commands, and dot prompt commands—in *macros* that you can later "play back" to repeat the same command sequences. The second method, which you can use at the dot prompt, involves assigning your own meanings to nine of the ten function keys and to the CTRL and SHIFT function key combinations. By using these techniques to automate frequently used procedures, you can make an application easier to use and improve both the speed and accuracy of many routine file maintenance tasks.

CHANGING dBASE IV SETTINGS

dBASE IV provides close to 100 settings, or options, that you can combine in different ways to create a personalized working environment. Many, including the DELIMITED, NEAR, and EXACT settings introduced in earlier chapters, are *toggles.* Like a push-button switch, they exist in one of two states: on or off. Some settings can take on a small, finite number of different values. For example, the date separator (the punctuation mark that separates the month, year, and day) can be a slash (/), a dash (-), or a period (.). In other cases, the value you enter is subject only to constraints imposed by your hardware or operating system software. For example, you can set the default disk drive to any drive that is physically present in your system, and you can set the display width for memo fields to any value between 8 and 255 characters (the maximum line length used on any printer supported by dBASE IV).

Two methods for changing dBASE IV settings were introduced in earlier chapters: using the menu invoked by choosing the **Settings** option on the Control Center **Tools** menu and typing individual SET commands at the dot prompt. dBASE IV provides the following five ways to edit the settings, each of which offers access to a different group of options:

- Using the **Settings** menu that is invoked when you select the **Settings** option on the Control Center **Tools** menu
- Typing individual SET commands at the dot prompt to change one setting at a time
- Using the SET menu that is invoked when you type SET at the dot prompt

- Using the DBSETUP program to create or edit the dBASE IV configuration file, CONFIG.DB
- Using a text editor to create or edit the CONFIG.DB file

The changes that you make using the first three methods last for the duration of your work session, whereas the settings established in the configuration file, CONFIG.DB, serve as new startup defaults for future work sessions with dBASE IV. Of the three methods that you can use from within dBASE IV to change settings for a single work session, the two dot prompt alternatives—typing individual SET commands and using the SET menu—provide access to more settings than the limited list you will find on the **Settings** menu accessed through the Control Center. Even if you generally prefer to work in the menu system, you may want to exit temporarily to the dot prompt to configure the working environment.

Because there are so many options and so many ways to combine them, it is unrealistic to try to memorize them all at once. As you work with dBASE IV, you can refer to the menu diagrams in both this chapter and Appendix B to review the various settings and determine which menus provide access to the options you need. Appendix D lists the dot prompt SET commands, and Appendix F covers the options that you can change through CONFIG.DB.

From the Menus

From the Control Center, you can change some of the environment settings and customize the display colors or monochrome display attributes through a menu that you invoke by selecting the **Settings** option from the **Tools** menu. Figure 18-1 diagrams the structure of the **Settings** menu bar. The **Options** menu provides access to 16 settings, which are listed in alphabetical order, together with the current status of each (Figure 18-1 shows the default settings). The **Display** menu should seem familiar—it is identical to the corresponding menu in the screen layout editor.

To change any setting that accepts only a finite number of values, you highlight it and press either ENTER or the spacebar to cycle through the choices. You can easily identify the settings that accept a range of values, because dBASE IV displays the currrent value within braces. To change one of these settings, you highlight it, press ENTER, and type in the new value. For numeric settings, after pressing ENTER to select the setting, you can use the UP ARROW and DOWN ARROW keys to increase or decrease the number by one.

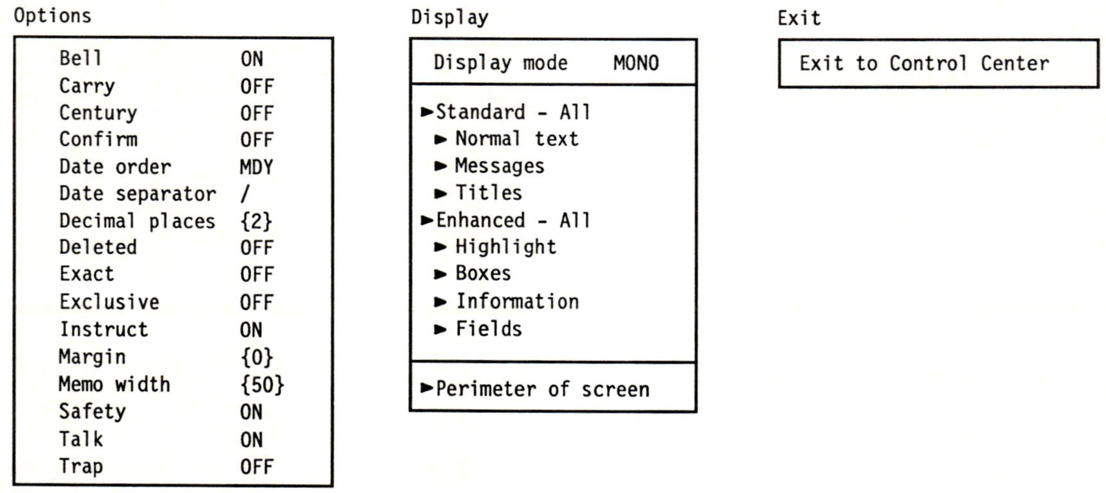

```
Options                          Display                       Exit
+------------------------+       +-----------------------+     +-------------------------+
| Bell            ON     |       | Display mode    MONO  |     | Exit to Control Center  |
| Carry           OFF    |       +-----------------------+     +-------------------------+
| Century         OFF    |       |►Standard - All        |
| Confirm         OFF    |       | ► Normal text         |
| Date order      MDY    |       | ► Messages            |
| Date separator  /      |       | ► Titles              |
| Decimal places  {2}    |       |►Enhanced - All        |
| Deleted         OFF    |       | ► Highlight           |
| Exact           OFF    |       | ► Boxes               |
| Exclusive       OFF    |       | ► Information         |
| Instruct        ON     |       | ► Fields              |
| Margin          {0}    |       +-----------------------+
| Memo width      {50}   |       |►Perimeter of screen   |
| Safety          ON     |       +-----------------------+
| Talk            ON     |
| Trap            OFF    |
+------------------------+
```

Figure 18-1.

The structure of the Settings menu

From the Dot Prompt

From the dot prompt, you can change the settings in two ways. You have already seen one method—typing individual SET commands. For the toggles, the SET commands take the following form:

SET *setting* ON

and

SET *setting* OFF

For example, by default dBASE IV sounds a "bell," or beeps, when you fill a field on the Edit or Browse screen, type a prohibited character (such as a letter in a numeric field), or enter an illegitimate value (such as an invalid date). You can turn off this beep with the following SET command:

```
SET BELL OFF
```

When a setting can take on values other than ON and OFF, the SET command takes the following form:

SET *setting* TO *value*

For example, you could increase the display width for memo fields from the default value of 50 characters to 70 with the following:

```
SET MEMOWIDTH TO 70
```

dBASE IV also offers a menu-driven SET command, which works like the **Settings** menu accessed through the Control Center but provides access to more settings. The SET menu is especially convenient when you want to change many settings at once or when you need a reminder of the available options. To invoke this menu from the dot prompt, type

```
SET
```

Figure 18-2 diagrams the structure of the SET menu. The only difference between this and the other dBASE IV menus is that the menu bar does not

```
Options

Alternate          OFF
Autosave           OFF
Bell               ON
Carry              OFF
Catalog
Century            OFF
Confirm            OFF
Currency sign      LEFT
Cursor             ON
Date order         MDY
Date separator     /
Decimal places     {2}
Deleted            OFF
Delimiters         OFF
Development        ON
Device             SCREEN
Encryption         ON
Escape             ON
Exact              OFF
Exclusive          OFF
Fields             OFF
Fullpath           OFF
Heading            ON
Help               ON
History            ON
Hours              12
Instruct           ON
Intensity          ON
Lock               ON
Margin             {0}
Memo width         {50}
Near               OFF
Pause              OFF
Precision          {16}
Print              OFF
Safety             ON
Scoreboard         ON
Space              ON
Status             OFF
Talk               ON
Title              ON
Trap               OFF
Unique             OFF
```

```
Display

Display mode     MONO

►Standard - All
  ► Normal text
  ► Messages
  ► Titles
►Enhanced - All
  ► Highlight
  ► Boxes
  ► Information
  ► Fields

►Perimeter of screen
```

```
Keys

F2          assist;
F3          list;
F4          dir;
F5          display structure;
F6          display status;
F7          display memory;
F8          display;
F9          append;
F10         edit;
CTRL-F1
CTRL-F2
CTRL-F3
CTRL-F4
CTRL-F5
CTRL-F6
CTRL-F7
CTRL-F8
CTRL-F9
CTRL-F10
SHIFT-F1
SHIFT-F2
SHIFT-F3
SHIFT-F4
SHIFT-F5
SHIFT-F6
SHIFT-F7
SHIFT-F8
SHIFT-F9
```

```
Disk

Default disk drive:              C
Disk drive search path           {}
OS Working drive/directory:      {C:\DBASE4}
```

```
Files

  Alternate  {}
  Device     {}
  Format     {}
► Index
```

Figure 18-2.

The structure of the SET menu

have an **Exit** option. To leave the menu and return to the dot prompt, you can press ESC or either of the standard "save and exit" keys: CTRL-END or CTRL-W. Note that pressing ESC is a "safe" exit—in contrast with its behavior in the Browse and Edit screens and the forms layout editors, dBASE IV does not discard your new settings if you exit by pressing ESC. The **Options** and **Display** menus work just like the corresponding menus on the **Settings** screen accessed through the Control Center **Tools** menu. The options are listed (together with their current values) in alphabetical order, and you can use the usual cursor movement keys to navigate through the list and make selections. The 43 options shown in Figure 18-2 cannot all fit on the screen at once, but if you press UP ARROW, DOWN ARROW, PGUP, PGDN, HOME, or END, the display scrolls to bring another part of the list into view.

The SET menu includes options to reprogram the function keys (this topic is covered later in this chapter) and to set the default disk drive, subdirectory, and search path. It also enables you to open auxiliary files—an *alternate file* (a text file that records screen output, a process that is described in Chapter 20), a screen form file (described as a "Format" file in the menu), or NDX index files. Because you can use a screen form file with more than one data base, you can choose a form without having a data base open; dBASE IV uses the specified form with any data bases that you open later in the work session. In contrast, you can only use an index with the data base for which it was constructed, and you must open a data base before you can open indexes. If you choose the **Index** option from the **Files** menu but you do not have a data base open, dBASE IV displays a pick list of available data bases; after you open one, it displays a pick list that includes only NDX indexes based on this file.

If you have more than one hard disk (or more than one partition on a high-capacity hard disk) or you want to store some data bases on floppy disks, you can use the **Default disk drive** option on the **Disk** menu to establish a new default drive and thus avoid having to specify the disk drive every time you open a file. The effect of choosing a new default drive is exactly the same as if you had logged onto the specified drive before you loaded dBASE IV.

The **Disk drive search path** option works like the DOS PATH command—it allows you to specify a list of subdirectories that dBASE IV should search when you attempt to open a file not found in the current subdirectory. This option is useful if you occasionally need to read a file stored in another subdirectory, but remember that dBASE IV uses the search path only to find and read existing files—it writes all new files in the current subdirectory. In order to specify a default subdirectory in which dBASE IV should read and write all files, you can use the **OS Working drive/directory** option. This option enables you to avoid having to switch subdirectories before you start up dBASE IV, or to switch to a different subdirectory during a work session without exiting to the operating system and reloading dBASE IV.

The Environment Option Settings

When you first look at the list of options displayed by the **Settings** or SET menu, or read the list of SET commands in Appendix D, you may be overwhelmed by the number of choices. Many of the options are of interest only to programmers, and the utility of others will not become apparent until you gain more experience with dBASE IV, but some settings are valuable for dBASE IV users at all levels. These options enable you to change aspects of the default working environment that you find irritating, to speed the data entry process, or to improve the accuracy of the data you enter.

The settings in the list that follows may be useful to you immediately (some were introduced in earlier chapters). All the options are available through SET commands at the dot prompt and from the dot prompt SET menu. Those that are also found on the **Settings** menu are marked with an asterisk. The default values are shown in parentheses.

- *AUTOSAVE (OFF)* When this setting is ON, dBASE IV updates the record count in the DBF file header immediately after you append a new record to a data base; when it is OFF, the record count is updated only when you close the file. By setting this option ON, you can reduce the risk of losing data if a power failure or hardware "crash" prevents you from closing a file properly before you exit dBASE IV.
- *BELL (ON)** When this setting is ON, dBASE IV sounds a bell (actually, a beep) when you fill a field or enter invalid data on the Edit or Browse screen.
- *CARRY (OFF)** When this setting is ON, dBASE IV carries forward the value entered into every field of a new record—including memo fields—to serve as the default value for the corresponding field in the next record.
- *CENTURY (OFF)** When this setting is ON, dBASE IV displays dates with 4-digit years.
- *CONFIRM (OFF)** When this setting is ON, you must always press ENTER to advance the cursor to the next field on the Edit or Browse

screen; when it is OFF, the cursor advances automatically when your entry fills a field.

- *DELETED (OFF)** When this setting is ON, dBASE IV ignores deleted records, except when a command accesses a record by number; when it is OFF, deleted records are included in all displays, reports, and calculations.
- *DELIMITERS (OFF)* When this setting is ON, the data entry areas in Edit, Browse, and custom screens are surrounded by punctuation marks. The default delimiter is a colon (:).
- *EXACT (OFF)** When this setting is ON, dBASE IV treats character strings as identical only if they are the same length, and you must specify the full key value in an index key search; when this setting is OFF, dBASE IV considers two strings equal if all characters up to the length of the shorter string match.
- *HEADING (ON)* When this setting is ON, dBASE IV includes the field names or expressions displayed by commands such as LIST, DISPLAY, and SUM at the top of the output as "column headings."
- *INSTRUCT (ON)** When this setting is ON, pressing ENTER with a file name highlighted in the Control Center invokes a dialog box; when it is OFF, dBASE IV automatically executes the default action—the one that it would display first in the dialog box. For example, when you press ENTER with a data base name highlighted, dBASE IV automatically opens the file or closes it if it is already open. If a report or label form name is highlighted, dBASE IV displays the **Print** menu. The other dialog box options are still available when this setting is OFF; you can press F2 (Data) to display data or SHIFT-F2 (Design) to invoke the appropriate layout editor and modify the highlighted file.
- *INTENSITY (ON)* When this setting is ON, dBASE IV distinguishes data entry areas (data base fields) from background text (the field name prompts) in Edit, Browse, and custom screens by using different colors or monochrome attributes; when it is OFF, data and background text take on the same visual attributes.
- *MEMOWIDTH (50)** This setting specifies the display width for memo fields in the output of commands such as LIST and the default width that dBASE IV assigns when you add a memo field to a custom screen or report form.

- *NEAR (OFF)* When this setting is ON, dBASE IV positions the record pointer on the record in which the index key would follow the search string after an unsuccessful index key search; when it is OFF, dBASE IV moves the record pointer to the end-of-file.
- *SAFETY (ON)** When this setting is ON, dBASE IV requests confirmation before it overwrites existing disk files.
- *SCOREBOARD (ON)* When this setting is ON, status indicators (such as "Ins" and "Caps") and error messages are displayed at the top of the screen if you suppressed the status bar by setting the STATUS option OFF.
- *STATUS (OFF)* When this setting is ON, dBASE IV uses the bottom three lines of the screen for a status display (the status bar, navigation line, and message line).

For all these settings, the wording of the menu option is identical or nearly identical to the equivalent dot prompt SET command. In other cases, the correspondence is not as close. For example, two menu options (on both the **Settings** and SET menus) control the display format for date fields and memory variables. **Date Order**, which by default is set to **MDY**, determines the display order of the month, day, and year. The **Date separator** option selects the punctuation that separates the month, day, and year; the default is a slash (/), but you can also choose a dash (-) or a period (.). From the dot prompt, the easiest way to set the date display format is to use the SET DATE command, which selects both the display order and separator punctuation mark and has the following syntax:

SET DATE TO *date display format*

The keywords that represent the date display formats are listed in Table 18-1. Note that the FRENCH and GERMAN formats are identical, as are AMERICAN and MDY. You could display dates in month/day/year order from the dot prompt, with dashes for separators, by using the following SET command:

```
SET DATE TO USA
```

In several cases, the dot prompt offers an additional choice that is not available through the menus. For example, the **Carry** option on the **Settings**

Name	Format
AMERICAN	*mm/dd/yy*
ANSI	*yy.mm.dd*
BRITISH	*dd/mm/yy*
FRENCH	*dd/mm/yy*
GERMAN	*dd.mm.yy*
ITALIAN	*dd-mm-yy*
JAPAN	*yy/mm/dd*
USA	*mm-dd-yy*
MDY	*mm/dd/yy*
DMY	*dd/mm/yy*
YMD	*yy/mm/dd*

Table 18-1.

dBASE IV Date Display Formats

and SET menus causes dBASE IV to carry over the value entered into every field of a new record to serve as the default value for the corresponding field in the next record. From the dot prompt, you can carry over fields selectively by using a variation of the SET CARRY command in which you list the fields that you want to retain from one new record to the next, as follows:

SET CARRY TO *field list*

When you elect to display delimiters to delineate the data entry areas on the Edit and Browse screens, the default delimiter is the colon. From the dot prompt, you can select another character or pair of characters with the SET DELIMITERS TO command, as follows:

SET DELIMITERS TO *delimiter character(s)*

If you specify one character, it is used at both the beginning and the end of the field; if you specify two, the first is displayed at the beginning and the second at the end. For example, you could substitute square brackets for the default delimiter (the colon) with the following command:

```
SET DELIMITERS TO "[]"
```

Although in principle each setting is independent of the others, be alert for possible interactions between settings that control related aspects of the working environment. For example, by default, INTENSITY is ON and fields are displayed in a different intensity (or in different colors) from background text, but on many monitors, the brightness of the inverse video display can be uncomfortable during long data entry sessions. If you use the SET INTENSITY OFF command to eliminate this difference, you should probably also SET DELIMITERS ON to make it easy to discern the beginning and the end of each field.

For many settings, the "best" choice is governed solely by personal style. For example, by default, dBASE IV beeps when you fill a field in Edit or Browse mode. Some people find the beep annoying, while others are reassured by this audible reminder that works like the bell on a typewriter signaling the end of a line. The nature of your data base may also play an important role in your decisions. When you update a file with short fields that are always filled in, you might SET CONFIRM OFF to eliminate an extra keystroke (pressing ENTER after each field). In a name-and-address data base, however, fields that are rarely filled (such as a street address) often alternate with fields that invariably are (such as the state abbreviation). You may prefer to SET CONFIRM ON if you find this inconsistency disconcerting.

The Display Options

You can customize the display mode and the colors or monochrome display attributes used throughout your work with dBASE IV by using the **Display** options accessed through the **Settings** menu or the SET menu, or by typing SET COLOR commands at the dot prompt. In a system that has both a color and a monochrome monitor, you can switch between the two, and if more than one video mode is available (for example, 43-line mode and 25-line mode on an EGA monitor), you can switch video modes as well.

You can set display colors or monochrome attributes at two levels of detail: in three major groups that correspond to the three major headings in the **Display** menu or for seven more specific types of information. If you install dBASE IV according to the standard procedure explained in Appendix A, the display attributes are set at the finer level of control.

The three major screen groups are defined as follows:

Standard	Most of the messages and text displayed by dBASE IV, including menu options, items in the Control Center panels, items in pick lists, and field name prompts in the full-screen edit modes
Enhanced	The borders that surround menus, Control Center panels, and pick lists; the status bar; and entered data in the full-screen edit modes
Perimeter	The narrow border of the screen that lies outside the 25-line by 80-column display area. By default, the border color is always set to black

You can further refine the color scheme by individually setting the foreground and background colors used to display seven more specific groups of screen items (as well as the Perimeter). The most important items in the seven groups follow (you can find a more complete list in the dBASE IV *Language Reference* manual under the SET COLOR command):

Normal text	Most of the messages and text displayed by dBASE IV, the background of the work surface in the layout editors, and the field name prompts on the Edit screen. By default, dBASE IV uses light characters on a dark background on a monochrome screen and bright white characters on a blue background on a color monitor
Messages	Menu options, items in the Control Center panels, items in pick lists, message and navigation line text, and text in error boxes and dialog boxes. By default, dBASE IV uses light characters on a dark background on a monochrome screen and white characters on a black background on a color monitor

Titles	Field name headings in LIST and DISPLAY output, field and column headings in the Browse screen and layout editors, and the borders of boxes on the Browse screen and in Query-by-Example. By default, dBASE IV uses bright, light characters on a dark background on a monochrome screen and white characters on a blue background on a color monitor
Highlight	The light-bar cursor in all menus and pick lists; file names and descriptions under the Control Center panels; and selected items on the layout editor work surfaces. By default, dBASE IV uses inverse video on a monochrome screen and yellow characters on a light blue background on a color monitor
Boxes	The borders of the Control Center panels, pick lists, dialog boxes, and error boxes. By default, dBASE IV uses inverse video on a monochrome screen and yellow characters on a light blue background on a color monitor
Information	The clock, the status bar, and the borders of help boxes. By default, dBASE IV uses inverse video on a monochrome screen and blue characters on a white background on a color monitor
Fields	All entered data, including fields on the Edit, Browse, and custom screens; and data entry areas displayed in dialog boxes that prompt you for file names and field names. By default, dBASE IV uses inverse video on a monochrome screen and black characters on a light blue background on a color monitor

From the Menus

You can use the **Display mode** option at the top of the **Display** menu to choose any available video display mode (dBASE IV displays only choices that are supported by the display hardware in your system). You can select **MONO**, **COLOR**, **EGA25** (25-line mode on an EGA or VGA monitor), **EGA43** (43-line mode on an EGA or VGA monitor), or **MONO43** (43-line mode on a monochrome monitor attached to an EGA or VGA adapter). dBASE IV does not support 50-line VGA mode. You can choose a single color for the Perimeter and set the foreground and background colors used for text in the Standard and Enhanced groups, or you can pick foreground and background colors for the seven more specific groups of screen items.

From the Dot Prompt

From the dot prompt, you can change the display mode and display colors or monochrome attributes by using SET COLOR and SET DISPLAY commands. In a system that has both a color and a monochrome monitor, you can switch between the two by using SET COLOR ON and SET COLOR OFF. If more than one video display mode is available, you can select any available mode with a SET DISPLAY command of the following form:

SET DISPLAY TO *video mode*

The *video mode* can be MONO, COLOR, EGA25 (25-line mode on an EGA or VGA monitor), EGA43 (43-line mode on an EGA or VGA monitor), or MONO43 (43-line mode on a monochrome monitor attached to an EGA or VGA adapter). dBASE IV does not support 50-line VGA mode.

You can customize the display colors by using the SET COLOR command. To control the colors of the three major screen groups, you use a command similiar to the following:

SET COLOR TO *standard, enhanced, perimeter*

The colors and monochrome attributes are identified by the letter codes listed in Table 18-2. Note that you can display underlining only in a true monochrome system—that is, with a monochrome or Hercules display card—not on a single-color monitor connected to a CGA, EGA, or VGA card. You can select a brighter form of most colors by adding a plus sign (+) to the color code or cause any color to blink by adding an asterisk (*). In some cases, however, the "brighter" color is distinctly different; for example, the "bright" version of brown, specified as GR+, is yellow.

You specify both the standard and enhanced colors in the SET COLOR command as a pair of color codes separated by a slash; the first code represents the foreground color and the second the background color (the perimeter is

Color	Standard Color Code	High Intensity Color Code
Black	N	
Blue	B	B+
Green	G	G+
Cyan (light blue)	BG	BG+
Gray	N+	
Red	R	R+
Magenta	RB	RB+
Brown	GR	
Yellow	GR+	
White	W	W+
Monochrome Attribute		
Bold (bright)	W+	
Underlined	U	
Inverse video	I	
Blinking	Add * to color code	

Table 18-2.

dBASE IV Color and Monochrome Display Attribute Codes

always a single color). For example, you could set the standard colors to white letters on a blue background and the enhanced colors to black letters on a cyan (light blue) background and leave the perimeter set to the default, black, with the following:

```
SET COLOR TO W/B, N/BG
```

You can also set foreground and background colors for any of the seven more detailed screen groups explained earlier in this section by using a slightly different form of the SET COLOR command:

SET COLOR OF *group* TO *colors*

You identify the *group* by a keyword that corresponds to its description on the **Display** menu—NORMAL, MESSAGES, TITLES, BOX, HIGHLIGHT, INFORMATION, or FIELDS—and you specify the colors in pairs, just as in the more general SET COLOR command. The following command sequence customizes the display colors for all seven groups of screen items:

```
SET COLOR OF NORMAL TO W/B
SET COLOR OF MESSAGES TO W/N
SET COLOR OF TITLES TO GR+/B
SET COLOR OF HIGHLIGHT TO W/R
SET COLOR OF BOX TO N/R
SET COLOR OF INFORMATION TO W+/R
SET COLOR OF FIELDS TO N/BG
```

The following SET COLOR commands establish a typical combination of monochrome display attributes:

```
SET COLOR OF NORMAL TO W/N
SET COLOR OF MESSAGES TO W/N
SET COLOR OF TITLES TO W+/N
SET COLOR OF HIGHLIGHT TO I
SET COLOR OF BOX TO W+/N
SET COLOR OF INFORMATION TO I
SET COLOR OF FIELDS TO U
```

USING THE CONFIG.DB FILE TO ESTABLISH THE DEFAULT ENVIRONMENT

When you change the dBASE IV default environment settings using any of the methods outlined in the previous section, the new settings remain in effect for the duration of your work session. You can change the default settings by storing your preferences in a configuration file called CONFIG.DB, which is analogous to the DOS configuration file, CONFIG.SYS.

The CONFIG.DB file is an ordinary ASCII text file with one command on each line. You can create or edit CONFIG.DB with any word processor or text editor that can read and write text files, including the dBASE IV program editor (which is covered in Chapter 21). If you prefer, you can use the menu-driven DBSETUP program to create or modify the CONFIG.DB file; this program is copied to your hard disk during the standard dBASE IV installation procedure detailed in Appendix A. You can run it immediately after installing dBASE IV, and you can rerun it at any time to change the default configuration.

Just as DOS reads CONFIG.SYS only when you boot your computer, dBASE IV checks for the CONFIG.DB file only when you start up the program. Later in a work session, you can override any of the settings established in CONFIG.DB by using the techniques described earlier in this chapter—by making selections from the **Settings** or SET menus, or by typing SET commands at the dot prompt. Remember also that if you edit the configuration file from within dBASE IV, you must exit and reload the program to see the effects of your changes.

If you load dBASE IV from a directory other than the one in which the program files are stored, it searches for CONFIG.DB first in the current subdirectory and then, if the file is not present, in the program directory. You can establish different default settings for different applications by storing each application in its own subdirectory and creating a different CONFIG.DB file in each one. If the configuration file is missing entirely, dBASE IV uses its internal default values for all the settings.

The commands in the CONFIG.DB file are similar to the equivalent dot prompt SET commands, but the syntax differs in several respects. SET commands have two common formats:

SET *setting value*

and

SET *setting* TO *value*

The equivalent CONFIG.DB commands take the form

setting = *value*

In some cases, there are other minor differences. For example, the following is a typical sequence of SET commands:

```
SET AUTOSAVE ON
SET BELL OFF
```

```
SET CONFIRM ON
SET DELETED ON
SET DELIMITERS ON
SET DELIMITERS TO "[]"
SET INTENSITY OFF
SET NEAR ON
SET STATUS ON
SET DIRECTORY TO C:\DBASE\SAMPLES
```

The options listed in the previous example, together with commands to customize the display colors, would appear as follows in CONFIG.DB:

```
AUTOSAVE = ON
BELL = OFF
CONFIRM = ON
DELETED = ON
DELIMITERS = ON
DELIMITERS = []
INTENSITY = OFF
NEAR = ON
STATUS = ON
DIRECTORY = C:\DBASE\SAMPLES
COLOR OF NORMAL = W/B
COLOR OF MESSAGES = W/N
COLOR OF TITLES = GR+/B
COLOR OF HIGHLIGHT = W/R
COLOR OF BOX = N/R
COLOR OF INFORMATION = W+/R
COLOR OF FIELDS = N/BG
```

There are several CONFIG.DB options that you cannot change from within dBASE IV, either from the dot prompt or from the **Settings** or SET menus, because the settings must be known to dBASE IV when the program is loaded. Although most of these options govern aspects of memory allocation that do not concern nonprogrammers, there is one you should know about. The COMMAND setting allows you to specify a dBASE IV command that is executed immediately when you load dBASE IV. For example, you could display a list of available data bases with the following entry:

```
COMMAND = DIR
```

The COMMAND command causes dBASE IV to display the Control Center menu when you start up the program, because the default CONFIG.DB file generated by the standard installation procedure contains the following line:

```
COMMAND = ASSIST
```

If you prefer to bypass the Control Center and do all your work at the dot prompt, you can remove this line from the CONFIG.DB file.

Using DBSETUP to Modify the CONFIG.DB File

You can edit an existing CONFIG.DB file or create a new one by using the DBSETUP program supplied with dBASE IV. As noted earlier in this chapter, dBASE IV copies the setup program onto your hard disk during the standard installation procedure to make it available later on. Even if you are running short on disk space, do not erase the DBSETUP program—the only way to copy it back to your hard disk is to reinstall dBASE IV. Because the files on the distribution disks are compressed, you cannot run the setup program directly from a floppy disk or use the DOS COPY command to transfer it back onto your hard disk. To run the setup program, type

```
DBSETUP
```

The DBSETUP menu bar has three options: **Config.db**, **DOS**, and **Exit**. To create or edit a CONFIG.DB file, select **Config.db** and then either **Modify existing CONFIG.DB** or **Create new CONFIG.DB**. If there is no CONFIG.DB file in the subdirectory from which you loaded DBSETUP, the program prompts you to enter the "Drive and directory from which to read the config.db file" and then displays a new menu.

The **Config.db** menu, which is diagrammed in Figure 18-3, provides access to almost all of the dBASE IV configuration settings. The arrangement of the options is somewhat different, but the menu works like the two settings menus described earlier in this chapter.

Editing the CONFIG.DB File Directly

As mentioned, you can edit or create the CONFIG.DB file with any text editor that can read and write text files, including the dBASE IV program editor, which is explained in Chapter 21. To use the dBASE IV editor, you could type the following command at the dot prompt:

```
MODIFY FILE CONFIG.DB
```

Whichever editor you use, remember that the CONFIG.DB file must be a plain ASCII text file without a document header or formatting commands. You must type each command on a separate line followed by a hard return. You can use any combination of uppercase and lowercase, and you can add blank spaces and blank lines to improve readability.

Printer Configuration Options

If you use the DBSETUP program to configure dBASE IV for your printer(s), you can choose up to four printers and designate one of the four as the default destination for all printed output. If you edit the CONFIG.DB file directly, you must add the equivalent commands to this file yourself. dBASE IV identifies the printers by number, and your selections are stored in the CONFIG.DB file, in commands like the following:

PRINTER *n* = *driver name* NAME *printer name* DEVICE *device name*

A printer driver is a file that contains instructions for accessing the fonts and other special features supported by your printer. The device name identifies the output port—the physical connector to which the printer is attached. The default device is the first parallel port, LPT1: (you must specify the output port only for printers that are not connected to LPT1:). In addition to the drivers you choose, two standard drivers are always available—GENERIC.PR2, which works with virtually any printer, and ASCII.PR2, which you can use to produce output with no printer control codes whatsoever. As noted in Chapter 13, this driver is particularly useful when you need to send report output to a text file on disk that you intend to format using other software (such as a word processor or desktop publishing program).

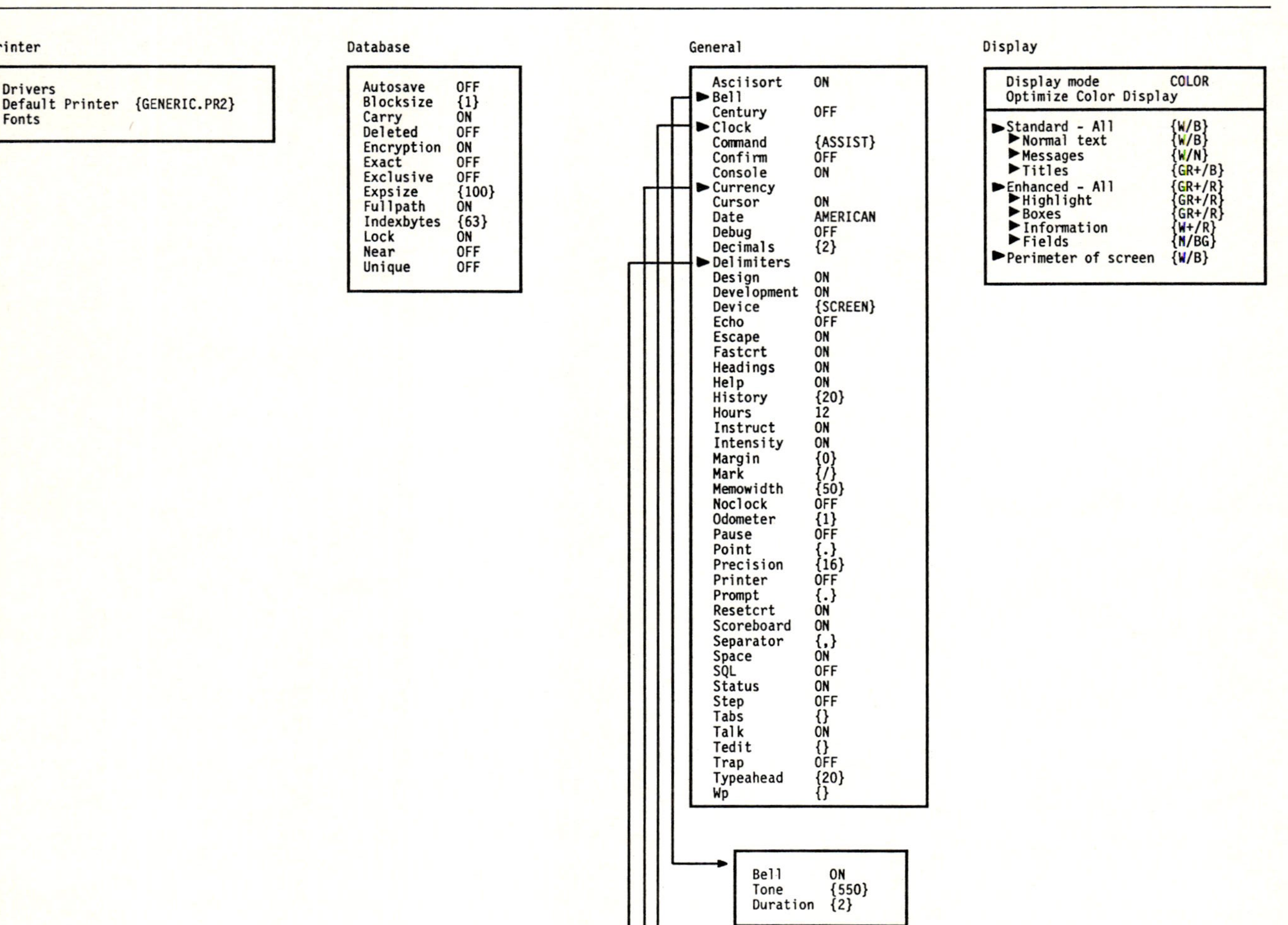
Printer
Drivers
Default Printer {GENERIC.PR2}
Fonts
Database
Autosave OFF
Blocksize {1}
Carry ON
Deleted OFF
Encryption ON
Exact OFF
Exclusive OFF
Expsize {100}
Fullpath ON
Indexbytes {63}
Lock ON
Near OFF
Unique OFF
General
Asciisort ON
Bell
Century OFF
Clock
Command {ASSIST}
Confirm OFF
Console ON
Currency
Cursor ON
Date AMERICAN
Debug OFF
Decimals {2}
Delimiters
Design ON
Development ON
Device {SCREEN}
Echo OFF
Escape ON
Fastcrt ON
Headings ON
Help ON
History {20}
Hours 12
Instruct ON
Intensity ON
Margin {0}
Mark {/}
Memowidth {50}
Noclock OFF
Odometer {1}
Pause OFF
Point {.}
Precision {16}
Printer OFF
Prompt {.}
Resetcrt ON
Scoreboard ON
Separator {,}
Space ON
SQL OFF
Status ON
Step OFF
Tabs {}
Talk ON
Tedit {}
Trap OFF
Typeahead {20}
Wp {}
Bell ON
Tone {550}
Duration {2}
Display
Display mode COLOR
Optimize Color Display
Standard - All {W/B}
Normal text {W/B}
Messages {W/N}
Titles {GR+/B}
Enhanced - All {GR+/R}
Highlight {GR+/R}
Boxes {GR+/R}
Information {W+/R}
Fields {N/BG}
Perimeter of screen {W/B}

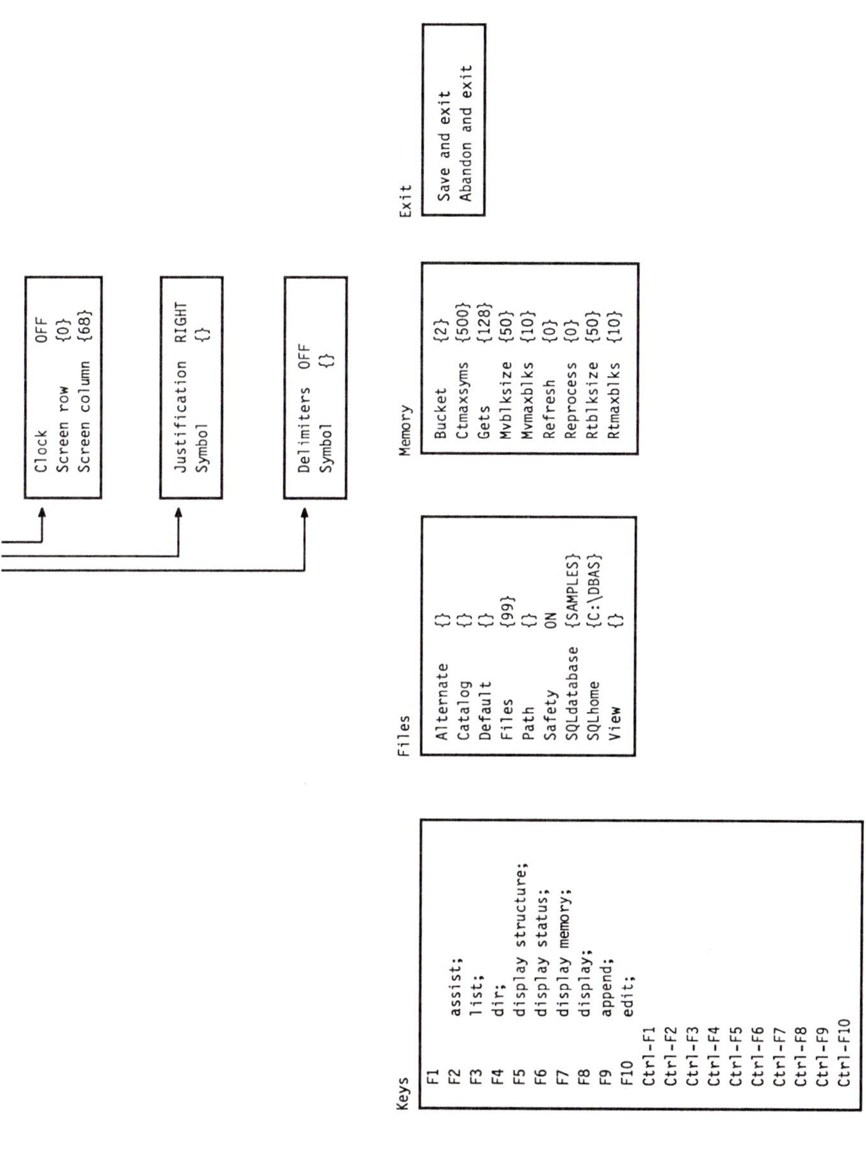

Figure 18-3.

The structure of the DBSETUP program Config.db menu

If you have more than one PRINTER command in the CONFIG.DB file, you can use the PDRIVER command to select one of the installed printers as the default output device. The following CONFIG.DB entries install two printers—a parallel Epson FX85 and a serial NEC Spinwriter—and select the Epson as the default printer:

```
PRINTER1 = FX85_1.PR2 NAME "Epson FX-185 Low resolution graphs"
PRINTER2 = NEC7710.PR2 NAME "NEC Spinwriter 7710" DEVICE COM1
PDRIVER = FX85_1.PR2
```

Even if you have only one printer, you may need to install multiple drivers, especially if you have a laser printer. For example, as noted in Chapter 14, you cannot use the standard HP Laserjet driver to print mailing labels, because this driver changes the vertical line spacing to 6.5 lines per inch in order to print 66 lines on an 11-inch page. Instead, you must use a printer driver that prints 60 lines per page at exactly 6 lines per inch. You also need a different driver to print in landscape mode at 6 lines per inch, and for some models, yet another to print in landscape mode at 6.5 lines per inch. You could install three drivers for the HP LaserJet II and select the first as the default with the following entries in CONFIG.DB:

```
PRINTER1 = HPLAS2I.PR2 NAME "HP LJII 6.5 lpi"
PRINTER2 = HPLAS260.PR2 NAME "HP LJII 6   lpi"
PRINTER3 = HPLA2L45.PR2 NAME "HP LJII land 6  lpi"
PDRIVER = HPLAS2I.PR2
```

If you have *any* PostScript printer, choose the Apple LaserWriter driver from the DBSETUP pick list; all PostScript printers use the same driver, which is called POSTSCRI.PR3.

You can use FONT commands in the CONFIG.DB file to access fonts or special print modes not directly supported by the dBASE IV printer drivers. Each FONT command specifies the printer control codes that turn the font or print attribute on and off. The syntax is as follows:

PRINTER *n* FONT *n* = *starting codes, ending codes NAME font name*

You must enter the starting and ending codes using the same notation explained in Chapter 13 for entering starting and ending control codes for a single print run on the **Control of printer screen** accessed through the **Print** menu. For example, you could define a special font for double-width print and another to access the near letter quality Sans Serif font on the Epson by placing the following FONT commands in CONFIG.DB:

```
PRINTER 1 FONT 1 = {ESC}W1, {ESC}W0 NAME "Double Width"
PRINTER 1 FONT 2 = {ESC}x1{ESC}k1, {ESC}x0 NAME "Sans Serif"
```

You can define up to five fonts for each printer; the font numbers determine the order in which dBASE IV lists the fonts in the bottom half of the dialog box invoked by selecting the **Style** option from the **Words** menu in the report and label layout editors. Note that if you install more than one printer driver, the drivers are entirely independent of each other. Thus, if you install multiple drivers to control the same laser printer, you must explicitly define the custom fonts you intend to use with each driver, even if some or all of them are the same. You might also want to install multiple copies of the *same* driver simply to gain access to more than five custom fonts. Keep in mind if you do this that only one printer driver can be active at a time, and that only the fonts defined for the active driver are available in the **Words** menu when you define a report or label form.

If you have a PostScript printer, you can access three fonts—Courier, Helvetica, and Times Roman. The font names are 1FONT, 2FONT, and 3FONT, and the starting control code for each is the font name followed by a space (you can specify the space by using its ASCII code, 32, enclosed in braces). For the ending code, you can enter the command to return to the font that you use as the default. For example, the following commands identify the PostScript printer driver and define two custom fonts, Helvetica and Times Roman; in both cases, the ending codes select the Courier font:

```
PRINTER1 = POSTSCRI.PR3 NAME "PostScript printer"
PRINTER 1 FONT 1 = 2FONT{32}, 1FONT{32} NAME "Helvetica"
PRINTER 1 FONT 2 = 3FONT{32}, 1FONT{32} NAME "Times Roman"
```

You can add printers and define new fonts by editing the CONFIG.DB file, but you may find it more convenient to use the DBSETUP program. This program allows you to select printer drivers from a pick list that displays the printer manufacturers and model names, so you do not have to remember the printer driver file names. To install printers, choose **Printers** from the main DBSETUP menu, and then use the **Drivers, Default Printer**, and **Fonts** options to select the drivers, choose the default driver, and set up custom fonts.

When you select **Drivers,** dBASE IV displays a table with four lines on which you enter the printer specifications: the name, driver name, and output port. You can choose the printer name from a pick list invoked by pressing SHIFT-F1 (Pick) with the cursor in the **Printer Name** column of this table. dBASE IV displays a pick list of printer manufacturers; you can choose one by highlighting it and pressing ENTER. dBASE IV displays another, more detailed list of printer models and associated driver files such as the one illustrated in Figure 18-4. If you cannot find your printer model on the list, you might try another model made by the same manufacturer or choose the name of a printer that yours emulates (uses the same control code commands). When you select a printer model (by pressing ENTER with the name highlighted), dBASE IV enters the printer and driver names in the appropriate columns in the printer list and moves the cursor to the **Device** column.

You can type in the ouput device name if you know it or choose a device from a pick list invoked by pressing SHIFT-F1 (Pick). If you have one parallel printer, it is probably connected to the LPT1: device, and if you have one serial printer, it is most likely hooked up to COM1:, the first "communications" port. Figure 18-5 illustrates the appearance of the screen after you have defined two printers: one serial and one parallel. When you have installed all of your printers, press CTRL-END to save the selections.

You can use the **Default Printer** option on the **Printer** menu to designate

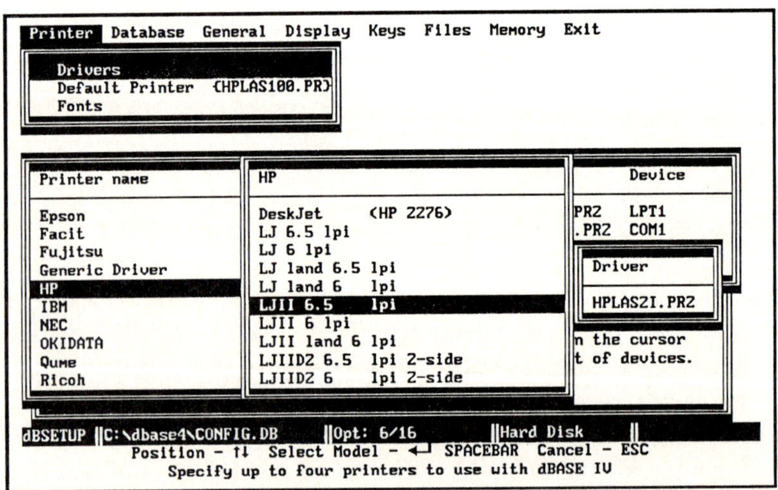

Figure 18-4.

Selecting a printer driver

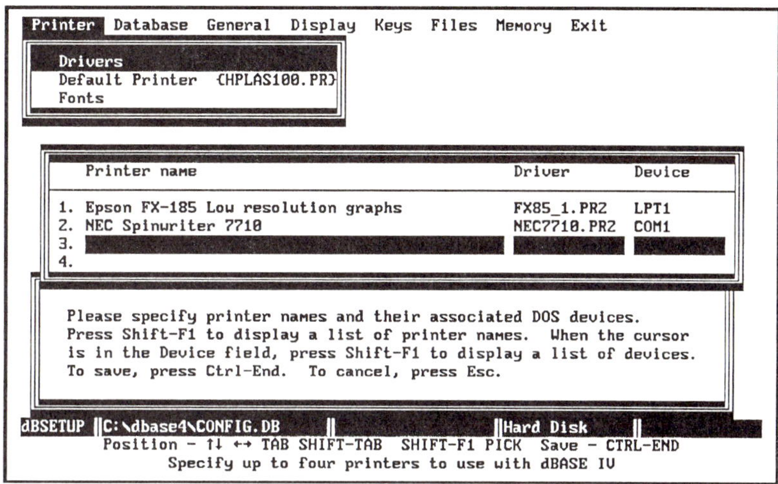

Figure 18-5.

Defining two printers

one of the installed printers as the default—the one that is used for all reports, labels, and printed lists unless you select another. When you choose this option, dBASE IV displays a pick list of the drivers that you have installed (not all available drivers), and allows you to select one from this list. If you do not choose a default printer, dBASE IV uses the generic driver, GENERIC.PR2, as the default.

When you select printers through DBSETUP, this program automatically installs the required driver files in the dBASE IV subdirectory on your hard disk. If you edit the CONFIG.DB file directly, you must also ensure that the required printer driver files are available. All of the dBASE IV printer drivers are stored in a single file called DRIVERS.EXE, which is copied to your hard disk when you install dBASE IV. You can extract individual printer drivers from this file if you know their names, by typing a command of the following form at the DOS prompt (not from within dBASE IV):

DRIVERS *driver name*

To extract more than one driver at a time, you can specify the *driver name* using the standard DOS wildcard characters: the question mark (?), which stands for any single character, and the asterisk (*), which stands for any group of characters. For example, you could extract all the HP LaserJet drivers with the following command:

```
DRIVERS HP*.*
```

Figure 18-6 lists a CONFIG.DB file originally created by DBSETUP that includes most of the configuration commands presented in this chapter.

```
*
*        dBASE IV Configuration File
*        Friday February 15, 1991
*

AUTOSAVE                = ON
COLOR OF NORMAL         = W/B
COLOR OF HIGHLIGHT      = W/R
COLOR OF MESSAGES       = W/N
COLOR OF TITLES         = GR+/B
COLOR OF BOX            = N/R
COLOR OF INFORMATION    = W+/R
COLOR OF FIELDS         = N/BG
COMMAND                 = ASSIST
CONFIRM                 = ON
DATE                    = USA
DELETED                 = ON
DISPLAY                 = EGA25
MEMOWIDTH               = 70
NEAR                    = ON
PDRIVER                 = FX85_1.PR2
PRINTER 1               = FX85_1.PR2 NAME "Epson FX-85"
PRINTER 1 FONT 1        = {ESC}W1, {ESC}W0 NAME "Double Width"
PRINTER 1 FONT 2        = {ESC}x1{ESC}k1, {ESC}x0 NAME "Sans Serif"
PRINTER 2               = HPLAS2I.PR2 NAME "HP LJII 6.5    lpi"
PRINTER 3               = HPLAS260.PR2 NAME "HP LJII 6 lpi"
PRINTER 4               = HPLS2L45.PR2 NAME "HP LJII land 6 lpi"
SAFETY                  = OFF
STATUS                  = ON
```

Figure 18-6.

The dBASE IV configuration file, CONFIG.DB

REPROGRAMMING THE FUNCTION KEYS

When you work in the menu system, you can use the function keys F1 through F10 and SHIFT-F1 through SHIFT-F10 as shortcuts to execute some of the most common file manipulation and editing commands. At the dot prompt, the function keys serve a similar purpose, although they represent different commands. dBASE IV assigns the following default meanings to function keys F1 through F10:

F1	HELP;
F2	ASSIST;
F3	LIST;
F4	DIR;
F5	DISPLAY STRUCTURE;
F6	DISPLAY STATUS;
F7	DISPLAY MEMORY;
F8	DISPLAY;
F9	APPEND;
F10	EDIT;

You can assign new meanings to nine of the ten function keys, F2 through F10, as well as SHIFT-F1 through SHIFT-F9 and CTRL-F1 through CTRL-F10. You cannot reprogram F1, which is reserved as the "Help" key; SHIFT-F10, which initiates and controls the recording of keyboard macros (macros are explained in the next section); or the ALT-function key combinations, which execute macros. Even if you have an enhanced keyboard, dBASE IV does not recognize F11, F12, SHIFT-F11, SHIFT-F12, CTRL-F11, and CTRL-F12. You can display the current function key assignments from the dot prompt by typing DISPLAY STATUS.

You can reassign a function key command through the DBSETUP program, by using the SET menu invoked from the dot prompt, by typing a SET FUNCTION command at the dot prompt, or by adding an entry to the CONFIG.DB file using a text editor. In the DBSETUP program or the SET menu, choose the **Keys** option, select the desired function key from the displayed list, and either edit the existing function key meaning or enter a new one. From the dot prompt, you use the SET FUNCTION command, which has the following syntax:

SET FUNCTION *key name* TO *character string*

For example, you could redefine the F2 key to type the character string "National Widgets, Inc.", the F3 key to open the Customer File and activate the ACCOUNT index tag, and SHIFT-F3 to switch to the ZIP index tag with the following commands:

```
SET FUNCTION F2 TO "National Widgets, Inc."
SET FUNCTION F3 TO "USE NWCUST ORDER ACCOUNT ALIAS CUSTOMER;"
SET FUNCTION SHIFT-F3 TO "SET ORDER TO ZIP;"
```

dBASE IV interprets a semicolon in a function key assignment as a hard return (the equivalent of pressing the ENTER key). The need for the semicolon will make sense if you keep in mind that a function key can represent *any sequence of keystrokes.* dBASE IV does not attempt to interpret these keystrokes in any way—it simply types them for you when you press the designated key. A function key might represent a frequently used character string (such as your company name), one command, several commands (up to a total of 238 characters), or part of a command. When a function key represents an entire command, you must include a semicolon to force dBASE IV to execute the command immediately, as if you had pressed ENTER. When a function key represents more than one command, each command (except perhaps the last) must end with a semicolon. For example, you could assign the F4 key to open the Customer File, specify a custom screen form to replace the Edit display, and begin editing records with the following command:

```
SET FUNCTION F4 TO "USE NWCUST ORDER ACCOUNT;SET FORMAT TO NWCFORM;EDIT;"
```

When a function key does not store a complete command, you often *do not* want dBASE IV to enter a hard return after typing the characters it represents. For example, after reassigning the string "National Widgets, Inc." to the F2 key, you might use this key to type the company name in report forms, where it would not necessarily be followed by a hard return. You can also use a function key to type part of a command. For example, you might want to use a LIST command to display the same set of fields from a data base but vary the record selection criteria. You could assign a function key to type the constant portion of the LIST command, as follows:

```
SET FUNCTION F5 TO "LIST ACCOUNT, COMPANY, TELEPHONE FOR "
```

When you press F5, dBASE IV types the LIST command (including the space after the keyword FOR) and stops; you can then type the condition that defines the selection criteria. If you ended the function key assignment with a semicolon, an error message would result when dBASE IV attempted to execute the incomplete command.

As noted earlier, you can replace the default function key meanings with your own assignments by making entries in the CONFIG.DB file. The syntax of the CONFIG.DB command is somewhat different from the equivalent SET FUNCTION command. For example, the following commands reprogram F2, F3, SHIFT-F3, and CTRL-F3:

```
SET FUNCTION F2 TO "National Widgets, Inc."
SET FUNCTION F3 TO "USE NWCUST ORDER ACCOUNT ALIAS CUSTOMER;"
SET FUNCTION SHIFT-F3 TO "SET ORDER TO ZIP;"
SET FUNCTION CTRL-F3 TO "SET ORDER TO STATECITY;"
```

The equivalent CONFIG.DB file commands are as follows:

```
F2 = "National Widgets, Inc."
F3 = "USE NWCUST ORDER ACCOUNT ALIAS CUSTOMER;"
SHIFT-F3 = "SET ORDER TO ZIP;"
CTRL-F3 = "SET ORDER TO STATECITY;"
```

USING KEYBOARD MACROS TO AUTOMATE YOUR WORK

When you work in the menu system, you cannot reprogram the function keys, but you can define macros to help automate frequently used command sequences. Like function keys, macros are short abbreviations—in this case, single letters or ALT-function key combinations—that represent longer sequences of keystrokes. Unlike function keys, macros are not limited to the printable text characters—a macro can represent *any sequences of keystrokes,* including text characters, commands, and menu navigation and option selection keystrokes.

For example, you could define a macro equivalent to the function key described in the previous section to type the character string "National Widgets, Inc." Another macro might store the keystrokes required to open a data base, select or build an index tag, and print a report from the Control Center.

You can define and use macros from the menu system and from the dot prompt, although macros that include commands as well as text generally do not execute in both working environments.

Macros offer more flexibility than function keys. dBASE IV can pause during macro execution to allow you to type a variable entry (such as a file name), and you can nest macros—one macro can call another. For example, you could define a macro to construct the page header band of a report; this macro could invoke the macro that types "National Widgets, Inc." dBASE IV stores macros in macro libraries, each of which can contain up to 35 macro definitions—one for each of the function keys ALT-F1 through ALT-F9 and one for each letter of the alphabet. You can build as many macro libraries as you need and segregate macros into groups according to their purpose or the data base application with which you plan to use them.

You can record or play back a macro from anywhere in the menu system or from the dot prompt. When you set up a new application, you may be able to predict some of the macros that you will need, but more often you will define macros "on the fly," when you are executing a procedure that you realize you have used before and will need to repeat in the future. For example, you may discover the need for a macro to type your company name as you are designing a report form.

To begin recording a macro from any of the dBASE IV working environments, press SHIFT-F10 (Macros). dBASE IV pops up a dialog box that offers two options: **Begin recording** and **Cancel.** When you select **Begin recording,** dBASE IV prompts you to "Press the key that will call this macro." You can press any single letter key or function key; you will later use this key in conjunction with the ALT-F10 key to play back the macro. If possible, try to assign a letter that is descriptive of the purpose or contents of the macro. After you specify the macro key, the prompt box disappears, but whenever the status display is on, dBASE IV displays a message on the navigation line below the status bar to remind you that it is recording your keystrokes: "Recording Macro; Press Shift-F10 E to end."

To end the macro definition, press SHIFT-F10 (Macros) again. dBASE IV displays a dialog box with three options: **End recording, Insert user-input break,** and **Continue recording.** When you select **End recording,** dBASE IV confirms with another message on the navigation line that "Macro recording has been finished." This message disappears when you press any key on the keyboard.

The easiest way to predefine macros that consist entirely of text is to invoke any of the layout editors (the report and screen form editors are convenient), record the macros you need as you type text on the work surface, and then exit without saving the form displayed on the work surface.

From the dot prompt or from any point in the menu system, you can execute a macro assigned to one of the function keys by holding down the ALT key and pressing the designated function key. Invoking a macro assigned to a letter key requires two keystrokes: first, press ALT-F10, and when dBASE IV prompts you to "Press an alphabetic key of macro to play back," press the designated single-letter key. From the dot prompt, you can also play back a macro by using the PLAY MACRO command:

PLAY MACRO *macro name*

The *macro name* is the single letter assigned to the macro or the name of the function key (F2, SHIFT-F2, and so on).

Keep in mind when you design macros that dBASE IV does not interpret the keystrokes stored in a macro in any way; it simply plays back the same keystrokes in the same order in which you pressed the keys when you recorded the macro. Because a macro can include cursor movement commands and menu navigation commands, you must be especially careful not to build macros that depend for proper operation on the state of the dBASE IV environment that existed when you defined them. This issue is far more important when you work in the Control Center than at the dot prompt, where most commands (and therefore, most macros) consist of text characters.

To illustrate the potential pitfalls, consider a macro that opens the National Widgets Customer File, displays the data on the Browse screen, and selects the ZIP code tag. To record this macro from the Control Center, you would begin with the cursor at the top of the **Data** panel. If the Customer File were the first file in the list, you might be tempted to open it by pressing DOWN ARROW to highlight the file name, ENTER to invoke the standard dialog box, RIGHT ARROW twice to highlight **Display data**, and then ENTER to select this option. If you later created a new data base that replaced the Customer File as the first file listed in the **Data** panel, the macro would open the wrong file.

When you define macros, avoid using the arrow keys. Type all file names and field names explicitly, and select menu options by letter. For example, a better way to open the Customer File while recording the macro in the previous example would be to type the name, NWCUST, press ENTER, and then press D to select **Display data** from the dialog box. If you also wanted to select the ZIP tag as the master index, you could then press ALT-O to pull down the

Organize menu on the Edit or Browse screen, press O to select **Order records by index** from this menu, and then type the name of the tag, ZIP, rather than using the cursor movement keys to select it from the pick list.

Obviously, the macro described in the previous example, which contains commands specific to the menu system, would not execute properly at the dot prompt. You could, however, define a macro that has exactly the same effect by recording the following keystrokes:

```
USE NWCUST ORDER ZIP
BROWSE
```

When you change the dBASE IV environment settings described earlier in this chapter, you should be alert for the possible impact these changes may have on existing macros. For example, if you changed the INSTRUCT setting from ON to OFF, the macro described earlier in this section to open the Customer File would fail because the D keystroke included in the macro to select **Display** from the dialog box that dBASE IV displays when INSTRUCT is ON is unnecessary; this keystroke would be played back on the Edit screen, overwriting the first character of the ACCOUNT field.

A macro can include any keystrokes, including those required to call another macro. To invoke one macro from within another, press the sequence of keys that you would use to activate the macro in any other context. For example, if you had defined a macro assigned to the N key that typed "National Widgets, Inc.", you could call this macro from within a macro that constructs a complete report page header band.

A macro can also include a pause for user input. By using this feature, you can design macros that are flexible enough to be used in similar but not identical situations. For example, consider again a macro that constructs the page header band in a report. All your report headers might share certain common features: the page number and date printed in certain positions, the company name centered in the middle of the page, and one or two additional title lines. To right-justify or center text, the page header macro must use the **Modify ruler** option on the **Words** menu to reset the right margin, but because your reports might vary in width, it would be preferable not to include in the macro all the keystrokes required to set a specific right margin.

To add a pause to a macro, press SHIFT-F10 (Macros), select **Insert user-input break** from the pop-up dialog box, and then continue typing, *beginning with the next keystroke that you want to record.* At times, the fact that you cannot press any keys during macro recording that you do not want included in the macro makes it difficult or impossible to record exactly the macro you want. For example, when you work at the dot prompt, you might want to record a macro that opens the Customer File, types the LIST command and a field list, pauses to allow you to enter either FOR or WHILE, and then resumes typing a condition that selects records. If you type the word "FOR" or "WHILE" after requesting the user-input break, it will be recorded in the macro; if you do not, the command will generate an error message (but the macro will be correct). If an error message would prevent you from recording the complete macro, you can include the necessary keystrokes, and edit the macro later to remove them, as described in the next section.

When you execute a macro that includes a user-input break, dBASE IV pauses when it reaches the break point and displays a message box that reminds you how to resume macro executions: "Macro playback suspended, press Shift-F10 to resume macro playback." You can type any commands or text that you want, and then press SHIFT-F10 (Macros) to continue playing back the keystrokes stored in the macro. When you play back a macro, you can cancel playback during a user-input break by pressing ESC.

You could use a user-input break to add flexibility to the macro that constructs a report page header band to vary the right margin setting. You could include in the macro the commands to pull down the **Words** menu and select the **Modify ruler** option, and you might even want to move the cursor to the column you would like to use as the default right margin (say, column 75 if you print most reports on 8 1/2- by 11-inch paper). Then press SHIFT-F10 (Macros), select **Insert user-input break**, and resume typing macro keystrokes: Press] to set the right margin, ENTER to save the new ruler line, and continue to build the page header. This macro design assumes that during the pause for user input, you will do nothing more than move the cursor within the ruler line to the correct right margin column for the report; the macro itself presses the key that sets the margin.

If you make a mistake while recording a short macro, the easiest way to correct the problem is to end recording and start over. When dBASE IV prompts you to "Press the key that will call this macro," type the same letter you used in the previous attempt. dBASE IV pops up a dialog box to ask for confirmation before overwriting the existing macro; if you are rerecording a macro deliberately, you can confirm your intentions and go ahead. As your macros grow longer, the prospect of starting over may seem less appealing, however. Instead, you can type the keystrokes necessary to correct the error;

these keystrokes will be recorded in the macro, but macro execution is fast enough that the slight delay should not present a problem. If you prefer, you can modify the macro to remove the extra keystrokes, using the macro editor explained in the next section.

Maintaining Macros and Macro Libraries

dBASE IV offers a comprehensive set of commands for manipulating macros and macro libraries. These commands are accessible only through the **Macros** option on the Control Center **Tools** menu, and even if you work primarily at the dot prompt, you will probably want to use these options to manage your macros. The structure of the **Macros** menu is diagrammed in Figure 18-7.

The **Begin recording, End recording, Insert user-input break,** and **Play** options are included in the **Macros** menu for convenience, but more often you will record and play back macros from other locations in the menu system or from the dot prompt, and control the recording process by pressing SHIFT-F10 (Macros) and then selecting the appropriate option from the dialog box.

When you select any menu option that manipulates existing macros—all the options except **Begin recording, Insert user-input break, Talk,** and the two library options—dBASE IV displays a list of available macros like the one shown in Figure 18-8, which tabulates the names and lengths (measured in keystrokes) of the defined macros. You select a macro from this list by pressing the key assigned to it, such as N for the macro that types "National Widgets, Inc."

The **Name** option enables you to replace the default single-letter macro name with a more descriptive name up to ten characters long. For example, you might name the N macro NATWIDGETS. dBASE IV displays the longer name, if you assigned one, in the pick list of available macros invoked by selecting the **Macros** menu options. If you rename a macro, you must use the new name in a PLAY MACRO command typed at the dot prompt. However, you can still execute the macro (either from the menu system or from the dot prompt) by pressing an ALT-function key combination or by pressing ALT-F10 followed by the single letter assigned to the macro.

You can edit a previously defined macro by selecting the **Modify** option, which invokes an editor that works just like the memo field editor. If you use this editor to modify or add to an existing macro, be careful, especially if you

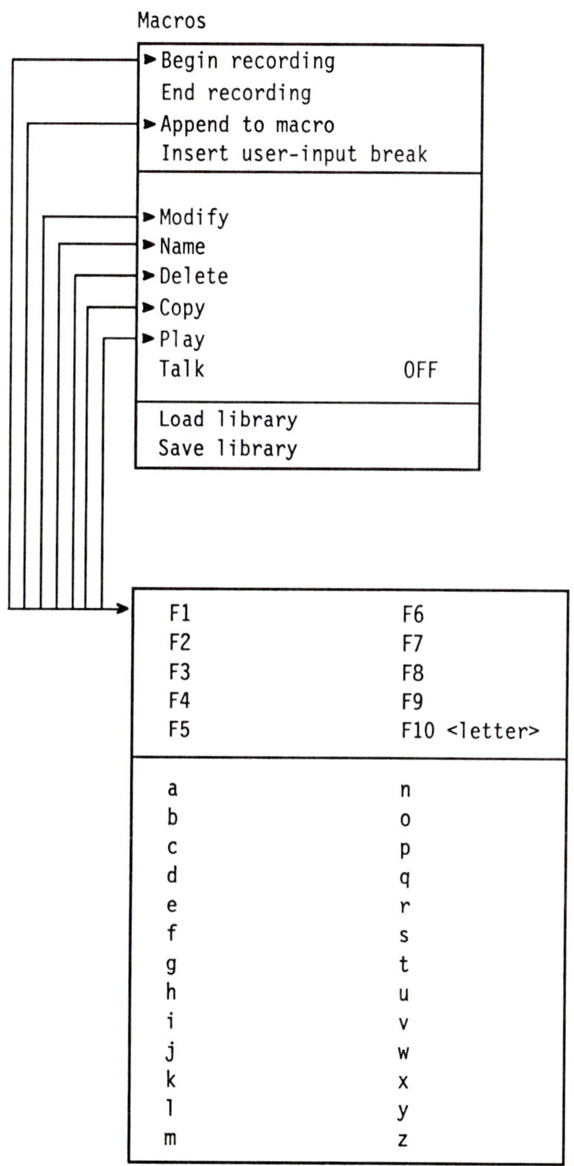

Figure 18-7.

The structure of the Macros menu

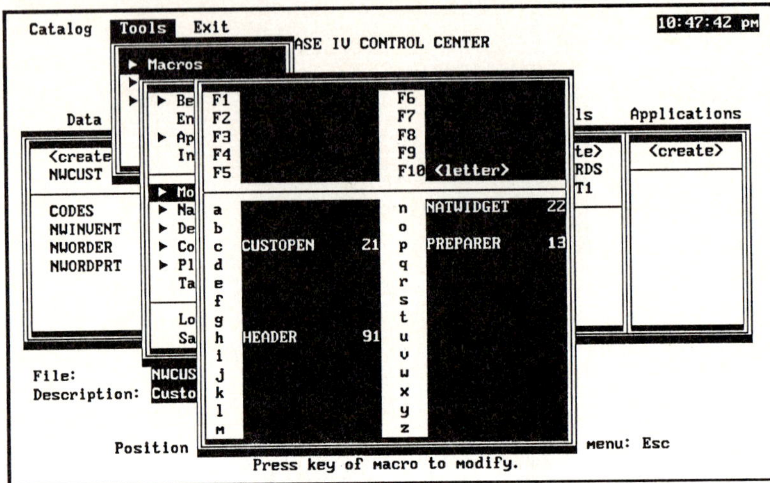

Figure 18-8.

Selecting a macro from a pick list

are not familiar with the keystroke sequence that you want to store in the macro. If you make a mistake or leave out a necessary command key, the macro will not execute correctly. When a macro "types" an erroneous command, dBASE IV behaves exactly as it would if you had pressed the same incorrect keys yourself—it displays an error message. If you are careful, however, the ability to edit an existing macro enables you to avoid rerecording a lengthy macro to make a minor modification.

When you edit a macro, you cannot press command and function keys alone, because these keys are used as command keys in the macro editor itself. Just as when you define printer command codes, you must represent all keys except the standard letters, numbers, and punctuation marks by using the special key names listed in Table 18-3. You can enter the key names—as well as other command keystrokes, file names, and field names—in any combination of uppercase and lowercase letters. Figure 18-9 illustrates the macro that displays the Customer File on the Browse screen and selects the ZIP tag as the master index.

dBASE IV inserts a hard return in the macro file whenever you press the ENTER key while recording the macro. When you edit a macro, you can insert additional hard returns to make the macro easier to read. When dBASE IV executes the macro, it ignores these hard returns and performs the equivalent

Key	Name
RIGHT ARROW	{Rightarrow}
LEFT ARROW	{Leftarrow}
UP ARROW	{Uparrow}
DOWN ARROW	{Downarrow}
HOME	{Home}
END	{End}
PGUP	{PgUp}
PGDN	{PgDn}
TAB	{Tab}
SHIFT-TAB	{Shift-Tab}
ENTER	{Enter}
ESC	{Esc}
BACKSPACE	{Backspace}
DEL	{Del}
INS	{Ins}
PRINT SCREEN	{PrtSc}
CTRL-*key*	{Ctrl-*key*}
ALT-*key*	{Alt-*key*}
SHIFT-*key*	{Shift-*key*}
F*n*	{F*n*}

Table 18-3.

Command Key Names Used in the Macro Editor

of pressing the ENTER key only when it encounters the special key name {Enter} in the macro definition. Note, however, that dBASE IV does play back all spaces stored in a macro, so you cannot include extra spaces in places where they would alter the meaning of the commands stored in the macro.

If all you need to do is *add* keystrokes to the end of an existing macro, it is easier to use the **Append to macro** option than to modify the macro with the dBASE IV macro editor. The additional keys that you press are then recorded and added to the ones already stored in the macro. Apart from its obvious purpose—adding to a macro functions that you did not originally foresee—you can use the **Append to macro** option to build a complex or lengthy macro in stages, by testing the macro before you add the next set of steps.

Because you must invoke the **Append to macro** option from the Control Center, you may end up adding extra keystrokes, which you can later remove using the macro editor invoked by the **Modify** option. Suppose, for example,

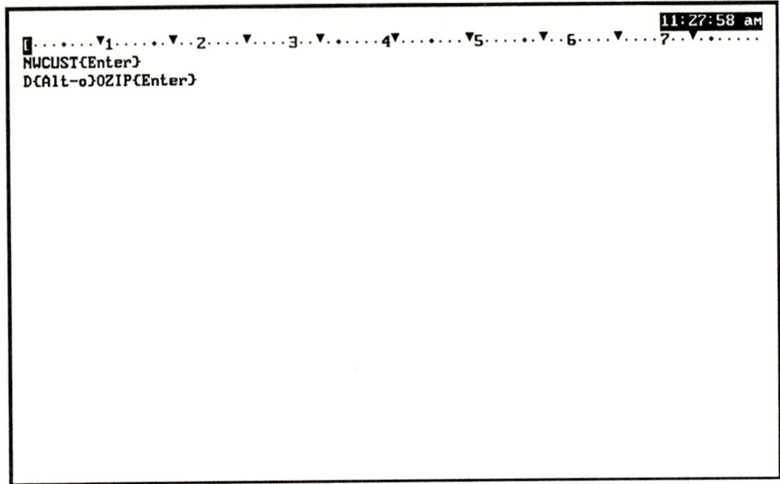

Figure 18-9.

Editing a macro

that you wanted to add commands to construct a page footer to a previously designed macro that builds the page header band in a report. When you recorded the original macro, you started and ended in the report layout editor, but to add onto the macro, you must begin at the Control Center. The keystrokes required to move from the Control Center to the report layout editor are added to the macro, and you must remove them later by editing the finished macro.

You can remove a macro from memory by using the **Delete** option; dBASE IV requests confirmation before removing the macro from the list. The **Copy** option enables you to generate a new macro based on an existing one. Duplicating an existing macro and then modifying or adding onto the copy is sometimes faster than creating a new macro from scratch. When you select the **Copy** option, dBASE IV displays the pick list of existing macros and prompts you first to "Press key for source macro" (the one you want to copy), to "Press key of destination" (the new macro you want to create), and finally to enter a name for the new macro. You can accept the default single letter or ALT-key name instead of entering a longer, more descriptive name.

dBASE IV retains macros in memory only for the duration of the current work session unless you save them on disk in a macro library. You can create a macro library by using the **Save library** option on the **Macros** menu and retrieve a previously saved library by selecting **Load library**. dBASE IV saves a macro library on disk in a file with the extension KEY (for "Keystroke macro library"). You can create as many macro libraries as you need to circumvent the limit of 35 macros in one library, to group macros by purpose or application, or to segregate macros used in the menu system from those you use at the dot prompt.

From the dot prompt, you can save the currently defined macros in a library by using the SAVE MACROS command, as follows:

SAVE MACROS TO *macro library file name*

To retrieve a previously saved macro library, you use the RESTORE MACROS command:

RESTORE MACROS FROM *macro library file name*

Designing macros is a little like programming—it enables you to automate a lengthy, tedious, or time-consuming process by storing the commands, menu options, and text entries required to carry out the operation so that dBASE IV can later repeat the sequence. By defining macros, you can avoid repetitive typing, reduce the likelihood that a careless error will prevent a crucial procedure from completing normally, and set up standard procedures that can be run by other users who are less familiar with dBASE IV or your application.

With these benefits come some of the same problems associated with programming, especially for novices. As your macros grow in both length and complexity, the probability increases that you will make errors. You must devise strategies for testing macros to ensure that they perform as expected and *debug* them—find the causes of the errors—when they do not. Because you record macros as you execute commands, most errors result not from errors in the component commands but from subsequent changes in the environment. For example, you might create a macro that opens the Customer File and prints labels using a label form called NWCUST1.LBL. If you later erased the label form and then tried to execute the macro, dBASE IV would either display an error message reporting that the label form file could be found or choose the wrong label form from the Control Center **Labels** panel.

The **Talk** option on the **Macros** menu can be helpful in tracking down elusive macro execution problems. When this option is set **ON** (it is **OFF** by default), dBASE IV monitors macro execution by displaying the keystrokes that make up the macro on the navigation line below the status bar, using the same special key names recognized by the macro editor (for example, {Enter} for the ENTER key). If the key names flash by too fast, you can press CTRL-S to pause execution temporarily and study the display, and then press CTRL-S again to resume execution. If you are baffled, you can often discover the source of a problem by using the **Print** option in the macro editor menu to generate a hard copy of the contents of a stubborn macro and then emulate macro execution by pressing the same keys yourself.

SUMMARY

This chapter introduced some detailed and sophisticated ways to personalize the dBASE IV working environment. None of the commands and strategies mentioned are essential for working with dBASE IV, however. If you find the details overwhelming, you can defer your experiments with configuration options, function keys, and macros until you feel more comfortable working with dBASE IV in the standard configuration. Even for an advanced user, the sheer number of options precludes memorizing all of them at the beginning. As you continue to learn and gain confidence, you might want to browse through the list of settings and options periodically as a reminder about which aspects of the working environment you can customize. When you begin to use the techniques presented in this chapter, you will find that the ability to customize the working environment for the requirements of a particular application, task, or user can help you work more productively and comfortably with dBASE IV.

CHAPTER NINETEEN

Managing Disk Files

As a data base application grows and matures, you will invariably amass more disk files than you might have anticipated based on the number of data bases in the application. A system with three main data bases, such as the National Widgets system, might easily generate dozens of disk files, including memo text files, the production MDX index files, NDX indexes, screen forms, report forms, label forms, view and update query files, programs (written by you or generated automatically by dBASE IV), and additional data bases that result from sorting, extracting, totaling, or archiving records derived from the original data files. The more disk files you accumulate, the more important it becomes to develop a coherent system for keeping track of the purpose and use of each.

One essential component of an effective file management system is a set of file naming conventions such as the scheme used in the National Widgets system. Although the guidelines you adopt may differ from those used in this book, you should strive to make your file names as descriptive of the contents as possible within the eight-character file name limit and to include in the names of auxiliary files, such as queries and report forms, a reference to the associated data base. This chapter introduces a more formal and far more flexible tool for grouping the files that make up an application—the file *catalog*. When you work in the menu system, dBASE IV builds and maintains one catalog automatically; at the dot prompt, the catalog is completely under your control. Users who alternate between the two working environments should be sure to read about both the menu-driven and dot prompt commands for using and updating catalogs to ensure that files created at the dot prompt are added to the current catalog.

dBASE IV also provides some help with the mechanics of managing disk files. A comprehensive menu-driven set of utilities enables you to display disk directories and copy, erase, rename, or display the contents of files. Using these file management tools is easy and convenient; you can perform routine file management tasks without leaving dBASE IV, and in some cases, the menu commands are more flexible and powerful than the corresponding DOS or OS/2 commands. When you work at the dot prompt, you can use commands that are roughly equivalent to the built-in DOS or OS/2 commands. You can execute any operating system command, batch file, or external program (provided that you have enough RAM installed in your computer) either from the menu system or from the dot prompt, without exiting from dBASE IV.

One reason that disk files proliferate as an application develops is that you may forget to erase files that you created in error or files that you no longer need, such as report forms designed for special purposes that you will never reprint. Another is the method dBASE IV uses to store and execute queries, applications, and report, label, and screen forms. You may recall that dBASE IV stores the specifications for a screen, label, or report form in two ways: as a file that can be interpreted by the layout editor used to create and edit the form and as a dBASE IV program. This program is compiled after you create or modify it (compiling is a translation process that is explained in Chapter 21), which yields yet another disk file, the one that is required to execute the instructions stored in the form. Queries require only two files—a generated program (the QBE file or UPD file) and its compiled form—but an application, as you will see in Chapter 22, can generate a multitude of files: one for each menu and pick list you define as well as two generated programs and their compiled versions. dBASE IV identifies each type of file by a unique extension. You will find a complete list of file extensions in Appendix G; you may want to refer to it frequently as you read this chapter.

Once you understand the purpose of each type of file, you can erase files selectively to free disk space and reduce the number of files in your directory listings. For example, in an emergency you can erase the generated programs and compiled programs to clear some disk space, because you can always regenerate them from the original forms. If you are sure that you no longer need to edit a form, you can erase the form file and the generated program, because only the compiled program is required to execute the form. However, it is always a good idea to save a copy of every form file you create, because you cannot edit the form without this file. Once an application is relatively stable, you can copy the form and generated program files onto a backup floppy disk and then erase them from your hard disk to save space.

This chapter describes a variety of techniques that you can use to manage disk files and suggests ways of combining these techniques into an effective disk file management strategy. It explains the inner workings of the catalog and describes the commands that you can use to maintain and update catalogs to group your files by application. This chapter also covers the dBASE IV file management commands as well as the methods that you can use to gain access to DOS commands and external programs.

Although dBASE IV provides a selection of file management tools, using these tools effectively requires some knowledge of your operating system (DOS or OS/2). In particular, you should understand the concept of the tree-structured directory and be somewhat familiar with the subdirectory structure on your hard disk. You should also know how to construct valid file and path names, and how to use the wildcard symbols (? and *) to manipulate files as a group.

USING CATALOGS TO GROUP THE FILES IN AN APPLICATION

A dBASE IV catalog is a list of all the files that make up an application. The catalog is an ordinary dBASE IV data base file, except that it has the extension CAT instead of DBF to distinguish it from the data bases that you create. You can maintain as many catalogs as you want; the files in each catalog may be physically located in more than one subdirectory, and a given file may appear in more than one catalog. This flexibility enables you to store each application in its own subdirectory and to share files when necessary without maintaining multiple copies of the data.

The Control Center can display files from only one catalog at a time, so when you are working with an application, you see only the relevant data bases and auxiliary files. Once you have established a catalog for each application, you do not have to remember where a file is located to open and use it, and users who are unfamiliar with your computer system or who do not understand the DOS subdirectory structure can work effectively with files stored in multiple subdirectories.

From the Menus

If you work in the menu system exclusively, dBASE IV automatically builds and maintains a catalog called UNTITLED.CAT in the subdirectory from which you load the program as well as a *master catalog* called CATALOG.CAT, which lists the catalogs in the current subdirectory. If there is more than one catalog in the directory from which you load dBASE IV, it opens the one that you used most recently. If there is no catalog, dBASE IV creates a new catalog called UNTITLED.CAT and reads into this catalog all the data bases, queries, screen forms, report forms, label forms, and applications in the subdirectory. By default, dBASE IV creates and maintains one catalog called UNTITLED.CAT in each subdirectory from which you load the software.

You can manipulate catalogs directly by using the options on the Control Center **Catalog** menu, which is diagrammed in Figure 19-1. To create a new catalog or activate a different catalog stored in the current subdirectory, select the **Use a different catalog** option, and then choose the catalog (or **<create>**) from a pick list. When you create a new catalog, it is empty, as are all the Control Center file panels.

Even if you maintain only one catalog in each subdirectory, you may want to assign a more descriptive name than UNTITLED. For example, you might want to rename the National Widgets catalog NW or NATWIDG. You can rename a catalog by using the **Modify catalog name** option on the **Catalog** menu. Be careful not to rename a catalog by using the DOS or dBASE IV RENAME command, because these methods do not update the catalog name

```
Catalog

 Use a different catalog
 Modify catalog name
 Edit description of catalog
 ---------------------------------------
 Add file to catalog
 Remove highlighted file from catalog
 Change description of highlighted file
```

Figure 19-1.

The structure of the Control Center Catalog menu

stored in the master catalog (CATALOG.CAT), which supplies the catalog names displayed in the pick list invoked by selecting the **Use a different catalog** option.

Like other DOS file names, a catalog name can have a maximum of 8 characters, but you can enter an 80-character description to identify the catalog. When you create a new catalog, dBASE IV prompts you to enter the description immediately after you type the name. You can enter or edit the description of an existing catalog by choosing the **Edit catalog description** option from the **Catalog** menu. When you select the **Use a different catalog** option to activate a new catalog, dBASE IV displays the description of the highlighted catalog name in a pop-up box, as illustrated in Figure 19-2, to help you choose the right catalog.

The **Add file to catalog** option enables you to add data bases, queries, and form files to the current catalog. You can use this option to add files created for an application stored in another subdirectory to the current catalog or to add a file to more than one catalog. This option is also useful when you do some of your work in the menu system and some at the dot prompt. By default, dBASE IV does not open a catalog when you work at the dot prompt, and it automatically closes the catalog when you exit the Control Center. As you will see later

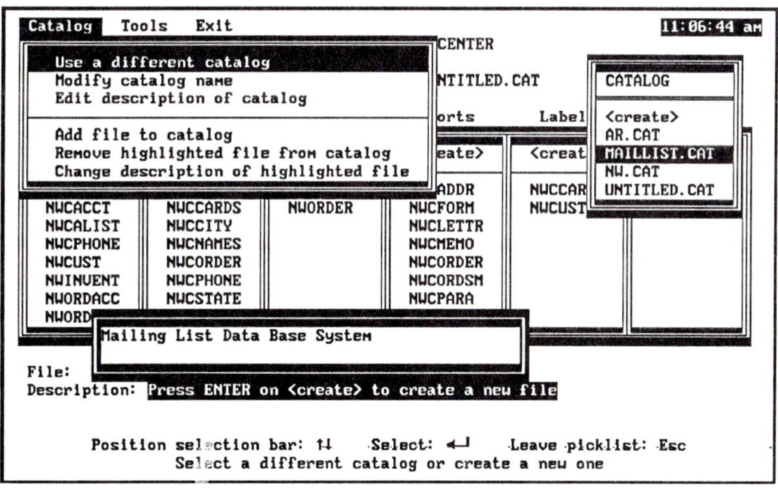

Figure 19-2.

Choosing a new catalog from a pick list

in this chapter, when you explicitly open a catalog from the dot prompt dBASE IV updates this catalog just as when you work in the menu system, but you can also use the **Add files to catalog** option to add files created at the dot prompt to the current catalog.

When you select the **Add file to catalog** option, dBASE IV displays a pick list of files *of the type that corresponds to the highlighted Control Center panel.* For example, if you select this option with the highlight in the **Data** panel, the list includes only data base files, identified by the DBF extension. Note that the pick lists displayed when any other panel is highlighted include both form files created by the layout editors (which are required to edit forms) and the compiled generated programs (the files required to execute the forms), but not the generated programs themselves. For example, the report pick list, which is illustrated in Figure 19-3, includes both FRM and FRO files.

Adding a data base file to the catalog does not automatically add related form files (queries, screen forms, report forms, and label forms) based on that data base. Even if you do add these forms to the catalog individually, dBASE IV does not move the form names above the dividing lines in the appropriate Control Center panels when you open the data base. Because dBASE IV records the association between a data base and its related forms in the catalog,

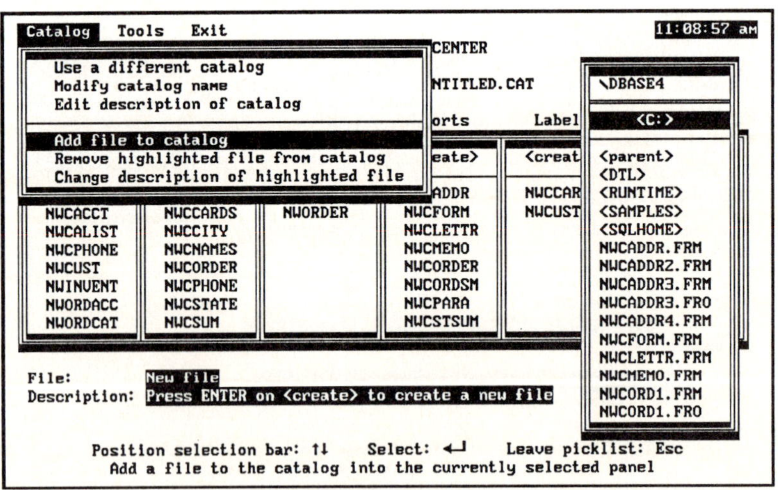

Figure 19-3.

Adding a file to the current catalog

this information is available only for those forms that you create or modify with a catalog active. If you want to update the catalog to reflect the linkage between a data base and a form file, you can open the data base and edit the form. Note that you cannot just open the form and immediately exit the form design work surface—you must make some change to force dBASE IV to update the catalog entry for the form. One simple trick you can use is to type a single character in any unoccupied space on the form and then erase this character before saving the form.

To edit a form, you must add the form file (the FRM, LBL, or SCR file) to the catalog; dBASE IV can regenerate and recompile the program based on this file. If you add only the compiled program to the catalog, you can execute but not edit the report, label, or screen form. Note that although dBASE IV does not display file extensions in the Control Center panels, the full path name, including disk drive, subdirectory, and extension, of the highlighted file is visible below the panels, along with the catalog description.

You can remove the highlighted file from the current catalog by selecting the **Remove highlighted file from catalog** option in the **Catalog** menu. This option is unavailable when the **<create>** option is highlighted or when there are no file names in the current panel. As always, when you issue a potentially destructive command, dBASE IV pops up a dialog box that asks you to confirm your intention to delete the indicated file: "Are you sure you want to remove this file from the catalog?" If you select **Yes**, dBASE IV deletes the catalog entry and asks "Do you also want to delete this file from the disk?" If you select **Yes** again, the file is erased from the disk and cannot be recovered. When you use this method to delete a file, dBASE IV erases only the file displayed in the panel (usually the LBL, FRM, or FMT file). If you are sure that you will no longer need the other disk files associated with a form (the generated program and the compiled program), you must use one of the other methods explained in this chapter to remove them from your hard disk.

You may have noticed that the **Layout** menu of each layout editor and file design work surface includes an option similar to the **Edit description of catalog** option. For example, the data base design screen **Layout** menu has an **Edit database description** option, and in the report layout editor, the corresponding option is **Edit description of report**. The description entered using any of these options is stored in the catalog entry, not in the file itself. When you use the **Add file to catalog** option on the Control Center **Catalog** menu to add a file to the current catalog, dBASE IV cannot determine whether the file is already in another catalog, so it prompts you to enter a new description.

dBASE IV displays the description below the file name under the Control Center file name panels when the file name is highlighted and in a separate pop-up window when you select a file from a pick list. The description is useful, because it enables you to describe the purpose or usage of a file in nontechnical terms that are readily comprehensible to users who are not familiar with your application. If you did not enter a description when you originally created a file, you can do so using the **Change description of highlighted file** option in the Control Center **Catalog** menu. If you have been following the examples in this book, you may want to go back and enter descriptions for some or all of the sample files.

From the Dot Prompt

When you work at the dot prompt, it is up to you to create and maintain data catalogs. When you exit the Control Center, dBASE IV closes the current catalog, and if you configure dBASE IV to bypass the Control Center, it does not open a catalog when you first start the program. If you work at the dot prompt exclusively, dBASE IV will never create a catalog unless you explicitly request one. If you alternate between the menu system and the dot prompt, or if several users of the same application prefer different working environments, you must add files that were created from the dot prompt with no catalog open to a catalog in order to make them accessible from the Control Center.

From the dot prompt, you can create a new catalog or open an existing one with the SET CATALOG command, as follows:

SET CATALOG TO *catalog file name*

You close a catalog with

```
SET CATALOG TO
```

When a catalog is open, dBASE IV checks the catalog every time you create or open a file, and if the specified file is not already present, it adds it to the catalog. When you open an existing file, dBASE IV prompts you to enter a description, also referred to as a title, which it stores in the catalog and displays in a pop-up box when you use the catalog to list available files of a given type (or, as was explained in the previous section, when you choose a file from a pick list). When you create a new file, dBASE IV does not prompt you for the title because all of the layout editors used to create files have an option on their **Layout** menus to enter the catalog description (on the data base design screen, this option is **Edit database description**). If you do not want to pause to enter the description every time you open a file that is not in the catalog, you can disable the prompt with

```
SET TITLE OFF
```

Because there is no objective way for dBASE IV to determine which files belong together, be sure to open the right catalog when you work with a given set of files. If you alternate between several applications in the course of a work session, this may entail typing SET CATALOG commands frequently. To open an occasional unrelated file without generating a catalog entry for this file, you can temporarily turn off the catalog update process with

```
SET CATALOG OFF
```

and reactivate it with

```
SET CATALOG ON
```

When a catalog is open, dBASE IV updates it automatically to reflect all changes in the group of files stored in the catalog. If you delete a file from the disk using the dBASE IV ERASE command, the corresponding catalog entry is also deleted, and if you change the name with RENAME, the catalog entry is modified to reflect the new name. When you activate a catalog, dBASE IV verifies that all the files in the catalog exist in the designated subdirectories and deletes any "orphan" catalog entries for files that you erased or renamed outside dBASE IV or when you did not have a catalog open.

From the menu system, you can use the **Add file to catalog** option to add files created at the dot prompt to the current catalog. From the dot prompt, the easiest way to add files to a catalog is to open the catalog with a SET CATALOG command, and then open each file in turn that you want to add to this catalog. If the TITLE setting is ON (as it is by default), dBASE IV prompts you to enter a description for each file you open. For example, you could use the following sequence of commands to add four of the National Widgets data base files to a catalog called NW:

```
SET CATALOG TO NW
USE NWCUST
USE NWORDER
USE NWINVENT
USE NWORDHST
```

If you also wanted to add queries, screen forms, report forms, and label forms to the catalog, you could open each of these files in turn before closing the associated data base and opening the next.

Whenever a catalog is open, even if you have used SET CATALOG OFF to disable the automatic update, you can use a *catalog query clause* in any command that opens files to display a list of the available files—those in the current catalog—of the appropriate type. To do this, you substitute a question mark for the file name. For example, you could display a list of data bases in the current catalog by typing

```
USE ?
```

In response to the catalog query clause, dBASE IV displays a pick list of file names and, in a separate pop-up box, the description (title) of the highlighted file. The pick list invoked by the previous USE command is illustrated in Figure 19-4. Because the description is so helpful for identifying the file you want, it is a good idea to enter a description for every file you catalog, even in small applications. You can open a file directly from the pick list by highlighting the name and pressing ENTER.

If you do not have a catalog open, using a query clause causes dBASE IV to display a pick list that includes *all* files of the appropriate type in the current subdirectory. Figure 19-5 illustrates the pick list of data bases invoked by typing USE ? without a catalog open. You can choose a file from the list, or you can switch to another disk drive or subdirectory by selecting the disk drive designator or subdirectory name. In effect, you can navigate through the subdirectory tree on any available disk drive to find the file you want. Note, however, that this process does not change the default disk drive or subdirectory.

The file selection pick lists displayed when a catalog is open are more selective and more helpful than the lists derived from the full disk directory, but the USE command in the previous example does not illustrate the full power of the catalog. As you know, you could easily determine which data bases belonged to the National Widgets system with a DIR command based on the naming conventions adopted for the files in the system. Because all the

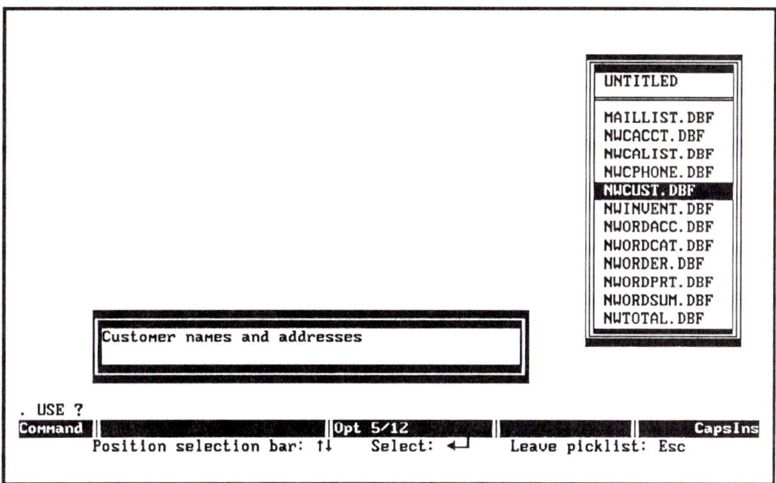

Figure 19-4.

Using a catalog query clause to open a file from the dot prompt

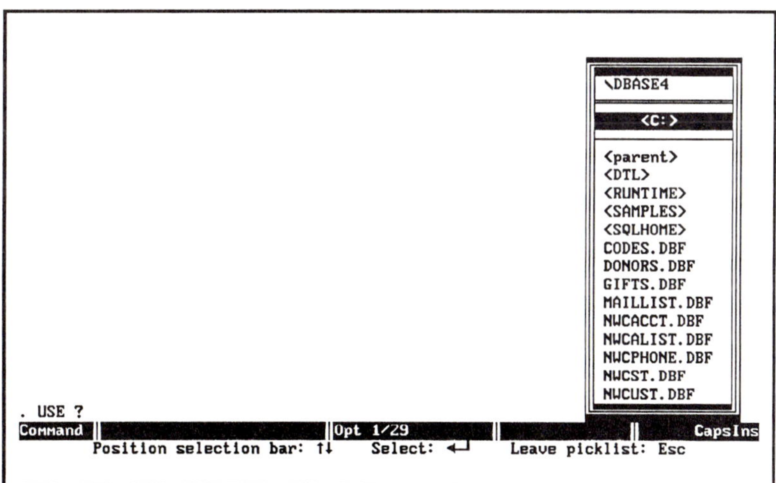

Figure 19-5.

Using a query clause from the dot prompt with no catalog open

National Widgets file names begin with NW, you could use a simple DIR command (the dBASE IV DIR command is covered in greater detail later in this chapter) to list the available data bases, as follows:

```
DIR NW*
```

A more significant advantage of the catalog is that it keeps track of which auxiliary files—NDX indexes, queries, and screen, report, and label form files—are associated with each data base. When you open a data base from the Control Center, dBASE IV checks the catalog to determine which file names to move above the lines in the other panels. The same information is available from the dot prompt when you use a query clause with a catalog open. For example, with the Customer File open, you could display a list of associated report forms by typing

```
MODIFY REPORT ?
```

or

```
REPORT FORM ?
```

If you want to open a catalog but have forgotten its name, you can use a catalog query clause in the SET CATALOG command, as follows:

```
SET CATALOG TO ?
```

To display the list of available catalogs as well as the associated descriptions, dBASE IV searches the master catalog (the catalog of catalogs in the current subdirectory) described earlier in this chapter.

The Structure of the Catalog File

As mentioned earlier in this chapter, the catalog is an ordinary dBASE IV data base file with the extension CAT instead of DBF. When you open a catalog with a SET CATALOG command, dBASE IV opens this data base in work area 10. The catalog remains open when you close "all" open files with the CLOSE DATABASES command. Note also that the catalog counts as an open data base file and as an open disk file; if you need to open ten other data bases or if you are approaching the limit your operating system places on the number of simultaneously open disk files, you may need to close the catalog at times to open another file.

When a catalog is open, you can select work area 10 and use the LIST, EDIT, or BROWSE command to examine or edit the catalog entries. You can also open a catalog with a USE command if it is not already open in work area 10, and update it as you would any other data base file, with commands such as APPEND, EDIT, BROWSE, and DELETE, but you should never change its structure (if you do, dBASE IV can no longer recognize the file as a catalog). Because of the CAT extension, dBASE IV does not include catalog files in the list of data bases displayed by the DIR command, and you must include the extension if you open a catalog with a USE command. You could open a catalog named NATWIDG with the following USE command:

```
USE NATWIDG.CAT
```

The structure of the catalog data base is listed in Figure 19-6. The fields are used as follows:

PATH	The file name and extension, and, if the file is not located in the current subdirectory, the disk drive and full path name
FILE_NAME	The file name and extension
ALIAS	The file name (excluding the extension)
TYPE	The standard extension that identifies the file type, regardless of the actual file extension
TITLE	For most files, a description of up to 80 characters; for NDX index files, the index key expression
CODE	A numerical code used to group files that are used together (for example, a data base and its related queries and form files). The CODE values are assigned sequentially and do not correspond in any way to the ten dBASE IV work areas
TAG	A four-character field provided to enable you to "tag" (mark) certain catalog entries for your own purposes; this field is not used at all by dBASE IV

```
Structure for database: C:\DBASE4\NW.CAT
Number of data records:       12
Date of last update   : 11/30/91
Field  Field Name  Type       Width    Dec    Index
    1  PATH        Character     70               N
    2  FILE_NAME   Character     12               N
    3  ALIAS       Character      8               N
    4  TYPE        Character      3               N
    5  TITLE       Character     80               N
    6  CODE        Numeric        3               N
    7  TAG         Character      4               N
** Total **                     181
```

Figure 19-6.

The structure of the catalog data base

Remember that because the catalog is an ordinary data base file, you can manipulate it using all the tools dBASE IV provides for working with data bases. For example, you can build an index to access the catalog data base in any order you wish, and you can generate a printout by using LIST TO PRINT or by defining report forms. You can combine these techniques to produce a printed list of the files that make up an application. For example, you might want to list each data base and its associated NDX indexes, query files, and report, label, and screen forms. To do this, you could build an index for the catalog based on the combination of CODE and TYPE and then list the relevant fields, as follows:

```
INDEX ON STR(CODE,3) + TYPE TAG CODETYPE
LIST CODE, TYPE, ALIAS, LEFT(TITLE,50) TO PRINT
```

If you prefer, you can produce a better-looking printout by defining a report form.

MANAGING DISK FILES

Every computerized application—word processing, accounting, or data base management—requires "disk housekeeping." You are undoubtedly aware of the need to create new files, but you must also know how to erase files that you no longer need, rename files, make copies of existing files—either in the same or different subdirectories—and perhaps most important of all, back up all the files you create (not just data base files) on floppy disks or magnetic tapes to guard against data loss in the event of a hardware or software failure.

dBASE IV allows you to carry out the fundamental file management tasks by executing standard DOS commands from within the program, by typing equivalent dBASE IV commands from the dot prompt, or by using a menu-driven set of DOS utilities. All these methods enable you to list, erase, rename, copy, and view files, but they provide different options, and each has advantages in some situations. Even if you work primarily at the dot prompt, you may want to read about the menu-driven DOS utilities, which enable you to carry out some operations more easily than you could by using the equivalent DOS and dBASE IV dot prompt commands.

From the Menus

dBASE IV provides a comprehensive set of file management utilities, which you access through the **DOS Utilities** option on the Control Center **Tools** menu. The initial screen that is displayed when you select this option is shown in Figure 19-7 and the structure of the menu bar is diagrammed in Figure 19-8. Like the Control Center, the DOS utilities screen is centered around a list of files, which is always displayed in the middle of the screen. By default, the list is arranged in alphabetical order by file name, and the display includes the following items for each file:

Name/Extension	The file name and extension as they would appear in the listing produced by the DOS DIR command
Size	The actual size of the file in bytes, or <DIR> for a subdirectory entry
Date & Time	The date and time that the file was last updated

Attrs — Any special attributes assigned to the file by the operating system. The attributes are represented by the following abbreviations:

- a — *Archive* The file has changed since the last time it was backed up with the BACKUP utility and should therefore be archived (backed up)
- h — *Hidden* The file is not displayed in the listing produced by the DOS DIR command
- r — *Read/only* DOS will not allow you to erase or modify the file
- s — *System* The file is part of the DOS operating system (System files are usually also hidden)

Space Used — The amount of disk space required to store the file, expressed in bytes; this is always a multiple of the cluster size (the smallest block of disk space that DOS can allocate). This entry is always the same as or larger than the number in the Size column

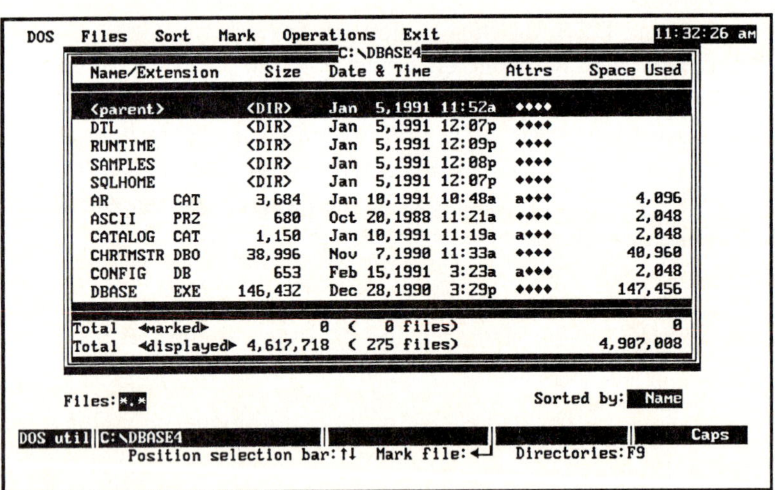

Figure 19-7.

The DOS utilities screen

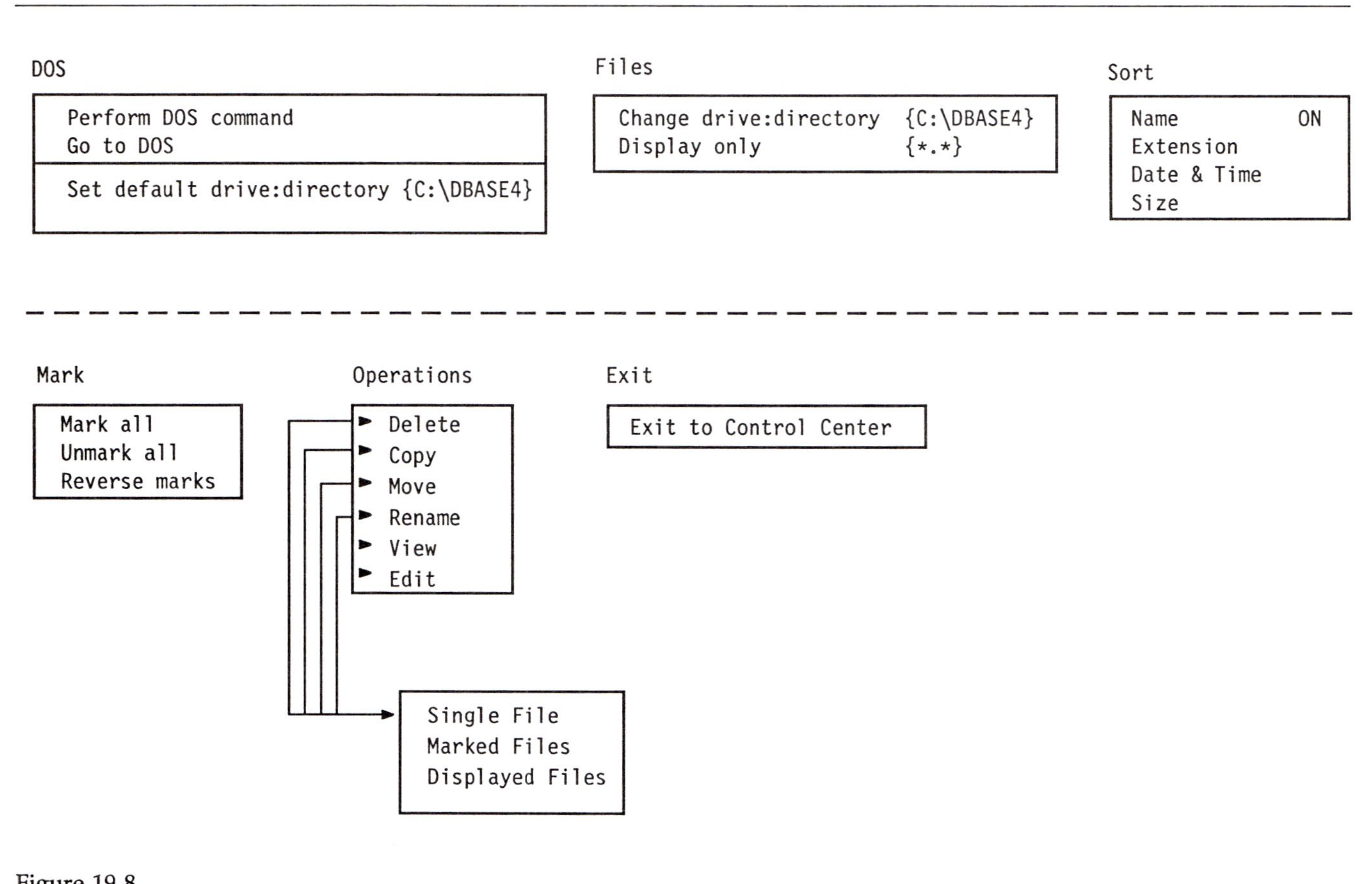

Figure 19-8.

The structure of the DOS utilities menu

Displaying File Directories

You can page through the file list on the DOS utilities screen as you would any other pick list—by using UP ARROW, DOWN ARROW, PGUP, PGDN, HOME, and END. The initial display includes all the files in the current subdirectory. To switch to a subdirectory that is below the current subdirectory in the DOS directory tree structure, you highlight the subdirectory name and press ENTER. You can move up one level in the subdirectory tree just as you do in other dBASE IV pick lists, by selecting **<parent>** from the list. If you are familiar with the subdirectory structure on your hard disk, you can move to another directory by selecting the **Change drive:directory** option on the **Files** menu. dBASE IV prompts you in a dialog box to enter the new drive and directory. You can type the path name, or you can press SHIFT-F1 (Pick) to display a graphical diagram of the subdirectory tree and then choose a subdirectory by highlighting the name and pressing ENTER.

You can also display the tree diagram, (shown in Figure 19-9) from the main DOS utilities screen by pressing F9 (Zoom). By default, dBASE IV displays the subdirectory structure of the current disk drive. To switch disk drives, you can either press SHIFT-F1 (Pick) again with the diagram displayed or highlight the disk

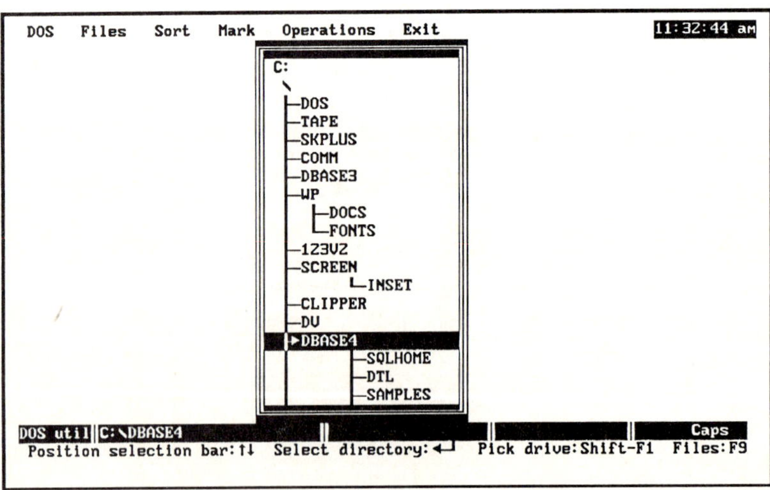

Figure 19-9.

The DOS utilities subdirectory tree diagram

drive designator at the top of the tree diagram, press ENTER, and then select the new drive from a pick list. Choosing a new drive and/or directory does not change the default drive or the currently logged subdirectory for the rest of your work session—it just governs the list of files displayed on the DOS utilities screen.

You can sort the directory listing on the DOS utilities screen by file name, extension, date, or size by selecting the appropriate option from the **Sort** menu. You might want to sort files by extension to group files of the same type, or sort them by date to see new files grouped together (perhaps to determine which files you created or changed since the last backup). You can only sort the file list by one attribute at a time, but you can sort more than once to view the list in any order you wish. When dBASE IV sorts file names, it moves each file only as far as is necessary to place the file in the proper group. Thus, if the listing is already sorted by name, sorting by extension produces a list that is sorted by extension and within each extension by file name.

You can use the **Display only** option on the **Files** menu to produce a more selective file listing. You identify the files you want by entering a file name pattern that includes the standard DOS wildcard characters: the question mark (?), which stands for any single character; and the asterisk (*), which stands for any group of characters. For example, you could display only data base files in the National Widgets system by using the pattern NW*.DB?, which selects both DBF and DBT files. The file name matching pattern remains in effect when you switch directories, but if you return to the Control Center and then select **DOS Utilities** again, dBASE IV reverts to the default listing, which includes *all the files in the current subdirectory*.

At the top of the frame that borders the file listing, dBASE IV displays the name of the subdirectory in which the listed files are stored. At the bottom, it displays the total number and size of the listed files (the total size is derived by summing the Space Used column) as well as the same totals for marked files (marking files will be explained shortly). Below the file name frame, dBASE IV displays the matching pattern that describes the file selection criteria and the order in which the listing is sorted. Knowing the total amount of disk space occupied by a group of files is especially convenient when you want to copy selected files to another subdirectory or to floppy disks. Based on the combined size of the files, you can decide whether you want to use COPY or BACKUP to copy a set of files onto floppy disks, determine whether to use a high-density or low-density disk, or verify that enough space remains on your hard disk before attempting to copy the files to another subdirectory.

File Operations

You can think of the commands and options explained in the previous section as the menu-driven equivalent of the DOS DIR ("directory") command (with several useful enhancements). The **Operations** menu on the DOS utilities screen enables you to carry out operations analogous to the DOS ERASE, COPY, RENAME, and TYPE commands and to *move* files to another directory (copy the files and then erase the originals), an operation for which there is no single equivalent DOS command.

dBASE IV allows you to mark files individually or in groups and then carry out some of the actions on the **Operations** menu on just the marked files. To mark one file or unmark a previously marked file, you highlight the file name and press ENTER. The mark appears as a small triangle to the left of the file name, as shown in Figure 19-10. You can mark all displayed files by selecting the **Mark all** option from the **Mark** menu or unmark all marked files by using the **Unmark all** option. The **Reverse marks** option unmarks all previously marked files and marks all those that were not marked. The easiest way to mark all files of a particular type, but continue to display all the files in a subdirectory, is to use the **Display only** option on the **Files** menu to display only the specified

```
DOS   Files   Sort   Mark   Operations   Exit                      11:37:35 am
                              C:\DBASE4
      Name/Extension      Size   Date & Time          Attrs    Space Used

     ▸NWCUST    DBF      5,974   Jan 10,1992 10:55a   a♦♦♦          6,144
      NWCUST    DBO     20,356   Jan  2,1992  9:55a   ♦♦♦♦         20,480
     ▸NWCUST    DBT      5,632   Jan  5,1992  1:17p   ♦♦♦♦          6,144
      NWCUST    FMO      2,648   Jan  9,1992  1:07p   a♦♦♦          4,096
      NWCUST    FMT      2,724   Jan  9,1992  1:07p   a♦♦♦          4,096
     ▸NWCUST    MDX     13,312   Jan  5,1992  1:17p   ♦♦♦♦         14,336
      NWCUST    PRG     21,170   Jan  2,1992  9:53a   ♦♦♦♦         22,528
      NWCUST    PRT      5,632   Dec 24,1991  1:43a   a♦♦♦          6,144
      NWCUST    SCR      3,880   Jan  9,1992  1:07p   a♦♦♦          4,096
      NWCUST1   FMT      1,721   Oct 27,1990  8:56a   ♦♦♦♦          2,048
      NWCUST1   LBG      3,938   Dec  7,1990  9:16a   ♦♦♦♦          4,096

     Total  ◂marked▸        24,918  (   3 files)                   26,624
     Total  ◂displayed▸  4,606,138  ( 273 files)                4,894,720

    Files: *.*                                         Sorted by:  Name

DOS util ║C:\DBASE4             ║              ║             ║       Caps
          Position selection bar: ↑↓   Mark file: ←┘   Directories: F9
```

Figure 19-10.

Marking files in the DOS utilities file listing

files, select the **Mark all** option from the **Mark** menu, and then select **Display only** and reset the file name pattern to *.*. Figure 19-11 illustrates the display that results from using this method to display all the National Widgets data base files (specified using the file name pattern NW*.DB?).

The **Delete, Copy, Rename,** and **Move** options on the **Operations** menu can act on a single file, on all marked files, or on all displayed files, and dBASE IV presents these three options in a pick list when you choose a file operation. If you choose **Single File**, dBASE IV processes only the highlighted file. You can select **Marked Files** to operate on only marked files (including marked files that are not currently displayed) or **Displayed Files** to process all displayed files (whether or not they are marked). Because you can mark files individually, the **DOS Utilities** menu enables you to use a single command to delete, copy, or move a group of files that do not have similar names (you cannot do this with the equivalent DOS commands). However, to rename more than one file at a time, you must be able to specify the new names as a file name pattern that includes wildcards.

The distinction between *marked* files and *displayed* files is an important one. Displayed files include all those that match the pattern specified using the **Display only** option on the **Files** menu (or all files in the current subdirectory if

```
DOS   Files   Sort   Mark   Operations   Exit                    11:46:24 am
                              C:\DBASE4
   Name/Extension      Size   Date & Time          Attrs   Space Used

   NWORDSUM DBF       1,102   Dec  3,1991  2:36a   ♦♦♦♦         2,048
   NWORDACC DBF         589   Dec  3,1991  2:44a   ♦♦♦♦         2,048
   NWORDCAT DBF         762   Dec  6,1991  3:14a   ♦♦♦♦         2,048
   NWINVENT DBF       2,546   Dec 29,1991 10:22a   a♦♦♦         4,096
  ►NWCUST   DBF       5,974   Jan 10,1992 10:55a   a♦♦♦         6,144
   NWCPHONE DBF       1,128   Nov  8,1991  7:13a   ♦♦♦♦         2,048
   NWCUST3  DBF       1,598   Jan  5,1992  1:07p   ♦♦♦♦         2,048
   NWORDER  DBF       2,665   Jan 10,1992 10:19a   a♦♦♦         4,096
   NWCACCT  DBF       6,046   Jan  5,1992  1:11p   a♦♦♦         6,144
  ►NWCUST   DBT       5,632   Jan  5,1992  1:17p   ♦♦♦♦         6,144
   NWCACCT  DBT      10,752   Jan  5,1992  1:11p   a♦♦♦        12,288

  Total  ◄marked►       11,606  (  2 files)                    12,288
  Total  ◄displayed►    41,045  ( 14 files)                    55,296

   Files: NW*.DB?                               Sorted by:  Extension

DOS util  C:\DBASE4                                                Caps
           Position selection bar:↑↓  Mark file:↵  Directories:F9
```

Figure 19-11.

Displaying the National Widgets data base files on the DOS utilities screen you did not use this option to specify another pattern); the file name matching pattern is displayed below the file name list. Marked files are those that you marked using one of the options explained earlier in this section, regardless of whether they are currently displayed. If you mark a group of files and then use the **Display only** option to change the list of files displayed on the screen, some of the marked files may no longer be visible, but they are affected by commands that operate on marked files. You can always confirm the number and total size of marked and displayed files by looking at the statistics displayed at the bottom of the file list.

When you select **Rename** from the **Operations** menu, dBASE IV prompts you for a new file name; as noted earlier, if you are renaming more than one file, you must enter the new names as a pattern that includes the DOS wildcard characters. For example, you could give all the National Widgets report form files the new prefix AB (to use these forms with a new application) by entering the new file name as AB*.FRM.

The **Copy** operation prompts you to enter a new drive and directory, and if you are copying multiple files, a file name pattern for the copies. You can type the drive and directory, or you can press SHIFT-F1 (Pick) to display the directory tree diagram and make your selection from this screen. To copy files to another drive or directory without changing the names, you can leave the file name blank. If you want to duplicate existing files under new names, either in the same or another directory, you must specify the file name pattern as well. For example, you could copy the National Widgets report form files to a subdirectory on drive D called ABSYSTEM and assign new names that begin with the AB prefix by specifying the drive and directory as D:\ABSYSTEM and the file name as AB*.FRM.

The **Move** operation combines the copy and delete operations. Just as when you copy files, dBASE IV prompts you to enter a new drive and directory (which you can type or select from the directory tree diagram) and a file name pattern, and then copies the specified files to the designated drive and subdirectory under the new names. After it completes the copy operation, dBASE IV deletes the original files. Even if you know how to use DOS commands to copy and erase files, the **Move** operation is convenient when the files you want to move do not all share a common file name prefix or extension and could not be copied and then erased with one COPY command followed by one ERASE command. Using the **DOS Utilities** menu, you can mark all the files you want to move and then specify that the **Move** command act on marked files.

The **View** command enables you to display the contents of any text file (you can view *any* file without damaging it, but the display will be incomprehensible for files other than text files). When you choose the **View** option, dBASE IV displays the first 20 lines of text from the highlighted file and enumerates your options on the message line at the bottom of the screen: "Display control: SPACEBAR:Next screenful, RETURN:Start/stop scroll." You can use the spacebar to display the contents of the file one screenful at a time, or use ENTER to start scrolling text continuously or freeze the display once it is scrolling. Just as when you use the DOS and dBASE IV TYPE commands, you cannot redisplay text that has scrolled off the top of the screen—you must repeat the **View** command to restart the display from the beginning of the file. At any point, you can press ESC to interrupt the listing and return to the file display screen.

The **Edit** option invokes the dBASE IV text editor to edit the highlighted file. This editor, which resembles the memo field editor, was designed for writing dBASE IV programs, and it is explained in detail in Chapter 21. As with the **View** command, it does not make sense to edit any files except text files, but unlike **View**, the editor does have the potential to damage nontext files such as external programs (programs with the extensions COM or EXE). dBASE IV reminds you of this fact by displaying the warning "must be a text file" as part of the message line prompt when you select the **Edit** option. However, it does allow you to edit any file (but not a directory entry). If you inadvertently load a nontext file into the editor, do not save the file—choose the **Abandon changes and exit** option from the text editor **Exit** menu.

Accessing DOS Commands

The options on the **DOS** menu enable you to execute a single DOS command, batch file, or external program, or exit temporarily to the operating system, where you can execute as many DOS commands as you want before returning to dBASE IV. When you select the **Perform DOS command** option, dBASE IV prompts you in a pop-up dialog box to "Enter DOS command:" After you type a command, dBASE IV clears the screen; executes the specified command, batch file, or program; and then displays a message on the navigation line below the status bar, instructing you to "Press any key to return to dBASE IV."

Although you should be able to run any built-in DOS command or batch file, you may not be able to run large external programs from within dBASE IV. You must have enough RAM *within the first 640K of memory*—the memory that is directly accessible to DOS—to load a second copy of the DOS command processor, COMMAND.COM (18K to 40K, depending on your DOS version), as well as the external program. Neither dBASE IV nor DOS can use expanded or extended memory for this purpose. If you try to run a program that requires more memory than you have available, you will receive an error message, either from the DOS command processor ("Program too big to fit in memory") or from the external program (for example, WordPerfect displays the error message "Insufficient memory to run WordPerfect").

If you want to execute more than two or three DOS commands, especially if you must switch directories between commands, you can use the **Go to DOS** option to exit temporarily from dBASE IV without closing open files or losing any active memory variables or environment settings. When you select this option, dBASE IV loads another copy of the DOS command processor (COMMAND.COM) into memory and relinquishes control to this new copy of DOS, which displays its own sign-on message. dBASE IV incorporates the messages "dBASE DOS Window" and 'Type "EXIT ↵" to return to dBASE' into the DOS prompt (normally, the C prompt). DOS thus redisplays a reminder that dBASE IV is still active after it executes each command you type to help ensure that you do not reboot or turn off the computer inadvertently without returning to dBASE IV to close any open data bases. Just as when you run DOS commands one at a time using the **Perform DOS command** option, you can execute DOS commands or run any program that fits in memory together with dBASE IV and DOS. (From the DOS prompt, you can use the DOS CHKDSK utility to verify exactly how much memory is available.)

To exit the DOS window and return to dBASE IV, type EXIT at the DOS prompt and press ENTER. dBASE IV redisplays the DOS utilities screen, with the working environment in exactly the same state as when you chose the **Go to DOS** option. Note that even if you switched to another directory while outside dBASE IV, the file list is exactly the same when you return as when you left. However, dBASE IV cannot keep track of which files on the DOS utilities screen were marked when you exit to DOS; if you have marked any files, it displays a dialog box to warn you "Accessing DOS will unmark all marked files" and allows you to choose **Proceed** to unmark the files and then go to DOS or **Cancel** to return to the file display. Also note that because dBASE IV cannot determine what commands you executed or what effects these commands or external programs might have had, it is your responsibility to ensure that you do not erase or rename any files from DOS that were open when you left dBASE IV.

The **Set default drive:directory** option on the **DOS** menu enables you to establish a new default disk drive and subdirectory for all your subsequent work, exactly as if you had logged onto that subdirectory before you loaded dBASE IV. You can type the directory name, or you can press SHIFT-F1 (Pick) to display the directory tree diagram and choose a subdirectory by pointing to it in the tree diagram and pressing ENTER.

From the Dot Prompt

If you are familiar with your operating system's commands and utility programs, you can execute these commands from within dBASE IV to perform some file management activities. The RUN command enables you to execute any DOS command, batch file, or program from within dBASE IV as long as you have enough memory in the first 640K—the memory available to DOS and to dBASE IV for running programs. You need 18 to 40K of memory to load COMMAND.COM, and for external programs (not built-in commands such as DIR, ERASE, and RENAME) enough RAM for the program. There are two ways to type the RUN command:

RUN *DOS command*

or

! *DOS command*

You can use a RUN command to display the disk directory in the standard DOS format, perhaps to check the date and time that the file was last modified without entering the menu system to use **DOS Utilities**. For example, to display a DOS directory of all the National Widgets label form files, you would use the following command:

```
RUN DIR NW*.LBL
```

dBASE IV provides equivalents for many of the DOS commands, all of which differ to some extent in syntax and capabilities from their DOS counterparts. Although the syntax may be more intuitive, in most cases the dBASE IV variants are more limited. In particular, the dBASE IV COPY, RENAME, and ERASE commands do not support wildcards—they can act on only one file at a time.

The dBASE IV COPY FILE command can copy files of any type (not just data base files) one at a time. If you use this command to copy a data base file that contains memo fields, remember to copy the DBT file as well as the DBF file. The syntax is as follows:

COPY FILE *old file name* TO *new file name*

You can use the ERASE or DELETE FILE command to erase a file, as follows:

ERASE *file name*

or

DELETE FILE *file name*

The RENAME command allows you to rename a file, as follows:

RENAME *old file name* TO *new file name*

The TYPE command is identical in syntax to the DOS equivalent:

TYPE *file name*

You can use the TYPE command to display the contents of any disk file, but the output will make sense only for text files. To direct the output to the printer or to a disk file, you can add the optional phrases TO PRINT or TO FILE (followed by a file name in the latter case), and you can add line numbers to the listing by including the optional keyword NUMBER.

If you are already familiar with DOS commands, the main advantage of the dBASE IV equivalents is speed. Because dBASE IV must load a new copy of the DOS command processor (COMMAND.COM) into memory to execute any external command or program, using the RUN command to execute a DOS command takes longer than executing the corresponding dBASE IV command. The chief advantage of the DOS commands is that they support wildcard characters in file names and can thus operate on groups of files, whereas the dBASE commands for copying, renaming, and erasing files act on only one file at a time. If you are learning file maintenance commands for the first time and you do not want to memorize two equivalent sets of commands, the DOS commands, which will serve you well in your work with other applications as well as dBASE IV, would be the better choice.

SUMMARY

You now have at your disposal an array of tools to group files in an application, identify the purpose or use of each file, and perform routine disk "housekeeping" activities such as copying, erasing, and renaming files. Some of these methods are nontechnical, such as choosing file names judiciously so that you can later discern the purpose or contents of a file from its name. Others, such as maintaining multiple catalogs, require that you understand more about how dBASE IV manages files.

For historical reasons, dBASE IV offers three alternatives for carrying out many file management tasks: using the **DOS Utilities** option on the Control Center **Tools** menu, running DOS commands and utility programs from within dBASE IV, and typing the dBASE IV equivalents for the DOS commands at the dot prompt. If you work primarily in the menu system, you may want to use the **DOS Utilities** options for managing disk files. From the dot prompt, the dBASE IV commands offer an advantage in speed, but they lack power and flexibility compared with the equivalent DOS commands. Regardless of which dBASE IV file management alternatives you use, you will benefit greatly in your work with dBASE IV and other application software by learning as much as you can about your operating system's directory structure, built-in commands, and file management utility programs.

CHAPTER TWENTY

Exchanging Data With Other Software

So far, this book has described only how to work with data created and updated entirely within dBASE. The time will come, however, when you need to exchange data with other software—perhaps software that runs on a different type of computer—to read data generated by another program into a dBASE IV data base, or to copy data from a data base file to an external file format. Although dBASE IV is a capable data base manager, it is probably not the only major application running on your computer, and it is not the best tool for every job. For example, calculation-intensive tasks are better left to spreadsheet programs and statistics packages, and although dBASE IV offers some basic word processing capabilities, you would probably not want to use it to produce documents of more than a few pages.

One of the ways that you can optimize your use of available software resources is to use each application program you own in its area of greatest strength. You might want to use a spreadsheet program to perform calculations on data derived from a dBASE IV data base file, insert the name and address fields from a mailing list data base into a personalized letter that requires the more sophisticated text formatting capabilities of your word processing or desktop publishing software, or read spreadsheet data into a dBASE IV data base to print formatted reports with group bands and summary statistics.

Although an increasing number of other programs can read a DBF file directly and dBASE IV can read and write a number of *external,* or *foreign,* file formats, you cannot assume that the solution to your data interchange problems will be easy, especially if you need to exchange data with other types of microcomputers (such as the Macintosh), or with minicomputers or mainframes. Data exchange can be a tricky proposition, because it often requires that you understand far more about how your data is physically stored on disk than is required to work with the same data within dBASE IV. You may also need to know quite a bit about the data structures and storage formats used by the "foreign" program, with which you may have little or no experience.

This chapter outlines some of the strategies you can use to import and export data. If you do not find the specific methods you need in the following discussion, your best line of defense is to arm yourself with as much detailed information as possible about the content and format of the data files you must read or write, and try to find an exchange format that is common to dBASE IV and the external program. Many of the strategies explained in this chapter involve creating a temporary data base to receive or transfer data and then modifying the structure of this file to fine-tune the format of the imported or exported file. Before you tackle a data exchange problem, you may want to refer to Chapter 16 to review the important concepts related to modifying the structure of a dBASE IV data base without losing data. In any event, be sure to back up your dBASE IV files before you experiment with a new data import procedure in case the test produces unanticipated—and undesirable—results.

READING AND WRITING EXTERNAL FILE FORMATS

As explained in Chapter 16, you can create a new dBASE IV data base by copying some or all of the data in an existing data base, and you can combine data base files by appending the records stored in one file into another. You can also copy data to several external file formats and append data created by other programs into a dBASE IV data base. The following is a list of supported formats:

Delimited	A text file in which the fields are separated by commas; character fields are surrounded (delimited) by spaces, quotes, or other punctuation marks; and there is a hard return at the end of each record
Fixed-length	Also known as System Data Format (SDF), a text file in which all fields are fixed in length, with no punctuation between fields, and with a hard return at the end of each record
Lotus 1-2-3	A Lotus worksheet file that can be read by 1-2-3 version 1A, 2, or 3 and Symphony, as well as by many other spreadsheet programs
Framework II	A Framework II data base frame, which can also be read by Framework III
RapidFile	A RapidFile data base
dBASE II	A dBASE II data base
dBASE III	A dBASE III or dBASE III PLUS data base
PFS:FILE	A PFS:FILE data base
VisiCalc	Also known as Data Interchange Format (DIF), a file format used by VisiCalc and other spreadsheets for data exchange
SYLK-Multiplan	Also known as Symbolic Link (SYLK) format, a file format used by Multiplan and other Microsoft programs for data exchange

When you work in the menu system, you can import or export an entire file using the **Import** or **Export** options on the Control Center **Tools** menu, or you can use the **Copy records from non-dBASE file** option on the data base design screen **Append** menu to read data into an open data base from an external file. From the dot prompt, you use the COPY, EXPORT, APPEND, and IMPORT commands. Table 20-1 lists the external file formats, the default file extensions for each, and the menu and dot prompt commands that support each format.

In some cases, a particular comand does not support one of the file formats because there is no need to do so. For example, dBASE IV can read a data base created by dBASE III or dBASE III PLUS directly, so there is no need for a special command to append records from a dBASE III or dBASE III PLUS data

File Format	TYPE Keyword	Extension	Menu Options	Dot Prompt Commands
Delimited	DELIMITED	TXT	**Export, Copy**	COPY, APPEND
Fixed-length	SDF	TXT	**Export, Copy**	COPY, APPEND
Lotus 1-2-3 ver 1A	WKS	WKS	**Export, Copy**	COPY, APPEND
Lotus 1-2-3 ver 2	WK1	WK1	**Import**	IMPORT
Framework II	FW2	FW2	**Export, Import, Copy**	COPY, EXPORT, APPEND, IMPORT
RapidFile	RPD	RPD	**Export, Import, Copy**	COPY, EXPORT, APPEND, IMPORT
dBASE II	DBASEII	DB2	**Export, Import, Copy**	COPY, EXPORT, APPEND, IMPORT
dBASE III	DBMEMO3	DBF		COPY
PFS:FILE	PFS	None	**Export, Import**	EXPORT, IMPORT
VisiCalc	DIF	DIF	**Export, Copy**	COPY, APPEND
SYLK-Multiplan	SYLK	None	**Export, Copy**	COPY, APPEND

Table 20-1.

File Formats, Default File Extensions, and Data Exchange Commands

base file. However, because dBASE IV stores memo fields differently, dBASE III and dBASE III PLUS cannot read a dBASE IV data base that contains memo fields; instead, you must copy the file to dBASE III format using a COPY command at the dot prompt. Similarly, Lotus versions 2 and 3 can read a WKS file (the version 1A worksheet format), so there is no need to export files to Lotus WK1 format or WK3 format. However, dBASE IV must be able to import worksheet files created under Lotus versions 2 and 3.

M From the Menus

When you work in the menu system, you use the **Export** option on the **Tools** menu to copy data stored in a dBASE IV data base to an external file format. When you choose this option, dBASE IV displays a pick list of external file formats. After you choose the format, it displays a pick list of data base files, and exports the entire data base you select. If another data base was open when you chose the **Export** option, dBASE IV closes this file, opens the file you want to export, and leaves this file open afterwards. dBASE IV exports the entire data base—all the fields and all the records—to the specified external format, so if you want to export selected fields or records, you must first generate a new data base that contains only the data you want to transfer. You can do this by defining a view query that describes the field and record selection criteria and using the **Write view as database file** option on the query design screen to copy the specified data to a true data base, which you can then export.

The operation of the **Import** option is similar. dBASE IV first displays a list of external file formats, and after you select a format, it displays a pick list of files of the specified type. dBASE IV identifies the format of an external file by its extension; to import a file that deviates from the standard file naming conventions listed in the **Import** menu and summarized in Table 20-1, you must first rename the file. No other advance preparation is required before you use the **Import** option; dBASE IV automatically creates a data base to receive the data, deriving the structure from that of the foreign file and assigning the same first name (with the standard DBF extension). dBASE IV imports all the data in the external file. If you need only some of the fields or records, you can either modify the structure of the new data base and then delete the unwanted records, or define a view query that describes the field and record selection criteria, and then use the **Write view as database file** option to create a new file that contains only the desired data.

The **Copy records from non-dBASE file** option on the data base design screen **Append** menu adds data to the active data base file from an external file. Unlike the **Import** option on the **Tools** menu, this option does not create the target data base, and it is up to you to ensure that the right dBASE IV file is open and that its structure is compatible with that of the incoming data. Exactly what constitutes "compatible" depends on the nature of the file you are importing. Special considerations for the various file types are described in greater detail in the remaining sections of this chapter.

D From the Dot Prompt

From the dot prompt, you can read data into a dBASE IV data base file using the APPEND and IMPORT commands, and write records to external file formats with COPY and EXPORT. Like the **Import** option on the Control Center

Tools menu, you can execute the dot prompt IMPORT command without having a data base open, because all the file formats supported by IMPORT include the structural information required to construct a matching dBASE IV data base file from scratch. Just as when you use the **Import** option, dBASE IV imports the entire external file; you must later delete any unneeded records or fields. In contrast, before you can use EXPORT, APPEND, or COPY, you must open a data base. These commands enable you to read or write files that contain only raw data with no structural information, and dBASE IV cannot build a new data base without a description of its structure.

You identify the type of file you want to read or write by adding a TYPE clause to the APPEND, COPY, IMPORT, or EXPORT command. The syntax is as follows:

COPY TO *file name* TYPE *file type*

or

EXPORT TO *file name* TYPE *file type*

or

APPEND FROM *file name* TYPE *file type*

or

IMPORT FROM *file name* TYPE *file type*

When you use the COPY or EXPORT command to write data to an external format, you can determine the order in which records are copied by sorting or indexing the source file. You can use any combination of a filter, scope, FOR, and WHILE clause to specify which records you want to copy. To transfer selected fields, you can add a FIELDS clause, which also determines the order of the fields in the imported or exported file. You cannot copy memo fields, and, as the keyword FIELDS implies, you can copy only whole fields, *not the results of evaluating expressions* based on data base fields. Ways to circumvent these limitations are covered later in this chapter.

COMPENSATING FOR DIFFERENCES IN FILE STRUCTURE

When you exchange data between dBASE IV and other data base programs using the **Import** and **Export** menu options or the equivalent IMPORT and

EXPORT commands at the dot prompt, dBASE IV handles most of the work of defining a data structure in the newly created file that matches the structure of the file that provides the data. Many of the file formats supported by these commands are used by other data base managers or spreadsheet programs, which all manipulate data in a structured format. When you import a text file, you must define the structure of the recipient data base yourself and ensure that it matches the incoming data.

In many cases, you must adjust the data that you import or export to compensate for differences in the file structures and data storage formats. For example, you may want to read a data file created by an accounting program that stores data in fixed-length format into an existing dBASE IV data base to print specialized reports. It would be an extraordinary coincidence if the structure of the accounting file exactly matched your dBASE IV file structure (that is, had all the same fields, in the same order, and of the same length and data type). Often, you must resolve the inconsistencies in dBASE IV, since most prepackaged software (accounting programs, for example, or mainframe data base software) does not allow you to alter the structures of the files it manipulates.

To solve problems like these, you can create a temporary, or intermediary, dBASE IV data base, and then adjust the structure of this file to match the requirements dictated by the external file format. You could use a procedure such as the following to transfer data into dBASE IV:

1. Back up the target dBASE IV data base if it already contains data.
2. Ensure that the structure of the temporary file matches the external file format.
3. Append data into the temporary file from the external file.
4. Change the structure and/or data in the temporary file so it matches the target dBASE IV file.
5. Append data from the temporary file into the target data base.

To transfer data from a dBASE IV data base to an external format, you can reverse these steps, as follows:

1. Back up the external file if it already exists.
2. Ensure that the structure of the temporary file matches the existing source data base.

3. Append data into the temporary file from the source data base.
4. Change the structure and/or data in the temporary data base so it matches the external file format.
5. Copy data from the temporary file to the external format.

If you do not have a clear description of the external file format, you can use any available tools to examine the file (or a sample file produced by exporting data from an existing dBASE IV data base to the specified format). You can use the DOS or dBASE IV TYPE command to display a text file on the screen or edit the file with any good word processor or text editor that can read and write ASCII text files, such as Brief, QEDIT, the WordPerfect Editor, the Norton Editor, or the Sidekick notepad. When you use a text editor to examine an unfamiliar file format, it is always prudent to work with a copy, not the original file, and to avoid saving the file.

When you devise a detailed method for implementing a particular data transfer, keep in mind which aspects of the structure are important. Neither the SDF nor delimited text file format includes field names, and in all cases, the dBASE IV fields must be arranged in the same order as the items in the foreign file. If you append data from one dBASE IV data base into another, the reverse is true: fields are matched solely by name, and can therefore differ in length, position, and even data type. Thus, you could append data from a text file or spreadsheet into a temporary file in which the fields have the same names as your target data base but occur in the same order as in the external file. You could then append this file into your target data base; in this step, dBASE IV matches the fields by name and rearranges them into the correct order.

In the delimited format, field widths are unimportant; dBASE IV removes trailing blank spaces when it writes data to a delimited file and adjusts incoming data from a delimited file to fit in the field widths defined in the target data base structure (by adding spaces to pad fields that are too short and by truncating fields that are too long). In an SDF file, however, fields are defined by their widths, so the widths of the fields in the data base that receives or supplies the data must match the external file format.

Sometimes, you will not only have to adjust the field sequence and widths but also combine or split fields to compensate for differences in the organization of the data. For example, National Widgets might need to copy the name and address fields from the Customer File to a text file for use by a program that expects to find the city, state, and ZIP code in a single field. All the methods dBASE IV provides to copy records can copy only whole fields, not complex expressions, so you cannot combine these three fields into a single string and include this string in the COPY command. The easiest way to solve this problem is by strategic use of calculated fields and temporary data bases.

From the Menus

Working in the menu system, you can export the results of evaluating expressions, in addition to single fields, by defining a view query that includes all the data base fields you want, together with calculated fields that perform the required data transformations. For example, you could create a calculated field called CITYSTATE, defined by the following expression:

```
TRIM(CITY) + ", " + STATE + "  " + ZIP
```

You could then use the **Write view as database file** option on the query design screen to create a data base that contains the CITYSTATE field (as well as other fields), and use the **Export** option on the **Tools** menu in the Control Center to export records from this file instead of the original data base. This strategy is easily extended to copying fields drawn from two or more related data bases—you can use the same **Write view as database file** option to copy data described by a multifile query to a single data base, which you could then export.

From the Dot Prompt

From the dot prompt, you can export the results of evaluating any legitimate dBASE IV expression by establishing the list of fields you want to transfer with a SET FIELDS command that includes one or more calculated fields, as in the following command sequence:

```
USE NWCUST
SET FIELDS TO CONTACT, COMPANY, ADDRESS,
  CITYSTATE = TRIM(CITY) + ", " + STATE + "  " + ZIP
```

To copy fields drawn from two or more related data bases, you could open the required files, link them with SET RELATION (and, if necessary, SET SKIP), use one or more SET FIELDS commands to establish a field list consisting of fields from two or more files, and then use a COPY or EXPORT command to create the external file.

Converting Data Types

When you copy records to a text file (a delimited or fixed-length file), dBASE IV writes dates in year/month/day order, with a full 4-digit year and no punctuation. For example, March 18, 1992 would become 19920318. If you prefer a different style for dates, such as the familiar American (*mm/dd/yy*) format or the character string "March 18, 1992", you can define a calculated field that uses one of the date conversion functions—DTOC (date-to-character) or MDY (month-day-year)—to convert the date to a character string in the desired format.

dBASE IV exports logical fields as the single characters "Y" (for .T.) and "N" (for .F.), but you can use the IIF function to transform a logical field to a more descriptive character string. For example, you could use the following expression to define a calculated field that converts the logical value CREDITOK to the string "Yes" or "No":

```
IIF(CREDITOK, "Yes", "No")
```

When you append data from an external file, you can use analogous techniques, also based on intermediary files—you can read the data into a data base file that matches the structure of the external file, add or delete fields so that the structure of this data base matches the eventual structure you want to obtain, and fill in any new fields with an update query or a REPLACE command.

For example, when you append data from a text file, dBASE IV recognizes dates only if they are in the same *yyyymmdd* format that it uses when it exports dates. If a date field in the text file you need to import is not in this format, you must read the date into a character field in an intermediary data base. This data base should also contain a true date field, placed, along with any other fields not present in the external file, *after* all the fields that directly correspond to fields in the text file. Next, you can use any of the techniques covered in Chapter 18 to set the dBASE IV date display format to match the appearance of the character string read in from the external file, import the data, and replace the true date field with the contents of the character field.

For example, suppose you needed to import dates stored in the format *mm-dd-yyyy* (03-18-1992 for March 18, 1992). After reading the date into a character field 10 characters long, you could turn the CENTURY setting ON to configure dBASE IV to express dates using 4-digit years and select USA as the date display format. Finally, use an update query or a REPLACE command to replace the true date field with the result of applying the CTOD (character-to-date) function to the character field.

When you import a text file, dBASE IV correctly interprets the single letters "Y" and "N" as logical values when you read them into a logical field. If the data in the text file was entered in some other format, such as "Yes" or "No" or as "1" or "0", you could import this data into a character field, add a new logical field to the structure, and replace the value of this field with .T. or .F. with an expression like the following (which assumes the character field is called YESNO):

```
IIF(YESNO = "Yes", .T., .F.)
```

IMPORTING AND EXPORTING TEXT FILES

Two of the standard text file formats—delimited and SDF—can be used to exchange data with a wide variety of programs, including those running on microcomputers that are incompatible with the IBM PC and on mini- and mainframe computers. In some cases, you can use one of these formats as a transfer medium between two programs when neither can directly read a data format that the other can produce. Because of their widespread use, these formats merit special attention, even if using them does not always represent the easiest or most direct way to exchange data with other software.

Using the Delimited Text File Format

A *delimited* file is an ASCII text file in which the fields are separated by commas, and character fields are surrounded (delimited) by punctuation marks. Although the standard delimiter is the double quotation mark ("), you can specify a different one. Because a carriage return ends every record, each record appears to begin on a new line on the screen when you use the dBASE IV or DOS TYPE command to display the contents of a delimited file.

You can read a delimited file into an existing Lotus 1-2-3 worksheet using the /File Import Numbers command sequence (or a similar command sequence with other spreadsheet programs). Many word processing programs that have mailmerge capabilities—such as WordStar and Microsoft Word—can read this format directly and combine the data base fields with fixed text to produce forms such as personalized letters. Some programs, including WordPerfect, which store their mailmerge files in a different format and cannot read delimited files directly, provide a utility program that can convert these files to their own proprietary formats.

Figure 20-1 illustrates the delimited file produced by the following command sequence, which copies selected fields from the National Widgets Customer File for customers who own IBM equipment:

```
USE NWCUST ORDER ACCOUNT
COPY TO NWIBM1 TYPE DELIMITED FIELDS ACCOUNT, COMPANY, ADDRESS, CITY, STATE,
   ZIP, CREDITOK, LASTORDER, TOTORDERS FOR "IBM" $ EQUIPMENT
```

A delimited file does not contain field names or any other explicit description of the file structure. Programs that read and write delimited files identify the fields by counting commas from the beginning of the record. Field 1 consists of all the characters up to the first comma, Field 2 all the characters between the first and second commas, and so on. The quotes surrounding character fields, which are not interpreted as part of the data, are necessary to distinguish embedded commas (as in "J. Thomas Johnson, CPA") from those used as field separators. Similarly, if a field is left blank, the comma that would normally follow the field remains as a place holder so that the next field is not mistaken for the missing item.

```
"Gina Aronoff","","601 First Street","Benicia","CA","94510",Y,19911214,1232.50
"Barbara Goddard","Ellis Manufacturing","832 130th N.E.","Bellevue","WA","98005",N,19920216,669.58
"Lisa Burns","The Image Makers","1900 Powell Street","Emeryville","CA","94608",Y,19871112,389.50
"Carolyn Sumner","J. Thomas Johnson, CPA","50 California Street","San Francisco","CA","94111",Y,19911206,368.42
"Richard Kelly","Kelly and Sons Furniture","14800 Bancroft Avenue","San Leandro","CA","94578",F,19920123,87.35
"Judy Barnes","Carol Klein, M.D.","1849 S.E. 40th Avenue","Portland","OR","97214",Y,19911228,1053.00
"Joan Mills","Lewis and Associates","460 Grand Avenue","Oakland","CA","94610",Y,19920120,3482.48
"Kathy McDonald","RapidType Secretarial Svc","2457 Union Street","San Francisco","CA","94123",Y,19920310,348.52
```

Figure 20-1.

A delimited file

If your data includes embedded quotation marks, or if the program with which you need to exchange data requires a different delimiter, you can override the default and specify your own delimiter character. When you choose the **Export** option from the Control Center **Tools** menu or the **Copy records from non-dBASE file** option from the data base design screen **Append** menu, dBASE IV displays a pick list of the 256 ASCII characters and allows you to choose one to use as the delimiter. The default (the double quote character) is highlighted initially, and you can press ENTER to retain this default. From the dot prompt, you must specify the delimiter in a COPY or APPEND command. For example, you could use the following command to read data into the National Widgets Customer File from a delimited file called CUSTOMER.TXT in which character fields are surrounded by slashes:

```
USE NWCUST
APPEND FROM CUSTOMER TYPE DELIMITED WITH /
```

Regardless of the delimiter, dBASE IV always separates fields with commas. You can eliminate both the delimiters and the field separators (the commas), and instead insert a single blank space between fields, by substituting the keyword BLANK for the delimiter as in the following:

```
USE NWCUST
COPY TO NWLETTER TYPE DELIMITED WITH BLANK
```

This format is most useful for copying numeric data. Many statistics and numerical analysis programs, including those that run on mainframes and minicomputers, can accept data in this format. It is generally inappropriate for character fields, however, since any blank spaces within a field would be interpreted as field separators.

When you append data from a delimited file into a data base, dBASE IV transfers fields from the text file one by one into the corresponding data base fields—all characters up to the first comma go into the first data base field, the characters between the first and second commas go into the second field, and so on. If the delimited file contains extra fields, the contents of these fields are lost; if the file contains fewer fields, the extra fields in the new data base records are left blank. Items in the delimited file that are shorter than the matching dBASE IV field width are padded with blank spaces; if any fields are too long, character data is truncated to fit, and numeric fields are replaced by asterisks to indicate a numeric overflow.

Using the Fixed-Length Text (SDF) File Format

A *fixed-length* text file is an ASCII text file in which each field occupies a fixed number of characters; each record is also therefore a fixed length. This format is referred to in the dBASE IV *Language Reference* manual as SDF, which is an acronym for System Data Format, a term used only by Ashton-Tate to describe this format. In a fixed-length file (as in the DBF file itself), there are no field separators or delimiters—each field is identified by its starting position in the record. If the entry in a field requires less than the full field width, it is padded with blank spaces. (Character fields are usually left-justified within the field width, while numeric fields are right-justified.) As in the delimited format, each record ends with a hard return.

Fixed-length files can be read by some word processors, including Microsoft Word, and they are used by many accounting programs and other data bases. Most data downloaded from mainframe data bases and online information utilities is in fixed-length format (although many mainframe files do not include the hard return that dBASE IV requires at the end of every record). Figure 20-2 illustrates the SDF file produced by a COPY command similar to the one used to illustrate the delimited file format:

```
USE NWCUST ORDER ACCOUNT
COPY TO NWIBM2 TYPE SDF FIELDS ACCOUNT, COMPANY, ADDRESS, CITY, STATE,
   ZIP, CREDITOK, LASTORDER, TOTORDERS FOR "IBM" $ EQUIPMENT
```

Because dBASE IV identifies fields in an SDF file by their positions in the record, the sequence and lengths of the fields common to both files must be identical when you append an SDF file into a dBASE IV data base. If the

```
Gina Aronoff                                601 First Street    Benicia        CA94510   Y19911214   1232.50
Barbara Goddard     Ellis Manufacturing     832 130th N.E.      Bellevue       WA98005   N19920216    669.58
Lisa Burns          The Image Makers        1900 Powell Street  Emeryville     CA94608   Y19871112    389.50
Carolyn Sumner      J. Thomas Johnson, CPA  50 California Street San Francisco CA94111   Y19911206    368.42
Richard Kelly       Kelly and Sons Furniture 14800 Bancroft Avenue San Leandro CA94578   F19920123     87.35
Judy Barnes         Carol Klein, M.D.       1849 S.E. 40th Avenue Portland     OR97214   Y19911228   1053.00
Joan Mills          Lewis and Associates    460 Grand Avenue    Oakland        CA94610   Y19920120   3482.48
Kathy McDonald      RapidType Secretarial Svc 2457 Union Street San Francisco  CA94123   Y19920310    348.52
```

Figure 20-2.

A fixed-length (SDF) file

fixed-length record is longer than the data base record, the extra data in the fixed-length file is lost; if the data base record is longer, the extra fields remain blank.

EXCHANGING DATA WITH SPREADSHEETS

Of the four formats intended for exchanging data with spreadsheets—DIF, SYLK, WKS, and WK1—only the two Lotus worksheet formats are in widespread use today. You can use the SYLK format (used in earlier versions of dBASE to exchange data with Microsoft's former Multiplan spreadsheet) to transfer data to Excel, but Excel can also read and write Lotus worksheet and dBASE III PLUS files (by the time this is published, it may support dBASE IV files as well). When you exchange data with a spreadsheet, each row in the spreadsheet corresponds to a record in the data base and each column corresponds to a field. If you are unfamiliar with spreadsheet software, you might think of the spreadsheet display as analogous to the Browse screen, with each record laid out horizontally and the fields lined up in columns.

When you export dBASE IV data to a Lotus WKS file, dBASE IV creates a new Lotus worksheet file with one record per row and each field in a separate column; it writes the field names into the first row of the spreadsheet as column headers. Memo fields are not converted, and logical fields are converted to labels ("Y" for .T. and "N" for .F.). In the new spreadsheet, all cells except those containing numeric fields are protected; if you enable protection for the spreadsheet, Lotus permits you to enter data only in columns derived from numeric fields. dBASE IV adjusts the column widths in the spreadsheet to match the field widths in the original data base, and you may want to widen columns to add spaces between adjacent data items or narrow them to fit more data on the screen. Figure 20-3 illustrates the Lotus spreadsheet generated from the National Widgets Inventory File.

If you want to add data from a dBASE IV file to a previously created worksheet, you can copy records to a delimited file instead of a WKS file and use the Lotus /File Import Numbers command sequence to read this file into the spreadsheet with the upper left corner of the imported data block at the cursor position. You could also export the data to a separate spreadsheet and read the data from this worksheet into another with the /File Combine command.

```
A1: [W6] 'CATEGORY                                                 READY

     A     B               C                D      E      F      G
1   CATEGOPARTNUDESCRIP                     VENDORCOST   PRICE
2   RIBBON270-11NEC 7700 Multistrike        NEC     3.20   5.45
3   RIBBON270-10NEC 7700 Cloth              NEC     3.20   5.45
4   RIBBON270-13NEC 3500 Cloth              NEC     5.50   9.95
5   RIBBON270-12NEC 3500 Multistrike        NEC     5.50   9.95
6   RIBBON240-51Epson FX-285, 286           EPSON   9.75  14.95
7   RIBBON250-30Okidata 80, 81, 82, 83      OKIDAT  1.50   2.95
8   RIBBON250-31Okidata 84, 94              OKIDAT  3.00   4.95
9   RIBBON240-50Epson MX-80, 85, FX-80,85EPSON      7.09  12.50
10  RIBBON240-52Epson EX-80, 100, Black     EPSON   3.60   5.95
11  RIBBON240-53Epson EX-80, 100, Color     EPSON   6.50  10.95
12  RIBBON260-20Apple Imagewriter II        APPLE   3.00   5.95
13  FORMS 803-2014-1/2 X 11" Green bar      MOORE  28.50  45.25
14  FORMS 803-2114-1/2 X 11" White          MOORE  24.00  42.50
15  FORMS 803-319-1/2 X 11" White           MOORE  24.50  37.50
16  FORMS 803-309-1/2 X 11" Green bar       MOORE  25.00  37.50
17  FORMS 820-203-1/2 x 1" Labels, 1-up     AVERY  14.50  21.95
18  FORMS 820-243-1/2 x 4" Labels, 4-up     AVERY  39.50  64.95
19  COVER 540-10Dust cover, Apple IIGS      COMCOV 16.50  24.95
20  COVER 540-11Dust cover, Mac Plus        COMCOV 18.50  29.95
10-Jan-91   11:48 AM                                          CAPS
```

Figure 20-3.

The spreadsheet created by exporting the Inventory File

When you append data from a Lotus spreadsheet, dBASE IV assumes that the data base begins in the upper left corner of the worksheet (cell A1), with no blank rows above the data and no blank columns to the left. If you use the IMPORT command or the **Import** menu option (rather than APPEND or the **Copy records from non-dBASE file** menu option), dBASE IV creates a data base with one field for each column that contains data. It uses the column letter designators—A, B, C, and so on—as field names, derives the field widths from the column widths in the spreadsheet, and assigns the character data type to all fields. When you use APPEND, dBASE IV transfers data from the spreadsheet into the data base, one column per field. If the spreadsheet has more columns than there are fields in the data base, the data in the extra spreadsheet columns is lost; if the data base has more fields, the ones lacking counterparts in the spreadsheet remain blank.

You can also convert dBASE IV data to Lotus spreadsheet format using the Lotus Translate utility, which offers some significant advantages. When dBASE IV creates a worksheet, it turns dates and logical fields into labels. You might not notice this at first because the "logical" columns display as "Y" and "N", and the labels derived from dates look just like the standard Lotus *dd-Mmm-yy* date display format. However, you cannot use the labels in formulas that depend on the spreadsheet's ability to carry out calcuations on true dates. The Lotus Translate utility converts dates to the Lotus storage form for dates ("date serial numbers"), and then assigns the standard display format. It converts logical fields to the functions @TRUE and @FALSE, which display as 1 and 0, respectively, and are treated as logical constants (just as .T. and .F. are in dBASE IV). Furthermore, it does not protect any cells in the converted worksheet.

Unfortunately, as of this writing, the Translate utility cannot read a dBASE IV data base file that includes memo fields. To use the Translate utility to import such a data base, you must first export the file to dBASE III PLUS format, either by using the COPY or EXPORT command or the **Export** menu option. Also note that dBASE IV cannot read the WK3 file format used by Lotus version 3. To import a version 3 spreadsheet, you must save the spreadsheet in WK1 format.

EXCHANGING DATA WITH PFS

Most of the special considerations that apply to reading and writing PFS:FILE (now called PFS Professional File) data bases are due to the different relationship between a data base and the custom screen used to update it in dBASE IV and PFS. In PFS, designing a screen form is an integral part of the data base definition process; accordingly, when you import a PFS file, dBASE IV automatically creates not only a dBASE IV data base structure but also a screen form file to draw an input screen that resembles the PFS screen layout.

If a screen form file is open when you export a data base to PFS, it determines both the structure of the PFS file and the screen layout used to update the data base in PFS. However, when you use the **Export** option on the Control Center **Tools** menu, you choose the data base from a pick list, and dBASE IV does not give you the opportunity to select a screen form. When you use the EXPORT command from the dot prompt, dBASE IV uses a form file (assuming one was opened with a previous SET FORMAT command) to determine which fields to copy to the PFS file and to design the PFS data entry screen. If no screen form is active, the PFS file will contain all the fields in the dBASE IV data base except the memo fields, and the screen layout will resemble the Edit screen. A PFS screen can contain only 21 rows; if all your existing dBASE IV screen forms use additional rows, you may need to edit one or create a new form.

If your data base contains a field that is unique, or nearly so, for each record—such as an ID code, an account number, or a part number—make sure that this is the first field on the screen, so that it becomes the first field in the PFS record. Unlike dBASE IV, PFS permits only one index for a data base file, always based on the first field. If the unique field does not come first in the dBASE IV file structure, you can either use a screen form file or a FIELDS clause in an EXPORT command from the dot prompt.

If you are unfamiliar with PFS, you should realize that this program imposes far less structure on its data than dBASE IV; it allows you to enter any type of data into any field and later treat the entry as either character or numeric when you define record selection criteria. You do not define field lengths explicitly—the data entry area for a field consists of all the space on the screen between the end of its prompt and the beginning of the next field.

When you import a PFS file into dBASE, all fields become character fields, and the width of each field is set to the number of spaces allocated for the field on the PFS entry screen (or 254 characters, whichever is fewer). In most cases, the resulting dBASE IV fields are much wider than necessary. Any data stored in PFS "Attachment Pages" is lost in the conversion; despite the similarity in purpose and use between Attachment Pages and memo fields, there is no way to transfer data between them, in either direction.

PFS does not require that you refer to fields by name, and the screen prompts may be much longer than the ten characters permitted for a dBASE IV field name. dBASE IV resolves this potential problem by assigning the names FIELD01, FIELD02, FIELD03, and so on, and using the PFS screen prompts in the matching screen form file. For any use except full-screen editing through the automatically generated custom screen, these "generic" field names are inconvenient. You can use MODIFY STRUCTURE to correct many of these problems without losing data. You can lengthen or shorten fields, rearrange the order of the fields, change data types, and even assign new field names, provided that you do not try to change field names when you make any other alterations in the structure.

If you do change field names to facilitate your work at the dot prompt, you can no longer use the screen form file created when you import the PFS file, because this form references fields by their original names (FIELD01, FIELD02, and so on). Furthermore, you cannot edit the screen form in the usual way, because dBASE IV generates only the FMT file—the dBASE IV program that is compiled and executed to draw the custom screen—and does not provide the SCR file that stores the image in a form accessible to the screen layout editor. Although the FMT file is an ASCII file that you can edit with a word processor or text editor, doing so requires more understanding of the commands it contains (@ . . . SAY . . . GET commands) than you are likely to possess at this stage in your experience with dBASE IV. You may prefer to abandon the format file and define a new one if necessary.

TRANSFERRING dBASE IV DATA TO WORD PROCESSING DOCUMENTS

The examples in this chapter illustrate ways to transfer data between dBASE IV and other applications that manipulate structured data. At times, you may want to create a text file that contains information derived from a dBASE IV data base but one that is treated as lines of text by another program such as a word processor. For example, you might want to incorporate dBASE IV data into a longer document produced using a word processor.

Chapter 13 described how to "print" a report or a set of labels to a disk file, which you can import into a word processing document. When you work at the dot prompt, you can export data displayed by commands such as LIST or DISPLAY by using an *alternate file,* an ASCII text file that records an exact duplicate of the data displayed on the screen. You open an alternate file with a SET command, as follows:

SET ALTERNATE TO *text file name*

Like other text files produced by dBASE IV, alternate files have the extension TXT, unless you explicitly override this default. To begin sending output to the text file, you type

```
SET ALTERNATE ON
```

To temporarily suspend recording in the alternate file, you use

```
SET ALTERNATE OFF
```

You can use SET ALTERNATE ON and SET ALTERNATE OFF as many times as needed during a work session to record output selectively. When you are finished, you close the file with

```
CLOSE ALTERNATE
```

Only *sequential* output—that is, output sent line by line to the output device, like the display produced by a LIST command—is copied to the alternate file; full-screen displays such as the Edit or Browse screens are not. If you want to copy to a text file the raw data in a dBASE IV data base file, without page titles or summary statistics, using an alternate file is often easier and faster than designing a report and printing the report to a disk file.

You can use an alternate file to capture the text stored in memo fields, which dBASE IV does not copy to the text files generated by the COPY and EXPORT commands. For example, the following command sequence creates an alternate file called NWCOMMNT, which contains the ACCOUNT and COMMENTS fields from the Customer File:

```
USE NWCUST ORDER ACCOUNT
SET ALTERNATE TO NWCOMMNT
SET ALTERNATE ON
LIST ACCOUNT, COMMENTS
CLOSE ALTERNATE
```

You can produce the same results by adding a TO FILE clause to the LIST command, as follows:

```
USE NWCUST ORDER ACCOUNT
LIST ACCOUNT, COMMENTS TO FILE NWCOMMNT
```

In this example, the two methods produce the same result. The advantage of the alternate file is that it can capture the output of more than one command, whereas each LIST TO FILE command creates a new output file on disk or overwrites an existing file with the same name.

You can also copy a single memo field to a text file with the COPY MEMO command. The syntax is as follows:

COPY MEMO *field name* TO *text file name*

By default, dBASE IV assigns the extension TXT to the text file that receives the output. To append text to an existing file rather than creating a new file, you add the keyword ADDITIVE to the COPY MEMO command. This command is ideal for exporting data from memo fields in separate records that you cannot describe by a single condition and thus cannot easily copy with a single LIST TO FILE command that includes a FOR clause.

SUMMARY

As you can see from the examples in this chapter, there are no hard and fast rules and few standard procedures for exchanging data between applications. To effect a particular data transfer, you may have to use a combination of methods presented in this chapter as well as others that are impossible to predict in advance. The existence of several data exchange formats helps, but in all but the most straightforward cases, you will need to experiment to determine the exact sequence of steps that yields the results you want.

In some cases, it may be easier to carry out the required changes in the external program, rather than in dBASE IV, especially if you (or your colleagues who need to use the data) are more familiar with that software. For example, you might prefer to copy an entire data base to a Lotus spreadsheet and rearrange the order, widths, and display formats of the columns within 1-2-3, rather than using a temporary dBASE IV data base file. Your best strategy when you approach a file format conversion problem is to learn as much as you can about all the standard data formats that can be read and created by dBASE IV and by your other application software so you can choose the optimal combination of transfer formats and conversion steps.

SET COMMANDS

SET PRINTER TO
[<*DOS device name*>/
FILE <*file name*>/
\\SPOOLER /\\CAPTURE]

SET PRINTER TO
\\<*computer name*>\<*printer name*>
= <*DOS device name*>

SET REFRESH TO <*number*>

SET RELATION TO
[<*key expression*>/<*expN*>
INTO <*alias*> [, <*key expression*>/
<*expN*> INTO <*alias*>] . . .]

SET REPROCESS TO <*number*>

SET SAFETY ON/off

SET SCOREBOARD ON/off

SET SEPARATOR TO <*character*>

SET SKIP TO [<*alias*> [, <*alias*>] . . .]

SET SPACE ON/off

SET SQL on/OFF

SET STATUS on/OFF

SET TALK ON/off

SET TITLE ON/off

SET TYPEAHEAD TO <*expN*>

SET UNIQUE on/OFF

SET VIEW TO <*query file name*>

SET WINDOW OF MEMO TO
<*window name*>

FUNCTIONS

&<*character variable*>
Value of named variable

ABS(<*expN*>)
Absolute value of *expN* (numeric)

ACCESS()
Access level of current user (numeric)

ACOS(<*expN*>)
Angle whose cosine is *expN* (number, radians)

ALIAS(<*work area*>)
Alias of data base open in *work area* (numeric)

ASC(<*expC*>)
Decimal ASCII code of first character in *expC* (numeric)

ASIN(<*expN*>)
Angle whose sine is *expN* (number, radians)

AT(<*expC1*>, <*expC2*>)
Starting position of *expC1* in *expC2* (numeric)

ATAN(<*expN*>)
Angle whose tangent is *expN* (number, radians)

ATN2(<*expN1*>, <*expN2*>)
Angle whose sine is *expN* (number, radians)

BAR()
Last selected bar from pop-up menu (numeric)

BOF([<*work area*>])
Is record pointer at beginning-of-file? (logical)

CALL(<*expC*> [, <*exp1*>/<*var1*>
[, <*exp2*>/<*var2*>]]. . .)
Expression computed by binary program

CDOW(<*expD*>)
Name of day of week (character)

CEILING(<*expN*>)
Smallest integer greater than or equal to *expN* (numeric)

CERROR()
Error number of last compiler error (numeric)

CHANGE()
Was current record changed by another user? (logical)

CHR(<*expN*>)
Character with ASCII code *expN* (character)

CMONTH(<*expD*>)
Name of month (character)

COL()
Current cursor column position (numeric)

COMPLETED()
Was transaction completed normally? (logical)

COS(<*expN*>)
Cosine of angle *expN* (numeric)

CTOD(<*expC*>)
Date that matches *expC* (date)

DATE()
System date (date)

DAY(<*expD*>)
Day of month (numeric)

DBF([<*work area*>])
Name of the data base open *work area* (character)

DELETED([<*work area*>])
Is current record marked for deletion? (logical)

DIFFERENCE(<*expC1*>, <*expC2*>)
Difference in Soundex codes between *expC1* and *expC2* (character)

DISKSPACE()
Free space on current drive (numeric)

DMY(<*expD*>)
Date in *dd Month yy* or *dd Month yyyy* format (character)

DOW(<*expD*>)
Day of week (numeric)

DTOC(<*expD*>)
Character string representation of *expD* (date)

DTOR(<*expN*>)
Angle in radians equivalent to *expN* degrees (numeric)

DTOS(<*expD*>)
Character string representation of *expD* in *yyyymmdd* format (character)

EOF([<*work area*>])
Is record pointer at end-of-file? (logical)

ERROR()
Error number of last execution error (numeric)

EXP(<*expN*>)
Result of raising *e* to the power *expN* (numeric)

FIELD(<*expN*> [, <*work area*>])
Name of field *expN* (character)

FILE(<*expC*>)
Is file *expC* present on disk? (logical)

FIXED(<*expN*>)
Fixed-point number equivalent to floating point number *expN* (numeric)

FKLABEL(<*expN*>)
Name of function key *expN* (character)

FKMAX()
Number of programmable function keys *expN* (numeric)

FLOAT <*expN*>
Floating-point number equivalent to the fixed point number *expN* (numeric)

FLOCK([<*work area*>])
Can file in *work area* be locked? (logical)

FLOOR(<*expN*>)
Largest integer smaller than or equal to *expN* (numeric)

FOUND(<*work area*>)
Was record found by index key search or LOCATE? (logical)

COMMANDS

PROTECT
QUIT
RECALL [<*scope*>] [FOR <*condition*>] [WHILE <*condition*>]
REINDEX
RELEASE [ALL [LIKE/EXCEPT <*skeleton*>]]/[<*memvar list*>]
RENAME <*old file name*> TO <*new file name*>
REPLACE [<*scope*>] [FOR <*condition*>] [WHILE <*condition*>] <*field1*> WITH <*exp1*> [ADDITIVE] [, <*field2*> WITH <*exp2*> ...]
REPORT FORM <*report form file*> [<*scope*>] [FOR <*condition*>] [WHILE <*condition*>] [TO PRINTER/ TO FILE <*file name*>] [NOEJECT] [PLAIN] [SUMMARY] [HEADING <*expC*>]
RESTORE FROM <*file name*> [ADDITIVE]
RESTORE MACROS FROM <*macro file*>
RESUME
ROLLBACK [<*data base name*>]
RUN/! <*DOS command*>
SAVE TO <*file name*> [ALL LIKE/EXCEPT <*skeleton*>]
SAVE MACROS TO <*macro file*>
SEEK <*exp*>
SELECT <*work area*>
SET
SKIP [<*expN*>] [IN <*work area*>]
SORT TO <*new file name*> ON <*field1*> [/A]/[/D] [/C] [, <*field2*> [/A]/[/D] [/C]...] [ASCENDING]/ [DESCENDING] [<*scope*>] [FOR <*condition*>] [WHILE <*condition*>]
STORE <*exp*> TO <*memvar list*>/ <*array element list*> <*memvar*>/ <*array element*> = <*exp*>
SUM [<*expN list*>] [TO <*memvarlist*>/ TO ARRAY <*array name*>] [<*scope*>] [FOR <*condition*>] [WHILE <*condition*>]
TOTAL ON <*key field*> TO <*file name*> [FIELDS <*field list*>] [<*scope*>] [FOR <*condition*>] [WHILE <*condition*>]
TYPE <*file name*> [TO PRINTER/TO FILE <*file name*>] [NUMBER]
UNLOCK [ALL/IN <*work area*>]
UPDATE ON <*key field*> FROM <*alias*> REPLACE <*field1*> WITH <*exp1*> [, <*field2*> WITH <*exp2*> ...] [RANDOM]
USE [<*file name*>] [IN <*work area*>] [[INDEX <*MDX and NDX index file list*>] [ORDER [TAG] <*NDX index*>/ <*MDX index tag*> [OF <*MDX file name*>]]] [ALIAS <*alias*>] [EXCLUSIVE] [NOUPDATE] [AGAIN]
ZAP

SET COMMANDS

SET ALTERNATE on/OFF
SET ALTERNATE TO [<*file name*>] [ADDITIVE]
SET AUTOSAVE on/OFF
SET BELL ON/off
SET BELL TO <*frequency*>, <*duration*>
SET BLOCKSIZE TO <*number*>
SET CARRY on/OFF
SET CARRY TO [<*field list*> [ADDITIVE]]
SET CATALOG on/OFF
SET CATALOG TO [<*catalog file name*>]
SET CENTURY on/OFF
SET CLOCK on/OFF
SET CLOCK TO [<*row*>, <*column*>]
SET COLOR ON/OFF
SET COLOR TO [<*standard foreground/background*>] [, <*enhanced foreground/ background*>] [, <*border*>]
SET COLOR OF NORMAL/ MESSAGES/TITLES/BOX/HIGHLIGHT/ INFORMATION/FIELDS TO [<*foreground/background*>] [, <*foreground/background*>]
SET CONFIRM on/OFF
SET CURRENCY TO [<*expC*>]
SET CURRENCY LEFT/right
SET DATE [TO] AMERICAN/ansi/ british/french/german/italian/japan/ usa/mdy/dmy/ymd
SET DECIMALS TO <*expN*>
SET DEFAULT TO <*drive*>[:]
SET DELETED on/OFF
SET DELIMITERS on/OFF
SET DELIMITERS TO [<*delimiter(s)*>]/[DEFAULT]
SET DEVELOPMENT ON/off
SET DISPLAY TO MONO/COLOR/ EGA25/EGA43/MONO43
SET ECHO on/OFF
SET ENCRYPTION ON/off
SET ESCAPE ON/off
SET EXACT on/OFF
SET EXCLUSIVE on/OFF
SET FIELDS on/OFF
SET FIELDS TO [<*field list*>]
SET FIELDS TO ALL [LIKE/EXCEPT <*skeleton*>]
SET FILTER TO [<*condition*>]
SET FORMAT TO [<*screen form file name*>]
SET FUNCTION <*key name*>/ <*key number*> TO <*expC*>
SET HEADING ON/off
SET HELP ON/off
SET HISTORY ON/off
SET HISTORY TO <*expN*>
SET HOURS TO 12/24
SET INDEX TO [<*index file list*> [ORDER [TAG] <*NDX index name*>/ <*MDX index tag name*> [OF <*MDX index file name*>]]]
SET INSTRUCT ON/off
SET INTENSITY ON/off
SET LOCK ON/off
SET MARGIN TO <*expN*>
SET MARK TO [<*character*>]
SET MEMOWIDTH TO <*expN*>
SET NEAR on/OFF
SET ODOMETER TO [<*expN*>]
SET ORDER TO [<*expN*>/ [TAG] <*index name*> [OF <*MDX index file name*>]]
SET PATH TO [<*path name list*>]
SET PAUSE on/OFF
SET POINT TO [<*character*>]
SET PRECISION TO [<*expN*>]

COMMANDS

BROWSE [FIELDS <field1> [/R] [/ <column width>]/
<calculated field name 1> = <exp1>
[, <field2> ...] ...] [NOINIT] [NOFOLLOW]
[NOAPPEND] [NOMENU] [NOEDIT]
[NODELETE] [NOCLEAR]
[COMPRESS] [FORMAT]
[LOCK <expN>] [WIDTH <expN>]
[FREEZE <field>]
[WINDOW <window name>]

CALCULATE [<exp list>]
[TO <memvar list>/ARRAY <array name>]
[<scope>] [FOR <condition>]
[WHILE <condition>]

CHANGE [FIELDS <field list>]
[<record number>] [<scope>]
[FOR <condition>]
[WHILE <condition>] [NOINIT] [NOFOLLOW]
[NOAPPEND] [NOMENU]
[NODELETE] [NOCLEAR]

CLEAR

CLEAR ALL/FIELDS/GETS/MEMORY/
MENUS/POPUPS/SCREENS/
TYPEAHEAD/WINDOWS

CLOSE ALL/ALTERNATE/DATABASES/
FORMAT/INDEXES/PROCEDURE

COMPILE <program name>
[RUNTIME]

CONTINUE

COPY TO <file name> [TYPE DBASEII/
DBMEMO3/DIF/FW2/RPD/SDF/SYLK
/WKS/DELIMITED [WITH
<delimiter>/BLANK]]
[[WITH] PRODUCTION] [FIELDS <field list>]
[<scope>] [FOR <condition>]
[WHILE <condition>]

COPY FILE <file1> TO <file2>

COPY INDEXES <NDX index file list>
[TO <MDX file name>]

COPY STRUCTURE TO <file name>
[[WITH] PRODUCTION]
[FIELDS <field list>]

COPY TO <file name> STRUCTURE
EXTENDED

COPY MEMO <memo field>
TO <file name> [ADDITIVE]

COPY TAG <tag name>
[OF <MDX file>] TO <NDX file>

COUNT [TO <memvar>] [<scope>]
[FOR <condition>]
[WHILE <condition>]

CREATE <data base name>

CREATE <data base name> FROM
<structure-extended file>

CREATE/MODIFY APPLICATION
<application file name>

CREATE/MODIFY LABEL
<label form name>

CREATE/MODIFY QUERY/VIEW
<query file name>

CREATE/MODIFY REPORT
<report form name>

CREATE/MODIFY SCREEN
<screen form name>

CREATE VIEW <view file name>
FROM ENVIRONMENT

DELETE [<scope>] [FOR <condition>]
[WHILE <condition>]

DELETE FILE <file name>

DELETE TAG <tag1>
[OF <MDX index file>/<NDX index file>]
[, <tag2> ...]

DIRECTORY/DIR [[ON] <drive>:] [[LIKE]
[<path>\] [<skeleton>]]

DISPLAY [<exp list>]
[FOR<condition>] [WHILE <condition>]
[<scope>] [OFF] [TO PRINTER/
TO FILE <file name>]

DISPLAY FILES [LIKE <skeleton>]
[TO PRINTER/TO FILE <file name>]

DISPLAY HISTORY [LAST <expN>]
[TO PRINTER/TO FILE <file name>]

DISPLAY MEMORY [TO PRINTER/
TO FILE <file name>]

DISPLAY STATUS [TO PRINTER/
TO FILE <file name>]

DISPLAY STRUCTURE
[IN <work area>]
[TO PRINTER/TO FILE <file name>]

DISPLAY USERS

DO <program name>/<procedure name>
[WITH <parameter list>]

EDIT [FIELDS <field list>]
[<record number>] [<scope>]
[FOR <condition>]
[WHILE <condition>] [NOINIT] [NOFOLLOW]
[NOAPPEND] [NOMENU]
[NODELETE] [NOCLEAR]

ERASE <file name>

EXPORT TO <file name> [TYPE] PFS/
DBASEII/FW2/RPD [FIELDS <field list>]
[<scope>] [FOR <condition>]
[WHILE <condition>]

FIND <character string>/<n>

GO/GOTO <expN>/BOTTOM/TOP
[IN <work area>]

HELP [<keyword>]

IMPORT FROM <file name> [TYPE]
PFS/DBASEII/FW2/RPD/WK1

INDEX ON <key expression>
TO <NDX file name>/
TAG <MDX index tag name> [OF <MDX file name>]
[UNIQUE] [DESCENDING]
[FOR <condition>]

INSERT [BEFORE]

JOIN WITH <alias> TO <file name>
FOR <condition> [FIELDS <field list>]

KEYBOARD <expC> [CLEAR]

LABEL FORM <label form file>
[<scope>] [FOR <condition>]
[WHILE <condition>]
[TO PRINTER/TO FILE <file name>]
[SAMPLE]

LIST [<exp list>] [<scope>]
[FOR <condition>] [WHILE <condition>]
[OFF] [TO PRINTER/
TO FILE <file name>]

LIST FILES [LIKE <skeleton>]
[TO PRINTER/TO FILE <file name>]

LIST HISTORY [LAST <expN>]
[TO PRINTER/TO FILE <file name>]

LIST MEMORY
[TO PRINTER/TO FILE <file name>]

LIST STATUS
[TO PRINTER/TO FILE <file name>]

LIST STRUCTURE [IN <work area>]
[TO PRINTER/TO FILE <file name>]

LIST USERS

LOCATE [<scope>] [FOR <condition>]
[WHILE <condition>]

LOGOUT

MODIFY APPLICATION
<application file name>

MODIFY COMMAND [<file name>]
[WINDOW <window name>]

MODIFY FILE [<file name>]
[WINDOW <window name>]

MODIFY LABEL <label form name>

MODIFY QUERY/VIEW
<query file name>

MODIFY REPORT <report form name>

MODIFY SCREEN <screen form name>

MODIFY STRUCTURE

PACK

PLAY MACRO <macro name>

CURSOR MOVEMENT AND COMMAND KEYS

Control Key	Command Key	Function
	ALT-*letter*	Activate menu system and pull down menu whose description begins with *letter*
	ENTER	Select highlighted option or item from active menu, panel, or pick list
CTRL-W	CTRL-END	Save changes and exit
CTRL-Q	ESC	Exit without saving changes
CTRL-E	UP ARROW	Move up one screen line
CTRL-X	DOWN ARROW or ENTER	Move down one screen line
CTRL-D	RIGHT ARROW	Move right one character or menu option
CTRL-S	LEFT ARROW	Move left one character or menu option
CTRL-I	TAB	Move to next field or column; in word wrap mode, move to next tab stop (Typeover mode) or insert a tab (Insert mode) or move left margin to next tab stop (Automatic indent enabled)
	SHIFT-TAB	Move to previous field or column; in word wrap mode, move to previous tab stop or move left margin to previous tab stop (Automatic indent enabled)
CTRL-F	CTRL-RIGHT ARROW	Move right one word or field
CTRL-A	CTRL-LEFT ARROW	Move left one word or field
CTRL-Z	HOME	Move to beginning of field (Edit), first field or column, or beginning of line
CTRL-B	END	Move to end of field (Edit), last field or column, or end of line
CTRL-C	PGDN	Display next screenful of data
CTRL-R	PGUP	Display previous screenful of data
	CTRL-PGDN	Move to bottom of file, work surface, or text
	CTRL-PGUP	Move to top of file, work surface, or text
CTRL-G	DEL	Delete character at cursor position or selected item
	BACKSPACE	Delete character to left of cursor
	CTRL-BACKSPACE	Delete word to left of cursor
CTRL-T		Delete characters from cursor to end of word
CTRL-Y		Delete characters from cursor to end of line, or entire line
CTRL-U		Mark record for deletion or clear deletion marker
CTRL-V	INS	Turn insert mode on (if off) or off (if on)
CTRL-N	ENTER	Insert a new line (Insert mode)
	CTRL-HOME	Invoke memo field editor (Browse and Edit)

FUNCTION KEYS

Key	Key Name	Meaning
F1	Help	Access online help system
F2	Data	Display Edit or Browse screen
F3	Previous	Move to previous item
F4	Next	Move to next item
F5	Field	Add or remove a field from a work surface
F6	Select	Mark a block of items
F7	Move	Move selected items
F8	Copy	Copy selected items
F9	Zoom	Expand or contract data entry or display area
F10	Menu	Activate menu system
SHIFT-F1	Pick	Display a pick list
SHIFT-F2	Design	Transfer to a design screen or layout editor
SHIFT-F3	Find Previous	Search backward for same string of characters
SHIFT-F4	Find Next	Search forward for same string of characters
SHIFT-F5	Find	Search for a string of characters
SHIFT-F6	Replace	Replace one string of characters with another
SHIFT-F7	Size	Change size of selected item
SHIFT-F8	Ditto	Copy data into current field from same field in previous record
SHIFT-F9	Quick Report	Print a Quick Report based on current data base or view
SHIFT-F10	Macro	Record a keystroke macro

COMMANDS

?/?? [<*exp1*> [PICTURE <*expC*>] [FUNCTION <*functions*>]
  [AT <*expN*>] [STYLE <*font number*>]] [, <*exp2*> . . .] . . .
??? [<*expC*>]
APPEND
APPEND FROM <*file name*> [TYPE DBASEII/DIF/FW2/RPD/
  SDF/SYLK/WKS/DELIMITED [WITH <*delimiter*>/BLANK]]
  [FOR <*condition*>]
APPEND MEMO <*memo field*> FROM <*file name*> [OVERWRITE]
ASSIST
AVERAGE [<*expN list*>] [TO <*memvar list*>/ARRAY <*array name*>]
  [<*scope*>] [FOR <*condition*>] [WHILE <*condition*>]
BEGIN TRANSACTION [<*path name*>] . . . END TRANSACTION

NO POSTAGE
NECESSARY
IF MAILED
IN THE
UNITED STATES

BUSINESS REPLY MAIL

First Class Permit NO. 3111 Berkeley, CA

Postage will be paid by addressee

Osborne **McGraw-Hill**
2600 Tenth Street
Berkeley, California 94710–9938

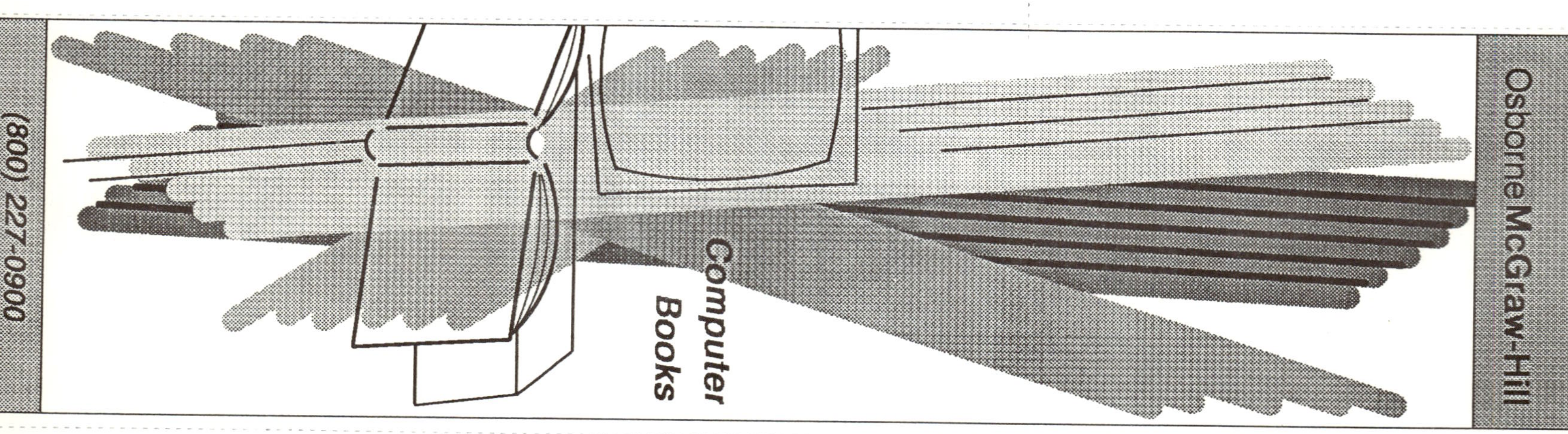

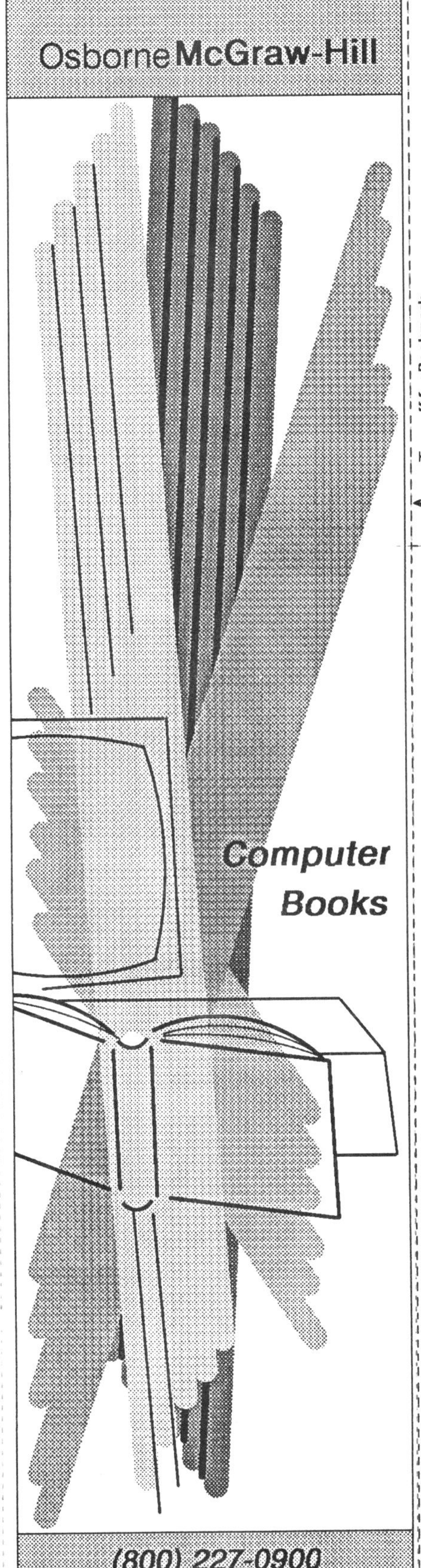

Tear off for Bookmark

▼ *You're important to us...*

We'd like to know what you're interested in, what kinds of books you're looking for, and what you thought about this book in particular.

Please fill out the attached card and mail it in. We'll do our best to keep you informed about Osborne's newest books and special offers.

YES, SEND ME A FREE COLOR CATALOG
of all Osborne/McGraw-Hill computer books.

Name:______________________ Title:______________

Company:____________________________________

Address:____________________________________

City:______________ State:__________ Zip:__________

I'M PARTICULARLY INTERESTED IN THE FOLLOWING *(Check all that apply)*

I use this software:
❒ Lotus 1-2-3
❒ Quattro
❒ dBASE
❒ WordPerfect
❒ Microsoft Word
❒ WordStar
❒ Others______________

I use this operating system:
❒ DOS
❒ OS/2
❒ UNIX
❒ Macintosh
❒ Others______________

I rate this book:
❒ Excellent ❒ Good ❒ Poor

I program in:
❒ C
❒ PASCAL
❒ BASIC
❒ Others______________

I chose this book because...
❒ Recognized author's name
❒ Osborne/McGraw-Hill's reputation
❒ Read book review
❒ Read Osborne catalog
❒ Saw advertisement in __________
❒ Found while browsing in store
❒ Found/recommended in library
❒ Required textbook
❒ Price
❒ Other______________

Comments____________________________________

____

Topics I would like to see covered in future books by Osborne/McGraw-Hill include:____________________________________

____

Print ISBN from the back cover here: 0-07-881_ _ _ - _

FUNCTIONS

REPLICATE(<*expC*>, <*expN*>)
ExpC repeated *expN* times (character)

RIGHT(<*expC*>, <*expN*>)
Rightmost *expN* characters of *expC* (character)

RLOCK([<*expN list*>] [, <*work area*>]) or LOCK( )
Can record be locked? (logical)

ROLLBACK( )
Did ROLLBACK command succeed in restoring data bases? (logical)

ROUND(<*expN1*>, <*expN2*>)
Result of rounding off *expN1* to *expN2* decimal places (numeric)

ROW( )
Current cursor row position (number)

RTOD(<*expN*>)
Number of degrees equivalent to *expN* radians (numeric)

RTRIM(<*expC*>)
ExpC with trailing blanks removed (character)

SEEK(<*exp*> [, <*expC*>])
Did an index key search or SEEK find a record? (logical)

SELECT( )
Highest numbered available work area (numeric)

SET(<*expC*>)
Status of SET option (character)

SIGN(<*expN*>)
1 if *expN* is positive, −1 if negative, or 0 if 0

SIN(<*expN*>)
Sine of the angle *expN* (numeric)

SOUNDEX(<*expC*>)
Soundex code for *expC* (character)

SPACE(<*expN*>)
String of *expN* blank spaces

SQRT(<*expN*>)
Square root of *expN* (numeric)

STR(<*expN1*> [, <*expN2*>] [, <*expN3*>])
Character string representation of *expN1*, *expN2* characters long, with *expN3* decimal places

STUFF(<*expC1*>, <*expN1*>, <*expN2*>, <*expC2*>)
Result of replacing *expN2* characters in *expC1*, starting at position *expN1*, with *expC2*

SUBSTR(<*expC*>, <*expN1*> [, <*expN2*>])
ExpN2 characters from *expC*, starting at position *expN1* (character)

TAG([<*MDX index file*>,] <*expN*> [, <*work area*>])
Name of index tag (character)

TAN(<*expN*>)
Tangent of angle *expN* (numeric)

TIME( )
Current system time (character)

TRANSFORM(<*exp*>, <*expC*>)
Result of formatting *exp* with picture function and/or template in <*expC*>

TRIM(<*expC*>)
ExpC with trailing blanks removed (character)

TYPE(<*expC*>)
Data type of expression *expC*

UPPER(<*expC*>)
Result of converting *expC* to all uppercase (character)

USER( )
Network login name of current user (character)

VAL(<*expC*>)
Number that matches character string *expC* (numeric)

VARREAD( )
Name of the variable collected by current @ . . . GET (character)

VERSION( )
Name of current dBASE IV version (character)

WINDOW( )
Name of active window

YEAR(<*date*>)
Four-digit year portion of date (numeric)

FUNCTIONS

FV(<*expN1*>, <*expN2*>, <*expN3*>)
Future value of investment with payment *expN1* at interest *expN2* for *expN3* payment periods (numeric)

GETENV(<*expC*>)
Operating system environment variable *expC* (character)

IIF(<*condition*>, <*exp1*>, <*exp2*>)
Exp1 if *condition* is .T., or *exp2* if *condition* is .F. (same data type as *exp1* and *exp2*)

INKEY([<*n*>])
Code for key pressed by user (numeric)

INT(<*expN*>)
Integer portion of *expN* (numeric)

ISALPHA(<*expC*>)
Is first character of *expC* alphabetic? (logical)

ISCOLOR()
Is a color display adapter present? (logical)

ISLOWER(<*expC*>)
Is first character of *expC* a lowercase letter? (logical)

ISMARKED([<*work area*>])
Is current record being updated in a transaction? (logical)

ISUPPER(<*expC*>)
Is first character of *expC* an uppercase letter? (logical)

KEY([<*MDX index file*>,] <*expN*> [, <*work area*>])
Index key expression of tag (character)

LASTKEY()
Code for last key pressed by user (numeric)

LEFT(<*expC*>, <*expN*>)
Leftmost *expN* characters of *expC* (character)

LEN(<*expC*>)
Length of *expC* (numeric)

LIKE(<*expC1*>, <*expC2*>)
Does value of *expC2* match pattern specified by *expC1*? (logical)

LINENO()
Line number of next program line to be executed (numeric)

LKSYS(<*expN*>)
Date, time, or user who placed last record or file lock (character)

LOCK([<*expN list*>] [, <*work area*>]) or RLOCK()
Can record be locked? (logical)

LOG(<*expN*>)
Natural (base *e*) logarithm of *expN* (numeric)

LOG10(<*expN*>)
Common (base 10) logarithm of *expN* (numeric)

LOOKUP(<*exp1*>, <*exp2*>, <*field name*>)
Result of evaluating *exp1* after looking up *exp2* in *field name*

LOWER(<*expC*>)
Result of converting *expC* to all lowercase (character)

LTRIM(<*expC*>)
ExpC with leading blanks removed (character)

LUPDATE([<*work area*>])
Date data base was last updated (date)

MAX(<*exp*>, <*exp*>)
Greater of the two input expressions (same data type as input expressions)

MDX(<*expN1*>/[, <*work area*>])
Name of MDX index file (character)

MDY(<*expD*>)
Date in *Month dd, yy* or *Month dd, yyyy* format (character)

MEMLINES(<*memo field name*>)
Number of lines in memo field (number)

MEMORY()
Amount of available RAM memory (number)

MENU()
Name of the last active bar menu (character)

MESSAGE()
Error message text of last execution error (number)

MIN(<*exp*>, <*exp*>)
Greater of the two input expressions (same data type as input expressions)

MLINE(<*memo field name*>, <*expN*>)
Line number *expN* from memo field (character)

MOD(<*expN1*>, <*expN2*>)
Remainder resulting from dividing *expN1* by *expN2* (numeric)

MONTH(<*expD*>)
Month portion of date (character)

NDX(<*expN*> [, <*work area*>])
Name of NDX index file (character)

NETWORK()
Is dBASE IV running on a network? (logical)

ORDER([<*work area*>])
Name of the master index tag or NDX index (character)

OS()
Name of current operating system (character)

PAD()
Name of last highlighted bar menu pad (character)

PAYMENT(<*expN1*>, <*expN2*>, <*expN3*>)
Periodic payment resulting from amortizing loan of *expN1* at interest rate *expN2* for *expN3* periods (numeric)

PCOL()
Current print head column position (number)

PI()
Value of pi (number)

POPUP()
Name of last active pop-up (character)

PRINTSTATUS()
Is printer turned on and ready to receive output? (logical)

PROGRAM()
Name of currently running procedure or program (character)

PROMPT()
Text displayed in last highlighted bar menu pad or pop-up bar (character)

PROW()
Current print head row position (numeric)

PV(<*expN1*>, <*expN2*>, <*expN3*>)
Present value of investment with payment *expN1* at interest *expN2* for *expN3* payment periods (numeric)

RAND([<*expN*>])
Random number between 0 and 1 (numeric)

READKEY()
Code of key user pressed to exit last READ (numeric)

RECCOUNT([<*work area*>])
Number of records in data base (numeric)

RECNO([<*work area*>])
Record number of current record (numeric)

RECSIZE([<*work area*>])
Record length of data base (numeric)

CHAPTER TWENTY-ONE

Writing Simple Programs

When you work with dBASE IV through the menu system or by typing commands at the dot prompt, you are using the program in an *interactive* mode: you select menu options or type commands one by one, and dBASE IV responds immediately by doing your bidding, displaying an error message and offering help, or prompting you for additional input such as a missing file name. The main advantages of the interactive mode are its flexibility and immediacy—you can execute commands as quickly as you can type them at the dot prompt or select the required menu options, and you can carry out varying ad hoc inquiries with little or no preparation.

The disadvantages of working in interactive mode will become apparent only after you have been using dBASE IV for a while. When an application has matured beyond the testing phase, and you have gone through several processing cycles without making major modifications in your procedures, it may seem as if you are repeatedly typing the same command sequences and that dBASE IV is taking longer and longer to do your bidding.

Some of this impatience stems from changes in your own frame of reference. As you grow more comfortable with data base concepts and with the

dBASE IV menu system and command syntax, devising procedures to carry out new tasks requires less effort, and repeating the same command sequences over and over seems more taxing. Because you may no longer clearly remember how long it took to perform the same operations manually, the computer might not seem as fast as it did the first time you accomplished in two minutes with a view query or a CALCULATE command what used to take two hours on a ten-key calculator. Other factors that contribute to your growing dissatisfaction with the computer's performance are more objective. As your files grow larger, operations that used to be virtually instantaneous may take minutes or even hours, and any process seems slower if you are sitting at the keyboard waiting for dBASE IV to finish executing a command so that you can issue the next one.

Chapter 18 introduced two ways to begin to overcome this frustration and automate some of your work with dBASE IV. By reprogramming function keys and defining keyboard macros, you can store multiple commands or menu navigation keystrokes such that you can repeat the same command sequences later by pressing just a few keys. This chapter explains how to further automate an application by combining commands into dBASE IV *programs.* In Chapter 22, you will learn how to use the dBASE IV applications generator to build a system of menus to link together the components of an application. You can call one of your own programs from a menu or batch process that you define, and you can do some programming entirely within the applications generator by *embedding* individual program statements in the application code generated by dBASE IV. Without having to learn many new commands or functions, you can use simple batch-type programs to automate frequently used procedures, and by doing so, you can realize substantial gains in processing efficiency and make better use of both human and computer time.

DO YOU REALLY WANT TO BECOME A PROGRAMMER?

The term "programming" has arcane and perhaps scary connotations for most people who view their computer hardware and software primarily as tools for getting a job done. At its simplest level, however, a program is nothing more than a set of instructions that directs the computer to carry out a series of operations in a specified order. In this sense, the macros and function key assignments explained in Chapter 18 are small programs, as are DOS *batch files,* such as the AUTOEXEC.BAT file that is executed every time you boot your

computer. If you have applied any of these techniques (in dBASE IV, DOS, or a spreadsheet or word processor with macro capabilities), you have already ventured into the world of programming.

The dBASE IV programming language is powerful and sophisticated enough that you can use it to develop complete menu-driven applications that look just like off-the-shelf packages written in languages such as COBOL, Pascal, or C. Not every user has the time, interest, or aptitude to become proficient enough to design commercial quality dBASE IV programs, and not every data base application demands this approach. Even if you never write programs that do more than what you could accomplish interactively, you can benefit in several important ways by combining the commands you already know into programs. You can

- Avoid the tedium of having to type the same command sequences repeatedly or select the same menu options
- Execute several consecutive commands without having to wait for each one to complete before issuing the next
- Reduce the chances that careless errors or omissions in a command sequence will compromise the integrity of your data bases
- Run time-consuming processes unattended when the computer is otherwise unoccupied
- Set up procedures that can be run by less experienced users

If you have been working with dBASE IV at the dot prompt, you are already familiar with the "grammar and syntax" of the dBASE IV command language, and the transition to using dBASE IV as a programming language can be very easy and natural. Many of the commands that you use at the dot prompt (as well as others not covered in this book) can be incorporated unchanged into your programs. If you have done all or most of your work with dBASE IV in the menu system, you must weigh the advantages of using programs to automate an application against the time required to master the requisite command vocabulary and syntax.

WRITING AND RUNNING dBASE IV PROGRAMS

A dBASE IV program is an ordinary text file that consists of one or more commands, each one typed just as you would enter it at the dot prompt, and

each ending with a hard return. When you write a program, you should use the extension PRG, the default dBASE IV program file extension, although dBASE IV uses different extensions for the programs it generates to execute queries, reports, labels, and screen forms (the dBASE IV file extensions are listed in Appendix G). You have already seen at least one example of a dBASE IV program, the NWCORDER.QBE query file listed in Figure 6-7.

The first time you run a program, dBASE IV *compiles* it, a process that translates it into a form called *pseudocode*, which is closer to the native language that dBASE IV uses internally than the original PRG file. In many programming languages, the compiled version of a program is called an *object file*, and dBASE IV gives compiled PRG files the extension DBO, for "dBASE object file." (The extensions for compiled versions of report, label, and screen form programs generated by dBASE IV consist of the first two letters of the form file extension plus an O—for example, FRO for a compiled FRG program generated from the FRM file produced using the report layout editor.) dBASE IV can execute a DBO file much faster than it can read, interpret, and execute the lines in the PRG file one by one (which is how earlier versions of dBASE ran programs). As it runs a program, dBASE IV displays the same prompts, status messages, dialog boxes, and error messages that the commands in the program would produce if you had typed them at the dot prompt.

As a detailed example, recall the methods presented in Chapter 17 for replacing the PRICE field in new Order File records with the standard prices stored in the Inventory File. If you wanted to process every order record, you could define an update query such as the one shown in Figure 17-13, which replaces the Order File PRICE field with the Inventory File PRICE field NWINVENT->PRICE and then replaces the SUBTOTAL field with PRICE * QUANTITY. From the dot prompt, you can use the following command sequence to open and link the files, read the prices into the new order records, and list the order records for which there is no match in the Inventory File:

```
USE NWORDER IN 1 ALIAS ORDER
USE NWINVENT IN 2 ORDER PARTNUMBER ALIAS INVENTORY
SELECT ORDER
SET RELATION TO PARTNUMBER INTO INVENTORY
REPLACE ALL PRICE WITH INVENTORY->PRICE, SUBTOTAL WITH PRICE * QUANTITY
LIST ACCOUNT, CATEGORY, PARTNUMBER FOR PARTNUMBER <> INVENTORY->PARTNUMBER
```

To write a program that contains the same instructions, you can create a text file, perhaps called NWOPRICE.PRG, that consists of six lines of text, one

for each command in the previous example, and each ending with a hard return. Writing the program, like defining the update query or typing the commands one by one from the dot prompt, requires that you understand how to work with multiple data bases, remember the syntax of several dBASE IV commands, and know quite a few details about the National Widgets files, including the following:

- The names of the Order and Inventory files
- The syntax of the USE command
- How to select work areas and open more than one data base at a time
- How to assign and use a file alias (this is not essential)
- How to link two files with SET RELATION
- The name of the Inventory File index tag used as the basis for the linkage
- The name of the common field used as the basis for the linkage
- How to access fields in an unselected work area by the combination of alias and field name
- The syntax of the REPLACE command
- The names of the fields you want to REPLACE and LIST
- How to test for Order File records for which there are no matching Inventory File records

If you also wanted to calculate the discount based on the quantity and dollar value of the order, add in sales tax, and compute the final invoice amount, you would need to understand additional commands and dBASE IV concepts, and have even more specific knowledge of the National Widgets files. To *use* a program, you need only remember the name of the PRG file and know how to start the program.

From the Menus

To run a program from the menu system, you highlight the program name in the Control Center **Applications** panel, press ENTER, and select **Run application**

from the dialog box. dBASE IV displays another dialog box to request confirmation: "Are you sure you want to run this application?" Note that, despite the wording of the prompts and the messages, the program need not be a complete menu-driven application, and it need not have been created with the dBASE IV applications generator.

From the Dot Prompt

To run a program from the dot prompt, you use the DO command, as follows:

DO *program name*

For example, to run the NWOPRICE.PRG program mentioned in the previous section, you would type

```
DO NWOPRICE
```

Notational and Typographical Conventions

When you write a program, keep in mind that you or one of your coworkers may some day have to understand it, add to it, or modify it. Even if you are the sole user, any measures you take to make your programs more readable and understandable will help a great deal when you edit a program several months after writing it and the details are no longer fresh in your mind.

You can type command lines in a dBASE IV program in any combination of uppercase and lowercase letters, just as you can at the dot prompt. When you write longer programs, it is advantageous to develop a consistent scheme for identifying file and variable names to make them stand out. For example, you could use lowercase letters for dBASE IV command words, uppercase letters for file and field names, and initial capital letters for memory variable names. This combination results in very clear, readable programs, because it conforms to normal English usage.

The dBASE IV documentation recommends that you use uppercase for command words (command verbs and keywords such as FOR and WHILE); initial capital letters for the names of data bases and other disk files, fields, index tags, programs, and procedures; and lowercase for the names of memory variables, menus, pop-ups, pick lists, and windows. For the most part, the programs generated by dBASE IV to execute applications (the applications generator is described in Chapter 22), reports, labels, and screen forms adhere to these conventions, although Query-by-Example does not (the QBE and UPD files generated from view and update queries are made up of all uppercase letters.) Regardless of your own preferences, there is a good reason to follow the dBASE IV conventions. If you later decide to learn more about programming and begin to modify the generated programs, you will already be familiar with the notational conventions, and your changes and additions will match the existing code.

Extra spaces are permitted anywhere within a command line, and you can use blank lines to separate groups of commands to identify them (to you, not to dBASE IV) as discrete functional units. Just as when you work at command level, extra spaces can make complex expressions and lists of file or field names easier to read and edit. When a command is too long to fit on one screen line, you may find it helpful to indent the continuation lines to distinguish them from new commands.

Comments are notes included in a program as a kind of internal documentation. You can use them to introduce a program section, explain a complex calculation, or elaborate on the logic behind a command or group of commands whose purpose might not be self-evident. When dBASE IV compiles a program, it ignores comments; they do not occupy any space in the compiled program and have no effect on execution speed. You can mark an entire line as a comment, by beginning the line with an asterisk (*), or add a comment to the end of any executable command (on the same line) by preceding it with two ampersands (&&).

It is a good idea to begin all but the shortest programs with a few comment lines that state the name of the program, a brief description of its purpose, your name, and perhaps the dates on which you wrote the program and last modified it. Including this information in the text of a program ensures that it is always visible when you edit the program or examine a printed copy. The following is the header added to the main program created by the dBASE IV applications generator (after customizing the defaults to include the author's name, copyright notice, and dBASE version):

```
******************************************************************************
* Program......: NW.PRG
* Author.......: Miriam Liskin
* Date.........: 11-30-90
* Notice.......: Copyright (C) 1990. All rights reserved.
* dBASE Ver....: dBASE IV version 1.1
* Generated by.: APGEN version 1.3
* Description..: National Widgets Customer and Order Tracking System
* Description..: Main routine for menu system
******************************************************************************
```

For short batch-type programs, a more concise header such as the following should suffice:

```
* NWOPRICE.PRG
* Program to read standard inventory prices into Order File
* Written:          11/21/90  M.Liskin
* Last revision:    06/12/91  M.Liskin
```

You may want to add a concluding comment line as well, so that when you later edit the program, you can verify that the text file was not accidentally truncated. This final line should include the name of the program and requires little or no other information. A comment like the following is adequate for most purposes:

```
* End of program NWOPRICE.PRG
```

Controlling the Screen Display During Program Execution

When you run a program, dBASE IV executes the commands it contains as if you had typed each one at the dot prompt and displays exactly the same messages on the screen in response to each. For example, a REPLACE command produces a status message that monitors the number of records processed, and a CALCULATE command displays the computed results on the screen (with headings above the values if the HEADING setting is ON). Figure 21-1 illustrates the appearance of the screen after you run NWOPRICE.PRG for the first time.

When you run programs that are longer than a few lines or that include many potentially long-running commands, such as INDEX, REPLACE, or CALCULATE, the standard messages displayed by dBASE IV may not be sufficient

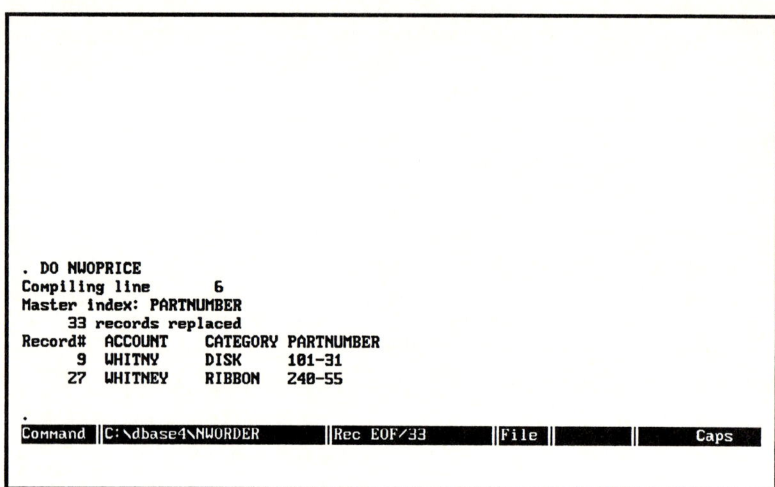

Figure 21-1.

Running a dBASE IV program

to keep you informed about exactly what the program is doing or how far it has progressed toward completion. For simple programs like the ones covered in this chapter, the most straightforward solution to this problem is to use the SET ECHO ON command, which causes dBASE IV to "echo," or display, each command line (except separate comment lines that begin with *) on the screen as it executes the command.

There is no equivalent option on either the **Settings** menu or the SET menu, perhaps because writing programs is closely related to working at the dot prompt and because testing is easier at the dot prompt than it is from the menu system. Although you can type SET ECHO ON at the dot prompt, it is more expedient to include it in the program and use a SET ECHO OFF command at the end of the program to restore the ECHO setting to the default. Figure 21-2 illustrates the appearance of the screen after you run the NWOPRICE.PRG program with the ECHO setting ON.

Controlling a Program's Environment

Every dBASE IV program you write, even the shortest, should set up its own working environment and restore the system to its prior state before it termi-

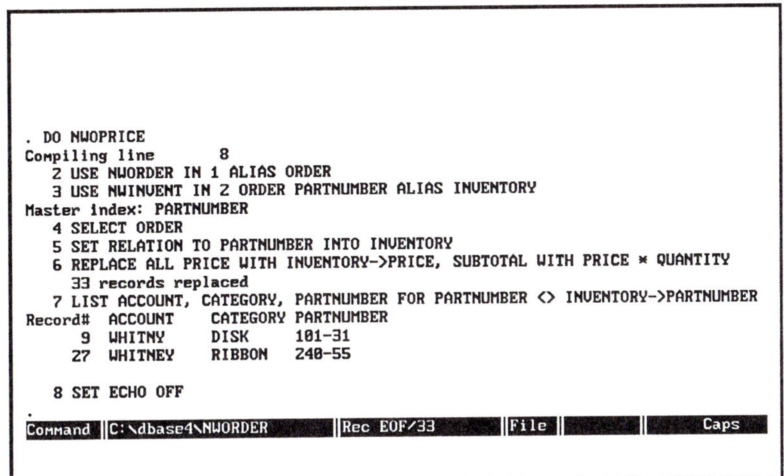

```
. DO NWOPRICE
Compiling line       8
   2 USE NWORDER IN 1 ALIAS ORDER
   3 USE NWINVENT IN 2 ORDER PARTNUMBER ALIAS INVENTORY
Master index: PARTNUMBER
   4 SELECT ORDER
   5 SET RELATION TO PARTNUMBER INTO INVENTORY
   6 REPLACE ALL PRICE WITH INVENTORY->PRICE, SUBTOTAL WITH PRICE * QUANTITY
     33 records replaced
   7 LIST ACCOUNT, CATEGORY, PARTNUMBER FOR PARTNUMBER <> INVENTORY->PARTNUMBER
Record#  ACCOUNT     CATEGORY PARTNUMBER
      9  WHITNY      DISK     101-31
     27  WHITNEY     RIBBON   240-55

   8 SET ECHO OFF
.
Command ║C:\dbase4\NWORDER       ║Rec EOF/33     ║File ║      ║        Caps
```

Figure 21-2.

Running a program with the ECHO setting ON

nates. You (or someone less knowledgeable) should be able to run a program without having to first open data bases or type preparatory SET commands, and then resume working afterward in a familiar environment. A program should open all the data bases it processes and close them afterward so you can leave it running unattended without risking damage to open files if a co-worker reboots or turns off the system, or a hardware or power failure occurs after the program has done its work.

If a program alters any SET options with commands such as SET DELETED ON, SET HEADING OFF, or SET STATUS OFF, it should reverse them if necessary to restore the settings that were previously in effect. dBASE IV provides a method for determining the current status of any SET option (the SET function), but using this function requires an understanding of programming that is beyond the scope of this book. A reasonable compromise is to return all settings to their default values or to the values established in the CONFIG.DB file.

Figure 21-3 shows a new, more complete, version of NWOPRICE.PRG that addresses all these issues. The program includes comment lines that explain each of the REPLACE commands and how the test for missing inventory items

```
* NWOPRICE.PRG
* PROGRAM TO READ STANDARD INVENTORY PRICES INTO ORDER FILE
* WRITTEN:           11/30/88      M.Liskin
* LAST REVISION:     12/02/88      M.Liskin

SET ECHO ON

* Open Order and Inventory Files, link by part number
USE NWorder IN 1 ALIAS Order
USE NWinvent IN 2 order Partnumber ALIAS Inventory
SELECT Order
SET RELATION TO Partnumber INTO Inventory

* Read Inventory Price field into order records
* that have no Price already
REPLACE Price WITH Inventory->Price FOR Price = 0

* Calculate SUBTOTAL
REPLACE ALL Subtotal WITH Price * Quantity

* Calculate DISCOUNT for orders over $50
REPLACE Discount WITH Subtotal * .10 FOR Subtotal >= 50

* Calculate final invoice amount
REPLACE ALL Invamount WITH Subtotal - Discount

* List orders with no matching Inventory records
*  (SET RELATION positions Inventory File to end-of-file)
LIST Account, Category, Partnumber;
  FOR Partnumber <> Inventory->Partnumber

CLOSE DATABASES
SET ECHO OFF

* End of program NWOPRICE.PRG
```

Figure 21-3.

A more readable version of NWOPRICE.PRG

works (the semicolon that breaks the LIST command is explained in the next section).

The program begins with a SET ECHO ON command that causes dBASE IV to display the remaining commands on the screen as the program runs and a

SET ECHO OFF command at the end to return the system to normal. The CLOSE DATABASES command closes both open files and selects work area 1 so that, when the program finishes, you can resume your work as if you had just started up dBASE IV.

USING THE dBASE IV TEXT EDITOR TO WRITE PROGRAMS

dBASE IV provides a simple text editor that enables you to write and edit programs without having to exit to DOS or load an external editor or word processor from within dBASE IV. If you become proficient enough at dBASE IV programming to develop complete applications or make extensive revisions to the programs that dBASE IV generates, you may want a more sophisticated editor, such as the Norton Editor, or one specifically designed for dBASE IV programming (such as the Brief/dBrief package), but for writing short programs and making occasional minor modifications to report or label programs, the built-in editor is more than adequate.

From the Menus

From the menu system, you can invoke the dBASE IV text editor to write a new program by highlighting the **<create>** option in the Control Center **Applications** panel and pressing ENTER. To edit an existing program, you can either highlight its name, press ENTER, and then select **Modify application** from the dialog box, or you can press SHIFT-F2 (Design) with the program name highlighted.

From the Dot Prompt

From the dot prompt, you invoke the dBASE IV text editor by typing

MODIFY COMMAND *program name*

or

MODIFY FILE *program name*

You can use these commands interchangeably. The wording of the more commonly used MODIFY COMMAND is derived from the original descrip-

tion of dBASE programs as *command files* during the early days of dBASE II. MODIFY FILE may seem more appropriate when you use the text editor to create or edit files that are not programs, such as CONFIG.DB.

If you do not include the name of the program, dBASE IV prompts you to "Enter filename:" If you use the MODIFY COMMAND variant, dBASE IV automatically supplies the extension PRG unless you override the default by including a different extension in the file name. When you invoke the editor by typing MODIFY FILE, you must always type the extension. Keep in mind that the programs generated by the report, label, and screen form editors have the extensions FRG, LBG, and FMT, respectively, and when you use the dBASE IV program editor to modify one of these files, you must include the extension explicitly in the file name.

Writing and Editing Programs

The dBASE IV program editor is closely related to the text editor used to enter and edit memo fields. The program editor makes use of the same full-screen editing and command keys and displays a similar menu bar, although many of the selections (such as the **Style**, **Display**, and **Position** options on the **Words** menu) are missing because they are not relevant to writing programs. Another noteworthy difference is that, when you invoke the dBASE IV text editor with the MODIFY COMMAND or MODIFY FILE command, word wrap mode is disabled. Instead of setting the right margin and allowing dBASE IV to word wrap your text to conform to this margin, you must enter all the line breaks yourself.

A dBASE IV command can be up to 1024 characters long and must end with a hard return generated by pressing ENTER. If you wish, you can type each command all on one line—that is, press ENTER only at the end of the command. When you type a long line or use the arrow keys to move the cursor "off the edge" of the screen in any direction, dBASE IV scrolls the display to follow the cursor. However, you may find that allowing long lines to extend beyond column 79 makes it harder to edit and print a program. To break a line at any point, you type a semicolon (;), press ENTER, and continue the command on the next line. The semicolon prevents dBASE IV from interpreting the hard return that follows as the end of the command. As you can see in the program listing in Figure 21-3, breaking a long line at a logical place, such as at the beginning of a FOR or WHILE clause, and indenting the continuation lines makes a program more readable.

Remember that dBASE IV ignores any characters to the right of a semicolon when it executes a program, so be sure to press ENTER immediately after typing the semicolon. Also, because the command continues with the very first character on the following line, make sure that you do not inadvertently omit any required spaces between the words in a command. For example, the REPLACE command that fills in the DISCOUNT field in the program in Figure 21-3 would generate an error message if it were split as follows:

```
REPLACE DISCOUNT WITH SUBTOTAL * .10;
FOR SUBTOTAL >=50
```

The problem is that when dBASE IV removes the semicolon and reconstructs the complete command from the two lines in the program, there is no space between the 0 at the end of the first line and the "F" at the beginning of the second. You could write this command correctly as

```
REPLACE DISCOUNT WITH SUBTOTAL * .10;
  FOR SUBTOTAL >=50
```

or

```
REPLACE DISCOUNT WITH SUBTOTAL * .10 ;
FOR SUBTOTAL >=50
```

You may prefer the former version, because indenting the second (and subsequent) lines makes it clear that these are continuation lines, not new commands.

Although dBASE IV displays a ruler line at the top of the screen, the **Words** menu does not include a **Modify ruler** option (because word wrap is disabled, resetting the right margin would have no effect.) You can use the **Hide ruler** option to remove the ruler from the screen and make room for two more lines of text, but the ruler, and the cursor that moves within the ruler to indicate your position as you type, serve as useful guides for lining up groups of indented lines.

You can save a new or edited program by selecting **Save changes and exit** from the **Exit** menu. This option returns you to the dot prompt or the Control Center, depending on which environment was active when you invoked the text editor. The **Run program** option on the **Exit** menu exits the editor, saves all changes, and immediately runs the program. This option is convenient during

the testing phase, when you write a program, test it, find problems, return to the editor to correct them, and then rerun the modified program. (Typically, you must repeat this cycle several times—often many times—before the program runs correctly.)

When you edit a program, your changes are applied to the original text file, the PRG file. Because dBASE IV does not execute the program file directly but compiles it and runs the compiled version, you will not see the effects of your changes until the program is recompiled. If you use the dBASE IV text editor to modify a program, dBASE IV erases the compiled program when you save your changes and exit from the editor, thereby ensuring that the program will be recompiled the next time you run it.

When you use an external editor to write programs, you may need to take measures to ensure that a modified program is recompiled. If the DEVELOPMENT setting is ON, as it is by default, dBASE IV compares the DOS date and time stamps on the program text file (the PRG file) and the compiled program (the DBO file) before executing a program. If the date and time on the PRG file are later, dBASE IV deduces that the program was modified after it was last compiled, and recompiles it. When the DEVELOPMENT setting is OFF, you must explicitly recompile a program after you modify it.

If you need to recompile a program manually, you do so from the dot prompt with the COMPILE command:

COMPILE *program name*

You can also force dBASE IV to recompile a program by erasing the compiled file (the DBO file).

Whenever you use the COMPILE command to compile a program, dBASE IV assigns the resulting file the extension DBO, the default extension for compiled PRG files. However, dBASE IV assumes the extensions FRO, LBO, and FMO for compiled report, label, and screen form files. If you edit one of the generated programs and then compile it explicitly, you must rename the newly compiled program to conform to the dBASE IV file name conventions (after you erase the old compiled program). The following example uses dBASE IV commands to accomplish this for a label-printing program:

```
COMPILE NWCUST1.LBG
ERASE NWCUST1.LBO
RENAME NWCUST1.DBO TO NWCUST1.LBO
```

You can print a program from within the text editor by using the **Print** menu, which is identical in most respects to the **Print** menu that is displayed when you print reports and labels. Only the direct actions listed in the first section of the menu are different: There is no option to view a program on screen, since that is the purpose of the text editor itself, and there is one additional option, **Line numbers**, which is not applicable to reports or labels. You can set this option to **Yes** to add line numbers to the printed program listing. When you print short programs, line numbers are usually unnecessary, but they can be helpful when you use the dBASE IV debugger (which is not discussed in this book) to find problems in a longer program.

Although the program editor lacks a provision for defining page headers or footers, dBASE IV automatically paginates program listings. It prints 63 lines per page to skip over the perforations on continuous-form paper and numbers the pages in the upper left corner. Figure 21-4 illustrates the printout of the NWOPRICE.PRG program, including the line numbers.

From the Dot Prompt

From the dot prompt, you can use the TYPE command to print a program. By default, the dBASE IV TYPE command (like its MS-DOS counterpart) displays the contents of a file on the screen, but you can route the output to the printer by adding the phrase TO PRINT. Because dBASE IV does not make any assumptions about the kind of file you are printing, you must specify the full file name, including the extension. You can add line numbers to the listing by including the keyword NUMBER. For example, you could print the program illustrated in Figure 21-3, NWOPRICE.PRG, with the following command:

```
TYPE NWOPRICE.PRG TO PRINT NUMBER
```

Just as when you print from within the program editor, dBASE IV automatically paginates the listing, but it uses a slightly different format: it prints 60 lines per page, with the file name and last modification date in the upper left corner, and the page number in the upper right corner. Figure 21-5 illustrates the listing produced by the TYPE command in the previous example.

```
Page #     1

* NWOPRICE.PRG
* PROGRAM TO READ STANDARD INVENTORY PRICES INTO ORDER FILE
* WRITTEN:          11/30/88       M.Liskin
* LAST REVISION:    12/02/88       M.Liskin
SET ECHO ON
* Open Order and Inventory Files, link by part number
USE NWorder IN 1 ALIAS Order
USE NWinvent IN 2 order Partnumber ALIAS Inventory
SELECT Order
SET RELATION TO Partnumber INTO Inventory
* Read Inventory Price field into order records
* that have no Price already
REPLACE Price WITH Inventory->Price FOR Price = 0
* Calculate SUBTOTAL
REPLACE ALL Subtotal WITH Price * Quantity
* Calculate DISCOUNT for orders over $50
REPLACE Discount WITH Subtotal * .10 FOR Subtotal >= 50
* Calculate final invoice amount
REPLACE ALL Invamount WITH Subtotal - Discount
* List orders with no matching Inventory records
*  (SET RELATION positions Inventory File to end-of-file)
LIST Account, Category, Partnumber;
  FOR Partnumber <> Inventory->Partnumber
CLOSE DATABASES
SET ECHO OFF
* End of program NWOPRICE.PRG
```

Figure 21-4.

Printing a program from the program editor

```
NWOPRICE.PRG 02/27/91                                                    1

* NWOPRICE.PRG
* PROGRAM TO READ STANDARD INVENTORY PRICES INTO ORDER FILE
* WRITTEN:          11/30/88      M.Liskin
* LAST REVISION:    12/02/88      M.Liskin

SET ECHO ON

* Open Order and Inventory Files, link by part number
USE NWorder IN 1 ALIAS Order
USE NWinvent IN 2 order Partnumber ALIAS Inventory
SELECT Order
SET RELATION TO Partnumber INTO Inventory

* Read Inventory Price field into order records
* that have no Price already
REPLACE Price WITH Inventory->Price FOR Price = 0

* Calculate SUBTOTAL
REPLACE ALL Subtotal WITH Price * Quantity

* Calculate DISCOUNT for orders over $50
REPLACE Discount WITH Subtotal * .10 FOR Subtotal >= 50

* Calculate final invoice amount
REPLACE ALL Invamount WITH Subtotal - Discount

* List orders with no matching Inventory records
*  (SET RELATION positions Inventory File to end-of-file)
LIST Account, Category, Partnumber;
  FOR Partnumber <> Inventory->Partnumber

CLOSE DATABASES
SET ECHO OFF

* End of program NWOPRICE.PRG
```

Figure 21-5.

Printing a program from the dot prompt

USING A WORD PROCESSOR TO WRITE PROGRAMS

As mentioned earlier in this chapter, you can use any word processor or text editor that can read and write ASCII text files to edit dBASE IV programs. These include editors specifically intended for programming, such as Brief/dBrief, the WordPerfect Editor, and the Norton Editor, as well as a number of popular word processors, such as WordStar, WordPerfect, Microsoft Word, and PC-Write. (Chapter 14 explained some of the considerations involved in determining if and how you can use your word processor to produce a text file with no "hidden" formatting codes or document headers.)

In principle, you can use the RUN command explained in Chapter 19 to access an external text editor from within dBASE IV, and you may be able to run some of the smaller programming editors in this way. By running the editor from inside dBASE IV, you can avoid having to exit dBASE IV repeatedly, load the word processor, load and save the program you are writing, exit the word processor, and reload dBASE IV. However, most sophisticated word processors are too large to run in this way. If you can run your editor from within dBASE IV, make sure that the editor resides in the same subdirectory or that the operating system can find it (either specify its full path name or use a DOS PATH command to include the subdirectory that contains the program in the DOS search path).

If you are sure that you will always want to use an external word processor to edit programs, you can place a TEDIT command in the CONFIG.DB file to cause dBASE IV to load the external editor whenever you execute a command that would normally invoke the dBASE IV text editor:

TEDIT = *program name*

If the program is stored in another subdirectory that is not part of the DOS search path, be sure to enter the full path name. For example, to substitute the Norton Editor, which is stored in a subdirectory called UTILITY on drive C for the dBASE IV text editor, you would use the following entry in CONFIG.DB:

```
TEDIT = C:\UTILITY\NE
```

The same memory and path search requirements that govern the use of the RUN command apply to TEDIT. dBASE IV automatically passes the name of the file you want to edit (the file name that is highlighted in the Control Center **Applications** panel or the name specified in a MODIFY COMMAND or MODIFY FILE command) to the external editor. If you can save a file and load a new one without exiting the word processor, you can also edit other files before you return to dBASE IV.

One of the best choices for a program editor, especially for short programs, is the editor or notepad of a RAM-resident utility such as Sidekick. A RAM-resident editor is convenient, because after the editor is loaded into memory (which is done only once, before you start up dBASE IV) and your program is loaded into the editor, you can call up the program almost instantly, make a change, and quickly save the modified program on disk. In contrast, every time you invoke the dBASE IV text editor to modify a program, a disk access is required to load part of the dBASE IV program into memory and read the program file into the editor. However, because dBASE IV uses nearly all the memory, even in a 640K system, you can use only the smaller RAM-resident editors in this way, and you may still have memory conflicts if you try to carry out complex operations that manipulate multiple files with the editor loaded.

Furthermore, you may have problems running some memory-resident software with dBASE IV. For example, some versions of Sidekick Plus are incompatible with the dBASE IV disk cache (the disk cache, which is used to speed up performance, is described in Appendix A). In some cases, you can resolve the conflict by disabling the disk cache, but you may not be willing to sacrifice performance just for the convenience of using a memory-resident text editor.

Also note that when you call an external editor from within dBASE IV, or when you use a memory-resident editor such as Sidekick, especially if you also use the dBASE IV disk cache, dBASE IV may not always recompile a program automatically after you modify it, even if the DEVELOPMENT setting is ON. You may need to experiment to determine whether this caution applies to you, but you should suspect this problem if you edit a program to fix an error and dBASE IV displays exactly the same error message the next time you run the program. When in doubt, it is always prudent to use a COMPILE command to recompile a program manually after you edit it.

TYPICAL APPLICATIONS FOR BATCH-TYPE PROGRAMS

When you begin to think about writing simple batch-type programs, the best way to choose which tasks to automate is to monitor your work and watch for command sequences that take a long time to execute or that you have to repeat many times in the course of a typical processing cycle. The brief summary of the advantages of programming presented earlier in this chapter can serve as

an informal guide to help you identify the operations that would benefit most from combining individual steps into short programs. Any of the following are good candidates for automation through programming:

- Command sequences that you must repeat many times during a typical month or year
- Command sequences that require little or no user input, especially ones that include several long-running commands
- Complex or lengthy command sequences in which an error or an omission could damage the integrity of the data bases
- Procedures that only some users understand how to carry out step by step

The remainder of this section presents three detailed examples, drawn from the National Widgets system, of the kind of programs you can write without mastering any new dBASE IV concepts. These programs are longer than the first six-line version of NWOPRICE.PRG presented at the very beginning of this chapter, but they all consist of commands that you already know if you have been working at the dot prompt, and they are typical of the types of operations in any application that stand to gain a great deal from automation. If you have been working primarily in the menu system, you may want to refer to earlier chapters to review the syntax of the dot prompt commands.

A Program That Reindexes the Data Bases

When you work with a data base that contains more than a few thousand records, constructing a new index or rebuilding an existing index can be slow, even on a fast hard disk. In any dBASE IV application, several situations call for rebuilding indexes, and they can all be improved by placing the indexing commands in a program. The first obvious candidate for automation is building an index that you do not maintain on a daily basis because you need it for a report that is printed infrequently. A simple version of this type of program might consist of just two or three commands—an INDEX command to build the required index tag or NDX index, a REPORT FORM or LABEL FORM command to produce the output, and possibly a command to delete the index tag or file afterward.

You may not always be able to print the report or labels unattended. With a laser printer, you might need to refill the paper tray several times during the print run, and if the paper or ribbon in a dot-matrix printer jams, you can lose more than your report—you can burn out the printhead. Nevertheless, you can save a great deal of time by writing a program that constructs all the indexes required for several reports, run this program in advance (or overnight), and print the reports when you are available to monitor the printer. This strategy is applicable to command sequences such as the end-of-month or end-of-year processing steps in an accounting application, which often require that you print numerous summary reports before you can "close" the accounting period. (If you use NDX indexes, you must remember to open these indexes with the data base if you need to make further changes to the data after you build the indexes and before you print the reports.)

Every dBASE IV system should also have, as part of its "disaster recovery" procedures, a program that rebuilds all the indexes associated with all the data bases. This program would allow you to return easily to normal operation after a hardware or software failure damages a production MDX file, and because you can easily reindex, you can save time and disks by not backing up the indexes. If a system crash forces you to recover the data bases from a set of backup disks, you can use the program to rebuild all the index tags and NDX indexes afterward.

The program in Figure 21-6, NWINDEX.PRG, rebuilds all the indexes normally used with the National Widgets system data bases. The SET SAFETY OFF command prevents dBASE IV from requesting permission to overwrite existing index tags or NDX index files, and the program uses the INDEX ON command rather than REINDEX so that it can reconstruct all the index tags, even if the production MDX file is damaged or missing. Note, however, that the SET SAFETY OFF command applies only to overwriting existing tags or files; if dBASE IV cannot find the production MDX file when it encounters the USE command in the program, it displays a dialog box that informs you "Production MDX file not found" and offers three options: **Cancel**, **Proceed**, and **Help**.

You can use a macro to circumvent this problem so you can run the reindexing program unattended. Chapter 18 described how to play back a previously recorded macro by typing a PLAY MACRO command at the dot prompt. You can also use this command in a program, but contrary to its behavior at the dot prompt, dBASE IV does not immediately type the keystrokes stored in the macro when it encounters the PLAY MACRO command. It reserves these keystrokes until your program solicits input and then plays them back, one keystroke for each character of input that the program requests.

```
* NWINDEX.PRG
* PROGRAM TO REBUILD ALL NATIONAL WIDGETS INDEXES
* WRITTEN:       12/05/88    M.Liskin
* LAST REVISED: 12/05/88    M.Liskin

SET ECHO ON
SET SAFETY OFF
RESTORE MACROS FROM NWprogrm
PLAY MACRO P

DELETE FILE NWcust.mdx
USE NWcust
INDEX ON ACCOUNT TAG ACCOUNT
INDEX ON Zip TAG Zip
INDEX ON State + UPPER(City) + Account TAG Statecity
INDEX ON State + STR({12/31/99}-Lastorder,5,0) TO NWclast

DELETE FILE NWorder.mdx
USE NWorder
INDEX ON Account TAG Account
INDEX ON Partnumber TAG Partnumber

DELETE FILE NWinvent.mdx
USE NWinvent
INDEX ON Partnumber TAG Partnumber
INDEX ON Category + Partnumber TAG Catpart

USE
SET ECHO OFF
SET SAFETY ON

* End of program NWINDEX.PRG
```

Figure 21-6.

A program that rebuilds all the National Widgets indexes

The NWINDEX.PRG program reindexes three data bases; for any or all of these, the production MDX file might be missing, causing dBASE IV to display the error dialog box. In order to respond to the dialog box, you can define a macro that consists of three P's (the key you would press to select **Proceed** and open the data base without the production MDX file) in either uppercase or lowercase. In this example, the macro is named P to suggest its contents, and it

is saved in a macro file called NWPROGRM.KEY. The RESTORE MACROS command in NWINDEX.PRG reads macros in this file into memory to make them available later in the program, and the PLAY MACRO command initiates the process.

Having invoked the macro, you must ensure that the keystrokes it stores are in fact used by the program. If the production MDX files were all present, and dBASE IV did not solicit any input while running the NWINDEX.PRG program, it would play back the keystrokes in the macro immediately after the program finished running. To avoid this problem, the NWINDEX.PRG program erases each production MDX file with a DELETE FILE command before it opens the associated data base so that dBASE IV always asks the questions for which the macro supplies the answers.

A Program That Calculates and Posts Orders

Any procedure that performs calculations or updates files is a good candidate for a dBASE IV program, especially if it involves lengthy or complex command sequences or commands that take a long time to execute. For example, Chapter 17 explained how to use the REPLACE command to calculate the numeric fields in the Order File and the UPDATE command to post data from a batch of orders to the year-to-date and total orders fields in the Customer File. In a real business application, these commands might form part of a longer sequence that carries out all the steps required to enter and post a new batch of orders.

In a typical processing cycle, you would begin by appending a new batch of records to the Order File. A few would include special prices entered individually, but for most, you could read in the standard prices from the Inventory File. You would then calculate the SUBTOTAL, DISCOUNT, and INVAMOUNT fields, and post the orders to the Customer File. When you perform the calculations, you can identify "new" records in the Order File by the fact that the computed fields are 0, with a condition such as the following:

```
REPLACE PRICE WITH INVENTORY->PRICE FOR PRICE = 0
```

As the Order File grows larger, this method will result in slower and slower performance. Using a conditional index based on exactly the same condition is a much better strategy. Even including the time required to build the index tag each time you run the program, this method is faster than using a FOR clause

or a filter, except in a very small data base. A final alternative is to enter new order records into a temporary file with the same structure as the Order File, use this file for the calculation and posting steps, append the records into the Order File, and then empty the temporary file to prepare for the next batch of orders.

Figure 21-7 lists NWOCALC.PRG, a program that uses the latter method to perform the Order File calculations and then update the Customer File. The program assumes that you have already entered the new orders into a temporary file called NWOTEMP.DBF, which has exactly the same structure as NWORDER.DBF. The easiest way to create this file is to copy the structure of the Order File, using the following commands:

```
USE NWORDER
COPY STRUCTURE TO NWOTEMP
```

The NWOCALC.PRG program opens three files: the Inventory File, the Customer File, and the Temporary Order File, which is assigned the alias ORDER to emphasize its equivalence to the Order File. A SET RELATION command links the Order File to the Inventory File by PARTNUMBER so that you can read the PRICE field from the Inventory File into the order records, and to the Customer File by ACCOUNT so that you can calculate sales tax based on the STATE field in the Customer File. The program then prints the order records for which there are no matching inventory records (if the printer is not turned on when you run the program, dBASE IV displays a message that prompts you to correct the problem, just as it would if you executed the PRINT command from the dot prompt).

Next, the NWOCALC.PRG program reads in the PRICE field from the Inventory File, just as in the NWOPRICE.PRG program explained earlier in this chapter, and then calculates the SUBTOTAL, DISCOUNT, and INVAMOUNT fields. National Widgets gives a 10 percent discount on any purchase for which the SUBTOTAL is $50 or more. The FOR clauses in the REPLACE commands that calculate the PRICE and DISCOUNT enter new values into these fields only if the current value is 0, and thus allow you to enter the price or discount manually. The calculation of the final invoice amount, INVAMOUNT, is also conditional, because National Widgets must charge sales tax only on orders in its own state, California. Because the Order File is linked to the Customer File by ACCOUNT code, the customer STATE field is available for use in the FOR clauses that differentiate between California and out-of-state customers.

```
* NWOCALC.PRG
* PROGRAM TO PROCESS A NEW BATCH OF ORDERS
* WRITTEN:          12/03/88      M.Liskin
* LAST REVISION:    12/04/88      M.Liskin

SET ECHO ON

* Open Order, Inventory, and Customer Files
* Link Order File to Inventory File by part number
* Link Order File to Customer File by account code
USE NWotemp IN 1 ALIAS Order
USE NWinvent IN 2 ORDER Partnumber ALIAS Inventory
USE NWcust IN 3 ORDER Account ALIAS Customer
SELECT Order
SET RELATION TO Partnumber INTO Inventory, Account INTO Customer

* Print orders with no matching Inventory records
LIST Account, Category, Partnumber TO PRINT;
  FOR Partnumber <> Inventory->Partnumber

* Read Inventory PRICE field into order records
* that have no PRICE already
REPLACE Price WITH Inventory->Price FOR Price = 0

* Calculate SUBTOTAL
REPLACE ALL Subtotal WITH Price * Quantity

* Calculate DISCOUNT for orders over $50
REPLACE Discount WITH Subtotal * .10;
  FOR Subtotal >= 50 .AND. Discount = 0

* Calculate final invoice amount,
* including California sales tax
REPLACE Invamount WITH Subtotal - Discount;
  FOR Customer->State <> "CA"
REPLACE Invamount WITH Subtotal - Discount +;
  .07 * (Subtotal - Discount) FOR Customer->State = "CA"

* Unlink files to speed up remaining steps
SET RELATION TO
```

Figure 21-7.

A program that performs order calculations and posts order records

```
* Update Customer File
SELECT Customer
UPDATE ON Account FROM Order RANDOM;
  REPLACE Lastorder WITH Order->Orderdate,;
  Ytdorders WITH Ytdorders + Order->Invamount,;
  Totorders WITH Totorders + Order->Invamount

* Add temporary file records into Order File
SELECT 1
USE NWorder
APPEND FROM NWotemp FOR Invamount > 0

* Delete all posted orders
USE NWotemp
DELETE FOR Invamount > 0
PACK

CLOSE DATABASES
SET ECHO OFF

* End of program NWOCALC.PRG
```

Figure 21-7.

A program that performs order calculations and posts order records (*continued*)

With the order calculations complete, the program cancels the relations set earlier. You do not have to link the Customer and Order files with SET RELATION to use the UPDATE command, and dBASE IV will read the Order File faster if it does not also have to reposition the record pointer in the Inventory File to match each order record. The UPDATE command in the NWOCALC.PRG program is identical to the command you would use at the dot prompt. After the update, the program opens the Order File in work area 1, thus closing the Temporary Order File, and appends the "posted" records. It then reopens the Temporary Order File and deletes the posted records.

The FOR clause in the APPEND command ensures that only records in which the INVAMOUNT field has a nonzero value are deleted from the Temporary Order File. Although the program prints order records for which there is no matching Inventory File record, it does not pause to allow you to

make corrections; in the mismatched records, the PRICE field, and therefore the SUBTOTAL and INVAMOUNT fields, will still have the value 0 when the program completes. These problem records should be left in the Temporary Order File so that you can easily identify them, correct the errors, and process them again the next time you run the NWOCALC.PRG program.

Finally, a PACK command removes the deleted records from the Temporary Order File. If you wanted to verify the results of the UPDATE before permanently removing posted records, you could omit the PACK step or make a backup copy of the temporary file before running the NWOCALC.PRG program.

If this program seems more complicated than carrying out the same steps at the dot prompt, it may be because you are not accustomed to thinking of the component commands as part of a single procedure. Most of the individual steps in NWOCALC.PRG were presented separately in earlier chapters, as illustrations of various dBASE IV concepts and commands, and the others, such as the conditional calculation of the INVAMOUNT field, draw on the same principles. In a real application, these commands are often combined into a single logical operation—in this case, entering and posting a batch of orders. When you design similar programs, remember that even if you understand the syntax and usage of all the individual commands, some forethought and planning are necessary to make sure that your program includes all the required steps executed in the correct sequence.

A Program That Compiles Statistics

The final program in this chapter carries out a series of statistical calculations on the Customer File using the CALCULATE command, which was introduced in Chapter 10. This program, NWCSTATS.PRG, which is shown in Figure 21-8, counts the number of customers who own IBM, Apple, Kaypro, and Compaq computers and accumulates the sum of the year-to-date and total orders in each group.

As noted in Chapter 10, these statistics represent the kind of management information that is difficult to obtain manually—exactly the type of ad hoc inquiry at which dBASE IV excels. But in a large file, the immediacy of the query process is diminished by the fact that computing the totals can be time-consuming. For every COUNT, SUM, AVERAGE, or CALCULATE command that includes a FOR clause, dBASE IV must read through the entire data base and test each record against the specified condition to determine whether it should be included in the statistics. You can often speed up the process by

```
* NWCSTATS.PRG
* PROGRAM TO CALCULATE CUSTOMER STATISTICS BY EQUIPMENT TYPE
* WRITTEN:       12/05/88    M.Liskin
* LAST REVISED:  02/22/91    M.Liskin

SET SAFETY OFF
SET ECHO ON
USE NWcust

INDEX ON Account TAG Account OF NWctemp FOR "IBM" $ UPPER(Equipment)
CALCULATE CNT(), SUM(Ytdorders), SUM(Totorders);
   TO mcountibm, mysumibm, mtsumibm

INDEX ON Account TAG Account OF NWctemp FOR "APPLE" $ UPPER(Equipment)
CALCULATE CNT(), SUM(Ytdorders), SUM(Totorders);
  TO mcountapp, mysumapp, mtsumapp

INDEX ON Account TAG Account OF NWctemp FOR "KAYPRO" $ UPPER(Equipment)
CALCULATE CNT(), SUM(Ytdorders), SUM(Totorders);
  TO mcountkay, mysumkay, mtsumkay

INDEX ON Account TAG Account OF NWctemp FOR "COMPAQ" $ UPPER(Equipment)
CALCULATE CNT(), SUM(Ytdorders), SUM(Totorders);
  TO mcountcom, mysumcom, mtsumcom

SAVE TO NWcstats

USE
SET ECHO OFF
SET SAFETY ON

* End of program NWCSTATS.PRG
```

Figure 21-8.

A program that calculates customer statistics by equipment type

building conditional indexes, but in a large data base, compiling the statistics may still be slow. Even Query-by-Example, which can group records and compute statistics for each group on one pass through the data base, cannot help in every instance, because you cannot always sort or build one index to group records in a way that speeds up all the computations.

For example, you cannot build one index for the National Widgets Customer File that expedites all the different searches based on the EQUIPMENT field. The names of the manufacturers might appear anywhere within the field, not just at the beginning, so you must use the substring operator to search for them. Also, some customers might own equipment in more than one category (say, both IBM and Compaq), and those records must be counted twice, on separate passes through the file.

You can use a single CALCULATE command to compute the count and sums (and other statistics not included in this simple example) for each type of equipment, and you can maximize processing speed by building and using conditional indexes, but even so, accumulating the desired statistics for four types of equipment requires four passes through the Customer File. Placing the commands in a program enables you to walk away from the computer and return after dBASE IV has computed all the statistics.

In order to ensure that the calculated results are available when you need them, the program stores the counts and sums in memory variables, which you can display on the screen by typing DISPLAY MEMORY or print with LIST MEMORY TO PRINT. When a program terminates, dBASE IV automatically *releases* (erases from memory) all memory variables created within the program, so NWOCALC.PRG also saves the memory variables on disk in a memory file called NWCSTATS.MEM. In a later work session, you could load the variables back into memory and display or print them with a command sequence such as the following:

```
RESTORE FROM NWCSTATS
LIST MEMORY TO PRINT
```

Three aspects of the commands that build the conditional indexes deserve special mention. First, when you use a conditional index solely to speed up the record selection process, the actual index key expression may be irrelevant, and you can use any key expression, preferably a short one. For example, the order in which dBASE IV reads the Customer File when it executes the NWCSTATS.PRG program makes no difference, and the program uses the same key expression—the ACCOUNT field—for each of the four indexes it builds. It also uses the same tag name—ACCOUNT—and the SET SAFETY OFF command at the beginning of the program ensures that dBASE IV does not ask for permission before overwriting the tag once it has been constructed by the first INDEX command.

Note also that the INDEX command places the new tag in a *nonproduction* MDX file. Placing temporary tags in a separate MDX index file keeps the production MDX file small, minimizes the number of tags it contains, and thus maximizes performance during data entry. You cannot use an NDX index file for this purpose, because dBASE IV does not allow you to specify a FOR clause in the INDEX command that builds an NDX file.

Finally, notice that the conditions in the FOR clauses convert the EQUIPMENT field to uppercase letters with the UPPER function to minimize the effect of inconsistent data entry on the accuracy of the statistics. Several people (or the same person at different times) may have entered data into the file using various combinations of uppercase and lowercase letters—for example, Kaypro, KAYPRO, and KayPro. If you convert the EQUIPMENT field to uppercase letters and search for all uppercase characters (using the substring operator) within this field, the actual combination of uppercase and lowercase characters in the EQUIPMENT field is immaterial. The UPPER function does not change the actual data stored in the Customer File—it simply converts the EQUIPMENT field to uppercase letters to carry out the comparison stated in the FOR clause.

TESTING AND DEBUGGING

No matter how proficient you are and how much experience with dBASE IV you have, it is impossible to work at the dot prompt without making mistakes, and you are even more likely to make errors in the programs you write. Finding the errors, or "bugs" in a program, a process known as *debugging,* can be a frightening prospect at first, because you are one step further removed from the command that caused the problem than when you work interactively.

The most common errors—and the easiest to find and correct—are syntax errors similar to the ones you might make at the dot prompt. You may use the wrong command verb; forget an essential phrase or option; use a clause not permitted in the command you are executing; misspell a dBASE IV command word, function name, data base field name, or memory variable name; or combine fields, memory variables, constants, functions, and operators incorrectly in a complex expression.

Many errors are detected by the dBASE IV compiler as a result of the syntax checking that is integral to the process of translating each line into the proper object file format. When the compiler finds an error, it displays the incorrect

command, an error message, and the line number. As illustrated in Figure 21-9, the dialog box displays the command that is responsible for the error—the DO command that called the program or the SET VIEW, REPORT FORM, LABEL FORM, or SET FORMAT command that invoked a program generated by dBASE IV—and offers you three choices: **Cancel**, **Edit**, and **Help**. If you can see the cause of the error, as is often the case for a spelling or typographical error, you can select **Cancel**, edit the program to fix the problem, and try running it again. If you select **Edit**, dBASE IV presents for editing the original command—the one displayed in the dialog box (usually a DO command), not, as you might expect, the faulty command line in the program. The **Help** option displays the table of contents for the dBASE IV help system.

Although the compiler can find syntax errors in a command line, it cannot detect mistakes in logic—problems caused by combining commands inappropriately. For example, a CALCULATE or LIST command that is syntactically correct would generate an error if you failed to open the right data base or select the right work area, because dBASE IV would not be able to find the fields listed in the command. When dBASE IV encounters an error during program execution, it pauses and displays the incorrect line (but not the line number), as well as the same error message that the erroneous command

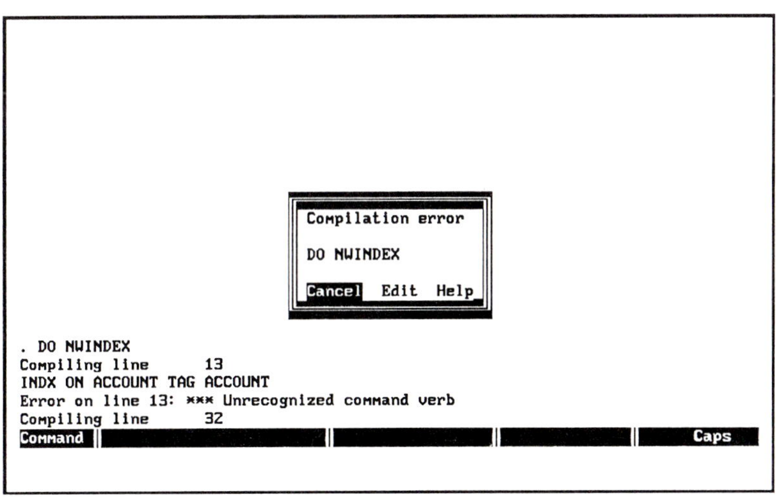

Figure 21-9.

An error message displayed during compilation

would generate if you had typed it at the dot prompt. If you failed to open the Order File in the NWINDEX.PRG program before building the PARTNUMBER tag, running the program would produce the display illustrated in Figure 21-10, because the Customer File (which remains open after the program builds its four indexes) does not contain a field called PARTNUMBER.

Because a line that is syntactically correct can generate an execution error, examining the error message and the offending line may not reveal the source of the problem. Whenever you run a new program, you should have at hand a printed listing of the program for reference as well as printouts of the structures and contents of any data bases opened by the program. If possible, records should be listed in the order in which dBASE IV processes them (either in a natural order or in a sequence determined by an index). When the cause of an error is not immediately obvious, seeing the bad command line in context and knowing what data dBASE IV was attempting to process when the program crashed can help you find the bug.

When dBASE IV encounters an error while running a program, it does not offer help. Instead, it gives you three choices: **Cancel**, **Ignore**, and **Suspend**. If you choose **Cancel**, dBASE IV stops running the program and returns you to the dot prompt or to the Control Center. It releases (erases from memory) any

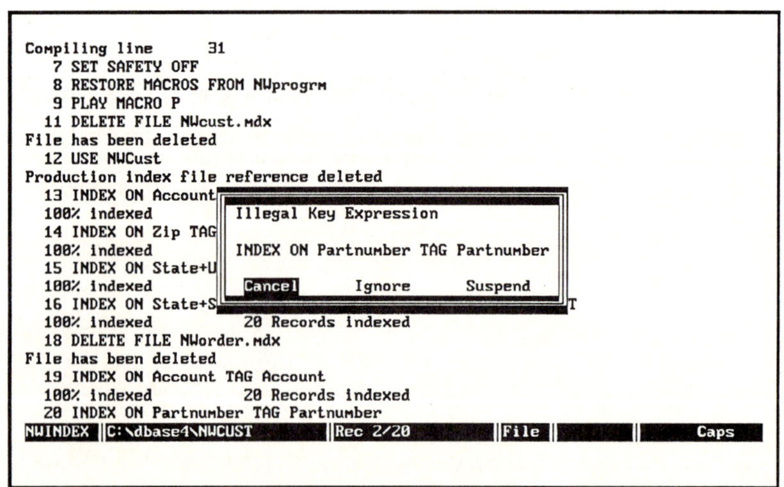

Figure 21-10.

An error message displayed during program execution

memory variables created by the program, but it leaves all data bases open, positioned exactly where they were when the error occurred. The **Ignore** option causes dBASE IV to bypass the line containing the error and execute the next command in the program.

If you select **Suspend**, dBASE IV temporarily pauses execution and returns you to the dot prompt. It does not release memory variables, and all data bases remain open, positioned exactly where they were when the error occurred. You can type any commands and then either pick up where the program left off by typing RESUME or terminate the program by typing CANCEL. Even if you started the program from the Control Center, dBASE IV displays the dot prompt when you suspend execution. If you then type CANCEL, dBASE IV returns you to the Control Center, just as it would if you had chosen **Cancel** from the error dialog box or if the program had completed normally.

In a simple program in which every step performs some essential processing on a data base file, you would rarely choose the **Ignore** option, since most commands depend for correct execution on the previous steps in the program. A possible exception is a LIST or DISPLAY command with a misspelled field name or a field not present in the active data base. Skipping this command would have no impact on subsequent program steps, and you might want to make a note of the error (perhaps by pressing PRTSC to print out the screen) and correct it at your leisure.

If the error is serious and you immediately recognize the cause, you can choose the **Cancel** option, edit the program to correct the error, and try running it again. You might also elect to suspend execution, type the corrected line from the dot prompt, and then type RESUME to continue running the program. By using this strategy, you might find several errors in one test run and correct them in a single editing session. Remember that retyping the command line at the dot prompt does not change the program—you must edit the PRG file to correct the problem permanently.

When the cause of an error is not immediately evident, you can suspend or cancel the program and type commands at the dot prompt to track down the bug. The **Suspend** option is generally preferable to **Cancel**, because suspending a program leaves the values of memory variables intact, and these values sometimes provide important clues to the source of the problem. In either case, all data bases remain positioned exactly where they were when the program crashed, and you can use DISPLAY STATUS, DISPLAY, LIST, or ? commands to answer the questions that might lead you to the source of the problem. When you are stumped, consider all of the following:

- Are the right data base files open?
- Is the right index tag or NDX index designated the master index?
- Is the right work area selected?
- Are file aliases specified when required?
- Is the record pointer positioned correctly in each open file?
- Are files linked correctly with SET RELATION and SET SKIP?
- Is the right FILTER condition in effect?
- Do all disk files and memory variables named in commands exist?

Once you have found the problem, the safest course if you suspended the program is to type CANCEL, edit the program to correct the error, and run it again. Knowing that you will start again from scratch, feel free to switch work areas and use commands that reposition the record pointer in your attempts to find the bug.

dBASE IV provides a more sophisticated *debugger,* a utility that executes a program line by line and offers commands specifically designed to help you track down elusive errors. The debugger presents four windows on the screen that display the program text, available debugger commands, status information that describes the active data base and the current record, and the values of selected fields, memory variables, or more complex expressions. If you are interested, you can read about the debugger in the dBASE IV documentation, but you probably will not need to use the debugger to test simple programs like the ones covered in this chapter.

When you make a syntax error, dBASE IV informs you of that fact in no uncertain terms, but *even if a new program runs to completion without generating an error message, do not assume that it has produced the correct results.* You might have stated a condition wrong, failed to position the record pointer correctly before executing a command that uses a WHILE clause, forgotten to cancel a filter, or executed a REPLACE command with the wrong data base selected (an error that could go unnoticed if the active file contains fields with the same names as the one you intended to process).

Whenever you write a new program, test it on a copy of your data base or, if your files are large, a smaller sample file, and verify that it correctly manipulates the data and produces the expected results. If you use a small test file, make sure that the sample data provides a wide range of input encompassing

all the possibilities that exist in the full data base. For every condition in a FOR or WHILE clause that tests the contents of a particular field, make sure that the test data includes some records in which the field is blank, some that satisfy the condition, and some that do not, even if some of these values "can't" occur in the real system. Devising strategic test conditions is important in assessing whether a program can cope with "impossible" values such as negative numbers or finding instances in which you used the wrong comparison operator in a condition, such as < (less than) when you really needed <= (less than or equal to).

You can often verify a program's performance by carrying out the same operation from the dot prompt, but if you adopt this approach, be sure to use a command sequence that is sufficiently different to uncover all the potential problems. For example, whenever you use a complex filter condition or FOR clause, you should verify the results, not by typing the same condition (which may be syntactically correct but select the wrong records) at the dot prompt, but by using a LIST or BROWSE command that displays the relevant fields from all the records in the data base so you can see that the right records were selected. In some cases, the only way to verify calculations is to perform the same computations on a hand-held calculator based on a printout of the contents of the data bases.

SUMMARY

The examples in this chapter barely scratch the surface of what you can do with dBASE IV programs by drawing on the commands that you already know how to use at the dot prompt. The programs presented here are detailed and are closely tied to the National Widgets sample system. At the same time, they are typical of the types of operations found in any application that are amenable to automation through simple batch-type programs.

You might try, as an exercise, to create these or other similar programs and test them on the National Widgets sample files. If you are working on a real data base application, you might also apply the same techniques to similar operations in your own system or begin to look for other procedures that could benefit from similar treatment. Once you have decided not to be intimidated by the prospect of writing programs, you can be on the lookout for command sequences that you could incorporate into short programs to improve the efficiency of your work with dBASE IV.

CHAPTER TWENTY-TWO

Creating Menu-Driven Applications

The first 17 chapters of this book described how to build all the components of a reasonably sophisticated data base system and carry out the fundamental data manipulation operations that made up the functional definition of data base management presented in Chapter 1. You now know how to create a data base structure and perform routine file maintenance activities—adding, viewing, editing, and deleting records—from the standard Edit and Browse screens or through custom screen forms. From the dot prompt or by using Query-by-Example, you can define field and record selection criteria to display or print only the data that is relevant in a given situation, and you can sort or use indexes to control the record processing sequence. You know how to produce a variety of printed forms, and you can carry out calculations based on information stored in one or more data base files. If you use the term "application" in a broad sense, to refer collectively to the data bases and related disk files that are used to solve a specific business problem, you already know how to create a dBASE IV application.

The introduction to programming in Chapter 21 served as a reminder of how much specialized knowledge is required to build and use a typical application. Even if you work entirely in the menu system, where you do not have to memorize command syntax or remember file names or field names, you must keep track of the purpose and use of each data base, query, and form file. When your application includes procedures that update many records in a data base, you must remember to carry out all the required steps in the correct order.

The solution to all these problems is automation. Chapters 18 and 21 introduced several methods for automating a dBASE IV application: assigning commands to function keys, recording commands or menu keystrokes in macros, and writing short batch-type programs. You can take another giant step toward automation by using the applications generator to link components that you have already created into a menu-driven system referred to in this chapter and in some of the dBASE IV documentation as an *application.*

When you design an application, you can make it easy for users who have little or no knowledge of dBASE IV to run your system by wording menu options in ordinary colloquial English, in the terminology of your business or profession, or even in idiosyncratic terms used only within your own organization. To run a menu-driven system created in the applications generator, the user only needs to know how to select items from menus and pick lists, and how to use the full-screen edit and browse modes to enter and update records.

You can use the applications generator without learning more about programming than you already know, but it does demand careful planning and attention to detail. You will find that some familiarity with dBASE IV command syntax is helpful, because many of the menu options and dialog box prompts use terminology derived from the dot prompt commands rather than the corresponding menu options. If you have been working primarily in the menu system, you may want to refer back to earlier chapters periodically to review the dot prompt sections that you skimmed or skipped entirely the first time through.

THE STRUCTURE OF A MENU-DRIVEN APPLICATION

The dBASE IV applications generator enables you to link the separate components of a data base application by defining a network of menus and pick lists

that look and work like the ones displayed by dBASE IV. The components of an application are called *objects*. You can define seven types of objects:

- *Application object* An object that stores the essential characteristics of the application and the text of an optional sign-on screen.
- *Horizontal bar menu* A menu in which the options are laid out across one or more screen lines, like the menus displayed at the top of the screen in the Control Center, in edit and browse modes, and in the dBASE IV layout editors (you need not place your menus at the top of the screen, however, and despite the name, they need not be horizontal).
- *Pop-up menu* A menu in which the options are arranged vertically on the screen, like the menus that appear when you select the options on the dBASE IV horizontal bar menus. You can display a pop-up menu independently or link it to a horizontal bar menu option so that it appears as a *pull-down* menu only when the bar menu option is selected.
- *Files list* A pick list of file names that match a specific pattern, such as NW*.DBF for the National Widgets data base files.
- *Structure list* A pick list of field names in the active data base or view.
- *Values list* A pick list of the values in one field in all records in the active data base or view.
- *Batch process* A series of steps that dBASE IV carries out in sequence, much like the simple programs described in Chapter 21.

dBASE IV stores each object you define in a separate disk file with an extension that identifies the type of object: APP for the main application object, BAR for a horizontal bar menu, POP for a pop-up menu, FIL for a files list, STR for a structure list, VAL for a values list, or BCH for a batch process. To run the application, dBASE IV generates two programs: one to start up the application and set up the working environment, and the other to display the main menu and carry out the actions assigned to the menu options.

Figure 22-1 diagrams the structure of a simple menu system for the National Widgets application (some of the components of this application are described in more detail in the examples in this chapter). The main menu of this application is a horizontal bar menu that has five options: **Update Data**, **Reports**,

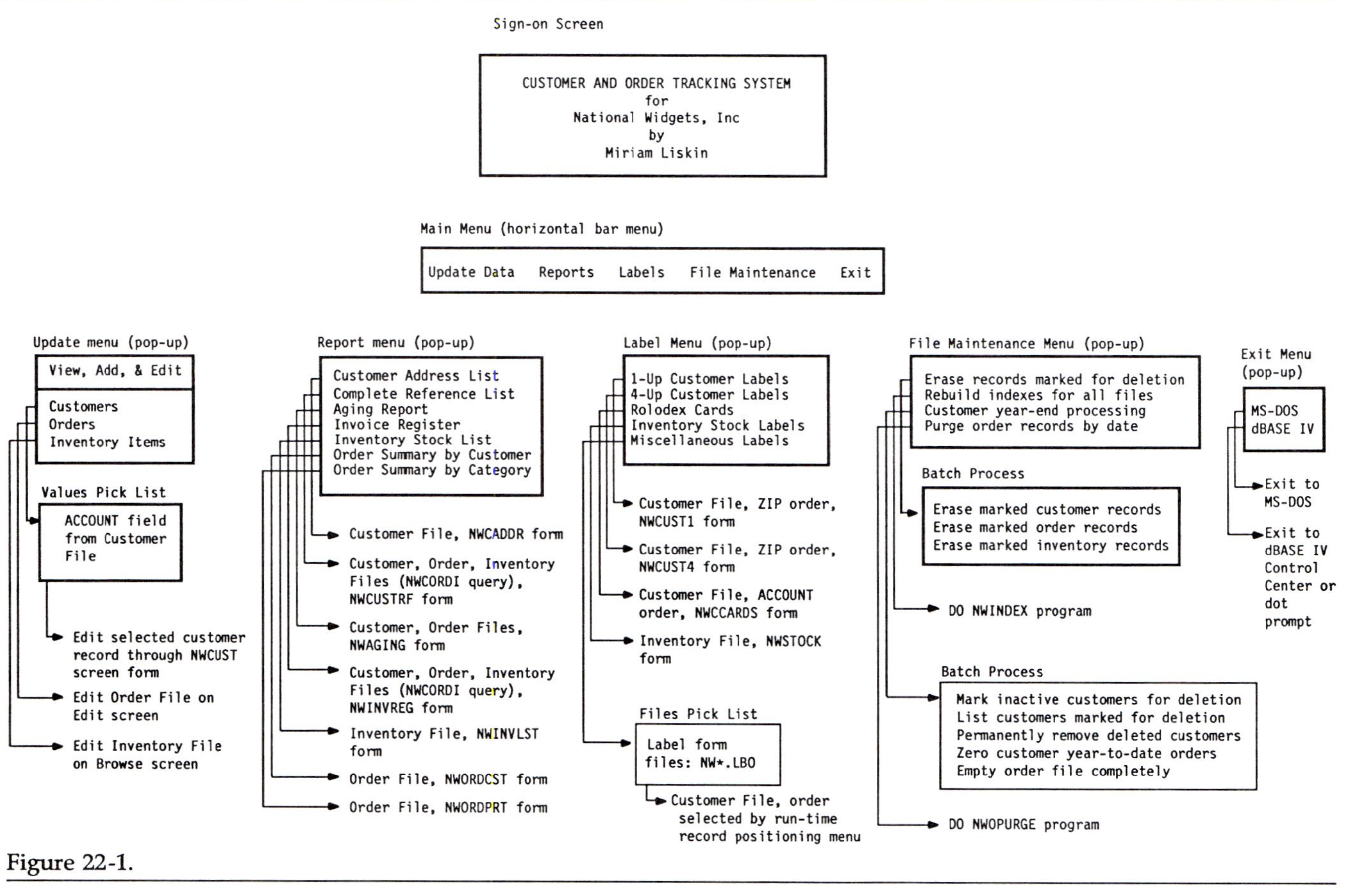

Figure 22-1.

The structure of the National Widgets application

Labels, **File Maintenance**, and **Exit**, all of which invoke pull-down menus. Some of the pop-up menu options result directly in a single action, while others call files lists or batch processes. To build this system, you must define the application object, one horizontal bar menu, five pop-up menus, one files list, one values list, and two batch processes.

dBASE IV offers considerable flexibility in how and when you define the components of an application. If you have already created and tested your data bases, queries, reports, labels, and screen forms, you can define the menus that bind these components into a unified system in one session (or more likely, a few sessions) with the applications generator. Alternatively, you can diagram the application on paper, create the menus in advance, and use the menu structure as an outline, or flowchart, to guide you as you define the data bases, queries, and forms called by the menu options.

You might even use the applications generator instead of the Control Center as your base of operations, because you can invoke many of the dBASE IV layout editors from the application design screen. Whenever dBASE IV prompts you for the name of a screen, report, or label form, you can press SHIFT-F1 (Pick) to display a pick list of available forms. The pick list always includes a **<create>** option, which transfers you to the appropriate layout editor to create a new form. You can also define a new data base, but not a view query, by selecting **<create>** from a pick list of data base names.

When you create a new application, you must define the application object first, but you can build the other objects in the menu system in any order. One strategy is to define all the objects first and then return to each (perhaps several times) to fill in the details. In this approach, you would first create the main menu and then the other menus, pick lists, and batch processes. Next, you would link each submenu to the higher level menu option that calls it, and finally, return to each menu and assign the action performed by each option. A different but equally valid approach would be to specify every detail of one menu, including the actions taken by all the options, before you move on to another.

USING THE APPLICATIONS GENERATOR

You build an application by defining certain overall characteristics, such as the main data base file and screen display colors, and then constructing the individual objects that make up the application. The applications generator work

surface resembles that of the report, label, and custom screen form layout editors, but there are a few significant differences. Foremost among these is the fact that the dBASE IV form layout editors can work with only one form at a time, whereas the applications generator enables you to place many objects on the work surface simultaneously and to move freely among them to make changes.

Each object on the application design work surface is an independent entity, even if it calls up or is called by another object. Every object is stored in a separate disk file, and you can use any object in any application. You may be able to call certain objects, such as files lists or pull-down menus that contain options for performing standard data base update operations, from several different applications. Note, however, that you can work on only one *application* at a time—you cannot place more than one application object on the work surface at the same time.

In many contexts, dBASE IV treats all objects on the application design work surface as equivalent, although the different types of objects perform very different functions in the completed application. If you wish (and if your computer has enough memory), you can place all the objects that make up an application onto the work surface at once. If you prefer to work in a less cluttered environment, you can load one or two objects at a time and remove them from the work surface when you are finished with them. The only limitation is that you cannot remove the application object from the work surface. Figure 22-2 illustrates the application design work surface with an application sign-on screen, a horizontal menu, a pull-down menu, and a values list displayed.

Each of the objects on the application design work surface is surrounded by a border, or *frame.* You can place objects anywhere on the work surface, but you can only type text or make entries within the boundaries of an object frame. To underscore this concept, the background of the application design screen is clear rather than patterned as in the other dBASE IV layout editors, but dBASE IV displays a dot every five spaces on every other line to help you position the objects you create. You cannot use double quotes (") in text that you type on the application design screen (in your menu options, help text screens, or message line prompts), because dBASE IV reserves this character for its own use in the programs generated to run the application. If you do use double quotes, dBASE IV displays an error message that reminds you to use one of the other allowable character string delimiters—"Double quotes here will cause problems - use single quotes or brackets"—and refuses to accept your entry.

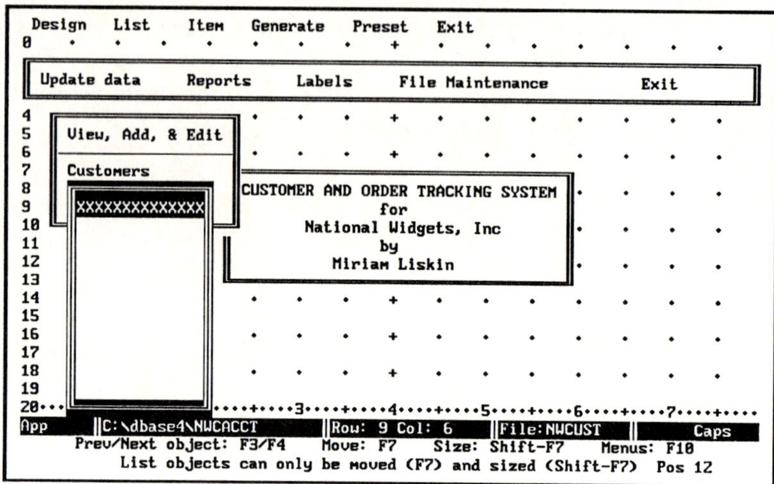

Figure 22-2.

The applications generator work surface with several objects displayed

There are several other minor differences: The ruler line appears just above the status bar instead of at the top of the screen, and the rows as well as the columns are numbered. By default, the last three lines of the application design screen are occupied by the status display, and as you define items on the work surface, dBASE IV displays the current row and column location in the third segment of the status bar. You can press F9 (Zoom) to suppress the status bar, and the applications generator menu as well, which leaves the full screen available for your application objects. The menu and status bar return temporarily whenever you select a menu option by pressing an ALT-key combination, and they disappear again when you return to the application design work surface.

When there are two or more objects on the work surface, you can move among them by pressing F4 (Next) and F3 (Previous). dBASE IV highlights the border of the current object so that you can easily distinguish it, even when a menu is pulled down and you cannot see the cursor on the work surface. Just as in the other layout editors, you can use SHIFT-F7 (Size) to resize an object and F7 (Move) to move either a whole object or one item within an object. Unlike the menu bars displayed in the other dBASE IV layout editors, the applications generator menu does not remain constant as you move among the objects on

the work surface. Four menu options—**Design, Generate, Preset,** and **Exit**—are always present, and two others change to reflect the nature of the currently selected object. The structure of the menu bar is diagrammed in Figure 22-3. The menus and options are shown in roughly the same order that you would use them to create a typical application.

From the Menus

You create, modify, and run applications through the **Applications** panel in the Control Center. You can create a new application by selecting the **<create>** option from the **Applications** panel or edit an existing application by highlighting its name, pressing ENTER, and selecting **Modify application** from the dialog box. You can also use the standard function key shortcut for opening a file and moving to the appropriate design work surface: highlight an application name and press SHIFT-F2 (Design). As always when you work from the Control Center, you need not name a new application until you save it.

From the Dot Prompt

From the dot prompt, you can invoke the applications generator by typing

CREATE APPLICATION *application name*

or

MODIFY APPLICATION *application name*

You can use the CREATE and MODIFY variations interchangeably, regardless of whether you are defining a new application or editing an existing one. If the application named in a CREATE APPLICATION command already exists, dBASE IV warns you in a pop-up dialog box and offers two options: **Modify** invokes the application design screen to modify the existing application, as if you had typed MODIFY APPLICATION. **Cancel** returns you to the dot prompt so you can retype the command with a new application name.

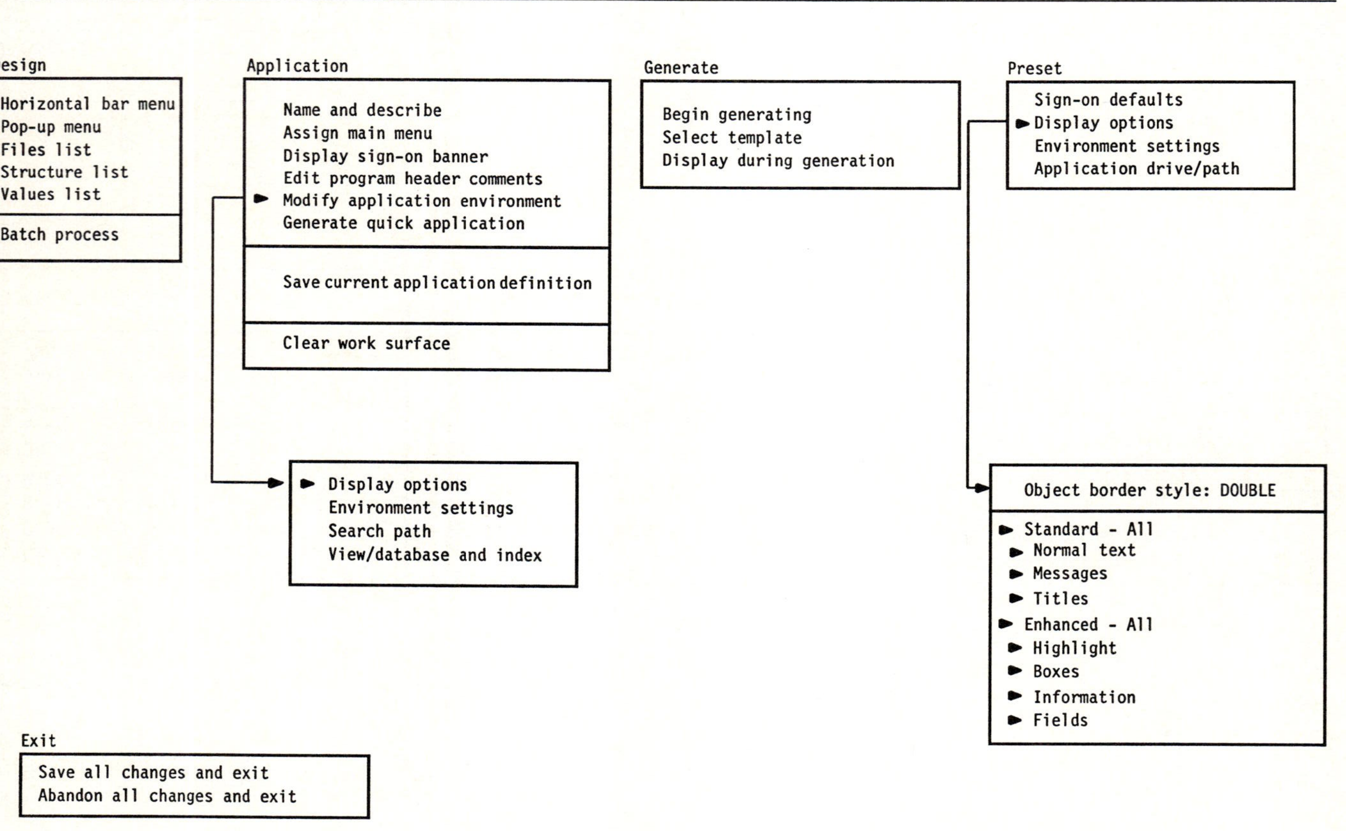

Figure 22-3.

The structure of the applications generator menu

OBJECT MENUS

```
Menu
 Name and describe
 Override assigned database or view
 Write help text
► Modify display options
► Embed code
 Attach pull-down menus
 ---
 Save current menu
 Put away current menu
 ---
 Clear work surface

List
 Name and describe
 Override assigned database or view
 Write help text
► Modify display options
► Embed code
 Identify files in list
 ---
 Save current list
 Put away current list
 ---
 Clear work surface

Batch
 Name and describe
 Override assigned database or view
► Embed code
 ---
 Save current batch process
 Put away current batch process
 ---
 Clear work surface
```

Figure 22-3.

The structure of the applications generator menu (*continued*)

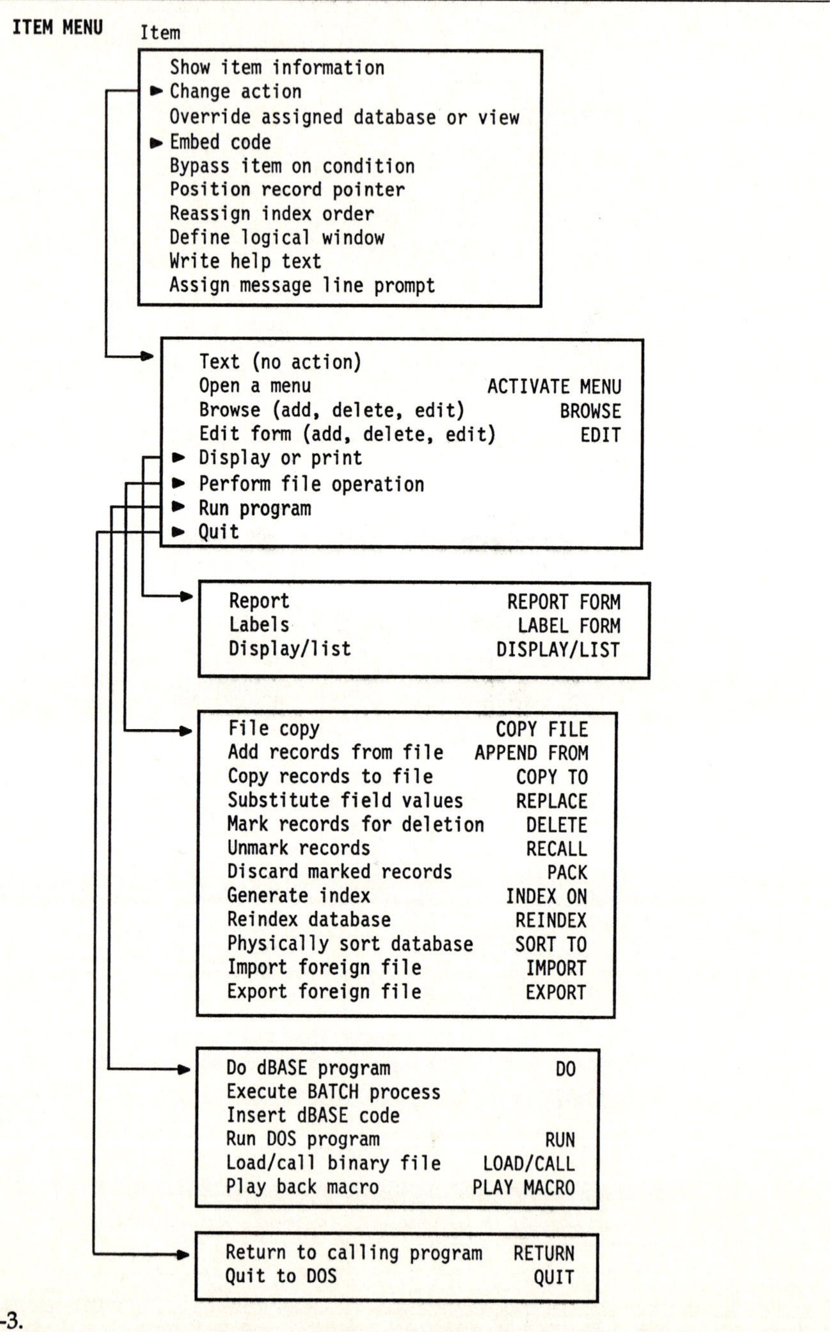

Figure 22-3.

The structure of the applications generator menu (*continued*)

When you work at the dot prompt, you must name new files as well as existing ones before you enter the layout editor used to create them. If you do not include an application name in the CREATE APPLICATION or MODIFY APPLICATION command, dBASE IV prompts you to enter one.

Defining the Application Object

The first step in constructing an application is to define the *application object,* which stores the overall characteristics of the application. When you invoke the applications generator to create a new application, dBASE IV displays a dialog box like the one shown in Figure 22-4 with the specifications for the National Widgets Customer System filled in. To define the application object, you must enter the following items:

- *Application name* A unique name, which dBASE IV assigns to the APP file that stores the application definition and to the main program generated to start up the application.
- *Description* A one-line description of the application (optional).

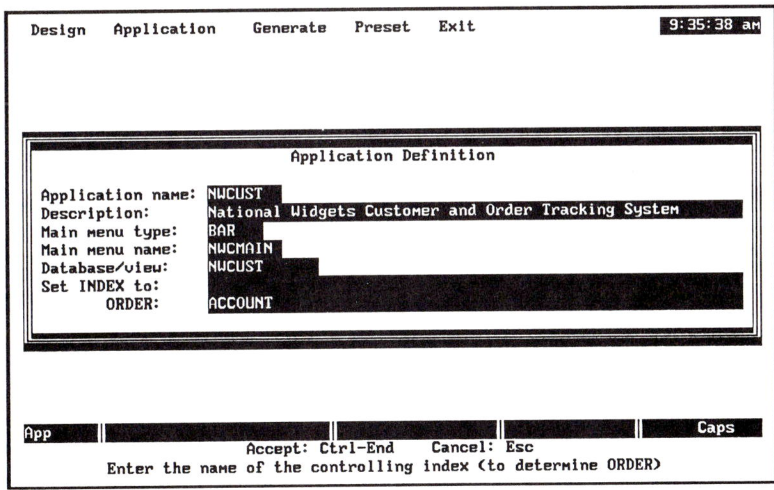

Figure 22-4.

Defining an application

- *Main menu type* The type of object that will serve as the main application menu; it can be a bar menu, a pop-up menu, or a batch process.
- *Main menu name* A unique name, which you must also assign to the disk file that stores the main menu object (which can be a bar menu, pop-up menu, or batch process). dBASE IV assigns the main menu name to the program that it generates to display this menu and execute the menu options or run the batch process. You can type any name (whether or not the named menu already exists) or press SHIFT-F1 (Pick) to select the name from a pick list of predefined objects of the appropriate type. However, you cannot use the same name as the name given the application as a whole, because dBASE IV uses this name for the application startup program (which calls the program that displays and executes the main menu).
- *Database/view* The default data base or view that dBASE IV opens before executing any menu option, unless you explicitly specify another. You can type any name (whether or not the named data base or view already exists) or press SHIFT-F1 (Pick) to select the name from a pick list of predefined data bases and view queries. If you type a view query name explicitly, you must include the QBE extension.
- *Set INDEX/ORDER to* The default NDX indexes that dBASE IV opens with the default data base, and the NDX index or MDX index tag that it uses as the default master index. This entry is optional; if you do not enter it, dBASE IV opens the default data base without activating an index. You need not name the production MDX file, which dBASE IV always opens. You can type NDX index file names explicitly, or press SHIFT-F1 (Pick) to select one or more from a pick list of existing NDX index files.

To save the application definition, press CTRL-END. dBASE IV displays a frame that represents the application object in the center of the screen and a reminder on the message line that you can "Type the text of your sign-on screen in the box above" (customizing the sign-on screen is described later in this chapter, in the section on establishing preset application defaults). You cannot return to the initial application definition screen later, but there are options on the **Application** menu (described later in this chapter) that allow you to change all the information that you entered when you first created the application. The application object must always remain on the work surface, but you can move or resize it like any other object.

Generating a Quick Application

The **Generate quick application** option on the **Application** menu enables you to generate a simple, limited application quickly and easily. Through a Quick Application, you can open and update only one data base, with a single master index (either an MDX tag or an NDX index), using one (optional) screen form, and you can produce output based on one report form and one label form.

To define a Quick Application, you select the **Generate quick application** option on the **Application** menu, and enter the specifications on a screen like the one shown in Figure 22-5. In addition to the data base, index, screen form, report form, and label form, you must enter a heading for the application main menu screen and, optionally, identify the author of the application. Just as when you define the application object, you can type each file name yourself or press SHIFT-F1 (Pick) to call up a pick list of files of the appropriate type.

When you press CTRL-END to save your specifications, dBASE IV displays a dialog box to ask whether you want to generate the application immediately. If you choose **No**, you can generate the Quick Application later in the same work session or in a later work session by selecting the **Generate quick application** option from the **Application** menu again. dBASE IV generates just one program (rather than the two generated to execute a standard application) to

```
Design  Application    Generate  Preset  Exit                         9:37:47 am
0                                                                                
1          Name and describe
2          Assign main menu
3          Display sign-on banner
4          Edit program header comments
5        ► Modify application environment
6          Generate quick application

  Database file:       NWCUST              Screen format file:  NWCUST
  Report format file:  NWCUSTRF            Label format file:   NWCUST1

  Set INDEX to:
        ORDER:        ACCOUNT

  Application author:          Miriam Liskin
  Application menu heading:    National Widgets Customer System

19
20•••+••••1••••+••••2••••+••••3••••+••••4••••+••••5••••+••••6••••+••••7••••+••••
App      C:\dbase4\NWQUICK                          File:NWCUST
                     Accept: Ctrl-End     Cancel: Esc
               Enter the menu heading for the quick application
```

Figure 22-5.

Defining a Quick Application

execute a Quick Application, and gives this program the same name as the application (and the usual PRG extension). If you created the National Widgets Customer File and at least some of the sample forms covered in earlier chapters, you may want to try generating and running the Quick Application described by the specifications in Figure 22-5.

Running a Quick Application

The main menu of every Quick Application is identical, except for the heading displayed at the top of the screen and the presence or absence of the **Reindex database** option, which is missing if you did not enter an index name when you defined the application. Figure 22-6 illustrates the main menu of the National Widgets Quick Application generated from the specifications in Figure 22-5. At the top of the screen, dBASE IV displays a banner that includes the current date, time, and the text you entered as the application menu heading when you defined the application; the main menu, which is always a pop-up menu, appears in the center. The Quick Application uses the display colors, frame style, environment settings, and other application defaults established through the **Preset** menu, which is covered later in this chapter.

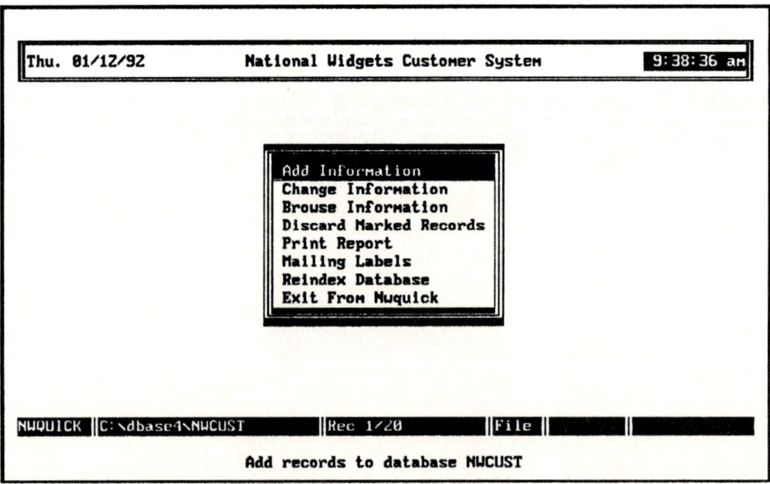

Figure 22-6.

Running a Quick Application

The **Add Information, Change Information,** and **Browse Information** options enable you to update the data base specified for the application. If you named a screen form when you defined the application, dBASE IV uses it for these three options; if not, it displays the standard Edit and Browse screens. The **Discard Marked Records** option packs the data base to erase records that were marked for deletion, and **Reindex Database** rebuilds all index tags and open NDX indexes.

When you select either **Print Report** or **Mailing Labels,** dBASE IV displays a standard pop-up menu of record positioning options as well as a reminder of the master index and the names of the first 16 fields in the data base structure. This screen is illustrated in Figure 22-7 for the Quick Application described by the specifications in Figure 22-5. The record positioning menu always appears in Quick Applications, but you can also request this menu in a custom application, before printing any report or listing.

To begin printing without moving the record pointer, you select **Done positioning** from the record positioning menu. The **Change index order** option on this menu enables you to choose a new master index from a pick list of available tags and NDX indexes like the one shown in Figure 22-8. To process records in the order in which they were entered, you can select **Natural Order** from the list. If an index is active, you can carry out an index key search by

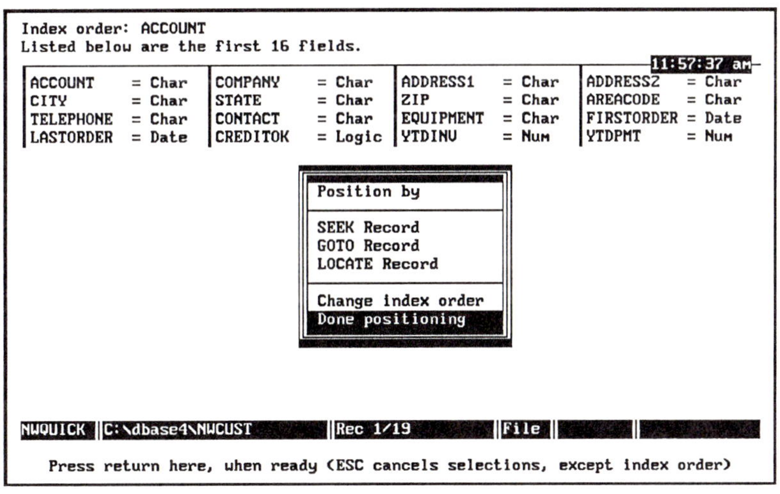

Figure 22-7.

The record positioning menu displayed when you print from a Quick Application

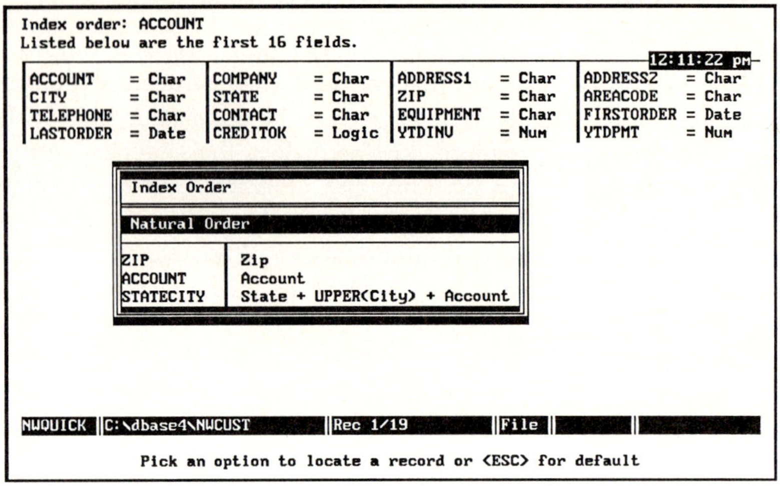

```
Index order: ACCOUNT
Listed below are the first 16 fields.
                                                                    12:11:22 pm
ACCOUNT    = Char  |COMPANY    = Char  |ADDRESS1   = Char  |ADDRESS2   = Char
CITY       = Char  |STATE      = Char  |ZIP        = Char  |AREACODE   = Char
TELEPHONE  = Char  |CONTACT    = Char  |EQUIPMENT  = Char  |FIRSTORDER = Date
LASTORDER  = Date  |CREDITOK   = Logic |YTDINV     = Num   |YTDPMT     = Num

          Index Order
          Natural Order
          ZIP        | Zip
          ACCOUNT    | Account
          STATECITY  | State + UPPER(City) + Account

NWQUICK |C:\dbase4\NWCUST       |Rec 1/19        |File |
          Pick an option to locate a record or <ESC> for default
```

Figure 22-8.

Selecting a new master index

selecting **SEEK Record** from the record positioning menu; this option is disabled when you process a file in natural order. You can use the **GOTO Record** option to move to the top or bottom of the file (if an index is active, these options move you to the record that corresponds to the first or last index entry), or to any record by number. The **LOCATE Record** option enables you to enter a scope, FOR clause, or WHILE clause, and then search for the first matching record.

If you exit from the record positioning menu by pressing ESC, dBASE IV cancels all your selections except the master index, which remains in effect until you change it explicitly (either from the record positioning menu or by using the **Order records by index** option on the **Organize** menu in Edit or Browse). If you exit by choosing the **Done positioning** option, dBASE IV positions the record pointer as you requested. In either case, it displays another pop-up menu that enables you to select the output device for the printout. You can always choose **Screen** or **Printer**; for labels, you can also select **Label Sample** option (which is displayed but is unavailable for reports) to request that dBASE IV print sample labels as an alignment guide before beginning to print the data. If you change your mind at this point, you can cancel the print job by choosing **Return** to go back to the main menu without producing any output.

GENERATING APPLICATION PROGRAMS

Like the report, label, and screen form layout editors, the applications generator generates dBASE IV programs that carry out the instructions you specify on the application design screen. When you run the application, dBASE IV compiles and executes these programs, just as it does the generated format files, report-printing programs, and label-printing programs, and the programs that you write. You can regenerate the application code as often as you like, and by generating the program at several interim stages of development, you can test the effects of some of your selections or fine-tune the appearance of the menus before you commit yourself to a given menu hierarchy or display style for the finished application.

To generate an application, you select the **Begin generating** option from the **Generate** menu. You do not need to retrieve all the objects in an application onto the work surface before you generate the programs. Each object contains all the information dBASE IV needs to find the other objects that it calls. Beginning with the application object, which always remains visible on the application design screen, dBASE IV can trace the complete chain of objects that make up an application.

Even a small application can require over 1000 lines of code (the program that executes a Quick Application is about 750 lines long), and the generation step can take some time, even on a fast hard disk. dBASE IV monitors the progress of the operation by counting lines in the third segment of the status bar. If you want to see the program statements as they are generated, you can select **Display during generation** from the **Generate** menu and set this option to **Yes** (the default is **No**). The program lines will scroll by faster than you can read them, but if you are familiar with the structure of the generated programs, you can often spot a section of interest before it disappears off the top of the screen. You can press CTRL-S at any point to pause the display momentarily and then press the same key to resume execution. After it finishes building the application programs, dBASE IV displays a message below the status bar to inform you: "Generation is complete. Press any key. . . ."

For each application, dBASE IV writes two program files: one, which has the same name as the application object, to start up the application and establish the working environment, and another, which has the same name as the main menu, that displays the main menu and executes the actions assigned to the main menu options (which may include running other menus). These two files both have the standard dBASE IV program extension, PRG, and both are required to run the application. The files created by the applications generator

to store menu, pick list, and batch process objects (the files with the extensions BAR, POP, FIL, STR, VAL, and BCH) are required only to modify the system on the application design screen.

Generating Documentation

dBASE IV generates an application (or any other program) by reading a file called a *template,* which contains a skeleton, or outline, of the finished program, and merging into the template the specific details that you enter on the application design screen to produce the final program that runs the application. If you changed the template (you can do so if you have the Developer's Edition of dBASE IV and you learn the template programming language), the same application design screen specifications could produce a very different finished product.

In addition to the standard template that builds the application program, dBASE IV provides a template that generates documentation—a text file containing a description of the application rather than dBASE IV program code to run the application. To use this template, you choose the **Select template** option from the **Generate** menu, and type DOCUMENT.GEN when dBASE IV prompts you for the template name. Although you can generate the program code from anywhere on the application design screen, you must select the application object before dBASE IV will allow you to switch templates. Also note that you cannot generate documentation for a Quick Application, presumably because the structure of all Quick Applications is the same and is adequately described by the specifications on the application definition screen and the dialog box invoked by selecting **Generate quick application** from the **Application** menu (which you can print by pressing PRTSC with the information displayed on the screen).

When you select the DOCUMENT.GEN template, dBASE IV displays a dialog box to ask whether you have an IBM graphics-compatible printer. If you type Y (for "Yes"), it uses continuous single- and double-line borders in the finished documentation to produce menu images that look just as they do on the screen. If you enter "N" (for "No"), dBASE IV substitutes dashes, vertical lines, and other symbols that any printer can reproduce. The documentation is stored in a file that has the same name as the application, and the extension DOC. You can print this file with a DOS or dBASE IV TYPE command or with any text editor or word processor that can read ASCII text files. Figure 22-9 illustrates the first few pages of the documentation for the National Widgets application.

```
Page: 1  Date: 2-27-91


Application Documentation for System: NW.PRG

Application Author: Miriam Liskin
Copyright Notice..: Copyright (C) 1991. All rights reserved.
dBASE Version.....: dBASE IV version 1.1


Display Application Sign-On Banner: Yes

Main Menu to Open : NWCMAIN.BAR

Sets for Application:
---------------------
  Bell         ON
  Carry        OFF
  Century      OFF
  Confirm      OFF
  Delimiters   OFF
  Display Size 25 lines
  Drive
  Escape       ON
  Path
  Safety       ON

Starting Colors for Application:
--------------------------------
 Color Settings:
   Text           : W+/B
   Heading        : W/B
   Highlight      : GR+/BG
   Box            : GR+/BG
   Messages       : W+/N
   Information    : B/W
   Fields         : N/BG

Database/View: NWCUST
Index Order: ACCOUNT

==============================================================================

Menu/Picklist definitions follow:
---------------------------------
```

Figure 22-9.

Documentation generated by the applications generator

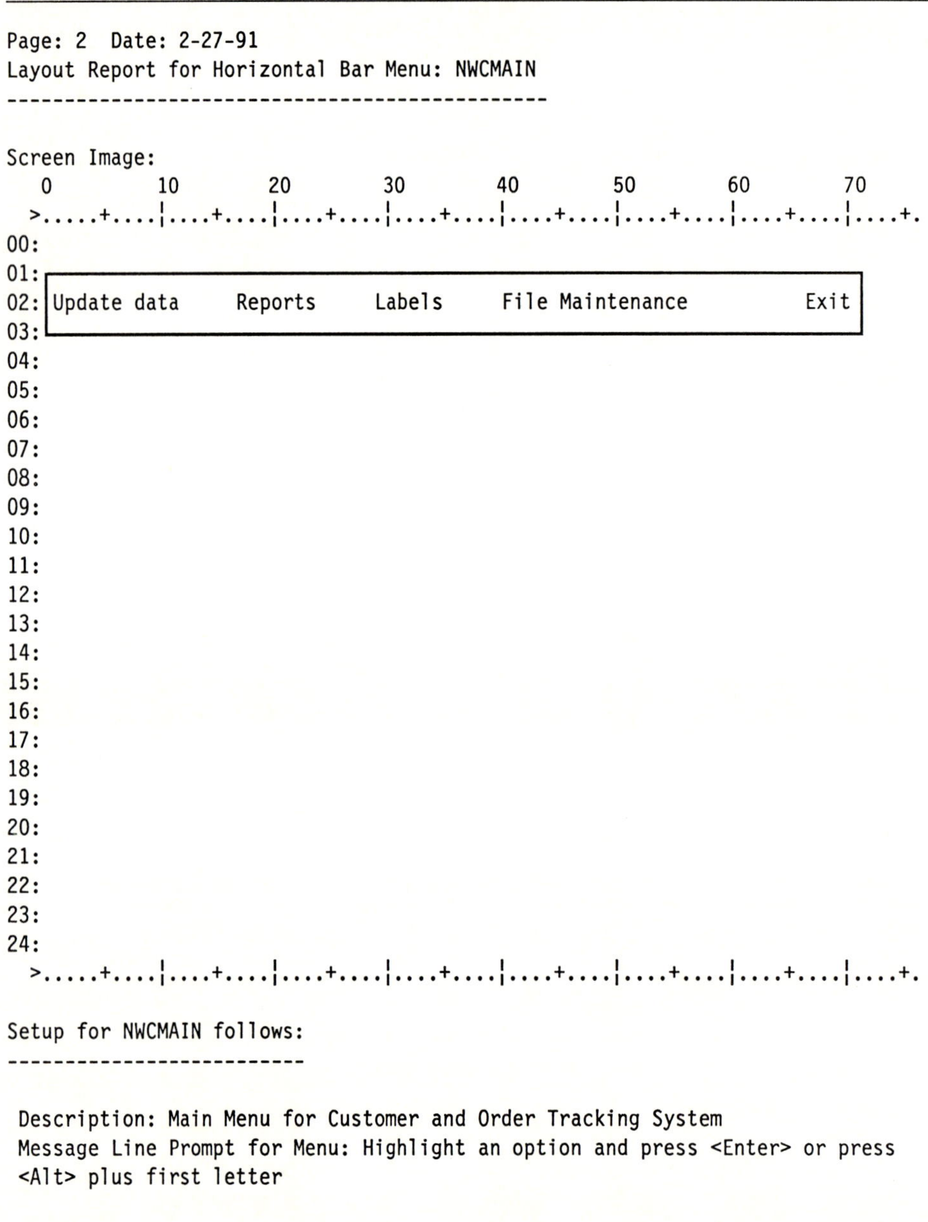

```
Page: 2  Date: 2-27-91
Layout Report for Horizontal Bar Menu: NWCMAIN
-----------------------------------------------

Screen Image:
   0         10        20        30        40        50        60        70
  >.....+....|....+....|....+....|....+....|....+....|....+....|....+....|....+.
00:
01:┌──────────────────────────────────────────────────────────────────────┐
02:│Update data      Reports      Labels      File Maintenance          Exit│
03:└──────────────────────────────────────────────────────────────────────┘
04:
05:
06:
07:
08:
09:
10:
11:
12:
13:
14:
15:
16:
17:
18:
19:
20:
21:
22:
23:
24:
  >.....+....|....+....|....+....|....+....|....+....|....+....|....+....|....+.

Setup for NWCMAIN follows:
--------------------------

 Description: Main Menu for Customer and Order Tracking System
 Message Line Prompt for Menu: Highlight an option and press <Enter> or press
 <Alt> plus first letter
```

Figure 22-9.

Documentation generated by the applications generator (*continued*)

```
Colors for Menu/Picklist:
-------------------------
 Color Settings:
   Text            : W+/B
   Heading         : W/B
   Highlight       : GR+/BG
   Box             : GR+/BG
   Messages        : W+/N
   Information     : B/W
   Fields          : N/BG

Bar actions for Menu NWCMAIN follow:
------------------------------------

Bar: 1
 Prompt: Update data
 Action: Open a Popup Menu Named: UPDATE
 Message Line Prompt for Item: Update a data base file

 Page: 3  Date: 2-27-91 12:09p
--------------------------------------------------------------------------------

Bar: 2
 Prompt: Reports
 Action: Open a Popup Menu Named: REPORTS
 Message Line Prompt for Item: Print lists and reports
--------------------------------------------------------------------------------

Bar: 3
 Prompt: Labels
 Action: Open a Popup Menu Named: LABELS
 Message Line Prompt for Item: Print labels, envelopes, and Rolodex cards
--------------------------------------------------------------------------------

Bar: 4
 Prompt: File Maintenance
 Action: Open a Popup Menu Named: MAINTAIN
 Message Line Prompt for Item: Carry out periodic file maintenance operations
--------------------------------------------------------------------------------

Bar: 5
 Prompt: Exit
 Action: Open a Popup Menu Named: EXIT
 Message Line Prompt for Item: Exit from this application to the dot prompt or to DOS
--------------------------------------------------------------------------------
```

Figure 22-9.

Documentation generated by the applications generator (*continued*)

```
Page: 4  Date: 2-27-91
Layout Report for Popup Menu: UPDATE
-----------------------------------

Screen Image:
   0         10        20        30        40        50        60        70
  >.....+....|....+....|....+....|....+....|....+....|....+....|....+....|....+.
00:
01:
02:
03:
04: ┌────────────────────┐
05: │ View, Add, & Edit  │
06: ├────────────────────┤
07: │ Customers          │
08: │ Orders             │
09: │ Inventory Items    │
10: └────────────────────┘
11:
12:
13:
14:
15:
16:
17:
18:
19:
20:
21:
22:
23:
24:
  >.....+....|....+....|....+....|....+....|....+....|....+....|....+....|....+.
Setup for UPDATE follows:
------------------------


Colors for Menu/Picklist:
------------------------
 Color Settings:
   Text           : W+/B
   Heading        : W/B
```

Figure 22-9.

Documentation generated by the applications generator (*continued*)

```
   Highlight      : GR+/BG
   Box            : GR+/BG
   Messages       : W+/N
   Information    : B/W
   Fields         : N/BG

Bar actions for Menu UPDATE follow:
-----------------------------------
Bar: 1
 Prompt: View, Add, & Edit
 Action: Text only defined for this option - NO ACTION
-------------------------------------------------------------------------------
```

Figure 22-9.

Documentation generated by the applications generator (*continued*)

The generated documentation is intended to serve as a concise reference to the structure, organization, and components of an application, not as instructions for learning how to use the application. The documentation is handy when you want to return to the applications generator to enhance or modify a complex application and you do not remember every detail of the menu structure or all the item actions. If you write applications that other people will use, you can use the generated documentation as an outline as you write the user-oriented documentation, which should include, at the very least, a brief summary of the purpose of each menu option and instructions for operating the parts of the system that are not self-explanatory.

RUNNING AN APPLICATION

You can run an application from the Control Center or from the dot prompt, and you can invoke dBASE IV in a way that automatically starts up your application so that you never have any direct contact with dBASE IV. To start up dBASE IV and immediately run an application (or any other dBASE IV program), you include the name of the application in the command line that you type to load dBASE IV. For example, to run the National Widgets application, you would type the following at the DOS prompt:

```
DBASE NWCUST
```

By entering a COMMAND command in the CONFIG.DB file, you can configure dBASE IV to run your application automatically every time you start up the program. The command is the same DO command that you type at the dot prompt to run the application. For example, to start up the National Widgets application automatically, you could use the following entry in the CONFIG.DB file:

```
COMMAND = DO NWCUST
```

From the Menus

To run an application from the Control Center, you select its name from the **Applications** panel, press ENTER, and then select **Run application** from the resulting dialog box. dBASE IV asks you to confirm your intentions by displaying the message, "Are you sure you want to run this application?" If the INSTRUCT setting is OFF, you can bypass this message and start up an application by pressing ENTER with the application name highlighted.

From the Dot Prompt

To run an application from the dot prompt, you use a DO command, just as you would to run any other program. For example, to run the National Widgets customer application, you would type

```
DO NWCUST
```

ESTABLISHING PRESET APPLICATION DEFAULTS

The **Preset** menu enables you to establish your own personalized application environment settings, in much the same way as the CONFIG.DB file enables you to customize the dBASE IV working environment. Note that the defaults you specify on the **Preset** menu apply only to *future* applications that you

create, not to the one you were working on when you modified the settings. Because you cannot invoke the application design screen without creating an application, the only way to customize the preset options to suit your personal preferences before you create your first real application is to define a "dummy" application, and then erase this application afterward. If you used a common prefix for the names of the application and its main menu, for example, XXAPP and XXMENU, you could erase all the application files with one DOS command, as follows:

```
ERASE XX*.*
```

When you define a new application, you can override any of the settings established through the **Preset** menu by using the **Modify application environment** option on the **Application** menu. Within an application, each menu *inherits* the default settings selected for the application as a whole, but you can override the defaults for any menu or list by using options on the menus that describe the individual menu or list object.

The **Sign-on defaults** option on the **Preset** menu allows you to enter three lines of text called **Application author, Copyright notice,** and **dBASE version.** dBASE IV includes three comment lines containing these entries in the comment *header* it places at the beginning of the generated application programs. Despite this usage, your entries for these three items need not conform to the prompts in the sign-on defaults dialog box, especially if you do not intend to read or modify the generated code.

By default, dBASE IV displays the application author, copyright notice, and dBASE version inside the sign-on screen frame, but you can change or add to the sign-on screen text (without affecting the comment header) by typing directly in the application object frame on the work surface. You can erase existing lines of text by pressing CTRL-Y, and insert new lines by pressing CTRL-N. These commands affect only the contents of the application object frame, not its size. You can use SHIFT-F7 (Size) to adjust the size of the frame, and F7 (Move) to position it anywhere on the screen. The sign-on screen for the National Widgets customer application is visible in the center of the screen pictured in Figure 22-2.

You can use the **Display options** menu to select the default **Object border style**—the type of border that surrounds menus and pick lists. You can choose **DOUBLE, SINGLE, PANEL** (a solid bar of color), or **NONE.** To create a horizontal bar menu that emulates the appearance of the dBASE IV main menu

bars, select **NONE**. Note, however, that even if you do not display an object frame, dBASE IV still reserves space for it on the work surface and does not allow you to move the object to any position where the invisible frame would be off the screen. You can set the foreground and background colors or monochrome display attributes for the two major screen regions (Standard and Enhanced) or for the seven more detailed regions that you can customize for dBASE IV as a whole by using the **Settings** menus described in Chapter 18.

The **Environment settings** option enables you to customize a few of the dBASE IV environment settings—BELL, CARRY, CENTURY, CONFIRM, ESCAPE, SAFETY, and DELIMITERS. All of these settings were described in Chapter 18, except ESCAPE, which determines whether you can interrupt a program by pressing ESC. When the ESCAPE setting is OFF, dBASE IV ignores the ESC key. You may be tempted to turn the ESCAPE setting OFF to help ensure that calculations and file update operations are completed without interruption, but you should use this option with caution. If pressing the ESC key fails to have its customary effect, a frustrated operator may turn off the computer or reboot—actions that can have disastrous consequences if data bases are open.

The settings accessible through the **Environment settings** option form a very limited subset of the dBASE IV environment settings. If you want to change other settings, you can do so by using the **Embed code** option, which is described in the next section, to run SET commands (exactly the same SET commands you would type at the dot prompt) *before* dBASE IV executes the main menu of your application.

The **Application drive/path** option enables you to select the default disk drive and search path for your application. These settings are equivalent to the **Default disk drive** and **Disk drive search path** options established overall for dBASE IV through the SET menu described in Chapter 18, or to the dot prompt SET DEFAULT and SET PATH commands. The applications generator does not offer an option that corresponds to the **OS Working drive/directory** option available through the SET menu, which enables you to choose a default disk drive and subdirectory at the same time (the equivalent of the dot prompt SET DIRECTORY command). Remember that dBASE IV uses the default drive for all files it reads and writes, whereas the search path is used only to search for files not found in the current subdirectory and has no influence on the location of new files that dBASE IV creates. Before you start up dBASE IV to run a generated application, you should therefore make sure that you log onto the right subdirectory on the application drive.

THE COMMON APPLICATIONS GENERATOR MENU OPTIONS

As noted earlier in this chapter, the applications generator menu bar includes four options that are always present, as well as others that vary, depending on what type of object is currently selected. The first option on the applications generator menu is always **Design**. The **Design** menu enables you to design a new object—a horizontal bar menu, pop-up menu, file, field, or values list, or batch process—or to load a previously created object onto the work surface. You use the **Generate** menu to generate the dBASE IV programs that execute the application or to create printed documentation that describes the application. The **Preset** menu, which was described in the previous section, enables you to choose the default frame style, display colors, environment settings, default disk drive, and search path for future applications. The **Exit** menu contains the usual **Save changes and exit** and **Abandon changes and exit** alternatives. If you select **Save changes and exit**, dBASE IV saves each object displayed on the work surface before returning you to the Control Center or the dot prompt.

The second option on the menu bar depends on the currently selected object—it is **Application** when the application object is selected, **Menu** when you are editing a horizontal bar menu or pop-up menu, **List** when you are working with a file, field, or values list, and **Batch** when you are defining a batch process. For all types of objects except the application object, an additional option— **Item**—appears in the third position of the main menu bar. The options on the **Application**, **Menu**, **List**, and **Batch** pull-down menus affect the object as a whole, and the options on the **Item** menu enable you to define the characteristics of individual items in the current menu, list, or batch process.

The complexity and plasticity of the menu system can be confusing at first, but although the main menu bar changes, the **Menu**, **List**, and **Batch** pull-down menus have a great deal in common. All of these menus include a **Name and describe** option, which enables you to enter a name for the disk file used to store the object, a brief description of the purpose of the object, and, for menus and lists, a default message line prompt that dBASE IV displays when you run the application and select the menu or list (for batch processes, which are not displayed on the screen in the finished application, the message line prompt option is absent).

Each object menu has an option to **Override assigned database or view** and specify a different view or data base and optionally, an MDX index tag or NDX index. The **Embed code** option enables you to enter up to 19 dBASE IV commands, typed exactly as you would at the dot prompt or in a dBASE IV

program, which dBASE IV executes either before or after the action associated with the selected item is carried out.

For menus and lists, you can select **Modify display options** to override the default frame style or display colors. You can use the **Write help text** option to define a help screen consisting of up to 19 lines of text, which dBASE IV displays when you press F1 (Help) with the item selected while running the finished application. Neither of these options is applicable to batch processes, which are not displayed as objects on the screen when you run the application.

Each object menu includes a **Save** option that enables you to save the current object on disk without leaving the application design screen or removing the object from the work surface. The easiest way to define a new menu or list that resembles an existing object of the same type is to load the previously defined object onto the work surface, modify it as required, use the **Name and describe** option on the object menu to assign a new name, and select **Save current menu** or **Save current list** to save the modified object under the new name. Note that dBASE IV retains the new name in memory, as you can see by looking at the file name displayed in the status bar when the object is selected, and applies all further changes that you make to the object to this new copy.

The **Put away** option allows you to remove the selected object from the work surface (dBASE IV saves the object first if it has changed since you saved it last). You may want to put some objects away to "clean up" the work surface, or you may be forced to remove objects if you get an "Insufficient memory" error message. Each object menu also has a **Clear work surface** option, which removes all objects except the main application object from the work surface. For each object that you have changed since you last saved it, dBASE IV displays a dialog box that informs you "The current frame has been modified" and offers two options: **Save changes** and **Abandon changes**.

The **Item** menu enables you to define the characteristics of individual items in the current menu or batch process, and to define collectively the items on a structure, files, or values list. The options on the **Item** menu also vary, depending on the type of objects, but many of the options are the same for all three types. The **Item** menu selections are described in detail later in this chapter.

As noted earlier, you can use the F4 (Next) and F3 (Previous) keys to move among the objects on the work surface. The application design screen differs from the other dBASE IV layout editors in that these keys are active even when a menu is pulled down, so you can select the same option in turn for two or more objects in succession without having to press ESC to close the current menu, press F4 (Next) or F3 (Previous) to select another object on the work surface, and then reactivate the menu system.

You can also press PGDN or PGUP to select the next or previous item within the current menu or batch process. For example, you can pull down the **Item** menu and define the individual menu items one after the other without exiting from the menu system and returning to the work surface. You can even use these keys with an option on the **Item** menu selected. For example, you could select **Assign message line prompt** from the **Item** menu, enter the text of the message line prompt for one menu item, press PGDN to move to the next item, enter its message line prompt, and so on. Whenever a menu object is selected, dBASE IV displays the text of the selected menu item in the third segment of the status bar, which remains visible on the screen even when the menu itself is covered by a dialog box or another menu.

Some of the object menus also include unique options that apply only to objects of the specified type. The **Application** menu contains options that enable you to change all of the settings you originally entered on the application definition screen when you first invoked the applications generator to create the application. The **Assign main menu** option enables you to select a new menu or batch process to serve as the application main menu, and the **Modify application environment** option allows you to override the default display colors and environment settings established through the **Preset** menu and to change the default view or data base and index.

The **Display sign-on banner** option on the **Application** menu determines whether dBASE IV displays the text in the application object frame as an initial sign-on screen when you run the finished application. If you choose **Yes** (the default), dBASE IV displays the frame, together with a message at the bottom of the screen that instructs the user to "Press ↵ to Continue." Setting this option to **No** causes dBASE IV to bypass the sign-on screen and display the main menu of the application immediately. The **Edit program header comments** option enables you to change the three lines of text that identify the author, copyright notice, and dBASE IV version in the comment lines added to the generated programs. As noted earlier in this chapter, dBASE IV also displays these three items in the sign-on screen frame unless you override this default by typing new text in the application object frame on the work surface.

When the current object is a horizontal bar menu, the **Menu** menu includes an **Attach pull-down menus** option, which links pop-up menus to horizontal bar menu options so that a pop-up menu is displayed (pulled down) whenever the corresponding bar menu option is highlighted. When the current object is a structure, files, or values list, the **List** menu has an option that enables you to identify the contents of the list (the file names, field names, or field values, respectively). These menu options are described in greater detail in the sections that describe how to create each type of object.

DEFINING A HORIZONTAL BAR MENU

To define a horizontal bar menu, you select **Horizontal bar menu** from the **Design** menu, and then choose **<create>** from the pick list of bar menu names. dBASE IV displays a menu definition dialog box analogous to the application definition screen, in which you enter a name for the disk file that will store the menu specifications and optionally, a brief description of the menu and a line of text that dBASE IV displays on the message line when you run the application and select the menu. This display is pictured in Figure 22-10 for the National Widgets system main menu. If you do not enter a message line prompt, dBASE IV uses a generic message that explains how to navigate through the menu and select options: "Position with ← → - <ENTER> to select choice - <F1> Help." Note also that you can define message line prompts for individual menu options, and dBASE IV displays the message associated with the menu only if there is no individual message for the selected option. Thus, if you assign a message line prompt to each menu option, you will never see the one assigned to the menu as a whole.

After you press CTRL-END to save the menu specifications, dBASE IV displays an empty menu frame, using the border style and colors defined in the **Preset**

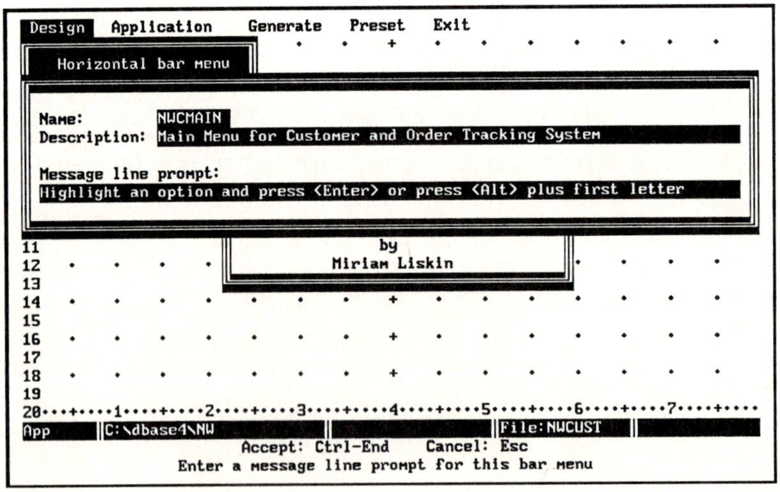

```
Design  Application   Generate   Preset   Exit
  Horizontal bar menu

  Name:        NWCMAIN
  Description: Main Menu for Customer and Order Tracking System

  Message line prompt:
  Highlight an option and press <Enter> or press <Alt> plus first letter

11                         by
12                    Miriam Liskin
13
14
15
16
17
18
19
20•••+••••1••••+••••2••••+••••3••••+••••4••••+••••5••••+••••6••••+••••7••••+••••
App      C:\dbase4\NW                         File:NWCUST
                 Accept: Ctrl-End    Cancel: Esc
            Enter a message line prompt for this bar menu
```

Figure 22-10.

Defining a horizontal bar menu

menu. By default, the frame occupies three lines (including the border) and appears at the top of the screen, but you can move or resize it using the standard function keys (SHIFT-F7 (Size) to resize the menu frame and F7 (Move) to move it). In most cases, you should move the menu down one line from the default location to leave row 0 free for dBASE IV status indicators. Remember also that a horizontal bar menu can be more than one line deep, that it need not extend all the way across the screen, and that it does not have to be horizontal. You might want to use a "vertical" bar menu to take advantage of the unique features of bar menus—the ALT-key method for selecting menu options or the ability to attach pull-down menus to the options. Remember, however, that the user must always press the LEFT ARROW and RIGHT ARROW keys to move among bar menu options, even if the menu is vertical.

To define a menu option, you move the cursor to the desired location, press F5, type the text of the option (which can be one or more words), and press F5 again. Use the LEFT ARROW and RIGHT ARROW keys to move to the location of the next menu option, and repeat the process as many times as necessary to define all your menu options. (As in the other dBASE IV layout editors, you press the F5 key to place an item on the work surface, although the usual name for this key, "Field", does not accurately describe the type of item.) The first letters of the menu options need not be unique, but if they are, you can select options by using ALT-key combinations when you run the application, just as you can when you work in the dBASE IV menu system. You cannot enter descriptive text in a bar menu frame, only menu options, and if you forget to press F5 before you begin to type a menu option, dBASE IV displays the error message "Text not allowed in Bar Menus."

When you are working on a horizontal bar menu, the second option in the applications generator menu bar is **Menu**, and this menu contains options to edit the bar menu specifications. Those options that are common to all the object menus are described later in this chapter. If you use a horizontal bar menu as the main menu of an application, each bar menu option may invoke another menu, usually a pop-up menu or a files list. You can set the **Attach pull-down menus** option to **Yes** to cause dBASE IV to automatically display—or pull down—the associated menu or list when you highlight a horizontal menu bar option while running the application. By default this option is set to **No**, and a pop-up menu appears only when you press ENTER to select the corresponding horizontal bar menu option.

DEFINING A POP-UP MENU

To define a pop-up menu, you select **Pop-up menu** from the **Design** menu, and then choose **<create>** from the pick list of menu names. Just as when you define a horizontal bar menu, dBASE IV prompts you to enter a name, description, and message line prompt for the pop-up menu. When you press CTRL-END to save the menu description, dBASE IV displays a menu frame (using the border style and colors defined in the **Preset** menu) in the center of the screen. Unlike bar menus, pop-up menus can contain both menu options and text; you differentiate between the two by assigning an action to each line that represents a menu option (by default, dBASE IV interprets all lines simply as displayed text). dBASE IV does not scroll the data entry area in the menu frame either horizontally or vertically, so you must resize the frame if the default size does not accommodate the text and menu options you want to enter.

You can use many of the standard function keys to edit the contents of a menu frame. For example, you can insert a blank line above the current line by pressing CTRL-N, and you can delete a line and pull the remaining lines up to fill the gap by pressing CTRL-Y. To move the highlighted line to a new position in the menu frame, press F7 (Move), and then select **Item only** from the dialog box that dBASE IV displays to ask, "Move entire frame or item only?" You then use the cursor keys to reposition the selected item, and press ENTER to confirm its new position. You cannot place an item over another line of text, so make sure to clear a blank line for the item you wish to move. To move an item from one menu frame to another, select the item, press F7 (Move), select **Item only** from the dialog box, press F3 (Previous) or F4 (Next) to select the target frame, use the arrow keys if necessary to position the item in the new frame, and finally, press ENTER to lock the item in place.

To move a menu frame and its contents as a unit, press F7 (Move), select **Entire frame** from the dialog box, use the arrow keys to reposition the menu frame, and press ENTER to confirm the new position. If you use the **Attach pull-down menus** option on the **Menu** menu to link pop-up menus to the associated options on a horizontal bar menu, you may want to move the pop-up menus so that they appear directly under the corresponding horizontal bar menu options, but the linkage between the menus does not depend on the position of either menu on the screen. To create a menu system that looks like the dBASE IV menus, you can define a horizontal bar menu with no borders and position the associated pull-down menus directly underneath.

Figure 22-11 illustrates the application design screen with the National Widgets system main menu and the pop-up attached to the **Update data** option on the work surface. This pop-up was resized to match the contents, and moved to a position right under the corresponding bar menu option; it contains two lines of text, followed by three options with assigned actions. To create a continuous line such as the one that separates the title "View, Add, & Edit" from the menu options (rather than a row of dashes), you can use the ALT key in combination with the numbers on the numeric keypad to enter the decimal ASCII code for the desired line-drawing character. For example, ALT-196 yields the continuous single-line character, and ALT-205 the double-line character.

DEFINING FILES, STRUCTURE, AND VALUES LISTS

The applications generator enables you to define three types of lists: files lists, structure lists, and values lists. In some contexts, you may want to display a list solely to provide information, but more often, you will take advantage of the

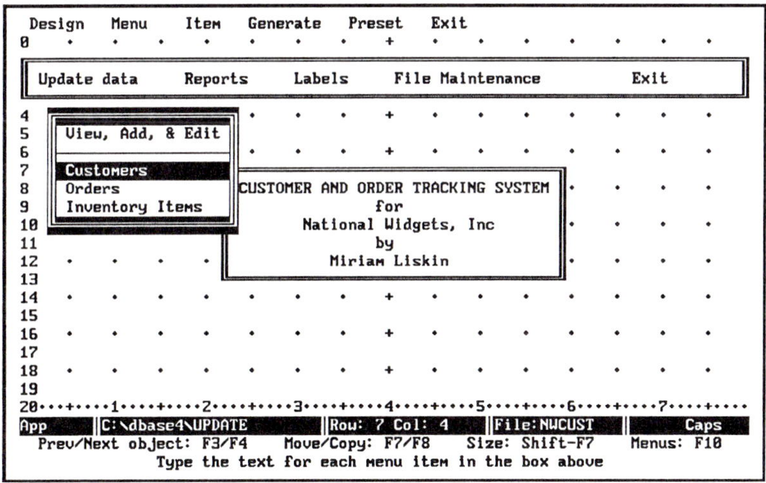

Figure 22-11.

A bar menu with an attached pull-down menu

fact that the lists you define function just like the pick lists displayed by dBASE IV. This property enables you to use lists much as you do menus, except that the lists are constructed dynamically by dBASE IV based on the environment when you run the application, rather than specified explicitly on the application design screen. For example, you could define a files list of label forms, invoked by one of the label printing options on an application menu. When you run the application, dBASE IV builds the list based on the label forms that are present on disk at that moment. Just as in a standard dBASE IV pick list, you can use the cursor movement keys to move through the files, structure, or values list, and press ENTER to choose an item from the list. dBASE IV stores the name of the selected item in a special memory variable called LISTVAL (for "list value"), which you can use in your application.

By using file pick lists, you can make your applications more general, more flexible, and less dependent on your own ability to predict the precise status of the working environment. A pick list adds flexibility to an application by enabling the users to access newly created forms from within the menu-driven application environment, but a pick list is not appropriate in every situation. Some of your label- and report-printing menu options should invoke specific forms, so that you and other users of your application can simply select a menu option such as "Aging Report" or "Four-across Labels for California Customers" rather than having to remember the name of each report or label form.

To define a list, you select **Files list, Structure list,** or **Values list** from the **Design** menu. After you enter the name, description, and message line prompt on the list definition screen, dBASE IV displays a list frame in the center of the screen. At the top of the frame is a row of X's that represents a list item, and below the status bar, dBASE IV displays a reminder that "List objects can only be moved (F7) and sized (Shift-F7)." You cannot type text in the list frame—dBASE IV supplies the fixed text and dividing lines, and fills in the list items automatically when you run the application. By default, the list frame is 14 characters wide—wide enough to display the items in a files or structure (field name) list, but you may want to expand it for a values list that displays the contents of a wider field. You can also make a list longer to accommodate more entries, but a list could easily include more entries than would fit on the screen, and when you run the application, you can use UP ARROW, DOWN ARROW, PGUP, PGDN, and the other standard cursor movement keys to scroll through a long list.

The **List** menu always includes an option for identifying the items that appear in the list frame when you run the application. For a files list, this option is **Identify files in list,** and you describe the files by entering a file name matching pattern that includes the standard wildcard characters—a question

mark (?) to represent a single character and an asterisk (*) to represent any group of characters. Thus, you could define a list that includes all the label forms in the National Widgets system by specifying the file name as NW*.LBO, or display a list of view queries by entering *.QBO. Note that in order to create a pick list of report, label, or screen form files, you *must* define the list in terms of the *compiled program files*—the LBO, FRO, FMO, or QBO files—rather than the original form files or generated program files. dBASE IV can *display* a list of files of any type, but unless you display compiled program files in the list, you must embed code or modify the generated application programs in order to process the selection properly.

The fields in a structure list are always drawn from the default data base or view, or from the data base or view assigned using the **Override assigned data base or view** option on the **List** menu. By default, dBASE IV includes all the fields in the data base or view, including calculated fields (in a view). If the structure list is attached to a horizontal bar menu option (that is, the list is pulled down automatically when you select a bar menu option), dBASE IV allows you to select one field from the list when you run the application. If the list is not attached to a bar menu option, you can use the **Identify fields in list** option in the **List** menu to choose which fields appear in the list. You can type the field names explicitly, separated by commas, or you can press SHIFT-F1 (Pick) to choose the field names from a pick list. In either case, the total length of the field name list is limited to 68 characters (the width of the data entry area on the screen). Whether you display all the fields or a smaller subset, dBASE IV allows you to select more than one field name from the list when you run the completed application.

For a values list, you use the **Identify field values in list** option in the **List** menu to select one field (which may be a calculated field) in the data base or view assigned to the list that will provide the values in the list. When you run the application, the list includes the value of the specified field for each record in the active data base or view. You can use a values list to enable the user of your application to select a record to edit or print, using a method described later in this chapter in the section on defining item actions.

DEFINING A BATCH PROCESS

A batch process is a series of steps that dBASE IV can carry out in sequence without user intervention. A batch process is similar to a dBASE IV program or

a keyboard macro, but you define it entirely within the applications generator by selecting items from menus. If you have done most of your work through the menu system, you may find it easier to create a batch process than to write the equivalent program, because defining a batch process does not require a formal understanding of dBASE IV command syntax. Nevertheless, some familiarity with the dot prompt command verbs is helpful, because dBASE IV displays these verbs on the menus that you use to define the batch steps, and the longer descriptions of the actions are phrased differently from the corresponding dBASE IV menu options.

To define a batch process, you select **Batch process** from the **Design** menu, and enter a file name for the batch and a brief description of its purpose on a batch process definition screen. Unlike a menu or list, a batch process presents no visible frame on the screen in the finished application. There is no need for a message line prompt or a help screen, and neither the batch process definition screen nor the batch item menu includes options to enter these items. dBASE IV executes a batch process "behind the scenes" and displays a standard message for each action; for example, when it executes a batch step that marks records for deletion, dBASE IV displays the message "Searching for DELETED records."

When you save a batch process definition, dBASE IV displays a frame in the center of the screen and prompts you to "Type descriptive text for each batch item in the box above." The text you enter is never displayed when you run the application—it serves solely as internal documentation of the actions carried out by the batch, and it should describe each step in terms that you will understand when you edit the batch process or read the printed documentation that dBASE IV generates for the application. For example, you might describe the steps in an "End-of-year processing" batch process for the Customer File as follows:

Mark inactive customers for deletion
List customers marked for deletion
Permanently remove deleted customers
Zero customer year-to-date orders
Empty order file completely

The steps you can include in a batch process are not limited to commands that operate on a file as a whole with no user intervention. For example, you could define a batch process that carries out the same order processing steps as the NWOCALC.PRG program described in Chapter 21. Before performing the order calculations and updating the Customer File, the batch process could

create a temporary order file by copying the structure of the Order File, display the Edit screen (or a custom form) to enable you to enter a new batch of order records into this file, and print a list of the orders for which there was no matching customer or inventory item.

You specify the command that dBASE IV uses to carry out each step in the batch process by using the **Change action** option on the **Item** menu, as described in the next section. Defining the action taken by a batch process step is exactly the same as identifying the action taken by a menu item, and indeed, you could define a menu that contains the individual actions in a batch process. Batch processes offer the same advantages as the simple batch-type programs described in Chapter 21: by calling a batch process from a menu, you can execute a series of commands in a predetermined sequence, often with no user intervention or keyboard input.

DESCRIBING MENU, LIST, AND BATCH ITEMS

The previous three sections of this chapter described how to use the object menus—the **Menu**, **List**, and **Batch** menus—to define the overall characteristics of menus, lists, and batch processes. Whenever a menu, list, or batch object is selected, the applications generator menu bar includes an **Item** option. For a menu or batch process, you use the options on the **Item** menu to describe each item that performs an action. For a list, the selections you make using the **Item** menu options apply to all of the items displayed in the list. This distinction reflects a fundamental difference between menus and batch processes, which contain independent items that can trigger different actions, and lists, in which all the items are equivalent. Although a list is similar in appearance to a menu, it is closer in function to a variable—when you run the application, dBASE IV carries out the single action specified for the list on a particular file, field, or value selected from the list, instead of on a file, field, or value entered explicitly on the application design screen.

The most important option in the **Item** menu is **Change action**, which enables you to define the action associated with a list, menu option, or batch process step. The actions are described in detail in the next section, followed by a section that discusses the other **Item** menu options. This organization parallels one common order in which you might build the components of a complex application: first define the menu and list objects, define the actions taken by each menu option (including actions that call other menus or lists), test the

application to make sure that it performs as expected, and then return to the application design screen to add amenities such as message line prompts and help screens. Note however, that some of the options on the **Item** menu—in particular, those that allow you to select a data base, choose the master index, and position the record pointer—are essential for proper performance of your menu options.

Defining Item Actions

The most important step in describing the items in a menu, list, or batch process is using the **Change action** option on the **Item** menu to specify the actions that you want dBASE IV to carry out when you run the application and select each item. For a menu or batch process, you assign an action to every item. For a files, structure, or values list, you assign a single action to the list, which dBASE IV executes when you select any item from the list.

When you pull down the **Item** menu, dBASE IV highlights the **Change action** option if you have already assigned an action to the selected menu item (otherwise, it highlights **Show item information**). When you select **Change action**, dBASE IV displays the list of actions pictured in Figure 22-12. The default action is **Text (no action)**, so you can include headings and descriptive text in a pop-up menu without having to take any special measures to identify them as such. When you run the finished application, dBASE IV displays items for which you have assigned an action in brighter characters than text items, and only allows you to highlight and select items with assigned actions.

The **Open a menu** option causes dBASE IV to activate another menu or list—a horizontal bar menu, pop-up menu, files list, structure list, or values list. The examples described thus far in this chapter require only two levels of menus—a horizontal bar menu with options that display pop-up menus—but in a large application, the menu hierarchy can be considerably more complex. For example, the **Print** option on the main horizontal bar menu could invoke another bar menu that has four options: **Accounting Reports**, **Management Reports**, **Labels**, and **Personalized Letters**. Each of these options might call a pop-up menu that lists the specific reports and types of labels, and one of the options on a report or label menu might display a files list of available report or label forms.

The **Browse** and **Edit** options invoke the Browse and Edit screens to view, add, or edit records in the data base assigned to the menu item. When you choose either of these actions, dBASE IV displays a dialog box that includes

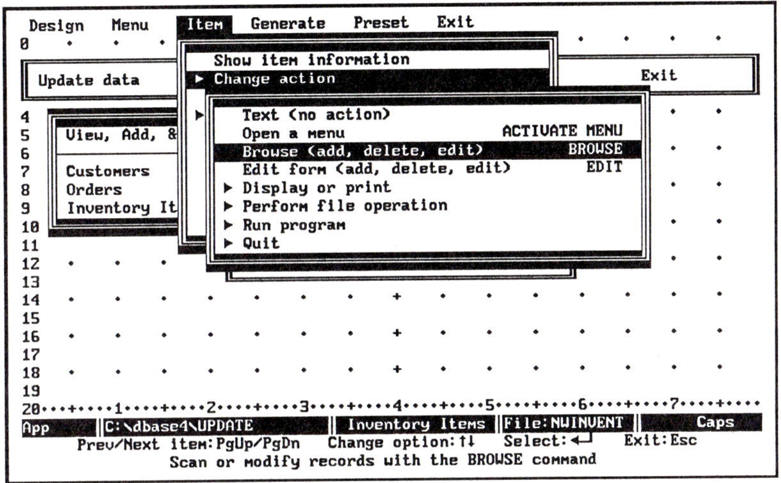

Figure 22-12.

Defining a menu action

options to customize many aspects of the Browse or Edit display. You may recognize these options from your prior work with dBASE IV, since many of the same options are available through the **Edit** and **Browse** menu bars or by adding keywords to an EDIT or BROWSE command typed at the dot prompt. The dot prompt keywords are displayed in uppercase letters in the dialog box, as you can see in Figure 22-13, which illustrates the browse dialog box with specifications for updating the Inventory File on the Browse screen filled in. If you do not understand what all of these options do, you may want to look up the keywords in the BROWSE and EDIT entries in Appendix C, or in the dBASE IV *Language Reference* manual.

For both the **Edit** and **Browse** actions, you can specify a field list, and you can define a filter condition to describe record selection criteria. You can name a screen form (called a "format file" as it is at the dot prompt) to substitute for the standard Browse or Edit screen. For the **Edit** action, you can also specify a scope, FOR clause, and WHILE clause (the BROWSE command does not support these options), and you can choose **EDIT** or **APPEND** as the initial data entry mode that dBASE IV uses when it first displays the Edit screen. For the **Browse** action, you can lock one or more fields at the left edge of the screen, specify the maximum column width, or use the **FREEZE edit for field** option to restrict editing to a single field.

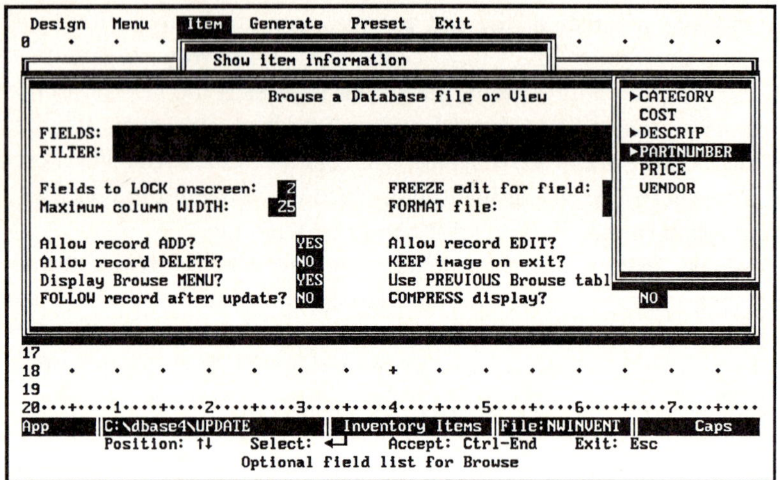
Design Menu Item Generate Preset Exit
Show item information
Browse a Database file or View
FIELDS:
FILTER:
Fields to LOCK onscreen: 2
Maximum column WIDTH: 25
FREEZE edit for field:
FORMAT file:
Allow record ADD? YES
Allow record DELETE? NO
Display Browse MENU? YES
FOLLOW record after update? NO
Allow record EDIT?
KEEP image on exit?
Use PREVIOUS Browse tabl
COMPRESS display? NO
▶CATEGORY
COST
▶DESCRIP
▶PARTNUMBER
PRICE
VENDOR
App C:\dbase4\UPDATE Inventory Items File:NWINVENT Caps
Position: ↑↓ Select: ←┘ Accept: Ctrl-End Exit: Esc
Optional field list for Browse

Figure 22-13.

Defining the Browse action

Additional options enable you to choose whether or not dBASE IV permits you to add records, edit (change) data, or delete records when you run the application. If you prohibit adding or deleting records, dBASE IV will not allow you to select the corresponding options from the **Records** menu on the Browse or Edit screen, and if you prohibit editing, dBASE IV treats every field as read/only. The remaining options determine whether dBASE IV allows you to activate the standard **Edit** or **Browse** menu, whether the record pointer should follow a record to its new position in the index when you change an index key field, and whether to retain the screen image or clear the screen after you exit from the full-screen edit mode.

The **Display or print** action enables you to print data using a report form or label form, or to display or print selected fields by executing the equivalent of a DISPLAY or LIST command. When you choose **REPORT FORM** or **LABEL FORM**, dBASE IV displays a dialog box in which you enter the report or label form name and select the output device. You can route report or label output to any of the three standard devices by selecting **SCREEN**, **PRINTER**, or **TEXT FILE**. If you select **ASK AT RUN TIME**, dBASE IV displays a menu of output devices similar to the one it uses in a Quick Application to allow you to choose the output destination "on the fly."

You can specify record selection criteria just as you do at the dot prompt—by entering any combination of a filter condition, scope, FOR clause,

and WHILE clause. However, your entry for each of these items can be only 68 characters long, whereas at the dot prompt, you are limited only by the total length of a command line (1024 characters). One way to circumvent this limitation is to predefine a view query that expresses the selection criteria and open this view instead of the underlying data base. You may also be able to define both a filter and a FOR clause that together define the selection criteria. Finally, you could use the **Embed code** option to embed a longer SET FILTER command *before* the display or print action is performed.

For reports (but not labels or lists), you can specify an additional line of heading text, choose between a report that prints full detail and a summary-only report (the report that dBASE IV would print if you closed the detail band before saving the report form or included the SUMMARY keyword in a REPORT FORM command typed at the dot prompt), suppress the page header and footer on all but the first page (as if you included the PLAIN keyword in a REPORT FORM command), and choose whether or not dBASE IV should eject the paper to the top of the next page before beginning to print. For labels, you can request that dBASE IV print samples to help you align the label stock in the printer.

The **DISPLAY/LIST** option produces the same output that you could generates by using a DISPLAY or LIST command at the dot prompt—LIST if you select **No** for the **PAUSE at full page/screen** option, or DISPLAY if you select **Yes**. The output device choices are the same as for reports or labels—**SCREEN, PRINTER, TEXT FILE,** and **ASK AT RUN TIME,** and you can choose whether or not you want the output to include record numbers. You can construct a field list, either by typing it or by selecting fields from a pick list invoked by pressing SHIFT-F1 (Pick) with the cursor in the data entry area next to the **FIELDS** prompt. Just as for reports and labels, you can specify record selection criteria by entering any combination of a filter condition, scope, FOR clause, and WHILE clause.

The **Perform file operation** option enables you to select dBASE IV commands that operate on all or some of the records in a data base. Figure 22-14 illustrates the file operations, which are listed, together with the equivalent dot prompt command verbs, in a pop-up menu. If you have been working at the dot prompt, most of these operations should seem familiar. The correspondence between the file operations and the dBASE IV menu system is more tenuous. Some of the file operations, such as **Import foreign file** and **Discard marked records**, are accessible through the menus, albeit under different names. Others, including **Copy records to file** and **Mark records for deletion,** would normally be carried out through update queries, not by executing single commands chosen from the menus.

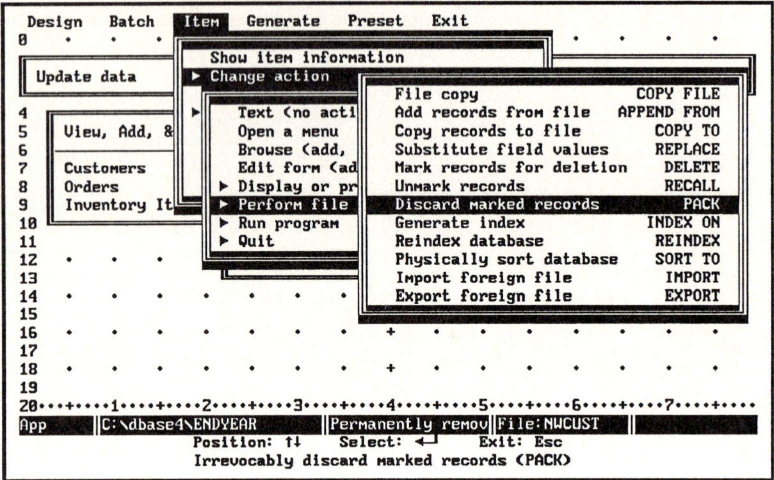

Figure 22-14.

Choosing a file operation action

When you select any file operation, dBASE IV prompts you to enter all the necessary command clauses, phrases, and options. When you choose a command that operates on data base records one by one, such as **Copy records to file** and **Mark records for deletion**, you can specify a field list when appropriate, and enter a scope, FOR clause, and WHILE clause to define selection criteria that govern which records are affected by the operation. When you run the application, all the commands that copy, create, or read files (such as **File copy** and **Import foreign file**) prompt you for file names when necessary and warn you that the file you create will overwrite an existing file with the same name.

All of the file operations are somewhat limited compared to the dot prompt or menu-driven equivalents. For example, you can specify only five sort keys rather than ten, and the **Substitute field values** option can replace the contents of only five fields at a time. If these limitations present problems, you can often overcome them by defining a batch process that repeats a file operation such as **Substitute field values** two or more times in succession. If you know the equivalent dot prompt command, you can assign the **Run program** action to the item instead of **Perform file operation,** and use the **Insert dBASE code** option to enter the less limited dot prompt command.

The **Run program** option enables you to call another program or batch process from within your application. The **Do dBASE program** option allows

you to run any dBASE IV program, such as the programs described in Chapter 21, and **Execute BATCH process** calls a batch process defined using the applications generator. **Insert dBASE code** calls up the same editor invoked by the **Embed code** option on the object or **Item** menus. You can enter up to 19 lines of dBASE IV code on this screen, in effect creating a small program from within the applications generator (you cannot, however, run the "program" independently from the dot prompt or the Control Center—you can use it only inside the application in which you defined it). You can use **Run DOS program** to run an external program, DOS command, or DOS batch file; and you can load or call a binary file (an assembly language program written specifically for this purpose), or play back a previously recorded keyboard macro.

The **Quit** action provides two exits from an application: **Return to calling program**, which returns you to the Control Center, the dot prompt, or another program that called your application, and **Quit to DOS**, which exits from dBASE IV to the operating system.

In many cases, there is more than one method for carrying out an action or series of actions in an application, and your choice may depend on how you have been using dBASE IV. For example, if you have been working primarily in the menu system, you might use a batch process such as the one cited in an example earlier in this chapter to carry out the end-of-year processing in the National Widgets system. To define the first step in the batch process, which marks inactive customers for deletion, you could assign the action **Mark records for deletion** and use the FOR clause DATE() – LASTORDER > 730 to select customers whose last order was more than two years ago, based on the current system date at the time the program is run.

The second step could call the **Display or print** action to print the list of customers marked for deletion, using an existing report form or a simple LIST command that includes the record numbers and several fields (perhaps ACCOUNT, COMPANY, CONTACT, LASTORDER, and TOTORDERS). You could use a FOR clause based on the DELETED function (which by itself evaluates to a valid condition—.T. if the current record is marked for deletion or .F. if it is not) to include only deleted records in this printout.

The third step, which erases deleted customers, could be carried out with the **Discard marked records** file operation. The fourth step, which zeros out the YTDORDERS field, could use the **Substitute field values** file operation to replace the YTDORDERS field with the value 0. For the last step, which empties the Order File, you could define another batch process with two steps, both carried out by file operations—**Mark records for deletion** and **Discard marked records**—and call this batch process from the first. For both the third

and fourth batch steps, you could use the **Override assigned data base or view** option to open the Order File instead of the default data base for the application (the Customer File).

If you are familiar with the dot prompt commands that carry out the end-of-year processing steps, you could use these commands instead of a batch process. To define the action assigned to the **End-of-year processing** option on the application's **File Maintenance** menu, choose **Run program**, and then **Insert dBASE code**. Seven lines of code are required, typed exactly as you would at the dot prompt:

```
USE NWCUST
DELETE FOR DATE() - LASTORDER > 730
LIST ACCOUNT, COMPANY, CONTACT, LASTORDER, TOTORDERS TO PRINT FOR DELETED()
PACK
REPLACE ALL YTDORDERS WITH 0
USE NWORDER
ZAP
```

As a third alternative, if you have already begun to write your own programs, you might write a simple program that consists of the same seven steps, and run this program from the application instead of inserting dBASE IV code directly.

Other Item Menu Options

The **Show item information** option displays a summary screen that includes the file name of the selected object, the text displayed for the selected menu or batch item, the view or data base and index assigned to the item, and a brief description of the action triggered by the item when you run the application. The summary screen resembles a dialog box with a single option, **OK**, which you select by pressing ENTER after reading the screen. You cannot change any of the items displayed on the information screen—if you discover a problem while reviewing a menu item, you must correct it using the same **Item** menu options that you used to define the item originally.

The **Override assigned database or view** option enables you to assign a different data base or view that dBASE IV opens before executing the action assigned to the selected menu option. Remember that by default, the data base or view assigned to a menu, list, or batch process is the one initially assigned to

the application as a whole, and the data base opened by a particular menu option is the one assigned to the menu, list, or batch process as a whole.

The **Override assigned database or view** option on the **Item** menu invokes a dialog box like the one pictured in Figure 22-15, which displays the name of the default view or data base and index. The cursor is positioned in the data entry area next to the prompt "For this item you may use values:" and you can press the spacebar to cycle through the three possible entries. The default is **ABOVE**, which retains the original view or data base. To enter a new view or data base and index, select **ENTERED BELOW**. Remember, if you type the name of a view explicitly rather than selecting it from a pick list, you must include the QBE extension. If you choose **IN EFFECT AT RUN TIME**, dBASE IV uses the data base or view that is already open (this data base may have been opened by a previous menu option or batch step, possibly through embedded code, or it may have been chosen from a pick list that your application displayed). If you want to open the default data base, but select a different index tag, you should use the **Reassign index order** option instead of **Override assigned database or view**.

You can use the **Position record pointer** option to reposition the record pointer in the active data base or view before carrying out the action specified for the item. There are four positioning methods, which you select from a

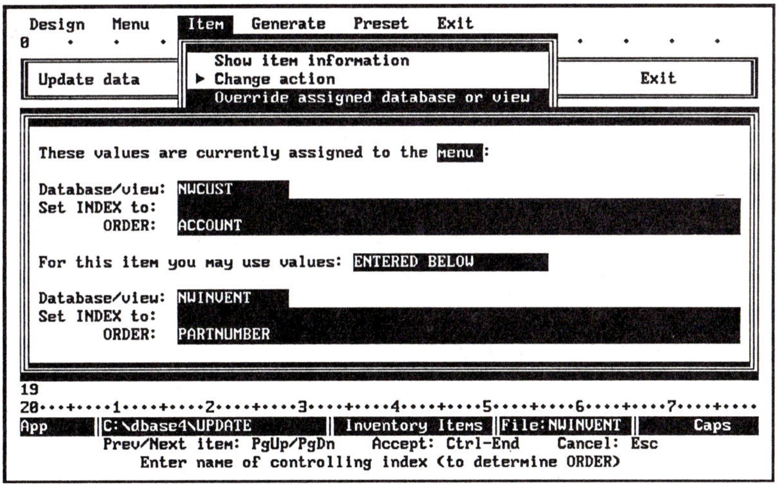

```
Design  Menu  Item  Generate  Preset  Exit
0                 Show item information
 Update data    ▶ Change action                                  Exit
                  Override assigned database or view

 These values are currently assigned to the menu :

 Database/view: NWCUST
 Set INDEX to:
        ORDER:  ACCOUNT

 For this item you may use values: ENTERED BELOW

 Database/view: NWINVENT
 Set INDEX to:
        ORDER:  PARTNUMBER

19
20•••+••••1••••+••••2••••+••••3••••+••••4••••+••••5••••+••••6••••+••••7••••+••••
App    C:\dbase4\UPDATE     Inventory Items  File:NWINVENT       Caps
        Prev/Next item: PgUp/PgDn    Accept: Ctrl-End    Cancel: Esc
             Enter name of controlling index (to determine ORDER)
```

Figure 22-15.

Overriding the default data base or view

dialog box like the one illustrated in Figure 22-16. The **SEEK** option executes an index key search for a specific key value. The **GOTO** option allows you to position the record pointer to the top or bottom of the file (by entering the keywords TOP or BOTTOM), or to a specific record, identified by number. The **LOCATE** option causes dBASE IV to search the file sequentially, as if you had typed a LOCATE command at the dot prompt. If you choose this option, you can define the search criteria by entering any combination of a scope, FOR clause, and WHILE clause. Note that both a scope and WHILE clause depend on the position of the record pointer, so you should use these options only if you know where the previous command or menu action left the record pointer.

The final choice, **Display POSITIONING MENU at RUN TIME**, causes dBASE IV to display a menu of positioning methods when you run the application, and allow you to select one "on the fly." The choices are the same as those displayed by the record positioning menu in the Quick Application: **SEEK, GOTO, LOCATE,** and **Change index order**. You can use this option for a menu item that displays data, to allow the users to select the first record, or for an option that prints a report or set of labels, to facilitate resuming from the point of interruption after a printer jam. However, it is appropriate only if the

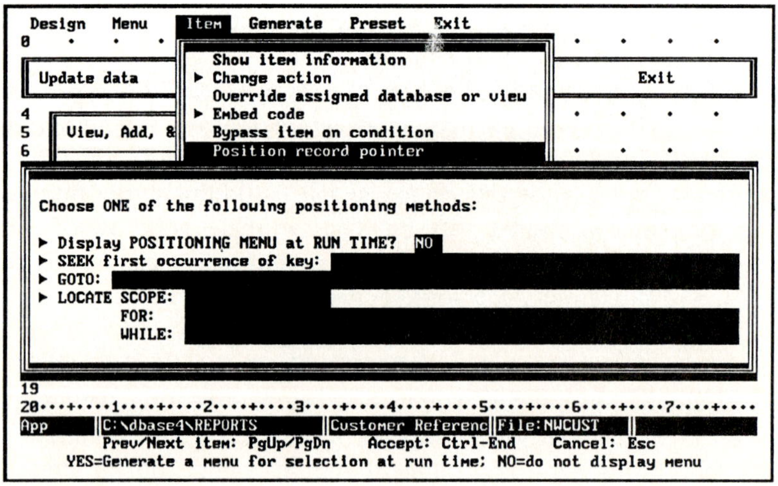

```
Design  Menu   Item  Generate  Preset  Exit
                Show item information
Update data     ▸ Change action                          Exit
                Override assigned database or view
                ▸ Embed code
  View, Add, &  Bypass item on condition
                Position record pointer

 Choose ONE of the following positioning methods:

 ▸ Display POSITIONING MENU at RUN TIME? NO
 ▸ SEEK first occurrence of key:
 ▸ GOTO:
 ▸ LOCATE SCOPE:
          FOR:
          WHILE:

App  ║C:\dbase4\REPORTS  ║Customer Referenc║File:NWCUST ║
       Prev/Next item: PgUp/PgDn   Accept: Ctrl-End   Cancel: Esc
   YES=Generate a menu for selection at run time; NO=do not display menu
```

Figure 22-16.

The record positioning options

users of your application are moderately knowledgeable about dBASE IV. They must understand the concept of the dBASE IV record pointer, know how to use the SEEK, GOTO, and LOCATE commands, and be able to construct valid scope, FOR, and WHILE clauses. The option to change the index order affords a welcome measure of flexibility—for example, you could print mailing labels in alphabetical order for a small label run or in ZIP code order for a mass mailing. However, this option can cause problems when producing the correct output depends on a particular master index, as it does in a report with group bands and subtotals.

The **Define logical window** option enables you to define a window of any arbitrary size, positioned anywhere on the screen, in which dBASE IV displays the output produced by the selected item. For example, if a menu option displays selected fields on the Browse screen, you could define a window just wide enough to accommodate the designated fields. You can choose the border style and display colors as well as the size and position of the window, but you must specify the colors with the same letter abbreviations that you would use in a SET COLOR command, rather than by making selections from a menu.

You can use the **Bypass item on condition** option to enter any legitimate condition (a dBASE IV expression that evaluates to .T. or .F.) that must be fulfilled to make the item available when you run the application. If you define a condition for a menu item, dBASE IV displays the item in dim text and does not allow you to select it whenever the condition evaluates to .F.. For a batch process action, dBASE IV simply evaluates the condition "behind the scenes" and executes the step only if the condition is .T..

The **Embed code** option enables you to enter up to 19 dBASE IV commands (program "code") that are executed either before or after performing the action associated with the item. If you know a little about the dBASE IV programming language, you can use this option to solicit additional user input or carry out more complex conditional tests, but you can make good use of embedded code even if you employ this option only to add a few commands that you already know. For example, you could embed a CLEAR command (which clears the screen) before executing a menu option that displays data in a window, so that the menu does not remain visible "behind" the display window. You might also embed several SET commands before executing your application main menu in order to customize aspects of the working environment that are not accessible through the **Environment settings** option on the **Preset** menu, and return to the default environment with SET commands embedded after the menu action is carried out.

You can use the **Assign message line prompt** option to enter one line of text that dBASE IV displays on the message line at the bottom of the screen when the item is selected. This option is available for menu and list items (dBASE IV does not display batch processes as objects on the screen when you run the application), but it is often unnecessary for list items, since you can display a message line prompt describing the list as part of the definition of the menu option that calls the list. For a menu option, you might enter a brief description of the usage or purpose of the menu option, a warning if the option has the potential to damage or erase data, or a reminder of which other options should be run before or after the selected option.

The **Write help text** option invokes a rudimentary line-oriented text editor that enables you to enter up to 19 lines of help text pertaining to the selected item. The editor is far less sophisticated than the dBASE IV text editors used to edit memo fields or programs—it does not support word wrap and offers no menu-driven editing commands—but it is adequate for constructing simple help screens. When you run the application, dBASE IV displays the text of the help screen if you press F1 (Help) with the item selected. Note that you can also define a help screen for a menu or list as a whole by selecting the corresponding option from the appropriate object menu. If there is no help screen defined for an individual menu item or for a list, dBASE IV displays the help screen that describes the menu or list; if there is no overall help screen either, dBASE IV displays the message "No help defined."

Processing Pick List Selections

One of the best features of the dBASE IV applications generator is that your application can display a pick list of files, fields, or values, and you can choose an item from the list when you run the application, just as you do when dBASE IV displays a pick list in response to a dot prompt command, the SHIFT-F1 (Pick) function key, or a selection from one of its menus. The procedure that you must use in order to process the list selection is a little complicated, and deserves further explanation.

The first step is to define both the list object and the menu object from which the list is called. You must assign the action itself—printing labels, editing a record, or displaying fields—to the list, using the **Change action** option on the **Item** menu. The menu option should simply display the list. For

example, you might want one of the label-printing options on the **Labels** menu in the National Widgets application to allow the user to select the label form from a files list. Although the pop-up menu option appears to describe the printing action, you must assign the **Open a menu** action to this option, and name the files list that displays the label forms as the menu to open. You then assign **Display or print** to the label files list.

One further detail is required in order to implement this technique: you must understand how dBASE IV identifies the item selected from a pick list in the generated program. Regardless of whether the item is a file name, field name, or field value, it is stored in a memory variable called LISTVAL; to process the selection, you substitute this variable for an explicit file name, field name, or field value. To choose an item from a values list, you can simply use the variable name LISTVAL in place of an explicit value. When you use LISTVAL to represent a file or field name, you must use the *macro substitution* symbol, &, to request that dBASE IV substitute *the value of the variable LISTVAL* (the name of the file or field) rather than the characters "LISTVAL", which form a legitimate file name or field name. For example, to print labels based on a form name selected from a pick list, you would enter the name of the label form like this:

```
&LISTVAL.
```

You can use a values list in an application to enable the user to easily search for a record before beginning an editing session, or to choose the first record to include in a report. For example, in the National Widgets system, the **Customers** option on the **Data Entry** menu might display a pick list of customer account codes before allowing the user to edit the Customer File through the Edit screen or a custom screen form. To implement this technique, you could define a values list based on the ACCOUNT field in the Customer File, and assign the action **Edit form (add, delete, edit)** to the list. To open the list, you would assign the action **Open a menu** (the predefined values list) to the **Customer File** option on the **Data Entry** menu.

When you run the application, selecting a value from the pick list of account codes does not cause dBASE IV to automatically position the record pointer in the Customer File to the corresponding record. To position the record pointer, you can use the **Position record pointer** option on the **Item** menu when you define the pick list of account codes: Select **SEEK first occurrence of key** as the positioning method, and enter the name of the variable LISTVAL instead of an explicit value as the key value to use in the SEEK. In

this context, you can use the variable name LISTVAL explicitly, rather than expanding it with the macro function (&), because the SEEK command can search for the value of *any expression,* and a reference to a memory variable constitutes a valid expression (one that evaluates to a character string).

SUMMARY

The dBASE IV applications generator is a powerful tool, and this chapter, despite its length, described only a fraction of its capabilities. The more you know about dBASE IV programming, the more you can get out of the applications generator, but even more important is an understanding of the basic "grammar and syntax" of the dBASE IV command language and an ability to think logically. If you have done most of your work in the menu system, you may want to review some of the explanations of dot prompt commands in earlier chapters to get a firmer grasp of command components such as scopes, FOR clauses, and WHILE clauses. Constructing a menu-driven application on the application design screen is a little like programming in a prompted environment—you must think out the flow of control and describe each step in terms that dBASE IV understands, but for the most part, you need not remember the exact syntax of each command or understand how to structure a long and complex program.

When you begin to use the applications generator, you may find the number and variety of menus and options overwhelming. Start with a simple application, build a few menus and lists, and gradually add more options. Regenerate the application programs after each revision, and test the menu options thoroughly. Without knowing any more about dBASE IV than you already do, you can use the applications generator to link the components of your applications into a menu-driven system and benefit from automation without having to learn to write complex dBASE IV programs.

CHAPTER TWENTY-THREE

Networking and Security

This chapter introduces two separate but related subjects: establishing a password-protected security system and running dBASE IV on a local area network (LAN). The connection between networking and security is in part historical, because multiuser software has migrated "down" from mainframe computers that support hundreds or even thousands of terminals. When all of a large organization's software and data files, some of which may contain highly sensitive information, are stored on the same computer, it is essential to be able to control which programs and data are available to each user. The same kinds of security considerations may also apply to a local area network in a corporate environment.

Although networking and security often go hand in hand, they are not inseparable. A single-user computer may require a security system if some staff members are prohibited from working with some of the programs or data base applications that coexist on the same hard disk. In contrast, many small companies or departments that use local area networks to enable several users to share expensive peripherals (such as a high-capacity hard disk or a laser

printer) or to update the same data bases simultaneously from several workstations may have no need to restrict access to any programs or data.

Whenever you run dBASE IV—or any other software—in a network environment, another type of security is of paramount importance: You must protect files from the damage that could result from two users trying to update the same data simultaneously. To guard against the potential dangers, which are described in detail in this chapter, dBASE IV allows you to *lock* an entire data base so that while one user is performing an operation that updates many records, users at other workstations cannot open the file. You can also lock individual records, so that more than one person can update the same data base (but not the same record) at the same time.

This chapter describes how to define a password-protection scheme tailored to the level of security that is appropriate for your organization. It introduces a variety of issues related to multiuser operation, outlines the potential conflicts that can arise in a network application, and offers some strategies for resolving these problems. Because of the many differences among the local area networks supported by dBASE IV and the variety of network configurations that may be installed in your organization, this book does not tell you how to configure your network or how to install dBASE IV on a network. This chapter assumes that the software is already installed and that you know how to start up the program and print from your workstation.

If you are following along with the examples in this book as a tutorial, note that it is impossible to experiment with the security system in a limited way that affects only the sample data bases, because you cannot establish password protection for any files without also restricting access to dBASE IV. A security system may already be in effect on your computer, and you may or may not be authorized to examine or change this system. If you can do so on your system, you may want to try some of the examples presented in this chapter or apply the same techniques to some of your own files. If you do, be sure to make a backup copy of the original sample data bases and any other files that you decide to protect.

PROTECTING A DATA BASE APPLICATION

dBASE IV enables you to implement a password-protected security system at several distinct levels. You can restrict access to dBASE IV itself so that a password is required to run the program, and you can exert a finer level of

control by limiting any user's access to certain data bases and individual fields within a data base. You do not have to establish the security system when you first install dBASE IV—you can add security at any time to a single-user or multiuser installation without having to reconfigure or reinstall the software.

To control access to dBASE IV, you define a *log-in profile* that includes a group name, log-in name, and password for each legitimate user. With the security system in effect, no one can run dBASE IV without entering a valid combination of these three items. To protect an individual data base, you define a *file access profile* that describes which users can carry out various operations, such as adding, updating, deleting, and viewing data. At the finest level of control, you can make certain fields read/only for some users and hide other fields entirely. When you protect a data base file, dBASE IV *encrypts,* or encodes, the DBF file, the matching DBT file (if the data base contains memo fields), and any associated index files. If you use the TYPE command to display an encrypted file, or examine it with a text editor or a disk inspection utility (such as the Norton Utilities or the DOS DEBUG program), the contents will be incomprehensible. To display the data in the file, dBASE IV must *decrypt* (decode) the contents, and this process slows performance somewhat.

You define and maintain the security system by using the menu-driven Protect utility, which is accessible from the Control Center or from the dot prompt.

From the Menus

To access the password-protection system from the Control Center, you select the **Protect** option from the **Tools** menu.

From the Dot Prompt

To move to the Protect screen from the dot prompt, you use the PROTECT command:

```
PROTECT
```

Using the Protect Utility

The dBASE IV security system is virtually unchanged from dBASE III PLUS, and the appearance of the menus and the mechanics of selecting options

therefore differ slightly from the rest of the dBASE IV menu system. To select an option, you highlight it and press ENTER. In response, dBASE IV displays a data entry area next to the prompt, marked with a small triangle, as you can see in Figure 23-1. Even if a value is already displayed next to the prompt, you must press ENTER before you can edit the entry or make a new one.

The arrangement of the "save" and "exit" options also differs somewhat from other dBASE IV menus, most of which have an option to save your work without exiting as well as a **Save changes and exit** option. In the Protect system, you always use the **Save** option on the **Exit** menu to save your work. After you select **Save**, the cursor advances automatically to the **Exit** option; you can either press ENTER to exit or move to another menu to resume working. To exit without saving your work, you must select **Abandon** from the **Exit** menu and then **Exit** (as it does when you choose **Save**, dBASE IV automatically highlights **Exit**). The structure of the **Protect** menu is diagrammed in Figure 23-2.

The Data Base Administrator

The person who manages the security system is called the *data base administrator.* dBASE IV uses a special password called the *administrator password*—in

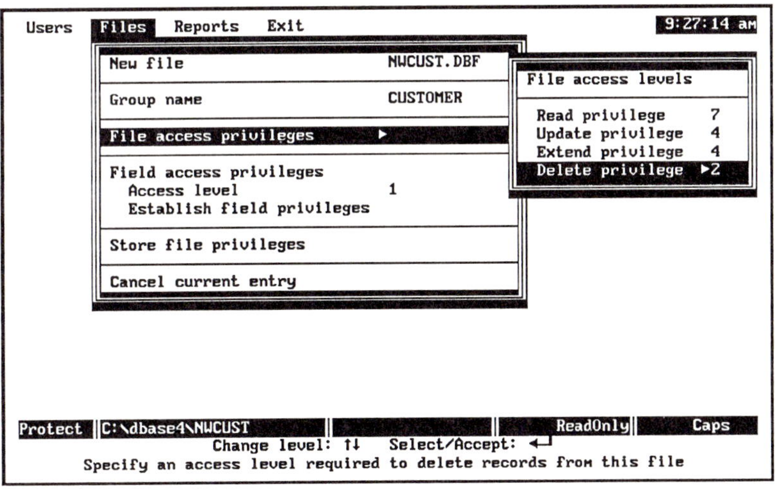

Figure 23-1.

Defining file access privileges

```
Users                              Files                                 Reports               Exit

+------------------------------+   +----------------------------------+  +------------------+  +---------+
| Login name                   |   | New file                         |  | User Information |  | Save    |
| Password                     |   +----------------------------------+  +------------------+  | Abandon |
| Group name                   |   | Group name                       |  | File Information |  | Exit    |
+------------------------------+   +----------------------------------+  +------------------+  +---------+
| Full Name                    |   | File access privileges           |
| Access level               1 |   +----------------------------------+
+------------------------------+   | Field access privileges          |
| Store user profile           |   |   Access level                 1 |
+------------------------------+   |   Establish field privileges     |
| Delete user from group       |   +----------------------------------+
+------------------------------+   | Store file privileges            |
                                   +----------------------------------+
                                   | Cancel current entry             |
                                   +----------------------------------+
```

Figure 23-2.

The structure of the Protect menu

theory known only to this person—to control access to the security system itself. In a small group or organization, the title of data base administrator may fall to the person who best understands dBASE IV, and several users may know the administrator password and have permission to protect their own data bases. In a larger organization, the data base administrator may be someone from the MIS department who is responsible for controlling access to all of the company's computers, not just the personal computers, and this person may exert tighter control over the dBASE IV security system.

Every time you enter the security system, dBASE IV displays a dialog box that prompts you to enter the administrator password. The password that you enter the *first* time you invoke the security system becomes the administrator password. To protect this password from prying eyes, dBASE IV does not display the characters you type, and because you cannot see what you are typing, you must verify a new administrator password by entering it a second time. The administrator password can be up to 16 characters long and can contain any characters; dBASE IV treats uppercase and lowercase letters as equivalent when you define the password and when you enter it later to access the security system again.

dBASE IV stores the administrator password on disk in encrypted form and provides no way to view or change the password once you have defined it. Every organization should ensure that the administrator password is written down (and stored in a secure location) in the event that the data base administrator forgets it or is unavailable or uncooperative when it is needed.

Controlling Access to dBASE IV

To control access to the dBASE IV program itself, you use the **Users** menu on the Protect screen to define a log-in profile for every legitimate user. The log-in profile consists of five items: log-in name, password, group name, full name, and access level. You define these items by selecting the similarly worded options from the **Users** menu. You can enter the components of the log-in profile in any combination of uppercase and lowercase; for all but the full name, case is not significant.

The *log-in name* is a short code of up to eight characters that identifies the individual user. It is customary, but not necessary, to assign unique log-in names, and because the password affords a higher level of security, there is no reason to make the log-in names cryptic or difficult to remember. Some common choices for log-in names are abbreviations derived from users' job titles or descriptions, first or last names, initials, and nicknames.

The *password* can be up to 16 characters long and should always be unique for each user, even if the log-in name is not. Whether the data base administrator assigns the passwords or whether the users choose their own is a matter of discretion and depends to some extent on the level of security required in your organization. A password should be difficult or impossible to guess, a stipulation that rules out most of the choices that first come to mind, such as names, nicknames, names of family members or pets, terms related to the user's job or hobbies, names of favorite songs, and any other words associated with the individual. However, passwords that consist of random sequences of 16 letters and numbers are unnecessarily difficult to remember. One good compromise is to use two or three common but unrelated English words, perhaps separated by punctuation marks, that fill or almost fill the allotted 16 characters, for example, "PLUM-ROSE-FERN" (not a good choice for someone known to be an avid gardener).

The *group name,* which can be up to eight characters long, is used to match users with the applications and data base files that they need to access. If you also assign a group name to a data base file (using commands described in the next section), dBASE IV permits only users who have a matching group name to open the file. In the National Widgets system, you might assign a group name such as NWACTREC or CUSTOMER to all the files in the accounts receivable system and use the group name MAILLIST for a separate set of mailing list data bases. To work with files in more than one group, a user must have two or more log-in profiles, each of which has a different group name (the log-in name and the password can be the same). If you do not assign specific file access privileges, the group name serves only as one of the three components of the log-in sequence that validates a user's permission to run dBASE IV.

The 24-character *full name* is an optional entry in the user log-in profile. You can enter the full name to identify the individual on the reports that document the security system, or you can use it to record the person's departmental association or relevant expertise. For example, you could use the full name to distinguish among members of the Data Processing, Accounting, and Marketing departments or to note a user's primary area of responsibility in running a particular application. dBASE IV does not display the full name during the log-in sequence or require that the user enter it; in fact, you can view or print it only from within the security system.

Each user profile includes an access level that can range from 1 (the highest and most powerful level) to 8 (the lowest level with the fewest privileges). This item is required, but because it automatically defaults to 1 (the highest level), you need not make an explicit entry unless you need to differentiate among users based on access levels. In combination with the file access levels assigned

through the **Files** menu (which is described in the next section), the access level determines which data base files a user can open and what operations dBASE IV permits the user to perform on a file as a whole or on individual fields. If you are implementing a security system only to guard against unauthorized entry into dBASE IV, you can retain the default access level, 1, for all users.

To save the log-in profile, you select the **Store user profile** option from the **Users** menu. To search for a previously defined user, you select the **Login name**, **Password**, and **Group name** options in turn, and enter the three components of the log-in profile that uniquely identify the desired user. dBASE IV displays a dialog box to advise you that the user is already on file: "User already exists, do you want to edit? (Y/N)." If you had inadvertently entered the log-in profile of an existing user, you can select **No** from the dialog box to return to entering new users. If you select **Yes**, you can modify the existing user profile or you can choose **Delete user from group** to delete the user.

dBASE IV stores user profiles in a file called DBSYSTEM.DB, which is encrypted to prevent a knowledgeable user from examining this file to discover the passwords and log-in names. The encryption scheme is based on the administrator password, without which you cannot access the Protect utility to view or print the log-in profiles.

Once you have defined the administrator password and at least one user profile, dBASE IV displays a log-in screen like the one shown in Figure 23-3 whenever you start up the program. You can type the log-in items in any combination of uppercase and lowercase letters (dBASE IV converts your entries to uppercase), and to make it more difficult for anyone to casually discover another user's log-in profile, dBASE IV does not display the password on the screen as you enter it. If you leave any of the three entries blank, dBASE IV exits immediately; otherwise, you have three tries to enter a valid log-in profile before dBASE IV returns you to the operating system.

When you work in the menu system, you must exit dBASE IV to allow another user to log in at the same workstation. From the dot prompt, you can use the LOGOUT command, which initiates a new log-in sequence, to relinquish control to another user without exiting. You might also want to log out and then log in again yourself if you use different log-in profiles to access files in several applications assigned to separate groups.

Controlling Access to Data Base Files

To control access to specific data base files and individual fields within files, you use the options on the **Files** menu to define a detailed access profile for

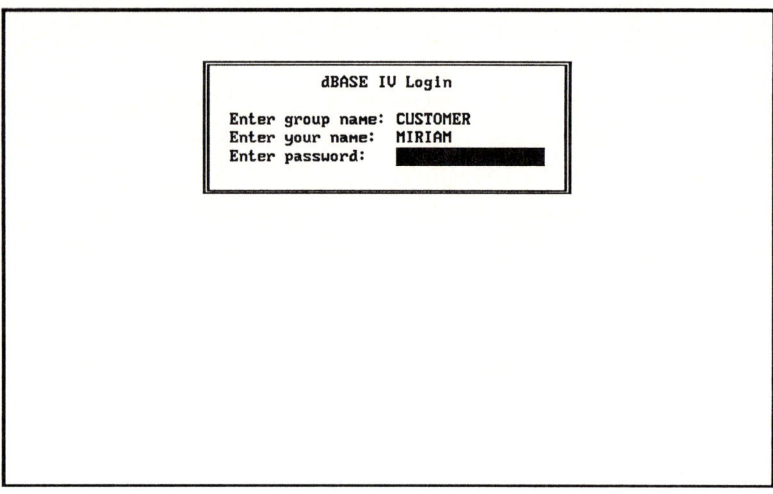

Figure 23-3.

The dBASE IV log-in screen

each data base you want to protect. At the very least, you must assign a group name, which dBASE IV matches with the group names in the user profiles to determine who is permitted to open the file.

You can define a more detailed protection scheme by designating the user access levels required to gain four different types of access to a file: to read (view) the file, update it (edit records), extend the file (add new records), and delete records. You define each access level by specifying the lowest, or least privileged, user access level that grants permission to perform the specified operation (the lowest access level corresponds to the highest numerical value). For example, in the National Widgets system, you might assign the following access levels for the Customer File:

Read privilege level	7
Update privilege level	4
Extend privilege level	4
Delete privilege level	2

According to this scheme, users with access levels 1 to 7 can read the file

(display data); levels 1 to 4 permit a user to update the file (edit records, execute update queries, and so on) and extend the file (add records); and only users at levels 1 or 2 can delete records. By default, dBASE IV assigns each new user an access level of 1 and sets all four file access levels to 8 so all users can access all data base files. If you need to segregate users and files into application groups without limiting the commands that any user can execute, you can simply assign each file a group name and retain the default access levels.

You define file access levels by selecting the **File access privileges** option on the **Files** menu, which invokes a dialog box like the one shown in Figure 23-1. The four options correspond to the four types of file access privileges. You can select each option for which you want to override the default privilege level by highlighting it and pressing ENTER, and then enter a new access level or adjust the number displayed by pressing the UP ARROW or DOWN ARROW. You can close the pick list, save your changes, and return to the **Files** menu by pressing LEFT ARROW, RIGHT ARROW, or ESC (even if you press ESC, dBASE IV saves your changes).

You can assign file privileges for only nine data bases at a time, but you do not have to exit the Protect utility to protect additional files—just select the **Save** option from the **Exit** menu to save your work, and then return to the **Files** or **Users** menu to continue defining access privileges.

When you exit the Protect utility after saving at least one user or file profile, dBASE IV stores the user profiles in DBSYSTEM.DB and makes an encrypted copy of each data base to which you assigned a group name. The encrypted data base file has the same first name as the original and the extension CRP. If the data base contains memo fields, dBASE IV copies the DBT file to an encrypted file with the extension CPT. If the data base is large, this process can take some time, and you must have enough room on your hard disk for both the original and encrypted copies of the data base.

dBASE IV does not encrypt existing MDX or NDX indexes, but does encrypt new indexes that you build for a protected data base, and encrypts existing indexes when you rebuild them. To encrypt an MDX or NDX index immediately, you can open the indexes with the data base from the dot prompt and use the REINDEX command to rebuild all open indexes. (There is no analogous menu option, although you can force dBASE IV to reindex by using the **Erase marked records** option on the **Organize** menu on the Edit, Browse, or data base design screen.) Because you can always reconstruct indexes based on information in the associated data bases, dBASE IV does not preserve the original MDX or NDX file when it creates an encrypted copy.

After dBASE IV encrypts a data base, it does not erase the unprotected DBF file (or the DBT file if the data base contains memo fields) from your hard disk.

In most cases, you will want to erase the DBF and DBT files and then substitute the encrypted file for the original by renaming the CRP and CPT files to the standard DBF and DBT extensions. As a precaution, you should back up the unencrypted files onto floppy disks or magnetic tapes before you erase them, but keep in mind that any subsequent changes made to the data base will not be reflected in this backup copy.

Working with Protected Data Bases

With a file access privilege scheme in effect, any command that might result in a forbidden action results in the "Unauthorized access level" error message. For example, dBASE IV displays this error message if you try to open a file with a group name that does not match the one that you entered when you logged on or if you try to execute a REPLACE command or an update query when you do not have update privileges for the active data base.

dBASE IV limits access only to data bases that you explicitly protected by defining access profiles. Other data bases, as well as new files that you create on the data base design screen, are not encrypted and are available to all users. The status of the ENCRYPTION setting, which is OFF by default, determines whether dBASE IV encrypts new files that you generate from protected files by using menu options or dot prompt commands that carry out operations such as sorting or copying records. When the ENCRYPTION setting is ON, all these commands generate encrypted files, and dBASE IV does not allow you to execute commands that invariably generate unencrypted files. For example, to copy or export data to a file in an external format, which cannot be encrypted, you must ensure that the ENCRYPTION setting is OFF.

You can change the status of the ENCRYPTION setting from the SET menu that is accessible from the dot prompt (but not from the **Settings** menu that is invoked when you select **Settings** from the Control Center **Tools** menu) or you can type the following SET commands at the dot prompt:

```
SET ENCRYPTION ON
```

or

```
SET ENCRYPTION OFF
```

Controlling Access to Data Base Fields

You can assign three different access privileges for any individual field in a data base—FULL, R/O (read/only), or NONE—and you can define a separate field access profile for each overall user access level. You must explicitly define privileges for each of the eight access levels (or at least for each level assigned to a user in your organization). If you assign restricted privileges for levels 2, 4, and 8, for example, users at privilege levels 1, 3, 5, 6, and 7 retain the default FULL access to all fields.

You must ensure that the field privilege levels you assign are consistent with the overall access levels specified for the data base. For example, in the scheme set forth in the previous section for the Customer File, an access level of 4 is required to update the data base. For users at access levels 5 through 8, the only field privileges that make sense are R/O and NONE. If the file and field privileges conflict, the overall file privileges take precedence; thus, if you granted FULL privileges to any Customer File fields for users with access levels 5, 6, 7, or 8, dBASE IV would only permit these users to view the data, just as if you had assigned R/O access. Even if you define an access profile for each field in a data base, you may still need to define the four privilege levels that make up the overall file access profile to prevent unauthorized users from executing commands that operate on the data base as a whole, such as deleting groups of records, erasing records marked for deletion, or emptying a data base with the ZAP command. Table 23-1 lists a field access privilege scheme for the National Widgets Customer File.

You define field access privileges using the two options in the **Field access privileges** section of the **Files** menu. First, select **Access level** and enter the user access level for which you want to define field privileges, and then select **Establish field privileges**. dBASE IV displays a pick list of fields like the one shown in Figure 23-4 for the Customer File. Note that the fields are listed in alphabetical order, not in the order in which they occur in the file structure; this discrepancy can be confusing if you are working from an annotated listing created by printing the file structure. To change a privilege for any field, you highlight the field name and press ENTER to cycle through the three choices. You can close the pick list and return to the **Files** menu by pressing either LEFT ARROW, RIGHT ARROW, or ESC (in all cases, dBASE IV saves your changes).

If you return to the Protect screen to edit a previously defined file access profile and attempt to select a protected file from the pick list displayed by the **New file** option on the **Files** menu, dBASE IV displays the error message "Database is encrypted" on the message line below the status bar. The only

Field	Levels 1, 2	Levels 3, 4	Levels 5, 6, 7	Level 8
ACCOUNT	FULL	R/O	R/O	NONE
COMPANY	FULL	FULL	R/O	NONE
ADDRESS	FULL	FULL	R/O	NONE
CITY	FULL	FULL	R/O	NONE
STATE	FULL	FULL	R/O	NONE
ZIP	FULL	FULL	R/O	NONE
TELEPHONE	FULL	FULL	R/O	NONE
CONTACT	FULL	FULL	R/O	NONE
EQUIPMENT	FULL	FULL	R/O	NONE
FIRSTORDER	FULL	R/O	R/O	NONE
LASTORDER	FULL	R/O	R/O	NONE
CREDITOK	FULL	R/O	NONE	NONE
YTDORDERS	FULL	R/O	NONE	NONE
TOTORDERS	FULL	R/O	NONE	NONE
COMMENTS	FULL	FULL	R/O	NONE

Table 23-1.

The Customer File Field Access Privileges

way to revise the access profile for a data base is to generate an unencrypted copy of the file, erase the encrypted data base, redefine the file privileges, and allow dBASE IV to encrypt the file again. If you do this, you must redefine *all* the file and field privileges, because your original specifications are unavailable (dBASE IV stores them in the encrypted data base, not in DBSYSTEM.DB).

When you update a data base for which field privileges were established, dBASE IV displays only fields for which you have either R/O or FULL privileges, and it uses the same colors or monochrome display attributes for R/O fields as it does for the field name prompts on the Edit and Browse screens (the background colors). Just as when you designate a field read/only in a custom

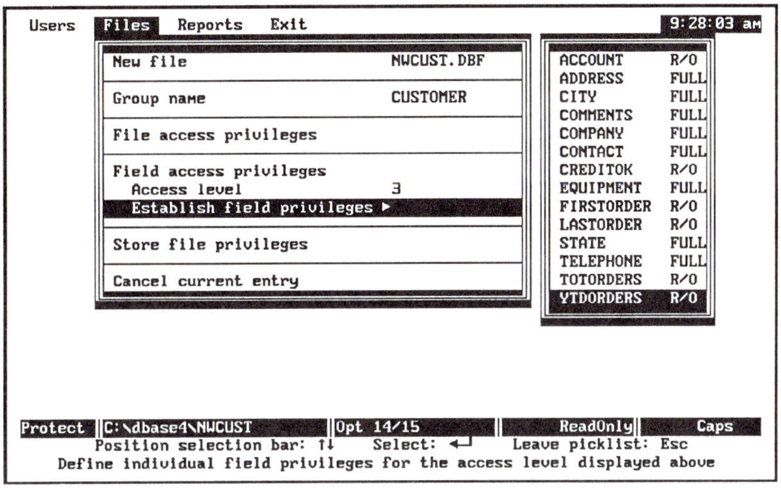

```
Users  Files  Reports  Exit                                   9:28:03 am

       New file                    NWCUST.DBF      ACCOUNT     R/O
                                                   ADDRESS     FULL
       Group name                  CUSTOMER        CITY        FULL
                                                   COMMENTS    FULL
       File access privileges                      COMPANY     FULL
                                                   CONTACT     FULL
       Field access privileges                     CREDITOK    R/O
         Access level              3               EQUIPMENT   FULL
         Establish field privileges ►              FIRSTORDER  R/O
                                                   LASTORDER   R/O
       Store file privileges                       STATE       FULL
                                                   TELEPHONE   FULL
       Cancel current entry                        TOTORDERS   R/O
                                                   YTDORDERS   R/O

Protect  C:\dbase4\NWCUST     Opt 14/15          ReadOnly      Caps
     Position selection bar: ↑↓    Select: ◄┘    Leave picklist: Esc
   Define individual field privileges for the access level displayed above
```

Figure 23-4.

Defining field access privileges

screen form or when you add the /R option to the field name in a list of fields to be displayed on the Edit or Browse screen, dBASE IV allows you to move the cursor into read/only fields, but not to make any changes.

When you work through the menu system or at the dot prompt, any attempt to perform a forbidden operation generates an error message, but the error message does not always accurately describe the true source of the problem. For example, unless you have FULL permission for a field, naming the field in a REPLACE command yields the "Variable not found" error message. This can be especially confusing if you have R/O permission, because you can see the field on the Edit and Browse screens (although you cannot change the data). If your permission is NONE, dBASE IV at least behaves consistently—it does not display the field in Edit or Browse, and for all intents and purposes, the field does not exist for you. If you use a screen form file that includes fields for which you do not have FULL permission, dBASE IV also displays the "Variable not found" error message. To avoid this problem, you may have to create several versions of each screen form file for users who have different access privileges.

In keeping with the field access privilege scheme, any data base or text file that you generate from a protected file contains only fields for which you have

R/O or FULL privileges in the original (regardless of the status of the ENCRYPTION setting). Since dBASE IV does not transfer the privilege scheme to the new file, you can use the COPY command to create a new data base, and you can edit fields in this data base for which you had only R/O privileges in the original. You cannot transfer the changes back to the original file, however.

Since dBASE IV stores the access profile for a data base in the data base file itself, you cannot define multiple profiles for different groups. To grant high-level access to the files in one application and more restricted privileges in another, you must define more than one log-in profile for a user: one profile for each application, with different access level numbers (the log-in names and passwords can be the same).

Documenting and Protecting the Security System

As mentioned, you should maintain a hard copy of the administrator password in case the data base administrator forgets the password, is out of the office when you need to modify the security system, or leaves your organization on unfriendly terms and refuses to disclose the password. Without the administrator password, you cannot access the Protect utility, and because the password is stored in the encrypted DBSYSTEM.DB file, you cannot retrieve this password by any other means. Depending on the overall security provisions in your organization, you may or may not need to store the password in a safe or in another secure location, on or off the premises, to prevent users from changing their own access levels and gaining access to sensitive information.

Some of the same considerations apply to documenting the details of the security system and generating unprotected copies of encrypted files. Be sure to document all user and file access profiles, not only to make it easier to retrieve a forgotten password but also in the event that the original designer of the security system is unavailable when you need this information.

You can generate a summary of the user or file access profile for a data base by selecting the **Reports** option on the Protect screen and then choosing either **User information** or **File information**. When you request the file report, dBASE IV displays a pick list of encrypted data bases. Because the pick list includes only files with the CRP extension, an extra step is required if you have already renamed an encrypted data base with the standard DBF extension: You must restore the CRP extension before you return to the Protect screen to print a file

access profile established earlier (ideally, you should print the reports from the Protect screen immediately after you first define the access profiles). After you select a file name from the pick list, dBASE IV prompts you in a pop-up dialog box to "Enter group name:" For both reports, dBASE IV allows you to route the output to the screen or the printer by prompting you in a dialog box: "Send report to the printer? (Y/N)." The reports for the National Widgets users and Customer File are illustrated in Figures 23-5 and 23-6.

Since access to encrypted files depends on the user profiles stored in the DBSYSTEM.DB file, you should back up this file separately from your daily backup in case the original and the routine backup files are damaged by a hardware failure. You may also want to create an unencrypted copy of each protected data base periodically, in case all existing copies of DBSYSTEM.DB are destroyed. A user who has FULL access to all the fields in a data base can make this copy with a command sequence like the following:

```
SET ENCRYPTION OFF
USE NWCUST
COPY TO NWCUST2
SET ENCRYPTION ON
```

Keep in mind that the effectiveness of any security system depends on the cooperation of the individuals involved. In a large organization where the network workstations are located far apart and users have little or no contact

```
User name Password         Group    Fullname                 Level
========= ================ ======== ======================== =====
MIRIAM    PLUM-ROSE-FERN   CUSTOMER Miriam Liskin              2
JACK      BOOK-GREEN-RADIO CUSTOMER John Garrison              4
BOOKKEEP  PENCIL-RADIO     CUSTOMER Leslie Bishop              2
OWNER     WINDY-RED-SWEET  CUSTOMER Kenneth G. Parker          1
MIRIAM    PLUM-ROSE-FERN   MAILLIST Miriam Liskin              5
JACK      BOOK-GREEN-RADIO MAILLIST John Garrison              2
BOOKKEEP  PENCIL-RADIO     MAILLIST Leslie Bishop              1
```

Figure 23-5.

The User Information report for the National Widgets system

```
Filename     C:\DBASE4\NWCUST.CRP
Group Name   CUSTOMER

 Read privilege   7
 Update privilege 4
 Extend privilege 4
 Delete privilege 2

                                   Access Levels
Fieldname       1     2     3     4     5     6     7     8
==========    ===== ===== ===== ===== ===== ===== ===== =====
ACCOUNT       FULL  FULL  R/O   R/O   R/O   R/O   R/O   NONE
COMPANY       FULL  FULL  FULL  FULL  R/O   R/O   R/O   NONE
ADDRESS       FULL  FULL  FULL  FULL  R/O   R/O   R/O   NONE
CITY          FULL  FULL  FULL  FULL  R/O   R/O   R/O   NONE
STATE         FULL  FULL  FULL  FULL  R/O   R/O   R/O   NONE
ZIP           FULL  FULL  FULL  FULL  R/O   R/O   R/O   NONE
TELEPHONE     FULL  FULL  FULL  FULL  R/O   R/O   R/O   NONE
CONTACT       FULL  FULL  FULL  FULL  R/O   R/O   R/O   NONE
EQUIPMENT     FULL  FULL  FULL  FULL  R/O   R/O   R/O   NONE
FIRSTORDER    FULL  FULL  R/O   R/O   R/O   R/O   R/O   NONE
LASTORDER     FULL  FULL  R/O   R/O   R/O   R/O   R/O   NONE
CREDITOK      FULL  FULL  R/O   R/O   NONE  NONE  NONE  NONE
YTDORDERS     FULL  FULL  R/O   R/O   NONE  NONE  NONE  NONE
TOTORDERS     FULL  FULL  R/O   R/O   NONE  NONE  NONE  NONE
COMMENTS      FULL  FULL  FULL  FULL  R/O   R/O   R/O   NONE
```

Figure 23-6.

The File Information report for the Customer File

with each other, this is generally not a problem. In smaller groups whose members consider themselves friends and view the security system as an insult or a burden, conflicts can arise. Any security system can become worthless if the users share their passwords to fill in for each other when someone is busy, sick, or otherwise absent from the office when a deadline approaches.

RUNNING dBASE IV ON A NETWORK

When you install dBASE IV on a local area network, users at more than one network workstation can use the program at the same time, and if the proper

precautions are observed, more than one user can access the same data bases and related auxiliary files simultaneously. For the most part, dBASE IV looks and works as it does in a single-user system, and in many cases you need not be concerned with the differences. dBASE IV automatically handles many of the conflicts that can arise when two or more users share programs and data files, either by resolving them or by displaying an appropriate error message. Nevertheless, some understanding of the potential problems will enable you to run dBASE IV on a network safely and efficiently and avoid much of the frustration and tension that can develop among users who are competing for the same system resources.

If several users share a copy of dBASE IV on the network, with the workstations dedicated to different applications that do not have common data base files, your only problem will be some degradation in performance when several users perform disk-intensive tasks at the same time. Cooperation among users—for example, running time-consuming tasks that require many disk accesses at lunchtime or overnight—can minimize this problem.

Several users can safely *read* a file simultaneously as long as no one changes data. For example, a user at one workstation could print a report based on the Customer, Order, and Inventory Files while another user executes a CALCULATE command or uses a query to compute statistics based on the Customer File with no risk to the data bases, indexes, report form, or query file.

Whether or not to allow one user to read a file while another updates it is less clear-cut, although this kind of simultaneous access will not damage the data bases. For example, in the National Widgets system, one user might want to print a report that calculates the profit margin on each order line item based on the PRICE field in the Order File and the COST field in the Inventory File. If another user were allowed to update the Inventory File at the same time, this user might change some of the costs and cause internal inconsistencies in the report: the profit margin for the same item sold at the same price would be different in records printed before and after the cost of the item was changed. You might not notice a problem like this one unless you examined the report carefully, and when you did, the reason for the discrepancy might not be apparent. (In this particular case, you could solve the problem by storing the item cost at the time of the sale in the Order File along with the selling price, but in other applications, this approach would result in storing a great deal of redundant data.)

Much more serious problems can arise when several users need to *update* the same data bases at the same time. While you perform certain operations that process an entire data base, it would be dangerous to allow any other

updates to the file. For example, if one user were allowed to add records to a data base or edit records while another built a new index for the file, the index might not contain an entry for every new record, and it would include incorrect entries for records in which the index key fields were changed after dBASE IV constructed the index entries. Similarly, it would be dangerous for one user to edit records while someone else at another workstation was erasing marked records from the file (running a PACK command). Between the time that the user who was editing the file read a record from the disk and the time this user saved the modified record, dBASE IV might move many records and assign them new record numbers, and the edited record would be written to the wrong place in the file, overwriting another valid record.

When you update individual records on the Browse or Edit screen, the potential problems are more subtle but equally serious. Viewing, editing, or deleting records in the same file is generally safe as long as no two users attempt to update the same record simultaneously. Suppose, however, that one of the National Widgets order entry clerks wanted to change a customer's telephone number while the bookkeeper edited the CREDITOK field. dBASE IV reads and saves data one record at a time. At each workstation, dBASE IV would read the requested customer record from the disk and present a copy of the data on the screen. Both users would make their changes in memory, and the one who saved the edited record first would lose his or her changes. If the clerk saved the record first, after changing the telephone number, and then the bookkeeper saved the record, which contained a different value for CREDITOK but the old phone number, this second copy of the customer record would overwrite the first, and the original telephone number would be restored.

The considerations involved in marking records for deletion and recalling deleted records are essentially the same, because deleting or undeleting a record sets or removes the deletion marker, which is stored in the record along with the fields defined in the structure. These dangers are particularly insidious, because you might not discover that some of your changes were lost until long after the damage had been done, by which time it would be very difficult to trace the chain of events that corrupted the data or determine how to correct the affected records.

Avoiding these potential disasters requires cooperation among the network operating system, the data base management software, and the users. For the most part, the operating system and dBASE IV attend to these matters "behind the scenes" and your role in the process can be minimal. The network operating systems that are supported by dBASE IV provide the means to *lock* an

entire file or a single record so that other users either cannot change the data or cannot access it at all. dBASE IV can access these network file- and record-locking capabilities, and for the most part it does so automatically (there are also explicit commands and functions that you can use from the menu system and the dot prompt) to protect a data base system from damage caused by multiple simultaneous updates.

Exclusive and Shared Access

dBASE IV allows you to open any type of file—a data base or any of the auxiliary files you use with data bases—either for *exclusive* or *shared* use. When you open a file in exclusive mode, no other user can open the file for any purpose, and there is no need to protect the file by locking it—any attempt by another user to access the file results in the "File in use by another" error message. When you open a file in shared mode, it is your responsibility to lock the file—or, for a data base file, lock individual records in the file—when necessary. By default, dBASE IV determines whether to open a file in exclusive or shared mode based on the potential of the command to change the contents of the file.

dBASE IV opens most files, including data bases, in shared mode whenever it is safe to do so. For example, dBASE IV opens a report, label, or screen form file in exclusive mode when you invoke the appropriate layout editor to modify the form, and in shared mode when you use the form solely to display or print data. MDX and NDX index files are always assigned the same mode as the associated data base file.

It is possible to override the default file-opening mode by using the EXCLUSIVE setting, which by default is OFF. You can change the status of this setting from the **Settings** menu accessed through the Control Center **Tools** menu, from the SET menu invoked from the dot prompt, or by typing a SET command from the dot prompt, as follows:

```
SET EXCLUSIVE ON
```

or

```
SET EXCLUSIVE OFF
```

Changing the status of the EXCLUSIVE setting has no effect on files that are already open. From the menus, the EXCLUSIVE setting is the only tool at your disposal for specifying the file-opening mode. At the dot prompt, you can open a data base file for exclusive use, regardless of the status of the EXCLUSIVE setting, by including the keyword EXCLUSIVE in the USE command. For example, you could open the National Widgets Customer File (and the production MDX file) in exclusive mode with the following command:

```
USE NWCUST ORDER ACCOUNT ALIAS CUSTOMER EXCLUSIVE
```

When a file is open in exclusive mode, dBASE IV displays the indicator "ExclLock" in the fifth segment of the status bar. Unfortunately, it does not include the status of the EXCLUSIVE setting in the list of environment settings displayed by the DISPLAY STATUS or LIST STATUS command.

You must open a data base in exclusive mode to carry out any command or operation that rewrites the file entirely, including modifying the structure, erasing records marked for deletion, and emptying the data base with the ZAP command. Exclusive use is required when you build a new tag in an MDX file or when you rebuild all indexes with the REINDEX command from the dot prompt. If you attempt to perform any of these operations on a data base that was opened in shared mode, dBASE IV pops up a dialog box to warn you, "File must be opened in exclusive mode." You can close the data base, reopen it in exclusive mode, and then retry the operation (you cannot open a file for exclusive use, however, if the file is already open at another workstation).

Occasionally, a conflict arises that can be resolved only by the users. Suppose that two users of the National Widgets data bases both needed to perform an operation that requires exclusive use of the Customer and Order files. If one user opens the Customer File first and the other opens the Order File at the same time, neither user will be able to gain exclusive access to the second required file. When the first user tries to open the Order File, it will already be open in exclusive mode at the second workstation, and when the second user tries to open the Customer File, it will be open in exclusive mode at the first. This situation, often called a *deadlock,* or *deadly embrace,* does not occur very often, but when it does, dBASE IV cannot resolve the conflict; it displays the "File in use by another" error message each time one of the two users tries to open the second data base. One of the users must recognize the problem and solve it by closing the file that is already open in exclusive mode at his or her workstation and thus relinquish it to the other user.

dBASE IV cannot tell you which user is updating the file you need, but from the dot prompt, you can determine who else is logged onto the network by typing

```
DISPLAY USERS
```

This command displays the user ID names established at the network operating system (the names that the users entered to log on to the network workstations).

Locking Shared Files

When you open a file in shared mode, it is your responsibility to prevent potential conflicts by locking either the entire file or, for a data base file, individual records whenever necessary. Although shared access is a concern with any type of file, the potential for data loss is far greater with data base files, which you are constantly updating, than for files such as report or label forms, which change less frequently.

dBASE IV helps you protect shared files by automatically locking files and records whenever you carry out a command or operation that requires a lock, and it releases the lock when it finishes executing the command. Which commands and operations require a file lock depends in part on the status of the LOCK setting. When this setting is ON (as it is by default), all the dot prompt commands listed in Table 23-2 (and equivalent menu options) trigger the automatic file lock. By changing the LOCK setting to OFF, you can disable the automatic file lock entirely for commands that only read data. For commands that read and write files, such as INDEX, turning the LOCK setting OFF causes dBASE IV to lock the file only during the writing phase; when it is reading data, dBASE IV unlocks the file.

If you change the status of the LOCK setting to OFF, it is your responsibility to ensure that multiple users do not perform updates that would compromise the accuracy of reports or calculations performed on the data. For example, if you allow a user at one workstation to print a report while another executes a REPLACE command, you must do so knowing that some records will be printed before they are affected by the REPLACE command and others will be printed afterward.

Command	Entity Locked	Disabled by SET LOCK OFF	Disabled by SET LOCK OFF During Read Phase
APPEND FROM	File	No	
AVERAGE	File	Yes	
BROWSE	Record	No	
CALCULATE	File	Yes	
CHANGE	Record	No	
COPY	File		Yes
COPY STRUCTURE	File		Yes
COPY TAG	File		Yes
COUNT	File	Yes	
DELETE (1 record)	Record	No	
DELETE	File	No	
EDIT	Record	No	
INDEX	File		Yes
JOIN	File		Yes
LABEL	File	Yes	
RECALL (1 record)	Record	No	
RECALL	File	No	
REPLACE (1 record)	Record	No	
REPLACE	File	No	
REPORT	File	Yes	
SET CATALOG ON	File	No	
SORT	File		Yes
SUM	File	Yes	
TOTAL	File		Yes
UPDATE	File	No	

Table 23-2.

Commands That Trigger an Automatic File Lock

When one user tries to lock a file that is already locked at another workstation (either by using an explicit locking command or by executing a command that triggers automatic record locking), dBASE IV repeatedly attempts to lock the file. By default, it displays a pop-up box with the message "File in use by another. Retrying lock, press ESC to cancel" and retries indefinitely to lock the file.

You can customize the number of retries by changing the REPROCESS setting to any number between 1 and 32,000. When you work at the dot prompt, dBASE IV attempts the lock the specified number of times and then redisplays the dot prompt. In Browse or Edit, dBASE IV displays the message, "Please wait, another user has locked this record or file" below the status bar as it executes the specified number of retries. If it cannot lock the file, dBASE IV displays the message "Unable to LOCK (Press SPACE)" below the status bar. When a data base is locked, dBASE IV displays the indicator "FileLock" in the fifth segment of the status bar, or at the top of the screen if the status display is turned off.

If you cannot lock a file after several retries, the wisest course of action may be to abandon the attempt and try again later. Be on the alert for a possible deadlock similar to the one described in the previous section. If two users both try to lock the same two files simultaneously, each may succeed in locking one only to find the other unavailable. You may want to check with other users on the network when you are locked out of a file for what seems like an unreasonably long time.

From the Dot Prompt

From the dot prompt, you can lock a file explicitly by using the FLOCK function. Unlike most other dBASE IV functions, the FLOCK function not only returns a value, but also performs an action—it attempts to lock the file, and returns the logical value .T. if the attempt succeeds or .F. if the file is already locked by another user. The easiest way to call the FLOCK function is to use the ? command to display the result of evaluating it, as in the following:

```
? FLOCK()
```

You can lock a file in an unselected work area by specifying the alias as input to the FLOCK function:

```
? FLOCK("CUSTOMER")
```

You can unlock the file in the currently selected work area by using the UNLOCK command:

```
UNLOCK
```

To release all file (and record) locks in all work areas, you use

```
UNLOCK ALL
```

Locking Shared Records

When you update a data base on the Edit or Browse screen (or substitute a custom screen form for the Edit screen), dBASE IV locks the current record when you type a change directly or choose a command that changes the record, such as **Mark record for deletion** or **Recall marked record**. Simply moving the cursor through the fields on the Browse or Edit screen does not trigger this automatic record lock. Because another user may have changed the record between the time you read it from the disk and the time you began typing your change, dBASE IV displays the warning message "Record may have been changed (press SPACE)." When you press the spacebar, dBASE IV discards your first keystroke (the one that triggered the record lock) and moves the cursor back to the beginning of the field you were editing. To avoid this inconvenience, you may want to lock a record explicitly, using commands described later in this section, as soon as you are sure that you need to edit the data.

If more than one data base is open, dBASE IV also locks any records in unselected work areas that are linked to the current record with SET RELATION. dBASE IV releases the record lock (unlocks the record or records) when you save your changes and move the record pointer to another record. You can determine whether a record is locked by looking at the fifth segment of the status bar (or the top line on the screen if the status display is turned off) where dBASE IV displays the indicator "RecLock" when the current record is locked.

If one user attempts to make a change to a record that is locked at another workstation, or to any record in a file that is locked at another workstation,

dBASE IV initiates a locking strategy similar to the file-locking procedure outlined in the previous section. If the REPROCESS setting retains its default value of 0, dBASE IV displays the message "Record in use by another. Retrying lock, press ESC to cancel" and tries indefinitely to lock the record. If the REPROCESS setting has any other value, dBASE IV retries the specified number of times while displaying the message, "Please wait, another user has locked this record or file." If it cannot lock the record, dBASE IV displays the message "Unable to LOCK (Press SPACE)" and returns you to the Edit or Browse screen.

Because many operations that require a file lock take a long time to complete, you may want to retry once or twice and then try again later if you find that a file you need is locked. In contrast, a record lock is likely to be released shortly, because an average typist requires only a minute or two to update a record on the Edit or Browse screen, and less than a minute to type a command such as REPLACE at the dot prompt. If your network and your fellow users are fast, you will generally gain access to any record you need after a short delay, unless the entire file is locked at another workstation. When you edit records in shared files, remember to *unlock* the record as soon as you are finished with your changes. Accidentally leaving a record locked on the Edit screen while you go to lunch can seriously inconvenience many other users on the network, who may need to edit the same record or to carry out an operation that requires locking the entire data base.

At times, you may want to lock a record explicitly *before* you begin editing. For example, when you work with a file that has 40 or 50 fields, updating a record may necessitate paging up and down on the Edit screen to study the contents before you edit any data, and you might want to lock the record in advance to ensure that it will be available when you begin typing your changes.

As noted earlier, when two users display the same record on the Edit or Browse screen, they are viewing separate copies of the data loaded into memory at the two workstations. When one user changes the record, dBASE IV updates the display at other workstations only when this user moves the record pointer and unlocks the record. You can reconfigure dBASE IV to refresh the display at a specified interval to reflect changes made at other workstations, but this involves using the CONVERT command to add a special network status field to the file structure, and it is beyond the scope of this book.

In a network environment, the summary screen displayed by the DISPLAY STATUS or LIST STATUS commands includes the status of all record and file locks, as illustrated in Figure 23-7 for the National Widgets Customer File.

```
Select area:  1, Database in Use: N:\DBASE\NWCUST.DBF    Alias: NWCUST
Production    MDX file:   N:\DBASE\NWCUST.MDX
          Index TAG:      ZIP  Key: ZIP
   Master Index TAG:      ACCOUNT  Key: ACCOUNT
          Index TAG:      FIRSTORDER  Key: FIRSTORDER (Descending)
          Index TAG:      STATECITY  Key: STATE+CITY+ACCOUNT
          Memo file:  N:\DBASE\NWCUST.DBT
          Lock list:        2  locked

Currently Selected Database:
Select area:  2, Database in Use: N:\DBASE\NWORDER.DBF    Alias: NWORDER
          Lock list:        2,      1,       3,      23  locked

    Related into: NWCUST
    Relation: ACCOUNT

File search path:
Default disk drive: N:
Print destination:  PRN:
Press any key to continue..._
Command ||C:\dbase4\NWORDER      ||Rec 2/33        ||File ||RecLock ||      CapsIns
```

Figure 23-7.

Using DISPLAY STATUS to view record locks

From the Menus

You can lock the current record from the Browse or Edit screen by selecting **Lock record** from the **Records** menu or by pressing CTRL-O. When a record is locked, the **Lock record** option disappears from the **Records** menu and is replaced by **Unlock record**. You can unlock the current record either by selecting this option or by pressing CTRL-O again. dBASE IV automatically unlocks the current record when you move the record pointer to another record, close the file, or exit to the operating system.

From the Dot Prompt

From the dot prompt, you can lock individual records with the RLOCK function, also called LOCK. Like the corresponding file-locking function, RLOCK performs an action *and* returns a value—it attempts to lock the specified record or records, and returns the value .T. if the record can be locked or .F. if it is

already locked by another user. You can call the RLOCK function by using the ? command to display the result of evaluating it, as in the following:

```
? RLOCK()
```

You can lock more than one record at a time by listing the record numbers, in the form of a character string enclosed in quotes, as input to the RLOCK function. For example, the following command would lock records 1, 2, and 3 in the current data base:

```
? RLOCK("1, 2, 3")
```

To lock records in a data base open in an unselected work area, you specify its alias as the second input to the RLOCK function. For example, if the Customer File were opened with the alias "CUSTOMER", you could lock records 1, 2, and 3 *from any work area* with the following command:

```
? RLOCK("1, 2, 3", "CUSTOMER")
```

dBASE IV automatically locks records that are linked to the current record with SET RELATION and SET SKIP. If you opened the Customer, Order, and Inventory files, selected the Order File work area, and used SET RELATION to link the Order File to the Customer File by ACCOUNT code and to the Inventory File by PARTNUMBER, dBASE IV would automatically lock the related Customer File and Inventory File records whenever you locked a record in the Order File.

Because you can lock more than one record at a time, dBASE IV does not unlock one record when you lock another. You can unlock a single record with the same UNLOCK command used to release a file lock, and you can unlock all locked records in the current work area with

```
UNLOCK ALL
```

To unlock records in an unselected work area, you specify the work area in the UNLOCK command:

```
UNLOCK ALL IN CUSTOMER
```

TRANSACTION PROCESSING

dBASE IV provides an additional facility —*transaction processing*—to help protect your data bases when a complex file update procedure fails to complete normally. Used in this sense, the term "transaction" means any sequence of commands that update one or more data base files. You identify the commands that constitute the transaction by surrounding them with BEGIN TRANSACTION and END TRANSACTION commands. Before the first command in the transaction, you type

```
BEGIN TRANSACTION
```

When you begin a transaction, dBASE IV stores the current status of the working environment—which data bases and indexes are open—in a *log file* on disk. In a single-user system, the log file is named TRANSLOG.LOG; on a network, dBASE IV creates a different log file for each user and assigns the user's network name (the one used to log onto the network, not the login name entered to gain access to dBASE IV if a security system is in effect) as the first name of the log file. dBASE IV also stores in the log file the contents of each data base record that you change, both before and after the change, so that the data bases can be restored to their original state if the transaction does not complete normally.

Although you can include most dBASE IV commands in a transaction, you cannot close files or overwrite existing disk files, because these commands would prevent dBASE IV from reversing the updates performed by the transaction. The CLOSE DATABASES, DELETE FILE, ERASE, MODIFY STRUCTURE, PACK, RENAME, and ZAP commands are always prohibited in a transaction, and COPY, COPY STRUCTURE, CREATE, EXPORT, IMPORT, INDEX, SET CATALOG, SET INDEX, SORT, TOTAL, and USE also generate errors if they close files or overwrite existing files. Because you cannot close a file, you must select a new work area for each file that you open during the transaction, even if you do not link the files or use them together in any way. Note also that dBASE IV ignores UNLOCK commands that you execute within a transaction; it unlocks all records and files locked in a transaction only after you end the transaction.

When you end a transaction, dBASE IV erases the log file. Be sure to take whatever measures are necessary to ensure that the transaction completed correctly before you indicate that the transaction is complete by typing

```
END TRANSACTION
```

dBASE IV runs somewhat more slowly when a transaction is in progress because of the time required to record every update in the log file. There is no limit to the number of commands that you can include in a transaction, but a lengthy transaction will result in a very large log file. By default, dBASE IV places the log file in the current subdirectory, but you can override the default by specifying a new subdirectory in the BEGIN TRANSACTION command, as in the following:

```
BEGIN TRANSACTION D:\DBASE4\DATA
```

If you are working on a network and you start up dBASE IV from the program directory on the file server, you can speed up performance by specifying a subdirectory on your local workstation hard disk, rather than allowing dBASE IV to write the log files on the server.

To restore the files to their original state based on the log file, you use the ROLLBACK command. While a transaction is in progress (before you type END TRANSACTION), the ROLLBACK command restores all open data bases; for the most part, ROLLBACK is executed this way from within dBASE IV programs. After the END TRANSACTION command, you can also specify a data base name in the ROLLBACK command to attempt to restore one data base at a time, as in the following:

```
ROLLBACK NWCUST
```

You can determine whether a rollback was successful by testing the value of the ROLLBACK function, which returns the logical value .T. if the data bases were successfully restored or .F. if the rollback failed. From the dot prompt, you can use a ? command to examine the value of this function, as follows:

```
? ROLLBACK()
```

If your system crashes in the middle of an incomplete transaction, dBASE IV displays a pop-up dialog box the next time you start up the program to remind you that a transaction is still pending: "** WARNING ** Uncompleted transaction found." This dialog box has one option—**Continue**—which you must select to acknowledge the warning, after which dBASE IV automatically rolls back the transaction. Because ROLLBACK may not be able to restore the data bases

if they were physically damaged, you should not use transaction processing as a substitute for regular backups. You may want to make an extra backup copy of your files before you begin a lengthy and complex sequence of file update commands if you are unsure about the outcome.

Transaction processing is intended primarily for use in dBASE IV programs running on networks. On a network, all shared files are susceptible to damage caused by failures in any part of the network. You may also find that after executing the first few steps of a lengthy procedure, a file you need is unavailable because another user has locked it or opened it in exclusive mode. If this happens, you could use the ROLLBACK command to reverse the steps you have already carried out and start again later. The same technique is also applicable in a single-user environment, where it can guard against errors that you make in your commands in addition to externally caused hardware or software failures.

SUMMARY

The information about security and networking presented in this chapter is intended to acquaint you with the issues and potential problems involved in sharing dBASE IV, and at times data bases and related auxiliary files, among two or more users. For some users, this chapter only scratches the surface (it does not, for example, describe how to install dBASE IV on a network), while others may find that they have no immediate need for the specific information presented in the networking section, because the automatic file and record locks placed by dBASE IV are adequate to handle potential conflicts. When you use dBASE IV on a network that connects many workstations, or when several users work intensively with the same set of files, either in the menu system or at the dot prompt, a little understanding will go a long way toward helping you interpret the error messages displayed by dBASE IV, enabling you to schedule your work so as to avoid many potential conflicts, and resolving them with a minimum of frustration and animosity when two or more users need the same system resources.

APPENDIX A

Installing dBASE IV

This appendix outlines the hardware and operating system requirements for running dBASE IV, describes in detail how to install the DOS version for single-user operation, and gives an overview of the multiuser installation. If you are installing dBASE IV on a local area network, you should also consult the dBASE IV documentation and the README.DOC file on the Installation Disk for additional details on how to prepare the network, how to install dBASE IV, and how to optimize performance on various types of workstations.

If dBASE IV is already running on your computer, you may want to skim the installation instructions, but do not skip this material entirely. To optimize performance and make full use of all of the program's capabilities, several preparatory steps are required to set up the DOS and dBASE IV working environment. It is a mistake to assume that this preparation was done correctly or at all. The standard installation procedure copies DBSETUP onto your hard disk, and you may want to rerun the setup program to tailor the dBASE IV environment to your personal preferences. (DBSETUP, a program that enables you to customize the display colors and many other aspects of the working environment, is covered in detail in Chapter 18.)

The installation program uses bar menus and dialog boxes identical to those displayed when you work in the dBASE IV menu system. If you are reading

this appendix first and have not yet used dBASE IV, you may not be familiar with the variety of cursor movement and command keys used to navigate through the menu system and make selections, but you can make do with just a few simple commands. You can select any menu or dialog box option by using the four arrow keys to highlight the option and then pressing ENTER. You can use the LEFT ARROW and RIGHT ARROW keys to move among the options on a horizontal bar menu (such as the one displayed when you choose the **Menu-driven** installation option) or in a dialog box. When selecting a horizontal bar menu invokes an associated pull-down menu, you can use UP ARROW and DOWN ARROW to highlight options on the pull-down menu.

When dBASE IV asks an open-ended question—for example, when it prompts you to enter the name of a subdirectory—it generally displays a default value, which you can accept by pressing ENTER. To override the default value, you can backspace to erase the displayed value and type your own entry, or you can use the LEFT ARROW and RIGHT ARROW keys to edit the default. As in most editors (including the dBASE IV full-screen edit modes), you can switch between typing in Insert mode and Overstrike mode by pressing INS, and you can delete the character at the cursor position by pressing DEL.

HARDWARE AND OPERATING SYSTEM REQUIREMENTS

dBASE IV runs on the IBM PC/XT; PC/AT; PS/2 models 30, 50, 60, and 80; Compaq 286 and 386; and other IBM-compatible computers. You need a hard disk and at least one 5 1/4-inch or 3 1/2-inch floppy drive. dBASE IV works with any combination of video card and monitor, and it supports the 43-line display mode of the EGA and VGA display adapters (but not 50-line mode on a VGA system). dBASE IV is compatible with PC-DOS or MS-DOS version 2.1, all versions of PC-DOS, MS-DOS or Compaq DOS 3, MS-DOS 4.01, and MS-DOS 5.0. The program is not copy-protected.

Although you do not need a printer to run dBASE IV, a printer is highly recommended. You can use any serial or parallel printer—dot matrix, ink jet, daisy wheel, or laser. dBASE IV can boldface and underline text on any printer; if there is a driver for your printer, you can also use italics, superscript, and subscript (provided that your printer can produce these type styles). Using the procedure described in Chapter 18, you can install up to five additional fonts, type sizes, or special print attributes if you know the printer codes required to initiate and terminate these print modes.

You must have at least 640K of RAM installed in your computer to run dBASE IV, and you must have at least 450K available in order to start up the program. That is, you must have 450K of memory free after loading the operating system, the network operating system or workstation software if you are running on a LAN, and any RAM-resident utilities. If you are close to this limit, you may find that although you can start up dBASE IV, you do not have enough memory to run DOS commands or external programs from within dBASE IV, open as many data base files as you need for your application, create complex reports, or use the applications generator. Some techniques for optimizing memory usage are presented later in this appendix.

dBASE IV occupies at least 3.5 megabytes of space on your hard disk, and if you install any of the optional files—the tutorial, sample files, RunTime, or template language—it can require as much as 7 megabytes. If you install all the options, you can erase some of them later to reclaim space, and you can erase the SQL files (which dBASE IV always installs). However, dBASE IV does not allow you to begin the installation unless you have 3.5 megabytes for the standard edition or 4 megabytes for the Developer's Edition.

CONFIGURING DOS FOR SINGLE-USER dBASE IV

To install single-user dBASE IV on your hard disk, you need subdirectories for the program and auxiliary files. You must also ensure that the DOS configuration file, CONFIG.SYS, is present in the root directory and that it contains a command to increase the number of files that the operating system can open simultaneously. On a single-user system, the installation program supplied with dBASE IV can carry out these preparatory steps for you, but if you prefer, you can do all or some of them yourself. When you install dBASE IV on a local area network, you must create all the required subdirectories in advance and assign the appropriate access privileges. Even if you allow dBASE IV to carry out all the configuration procedures for you, you should understand why they are important and how dBASE IV interacts with the operating system to access the hard disk and open files.

Creating a Subdirectory for dBASE IV

The standard installation procedure can copy the dBASE IV program files to any subdirectory on any available hard drive. Using a DOS PATH command, you can access dBASE IV from any disk drive and subdirectory, so you can

create additional subdirectories in which to store your data bases and other auxiliary files, and switch to the appropriate subdirectory before you start up the program. dBASE IV supports its own directory search command (analogous to the DOS PATH command) that enables it to find files in other subdirectories, it allows you to choose a new default drive or default subdirectory at any time, and it recognizes full DOS path names, so you can read or write files anywhere on your hard disk.

All the examples in this book assume that both the dBASE IV program and the sample data bases are stored on a hard disk called drive C, in a subdirectory named DBASE4, which is located directly under the root directory (the full path name of this subdirectory is C:\DBASE4). If you want to install dBASE IV on a different drive or subdirectory, remember to make the appropriate substitutions when you install and run the program. Most dBASE IV applications, even relatively simple ones, generate many disk files, and you can improve performance significantly by creating a separate subdirectory for each application, because all DOS disk accesses slow down dramatically when the number of files in a subdirectory exceeds about 120.

As noted earlier, the installation program described later in this chapter can create the subdirectories required for the dBASE IV program files and optional files if they do not already exist. If you prefer, you can create the dBASE IV subdirectory in advance using the DOS MD or MKDIR ("make directory") command. To create a subdirectory called DBASE4 under the root directory on drive C, you could type the following command, from any drive or subdirectory:

```
MD C:\DBASE4
```

You do not have to log on to this subdirectory (make it the current subdirectory) to run the installation program.

The CONFIG.SYS File

The DOS configuration file, CONFIG.SYS, contains commands for customizing certain aspects of the DOS working environment. The CONFIG.SYS file is a text file that contains one or more commands, each on a separate line, and each ending with a hard return. You can create or edit this file with any word processor or text editor that can read and write ASCII text files—files containing only standard keyboard characters, such as letters, numbers, and punctua-

tion marks, with no embedded word processing or formatting commands. If you do not have another editor that can create a text file, you can use the dBASE IV program editor (covered in Chapter 21) for this purpose.

DOS checks for the presence of a CONFIG.SYS file and reads its contents when—and only when—you boot your computer, either by turning on the power or pressing ALT-CTRL-DEL. Because DOS reads the configuration file only at startup, *CONFIG.SYS must be located in the root directory of the disk from which you boot your computer,* not in the subdirectory that contains the DOS utility programs, the subdirectory in which dBASE IV is located, or in any other subdirectory. In most cases, you boot your computer directly from the hard disk, and the CONFIG.SYS file must be in the root directory of the first (or only) logical drive, usually drive C. If you boot from a floppy disk, even if you log on to a hard disk immediately, CONFIG.SYS must be in the root directory of the boot floppy. If you modify the CONFIG.SYS file, you must reboot your computer to see your changes take effect.

The most important CONFIG.SYS entry for dBASE IV users is the FILES command, which specifies the maximum number of disk files that the operating system can open simultaneously. dBASE IV allows you to open up to 99 disk files at once—10 data base files and auxiliary files such as indexes, screen form files, and report and label form files—but without special instructions in the CONFIG.SYS file, DOS imposes a more stringent limitation. By default, DOS sets aside enough memory to store the names of 8 open files. However, to the operating system, the process of reading and writing disk files is the same as transferring data to or from physical devices such as the keyboard, monitor, printer, and communications ports. DOS reserves five file names for these physical devices, which leaves only three for disk files.

You can use the FILES command in the CONFIG.SYS file to increase up to 255 the number of file and device names permitted by DOS. Under DOS versions earlier than 3.3, any one application program can access only 20 files (a local area network would require more than 20 total files, but no more than 20 could be open at one workstation). All dBASE IV users should increase the number of open files to at least 20, and if you have DOS 3.3 or later, 40 (the value used by the installation program) is a good initial choice. When you modify the CONFIG.SYS file yourself, make sure that it contains one of the following commands:

```
FILES = 20
```

or

```
FILES = 40
```

If you allow the dBASE IV installation program to update the CONFIG.SYS file, it also checks for the presence of a BUFFERS command, which determines how much memory is allocated for disk buffers. Increasing this setting (you can specify any value between 1 and 99) can reduce the number of disk accesses required to retrieve the same data repeatedly, but it also reduces available memory. If you cannot use the dBASE IV disk cache (which is described later in this appendix), you can fine-tune hard disk performance by experimenting with the BUFFERS setting. If you do use the disk cache, which serves the same purpose and will result in a much larger performance improvement, you can assign a low value (3 to 5) to the BUFFERS setting. If you allow the installation program to update your CONFIG.SYS file, it ensures that BUFFERS is set to at least 15. To request 5 buffers, you would use the following command in the CONFIG.SYS file:

```
BUFFERS = 5
```

The CONFIG.SYS file may also contain commands to customize other aspects of the DOS environment, including the number of disk drives in your system, the date and time format, and how often DOS checks the keyboard to determine whether you have pressed CTRL-BREAK to interrupt the current process. It also frequently contains DEVICE commands that identify *device drivers*—small programs that are loaded into memory with DOS when you boot your system. Device drivers are commonly used to manage memory and to enable the operating system to communicate with peripheral devices such as video display adapters, mice, external hard disks, tape backup units, and other mass storage subsystems. DEVICE commands, if present, are essential for the proper functioning of your hardware and other application software. The standard installation procedure adds or modifies only the FILES and BUFFERS commands; it leaves any other CONFIG.SYS commands unchanged. If you set up the DOS environment yourself, check for the presence of a CONFIG.SYS file and modify its contents if necessary, rather than re-creating this file from scratch or overwriting the original.

Setting the Date and Time

All IBM and compatible computers have a clock that runs as long as the power is on, and almost all AT-compatibles, 80386-based computers, and PS/2 systems

have a battery-powered clock that keeps time even when the computer is turned off. Whenever you create or update a file, DOS records the current date and time in the file's directory entry along with the file name and size. This information can help you determine which in a group of related files is the most recent version. Within dBASE IV, the current date and time are available through built-in functions for use in calculations and for printing on reports. It is therefore to your advantage to make sure that the date and time are always set correctly.

You can view the date and time, and reset them for the duration of a work session, using the DOS DATE and TIME commands. To set the date, type

```
DATE
```

DOS displays the current date and prompts you to enter a new date. You enter the date in month/day/year format, using either slashes or dashes as punctuation. Although DOS includes the day of the week in the date display format, do not enter the day when you set the date—DOS calculates it when it displays the date. To set the time, you use the TIME command and enter the time in hours:minutes:seconds format based on a 24-hour clock.

If you find that the "current" date is always "Tue 1-01-1980" before you reset it, you can deduce that your computer does not have a battery-powered clock, and you must use the DOS DATE and TIME commands to set the system clock every time you boot your computer. The easiest way to do this is to add the DATE and TIME commands to your AUTOEXEC.BAT file so that you do not have to remember to type them at the DOS prompt every time you start up your computer.

Using a Serial Printer

Chapter 18 described how to use the DBSETUP program to install up to four printers for use with dBASE IV, and to specify the output port for each printer. dBASE IV can route output to any port, and if you have both a serial and a parallel printer, it can switch between ports. However, it does not initialize the serial port. If one of your printers (or your only printer) is connected to a serial port (an output port known as COM1: or COM2:), an extra step is required before you can use this printer through dBASE IV: You must use the DOS

MODE command to set the baud rate (the speed at which data is sent to the printer) and other communications parameters. Assuming that your printer accepts data at 1200 baud, the required MODE command is as follows:

```
MODE COM1: 1200,N,8,1,P
```

For baud rates other than 1200, you can make the appropriate substitution. You may already be accustomed to using this MODE command, as well as another that redirects printed output from the default output device (the parallel port called LPT1:) to the serial, or communications, port. With dBASE IV, you do not need the second MODE command, because dBASE IV can select the right output port based on the information that you enter when you install your printers.

You can either type the MODE command at the DOS prompt or place it in your AUTOEXEC.BAT file so that it is executed every time you boot your computer. Make sure that MODE.COM is available, either in the root directory or in a subdirectory made accessible through a DOS PATH command. If you have enough memory in your computer, you can execute the MODE command from within dBASE IV, but you will probably find it more convenient to take care of this "housekeeping" chore from DOS, before you start up dBASE IV.

BACKING UP THE dBASE IV PROGRAM DISKS

dBASE IV is distributed on 5 1/4-inch or 3 1/2-inch floppy disks; the number of distribution disks depends on the disk format and on whether you purchased the standard version or the Developer's Edition. In all cases, your disk package should include an Installation Disk, the System Disks that contain the dBASE IV program files, and additional disks with the sample files, on-disk tutorial, and, if you have the Developer's Edition, the RunTime files and template language. The distribution disks are not copy-protected, and you should be sure to make backup copies. If you back up the disks *after* you install, the registration information will be stored on the backup copy of System Disk #1, and you will not have to re-enter this data if you reinstall dBASE IV from the backups. You can have an extra margin of safety, however, if you make the copies before you install dBASE IV.

The easiest way to ensure that the backup copy of each disk is complete is to use the DOS DISKCOPY utility, which copies a disk track by track, regardless of the subdirectory structure or data stored on the disk. If you have two floppy disk drives of the same capacity, you can place the disk you want to copy in one drive, such as drive A, a blank disk (which need not be formatted) in the other, drive B, and type

```
DISKCOPY A: B:
```

If for some reason you accidentally reverse the disk drive specifications, DISKCOPY will copy the contents of the blank disk onto the disk you wanted to copy. To guard against this possibility, *always write-protect the original disk when you use DISKCOPY.* Remember to remove the write-protect tab from System Disk #1 before you begin the installation procedure so that dBASE IV can write your registration information on this disk.

If you have only one floppy drive, it is not convenient to copy directly from one floppy disk to another, but with patience, you can do it. If you specify the same drive twice, DOS assumes that the source and destination disks will alternate in the same drive and prompts you to switch disks when necessary. Make sure to write-protect the original disk when you use this method (to guard against losing track and inserting the wrong disk), and then type

```
DISKCOPY A: A:
```

DOS reads as much data from the source disk as it can fit into memory, prompts you to switch disks, copies the data in memory onto the target disk, and then requests the source disk again.

OPTIMIZING MEMORY USAGE AND PERFORMANCE

dBASE IV version 1.1 offers significant improvements over version 1.0 in both memory utilization and performance, and provides more options for configuring the software to optimize performance under different conditions. A good understanding of the factors that affect performance is essential to enable you to fine-tune dBASE IV to match your hardware, operating system, and preferred working environment.

Optimizing Memory Usage

Like version 1.0, dBASE IV version 1.1 uses only standard DOS memory (not expanded or extended memory) for itself and for your data bases, indexes, and other application files. The minimum free RAM required to start up the program is around 450K, so you may be able to run dBASE IV with some small memory-resident utilities loaded. However, the amount of available memory has a strong influence on performance: the more memory is available, the faster your system will run.

The most important single thing that you can do to improve performance is to maximize the amount of memory that is available to DOS, and thereby to dBASE IV. In a standard DOS environment, this means reducing the amount of memory allocated to DOS services or utility programs. You can also make additional memory available to DOS by using memory managers such as QEMM or 386Max, which remap unused memory between 640K and 1 megabyte (for example, memory set aside for a video adapter that is not physically present in your system) so that this memory behaves exactly like the first 640K.

dBASE IV uses memory to manage its own overlays as well as to store your data, memory variables, forms, and programs (if you write programs or use the applications generator). You have some control over how to allocate memory for these various functions through the DOS environment variable DBHEAP, which represents the percentage of available memory that dBASE IV uses for running application programs. DBHEAP can take on any value between 0 and 100, and the default is 50. For example, you could request that 30 percent of available memory be devoted to running programs with the following command:

```
SET DBHEAP=30
```

Remember that DBHEAP is a DOS environment variable, not a dBASE IV setting, although the DOS command SET is the same as the dBASE IV command verb. You must assign values to DOS environment variables from outside of dBASE IV—from the DOS prompt or from a DOS batch file (such as the AUTOEXEC.BAT file); you cannot execute a DOS SET command with the RUN command from the dBASE IV dot prompt.

When DBHEAP is assigned a relatively low value, more memory is allocated to dBASE IV overlays, so that moving from one menu or editor to another requires fewer disk accesses, and performance improves in the Control Center,

the layout editors, and the Edit and Browse screens. When DBHEAP is relatively high, more memory is used for program code, data bases, memory variables, windows, and menus and most application programs (including programs generated by the applications generator) run faster overall. If you work primarily in the menu system, you might try values of DBHEAP between 30 and 50; for working at the dot prompt or running application programs, 80 or 90 will yield somewhat faster performance and reduce the likelihood of encountering "Insufficient memory" errors. Keep in mind, however, that all of the full-screen editors—including Edit, Browse, and the form layout editors—are considered to be part of the menu system. Thus, even if you work primarily at the dot prompt, you should choose a low value for DBHEAP if you anticipate making heavy use of any of these editors during a work session.

The dBASE IV Disk Cache

dBASE IV version 1.1 achieves most of its performance gains over version 1.0 by means of a *disk cache program* that can make use of either expanded or extended memory. The disk cache program does not enable dBASE IV to add expanded or extended memory directly to the available memory pool (which is drawn entirely from standard memory available to DOS), but it can significantly reduce the number of times dBASE IV must read the hard disk. In a system with no expanded or extended memory, version 1.1 runs only a little faster than version 1.0. Performance will improve somewhat if you can use any memory at all for disk caching, and it will improve dramatically if you can devote between one and 1.5 megabytes to the cache.

In general, disk cache programs work by storing data or program code read from the disk in expanded or extended memory. The next time the same information is required, the cache manager transfers it from the cache area in expanded or extended memory into standard DOS memory, rather than forcing the operating system to reread the hard disk. The concept of disk caching is not new or unique to dBASE IV. The DOS BUFFERS command in CONFIG .SYS, introduced earlier in this appendix, allocates a portion of the first 640K of memory as a disk cache, and other operating systems and utility packages may provide disk caching as well.

You should never run two different disk cache programs at the same time—conflicts between incompatible memory managers can corrupt the disk directory or cause the system to hang up. If you have another disk cache

program, such as the SMARTDRV software provided with Windows, you may want to try using it instead of the dBASE IV cache. Note that although the dBASE IV cache is compatible with the caching mediated by the DOS BUFFERS command, you can set BUFFERS to a small number (3 to 5) if you are using *any* other disk cache, and thereby maximize the amount of memory available to DOS.

You should also be wary of potential conflicts between the dBASE IV disk cache and other memory-resident programs. For example, some versions of Sidekick are incompatible with some versions of the disk cache. You may be able to resolve the problem by running a utility called DBCINIT.EXE, provided with dBASE IV, before you load the memory-resident program. You can do this by typing DBCINIT from the DOS prompt or by including this command in your AUTOEXEC.BAT file. (As with any other program, you must ensure that the operating system can find the DBCINIT.EXE program, either by establishing a search path before you type the command or by including the disk drive and subdirectory in your command line.) You can also invoke DBCINIT.EXE as a device driver by adding the following line to your CONFIG.SYS file (assuming that the dBASE IV program directory is located on drive C and is called DBASE4):

```
DEVICE=C:\DBASE4\DBCINIT.EXE
```

Regardless of the method you use to load DBCINIT.EXE, keep in mind that it must be run after you load any hard disk or RAM disk device drivers, but before the memory-resident utility that conflicts with the dBASE IV cache. Note that DBCINIT.EXE will not resolve every conflict between the dBASE IV cache and memory-resident programs, and in some cases, it can *cause* problems (for example, with some versions of Sidekick Plus). Whenever you are experiencing otherwise inexplicable problems with dBASE IV, you might try disabling the disk cache or removing all RAM-resident programs from memory before you start up the program.

The dBASE IV disk caching software cannot cache the hard disk used as the file server on a local area network, but it does work on a local hard disk installed in a network workstation. To make use of caching on a workstation, you must copy the dBASE IV overlay and resource files onto the local hard disk and install the disk cache on the workstation. If you do not have expanded or extended memory in the workstation computers, you can still improve performance somewhat by copying the dBASE IV overlay and resource files onto the local hard disk. In either case, you must place the local subdirectory that

contains these files *before* the dBASE IV subdirectory on the file server in the DOS search path. This ensures that when you work in any other directory on the file server, the operating system searches for dBASE IV program files on the local hard disk in the workstation before looking on the file server.

The installation program allows you to choose whether or not to install the cache, and to specify which type of memory to use—either extended or expanded. You can also use a batch file called CACHEDB.BAT, which is supplied with dBASE IV and copied onto your hard disk by the installation program, to configure the cache later. If you are unsure about which type of memory is present in your computer, you can try one chosen at random, and switch to the other if necessary later on. If you have an 8086-, 8088-, or 80286-based system with an extra memory board, you probably have *expanded* memory (although some expanded memory boards can be set up to provide extended memory on 80286-based machines). If you have an 80386- or 80486-based system, you have *extended* memory, but you may be using a memory manager such as QEMM or 386MAX to configure this memory to emulate expanded memory. When you start up dBASE IV, it displays a warning message and does not load the disk cache if it does not find any memory of the specified type. The program will run without the cache, but performance will suffer.

Note also that there are several cache options that you cannot establish during installation—you must set them while the cache software is running. Foremost among these are the options that determine how often dBASE IV writes changed data back to the hard disk. By default, the cache uses *staged writes*—it updates the hard disk based on data retained in memory when the system is idle. You can gain an additional measure of security by switching to a system called *write through hard,* in which the cache software writes all changes to disk immediately (but continues to read data from the memory allocated to the cache whenever possible). When you use the cache in this way, performance will be somewhat slower, because more frequent disk accesses are required, but there is less likelihood that you will lose data if the system crashes, and you may have less trouble with memory-resident editors. To select the write through hard cache option, type the following command from the dot prompt (you cannot run the cache configuration program from the Control Center):

```
RUN DBCACHE/W
```

To return to using staged writes, you can type

```
RUN DBCACHE/S
```

If you always want to use the write through hard method, you can use a COMMAND entry in CONFIG.DB to instruct dBASE IV to run the DBCACHE command every time you start up the program (the CONFIG.DB file and the COMMAND command are described in Chapter 18). Note, however, that you can only invoke one command automatically, so you cannot easily run the DBCACHE command and then automatically invoke the ASSIST command to start up the Control Center each time you run dBASE IV. If you use the COMMAND entry in CONFIG.DB to set cache configuration options, you must type ASSIST at the dot prompt or press F2 (Assist) to activate the Control Center.

The specific method that you use to reconfigure the dBASE IV disk cache after the initial installation may vary somewhat, depending on when you purchased your copy of version 1.1. The cache also offers other configuration options in addition to the staged writes and write through hard settings, all of which must be set with the DBCACHE command while the cache software is running. Be sure to check the documentation packaged with dBASE IV for other specific instructions on installing and configuring the disk cache software. The documentation and README.DOC files provided with version 1.1 also describe in more detail how to configure dBASE IV for optimal performance on a local area network and how to install disk caching on workstations with expanded or extended memory and a local hard disk.

Using a RAM Disk to Improve Performance

Another way to substitute fast memory transfers for slower disk read operations is to use a RAM disk program, which allocates a certain amount of expanded or extended memory to emulate a disk drive. Even with the disk cache, if you have RAM disk software that enables you to create a RAM disk of 500K to 1 megabyte, you can further improve the performance of dBASE IV by using the TMP or DBTMP environment variable to request that dBASE IV write its temporary files on this simulated disk drive. For example, if your RAM disk is identified as drive F, you could use the following command, executed at the DOS prompt or from the AUTOEXEC.BAT file:

```
SET DBTMP=F:\
```

INSTALLING dBASE IV

When you install dBASE IV for single-user operation, the installation program can create all required subdirectories, and with your permission, it can update your CONFIG.SYS and AUTOEXEC.BAT files. If you prefer to modify these files yourself (for example, to request more than the default 40 files), you can do so before you begin the installation, or you can edit either file afterward. If you want to install the multiuser version, you must first create all required subdirectories and use the appropriate network operating system commands or utility programs to make the program directory shareable and to ensure that you have access privileges that allow you to complete the installation. If you do not always start up the network—that is, if you can run your computer either as a stand-alone system or connected to the network—make sure to do so before you begin the installation.

If you have a copy-protected version of dBASE III or III PLUS on your hard disk, you should "uninstall" it, using the utility program supplied with the earlier version of dBASE, before you try to install dBASE IV. If you wish, you can leave an unprotected copy of single-user dBASE III PLUS or an earlier version of dBASE IV on your hard disk, but you must install dBASE IV version 1.1 in a different subdirectory. Two multiuser versions of dBASE cannot coexist on the same hard drive, but if your hard disk is partitioned into multiple volumes that you access as different *logical drives* (by typing different drive letters), you can maintain multiple multiuser copies of dBASE by placing them on different logical drives (for example, multiuser dBASE III PLUS on drive C and multiuser dBASE IV on drive D).

To begin the installation, place the Installation Disk (the disk numbered 0) in your floppy disk drive (usually drive A or B), and log on to the floppy drive by typing

```
A:
```

To start the installation program, type

```
INSTALL
```

dBASE IV displays a sign-on screen that summarizes the terms of the licensing agreement and prompts you on the message line to "Press ↵ to Continue." The first time you run the installation program, you must identify

this copy of dBASE IV as your own by filling out a registration screen on which you enter your name (or in a large company, perhaps your department or job title), company name, and serial number. If you are installing a new copy of dBASE IV, you will find the serial number on System Disk #1 or on the Installation Disk. If you are upgrading from dBASE IV version 1.0, you can use the serial number on the appropriate version 1.0 distribution disk. The registration information that you enter is prominently displayed on the dBASE IV sign-on screen every time you start up the program. Although this does not prevent someone else from copying and using your copy of dBASE IV, it does enable Ashton-Tate to identify the rightful owner if someone with an illegal copy calls Technical Support.

Type the registration information carefully, because once you have saved it, there is no way to change it later. When the three items are complete and correct, press CTRL-END to save your entries and proceed with the installation. If you enter the wrong serial number, dBASE IV will detect the error, issue a warning, and wait until you enter the correct serial number. After accepting the registration information, dBASE IV displays a summary screen that describes the three installation options. This screen is pictured in Figure A-1.

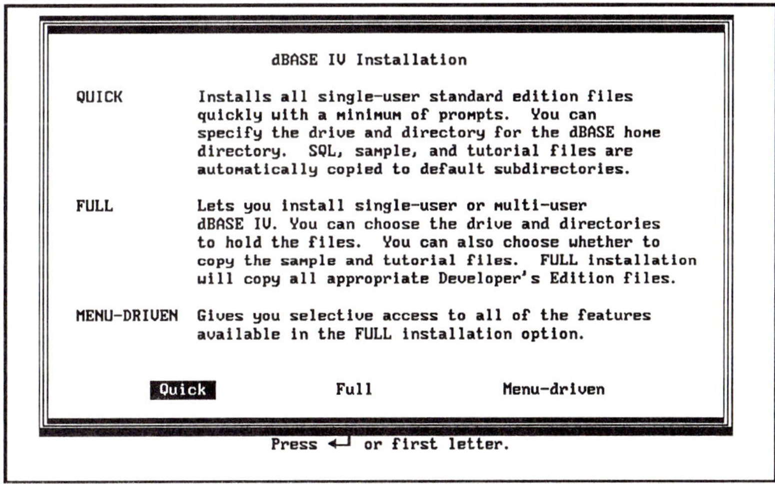

Figure A-1.

The installation options

In all cases, the installation progam copies the dBASE IV program files to a subdirectory of your choice on the hard disk. The default subdirectory for the program files is always C:\DBASE, but you can edit this entry or backspace over it to erase the default from the dialog box and enter a different drive and subdirectory. The installation program also copies the DBSETUP program and the printer driver file to the program directory so that you can reconfigure the working environment at any time.

dBASE IV does not allow you to begin the installation unless you have enough room on the specified drive for the program files and SQL files (approximately 3.5 megabytes for the standard version or 4 megabytes for the Developer's Edition). If you do not have enough space, the installation program allows you to select another drive or exit to DOS, presumably to erase other files and free some space before you try the installation again. The installation program also issues a warning if any version of dBASE is already present in the selected directory and allows you to overwrite the previously installed version (which may be dBASE IV or an earlier version) or select another directory. You cannot overwrite a copy-protected version of dBASE III or dBASE III PLUS. You must exit to DOS and use the UNINSTAL program provided with the earlier version of dBASE to remove it from your hard disk.

In a single-user installation, dBASE IV always gives you the option to activate the disk cache, using either expanded or extended memory. To turn on caching, choose **Yes** from the dialog box that asks "Do you wish to install caching for extended/expanded memory?" and then choose extended or expanded (LIM) memory. If you are unsure of how to answer this question, you can either try one and see if it works, or you can bypass the cache installation and configure the disk cache later.

If you choose **Quick** from the menu of installation options, dBASE IV automatically installs the sample files, tutorial, and SQL files, placing them in subdirectories called SAMPLES, DBTUTOR, and SQLHOME, respectively; these subdirectories are located under the main dBASE IV program directory.

When you choose the **Full** installation option, dBASE IV allows you to choose either a single-user or multiuser installation. After you enter the drive and directory in which to install dBASE IV, the installation program prompts you for the drive and directory for the SQL files. The proposed default for the SQL directory is always a subdirectory called SQLHOME, located directly under the main dBASE IV program directory.

After copying the program files and SQL files, the installation program presents a series of dialog boxes that allow you to install any or all of the optional files. Depending on your version of dBASE IV, you can install the

sample files, tutorial, RunTime, and template language into any subdirectory on any disk drive. By default, the installation program copies the RunTime files into the dBASE IV program directory, and creates subdirectories under the program directory for the samples, tutorial, and template language files named SAMPLES, DBTUTOR, and DTL, respectively.

If you install a single-user copy of dBASE IV using either the **Quick** or **Full** installation option, dBASE IV also offers to update the AUTOEXEC.BAT and CONFIG.SYS files as described earlier in this appendix. Remember that if you allow dBASE IV to modify the CONFIG.SYS or AUTOEXEC.BAT file, you must reboot your computer to see the effects of the changes.

If you choose the **Menu-driven** installation option, dBASE IV allows you to carry out any or all of the steps included in the Full installation by selecting options one at a time from a menu, and to specify all of the drives and subdirectories for the required and optional files. You might choose this option initially if you want to skip most of the optional steps. You can also use the **Menu-driven** option to install additional files that you bypassed when you originally installed dBASE IV, to finish an installation that you could not complete because you did not have enough free disk space, or to request that dBASE IV modify your AUTOEXEC.BAT or CONFIG.SYS files if you skipped this step previously. When you choose the **Menu-driven** installation option, dBASE IV displays a horizontal bar menu at the top of the screen with three options: **Install**, **DOS**, and **Exit**. The structure of this menu is illustrated in Figure A-2.

To begin copying the dBASE IV program files, choose the **Install dBASE IV** option from the **Install** menu. To install any of the optional files, select **Transfer other files** from the **Install** menu. You can choose items from this menu one at a time, in any order you wish, to install only the options you want. In each case, dBASE IV prompts you for the directory in which dBASE IV is located, and then for the subdirectory in which to place the optional files.

If you use either the full or menu-driven installation to copy the RunTime files to your hard disk, the installation program refuses to begin copying files unless you have approximately 2.1 megabytes of disk space on the designated drive. If you do not have this much space free, it displays a dialog box that offers two options: **Change Target Drive** and **Abandon**. You can either enter another drive, which is used for the RunTime files and, if you are carrying out a full installation, all subsequent optional files as well, or you can abandon the RunTime installation.

If you run out of disk space while the installation program is copying any of the other optional files—the sample files, tutorial, or template language,

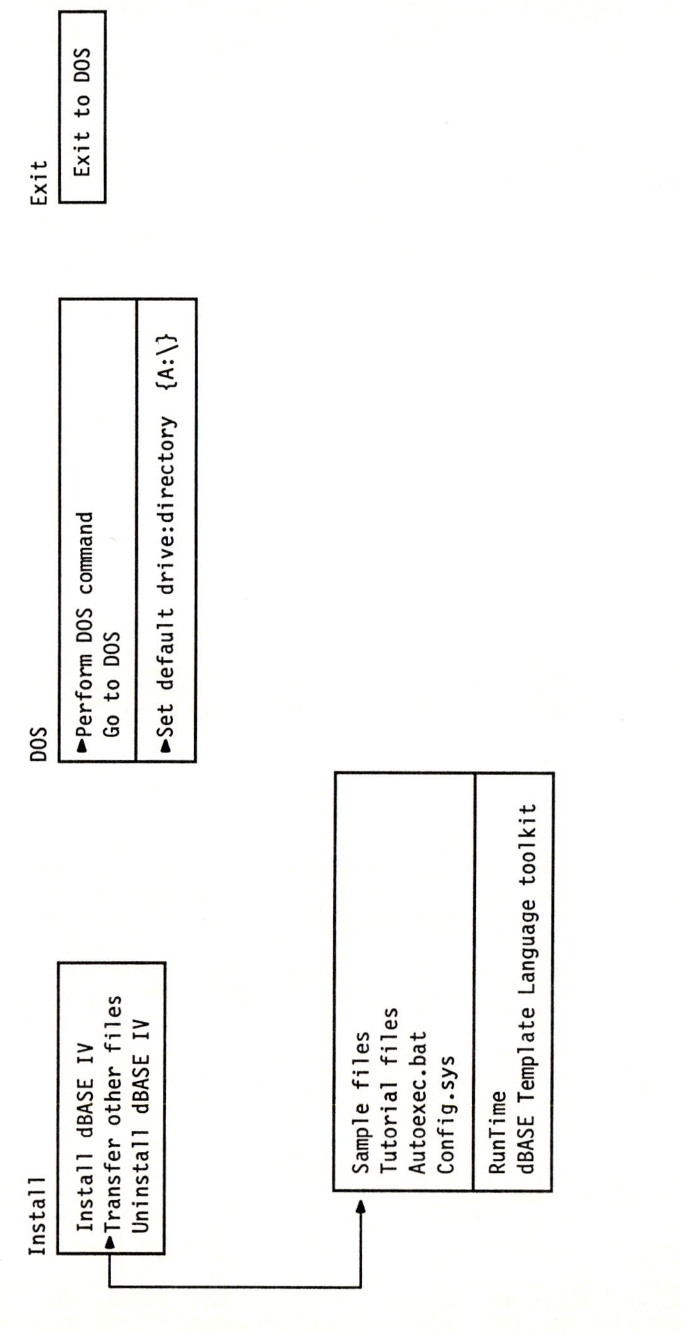

Figure A-2.

The structure of the Install menu

dBASE IV displays a "Disk full" error and returns you either to DOS or to the installation menu. After clearing additional space, you can rerun the installation program and use the **Menu-driven** installation option to recopy just the desired files.

When the single-user installation process completes normally, dBASE IV displays the message "The installation of dBASE IV is complete. To modify the Config.db file for dBASE IV use the DBSETUP utility now installed on your dBASE directory" and prompts you to press ENTER to continue. After it finishes a multiuser installation, dBASE IV displays the message "You may now add dBASE IV users to this network. If you choose to add users now, the dBASE IV Adduser4 program will be invoked for you." If you have the Developer's Edition of dBASE IV, up to three workstations can access dBASE IV simultaneously without any further preparation. The ADDUSER4 program allows you to add network support for more users, based on a Lan Pack or an additional copy of dBASE IV. You can also run this program separately, from the DOS prompt, to add users to your network at a later date.

APPENDIX B

Menu Tree Diagrams

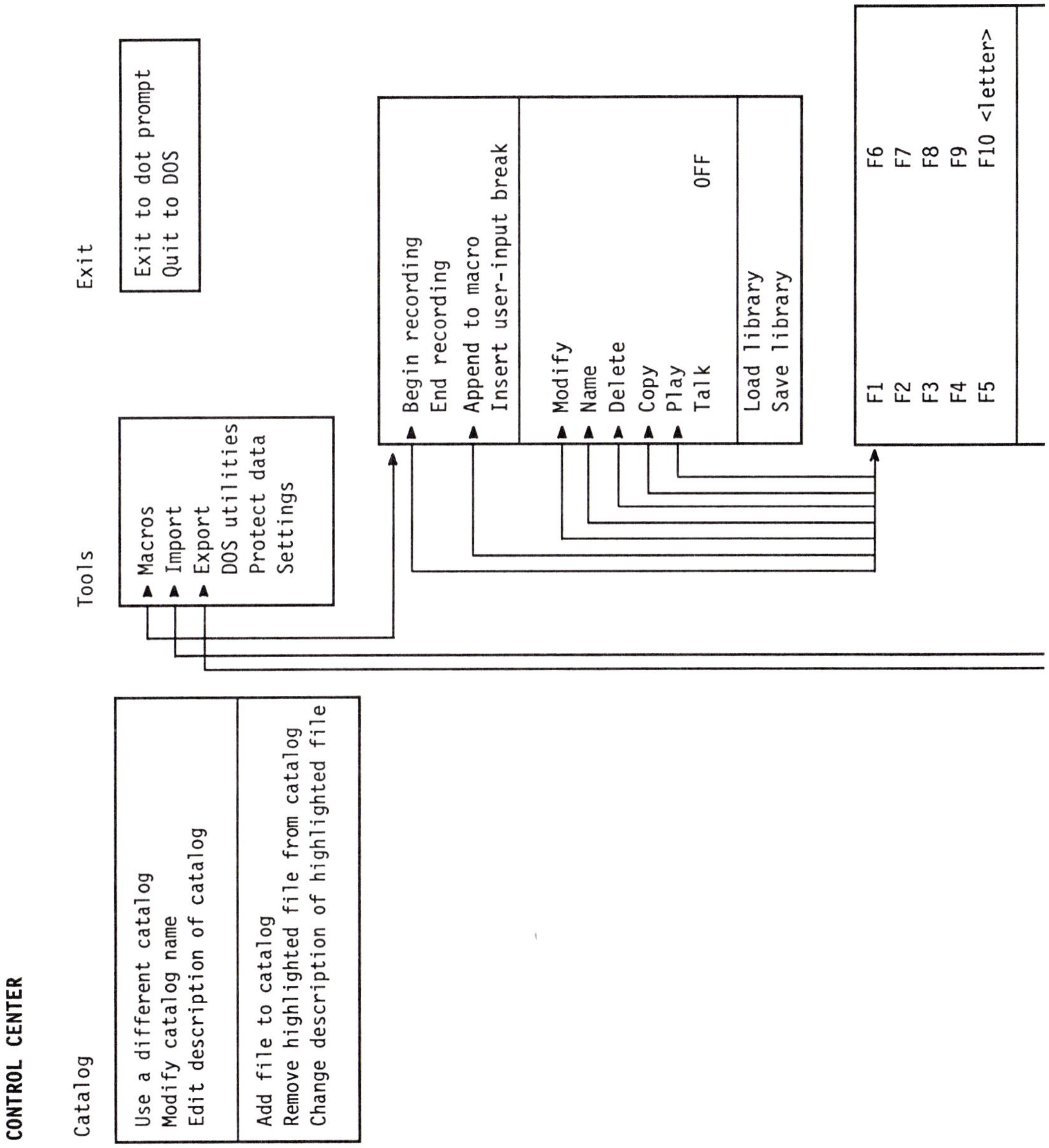

CONTROL CENTER

Catalog

Use a different catalog
Modify catalog name
Edit description of catalog

Add file to catalog
Remove highlighted file from catalog
Change description of highlighted file

Tools

► Macros
► Import
► Export
DOS utilities
Protect data
Settings

Exit

Exit to dot prompt
Quit to DOS

► Begin recording
End recording
► Append to macro
Insert user-input break

► Modify
► Name
► Delete
► Copy
► Play
Talk OFF

Load library
Save library

F1	F6
F2	F7
F3	F8
F4	F9
F5	F10 <letter>

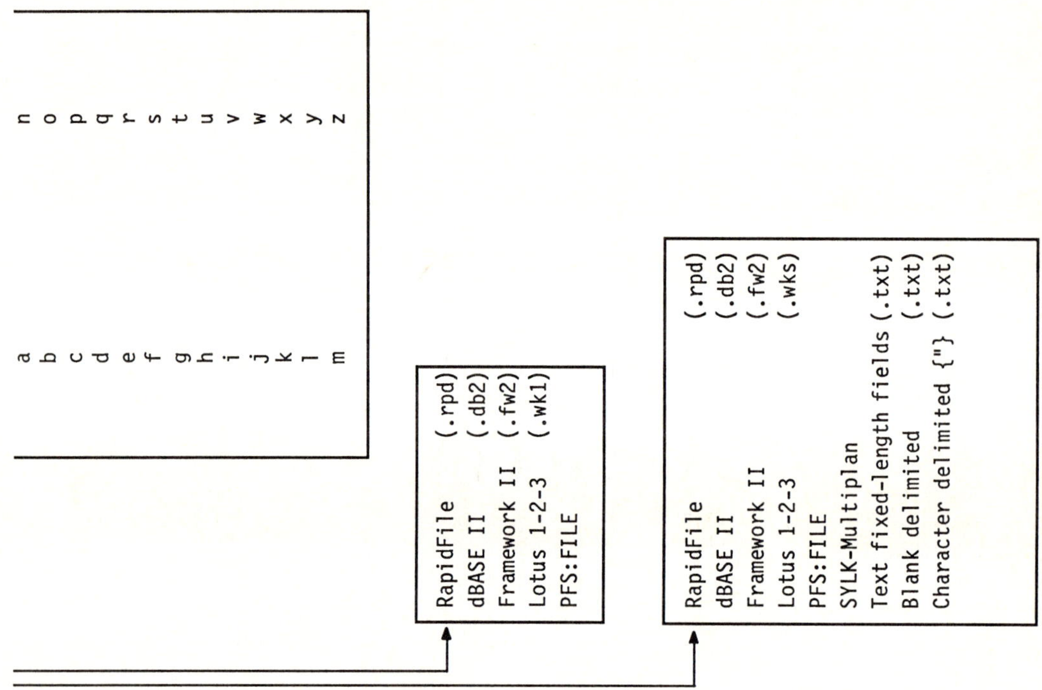

a
b
c
d
e
f
g
h
i
j
k
l
m
n
o
p
q
r
s
t
u
v
w
x
y
z
RapidFile (.rpd)
dBASE II (.db2)
Framework II (.fw2)
Lotus 1-2-3 (.wk1)
PFS:FILE
RapidFile (.rpd)
dBASE II (.db2)
Framework II (.fw2)
Lotus 1-2-3 (.wks)
PFS:FILE
SYLK-Multiplan
Text fixed-length fields (.txt)
Blank delimited (.txt)
Character delimited {"} (.txt)

BROWSE/EDIT

Records

```
  Undo change to record
  ---------------------------------
  Add new records
  Mark record for deletion
  Blank record
  Lock record
  Follow record to new position
```

Organize

```
► Create new index
► Modify existing index
  Order records by index
  Activate .NDX index file
  Include .NDX index file
  Remove unwanted index tag
  -------------------------------
  Sort database on field list
  Unmark all records
  Erase marked records
```

Fields

```
  Lock fields on left   {0}
  Blank field
  Freeze field          {}
► Size field
```

Go To

```
  Top record
  Last record
  Record number          {0}
  Skip                   {10}
  -------------------------------
  Index key search
  Forward search         {}
  Backward search        {}
  Match capitalization   YES
```

Exit

```
  Exit
  Transfer to Query Design
```

Note: The **Fields** menu is present only in Browse, not in Edit

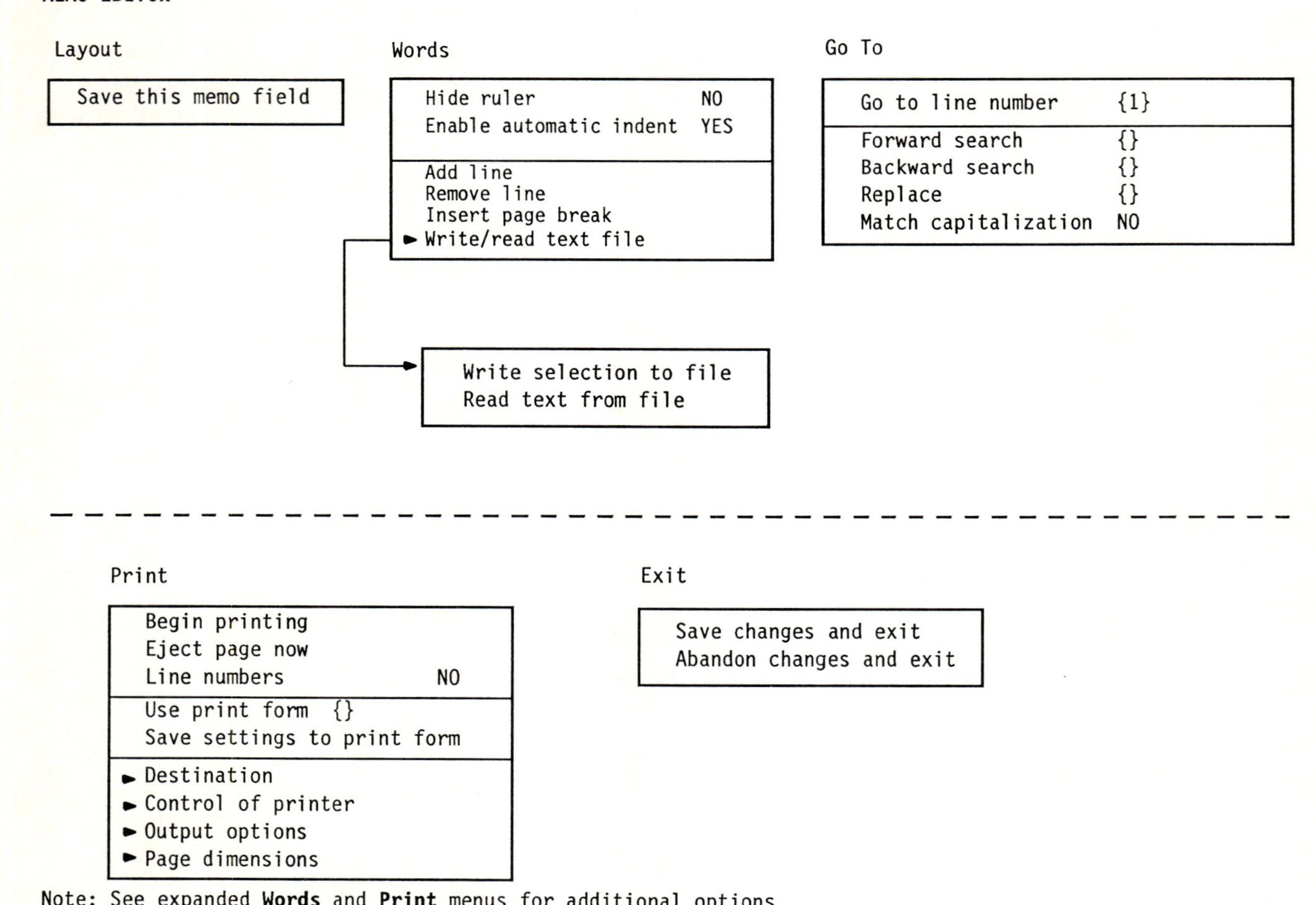

Note: See expanded **Words** and **Print** menus for additional options

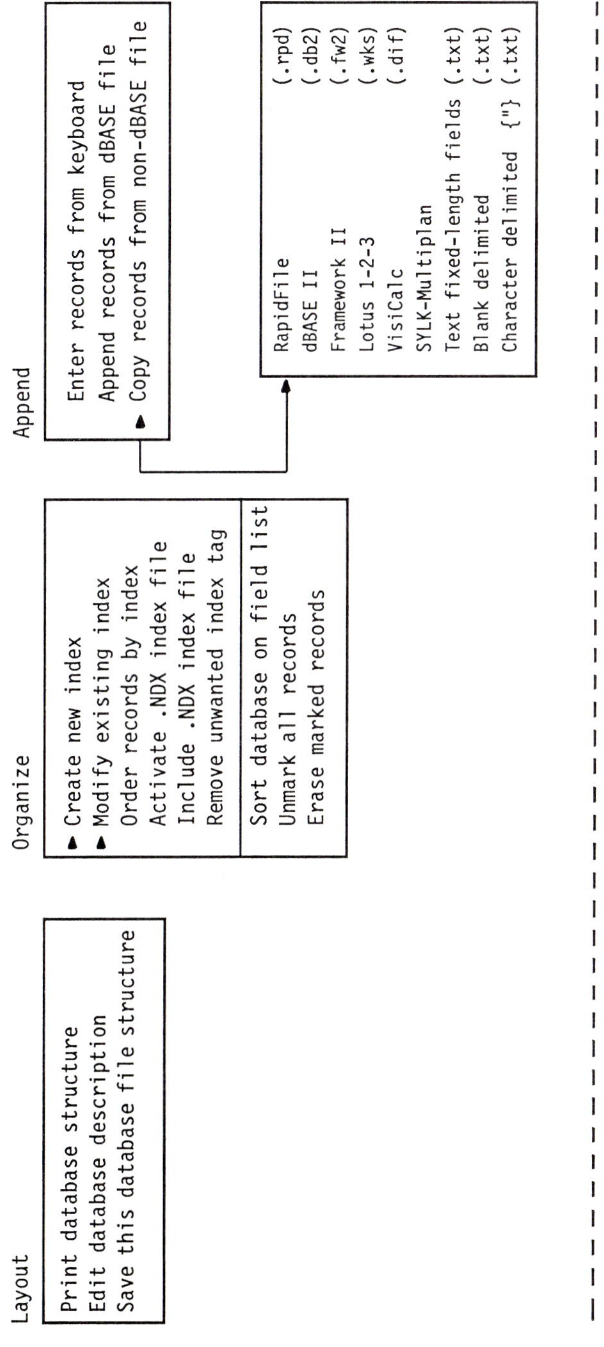
DATA BASE DESIGN
Layout
Print database structure
Edit database description
Save this database file structure
Organize
Create new index
Modify existing index
Order records by index
Activate .NDX index file
Include .NDX index file
Remove unwanted index tag
Sort database on field list
Unmark all records
Erase marked records
Append
Enter records from keyboard
Append records from dBASE file
Copy records from non-dBASE file
RapidFile (.rpd)
dBASE II (.db2)
Framework II (.fw2)
Lotus 1-2-3 (.wks)
VisiCalc (.dif)
SYLK-Multiplan
Text fixed-length fields (.txt)
Blank delimited (.txt)
Character delimited {"} (.txt)
Go To
Top field
Last field
Field number
Exit
Save changes and exit
Abandon changes and exit

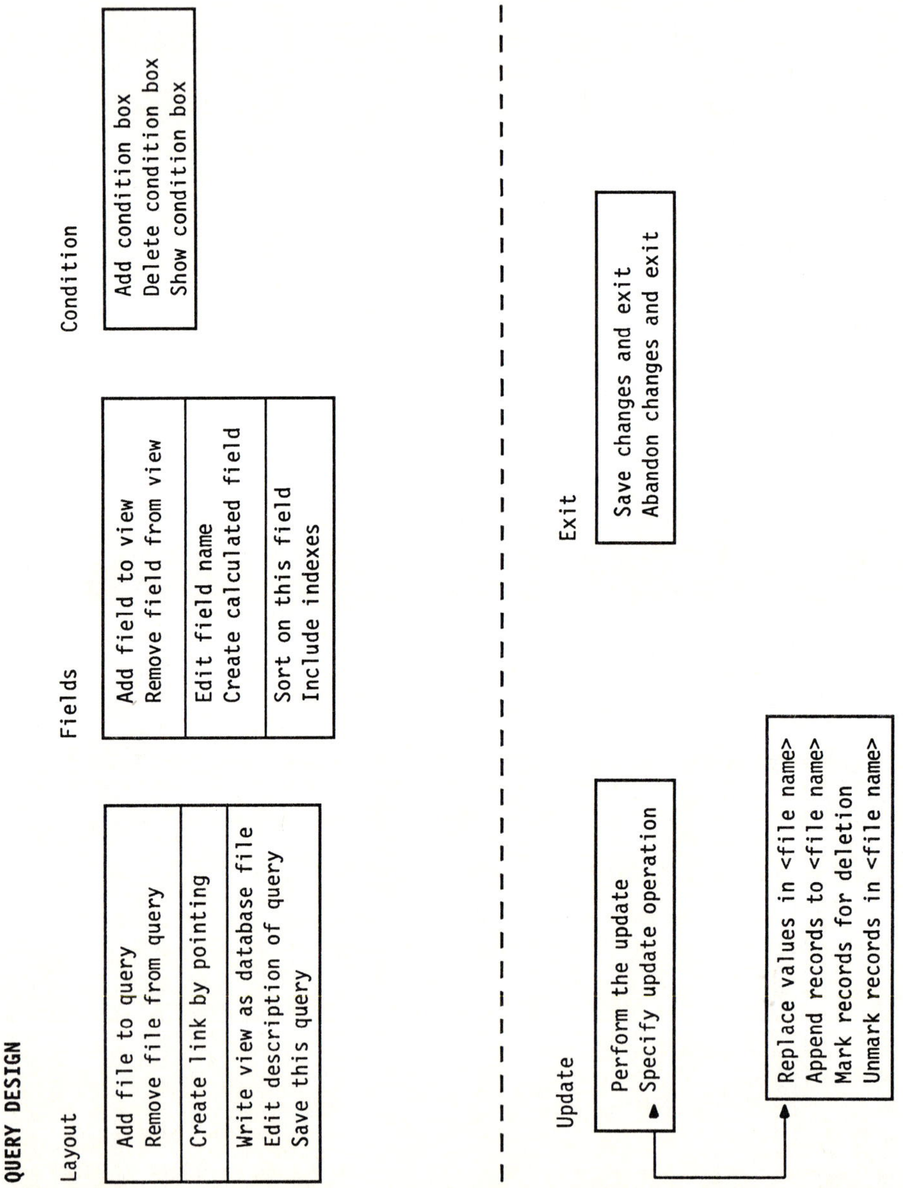

QUERY DESIGN

Layout

- Add file to query
- Remove file from query

- Create link by pointing

- Write view as database file
- Edit description of query
- Save this query

Fields

- Add field to view
- Remove field from view

- Edit field name
- Create calculated field

- Sort on this field
- Include indexes

Condition

- Add condition box
- Delete condition box
- Show condition box

Update

- Perform the update
- Specify update operation
  - Replace values in <file name>
  - Append records to <file name>
  - Mark records for deletion
  - Unmark records in <file name>

Exit

- Save changes and exit
- Abandon changes and exit

LABEL DESIGN

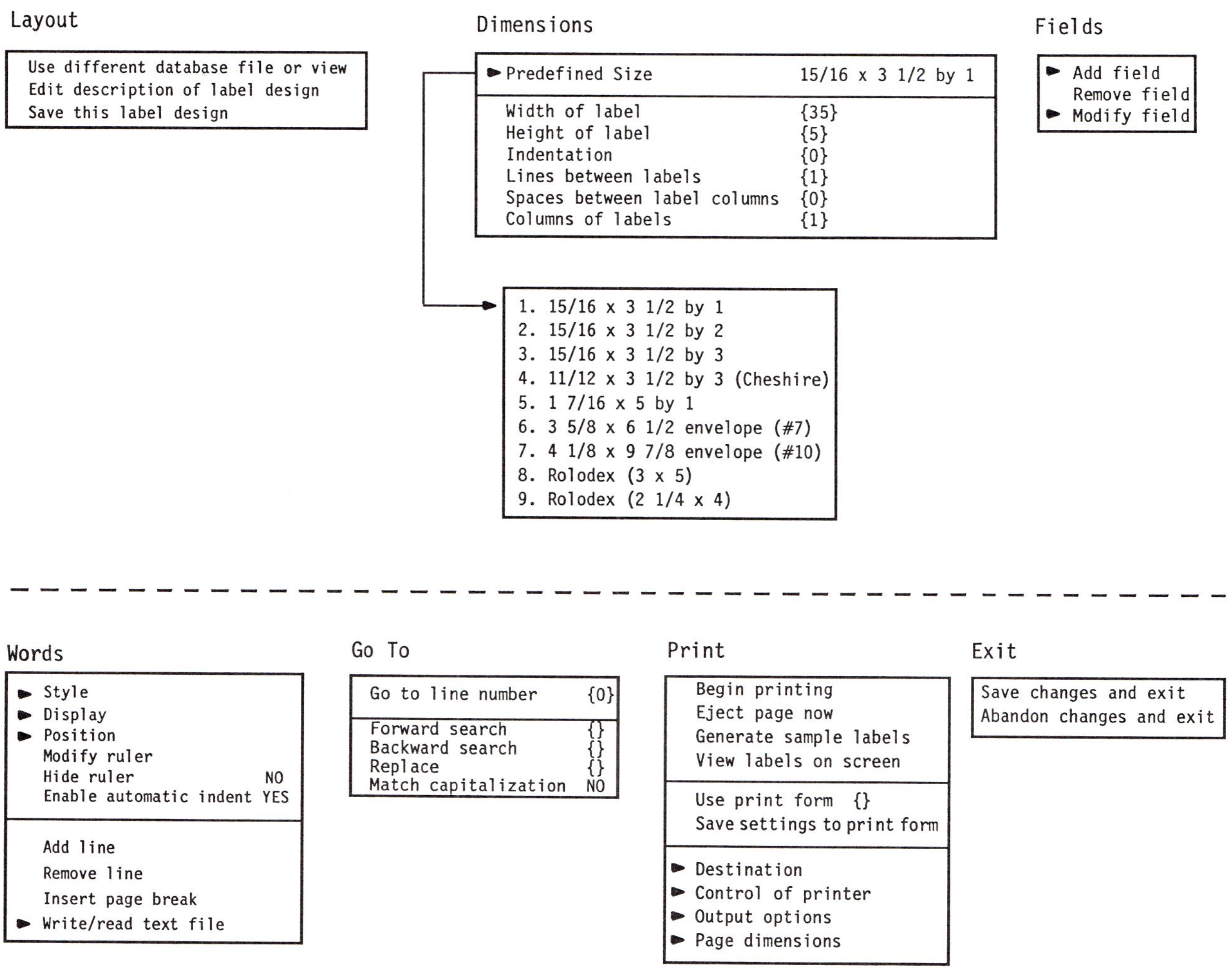

Layout

```
Use different database file or view
Edit description of label design
Save this label design
```

Dimensions

```
► Predefined Size                 15/16 x 3 1/2 by 1
-----------------------------------------------------
  Width of label                  {35}
  Height of label                 {5}
  Indentation                     {0}
  Lines between labels            {1}
  Spaces between label columns    {0}
  Columns of labels               {1}
```

Predefined Size options:

```
1. 15/16 x 3 1/2 by 1
2. 15/16 x 3 1/2 by 2
3. 15/16 x 3 1/2 by 3
4. 11/12 x 3 1/2 by 3 (Cheshire)
5. 1 7/16 x 5 by 1
6. 3 5/8 x 6 1/2 envelope (#7)
7. 4 1/8 x 9 7/8 envelope (#10)
8. Rolodex (3 x 5)
9. Rolodex (2 1/4 x 4)
```

Fields

```
► Add field
  Remove field
► Modify field
```

Words

```
► Style
► Display
► Position
  Modify ruler
  Hide ruler                    NO
  Enable automatic indent       YES
---------------------------------
  Add line
  Remove line
  Insert page break
► Write/read text file
```

Go To

```
Go to line number       {0}
---------------------------
Forward search          {}
Backward search         {}
Replace                 {}
Match capitalization    NO
```

Print

```
  Begin printing
  Eject page now
  Generate sample labels
  View labels on screen
------------------------------
  Use print form  {}
  Save settings to print form
------------------------------
► Destination
► Control of printer
► Output options
► Page dimensions
```

Exit

```
Save changes and exit
Abandon changes and exit
```

Note: See expanded **Words** and **Print** menus for additional options

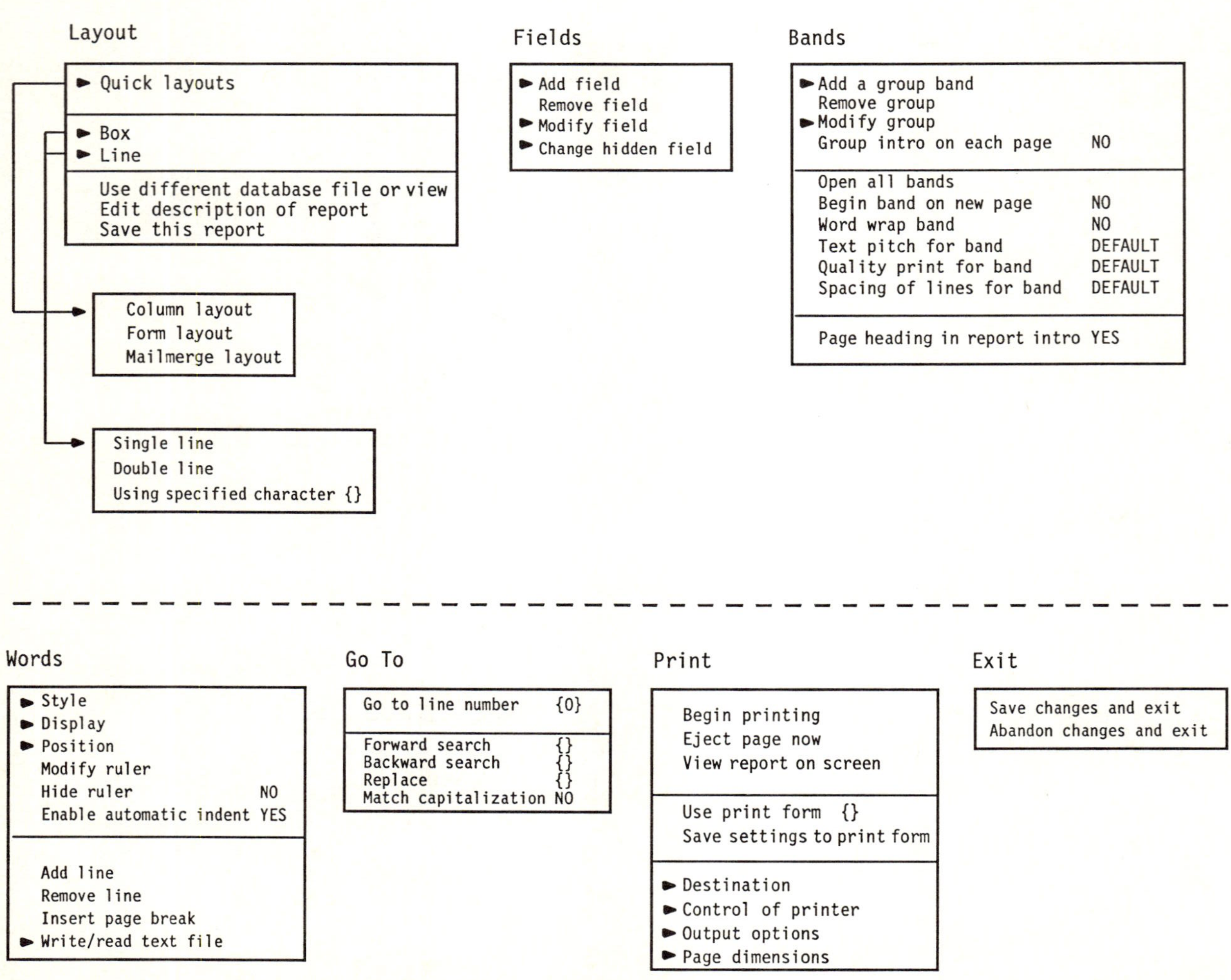
REPORT DESIGN
Layout
Quick layouts
Box
Line
Use different database file or view
Edit description of report
Save this report
Column layout
Form layout
Mailmerge layout
Single line
Double line
Using specified character {}
Fields
Add field
Remove field
Modify field
Change hidden field
Bands
Add a group band
Remove group
Modify group
Group intro on each page NO
Open all bands
Begin band on new page NO
Word wrap band NO
Text pitch for band DEFAULT
Quality print for band DEFAULT
Spacing of lines for band DEFAULT
Page heading in report intro YES
Words
Style
Display
Position
Modify ruler
Hide ruler NO
Enable automatic indent YES
Add line
Remove line
Insert page break
Write/read text file
Go To
Go to line number {0}
Forward search {}
Backward search {}
Replace {}
Match capitalization NO
Print
Begin printing
Eject page now
View report on screen
Use print form {}
Save settings to print form
Destination
Control of printer
Output options
Page dimensions
Exit
Save changes and exit
Abandon changes and exit
Note: See expanded Words and Print menus for additional options

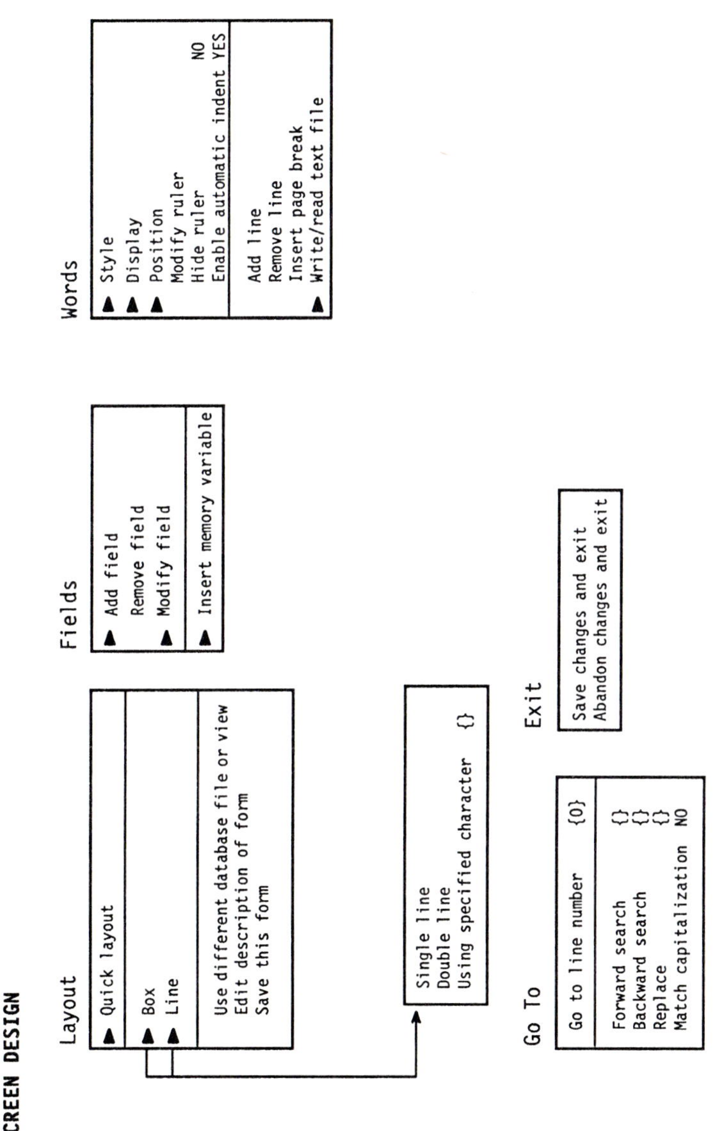
SCREEN DESIGN
Layout
Quick layout
Box
Line
Use different database file or view
Edit description of form
Save this form
Single line
Double line
Using specified character {}
Fields
Add field
Remove field
Modify field
Insert memory variable
Words
Style
Display
Position
Modify ruler
Hide ruler NO
Enable automatic indent YES
Add line
Remove line
Insert page break
Write/read text file
Go To
Go to line number {0}
Forward search {}
Backward search {}
Replace {}
Match capitalization NO
Exit
Save changes and exit
Abandon changes and exit
Note: See expanded Words menu for additional options

WORDS

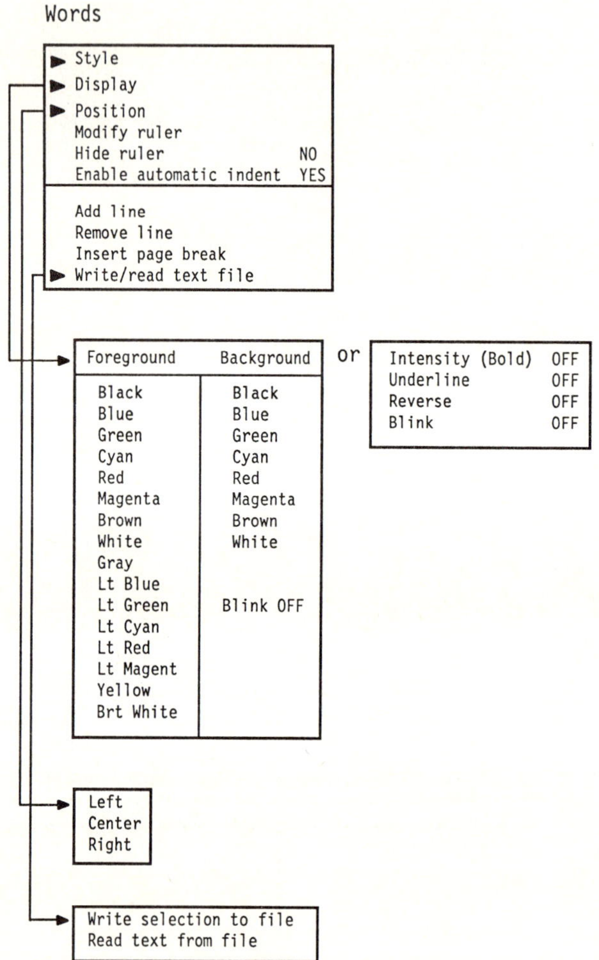
Words
Style
Display
Position
Modify ruler
Hide ruler NO
Enable automatic indent YES
Add line
Remove line
Insert page break
Write/read text file
Foreground
Background
Black
Blue
Green
Cyan
Red
Magenta
Brown
White
Gray
Lt Blue
Lt Green
Lt Cyan
Lt Red
Lt Magent
Yellow
Brt White
Black
Blue
Green
Cyan
Red
Magenta
Brown
White
Blink OFF
or
Intensity (Bold) OFF
Underline OFF
Reverse OFF
Blink OFF
Left
Center
Right
Write selection to file
Read text from file

PRINT

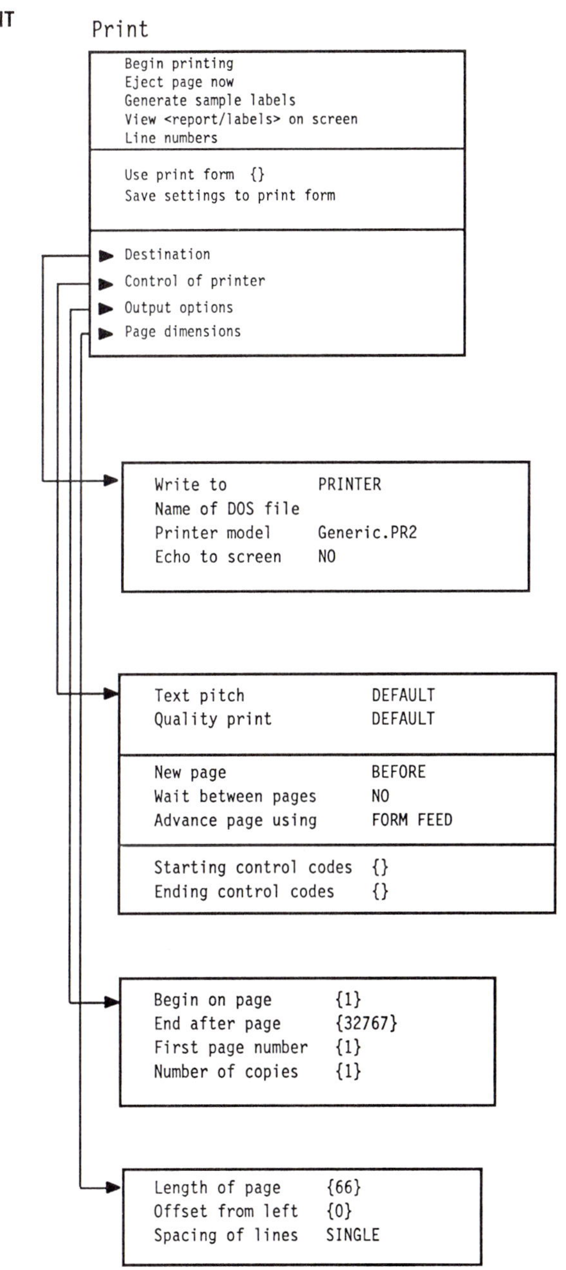

Notes: **Generate sample labels** option appears only on label design screen.
Line numbers option appears only in program editor.

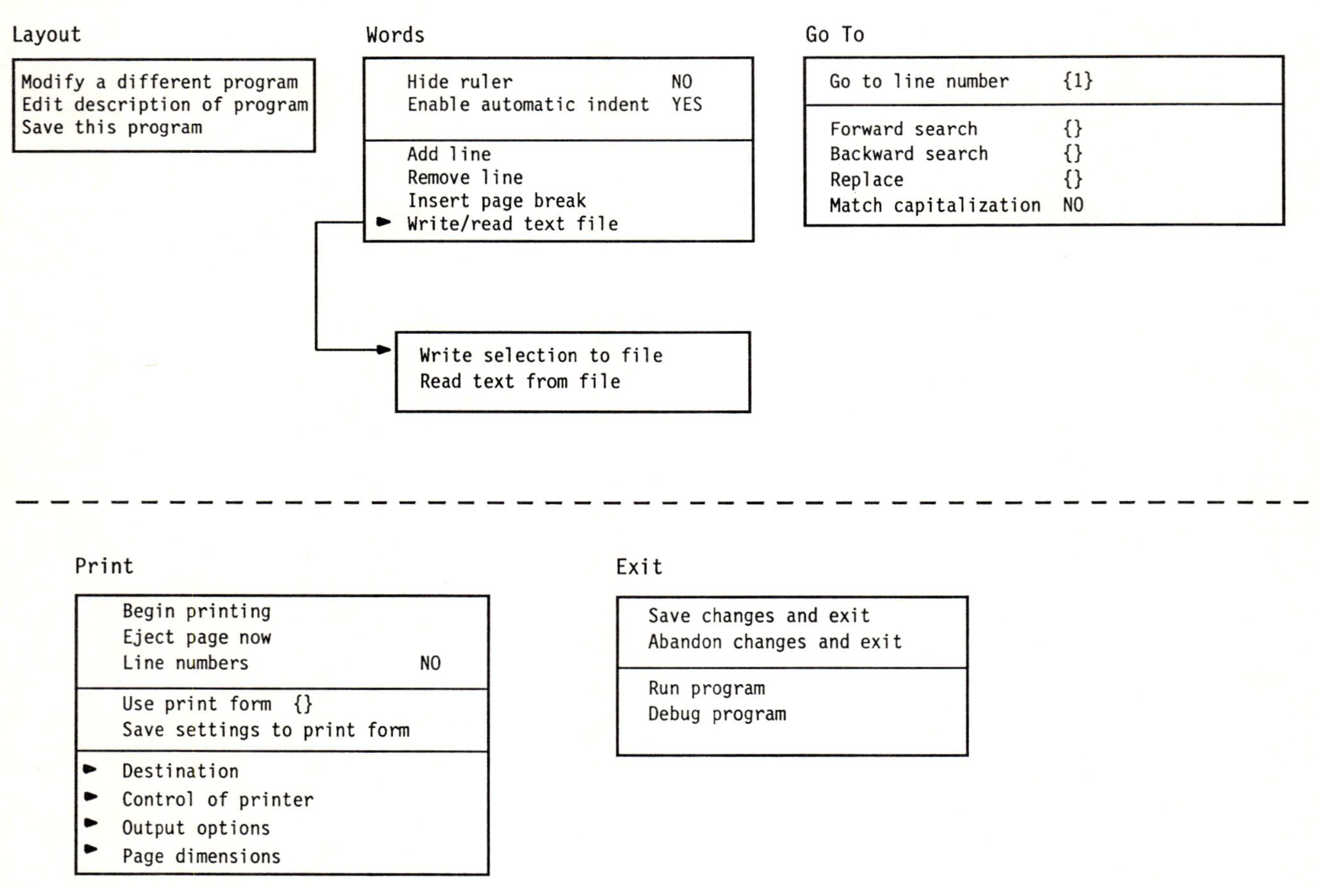

Note: See expanded **Words** and **Print** menus for additional options

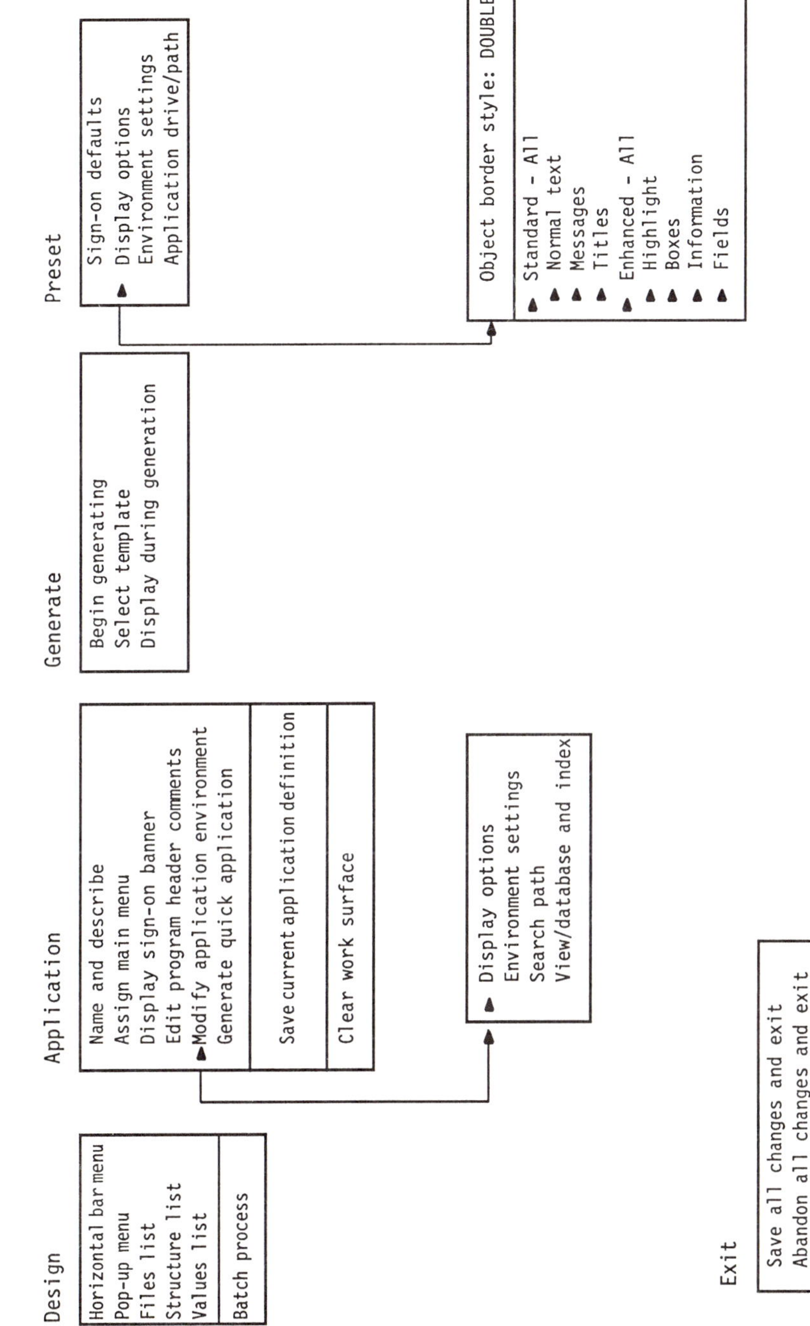
APPLICATION DESIGN
Design
Horizontal bar menu
Pop-up menu
Files list
Structure list
Values list
Batch process
Application
Name and describe
Assign main menu
Display sign-on banner
Edit program header comments
Modify application environment
Generate quick application
Save current application definition
Clear work surface
Display options
Environment settings
Search path
View/database and index
Generate
Begin generating
Select template
Display during generation
Preset
Sign-on defaults
Display options
Environment settings
Application drive/path
Object border style: DOUBLE
Standard - All
Normal text
Messages
Titles
Enhanced - All
Highlight
Boxes
Information
Fields
Exit
Save all changes and exit
Abandon all changes and exit

ITEM MENU

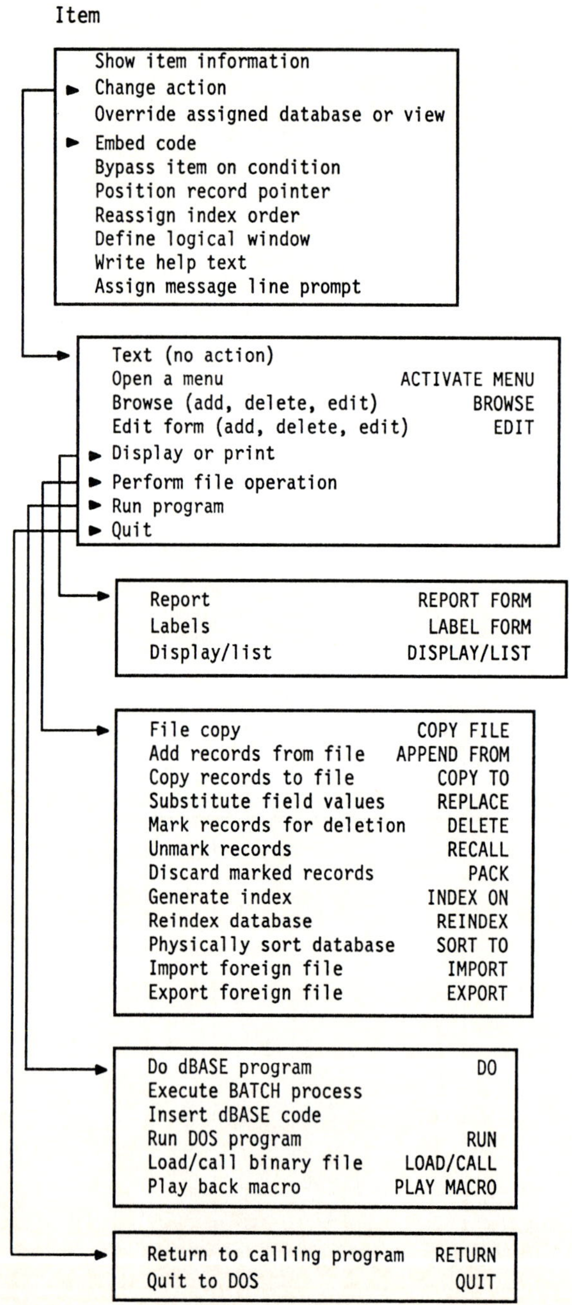
Item
Show item information
Change action
Override assigned database or view
Embed code
Bypass item on condition
Position record pointer
Reassign index order
Define logical window
Write help text
Assign message line prompt
Text (no action)
Open a menu ACTIVATE MENU
Browse (add, delete, edit) BROWSE
Edit form (add, delete, edit) EDIT
Display or print
Perform file operation
Run program
Quit
Report REPORT FORM
Labels LABEL FORM
Display/list DISPLAY/LIST
File copy COPY FILE
Add records from file APPEND FROM
Copy records to file COPY TO
Substitute field values REPLACE
Mark records for deletion DELETE
Unmark records RECALL
Discard marked records PACK
Generate index INDEX ON
Reindex database REINDEX
Physically sort database SORT TO
Import foreign file IMPORT
Export foreign file EXPORT
Do dBASE program DO
Execute BATCH process
Insert dBASE code
Run DOS program RUN
Load/call binary file LOAD/CALL
Play back macro PLAY MACRO
Return to calling program RETURN
Quit to DOS QUIT

OBJECT MENUS

Menu

```
  Name and describe
  Override assigned database or view
  Write help text
► Modify display options
► Embed code
  Attach pull-down menus
  ------------------------------------
  Save current menu
  Put away current menu
  ------------------------------------
  Clear work surface
```

List

```
  Name and describe
  Override assigned database or view
  Write help text
► Modify display options
► Embed code
  Identify files in list
  ------------------------------------
  Save current list
  Put away current list
  ------------------------------------
  Clear work surface
```

Batch

```
  Name and describe
  Override assigned database or view
► Embed code
  ------------------------------------
  Save current batch process
  Put away current batch process
  ------------------------------------
  Clear work surface
```

SETTINGS

Options

Bell	ON
Carry	OFF
Century	OFF
Confirm	OFF
Date order	MDY
Date separator	/
Decimal places	{2}
Deleted	OFF
Exact	OFF
Exclusive	OFF
Instruct	ON
Margin	{0}
Memo width	{50}
Safety	ON
Talk	ON
Trap	OFF

Display

Display mode MONO

- ► Standard - All
  - ► Normal text
  - ► Messages
  - ► Titles
- ► Enhanced - All
  - ► Highlight
  - ► Boxes
  - ► Information
  - ► Fields
- ► Perimeter of screen

Exit

Exit to Control Center

SET

Options

```
Alternate         OFF
Autosave          OFF
Bell              ON
Carry             OFF
Catalog
Century           OFF
Confirm           OFF
Currency sign     LEFT
Cursor            ON
Date order        MDY
Date separator    /
Decimal places    {2}
Deleted           OFF
Delimiters        OFF
Development       ON
Device            SCREEN
Encryption        ON
Escape            ON
Exact             OFF
Exclusive         OFF
Fields            OFF
Fullpath          OFF
Heading           ON
Help              ON
History           ON
Hours             12
Instruct          ON
Intensity         ON
Lock              ON
Margin            {0}
Memo width        {50}
Near              OFF
Pause             OFF
Precision         {16}
Print             OFF
Safety            ON
Scoreboard        ON
Space             ON
Status            OFF
Talk              ON
Title             ON
Trap              OFF
Unique            OFF
```

Display

```
   Display mode  MONO

► Standard - All
  ► Normal text
  ► Messages
  ► Titles
► Enhanced - All
  ► Highlight
  ► Boxes
  ► Information
  ► Fields

► Perimeter of screen
```

Keys

```
F2         assist;
F3         list;
F4         dir;
F5         display structure;
F6         display status;
F7         display memory;
F8         display;
F9         append;
F10        edit;
CTRL-F1
CTRL-F2
CTRL-F3
CTRL-F4
CTRL-F5
CTRL-F6
CTRL-F7
CTRL-F8
CTRL-F9
CTRL-F10
SHIFT-F1
SHIFT-F2
SHIFT-F3
SHIFT-F4
SHIFT-F5
SHIFT-F6
SHIFT-F7
SHIFT-F8
SHIFT-F9
```

Disk

```
Default disk drive:            C
Disk drive search path         {}
OS Working drive/directory:    {C:\DBASE4}
```

Files

```
   Alternate   {}
   Device      {}
   Format      {}
►  Index
```

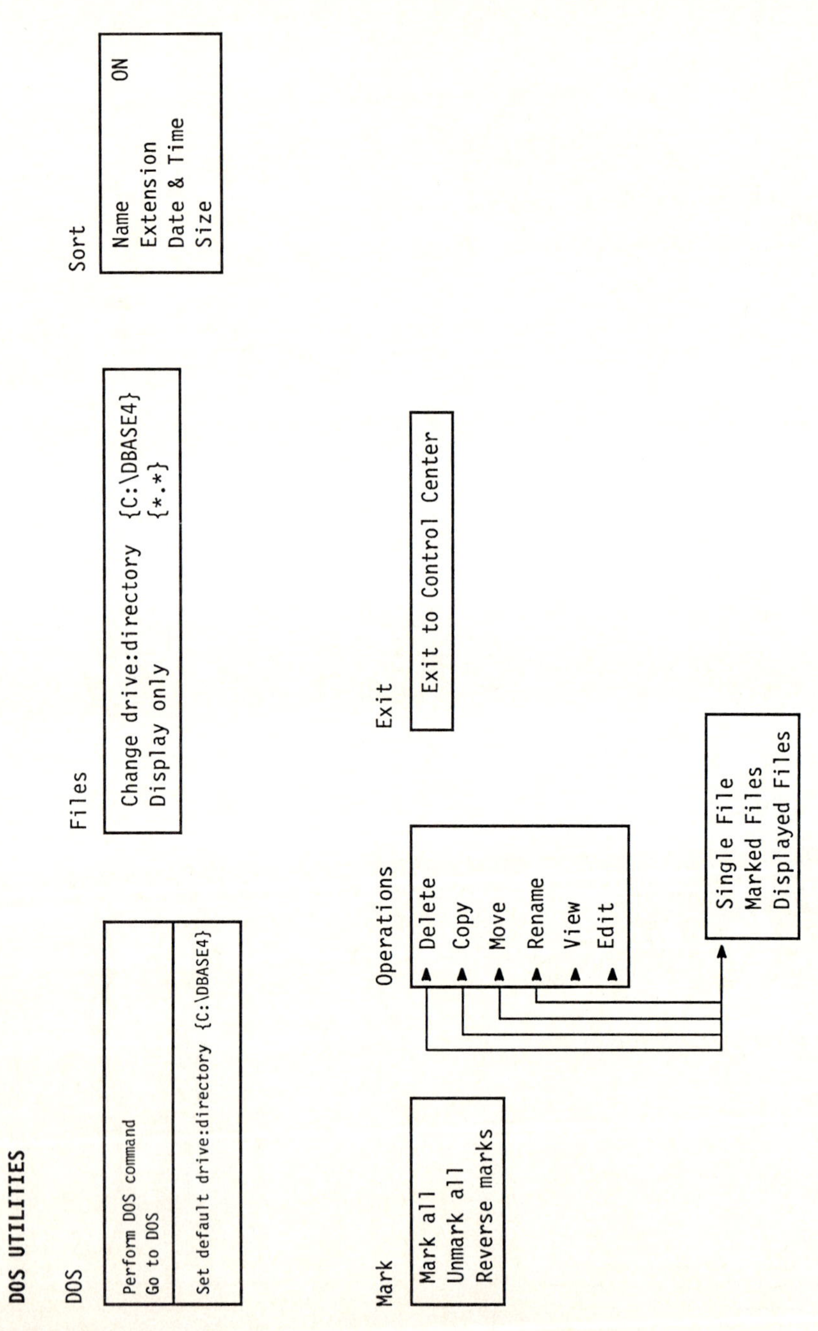
DOS UTILITIES
DOS
Perform DOS command
Go to DOS
Set default drive:directory {C:\DBASE4}
Files
Change drive:directory {C:\DBASE4}
Display only {*.*}
Sort
Name ON
Extension
Date & Time
Size
Mark
Mark all
Unmark all
Reverse marks
Operations
Delete
Copy
Move
Rename
View
Edit
Single File
Marked Files
Displayed Files
Exit
Exit to Control Center

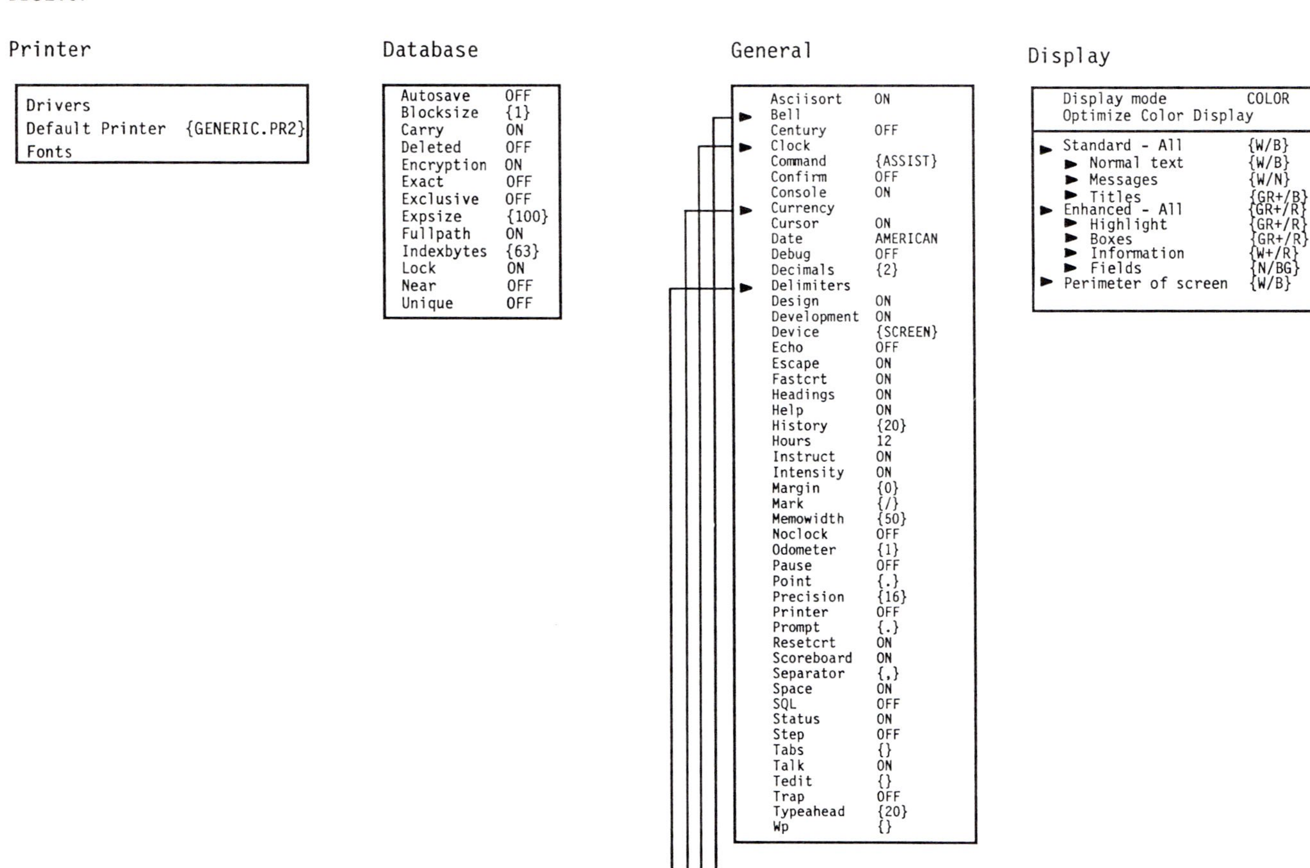
DBSETUP
Printer
Drivers
Default Printer {GENERIC.PR2}
Fonts
Database
Autosave OFF
Blocksize {1}
Carry ON
Deleted OFF
Encryption ON
Exact OFF
Exclusive OFF
Expsize {100}
Fullpath ON
Indexbytes {63}
Lock ON
Near OFF
Unique OFF
General
Asciisort ON
Bell
Century OFF
Clock
Command {ASSIST}
Confirm OFF
Console ON
Currency
Cursor ON
Date AMERICAN
Debug OFF
Decimals {2}
Delimiters
Design ON
Development ON
Device {SCREEN}
Echo OFF
Escape ON
Fastcrt ON
Headings ON
Help ON
History {20}
Hours 12
Instruct ON
Intensity ON
Margin {0}
Mark {/}
Memowidth {50}
Noclock OFF
Odometer {1}
Pause OFF
Point {.}
Precision {16}
Printer OFF
Prompt {.}
Resetcrt ON
Scoreboard ON
Separator {,}
Space ON
SQL OFF
Status ON
Step OFF
Tabs {}
Talk ON
Tedit {}
Trap OFF
Typeahead {20}
Wp {}
Bell ON
Tone {550}
Duration {2}
Display
Display mode COLOR
Optimize Color Display
Standard - All {W/B}
Normal text {W/B}
Messages {W/N}
Titles {GR+/B}
Enhanced - All {GR+/R}
Highlight {GR+/R}
Boxes {GR+/R}
Information {W+/R}
Fields {N/BG}
Perimeter of screen {W/B}

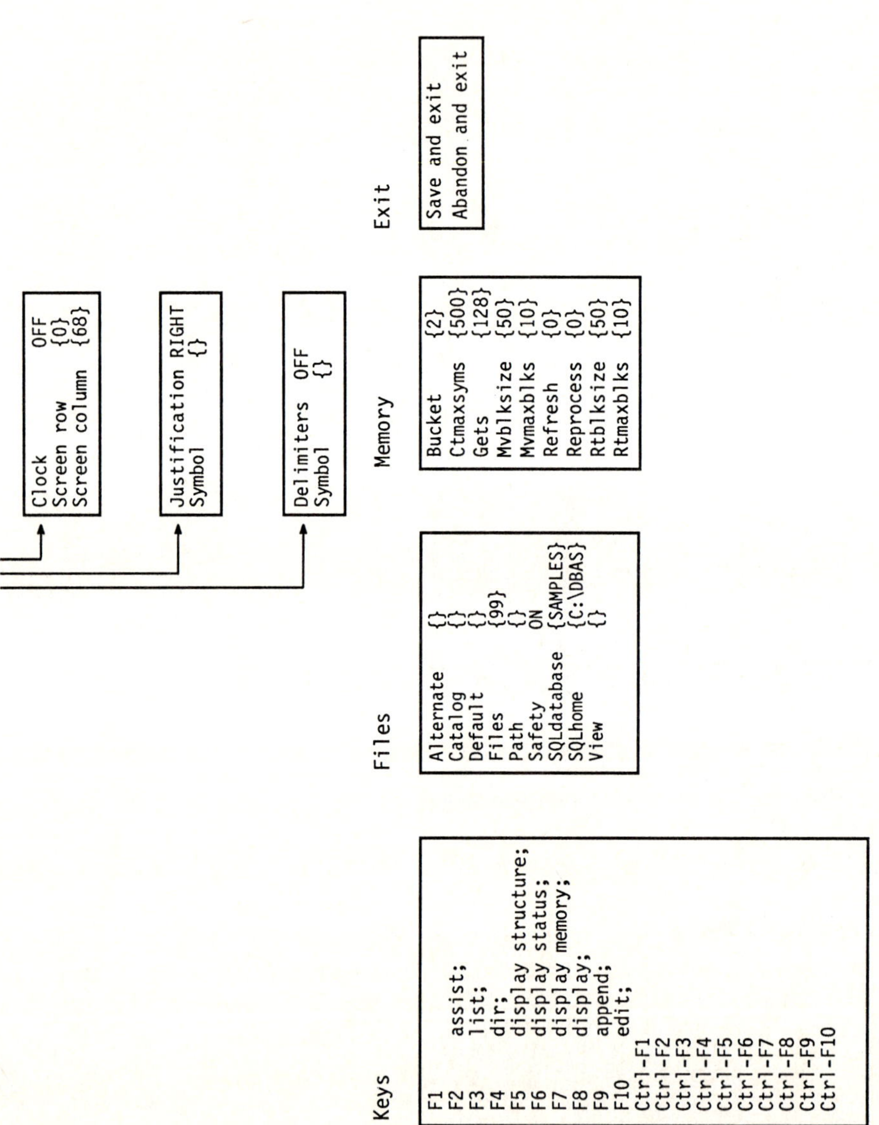
Clock OFF
Screen row {0}
Screen column {68}
Justification RIGHT
Symbol {}
Delimiters OFF
Symbol {}
Keys
F1 assist;
F2 list;
F3 dir;
F4 display structure;
F5 display status;
F6 display memory;
F7 display;
F8 append;
F9 edit;
F10
Ctrl-F1
Ctrl-F2
Ctrl-F3
Ctrl-F4
Ctrl-F5
Ctrl-F6
Ctrl-F7
Ctrl-F8
Ctrl-F9
Ctrl-F10
Files
Alternate {}
Catalog {}
Default {}
Files {99}
Path {}
Safety ON
SQLdatabase {SAMPLES}
SQLhome {C:\DBAS}
View {}
Memory
Bucket {2}
Ctmaxsyms {500}
Gets {128}
Mvblksize {50}
Mvmaxblks {10}
Refresh {0}
Reprocess {0}
Rtblksize {50}
Rtmaxblks {10}
Exit
Save and exit
Abandon and exit

PROTECT

Users

```
Login name
Password
Group name
-------------------------
Full Name
Access level        1
-------------------------
Store user profile
-------------------------
Delete user from group
```

Files

```
New file
------------------------------
Group name
------------------------------
File access privileges
------------------------------
Field access privileges
  Access level                1
  Establish field privileges
------------------------------
Store file privileges
------------------------------
Cancel current entry
```

Reports

```
User Information
----------------
File Information
```

Exit

```
Save
Abandon
Exit
```

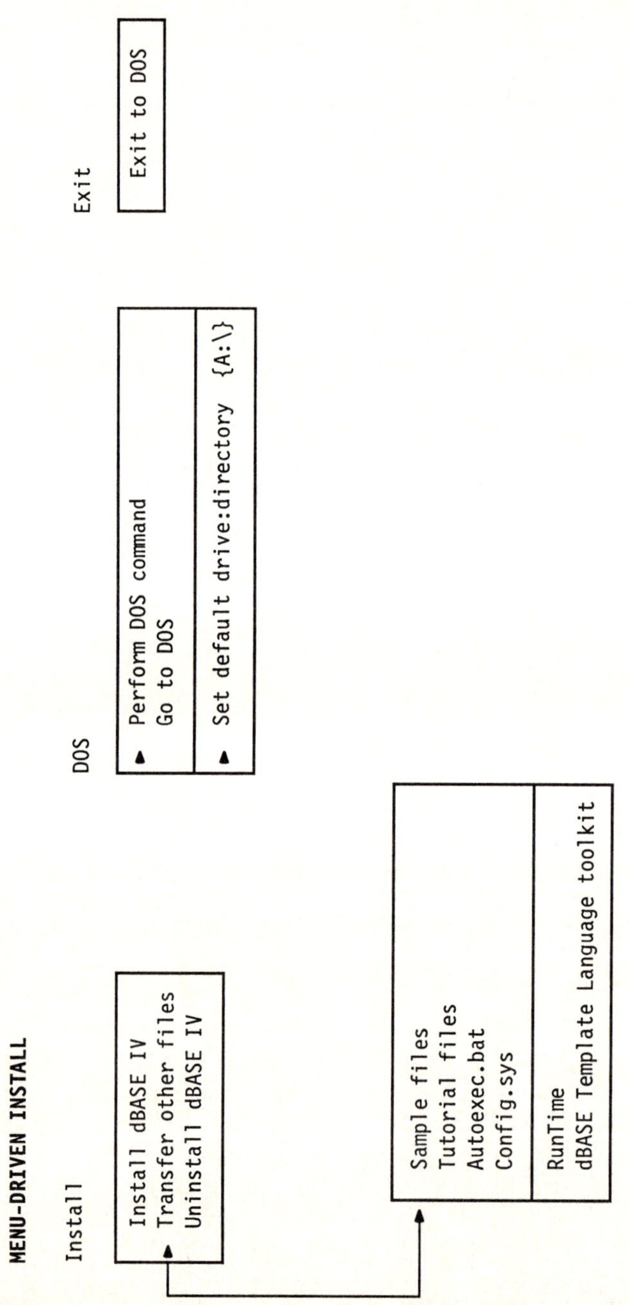
MENU-DRIVEN INSTALL
Install
Install dBASE IV
Transfer other files
Uninstall dBASE IV
Sample files
Tutorial files
Autoexec.bat
Config.sys
RunTime
dBASE Template Language toolkit
DOS
Perform DOS command
Go to DOS
Set default drive:directory {A:\}
Exit
Exit to DOS

APPENDIX C

Command Syntax Notation Guide

This appendix is a glossary of some common terms used in the dBASE IV documentation and in the command syntax notation used in Appendixes D, E, and F, which summarize the dBASE IV commands, functions, and environment configuration settings.

These appendixes use the same standard notation as the dBASE IV *Language Reference* manual. UPPERCASE is used for all dBASE IV keywords (words that are part of the dBASE IV command vocabulary), including command verbs; function names; words like FOR, WHILE, and TO, which introduce command clauses; and command options like OFF, NOEDIT, and DELIMITED. When you work at the dot prompt, you can type keywords in any combination of uppercase and lowercase. You can abbreviate all keywords, provided that you type at least the first four characters, and, if you type more than four characters, that they are consecutive. For example, you could abbreviate DELIMITED as DELI or DELIM, but not DELIT.

Optional command components are enclosed in square brackets ([ ]). When you use these options, remember not to type the brackets. An ellipsis (...)

indicates that a clause or phrase can be repeated more than once in a command. Two or more equivalent command alternatives are separated by a slash (/) if any one, but only one, is permitted. When alternative options are listed for commands that accept a finite number of possible entries (such as ON and OFF for many of the environment settings), the default value is printed in UPPERCASE, with the alternate value or values in lowercase. For example, the command to turn the computer's bell (beeper) on or off is written as SET BELL ON/off.

Substitutions are printed in *lowercase italics* and enclosed in angle brackets (< >). When you use these commands, remember not to type the brackets or the exact words printed between the brackets; instead, you should make the appropriate substitution. For example, the command to create a new data base is listed as CREATE <*data base name*>. To create the National Widgets Customer File, you would type CREATE NWCUST.

Every dBASE IV command must begin with a verb, but in most cases, you may type the other command components—the various clauses and options—in any order. The order used in the command summary in Appendix D was chosen so that the commands would read as much like English sentences as possible.

The terms and substitution items are as follows:

?: Query clause symbol, which you can substitute for a file name in any command that opens a disk file to invoke a pick list of files of the appropriate type. If a catalog is open, the list includes only files in the catalog, and another pop-up box displays the catalog description of the file that is highlighted in the pick list. If no catalog is open, the list includes all files of the specified type in the current subdirectory, but dBASE IV allows you to navigate through the disk directory structure and display files on any available drive in any subdirectory.

alias: An optional alternate name for a data base. The alias can be up to ten characters long and can contain an embedded underscore (_). If you do not assign an alias in the USE command that opens the file, dBASE IV assigns the file name as the alias. You can always use the letter that represents the work area (A, B, and so on) as an additional file alias, whether or not you assigned an alias explicitly in the USE command. Some commands require that you use the alias rather than the file name.

alias—>field: A field in a data base open in any work area; you must use this notation to refer to fields in work areas other than the currently selected work area.

application: A menu-driven system (often created by using the applications generator) for entering, updating, displaying, and printing data. This term is also used in a more general sense to describe a set of related data bases and auxiliary files that collectively solve a business problem.

attribute: A characteristic of displayed or printed data. On a color screen, this term refers to the display colors; on a monochrome screen, the attributes are inverse video, bold (bright), and underlining. Printer attributes include boldfacing, underlining, and other special fonts and print modes.

border: The region of the screen outside the 25-line by 80-column display area (or 43-line by 80-column on an EGA or VGA monitor). Also called the *perimeter.*

border characters: The ASCII codes for the characters used to form a custom border, or frame, around a screen menu or window. The characters are listed in the following order: top, bottom, left side, right side, upper left corner, upper right corner, lower left corner, and lower right corner.

character string: Any sequence of characters, enclosed in single quotes ('), double quotes ("), or square brackets ([ ]).

column: A screen or printer column (horizontal) coordinate. Columns are numbered from left to right, beginning with 0.

condition: A logical expression that evaluates to .T. (true) or .F. (false).

current: Used to describe the disk drive and subdirectory from which dBASE IV was loaded, the selected work area, the data base file open in the selected work area, or the record at the position of the dBASE IV record pointer.

delimiter: Punctuation mark or marks used to enclose character strings or fields on the screen.

drive: A disk drive designator (A, B, C, and so on), followed by a colon (:) if it forms part of a file name.

enhanced display area: All the data entry areas on the screen (regions in which you enter data base fields and respond to questions or prompts).

exp: Any syntactically valid dBASE IV expression composed of data base fields, memory variables, functions, constants, and operators.

expC: An expression that evaluates to a character string.

expD: An expression that evaluates to a date.

expL: An expression that evaluates to a logical value (.T. or .F.).

expN: An expression that evaluates to a number.

field or *field name:* The name of a field in the data base open in the currently selected work area.

file name: A valid DOS or OS/2 file name. You must include the disk drive if the file does not reside on the default drive, and specify the full path name if the file is not in the current subdirectory (unless you have used the SET DEFAULT or SET DIRECTORY commands to change the default drive or subdirectory, or used a SET PATH command to specify a search path for files not in the current subdirectory). Any command that manipulates a particular type of file (for example, USE, which opens a data base file, or SAVE, which creates a memory variable file) assumes the standard dBASE IV extension unless you override it by explicitly typing the extension. In commands that may operate on any type of disk file (for example, ERASE or RENAME) you must always include the extension. The standard file extensions are listed in Appendix G.

file type: A keyword that identifies one of the external, or foreign file formats that dBASE IV can read or write.

index: An auxiliary file that enables dBASE IV to process records in a sequence that differs from the physical order of the records.

key or *key expression:* The field or expression used as the basis for indexing or sorting a data base file.

keyword: A word recognized by dBASE IV as part of its command vocabulary; keywords include command verbs, function names, and other words used in commands.

list: One or more items of the same type (fields, files, expressions, indexes, and so on) separated by commas.

master index: The index tag or NDX index that currently governs the order in which dBASE IV processes records and that is used as the basis for index key searches.

memvar: A memory variable (a temporary variable retained in memory during a work session).

MDX index: A multiple index file that contains indexing information for up to 47 separate key expressions.

n: A number.

NDX index: A stand-alone index file that contains indexing information for one key expression.

path: A DOS path name (the path through the subdirectory structure from the current subdirectory to the specified file) followed by a backslash (\).

picture function: A symbol that governs the overall format of data displayed on a custom data entry screen or printed on a report or label.

record pointer: An indicator that keeps track of the current record. dBASE IV maintains a separate record pointer in each active work area.

row: A screen or printer row (vertical) coordinate. Rows are numbered from top to bottom, beginning with 0.

scope: The range of records in a data base that you want dBASE IV to act on when it executes the current command. The valid scopes are

ALL	All the records in the current data base
RECORD <*expN*>	A single record, the one with a record number equal to the value of *expN*
NEXT <*expN*>	A number of records equal to the value of *expN*, beginning with and including the current record
REST	All the remaining records in the file, beginning with and including the current record

In interpreting the *scope*, dBASE IV takes into consideration any factors that affect the sequence or the range of records to be processed, including the master index, a filter if one is active, and the status of the DELETED option. For example, with a filter in effect and the DELETED setting ON, REST means the remaining records that are not marked for deletion and that satisfy the filter condition.

skeleton: A pattern of letters and wildcard symbols that a file name or variable name must match. The two wildcard characters are ?, which stands for any single character, and *, which substitutes for any combination of characters.

source file: The file that provides the data when a dBASE IV command or operation updates one file based on data stored in another.

standard display area: All the areas of the screen used to display text, including field name prompts, headings, and read/only fields.

tag: The name assigned to one of the key expressions in an MDX index file.

target file: The file that is updated by a dBASE IV command or operation (which may or may not involve a second file).

template: A string of symbols, one for each character position in a field or memory variable, that governs the format of the variable character by character on a custom data entry screen, report, or label.

variable: A memory variable or a data base field.

work area: One of ten memory regions in which you can open data bases. You can express the work area as a number (1 to 10) or letter (A to J). You can also use any expression that evaluates to a legitimate work area designator (a number, single letter, or character string that represents an alias).

APPENDIX D

Command Syntax Summary

This appendix contains a brief summary of the dBASE IV commands, listed in alphabetical order. This appendix is intended to serve as a reference for looking up the exact syntax of a command or for confirming which options are available, not as a learning guide. It does not include usage suggestions or examples for every command, and it does not describe in detail the use of the full-screen edit modes invoked by commands such as BROWSE and EDIT, the layout editors invoked by commands such as CREATE/MODIFY REPORT, or the online help system. Commands and command options that are intended primarily for use in dBASE IV programs are listed, marked with an asterisk (*), but only the ones that are readily applicable to working at the dot prompt are explained in detail.

?/?? [<*exp1*> [PICTURE <*expC*>] [FUNCTION <*functions*>]
[AT <*expN*>] [STYLE <*font number*>]] [, <*exp2*> ...] ...

??? [<*expC*>]

Displays (if the CONSOLE setting is ON) and/or prints (if the PRINTER setting is ON) the listed expressions. If the SPACE setting is ON, the items are separated by single spaces. The ? variation first issues a hard return and thus displays or prints the expressions on the next available line. ?? displays the listed expressions beginning at the current cursor position (on the screen) or the current printhead position. The PICTURE, FUNCTION, AT, and STYLE options, which enable you to format and position data, are used primarily in dBASE IV programs.

??? sends the specified character string to the printer without moving the printhead or updating the printer's internal row and column counters. This command is useful for sending control codes to the printer to access special type styles or fonts not directly supported by a dBASE IV printer driver. The easiest way to send control characters to the printer is to express them using the abbreviations listed in Table 13-1.

---

* @ <*row*>, <*column*> [SAY <*exp*> [PICTURE <*template*>]
[FUNCTION <*functions*>]]
[GET <*variable*> [PICTURE <*template*>] [FUNCTION <*functions*>]
[RANGE [REQUIRED] <*exp1*>, <*exp2*>]
[VALID [REQUIRED] <*condition*> [ERROR <*expC*>]]
[WHEN <*condition*>] [DEFAULT <*exp*>] [MESSAGE <*expC*>]]
[[OPEN] WINDOW <*window name*>]
[COLOR [<*standard foreground/background*>
[, <*enhanced foreground/background*>]]]

* @ <*row1*>, <*column1*> CLEAR [TO <*row2*>, <*column2*>]

* @ <*row1*>, <*column1*> FILL TO <*row2*>, <*column2*>
[COLOR <*foreground/background*>]

* @ <*row1*>, <*column1*> TO <*row2*>, <*column2*>
[DOUBLE/PANEL/<*border characters*>]
[COLOR <*foreground/background*>]

---

* ACCEPT [<*expC*>] TO <*memvar*>

---

* **ACTIVATE MENU <*menu name*> [PAD <*pad name*>]**

---

* **ACTIVATE POPUP <*popup name*>**

---

* **ACTIVATE SCREEN**

---

* **ACTIVATE WINDOW <*window name list*>/ALL**

APPEND

* **APPEND BLANK**

* **APPEND FROM ARRAY <*array name*> [FOR <*condition*>]**

APPEND FROM <*file name*> [FOR <*condition*>] [TYPE DBASEII/DIF/FW2/RPD/SDF/SYLK/WKS/DELIMITED [WITH <*delimiter*>/BLANK]]

APPEND MEMO <*memo field*> FROM <*file name*> [OVERWRITE]

APPEND invokes the full-screen edit mode to enable you to add new records one at a time to the active data base.

APPEND FROM adds records from the named file (the source file) to the active data base. If you specify a *condition,* it must refer only to fields that are common to both data bases. Unless the DELETED setting is ON, dBASE IV appends records that are marked for deletion, and does not mark them as deleted in the target file. dBASE IV updates all MDX tags and open NDX indexes to reflect the new records. Data is transferred between two DBF files by matching identically named fields; the field lengths, sequence, and data types can differ. When you append data from a file other than a DBF file, you must ensure that the structure of the active data base file matches the incoming data.

The SDF ("System Data Format") option identifies the source file as a fixed-length text file with a hard return at the end of each record. The DELIMITED option identifies the source file as a text file in which the fields are surrounded by delimiters and separated by commas, with a hard return at the end of each record. If the source file uses a delimiter other than the default double quotes, you must specify the delimiter in a WITH clause. The DELIMITED WITH BLANK option identifies a file in which the fields are separated by single spaces, with no delimiters.

When you append data from DIF ("Data Interchange Format"), SYLK (Multiplan "Symbolic Link"), or WKS (Lotus Worksheet) files, the rows in the spreadsheet become records in the data base, with each column supplying data for a field.

APPEND MEMO appends the contents of the named file into the specified memo field in the current record in the active data base. If you include the OVERWRITE option, dBASE IV replaces the existing memo text with the contents of the external file rather than adding the new text to the end.

ASSIST

Invokes the menu-driven mode of operation for dBASE IV and displays the Control Center menu.

AVERAGE [<*expN list*>] [TO <*memvar list*>/ARRAY <*array name*>] [<*scope*>] [FOR <*condition*>] [WHILE <*condition*>]

Calculates the average value for each expression in the list for the range of records in the active data base defined by the *scope* and *conditions.* If you do not list any expressions, dBASE IV averages all numeric fields, and if you do not specify a *scope,* dBASE IV averages all records. If the TALK setting is ON, dBASE IV displays the averages on the screen, and if the HEADING setting is ON, it displays the *expressions* above the results. If you specify a list of memory variables, dBASE IV creates the named numeric variables to store the averages. Alternatively, you can specify the name of a previously declared one-dimensional array to store the averages.

BEGIN TRANSACTION [<*path name*>] . . . END TRANSACTION

Identifies the commands between BEGIN TRANSACTION and END TRANSACTION as a *transaction,* which dBASE IV can reverse if it is not completed normally. A transaction can consist of any number of commands, but it cannot include commands that close open files or overwrite existing disk files. While a transaction is in progress, whenever you type a command that changes a record in an open data base, dBASE IV records the previous contents of the record in a log file, which is stored in the current subdirectory if you do not specify another *path name.* To restore the files to their original state based on the log file, you use the ROLLBACK command. When you type END TRANSACTION to indicate that the transaction is complete, dBASE IV erases the log file. ROLLBACK cannot always restore a data base, so you should back up your data bases before you begin a lengthy and complex sequence of file update commands.

BROWSE [FIELDS <*field1*> [/R] [/<*column width*>]/
<*calculated field name 1*> = <*exp1*> [, <*field2*> . . .] . . .]
[NOINIT] [NOFOLLOW] [NOAPPEND] [NOMENU] [NOEDIT]
[NODELETE] [NOCLEAR] [COMPRESS] [FORMAT] [LOCK <*expN*>]
[WIDTH <*expN*>] [FREEZE <*field*>] [WINDOW <*window name*>]

Invokes the full-screen Browse mode in which records are displayed one on each line, with the fields aligned in columns. The first record displayed is the current record. You can switch to the Edit screen by pressing F2 (Data). The other cursor movement and command keys and Browse menu options are described in Chapter 4. If you include a FIELDS clause, dBASE IV displays only the named fields and calculated fields, in the specified order. The /R option designates a field as read/only (you cannot edit the data), and */column width* changes the display width for the field to any number between 4 (for character fields) or 8 (for date fields) and 100.

The LOCK clause instructs dBASE IV to "lock" the first *expN* fields in the structure so that they remain fixed at the left side of the screen as you pan the display, and the FREEZE option restricts editing to the specified field. The

WIDTH option specifies the maximum display width for all character fields; dBASE IV scrolls longer fields within the data entry area so you can view and edit the entire field. COMPRESS causes dBASE IV to superimpose the column titles on the top border of the Browse frame, leaving two more lines free for data.

The NOAPPEND option prevents you from adding new records, NODELETE prevents you from deleting records, and NOEDIT prevents you from changing data in existing records (but not from adding or deleting records). NOMENU disables the standard Browse menu bar.

The NOFOLLOW option controls the position of the record pointer after you edit the key fields in the master index. Normally, the record pointer remains positioned at the same record after you change the index key field, and dBASE IV redraws the screen with this record at the top. Since the record has moved in the index, the records that follow will no longer be the same ones as before the change. NOFOLLOW causes dBASE IV to reposition the record pointer to the record originally displayed below the one that was changed, so that the screen display remains constant except for the disappearance of the altered record.

The FORMAT option causes dBASE IV to use the active format file to control data formatting and validation (but not, as on the Edit screen, the screen layout). The WINDOW option names a previously defined screen window that controls the size of the Browse frame and the display colors. NOCLEAR prevents dBASE IV from clearing the screen when you exit from the Browse screen to the dot prompt, so that the data remains visible as you type your next command. NOINIT causes dBASE IV to display the Browse screen with the same configuration (fields, field widths, locked and frozen fields, and so on) established for the last Browse command in the current work session.

CALCULATE [<*exp list*>] [TO <*memvar list*>/ARRAY <*array name*>] [<*scope*>] [FOR <*condition*>] [WHILE <*condition*>]

Calculates the specified statistics for each expression in the list for the range of records in the active data base defined by the *scope* and *conditions*. The *exp list* can include any combination of eight functions: AVG(<*expN*>), CNT(), MAX(<*exp*>), MIN(<*exp*>), NPV(<*rate*>, <*cash flows*>, <*initial investment*>), STD(<*expN*>, SUM(<*expN*>, VAR(<*expN*>).

If you do not specify a *scope,* dBASE IV includes all records in the calculation. If the TALK setting is ON, dBASE IV displays the calculated results on the screen, and if the HEADING setting is ON, it displays the *expressions* above the results. If you specify a list of memory variables, dBASE IV creates the named numeric variables to store the calculated statistics Alternatively, you can specify the name of a previously declared one-dimensional array to store the results of the calculations.

---

* **CALL <*binary module name*> [WITH <*exp list*>]**

---

* **CANCEL**

CHANGE [FIELDS <*field list*>] [<*record number*>] [<*scope*>] [FOR <*condition*>] [WHILE <*condition*>] [NOINIT] [NOFOLLOW] [NOAPPEND] [NOEDIT] [NOMENU] [NODELETE] [NOCLEAR]

Invokes the full-screen edit mode to edit the specified fields in the range of records defined by the *scope* and *conditions.* If you do not specify a *scope,* dBASE IV assumes ALL. CHANGE is identical to EDIT.

CLEAR

CLEAR ALL/FIELDS/GETS/MEMORY/MENUS/POPUPS/SCREENS/ TYPEAHEAD/WINDOWS

CLEAR erases the screen, leaving the cursor positioned in the lower left corner.

CLEAR ALL closes all open data base files, indexes, and format files, as well as the catalog file if one is open, and selects work area 1. dBASE IV also releases all memory variables (except system memory variables), all array elements, and all popups, menus, and windows.

CLEAR FIELDS cancels a field list established with a SET FIELDS command, and turns off the field list as if you had typed SET FIELDS OFF.

CLOSE ALL/ALTERNATE/DATABASES/FORMAT/INDEXES/PROCEDURE

Closes all files of the specified type.

CLOSE ALL closes all data bases and auxiliary files, and selects work area 1.

CLOSE ALTERNATE (exactly like SET ALTERNATE OFF, followed by SET ALTERNATE TO) closes the current alternate file.

CLOSE DATABASES closes all data bases, indexes, and format files in all ten work areas, except the catalog file if one is open in work area 10, and selects work area 1.

CLOSE FORMAT (exactly like SET FORMAT TO) closes the format file in the current work area.

CLOSE INDEXES (exactly like SET INDEX TO) closes all NDX indexes and nonproduction MDX indexes in the current work area.

COMPILE <*program name*> [RUNTIME]

Compiles the specified program file. You must specify the extension if it differs from the default PRG (the programs generated by QBE and by the dBASE IV report, label, and screen form layout editors all have different extensions), and it always produces a file with the extension DBO (dBASE IV requires different extensions for the compiled versions of programs generated by QBE and by the report, label, and screen form editors).

CONTINUE

Searches the active data base, starting with the current record, for the next record that satisfies the condition in the most recent LOCATE command executed in the current work area, and leaves the record pointer positioned on that record. If the TALK setting is ON, dBASE IV displays the record number. If no matching record is found within the *scope* specified in the LOCATE command (ALL by default), dBASE IV displays the message "End of locate scope."

---

* **CONVERT [TO <*expN*>]**

COPY TO <*file name*> [[WITH] PRODUCTION] [FIELDS <*field list*>] [<*scope*>] [FOR <*condition*>] [WHILE <*condition*>] [TYPE DBASEII/DBMEMO3/DIF/FW2/RPD/SDF/SYLK/WKS/ DELIMITED [WITH <*delimiter*>/BLANK]]

COPY FILE <*file1*> TO <*file2*>

COPY INDEXES <*NDX index file list*> [TO <*MDX file name*>]

COPY STRUCTURE TO <*file name*> [[WITH] PRODUCTION] [FIELDS <*field list*>]

COPY TO <*file name*> STRUCTURE EXTENDED

COPY MEMO <*memo field*> TO <*file name*> [ADDITIVE]

COPY TAG <*tag name*> [OF <*MDX file name*>] TO <*NDX file name*>

* **COPY TO ARRAY <*array name*> [FIELDS <*field list*>] [<*scope*>] [FOR <*condition*>] [WHILE <*condition*>]**

Copies the range of records from the active data base defined by the *scope* and *condition* to a new file, which dBASE IV creates, or overwrites if it already exists. dBASE IV copies records that are marked for deletion unless the DELETED setting is ON. If you do not specify a *scope,* dBASE IV copies all the records. If you include a *field list,* dBASE IV copies only the named fields, in the specified order; otherwise, dBASE IV copies all fields if the new file is a DBF file, or all fields except memo fields if the new file is in an external format. When you copy records to a DBF file and include the WITH PRODUCTION clause, dBASE IV also builds a production MDX index file for the new data base, with the same tags as the original.

The SDF ("System Data Format") option identifies the new file as a fixed-length text file with a hard return at the end of each record. The DELIMITED option identifies the new file as a text file in which the fields are surrounded by delimiters and separated by commas, with a hard return at the end of each

record. To create a file that uses a delimiter other than the default double quotes, you must specify the delimiter in a WITH clause. The DELIMITED WITH BLANK option creates a file in which the fields are separated by single spaces, with no delimiters.

When you copy data to DIF ("Data Interchange Format"), SYLK (Multiplan "Symbolic Link"), or WKS (Lotus Worksheet) files, each record in the data base becomes a row in the spreadsheet and each field supplies data for one column. dBASE IV enters the field names into the first row of the spreadsheet as column titles.

COPY FILE <*file1*> TO <*file2*> creates a copy of *file1* under the name *file2.* You can use this command to copy any disk file, so you must specify the full name, including the extension (and path, if the file is not in the current subdirectory). If you copy a DBF file that contains memo fields, you must remember to copy the DBT file with a second COPY FILE command. You cannot copy an MDX index file because it includes a reference to the name of the associated data base file; you must either recreate it from scratch by rebuilding the index tags, or use the COPY TO command and include the WITH PRODUCTION clause, instead of using COPY FILE.

COPY INDEXES copies the index information in the named NDX index files into the specified MDX index file, or into the production MDX file if you do not include an MDX file name in the COPY command. In either case, dBASE IV creates the MDX file if it does not already exist.

COPY STRUCTURE creates an empty data base file containing the fields listed in the *field list* in the specified order, or all of the fields in the current file if you do not include a *field list.* If you include the WITH PRODUCTION clause, dBASE IV creates a production MDX file for the new data base file, with the same tags as the original.

The STRUCTURE EXTENDED option creates a structure-extended file instead of creating a data base with the same structure. The *structure-extended file* is a data base that has one record for each field in the active file, with five fields, named FIELD_NAME, FIELD_TYPE, FIELD_LEN, FIELD_DEC, and FIELD_IDX, which contain the names, types, lengths, number of decimal places, and index status of the fields. You can edit the structure-extended file if necessary, and then use this file to create a new data base with the CREATE FROM command.

COPY MEMO copies the contents of the named memo field in the current record in the active data base to the specified file, which is given the extension TXT if you do not specify a different one. If the named file already exists,

dBASE IV overwrites it unless you include the ADDITIVE option to append the memo text to the existing file.

COPY TAG copies the index information in the named MDX index tag to create the named NDX index file. dBASE IV assumes that the tag is in the production MDX file if you do not specify another.

COUNT [TO <*memvar*>] [<*scope*>] [FOR <*condition*>] [WHILE <*condition*>]

Counts the number of records in the active data base in the range defined by the *scope* and *conditions.* If you do not specify a *scope,* dBASE IV counts all the records. If the TALK setting is ON, dBASE IV displays the count on the screen. If you specify a memory variable, dBASE IV creates the named numeric variable to store the count.

CREATE <*data base name*>

CREATE <*data base name*> FROM <*structure-extended file*>

CREATE invokes the data base design screen to enable you to define a new data base file by entering the name, data type, length, number of decimal places (for numeric and float fields), and index status for up to 255 fields, which can total up to 4000 bytes.

If you include the FROM option, dBASE IV derives the structure of the new file from the contents of the named structure-extended file. This file is a data base that has one record for each field in the structure it describes, with five fields, named FIELD_NAME, FIELD_TYPE, FIELD_LEN, FIELD_DEC, and FIELD_IDX, which contain the names, types, lengths, number of decimal places, and index status of the fields. The file is usually generated by using a COPY command that includes the STRUCTURE EXTENDED option, but you can create and update a structure-extended file just as you would any other data base, provided that you adhere to the five standard field names.

CREATE/MODIFY APPLICATION *<application file name>*

Invokes the applications generator to define an application—a set of linked menus, pick lists, and batch processes that enables you to work with a data base system in a menu-driven environment.

CREATE/MODIFY LABEL *<label form name>*

Invokes a specialized layout editor to define a new label form or modify an existing label form. If you do not specify the *label form name,* dBASE IV prompts you to enter it. If no data base is open in the selected work area, dBASE IV prompts you for a file name and then opens the specified data base.

CREATE/MODIFY QUERY/VIEW *<query file name>*

Invokes the query design screen to define a view query, which displays data derived from one or more data bases, or an update query, which updates a data base by adding records, replacing fields, deleting records, or undeleting records.

CREATE/MODIFY REPORT *<report form name>*

Invokes a specialized layout editor to define a new report form or modify an existing report form. If you do not specify the *report form name,* dBASE IV prompts you to enter it. If no data base is open in the selected work area, dBASE IV prompts you for a file name and then opens the specified data base.

CREATE/MODIFY SCREEN *<screen form name>*

Invokes a specialized layout editor to define a new screen form that substitutes for the standard Edit screen, or to modify an existing screen form. If you do not

specify the *screen form name,* dBASE IV prompts you to enter it. If no data base is open in the selected work area, dBASE IV prompts you for a file name and then opens the specified data base.

CREATE VIEW <*view file name*> FROM ENVIRONMENT

Creates a dBASE III PLUS-compatible view file based on the current environment. The view file, which has the extension VUE, stores the names and work areas of one or more data base files and indexes, the relations that link them, the selected work area, the field list, a format file, and a filter condition currently in effect. If you used SET SKIP in addition to SET RELATION to link files, this information is *not* stored in the VUE file.

You can later restore the working environment from the view file by using the SET VIEW TO <*view file name*> command.

---

* **DEACTIVATE MENU**

---

* **DEACTIVATE POPUP**

---

* **DEACTIVATE WINDOW <*window name list*>/ALL**

---

* **DEBUG <*program name*>/<*procedure name*> [WITH <*parameter list*>]**

---

* **DECLARE <*array1*> [{<*rows*>,} <*columns*>]**
[, <*array2*> [{<*rows*>,} <*columns*>]] . . .

---

* **DEFINE BAR <*line number*> OF <*popup name*> PROMPT <*expC*>
[MESSAGE <*expC*>] [SKIP [FOR <*condition*>]]**

---

* **DEFINE BOX FROM <*column1*> TO <*column2*> HEIGHT <*expN*>
[AT LINE <*line*>] [SINGLE/DOUBLE/<*border characters*>]**

---

* **DEFINE MENU <*menu name*> [MESSAGE <*expC*>]**

---

* **DEFINE PAD <*pad name*> OF <*menu name*> PROMPT <*expC*>
[AT <*row*>, <*column*>] [MESSAGE <*expC*>]**

---

* **DEFINE POPUP <*popup name*> FROM <*row1*>, <*column1*>
[TO <*row2*>, <*column2*>] [PROMPT FIELD <*field name*>
/PROMPT FILES [LIKE <*skeleton*>]/PROMPT STRUCTURE]
[MESSAGE <*expC*>]**

---

* **DEFINE WINDOW <*window name*> FROM <*row1*>, <*column1*>
TO <*row2*>, <*column2*> [DOUBLE/PANEL/NONE/<*border characters*>]
[COLOR [<*standard foreground/background*>]
[, <*enhanced foreground/background*>] [, <*frame*>]]**

DELETE [<*scope*>] [FOR <*condition*>] [WHILE <*condition*>]

DELETE FILE <*file name*>

**DELETE TAG <*tag1*> [OF <*MDX index file*>/<*NDX index file*>]
[, <*tag2*> ...]**

DELETE marks for deletion the records in the active data base in the range defined by the *scope* and *conditions.* If you do not specify a *scope,* dBASE IV deletes only the current record. dBASE IV identifies deleted records by displaying an asterisk (*) next to the record number in the output of LIST and DISPLAY commands, and by displaying the "Del" indicator in the status bar (or on the top line of the screen if the STATUS setting is OFF and the SCOREBOARD setting is ON) on the Browse and Edit screens.

You must use the PACK command or the **Erase marked records** menu option to physically remove records that are marked for deletion and recover the space they occupied. Until you PACK a file, you can recover records marked for deletion with the RECALL command or the **Unmark all records** menu option. When the DELETED setting is ON, dBASE IV ignores deleted records except when you specify the record number explicitly in a command.

DELETE FILE is identical to ERASE.

DELETE TAG deletes the specified index tags (however, dBASE IV does not reclaim the disk space they occupied until you PACK the data base). If you do not include an index file name for any tag, dBASE IV searches for the tag in the production MDX file. If you name an NDX index, dBASE IV closes the specified index, but does not erase the NDX file from the disk. You can use this command to close one NDX file while leaving several others open without having to use the slower SET INDEX command (which would close all the NDX indexes and reopen the ones you named).

DIRECTORY/DIR [[ON] <*drive*>:] [[LIKE] [<*path*>\] [<*skeleton*>]]

Displays a directory of the specified files. If you do not include a *drive, path,* or file name *skeleton,* dBASE IV lists only data base files, and the display includes, for each file, the number of records, date of last update, and file size. If you do include a *drive, path,* or file name *skeleton,* dBASE IV displays files four across, in a format that resembles the listing produced by adding the /W (wide) option to a DOS DIR command. When it executes the DIRECTORY command, dBASE IV ignores any search path established with the SET PATH command; if you do not specify a *path,* it displays files from the drive specified with SET DEFAULT, the directory specified with SET DIRECTORY, or the current subdirectory.

DISPLAY [<*exp list*>] [FOR <*condition*>] [WHILE <*condition*>] [<*scope*>] [OFF] [TO PRINTER/TO FILE <*file name*>]

The DISPLAY command is identical to LIST, except that DISPLAY assumes a default *scope* of one record (the one at the current position of the record pointer), whereas LIST assumes a *scope* of ALL. Also, when you use a DISPLAY command, dBASE IV pauses when the screen is full and prompts you to "Press any key to continue..." whereas LIST causes dBASE IV to scroll data continuously and is thus more convenient when you route the output to the printer or to a text file.

DISPLAY FILES [LIKE <*skeleton*>] [TO PRINTER/TO FILE <*file name*>]

This command is identical to DIR, except that the optional TO PRINTER phrase causes dBASE IV to echo the screen display to the printer.

DISPLAY HISTORY [LAST <*expN*>] [TO PRINTER/TO FILE <*file name*>]

This command is identical to LIST HISTORY, except that dBASE IV pauses the display when the screen is full and prompts you to "Press any key to continue...."

DISPLAY MEMORY [TO PRINTER/TO FILE <*file name*>]

This command is identical to LIST MEMORY, except that dBASE IV pauses the display when the screen is full and prompts you to "Press any key to continuc...."

DISPLAY STATUS [TO PRINTER/TO FILE <*file name*>]

This command is identical to LIST STATUS, except that dBASE IV pauses the display when the screen is full and prompts you to "Press any key to continue . . . ."

DISPLAY STRUCTURE [IN <*work area*>] [TO PRINTER/ TO FILE <*file name*>]

This command is identical to LIST STRUCTURE, except that dBASE IV pauses the display when the screen is full and prompts you to "Press any key to continue . . . ."

DISPLAY USERS

This command is identical to LIST USERS, except that dBASE IV pauses the display when the screen is full and prompts you to "Press any key to continue . . . ."

DO <*program name*>/<*procedure name*> [WITH <*parameter list*>]

Runs the specified dBASE IV program or procedure. The first time you run a program, and every time you modify it if the DEVELOPMENT setting is ON, dBASE IV automatically compiles the program and executes the compiled file. When a program or procedure terminates, dBASE IV returns you to the dot prompt.

---

* **DO CASE . . . ENDCASE**

---

* **DO WHILE . . . ENDDO**

EDIT [FIELDS <*field list*>] [<*record number*>] [<*scope*>] [FOR <*condition*>] [WHILE <*condition*>] [NOINIT] [NOFOLLOW] [NOAPPEND] [NOEDIT] [NOMENU] [NODELETE] [NOCLEAR]

Invokes the full-screen edit mode to edit the specified fields in the range of records defined by the *scope* and *conditions.* If you do not specify a *scope,* dBASE IV assumes ALL. You can switch to the Browse screen by pressing F2 (Data). The other cursor movement and command keys and **Edit** menu options are described in Chapter 4. If you include a FIELDS clause, dBASE IV displays only the named fields and calculated fields, in the specified order.

The NOAPPEND option prevents you from adding new records, NODELETE prevents you from deleting records, and NOEDIT prevents you from changing data in existing records (but not from adding or deleting records). NOMENU disables the standard **Edit** menu bar.

The NOFOLLOW option controls the position of the record pointer after you edit the key fields in the master index. Normally, the record pointer remains positioned at the same record after you change the index key field, and dBASE IV redraws the screen with this record at the top. Since the record has moved in the index, the records that follow will no longer be the same ones as before the change. NOFOLLOW causes dBASE IV to reposition the record pointer to the record originally displayed below the one that was changed, so that the screen display remains constant except for the disappearance of the altered record.

NOCLEAR prevents dBASE IV from clearing the screen when you exit from the Edit screen to the dot prompt, so that the data remains visible as you type your next command. NOINIT causes dBASE IV to display the Edit screen with the same configuration (the same fields, and the same options selected) established for the last Edit command in the current work session.

EDIT is identical to CHANGE.

---

* **EJECT**

* **EJECT PAGE**

ERASE <*file name*>

Erases the specified file from the disk. You can use this command to erase any disk file, so you must specify the full name, including the extension (and path, if the file is not in the current subdirectory). If you erase a DBF file, you must remember to also erase any associated auxiliary files—the DBT file if the data base contains memo fields, the production MDX file, and other MDX and NDX index files. The ERASE command does not accept wildcard characters in the file name specification, so you can erase only one file at a time. dBASE IV does not allow you to erase a file that is currently open.

---

* **EXIT**

EXPORT TO <*file name*> [TYPE] PFS/DBASEII/FW2/RPD
[FIELDS <*field list*>] [<*scope*>] [FOR <*condition*>]
[WHILE <*condition*>]

Exports data from the named fields in the range of records in the active data base specified by the *scope* and *conditions* to a file in the designated format. If you do not specify a *scope,* dBASE IV assumes ALL. When you export to PFS:FILE format, dBASE IV uses a screen form file if one is open to design the PFS screen layout; otherwise, the PFS screen resembles the standard dBASE IV Edit screen. When you export to FW2 (Framework) format, dBASE IV creates a data base frame.

FIND <*character string*>/<*n*>

Searches for the specified character string or number in the master index for the active data base. If the index is based on a character string, you need not enclose a literal search string in quotation marks unless it includes leading blank spaces. When the search string is stored in a memory variable, you must precede the variable name with the macro symbol (&) so that dBASE IV searches for the *value* of the variable rather than the characters that make up its

name. If the index is based on a numeric field, you must specify the key value as a numeric constant, not by storing it in a memory variable. In every other respect, FIND works like SEEK.

---

* **FUNCTION <*function name*> ... RETURN <*exp*>**

GO/GOTO <*expN*>/BOTTOM/TOP [IN <*work area*>]

Positions the record pointer in a data base to the specified record. If you do not specify another file (by its alias), dBASE IV moves the record pointer in the active file (the one open in the currently selected work area). GOTO BOTTOM positions the record pointer to the last record in the file or, with an index open, at the last record in indexed order. GOTO TOP positions the record pointer to the first record in the file or, with an index open, to the first record in indexed order. If the DELETED setting is ON or if a filter is in effect, GOTO TOP and GOTO BOTTOM position the record pointer to the first or last record that satisfies all of the specified conditions; however, you may still use GOTO to move directly to any record by number.

HELP [<*keyword*>]

Invokes the dBASE IV online help system and displays a screen of help text that summarizes the syntax and usage of the specified keyword. HELP with no keyword calls up the main Table of Contents screen for the Dot Prompt section of the help system.

---

* **IF ... ELSE ... ENDIF**

IMPORT FROM <*file name*> [TYPE] PFS/DBASEII/FW2/RPD/WK1

Imports data from the named external file, and creates a data base with a matching structure. When you import a PFS file, dBASE IV also creates a format file to draw a data entry screen that resembles the PFS screen layout; however, it does not create a matching screen form (SCR) file, so you cannot modify the screen layout with the screen form layout editor (you must edit the format file directly). When you import a Lotus worksheet file, each row in the spreadsheet becomes a record in the data base, and each column supplies data for one field.

INDEX ON <*key expression*> TO <*NDX file name*>
/TAG <*MDX index tag name*> [OF <*MDX file name*>] [UNIQUE]
[DESCENDING] [FOR <*condition*>]

Builds an MDX index tag or an NDX index file for the active data base based on the specified *key expression.* If you omit the *key expression* or *file name,* dBASE IV prompts you to enter them. The *key expression* can be up to 220 characters long; the key itself (the result of evaluating the key expression) is limited to 100 characters.

An MDX file can contain up to 47 index tags. dBASE IV adds each new tag to the production MDX file unless you specify another MDX file name in the INDEX command. In either case, dBASE IV creates the MDX file if it does not already exist. After building an index, dBASE IV leaves it open, as the master index for the active data base, and positions the record pointer to the top of the index. After building an NDX index, dBASE IV closes all other open indexes except the production MDX file.

An index can be based on a single character, numeric, or date field, resulting in alphabetical, numeric, or calendar date order, respectively. You can also combine fields of different data types to form the key expression, provided that all are converted to character strings (using the DTOS function for dates and the STR function for numeric fields). You can index in descending order with respect to the entire key expression by adding the keyword DESCENDING to the INDEX command.

If you include the UNIQUE keyword, only the first record in a group that shares the same value for the *key expression* is represented in the index. Thereafter, whenever the file is opened with this index, it will appear to contain unique index keys.

If you include the optional FOR clause, which is permitted only for MDX index tags, the result is a *conditional index*, which references only records that satisfy the specified condition. Building a conditional index is often the fastest way to access a small subset of records in a large data base.

---

* **INPUT [<*expC*>] TO <*memvar*>**

INSERT [BEFORE]

* **INSERT BLANK**

INSERT adds a new record to the active data base, using the standard dBASE IV Edit screen. dBASE IV inserts the new record after the current record unless you include the BEFORE keyword. If no index is active, dBASE IV moves all of the remaining records down to make room for the new entry, a process that can be very slow in a large data base. If the CARRY setting is ON, all fields in the new record take their default values from the current record, or from the previous record if you specified the BEFORE option.

A faster alternative is to use an index to access the file in the desired order and allow dBASE IV to add new records to the end of the file. dBASE IV does this automatically if you use the INSERT command with a master index active.

JOIN WITH <*alias*> TO <*file name*> FOR <*condition*>
[FIELDS <*field list*>]

Creates a new data base file based on the contents of the active data base and a second file, which is open in another work area and is specified by its *alias*. For

each record in the active data base, dBASE IV reads every record in the second file, and adds a record to the new data base for each pair of records from the two files that satisfies the *condition.*

If you include a *field list,* this list determines the structure of the new file. Otherwise, this file contains all of the fields from the active file, together with as many fields as possible from the second (subject to the limitation of 255 fields in a data base). Duplicate fields (identified by name) are represented only once in the resulting file, and dBASE IV ignores memo fields when it executes a JOIN command.

Because dBASE IV reads through the entire second file for each record in the active file, executing a JOIN command can be very time-consuming. In many cases, you can create the same data base faster by linking the two original files with SET RELATION and SET SKIP, and then using a COPY command, or by defining a view query and using the **Write view as database file** option to save the data described by the view in a new file.

KEYBOARD <*expC*> [CLEAR]

LABEL FORM <*label form file*> [<*scope*>] [FOR <*condition*>] [WHILE <*condition*>] [TO PRINTER/TO FILE <*file name*>] [SAMPLE]

Prints labels based on data in the active data base or view, using the specified label form file, for the range of records defined by the *scope* and *conditions.* If you do not specify a *scope,* dBASE IV assumes ALL. If the label form references fields from more than one data base, all of the necessary data base and index files must be open and the files must be linked with SET RELATION and SET SKIP if necessary (you can open the files by defining a view query or by typing commands at the dot prompt).

If you include TO PRINTER, dBASE IV prints the labels as well as displaying them on the screen. The TO FILE option routes the output to a disk file to generate an exact image of the printed labels. If you include the SAMPLE option, dBASE IV prints sample labels—rows of X's that occupy the same amount of space as a label—to help you to align the label stock in the printer. You can select the output device and control other aspects of the print job by storing the settings in a *print form.* To activate a print form from the dot

prompt, you must assign its name to the system memory variable _PFORM.

LIST [<*exp list*>] [<*scope*>] [FOR <*condition*>] [WHILE <*condition*>] [OFF] [TO PRINTER/TO FILE <*file name*>]

Displays the specified expressions for the range of records in the active data base defined by the *scope* and *conditions.* If you do not specify a *scope,* dBASE IV assumes ALL, and if you do not include an *exp list,* dBASE IV lists all fields. If the HEADING setting is ON, dBASE IV displays the specified expressions as column titles, in the same mixture of uppercase and lowercase used in the LIST command. dBASE IV displays the contents of memo fields only if you include the field names in the *exp list*; otherwise, they are represented by *memo markers*—"MEMO" for fields that contain text, or "memo" for empty memo fields. dBASE IV includes record numbers in the display unless you include the OFF option.

If you include the clause TO PRINTER, dBASE IV echoes the screen display to the printer, and the clause TO FILE routes the output to a disk file to generate a text file that contains one line for each record (even if dBASE IV wrapped the data onto multiple lines on the screen).

This command is similar to DISPLAY, except that the default scope is ALL rather than one record, and dBASE IV does not pause the display when the screen is full; thus, LIST is more convenient than DISPLAY when you route the output to the printer or to a text file.

LIST FILES [LIKE <*skeleton*>] [TO PRINTER/TO FILE <*file name*>]

This command is identical to the DIR command.

LIST HISTORY [LAST <*expN*>] [TO PRINTER/TO FILE <*file name*>]

Displays a list of the commands in history, normally 20 unless you have increased this number with a SET HISTORY command. If you include the LAST clause, dBASE IV displays the specified number of commands, taken from the

bottom of the list. If you include TO PRINTER, dBASE IV echoes the screen display to the printer, and the TO FILE option routes the output to a disk file to generate an exact image of the screen display. This command is identical to DISPLAY HISTORY, except that LIST HISTORY scrolls data continuously and is thus more convenient when you route the output to the printer or to a text file.

LIST MEMORY [TO PRINTER/TO FILE <*file name*>]

Displays a summary of all active memory variables and arrays that you have created during the current work session, all system memory variables, and memory allocated for active windows, pop-ups, menus, and pads. For each memory variable, the display includes the name, status (public or private), data type, stored value, the program (if any) that created the variable, and for numeric variables, the display value (which may include fewer decimal places than the stored value).

The display includes a summary of the number of variables defined, the amount of memory (in bytes) they occupy, and the number and size of the variables that you may still create, based on the memory allocated for memory variables in the CONFIG.DB file (using the MVBLKSIZE, MVMAXBLKS, RTBLKSIZE, and RTMAXBLKS settings).

If you include the TO PRINTER clause, dBASE IV echoes the screen display to the printer, and the TO FILE option routes the output to a disk file to generate an exact image of the screen display. This command is identical to DISPLAY MEMORY, except that LIST MEMORY scrolls data continuously and is thus more convenient when you route the output to the printer or to a text file.

LIST STATUS [TO PRINTER/TO FILE <*file name*>]

Displays information about the current status of the working environment. For each active work area, the display includes the name and alias of the open data base; the name of the DBT file if the data base contains memo fields; whether the file is marked read/only; all open index names (MDX index tags and NDX index files), key expressions, and, if applicable, the UNIQUE and DESCENDING attributes; the name of any open format file; the filter condition if one is in

effect, and any linkages established with SET RELATION and SET SKIP. In a network environment, the display includes any file locks currently in effect and a list of any records that are locked.

The status display also includes the file search path, the default disk drive, any binary files loaded into memory, the left margin and destination port or device for printed output, the screen update interval established with SET REFRESH, the number of retries established with SET REPROCESS, the currently selected work area and total number of files open, the currency and delimiter symbols, and "traps" established with ON ERROR, ON KEY, and other similar commands. Finally, dBASE IV lists the status of most of the environment settings and the current function key assignments.

If you include TO PRINTER, dBASE IV echoes the screen display to the printer, and the TO FILE option routes the output to a disk file to generate an exact image of the screen display. This command is identical to DISPLAY STATUS, except that LIST STATUS scrolls data continuously and is thus more convenient when you route the output to the printer or to a text file.

LIST STRUCTURE [IN <*work area*>] [TO PRINTER/TO FILE <*file name*>]

Displays the structure of the active data base file, or a data base open in another work area, which you identify by its alias. For each field, the display includes the name, data type, length, number of decimal places (for numeric and float fields), and index key status. If you established a field list with SET FIELDS commands, the fields in the list are marked with the > symbol. dBASE IV also displays the number of records in the file, the date of the last update, and the total record length (the sum of the field lengths plus the one character used for the deletion marker).

If you include the TO PRINTER clause, dBASE IV echoes the screen display to the printer, and the TO FILE option routes the output to a disk file to generate an exact image of the screen display. This command is identical to DISPLAY STRUCTURE, except that LIST STRUCTURE scrolls data continuously and is thus more convenient when you route the output to the printer or to a text file.

LIST USERS

In a network environment, displays a list of the network workstation names of the users currently logged onto dBASE IV, with the currently logged user marked with the < symbol.

---

* **LOAD** ***<binary file name>***

LOCATE [*<scope>*] [FOR *<condition>*] [WHILE *<condition>*]

Searches the range of records in the active data base defined by the *scope* and WHILE clause for the first record that matches the specified *condition.* If you do not specify a *scope,* dBASE IV assumes ALL. If dBASE IV finds a matching record, it positions the record pointer on this record; if the TALK setting is ON, dBASE IV displays the record number. You can use the CONTINUE command to search for additional records that satisfy the *condition* specified in the previous LOCATE command in the selected work area. (You can execute a different LOCATE command in each active work area, and dBASE IV uses the appropriate condition in a subsequent CONTINUE command.) When dBASE IV cannot find a matching record after a LOCATE or CONTINUE command, it displays an "End of locate scope" message, and assigns the value .F. to the FOUND function.

LOGOUT

When a password-protected security system defined through the PROTECT utility is in effect, this command closes all open files and presents a new log-in screen, exactly as if you had QUIT and reentered dBASE IV.

---

* **LOOP**

MODIFY APPLICATION *<application file name>*

This command is identical to CREATE APPLICATION.

MODIFY COMMAND [*<file name>*] [WINDOW *<window name>*]

MODIFY FILE [*<file name>*] [WINDOW *<window name>*]

Invokes the dBASE IV text editor to create or edit a text file. If you do not specify the *file name,* dBASE IV prompts you to enter it. When you use the MODIFY COMMAND variation, dBASE IV assumes that you want to edit a program file with the extension PRG; to edit a file with a different extension (for example, a format file or program generated by dBASE IV), you must specify the extension explicitly. When you use the MODIFY FILE variant, dBASE IV makes no assumptions about the file you want to edit, so you must always provide the full file name, including extension.

The dBASE IV text editor supports lines up to 1024 characters long and permits up to 32,000 lines in a file, subject to the more restrictive limitations imposed by available memory and disk space. The editor occupies the full screen unless you specify a smaller (previously defined) window in the WINDOW clause.

You can use the TEDIT option in CONFIG.DB (TEDIT = *<program name>*) to substitute an external editor or word processor for the dBASE IV editor (provided that you have enough RAM in your system to load COMMAND .COM and the editor into memory together with dBASE IV) so that the MODIFY COMMAND command calls the external editor instead of the dBASE IV text editor.

MODIFY LABEL *<label form name>*

This command is identical to CREATE LABEL.

MODIFY QUERY/VIEW *<query file name>*

This command is identical to CREATE QUERY/VIEW.

MODIFY REPORT *<report form name>*

This command is identical to CREATE REPORT.

MODIFY SCREEN *<screen form name>*

This command is identical to CREATE SCREEN.

MODIFY STRUCTURE *<data base file name>*

Invokes the data base design screen to enable you to modify the structure of the active data base and adjust all existing records to match the new structure. dBASE IV creates a temporary copy of the file structure, to which you make your changes, and then appends the data from the original file into the new structure. The original data base file is renamed with a BAK (backup) extension, and the original memo text file (if any) with a TBK extension.

The same rules that govern the APPEND FROM command apply to transferring data from the backup file to the new structure. You can change field lengths, add or delete fields, or change the data type of a field without losing data (provided that the contents of the field are consistent with the new type). If you shorten a character field, dBASE IV truncates the data to fit, whereas when numeric data is too long for a field, dBASE IV replaces the field value with asterisks to indicate a numeric overflow. If you delete a field, the data is lost, and if you add a new field, it will be blank in every record. You can change field names, provided that you do not make any other changes at the same time. If you change a field that forms part of an index key expression in the production MDX file, dBASE IV rebuilds the tag; if you delete an index key field, dBASE IV deletes the tag.

---

* **MOVE WINDOW** ***<window name>*** **TO** ***<row>, <column>***
/BY ***<row difference>, <column difference>***

---

* **NOTE/*/&&**

NOTE and *, when placed at the beginning of a program statement, identify the statement as a comment (nonexecutable) line in a dBASE IV program. && identifies the characters that follow on a line as a comment, so you can use this variant to include a comment on the same line as an executable program statement.

---

* **ON ERROR/ESCAPE/KEY [LABEL** ***<key label name>*** **] [** ***<command>*** **]**

---

* **ON PAD** ***<pad name>*** **OF** ***<menu name>*** **[ACTIVATE POPUP**
<popup name> **]**

---

* **ON PAGE [AT LINE** ***<expN>*** ***<command>*** **]**

---

* **ON READERROR [** ***<command>*** **]**

---

* **ON SELECTION PAD** ***<pad name>*** **OF** ***<menu name>*** **[** ***<command>*** **]**

---

* **ON SELECTION POPUP** ***<popup name>*** **/ALL [** ***<command>*** **]**

PACK

Permanently removes from the active data base all records previously marked for deletion. dBASE IV automatically rebuilds all tags in the production MDX file and any other MDX and NDX indexes that are open, and reclaims the space formerly occupied by deleted tags. After you execute a PACK command, there is no way to recover the deleted records. PACK reclaims the disk space formerly occupied by the deleted records, but dBASE IV updates the file size and number of records on disk (and therefore reports them correctly when you type a DIR command) only after you close the file.

---

* **PARAMETERS <*exp list*>**

PLAY MACRO <*macro name*>

Plays back the keystrokes stored in the named macro, which must be in memory. If the macro was created in a previous work session and saved in a macro library file, you must issue a RESTORE MACROS command before you can execute any of the macros stored in the file. You can use the PLAY MACRO command to execute any macro from the dot prompt or from a dBASE IV program, but macros recorded from the menu system that contain menu command keystrokes will not execute properly from the dot prompt. When you invoke a macro from within a program, dBASE IV does not play back the keystrokes stored in the macro until the program requests input from the user.

---

* **PRINTJOB . . . ENDPRINTJOB**

---

* **PRIVATE [ALL [LIKE <*skeleton*>]]/[<*memvar list*>]**

---

* **PROCEDURE <*procedure name*> . . . RETURN**

PROTECT

Invokes the menu-driven Protect utility, which enables you to define and implement a password-protected security system for controlling access to dBASE IV, to specific data base files, and to specific fields in these files.

---

* **PUBLIC <*memvar list*>/[ARRAY <*array element list*>]**

QUIT

Closes all open disk files and exits from dBASE IV to the operating system.

---

* **READ [SAVE]**

RECALL [<*scope*>] [FOR <*condition*>] [WHILE <*condition*>]

Recovers ("undeletes") all of the records marked for deletion in the current data base in the range of records defined by the *scope* and *conditions.* If you do not specify a *scope,* dBASE IV recalls only the current record.

REINDEX

Rebuilds all of the tags in the production MDX file, and any other MDX and NDX indexes that are open in the current work area, based on the key expressions stored in the index files. If an index was originally created with the UNIQUE setting ON or if the index was assigned the UNIQUE attribute, the reconstructed index will also have this attribute. If an MDX or NDX index file is

physically damaged, dBASE IV may not be able to read the key expressions, and you must rebuild the indexes from scratch by using the INDEX command instead of using REINDEX.

RELEASE [ALL [LIKE/EXCEPT <*skeleton*>]]/[<*memvar list*>]

Erases from memory the specified memory variables and frees the space so that you can define additional variables.

---

* **RELEASE MODULE [<*module name list*>]/MENUS [<*menu name list*>]
/POPUPS [<*popup name list*>]/SCREENS [<*screen name list*>]
/WINDOWS [<*window name list*>]**

RENAME <*old file name*> TO <*new file name*>

Renames the specified file. You can use this command to rename any disk file, so you must specify the full name, including the extension. When it executes the RENAME command, dBASE IV ignores any search path established with the SET PATH command; if you do not specify a *path,* it displays files from the drive specified with SET DEFAULT, the directory specified with SET DIRECTORY, or from the current subdirectory. If you rename a DBF file that contains memo fields, you must remember to rename the DBT file as well. You cannot rename an MDX index file because it includes a reference to the name of the associated data base file; you must recreate it from scratch by rebuilding the index tags. RENAME does not accept wildcard characters, so you can rename only one file at a time. dBASE IV does not allow you to rename a file that is currently open.

**REPLACE [<*scope*>] [FOR <*condition*>] [WHILE <*condition*>]
<*field1*> WITH <*exp1*> [ADDITIVE] [,<*field2*> WITH <*exp2*> . . .]**

* **REPLACE FROM ARRAY <*array name*> [FIELDS <*field list*>] [<*scope*>]
[FOR <*condition*>] [WHILE <*condition*>]**

Substitutes the results of evaluating the listed expressions for the current values of the specified fields, for the range of records in the active data base defined by the *scope* and *conditions.* If you do not specify a *scope,* dBASE IV performs the replacements only in the current record. The ADDITIVE keyword applies only to memo fields, and causes dBASE IV to append the result of evaluating the specified expression to the existing memo text instead of replacing it.

dBASE IV automatically updates all index tags in the production MDX file and all other open indexes to reflect changes to the key fields effected with a REPLACE command. When you use REPLACE to change fields that make up all or part of the master index key expression, dBASE IV temporarily disables the index update process while it executes the command, and then rebuilds the index tag from scratch afterward.

REPORT FORM <*report form file*> [<*scope*>] [FOR <*condition*>] [WHILE <*condition*>] [TO PRINTER/TO FILE <*file name*>] [NOEJECT] [PLAIN] [SUMMARY] [HEADING <*expC*>]

Prints a report based on data in the active data base or view, using the specified label form file, for the range of records defined by the *scope* and *conditions.* If you do not specify a *scope,* dBASE IV assumes ALL. If the report form references fields from more than one data base, all of the necessary data base and index files must be open and the files must be linked with SET RELATION and SET SKIP if necessary (you can open the files by defining a view query or by typing commands at the dot prompt). If you include the clause TO PRINTER, dBASE IV prints the report as well as displaying it on the screen, and the TO FILE option routes the output to a disk file to generate an exact image of the printed report.

The HEADING clause specifies an optional extra heading line that is printed, centered, on the first line of each page. NOEJECT suppresses the default page eject dBASE IV normally sends to the printer before beginning the report. PLAIN suppresses the page header band on all pages except the first, and the page footer band on all pages except the last. SUMMARY suppresses the detail band; you can specify this option for a report that includes group bands in order to print only the group intro bands and the summary statistics defined in the group summary bands. You can select the output device and control other aspects of the print job by storing the settings in a *print form.* To

activate a print form from the dot pompt, you must assign its name to the system memory variable _PFORM.

---

* **RESET [IN <*work area*>]**

RESTORE FROM <*file name*> [ADDITIVE]

Loads the variables in the specified memory file into memory to make them available during the current work session. dBASE IV first releases (erases from memory) any existing memory variables, unless you include the ADDITIVE option. (You can save memory variables with the SAVE command.)

RESTORE MACROS FROM <*macro file*>

Loads the macro definitions stored in the specified macro library file into memory to make them available during the current work session. (You can save macros with the SAVE MACROS command.)

RESTORE SCREEN FROM <*screen name*>

---

* **RESTORE WINDOW <*window name list*>/ALL FROM <*file name*>**

RESUME

Continues execution of a program that you previously interrupted by pressing the ESC key and then selecting **Suspend** (rather than **Cancel**) from the dialog

box. dBASE IV resumes execution with the command following the one that was running when you interrupted the program.

---

* **RETRY**

---

* **RETURN [<*expression*>/TO MASTER/TO <*procedure name*>]**

ROLLBACK [<*data base name*>]

Restores one or more data bases to their original state when a transaction—a series of commands executed between BEGIN TRANSACTION and END TRANSACTION commands—fails to complete normally. While the transaction is still in progress (before you type END TRANSACTION), you cannot include a data base name in the command, and dBASE IV rolls back all data bases affected by the transaction. After the END TRANSACTION command, you can include the optional data base name to process only the designated file. ROLLBACK cannot always restore a data base, so you should back up your data bases before you begin a lengthy and complex sequence of file update commands.

RUN/! <*DOS command*>

Executes the specified DOS command, batch file, or program. COMMAND .COM must be available, either in the root directory of the disk from which you boot your system or, under DOS version 3.0 or later, in any subdirectory identified to DOS with a SET COMSPEC command. You must have enough RAM in your computer to load COMMAND.COM and the external program (if any) into memory together with dBASE IV.

SAVE TO <*file name*> [ALL LIKE/EXCEPT <*skeleton*>]

Saves the specified memory variables on disk in the named memory variable file to make them available in future work sessions. If you include the ALL LIKE clause, dBASE IV saves only memory variables with names that match the *skeleton,* which can include the standard wildcard characters, ? and *. If you include the ALL EXCEPT clause, dBASE IV saves all memory variables except those with names that match the *skeleton.* You can retrieve the memory variables with the RESTORE command.

SAVE MACROS TO <*macro file*>

Saves all currently defined macros on disk in the named macro library file to make them available in future work sessions. You can retrieve the macros with the RESTORE MACROS command.

SAVE SCREEN TO <*screen name*>

---

* **SAVE WINDOW <*window name list*>/ALL TO <*window file name*>**

---

* **SCAN [<*scope*>] [FOR <*condition*>] [WHILE <*condition*>]...
ENDSCAN**

SEEK <*exp*>

Searches for the result of evaluating the specified expression in the master index for the active data base. If the EXACT setting is OFF, you may search for

a partial index key value, but the portion you specify must start at the beginning of the field. SEEK is similar to FIND, except that FIND can accept only a single numeric or character string constant as its object, whereas SEEK can accept any valid expression.

If the search succeeds, dBASE IV positions the record pointer on the first record in which the master index key matches the value of the *expression* and sets the FOUND function to .T. and the EOF (end-of-file) function to .F.. If there is no matching record, dBASE IV displays the message "Find not successful." If the NEAR setting is OFF, it positions the data base at the end-of-file, and sets the EOF function to .T. and FOUND to .F.. If the NEAR setting is ON, dBASE IV positions the record pointer to the record with the first key value that follows the search string and sets both EOF and FOUND to .F..

SELECT <*work area*>

Switches to the specified work area. You can always select a work area by number (1 to 10) or by letter (A to J), and if a data base is open in a work area, you can also select the work area by the file's alias. dBASE IV maintains a separate record pointer in each active work area, and when you select one work area, any data bases open in other work areas remain positioned exactly where they were. You can access fields from data bases open in unselected work areas by using the notation <*alias*>—><*field name*>.

SET

Invokes a menu system for viewing and changing many of the dBASE IV environment settings. The options are described individually later in this appendix.

---

* **SHOW MENU <*menu name*> [PAD <*pad name*>]**

---

* **SHOW POPUP <*popup name*>**

SKIP [<*expN*>] [IN <*work area*>]

Moves the record pointer forward (if *expN* is positive) or backward (if *expN* is negative) the specified number of records; a SKIP command with no *expN* moves the pointer forward one record. If you do not specify another file (by its alias), dBASE IV moves the record pointer in the file open in the currently selected work area. If a master index is assigned, dBASE IV moves the record pointer relative to the index: it moves forward or backward in the index *expN* entries and then repositions the record pointer to the corresponding record. If the DELETED setting is ON or if a filter is in effect, only records that satisfy all the filter conditions are counted.

If a SKIP command moves the record pointer past the last record in a file, dBASE IV leaves the pointer positioned at a blank record (which is *not* actually added to the file), and sets the EOF (end-of-file) function to .T.. If you SKIP backward past the first record in the file, dBASE IV leaves the record pointer positioned at the first record in the file and sets the BOF (beginning-of-file) function to .T..

SORT TO <*new file name*> ON <*field1*> [/A]/[/D] [/C]
[, <*field2*> [/A]/[/D] [/C] . . .] [ASCENDING]/[DESCENDING]
[<*scope*>] [FOR <*condition*>] [WHILE <*condition*>]

Creates a new data base file containing the range of records from the active data base defined by the *scope* and *conditions.* You may sort on up to ten fields. The first field determines the major sort order, within which records are sorted according to the second field, and so on.

For each sort key field, you may specify three optional parameters: /A for ascending (low-to-high) ASCII order, /D for descending ASCII (high-to-low) order, and /C for *case-independence,* which causes dBASE IV to treat the uppercase and lowercase versions of a letter as equivalent. (By default, the sort order parallels the sequence of the ASCII character codes, and all of the uppercase letters precede all of the lowercase letters.) If you combine the A or D options

with the C option, only one slash is required—for example, /AC. The keyword ASCENDING or DESCENDING specifies the overall sort order for all fields not explicitly qualified with /A or /D.

You can sort on any combination of numeric, character, and date fields, but you cannot sort on logical or memo fields, and the sort keys must be whole fields, not expressions. To create a file sorted on a more complex expression, you can build an index based on the desired expression, designate the index as the master index, and then copy the file.

STORE <*exp*> TO <*memvar list*>/<*array element list*>
<*memvar*>/<*array element*> = <*exp*>

STORE creates the named variables and assigns them the initial values and data types specified by the *expression.* You must define an array by using the DECLARE command before you use STORE to assign the initial values. Assigning a new value to an existing memory variable or array element has the same effect as re-creating the variable from scratch with the new value. If you use the equal sign syntax, you can create only one memory variable or array element at a time.

SUM [<*expN list*>] [TO <*memvar list*>/TO ARRAY <*array name*>] [<*scope*>] [FOR <*condition*>] [WHILE <*condition*>]

Calculates the sum for each expression in the list for the range of records in the active data base defined by the *scope* and *conditions.* If you do not list any expressions, dBASE IV sums all numeric fields, and if you do not specify a *scope,* dBASE IV sums all records. If the TALK setting is ON, dBASE IV displays the sums on the screen, and if the HEADING setting is ON, it displays the *expressions* above the sums. If you specify a list of memory variables, dBASE IV creates the named numeric variables to store the sums. Alternatively, you can specify the name of a previously declared one-dimensional array to store the sums.

*** SUSPEND**

*** TEXT . . . ENDTEXT**

TOTAL ON <*key field*> TO <*file name*> [FIELDS <*field list*>] [<*scope*>] [FOR <*condition*>] [WHILE <*condition*>]

Creates a new data base containing summarized data for the specified numeric fields in the active data base for the range of records defined by the *scope* and *conditions.* The active file must be either sorted or indexed on the *key field.* If you do not specify a *field list,* dBASE IV totals all numeric fields. The new file has the same structure as the active data base, except that memo fields are not included. Each record in the new file contains totals for a group of records in the active file with the same value in the *key field.* If the numeric fields are not large enough to accommodate the totals, dBASE IV fills the fields with asterisks to indicate a numeric overflow.

TYPE <*file name*> [TO PRINTER/TO FILE <*file name*>] [NUMBER]

Displays the contents of the specified file on the screen. If you include TO PRINTER, dBASE IV prints the file as well as displaying it on the screen. If you include the NUMBER option, dBASE IV adds line numbers to the listing.

UNLOCK [ALL/IN <*work area*>]

In a network environment, releases the most recent file lock (if the most recent locking command locked a file) or all the record locks in the current work area (if the most recent locking command locked a record) that were placed by the

user who typed the UNLOCK command. UNLOCK ALL unlocks all files and fields locked by the current user in all work areas.

UPDATE ON <*key field*> FROM <*alias*> REPLACE <*field1*>
WITH <*exp1*> [, <*field2*> WITH <*exp2*> . . .] [RANDOM]

Updates the active data base based on information in a second file, which is open in another work area and is specified by its *alias.* Records are matched up based on the contents of the *key field,* which must be present in both files. One way to execute the UPDATE command is to sort or index both files based on the common key field; a faster way is to index the active data base on the *key field* and include the RANDOM keyword in the command to indicate that the file that supplies the data is in *random* order with respect to the common *key field.* For each record in the file that provides the data, dBASE IV replaces the designated fields in the matching record in the active file with the specified expressions, which may include references to any fields in either file.

USE [<*file name*>] [IN <*work area*>]
[[INDEX <*MDX and NDX index file list*>]
[ORDER [TAG] <*NDX index*>/<*MDX index tag*>
[OF <*MDX file name*>]]] [ALIAS <*alias*>] [EXCLUSIVE]
[NOUPDATE] [AGAIN]

Opens the specified data base in the designated work area, or in the currently selected work area if you do not specify another. dBASE IV always opens the production MDX file if one exists; in addition, you can open up to 10 other MDX and NDX index files for a total of up to 47 key expressions. If you do not specify an alias, dBASE IV automatically assigns the file name as the alias. If you do assign an alias, you must use either the alias (or the alternative alias A, B, and so on) in place of the file name in the standard <*alias*>—><*field name*> notation for referring to fields in unselected work areas. If you include the NOUPDATE option, dBASE IV does not allow you to update the data base by adding, deleting, or changing records. USE, with no file name, closes the data base and all associated index and format files in the current work area.

If you include an ORDER clause, the specified MDX index tag or NDX index file becomes the *master index*—the one that controls the display order of the records and the one that you can use to find records with index key search commands. If you open at least one NDX index with the data base, the first NDX index named becomes the master index (unless an ORDER clause overrides this selection). Without an explicit index key reference, dBASE IV processes the data base in natural order—the order in which records were entered—and positions the data base on the first record. If you do assign a master index, dBASE IV positions the data base on the record corresponding to the first entry in this index. Whether or not you assign a master index, dBASE IV updates all open indexes to replace changes that you make to the index key fields.

In a network environment, if you include the EXCLUSIVE keyword, dBASE IV opens the file for exclusive rather than shared use, and only one work station at a time may access the file. This is equivalent to issuing a SET EXCLUSIVE ON command prior to opening the file. You must open a file for exclusive use in order to run commands that affect the entire data base, including INSERT, MODIFY STRUCTURE, PACK, REINDEX, and ZAP.

*** WAIT [<*expC*>] [TO <*memvar*>]**

ZAP

Empties the current data base of all records. This command is equivalent to DELETE ALL, followed by PACK. ZAP operates much faster because dBASE IV does not actually read and delete every record, but instead places an end-of-file marker at the beginning of the file and resets the record count to 0. dBASE IV also reinitializes any indexes opened with the data base to match the new empty file.

SET COMMANDS

SET ALTERNATE on/OFF

SET ALTERNATE TO [<*file name*>] [ADDITIVE]

SET ALTERNATE TO < *file name*> opens the specified text file. Once the file is open, SET ALTERNATE ON causes dBASE IV to record all *streaming,* or *sequential,* screen output (data that is displayed line by line, not by full-screen commands such as Edit and Browse) in the text file. If the named text file already exists, dBASE IV erases it and recreates it from scratch unless you include the ADDITIVE option.

SET ALTERNATE OFF temporarily suspends recording without closing the alternate file. You may SET ALTERNATE ON and OFF as many times as necessary during a work session. To close the text file, use CLOSE ALTERNATE or SET ALTERNATE TO after the last SET ALTERNATE OFF command.

SET AUTOSAVE on/OFF

Determines whether or not dBASE IV immediately saves all changes made to a database file on disk and updates the DOS disk directory. When AUTOSAVE is OFF, new records, changes, and the information in the file header (most importantly, the record count), are buffered in memory. When AUTOSAVE is ON, all these updates are stored on disk immediately, and there is less risk that you will lose data if you fail to close the data base properly due to a hardware or software failure.

SET BELL ON/off

SET BELL TO <*frequency*>, <*duration*>

SET BELL ON/off determines whether or not dBASE IV sounds the computer's bell (beeper) when you completely fill a field on the Edit or Browse screen or when you make an error (for example, typing an invalid date or entering alphabetic characters into a numeric field).

SET BELL TO enables you to customize the sound of the bell (beeper) by setting the frequency and duration of the tone. The frequency is expressed in Hz (cycles per second), and the duration is expressed in clock "ticks." The default frequency is 512 Hz, and you may specify any number between 19 and 10,000. The default duration is 2 ticks, and you may specify any number between 2 and 19.

SET BLOCKSIZE TO <*number*>

Determines the size of the blocks in which dBASE IV allocates disk space for memo fields and MDX index tags, expressed as a multiple of 512 bytes. The default value is 1, and you may specify any number between 1 (512 bytes) and 32 (16K). A larger block size will improve performance if the average size of your memo fields is large, but setting the block size too large wastes disk space. After you change this setting, you must use MODIFY STRUCTURE or COPY to rewrite existing memo fields using the new block size.

---

* **SET BORDER TO [SINGLE/double/panel/none/<*border characters*>]**

SET CARRY on/OFF

SET CARRY TO [<*field list*> [ADDITIVE]]

SET CARRY on/OFF determines whether dBASE IV carries forward the value you enter into every field of a new record—including memo fields—to serve as the default value for the corresponding field in the next new record. SET CARRY TO *field list* turns the CARRY setting ON, and also causes dBASE IV to carry over only the listed fields. The ADDITIVE option adds fields to the list specified in a previous SET CARRY command rather than substituting a new field list. The status of the CARRY setting affects only records added on the Edit (Append) and Browse screens; even after a SET CARRY ON command, all of the fields in a record added with an APPEND BLANK or INSERT BLANK

command are blank. SET CARRY TO, with no field list, cancels any field list established by a previous SET CARRY command.

SET CATALOG on/OFF

SET CATALOG TO [<*catalog file name*>]

SET CATALOG TO <*catalog file name*> opens the specified catalog data base in work area 10, or creates it if it does not exist. A catalog is a standard dBASE IV data base file distinguished by its extension—CAT instead of DBF. You can open, display, and update a catalog from the dot prompt as long as you do not change the structure.

The catalog records all files opened or created while it is active, as well as some of the associations between files (for example, which data base was open when a report, label, or screen form was designed). When you work in the Control Center, a catalog is always open, and only the files in the active catalog appear in the file panels and in pick lists. At the dot prompt, when a catalog is open, the file query clause—substituting a "?" where dBASE IV expects a file name—displays only files of the relevant type in the active catalog. If a data base is open, the list of index, report, label, or other auxiliary files displayed by a query clause includes only files that are associated with the active data base.

dBASE IV updates the active catalog automatically when you create, rename, or delete files. When it adds a new file to the catalog, unless you have SET TITLE OFF, dBASE IV prompts you to enter an 80-character description for the file, which is displayed below the file name under the Control Center panels, and in a separate pop-up box when you use a query clause or choose files from a pick list.

SET CATALOG OFF temporarily disables the catalog update process, and SET CATALOG ON reactivates it. SET CATALOG TO, with no catalog name specified, closes the active catalog without opening another.

SET CENTURY on/OFF

Determines whether dates are displayed and entered with 4-digit years. When the CENTURY setting is OFF, dBASE IV assumes that the century is 1900 and displays the year as 2 digits, but it stores the century and uses it in

calculations that involve dates in another century. When the CENTURY setting is ON, all dates are displayed and entered with 4-digit years.

SET CLOCK on/OFF

SET CLOCK TO [<*row*>, <*column*>]

SET CLOCK on/OFF determines whether dBASE IV always displays the clock on the screen. SET CLOCK TO determines the row and column position of the clock. In the Control Center and the full-screen edit modes and layout editors, the clock is always present, regardless of the status of this setting, and it is always positioned at row 0, column 69.

SET COLOR ON/OFF

SET COLOR TO [<*standard foreground/background*>]
[, <*enhanced foreground/background*>] [, <*border*>]

SET COLOR OF NORMAL/MESSAGES/TITLES/BOX/HIGHLIGHT/
INFORMATION/FIELDS TO [<*foreground/background*>]
[, <*foreground/background*>]

SET COLOR ON/OFF selects between color and monochrome screens if both are present. The default value corresponds to the monitor in use when you started up dBASE IV.

SET COLOR TO determines the colors or monochrome display attributes used for three broad groups of screen items: the *standard* area (information displayed by dBASE IV), the *enhanced* area (entered data), and the *border* (the area of the screen outside the 25-line by 80-column or 43-line by 80-column display area). SET COLOR OF enables you to select display colors for seven more specific groups of screen items (these groups are described in Chapter 18). SET COLOR TO, with no color abbreviations specified, resets the display colors to the internal dBASE IV defaults. The color and monochrome attribute abbreviations are listed in Table 18-2.

SET CONFIRM on/OFF

Determines whether you must confirm each field entry by pressing ENTER. When the CONFIRM setting is ON, dBASE IV does not advance the cursor automatically to the next item when you fill a field completely—you must always press ENTER.

---

* **SET CONSOLE ON/off**

SET CURRENCY TO [<*expC*>]

SET CURRENCY LEFT/right

SET CURRENCY TO establishes the currency symbol that dBASE IV displays or prints with numbers assigned the $ picture function or a template that includes the $ symbol. SET CURRENCY LEFT/right determines whether dBASE IV positions the currency symbol to the left or right of the number. The currency symbol may be any character string up to nine characters long. SET CURRENCY TO, with no symbol specified, resets the currency symbol to the default dollar sign ($).

---

* **SET CURSOR ON/off**

SET DATE [TO] AMERICAN/ansi/british/french/german/italian/japan/ usa/mdy/dmy/ymd

Establishes the display format for date fields and memory variables. No matter which display format is in effect, dBASE IV can carry out date arithmetic and date comparisons, and it can SORT or INDEX on a date field in correct chronological order. If the CENTURY setting is ON, all the date formats display

and collect dates with 4-digit years; if it is OFF, the year is displayed with 2 digits. The formats are listed in Table 18-1.

---

* **SET DBTRAP ON/off**

---

* **SET DEBUG on/OFF**

SET DECIMALS TO <*expN*>

Determines the number of decimal places displayed or printed in numbers that result from evaluating expressions involving multiplication, division or any mathematical, trigonometric, or financial functions. The default is 2, and you may specify any value between 0 and 18.

SET DEFAULT TO <*drive*>[:]

Establishes the default disk drive that dBASE IV uses to read and write all disk files unless a different drive is explicitly included in the file name. This command has the same effect as logging onto the designated drive before loading dBASE IV.

SET DELETED on/OFF

Determines whether dBASE IV processes records that are marked for deletion. When the DELETED setting is ON, dBASE IV ignores deleted records except when you specify the record number explicitly (for example, in a GOTO command or a command with a scope of a single record). The SET DELETED ON command does not automatically reposition the record pointer to the first

nondeleted record; if you execute this command with a data base open, you should follow it with GOTO TOP, SKIP, or any other command that repositions the record pointer.

SET DELIMITERS on/OFF

SET DELIMITERS TO [<*delimiter(s)*>]/[DEFAULT]

SET DELIMITERS ON/OFF determines whether dBASE IV surrounds data entry areas with delimiters. SET DELIMITERS TO designates the actual delimiter character(s). You may specify either one or two characters, enclosed in quotes. If you specify one, dBASE IV uses this character as both the beginning and ending delimiter; if you specify two, it uses the first as the beginning delimiter and the second as the ending delimiter. The default delimiter, which dBASE IV uses if you SET DELIMITERS ON without assigning a new delimiter, is the colon (:). The DEFAULT option restores this default delimiter after a previous SET DELIMITERS TO command.

---

* **SET DESIGN ON/off**

SET DEVELOPMENT ON/off

Determines whether dBASE IV compares the date and time stamps on an original (source) program and the compiled (object) program every time you execute the program. When the DEVELOPMENT setting is ON, dBASE IV recompiles a program automatically if it has changed since the last compilation; if this seting is OFF, you must use an explicit COMPILE command.

---

* **SET DEVICE TO SCREEN/printer/file <*file name*>**

SET DIRECTORY TO <*path*>

Establishes the default disk drive and subdirectory that dBASE IV uses to read and write all disk files unless a different drive is explicitly included in the file name. This command has the same effect as logging onto the designated drive and switching to the designated subdirectory before loading dBASE IV.

SET DISPLAY TO MONO/COLOR/EGA25/EGA43/MONO43

Selects the monitor or display mode in a system that has two monitors or supports more than one display mode.

SET ECHO on/OFF

Determines whether dBASE IV echoes command lines in programs to the screen as they are executed. You can use this option to monitor the progress of a long-running program or to trace execution while you test and debug the program.

SET ENCRYPTION ON/off

Determines whether dBASE IV encrypts new files created by copying or sorting existing data bases that are encrypted. The status of the ENCRYPTION setting has no effect on new files that you define on the data base design screen; you must encrypt new files by using the PROTECT command from the dot prompt or the **Protect** option on the Control Center **Tools** menu. You cannot copy or export a protected data base file to any of the external file formats supported by dBASE IV unless the ENCRYPTION setting is OFF.

SET ESCAPE ON/off

Determines whether you can interrupt a dBASE IV command by pressing the ESC key. When the ESCAPE setting is OFF, the only way to abort a long-running command is to reboot or turn off the computer.

SET EXACT on/OFF

Determines whether character strings must be the same length and have the same value to be considered equal. When the EXACT setting is OFF, dBASE IV considers two strings equal if they are equal up to the length of the shorter string. This setting also determines whether you can retrieve a record based on a partial key value in an index key search; when EXACT is ON, you must specify the full key value.

SET EXCLUSIVE on/OFF

In a network environment, determines whether files are opened in exclusive or shared mode. The file open mode is determined by the status of the EXCLUSIVE setting at the time a file is opened, even if you subsequently issue a new SET EXCLUSIVE command. Any file opened with the EXCLUSIVE setting ON can only be accessed by one user at a time. You can also open a data base file for exclusive use by including the EXCLUSIVE keyword in the USE command.

SET FIELDS on/OFF

SET FIELDS TO [<*field list*>]

SET FIELDS TO ALL [LIKE/EXCEPT <*skeleton*>]

SET FIELDS TO <*field list*> specifies a list of fields from one or more open data bases to make them accessible to dBASE IV commands that accept a field list (APPEND, AVERAGE, BROWSE CALCULATE, CHANGE, CREATE VIEW

FROM ENVIRONMENT, COPY, COPY STRUCTURE, DISPLAY, EDIT, EXPORT, JOIN, LIST, SUM, and TOTAL). You can designate a field read/only by adding /R after the field name, and you can include calculated fields in the list by naming them and supplying the expression used to calculate the field, in the form <*name*> = <*exp*>. Successive SET FIELDS commands add to the field list, so the number of fields that you can access is not limited by the 1024-character command length limit. Even with a field list in effect, you can name any field in any open data base in a FOR clause, SET FILTER command, an index key expression, or the expression that links two files in a SET RELATION command.

SET FIELDS TO ALL sets the field list to all fields in the current data base, and no others. To access all fields from the current data base, together with selected fields from other work areas, you must therefore type the SET FIELDS TO ALL command before the SET FIELDS commands that identify the other fields. To access fields from more than one file in a meaningful way, the files must share a common key and they must be linked with SET RELATION, and SET SKIP if necessary.

SET FIELDS TO ALL LIKE/EXCEPT <*skeleton*> enables you to select multiple fields in one command by specifying the field name as a *skeleton* that includes the standard wildcard characters—a question mark (?) to represent one character and an asterisk (*) to represent any group of characters.

SET FIELDS ON activates the field list defined with SET FIELDS commands, and SET FIELDS OFF temporarily disables the field list.

SET FILTER TO [<*condition*>]

Establishes a condition that determines which records dBASE IV processes in subsequent commands. With a filter in effect, dBASE IV ignores records that do not satisfy the filter condition, except when you specify the record number explicitly (for example, in a GOTO command, or a command with a scope of a single record).

All commands that position the record pointer act relative to the filter, but the SET FILTER command itself does not reposition the record pointer, even if the current record does not pass the filter condition. You should therefore always follow this command with GOTO TOP, SKIP, or any other command that repositions the record pointer. You can define a separate filter in each active work area, and you can include references to fields in unselected work

areas in any filter condition. dBASE IV takes all active filters into account when it processes records, but a multifile filter will select meaningful data only if the files are linked with SET RELATION and if necessary, SET SKIP.

SET FILTER TO, with no condition, cancels the filter in the current work area. If a FILTER depends on fields in more than one file, be sure to cancel the filter before closing any of the files.

SET FORMAT TO [<*screen form file name*>]

Opens a screen form file that draws a formatted data entry screen to substitute for the standard Edit screen. The data formatting and validation rules established through the format file remain in effect when you switch to Browse mode, although the form file does not alter the layout of the Browse screen. SET FORMAT TO, with no file name, closes the screen form file open in the current work area.

---

* **SET FULLPATH on/OFF**

SET FUNCTION <*key name*>/<*key number*> TO <*expC*>

Assigns a new meaning to one of the programmable function keys. You can reassign the meanings of function keys F2 through F10, SHIFT-F1 through SHIFT-F9, and CTRL-F1 through CTRL-F10. You cannot reprogram F1, which invokes the dBASE IV online help system, SHIFT-F10, which controls the recording of keyboard macros, or any of the ALT-function key combinations, which are reserved for executing macros. A function key assignment can be any arbitrary sequence of up to 238 characters; it can be a frequently used character string, part of a command, a complete command, or more than one command. You can use a semicolon (;) to symbolize a hard return in the function key assignment, and thus cause dBASE IV to perform the equivalent of pressing the ENTER key.

SET HEADING ON/off

Determines whether dBASE IV displays column headings together with the output of the LIST, DISPLAY, SUM, AVERAGE, and CALCULATE commands. When this setting is ON, dBASE IV displays the field names, variable names, or expressions as column headings, in the same mixture of uppercase and lowercase that you typed them in the command. The width of each column of data on the screen is the width of the field defined in the structure or the width of the column heading, whichever is greater.

SET HELP ON/off

Determines whether dBASE IV responds to syntax errors at the dot prompt by displaying a dialog box that offers options to cancel the command, edit and resubmit the command, or invoke the online help system and display the help screen that summarizes the syntax of the verb in the erroneous command. When the HELP setting is OFF, dBASE IV simply displays an error message and immediately returns you to the dot prompt.

SET HISTORY ON/off

SET HISTORY TO <*expN*>

SET HISTORY TO *expN* determines the number of commands that are retained in the history list when you work at the dot prompt. You can retrieve, edit, and resubmit any commands in history. The default is 20, and you may specify any value between 0 and 16,000. SET HISTORY OFF temporarily disables the history feature without clearing the current history list, and SET HISTORY ON turns it back on.

SET HOURS TO 12/24

Determines whether the time displayed on the screen when you work in the menu system uses a 12-hour clock (the default) or a 24-hour clock.

SET INDEX TO [?/<*index file list*> [ORDER [TAG] <*NDX index name*> /<*MDX index tag name*> [OF <*MDX index file name*>]]]

Opens the specified index file(s) together with the current data base. You may open up to ten index files (any combination of MDX and NDX files) with a total of up to 47 keys for each data base, all of which are updated to reflect new entries and changes made to the key fields. dBASE IV always opens the production MDX file, so you need not name this file in a SET INDEX command. SET INDEX TO, with no list of index files, closes all indexes in the current work area.

The master index is the one that determines the order in which dBASE IV processes records, and is the only index that you can use to retrieve records with index key search commands. If the index named first in the *index file list* is an NDX index, it becomes the master index. Regardless of the mixture of MDX and NDX indexes, you can specify the master index by including the optional ORDER clause. To select a tag in an MDX index other than the production MDX file, you must name the MDX file in an OF clause. The SET INDEX command positions the data base to the record that matches the first index entry in the master index.

SET INSTRUCT ON/off

Determines whether dBASE IV displays a dialog box when you highlight a file name in the Control Center and press ENTER. When the INSTRUCT setting is OFF, dBASE IV automatically performs the action specified by the first option in the dialog box—opening or closing a data base or view, printing a report or set of labels, or running a program or application. To execute the other dialog box options, you can press a function key—F2 (Data) to view data or SHIFT-F2 (Design) to move to the appropriate layout editor.

SET INTENSITY ON/off

Determines whether dBASE IV uses the same colors or monochrome attributes for the standard display area (displayed data) and the enhanced display area (entered data). SET INTENSITY OFF eliminates the difference between these two screen groups and uses the colors selected for the standard area for the enhanced area as well.

SET LOCK ON/off

Determines whether dBASE IV automatically locks a file or record before executing certain commands that read but do not write to a file. When the LOCK setting is OFF, dBASE IV allows multiple users to access a file that would otherwise be locked, and it is up to you to ensure that multiple access does not compromise the accuracy of calculations or report data. The affected commands include AVERAGE, CALCULATE, COUNT, LABEL, REPORT, and SUM. When you use COPY, INDEX, JOIN, SORT, or TOTAL with the LOCK setting OFF, dBASE IV locks the file only while it is writing data, not during the reading phase.

SET MARGIN TO <*expN*>

Establishes a left margin (page offset) that dBASE IV uses for all printed output, including reports and the output of LIST TO PRINT and DISPLAY TO PRINT commands. The default is 0, and you can specify any value consistent with the page width. For reports and labels, dBASE IV adds the value of the MARGIN setting to the margin specified in the report or label form.

SET MARK TO [<*character*>]

Determines the character that dBASE IV uses to separate the month, day, and year in dates. The character must be enclosed in quotation marks in the SET

MARK command. SET MARK TO, with no mark character specified, restores the default mark, the slash (/).

SET MEMOWIDTH TO <*expN*>

Determines the display width for memo fields in LIST, DISPLAY, and ? commands, and the default template width assigned when you place a memo field on a report, label, or screen form. The default is 50, and you may specify any value between 8 and 32,000.

---

* **SET MESSAGE TO [<*expC*> [AT <*row*>[, <*column*>]]]**

SET NEAR on/OFF

Determines where dBASE IV positions the record pointer after an unsuccessful SEEK command. When the NEAR setting is OFF, dBASE IV moves the record pointer to the end-of-file (past the last record), and sets the FOUND function to .F. and EOF (end-of-file) to .T.. When NEAR is ON, dBASE IV displays the usual "Find not successful" message and sets FOUND to .F., but it positions the record pointer on the record with the first key value that follows the search string. This setting does not affect index key searches carried out through the menu system, where dBASE IV always returns the record pointer to its prior position after an unsuccessful index key search.

SET ODOMETER TO [<*expN*>]

Determines how often dBASE IV updates the display of the number of records processed by such commands as APPEND, COPY, and COUNT. dBASE IV updates the display every *expN* records. Higher values for ODOMETER will

result in slightly faster command execution. The default is 1, and you may specify any value between 1 and 200.

SET ORDER TO [<*expN*>/[TAG] <*index name*>
[OF <*MDX index file name*>]]

Determines which of the open NDX indexes or MDX index tags is the master index for the data base in the selected work area (the index that controls the order in which records are processed and the one used as the basis for index key search commands). To select a tag in an MDX index other than the production MDX file, you must name the MDX file in an OF clause.

The SET ORDER TO *expN* variation is permitted only when no MDX indexes are open; the expression evaluates to a number that corresponds to the position of the desired NDX index in the index list specified in the command (USE or SET INDEX TO) that originally opened the indexes.

SET ORDER TO causes dBASE IV to process the file in sequential order, as if no indexes were open; however, all open indexes are still updated to reflect changes to the data base. SET ORDER switches master indexes faster than SET INDEX, if the index you want is already open, because dBASE IV does not have to open or close any files.

SET PATH TO [<*path name list*>]

Establishes the search path used by dBASE IV to look for existing disk files not found in the current subdirectory, just as the DOS PATH command establishes a search path for the operating system. However, the SET PATH command has no effect on where dBASE IV creates new files or on the files accessible to commands such as DIR, DELETE FILE, ERASE, RENAME, and SET ALTERNATE TO. These commands, and the commands that create files, use the drive specified with SET DEFAULT, the directory specified with SET DIRECTORY, or the current subdirectory if you do not specify a path name. SET PATH TO, with no path names listed, cancels any previously established search path.

SET PAUSE on/OFF

Determines whether dBASE IV pauses after each screenful of data displayed by the SELECT command in SQL mode (as DISPLAY, but not LIST does).

SET POINT TO [<*character*>]

Determines the decimal point character that dBASE IV displays in numeric fields and memory variables; the point character is usually a period (.) in the United States, and a comma (,) in Europe. You must enclose the point character in quotation marks in the SET POINT command. SET POINT TO, with no character specified, restores the default decimal point character, the period (.).

SET PRECISION TO [<*expN*>]

Determines the number of significant digits dBASE IV uses in mathematical calculations involving fixed-point (data type numeric) numbers. The number of decimal places that dBASE IV *displays* is determined by the value of the DECIMALS setting. The default is 16, and you may specify any value between 10 and 20.

---

* **SET PRINTER on/OFF**

SET PRINTER TO [<*DOS device name*>/FILE <*file name*>/ \\SPOOLER/\\CAPTURE]

SET PRINTER TO \\<*computer name*>\<*printer name*> = <*DOS device name*>

SET PRINTER TO *DOS device name* selects the local printer, identified by the DOS name of the output port (for example, LPT1: or COM1:), to be used for printed output. The default port is LPT1:. This command has the same effect as

the equivalent DOS MODE command that redirects printer output, and you can substitute a MODE command, executed before you load dBASE IV or from within dBASE IV with a RUN command. Before you redirect output to a serial printer, you must use a separate MODE command to set the baud rate and other communications parameters.

In a network environment, SET PRINTER TO \\ *computer name*\ *printer name* = *DOS device name* routes output to a network printer via the network print spooler. The *computer name* is the network name for the file server, and the *printer name* is the network name for the printer. The *destination* is the shared printer port, identified by its device name (LPT1:, LPT2:, or LPT3:).

SET PRINTER TO FILE routes printer output to a disk file that you can later print or incorporate into a document, spreadsheet, or other external file.

SET PRINTER TO resets the destination for printed output to the default printer assigned at the operating system level. In a network environment, it also initiates printing to empty the print spooler file.

*** SET PROCEDURE TO [<*procedure file name*>]**

SET REFRESH TO <*number*>

Specifies the interval, in seconds, at which dBASE IV updates data displayed on the Edit or Browse screen at each workstation in a network to reflect changes made by other users. The default is 0 (which disables the refresh process), and you may specify any value between 0 and 3,600.

SET RELATION TO [<*key expression*>/<*expN*> INTO <*alias*>
[, <*key expression*>/<*expN*> INTO <*alias*>]...]

Establishes a relationship between the data base open in the selected work area and one or more data bases open in any other work areas, which are identified by their aliases. You can base any relation either on record numbers or on a common key expression. Once the files are linked, all commands that move the

record pointer in the selected work area also reposition the record pointers in each of the related files to the first matching record. SET RELATION TO, with no RELATION specified, cancels any relations that were set from the current work area.

If you specify a numeric expression in the SET RELATION command, dBASE IV moves the record pointer in the related file to the record with the record number equal to the result of evaluating the numeric expression. To link the files by record number, specify RECNO() as the numeric expression.

In order for you to link two files by a common *key expression,* the fields that make up the expression must be present in both files (although they need not have the same names), the related file must be indexed on this expression, and the index tag or file must be designated the master index. Once the files are linked, moving the record pointer in the first file causes dBASE IV to automatically position the related file to the first record with the specified value of the key expression, exactly as if you had carried out an index key search.

If dBASE IV fails to find a match in the related file, it positions the record pointer in this file to the end-of-file, and sets the EOF (end-of-file) function to .T. and FOUND to .F. (regardless of the status of the NEAR setting).

SET REPROCESS TO <*number*>

In a network environment, specifies how many times dBASE IV attempts to lock a file or record that is locked at another workstation before displaying an error message. If REPROCESS is 0, dBASE IV displays an informative message and retries indefinitely, but you can interrupt by pressing ESC if you do not want to wait until the record becomes available. When this setting is −1, dBASE IV retries indefinitely without displaying a message (you would generally do this only in a program, where you can provide your own). The default is 0, and you may specify any value between −1 and 32,000.

SET SAFETY ON/off

Determines whether dBASE IV displays a warning message and requests confirmation before executing any command (such as COPY, INDEX, or SORT)

that would overwrite an existing disk file, and before executing the ZAP command (which empties a file).

SET SCOREBOARD ON/off

Determines whether or not dBASE IV displays status indicators (such as "Del" and "Ins") and error messages (for example, when an invalid date is entered) on the top line of the screen when the STATUS setting is OFF. When the STATUS setting is ON, the indicators are displayed in the status bar, and error messages appear on line 24; when the STATUS setting is OFF, all the scoreboard information is displayed on line 0. If the STATUS and SCOREBOARD settings are both OFF, the error messages are not displayed, but dBASE IV still refuses to allow the cursor to advance beyond a field that contains invalid data until you correct the entry.

SET SEPARATOR TO <*character*>

Determines the character used to separate thousands in numeric fields and memory variables; the separator character is usually a comma (,) in the United States, and a period (.) in Europe. The character must be enclosed in quotation marks in the SET SEPARATOR command. SET SEPARATOR TO, with no character specified, restores the default separator character, the comma (,).

SET SKIP TO [<*alias*> [, <*alias*>]...]

Used in conjunction with SET RELATION, this setting enables you to access as a group all the records in a data base open in an unselected work area that match each record in the active data base (that is, that have the same contents in the key fields). The related files are identified by alias in the SET SKIP command, and must already be linked to the active data base with SET RELATION. The SKIP setting causes dBASE IV to move the record pointer

through the set of related records in each linked file before advancing to the next record in the active data base.

SET SPACE ON/off

Determines whether dBASE IV adds a space between the expressions displayed with a ? command. When this setting is OFF, dBASE IV displays the expressions with no intervening spaces.

SET SQL on/OFF

Invokes the SQL mode of operation, in which you type SQL commands for defining and updating data bases, mixed with dBASE IV commands and functions for which there are no direct counterparts in SQL.

SET STATUS on/OFF

Determines whether dBASE IV uses the last three lines on the screen for a status display. The *status bar* on line 22 displays the current disk drive, data base or view if one is open, the current record, command, or option, and information about the current environment—whether the current record is deleted or locked, and the status of the INS, NUM LOCK, and CAPS LOCK keys. Line 23, the *navigation line*, displays a brief description of some relevant command and cursor movement keys, and line 24, the *message line*, describes the highlighted command or option, or displays additional information about available options. A screen form file designed for use with the STATUS setting ON should not display data on lines 22 through 24. Regardless of the STATUS setting, the status display is always present in the layout editors, and it is never displayed in the Control Center.

---

* **SET STEP on/OFF**

SET TALK ON/off

Determines whether dBASE IV displays the results of the actions it takes in response to your commands, including the values of newly created memory variables, the results computed by SUM, COUNT, AVERAGE, and CALCULATE, the record number of the new current record after a SKIP, GOTO, or LOCATE command, and the status messages that monitor the progress of commands that process entire data bases (such as INDEX, DELETE, COPY, COUNT, and REPLACE).

SET TITLE ON/off

Determines whether dBASE IV prompts you for a title, or description, for each new file that it adds to the current catalog. When the TITLE setting is OFF, dBASE IV still adds files to an open catalog, but the TITLE field in the catalog data base remains blank.

---

* **SET TRAP on/OFF**

SET TYPEAHEAD TO *<expN>*

Specifies the number of keystrokes stored in the typeahead buffer. The default is 20, and you may specify any value between 0 (which disables the typeahead buffer) and 32,000.

SET UNIQUE on/OFF

Determines whether an index can contain duplicate key entries. All indexes constructed with this setting ON will include only one entry for any given key value. You can achieve the same result for one index by adding the UNIQUE keyword to an INDEX command typed at the dot prompt or by setting the **Display first duplicate key only** option to **Yes** when building an index from the data base design screen. An index constructed with the UNIQUE setting ON retains the unique attribute even after you turn UNIQUE OFF.

You can use a unique index to determine if the data base itself contains any duplicate key values (by comparing the number of records indexed, which dBASE IV displays after completing the index, to the total number of records in the file) or to prepare a list of all of the possible unique key values (by making a unique index the master index and then listing the relevant fields or copying them to another file).

SET VIEW TO <*query file name*>

Executes the instructions stored in a view query file, which may entail opening one or more data bases, linking them with SET RELATION and SET SKIP, selecting or building an index or sorting the data, and selecting the fields and records in the view. When a query is active, it appears that you are viewing a data base file that contains only the data described by the query, but in fact, the data in the view is derived from the component data bases.

---

* **SET WINDOW OF MEMO TO <*window name*>**

APPENDIX E

dBASE IV Functions

All dBASE IV functions are expressed as the name of the function followed by the input(s) to the function (also referred to as *arguments)* in parentheses. Even if the function requires no explicit input, you must type the parentheses to distinguish the function from a field or memory variable with the same name. A function is considered to have the same data type as the output it produces, and it may be used anywhere that dBASE IV permits an expression of that type. The listing for each function describes the type of input the function requires and the data type of the function's output.

The examples in this appendix consist of ? commands that you could type at the dot prompt to test the output of the functions, printed in **UPPERCASE BOLDFACE** type, followed by the data that dBASE IV would display in response, printed in normal type. Many of the examples assume that the National Widgets Customer File is open, and is positioned at the first record; several examples also use the Order File and/or Inventory File.

This appendix includes all the dBASE IV functions, but functions that are used only or primarily in dBASE IV programs are marked with an asterisk and listed with only a minimal explanation. You can find a description of all the functions in the dBASE IV *Language Reference* manual.

& <*character variable*>

Substitute the *value* of the named variable for the variable name. The macro can be used to provide variable input in contexts in which dBASE IV expects a field name or condition. It is recommended that you end the macro expression with a period (.).

Example:

```
STORE "FOR CITY = 'San Francisco'" TO MCONDITION
LIST ACCOUNT, COMPANY, CITY &MCONDITION.
Record#  ACCOUNT    COMPANY
      6  RAPIDTYPE  RapidType Secretarial Svc San Francisco
     13  JOHNSON    J. Thomas Johnson, CPA    San Francisco
     17  HRINSURANC H & R Insurance           San Francisco
```

ABS(<*expN*>)

Input: Numeric expression
Output: Number

Evaluates to the absolute value of the numeric expression. The absolute value of a negative number is the positive number with the same magnitude; the absolute value of a positive number is identical to the number itself.

* **ACCESS()**

Input: None
Output: Number

When a password-protected security system is in effect, evaluates to the access level assigned to the current user.

ACOS(<*expN*>)

Input: Numeric expression
Output: Number

Evaluates to the angle whose cosine equals the number specified as input. The input to the ACOS function must be a number or numeric expression that evaluates to a number between −1.0 and +1.0. The output is an angle expressed in radians.

*** ALIAS(<*work area*>)**

Input: Numeric expression (optional)
Output: Character string

Evaluates to the alias of the data base open in the specified work area.

ASC(<*expC*>)

Input: Character string expression
Output: Number

Evaluates to the decimal (base 10) ASCII code of the first character in the character string expression.

Examples:

```
? ASC("LEWIS")
        76
? ACCOUNT
LEWIS
? ASC(ACCOUNT)
        76
```

ASIN(<*expN*>)

Input: Numeric expression
Output: Number

Evaluates to the angle whose sine equals the number specified as input. The input to the ASIN function must be a number or numeric expression that evaluates to a number between −1.0 and +1.0. The output is an angle expressed in radians.

AT(<*expC1*>, <*expC2*>)

Input: Character string expression, character string expression
Output: Number

Evaluates to the starting position of *expC1* in *expC2,* or to 0 if the first string is not found anywhere within the second.

Example:

```
? COMPANY
Lewis and Associates
? AT("and", COMPANY)
         7
```

ATAN(<*expN*>)

Input: Numeric expression
Output: Number

Evaluates to the angle whose tangent equals the number specified as input. The output is an angle expressed in radians.

ATN2(<*expN1*>, <*expN2*>)

Input: Numeric expression, numeric expression
Output: Number

Evaluates to the angle whose sine equals the value of the first numeric expression specified as input, and whose cosine equals the value of the second. The output is an angle expressed in radians.

* **BAR()**

Input: None
Output: Number

Evaluates to a number that identifies the most recently selected bar from an active pop-up menu.

* **BOF([<*work area*>])**

Input: Numeric or character expression (optional)
Output: Logical value

Evaluates to a logical value that indicates whether the record pointer is positioned at the beginning-of-file.

* **CALL(<*expC*> [, <*exp1*>/<*var1*> [, <*exp2*>/<*var2*>]]...)**

Input: Character string expression, 1 to 7 character string expressions or memory variable names
Output: Expression

Evaluates to the value returned by a binary routine previously placed in memory with the LOAD command.

CDOW(<*expD*>)

Input: Date expression
Output: Character string

Evaluates to a character string containing the name of the day of the week that corresponds to the specified date.

Examples:

```
? LASTORDER
01/20/91
? CDOW(LASTORDER)
Sunday
? CDOW(LASTORDER+30)
Tuesday
```

CEILING(<*expN*>)

Input: Numeric expression
Output: Number

Evaluates to the smallest integer that is greater than or equal to the result of evaluating the numeric expression.

Examples:

```
? YTDORDERS
  494.81
? CEILING(YTDORDERS)
     495
? CEILING(-5.62)
    -5
```

* CERROR()

Input: None
Output: Number

Evaluates to the error number of the last compiler error.

* CHANGE()

Input: None
Output: Logical value

On a network, evaluates to a logical value that indicates whether the current record was changed by another user since it was read from disk.

CHR(<*expN*>)

Input: Numeric expression
Output: Character

Evaluates to a character string that consists of the single character specified by the decimal ASCII code represented by the numeric expression. You can use this function to express control characters (characters with ASCII codes below 32) and graphics characters.

Example:

```
? CHR(65)
A
```

CMONTH(<*expD*>)

Input: Date expression
Output: Character string

Evaluates to a character string containing the name of the month that corresponds to the specified date.

Example:

```
? LASTORDER
01/20/91
? CMONTH(LASTORDER)
January
```

* COL()

Input: None

Output: Number

Evaluates to the current cursor column position on the screen.

* **COMPLETED()**

Input: None
Output: Logical value

Evaluates to a logical value that indicates whether a transaction completed normally.

COS(<*expN*>)

Input: Numeric expression
Output: Number

Evaluates to the cosine of the angle represented by the number specified as input. The angle must be expressed in radians.

CTOD(<*expC*>)

Input: Character expression
Output: Date

Evaluates to a true date that matches the character string representation of the date supplied as input.

DATE()

Input: None
Output: Date

Evaluates to the system date as obtained from the operating system.

DAY(<*expD*>)

Input: Date expression
Output: Number

Evaluates to a number that represents the day of the month in the specified date.

Example:

```
? LASTORDER
01/20/91
? DAY(LASTORDER)
       20
```

* **DBF([<*work area*>])**

Input: Numeric or character expression (optional)
Output: Character string

Evaluates to the name of the data base open in the specified work area.

DELETED([<*work area*>])

Input: Character string (optional)
Output: Logical value

Evaluates to .T. if the current record is marked for deletion, or .F. if it is not. If you do not specify a <*work area*>, dBASE IV tests the record in the currently selected work area.

DIFFERENCE(<*expC1*>, <*expC2*>)

Input: Character expression, character expression
Output: Number

Evaluates to a number that represents the difference in Soundex codes between *expC1* and *expC2* (see the entry for the SOUNDEX function for an explanation of how Soundex codes are calculated). The DIFFERENCE function evaluates to 4 if the two Soundex codes are identical, or 0 if the two codes have no characters in common. You can use Soundex codes to retrieve records when you are unsure of the spelling of an entry or when the data was not entered consistently.

Example:

```
LIST ACCOUNT, COMPANY, CITY FOR DIFFERENCE("Berkly", CITY) = 4
Record# ACCOUNT    COMPANY                     CITY
      2 ABCPLUMB   ABC Plumbing                Berkeley
      9 GREENTHUMB Green Thumb Landscaping     Berkeley
     10 HOMEMOVIES Home Movies Video Rentals Berkeley
```

DISKSPACE()

Input: None
Output: Number

Evaluates to the number of bytes of free space that remain on the disk in the current drive. You can use this function to test whether you have enough space to sort or copy a data base. To determine the disk space remaining on a drive other than the current drive, you must reset the default drive with the SET DEFAULT command.

Example:

```
SET DEFAULT TO A:
? DISKSPACE()
          101584
SET DEFAULT TO C:
RUN COPY NWCUST.DB? A:
```

DMY(<*expD*>)

Input: Date expression

Output: Character string

Evaluates to a character string that represents the specified date, in *dd Month yy* or *dd Month yyyy* format (the year is displayed as four digits if the CENTURY setting is ON, or as two digits if it is OFF).

Example:

```
? LASTORDER
01/20/91
? DMY(LASTORDER)
20 January 91
SET CENTURY ON
? DMY(LASTORDER)
20 January 1991
```

DOW(<*expD*>)

Input: Date expression
Output: Number

Evaluates to a number that represents the day of the week of the specified date (Sunday is day 1).

Example:

```
? LASTORDER
01/20/91
? CDOW(LASTORDER)
         1
```

DTOC(<*expD*>)

Input: Date expression
Output: Character string

Evaluates to a character string representation of the date expression supplied as input. You can use this function to convert a date to a character string in order to concatenate it with another character string to display or print it.

Example:

```
? LASTORDER
01/20/91
? "Last order date: " + DTOC(LASTORDER)
Last order date: 01/20/91
```

DTOR(<*expN*>)

Input: Numeric expression
Output: Number

Evaluates to the angle, expressed in radians, equivalent to the number of degrees specified by the numeric expression.

DTOS(<*expD*>)

Input: Date expression
Output: Character string

Evaluates to a character string representation of the date expression supplied as input, in *yyyymmdd* format. You can use this function to convert a date to a character string in order to concatenate it with another character string (typically in an index key expression) while preserving chronological order.

Examples:

```
? LASTORDER
01/20/91
? DTOS(LASTORDER)
19910120
INDEX ON STATE + DTOS(LASTORDER) TAG STATEORDER
```

* **EOF([<*work area*>])**

Input: Numeric or character expression (optional)
Output: Logical value

Evaluates to a logical value that indicates whether the record pointer is positioned at the end-of-file.

* **ERROR()**

Input: None
Output: Number

Evaluates to the error number of the last execution error.

EXP(<*expN*>)

Input: Numeric expression
Output: Number

Evaluates to the result of raising *e* (the base for natural logarithms) to the power specified by the numeric expression.

* **FIELD(<*expN*> [, <*work area*>])**

Input: Numeric expression, numeric or character expression (optional)
Output: Character string

Evaluates to the name of the specified field.

* **FILE(<*expC*>)**

Input: Character expression
Output: Logical value

Evaluates to a logical value that indicates whether the specified file is present on disk.

FIXED(<*expN*>)

Input: Numeric expression
Output: Number

Evaluates to a fixed-point number equivalent to the floating-point number specified as input.

* **FKLABEL(<*expN*>)**

Input: Numeric expression
Output: Character string

Evaluates to the name of the specified programmable function key.

* **FKMAX()**

Input: None
Output: Number

Evaluates to the number of programmable function keys on the keyboard.

FLOAT<*expN*>

Input: Numeric expression
Output: Number

Evaluates to a floating-point number equivalent to the fixed-point number specified as input.

FLOCK([<*work area*>])

Input: Character string (optional)
Output: Logical value

Evaluates to .T. if it is possible to lock the file that is open in the currently selected work area, or .F. if the attempt fails because another user has already locked the file. This function simultaneously tests the status and attempts to lock the file. When a file is locked, other users can view, but not update the data. In a single-user system, FLOCK() always evaluates to .T. You can unlock a file with the UNLOCK command, by closing the file, or by exiting from dBASE IV.

FLOOR(<*expN*>)

Input: Numeric expression
Output: Number

Evaluates to the largest integer that is smaller than or equal to the numeric expression.

Examples:

```
? YTDORDERS
  494.81
? FLOOR(YTDORDERS)
     494
? FLOOR(-5.62)
      -6
```

* **FOUND([<*work area*>])**

Input: Numeric or character expression (optional)
Output: Logical value

Evaluates to a logical value that indicates whether an index key search, a SET RELATION command, or a LOCATE command succeeded in finding a record.

FV(<*expN1*>, <*expN2*>, <*expN3*>)

Input: Numeric expression, numeric expression, numeric expression
Output: Number

Evaluates to a number that represents the future value of an investment. The result of evaluating *expN1* represents the payment made each period, *expN2* represents the periodic interest rate, and *expN3* evaluates to the number of payment periods. (Note that if the period is one month, the interest rate must be the monthly rate, or the annual rate divided by 12.)

Example:

```
? FV(50.00, .12/12, 60)
    4083.48
```

* GETENV(<*expC*>)

Input: Character expression
Output: Character string

Evaluates to the specified operating system environment variable.

IIF(<*condition*>, <*exp1*>, <*exp2*>)

Input: Logical expression, expression, expression
Output: Same data type as expressions 1 and 2

Evaluates to *exp1* if the *condition* is .T., or to *exp2* if the *condition* is .F.. The two expressions may be of any data type, but they must be of the same data type. This function is useful for processing, displaying, or printing fields or text conditionally.

Example:

```
? YTDORDERS, TOTORDERS
    494.81    3482.48
? IIF(TOTORDERS <> 0, YTDORDERS/TOTORDERS, 0)
         0.14
? CREDITOK
```

```
.T.
? IIF(CREDITOK, "OK to grant credit", "Credit denied")
OK to grant credit
```

* INKEY([<*n*>])

Input: Number (optional)
Output: Number

Evaluates to a number that corresponds to the key pressed by the user.

INT(<*expN*>)

Input: Numeric expression
Output: Number

Evaluates to the integer portion of the number represented by *expN* (the result of dropping any digits beyond the decimal point). To round off a number to the nearest integer, use the ROUND function instead.

Example:

```
? INT(YTDORDERS)
      494
? INT(-5.62)
       -5
```

* ISALPHA(<*expC*>)

Input: Character expression
Output: Logical value

Evaluates to a logical value that indicates whether the first character of the specified expression is alphabetic (A through Z or a through z).

*** ISCOLOR()**

Input: None
Output: Logical value

Evaluates to a logical value that indicates whether a color display adapter is present.

*** ISLOWER(<*expC*>)**

Input: Character expression
Output: Logical value

Evaluates to a logical value that indicates whether the first character of the specified expression is a lowercase letter.

*** ISMARKED([<*work area*>])**

Input: Numeric or character expression
Output: Logical value

Evaluates to a logical value that indicates whether the current record is being updated in a transaction.

*** ISUPPER(<*expC*>)**

Input: Character expression
Output: Logical value

Evaluates to a logical value that indicates whether the first character of the specified expression is an uppercase letter.

*** KEY([<*MDX index file*>,] <*expN*> [, <*work area*>])**

Input: Character expression, numeric expression, numeric or character expression

Output: Character string

Evaluates to the index key expression for the specified tag.

* LASTKEY()

Input: None
Output: Number

Evaluates to a number that corresponds to the last key pressed by the user.

LEFT(<*expC*>, <*expN*>)

Input: Character string expression, numeric expression
Output: Character string

Evaluates to a substring (part of a string) of the character string represented by *expC*. The substring begins with the first (leftmost) character, and the length is specified by *expN*. If the requested length exceeds the length of the original character string, the substring consists of the full string.

Example:

```
? COMPANY
Lewis and Associates
? LEFT(COMPANY, 5)
Lewis
```

LEN(<*expC*>)

Input: Character string expression
Output: Number

Evaluates to the length of the character string that results from evaluating the character string expression. The length of a data base field is always the full field width, but you can use the TRIM function to eliminate trailing blanks.

Example:

```
LIST ACCOUNT, COMPANY FOR LEN(TRIM(COMPANY)) > 20
Record# ACCOUNT    COMPANY
      6 RAPIDTYPE  RapidType Secretarial Svc
      8 KELLY      Kelly and Sons Furniture
      9 GREENTHUMB Green Thumb Landscaping
     10 HOMEMOVIES Home Movies Video Rentals
     11 SHAPEUP    Shape Up Fitness Center
     12 FLOORPLAN  Floor Plan Carpet Center
     13 JOHNSON    J. Thomas Johnson, CPA
     16 WHITNEY    Financial Planning Svcs.
```

LIKE(*<expC1>, <expC2>)*

Input: Character expression, character expression
Output: Logical value

Evaluates to .T. if the result of evaluating *expC2* matches the pattern specified by *expC1*. The pattern can include the two DOS wildcards, a question mark (?) to represent any single character and an asterisk (*) to represent any group of characters.

Example:

```
LIST ACCOUNT, LASTORDER FOR LIKE("02/??/91", DTOC(LASTORDER))
Record# ACCOUNT    LASTORDER
      4 MTK        02/03/91
     16 WHITNEY    02/13/91
     18 DELTADESGN 02/23/91
```

* LINENO()

Input: None
Output: Number

Evaluates to the line number of the next program line to be executed.

*** LKSYS(<*expN*>)**

Input: Numeric expression
Output: Character string

On a network, evaluates to the date, time, or user who placed the last record or file lock.

LOCK([<*expN list*>] [, <*work area*>]) or RLOCK()

Input: Numeric expression list, character string (optional)
Output: Logical value

Evaluates to .T. if it is possible to lock the current record in the active data base, or .F. if another user has already locked the record. This function simultaneously tests the status and attempts to lock the record. When a record is locked, other users can view, but not update the fields. In a single-user system, LOCK() always evaluates to .T.. You can unlock a record with the UNLOCK command or by closing the data base or exiting from dBASE IV.

LOG(<*expN*>)

Input: Numeric expression
Output: Number

Evaluates to the natural (base *e*) logarithm of the number represented by the numeric expression.

LOG10(<*expN*>)

Input: Numeric expression
Output: Number

Evaluates to the common (base 10) logarithm of the number represented by the numeric expression.

LOOKUP(<*exp1*>, <*exp2*>, <*field name*>)

Input: Expression, expression, field name
Output: Expression

Looks up the result of evaluating *exp2* in the field specified as input, and yields as output the value of *exp1*. If *field name* includes a reference to an unselected data base, the lookup is performed in that work area. If *exp2* is a valid index key expression in the master index for the file in which you are performing the lookup, dBASE IV uses a fast index key search; otherwise, it searches the file sequentially. In either case, the record pointer in the file in which you performed the lookup remains where it is positioned by the search. You can use this function to validate an entry in one file by looking it up in another even when you do not have an index that would enable you to do a fast index key search.

Example:

```
USE NWORDER
? ACCOUNT
ABCPLUMB
USE NWCUST IN 2 ALIAS CUSTOMER
? LOOKUP(CUSTOMER->COMPANY, ACCOUNT, CUSTOMER->ACCOUNT)
ABC Plumbing
```

LOWER(<*expC*>)

Input: Character string expression
Output: Character string

Evaluates to the result of converting the character string expression to all lowercase. You can use this function to convert a character string entered in various mixtures of uppercase and lowercase to a consistent format for comparison to another variable or constant.

Example:

```
LOCATE FOR "kaypro" $ LOWER(EQUIPMENT)
Record =          2
? EQUIPMENT
Kaypro 4, Kaypro 10, Kaypro 286 PC, Epson FX-286 printer
```

LTRIM(<*expC*>)

Input: Character string expression
Output: Character string

Evaluates to the character string that results from removing all leading blanks from *expC*. This function is useful for removing leading blanks created when you convert a numeric expression to a character string with the STR function.

Example:

```
? "Year-to-date orders: $" + LTRIM(STR(YTDORDERS, 10, 2))
Year-to-date orders: $494.81
```

* **LUPDATE([<*work area*>])**

Input: Numeric or character expression
Output: Date

Evaluates to the date the specified data base was last updated.

MAX(<*exp*>, <*exp*>)

Input: Expression, Expression
Output: Number, date, or character string

Evaluates to the number, date, or character string represented by the greater of the two expressions specified as input. The two expressions may be character

strings, dates, or numbers, but they must be of the same data type. You can use this function to process, display, or print fields conditionally.

Example:

```
USE NWORDER
REPLACE ALL DISCOUNT WITH MAX(SUBTOTAL*.15, 5.00)
```

* MDX(<*expN1*>/[, <*work area*>])

Input: Numeric expression, numeric or character expression
Output: Character string

Evaluates to the name of the specified MDX index file.

MDY(<*expD*>)

Input: Date expression
Output: Character string

Evaluates to a character string that represents the specified date, in *Month dd, yy* or *Month dd, yyyy* format (the year is displayed as 4 digits if the CENTURY setting is ON, or as 2 digits if it is OFF).

Examples:

```
? LASTORDER
01/20/91
? MDY(LASTORDER)
January 20, 91
SET CENTURY ON
? MDY(LASTORDER)
January 20, 1991
```

* MEMLINES(<*memo field name*>)

Input: Character string expression
Output: Number

Evaluates to the number of lines in the specified memo field, based on the width established with the MEMOWIDTH setting.

MEMORY()

Input: None
Output: Number

Evaluates to the amount of available RAM, in kilobytes. You can use this function to determine whether you have enough free memory to run an external program from within dBASE IV, or to gauge the impact of RAM-resident utility programs loaded before you started up dBASE IV.

* **MENU()**

Input: None
Output: Character string

Evaluates to the name of the last active bar menu.

* **MESSAGE()**

Input: None
Output: Character string

Evaluates to the error message text that corresponds to the last execution error.

MIN(<*exp*>, <*exp*>)

Input: Expression, expression
Output: Number, date, or character string

Evaluates to the number, date, or character string represented by the smaller of the two expressions specified as input. The two expressions may be character

strings, dates, or numbers, but they must be of the same data type. You can use this function to process, display, or print fields conditionally.

Example:

```
USE NWORDER
REPLACE ALL DISCOUNT WITH MIN(SUBTOTAL * .15, 10.00)
```

* MLINE(<*memo field name*>, <*expN*>)

Input: Character string expression, numeric expression
Output: Character string

Evaluates to the specified line from the specified memo field.

MOD(<*expN1*>, <*expN2*>)

Input: Numeric expression, numeric expression
Output: Number

Evaluates to the remainder that results from dividing *expN1* by *expN2*. This function is useful for converting between different units of measure, for example, for converting inches to feet and inches, or days to years and days.

Example:

```
STORE DATE() - LASTORDER TO MTIME
     372
STORE INT(MTIME/365) TO MYEARS
       1
STORE MOD(MTIME, 365) TO MDAYS
       7
```

MONTH(<*expD*>)

Input: Date expression
Output: Number

Evaluates to a number that represents the month in the specified date.

Example:

```
? LASTORDER
01/20/91
? MONTH(LASTORDER)
        1
```

*** NDX(<*expN*> [, <*work area*>])**

Input: Numeric expression, numeric or character expression (optional)
Output: Character string

Evaluates to the name of the specified NDX index file.

*** NETWORK()**

Input: None
Output: Logical value

Evaluates to a logical value that indicates whether dBASE IV is running on a network.

*** ORDER([<*work area*>])**

Input: Numeric or character expression (optional)
Output: Character string

Evaluates to the name of the master index tag or NDX index for the specified data base.

*** OS()**

Input: None

Output: Character string

Evaluates to the name of the current operating system.

* PAD()

Input: None
Output: Character string

Evaluates to the name of the last highlighted bar menu pad.

PAYMENT(<*expN1*>, <*expN2*>, <*expN3*>)

Input: Numeric expression, numeric expression, numeric expression
Output: Number

Evaluates to the periodic payment that results from amortizing the loan amount specified by *expN1* at an interest rate specified by *expN2* for a number of periods specified by *expN3*. (Note that if the period is one month, the interest rate must be the monthly rate, or the annual rate divided by 12.)

Example:

```
? PAYMENT(5000.00, .12/12, 48)
         131.67
```

* PCOL()

Input: None
Output: Number

Evaluates to the current printhead column position.

PI()

Input: None
Output: Number

This function evaluates to the value of pi (the ratio of a circumference of a circle to its diameter).

* **POPUP()**

Input: None
Output: Character string

Evaluates to the name of the last active pop-up.

* **PRINTSTATUS()**

Input: None
Output: Logical value

Evaluates to a logical value that indicates whether the printer is turned on and ready to receive output.

* **PROGRAM()**

Input: None
Output: Character string

Evaluates to the name of the currently running procedure (or program).

* **PROMPT()**

Input: None
Output: Character string

Evaluates to the text displayed in the last highlighted bar menu pad or pop-up bar.

* PROW()

Input: None
Output: Number

Evaluates to the current printhead row position.

PV(<*expN1*>, <*expN2*>, <*expN3*>)

Input: Numeric expression, numeric expression, numeric expression
Output: Number

Evaluates to a number that represents the present value of an investment. The first numeric expression specified as input represents the payment made each period, *expN2* represents the periodic interest rate, and *expN3* represents the number of payment periods. (Note that if the period is one month, the interest rate must be the monthly rate, or the annual rate divided by 12.)

Example:

```
? PV(50.00, .12/12, 60)
    2247.75
```

* RAND([<*expN*>])

Input: Numeric expression (optional)
Output: Number

Evaluates to a random number between 0 and 1.

* READKEY()

Input: None
Output: Number

Evaluates to a number corresponding to the key the user pressed to exit the last READ.

RECCOUNT([<*work area*>])

Input: Numeric or character string expression (optional)
Output: Number

Evaluates to the number of records in the data base open in the specified work area, or, if you do not include a work area, in the currently selected work area.

RECNO([<*work area*>])

Input: Numeric or character string expression (optional)
Output: Number

Evaluates to the record number at the position of the record pointer in the data base open in the specified work area, or, if you do not include a work area, in the currently selected work area. If the data base is positioned past the end-of-file, RECNO() evaluates to 1 greater than the number of records in the file. This means that if the data base is empty, RECNO() has the value 1.

RECSIZE([<*work area*>])

Input: Numeric or character string expression (optional)
Output: Number

Evaluates to the record length of the data base in the currently selected work area. You can use this function together with the RECCOUNT() function to calculate the approximate size of a data base (not including the space occupied by the file header or memo fields).

REPLICATE(<*expC*>, <*expN*>)

Input: Character string expression, numeric expression
Output: Character string

Evaluates to a character string that consists of the character string specified as input, repeated a number of times equal to the value of the numeric expression.

Examples:

```
? REPLICATE("-*", 5)
-*-*-*-*-*
? REPLICATE(CHR(205), 5)
═════
```

RIGHT(<*expC*>, <*expN*>)

Input: Character string expression, numeric expression
Output: Character string

Evaluates to a substring (part of a string) of the character string represented by the expression providing the input. The length of the substring is specified by the numeric expression, and the substring is taken from the right side of the original string. If the requested length exceeds the length of the original character string, the substring consists of the full string.

Example:

```
? COMPANY
Lewis and Associates
? RIGHT(TRIM(COMPANY), 10)
Associates
```

RLOCK([<*expN list*>] [, <*work area*>]) or LOCK()

Input: Numeric expression list, numeric or character string (optional)
Output: Logical value

RLOCK() is identical to LOCK() and is provided for parity with the FLOCK() function.

* ROLLBACK()

Input: None
Output: Logical value

Evaluates to a logical value that indicates whether a ROLLBACK command succeeded in restoring the data bases to their status before a transaction began.

ROUND(<*expN1*>, <*expN2*>)

Input: Numeric expression, numeric expression
Output: Number

Evaluates to the result of rounding off *expN1* to the number of decimal places specified *expN2.* If *expN2* is a negative number, the specified number of digits to the *left* of the decimal point are rounded off.

Examples:

```
? YTDORDERS
    494.81
? ROUND(YTDORDERS, 1)
       494.80
? ROUND(YTDORDERS, 0)
       495
? ROUND(YTDORDERS, -2)
       500
```

* ROW()

Input: None
Output: Number

Evaluates to the current cursor row position on the screen.

RTOD(<*expN*>)

Input: Numeric expression
Output: Number

Evaluates to the angle, expressed in degrees, equivalent to the number of radians specified by the numeric expression.

RTRIM(<*expC*>)

Input: Character expression
Output: Character string

RTRIM is identical to TRIM and is provided for parity with the LTRIM function.

RUN(<*expC*>)

Input: Character expression
Output: Number

Evaluates to the result code returned by the operating system after executing the command or program specified as input.

SEEK(<*exp*> [, <*expC*>])

Input: Expression, character expression
Output: Logical value

Evaluates to .T. if an index key search (a SEEK command) for the first expression succeeds in finding a record in the current master index. The second input must evaluate to the alias of the data base in which you want to perform an index key search; if this input is omitted, dBASE IV executes the SEEK in the currently selected work area. In either case, the record pointer remains where it

is positioned by the SEEK command. You can use this function to validate an entry in one file by looking it up in another.

Example:

```
USE NWORDER
? ACCOUNT
ABCPLUMB
USE NWCUST IN 2 ORDER ACCOUNT ALIAS CUSTOMER
? SEEK(ACCOUNT, "CUSTOMER")
.T.
```

* SELECT()

Input: None
Output: Number

Evaluates to a number corresponding to the highest numbered available work area.

SET(<*expC*>)

Input: Character expression
Output: Character string

Evaluates to a character string that represents the status of the SET option specified as input (dBASE IV does not accept all of the settings as input to this function). You can use this function to quickly determine the status of one of the SET options, or to verify the status of an option that is not displayed by DISPLAY STATUS.

Examples:

```
? SET("BELL")
ON
? SET("DELIMITERS")
```

```
OFF
? SET("MEMOWIDTH")
        50
```

SIGN(<*expN*>)

Input: Numeric expression
Output: Number

Evaluates to 1 if the numeric expression represents a positive number, −1 if it is negative, or 0 if it is 0.

SIN(<*expN*>)

Input: Numeric expression
Output: Number

Evaluates to the sine of the angle represented by the number specified as input. The angle must be expressed in radians.

SOUNDEX(<*expC*>)

Input: Character string expression
Output: Character string

Evaluates to a four-character string that represents the way *expC* "sounds." The code consists of the first letter of the expression plus a number calculated by dropping vowels and other letters with unclear or varied pronunciation, and assigning the same numeric code to letters with similar pronunciation. You can use Soundex codes to retrieve records when you are unsure of the spelling of an entry or when the data was not entered consistently.

Example:

```
? SOUNDEX("Louis")
L200
USE NWCUST
LOCATE FOR SOUNDEX(COMPANY) = SOUNDEX("Louis")
Record =          3
? COMPANY
Lewis and Associates
```

SPACE(<*expN*>)

Input: Numeric expression
Output: Character string

Evaluates to a character string consisting of the number of blank spaces specified by *expN*. You can use this function to initialize a blank character memory variable or specify a blank string in a comparison without having to count spaces.

SQRT(<*expN*>)

Input: Numeric expression
Output: Number

Evaluates to the square root of the number represented by the numeric expression.

STR(<*expN1*> [, <*expN2*>] [, <*expN3*>])

Input: Numeric expression, numeric expression, numeric expression
Output: Character string

Evaluates to a character string representation of the number that results from evaluating *expN1*. The length of the string is specified by *expN2*, and the

number of decimal places by *expN3*. If you omit the length, dBASE IV assumes that it is 10, and if you omit the number of decimal places, dBASE IV assumes 0. You can use this function to convert a number to a character string in order to concatenate it with another character string to display or print it, or use it in an index key expression.

Example:

```
INDEX ON STATE + STR(YTDORDERS, 10, 2) TAG STATEYTD
```

* STUFF(<*expC1*>, <*expN1*>, <*expN2*>, <*expC2*>)

Input: Character string expression, numeric expression, numeric expression, character string expression
Output: Character string

Evaluates to the result of replacing the specified characters in one character string with another string.

SUBSTR(<*expC*>, <*expN1*> [, <*expN2*>])

Input: Character string expression, numeric expression, numeric expression
Output: Character string

Evaluates to the substring (part of a string) of the specified character string that begins at the position represented by *expN*. If a second numeric expression is included, it specifies the length of the substring. If the length is omitted, dBASE IV assumes that the substring begins at the designated starting position and includes all of the remaining characters in the original string.

Examples:

```
? COMPANY
Lewis and Associates
? SUBSTR(COMPANY, 7, 3)
and
```

* **TAG([<*MDX index file*>,] <*expN*> [, <*work area*>])**

Input: Character expression, numeric expression, numeric or character expression
Output: Character string

Evaluates to the name of the specified tag in the specified MDX file.

TAN(<*expN*>)

Input: Numeric expression
Output: Number

Evaluates to the tangent of the angle represented by the number specified as input. The angle must be expressed in radians.

TIME()

Input: None
Output: Character string

Evaluates to a character string representation of the current system time.

* **TRANSFORM(<*exp*>, <*expC*>)**

Input: Expression
Output: Character string

Evaluates to the result of formatting the specified expression with a picture function and/or template represented by <*expC*>.

TRIM(<*expC*>)

Input: Character string expression
Output: Character string

Evaluates to the character string that results from removing all trailing blanks from *expC*. This function is identical to RTRIM.

*** TYPE(<*expC*>)**

Input: Character expression
Output: Character

Evaluates to a character that represents the data type of the specified expression.

UPPER(<*expC*>)

Input: Character string expression
Output: Character string

Evaluates to the result of converting the specified character string expression to all uppercase. You can use this function to convert a character string entered in a mixture of uppercase and lowercase to a consistent format for comparison to another variable or constant.

Examples:

```
LOCATE FOR "KAYPRO" $ UPPER(EQUIPMENT)
Record =        2
? EQUIPMENT
Kaypro 4, Kaypro 10, Kaypro 286 PC, Epson FX-286 printer
```

*** USER()**

Input: None
Output: Character string

On a network, evaluates to the network login name of the current user.

VAL(<*expC*>)

Input: Character string expression
Output: Number

Evaluates to a true number that matches the character string representation of the number supplied as input.

* **VARREAD()**

Input: None
Output: Character string

Evaluates to the name of the variable collected by the current @ . . . GET.

* **VERSION()**

Input: None
Output: Character string

Evaluates to the name of the current dBASE IV version.

* **WINDOW()**

Input: None
Output: Character string

Evaluates to the name of the currently active screen window.

YEAR(<*date*>)

Input: Date expression
Output: Number

Evaluates to a 4-digit number that represents the year in the specified date.

Example:

```
? LASTORDER
01/20/91
? YEAR(LASTORDER)
1991
```

APPENDIX F

The CONFIG.DB File

The CONFIG.DB file is a configuration file that establishes defaults for the dBASE IV environment settings; you can use this file to customize the default environment to suit your personal preferences. CONFIG.DB is an ASCII text file that consists of one or more command lines, each of which controls one environment setting. If this file is present in the subdirectory from which you load dBASE IV, the dBASE IV program directory, or a subdirectory specified in a DOS PATH command, the settings it contains are automatically placed in effect when you start up the program. dBASE IV uses its internal default values for settings not explicitly mentioned in CONFIG.DB.

You can create or modify the CONFIG.DB file by using the menu-driven DBSETUP program supplied with dBASE IV or by making the changes directly with any word processor or editor that can read and write ASCII files, including the dBASE IV program editor. (These methods are described in Chapter 18.) If you change the configuration file from within dBASE IV, you must exit and reload the program to see the effects of your changes.

You can also change most of the environment settings—for the duration of the current work session—by using the **Settings** menu accessed through the Control Center **Tools** menu, by using the SET menu invoked from the dot prompt, by typing individual SET commands at the dot prompt, or by entering

SET commands into a dBASE IV program. The syntax for the CONFIG.DB entries that have SET equivalents is listed here without further explanation, except for several minor differences that are noted below the commands. See Appendix D for a more complete explanation of all of the SET commands.

The settings that you *cannot* change from within dBASE IV govern aspects of the environment that must be known when the program is first loaded, such as the amount of RAM to allocate for memory buffers (temporary storage areas). These options are marked with an asterisk (*) and are explained in this appendix. There are also some SET commands that have no CONFIG.DB equivalents. These include all of the commands that you can execute only if a data base is open, such as SET FIELDS and SET FILTER, as well as others that would not normally be set to a single value for an entire work session: SET MESSAGE, SET PRINTER, and SET TITLE.

The syntax used in CONFIG.DB is different from the syntax of the corresponding SET options. The general format for a CONFIG.DB entry is

<*option*> = <*value*>

instead of

SET <*option*> <*value*>

or

SET <*option*> TO <*value*>

As in the descriptions of the SET options in Appendix D, the default values of settings with a finite number of possible values (typically, ON or OFF) are printed here in uppercase.

ALTERNATE = <*file name*>

This command is equivalent to the two SET commands

SET ALTERNATE TO <*file name*>
SET ALTERNATE ON

AUTOSAVE = on/OFF

BELL = ON/off

BELL = <*frequency*>, <*duration*>

BLOCKSIZE = <*number*>

BORDER = SINGLE/double/panel/none/<*border characters*>

* **BUCKET = <*number*>**

This option specifies the amount of memory (expressed in kilobytes) reserved by dBASE IV for PICTURE, FUNCTION, and RANGE clauses in @... SAY... GET commands in programs and screen form files. The default is 2, and you may specify any number between 1 and 31. You should increase this number if you experience inexplicable problems while entering data through screen form files (or with @... SAY... GET commands in dBASE IV programs).

CARRY = on/OFF

CATALOG = on/OFF

The CATALOG setting applies only to the dot prompt mode of operation. Regardless of the setting established in CONFIG.DB, dBASE IV always opens a catalog when you work in the Control Center menu system.

CATALOG = <*file name*>

CENTURY = on/OFF

CLOCK = on/OFF

CLOCK = <*row*>, <*column*>

COLOR = ON/OFF

The default value is determined when you install dBASE IV, depending on the display adapter that is physically present in your computer.

COLOR = <*standard foreground/standard background*>, <*enhanced foreground/enhanced background*>, <*border*>

COLOR OF NORMAL = <*foreground/background*>

COLOR OF TITLE = <*foreground/background*>

COLOR OF MESSAGES = <*foreground/background*>

COLOR OF BOX = <*foreground/background*>

COLOR OF INFORMATION = <*foreground/background*>

COLOR OF HIGHLIGHT = <*foreground/background*>

COLOR OF FIELDS = <*foreground/background*>

* **COMMAND = <*command*>**

This setting specifies a command that dBASE IV runs automatically when you first start up the program. The default CONFIG.DB file provided with dBASE IV contains the line COMMAND = ASSIST, which causes dBASE IV to display the Control Center menu when you load the software. You can use a COMMAND command such as COMMAND = DO NW to run the main menu program of a dBASE IV application. If you name a different command file when you load dBASE IV by typing DBASE <*program name*>, dBASE IV runs this program instead of the one named in CONFIG.DB.

CONFIRM = on/OFF

CONSOLE = ON/off

* **CTMAXSYMS = <*number*>**

This setting determines the number of *symbols*—memory variable, field, program, and procedure names—permitted when you compile a dBASE IV program. You should increase this value if you see the error message "Exceeded maximum number of compile time symbols" while dBASE IV compiles a program. The default is 500, and you may specify any number between 1 and 5000.

CURRENCY = <*symbol*>

CURRENCY = LEFT/right

DATE = AMERICAN/ansi/british/french/german/italian/japan/usa/mdy/ dmy/ymd

DBTRAP = ON/off

DEBUG = on/OFF

DECIMALS = <*number*>

DEFAULT = <*disk drive*>

DELETED = on/OFF

DELIMITERS = on/OFF

DELIMITERS = <*delimiter character(s)*>

The delimiter characters must *not* be enclosed in quotes, as they are in the equivalent SET command.

DESIGN = ON/off

DEVELOPMENT = ON/off

DEVICE = SCREEN/printer/file <*file name*>

DIRECTORY = <*path name*>

DISPLAY = MONO/COLOR/EGA25/EGA43/MONO43

The default value is determined when you install dBASE IV, depending on the display adapter that is physically present in your computer.

* DO = *<number>*

This setting establishes the number of nested program calls (DO commands) permitted in dBASE IV programs. The default value is 20, and you may specify any number between 1 and 256.

ECHO = on/OFF

ENCRYPTION = ON/off

ESCAPE = ON/off

EXACT = on/OFF

dBASE IV turns this setting ON while it executes queries.

EXCLUSIVE = on/OFF

* **EXPSIZE = *<number>***

This setting specifies the size of the memory buffer dBASE IV uses to interpret expressions. You should increase this number if you see the error message "EVAL work area overflow." The default value is 100, and you may specify any number between 100 and 2000.

* **FASTCRT = ON/off**

This setting specifies whether dBASE IV should use a fast method for redrawing the display screen. On some older CGA color display systems, the fast redraw produces "snow," and setting FASTCRT to OFF solves the problem by substituting a slower screen redraw method for the default fast redraw. When you use the DBSETUP program to create or modify the CONFIG.DB file, you can select the **Optimize color display** option on the **Display** menu to perform a test that determines whether this slow redraw is necessary. The FASTCRT setting should always be OFF for EGA, VGA, and Hercules-compatible monochrome video adapters, which can handle the faster redraw method.

* **FILES = <*number*>**

This setting determines the maximum number of disk files that you may open simultaneously. When the FILES settings differ in the DOS configuration file (CONFIG.SYS) and the dBASE IV configuration file (CONFIG.DB), the smaller of the two governs the maximum number of open files. The default value is 99, and you may specify any number between 15 and 99.

FULLPATH = on/OFF

FUNCTION <*key name*> = <*character string*>

* **GETS = <*number*>**

This setting determines the number of GETs that you may collect between READ, CLEAR GETS, or CLEAR commands. The default is 128, and you may specify any number between 35 and 1023.

HEADING = ON/off

HELP = ON/off

HISTORY = ON/off

HISTORY = <*number*>

HOURS = 12/24

The default is 12.

* **INDEXBYTES = <*number*>**

This setting determines the amount of memory, expressed in kilobytes, allocated for the index file memory buffer. The number of index file blocks (units of storage in the index file) that dBASE IV can read into memory at once is determined both by the INDEXBYTES setting and the BLOCKSIZE setting,

which specifies the size of a block. When your index key expressions are long and complex, you can improve performance by increasing the INDEXBYTES setting. The default value is 2, and you may specify any number between 2 and 128.

INSTRUCT = ON/off

INTENSITY = ON/off

LOCK = ON/off

MARGIN = *<number>*

MEMOWIDTH = *<number>*

MENUS = ON/off

* **MVBLKSIZE**

This setting determines the number of memory variables in a block (you can use the MVMAXBLKS setting to establish the number of blocks permitted). The default is 50, and you may specify any number between 25 and 100.

* **MVMAXBLKS**

This setting determines the number of blocks of memory allocated for storing memory variables (you can use the MVBLKSIZE setting to establish the size of one block). The default is 10, and you may specify any number between 1 and 150.

NEAR = on/OFF

ODOMETER = *<number>*

PATH = *<path name list>*

PAUSE = on/OFF

* **PDRIVER = *<printer driver name>***

This setting identifies the printer driver that dBASE IV uses as the default for printed output if you do not select another driver for an individual print job.

POINT = <*decimal point character*>

PRECISION = <*number*>

PRINTER = on/OFF

PRINTER = PRN/lpt1/lpt2/lpt3/com1/com2

* **PRINTER <*number*> = <*driver name*> NAME <*printer name*> DEVICE <*device name*>**

This setting identifies a printer driver to make it available as an output device. You may specify up to four printer drivers in addition to the "generic" driver, which is always available. Printer installation is described in Chapter 18.

* **PRINTER <*number*> FONT <*number*> = <*starting codes*>, <*ending codes*> NAME <*font name*>**

This setting specifies the codes required to turn a special font or print mode on and off for one of the printers identified in a PRINTER command. You may specify up to five fonts for each printer, using notation described in Chapter 18.

* **PROMPT = <*character string*>**

This option changes the dBASE IV command prompt from the standard dot (.) to the specified character string.

REFRESH = <*number*>

REPROCESS = <*number*>

* **RESETCRT = ON/off**

This setting determines whether, after running an external program, dBASE IV automatically resets the display mode to the mode that was previously in effect.

* **RTBLKSIZE**

This setting determines the size of the memory blocks used for storing the names of memory variables, fields, and procedures when a program is running (the RTMAXBLKS setting establishes the number of blocks permitted). The default is 50, and you may specify any number between 25 and 100.

* **RTMAXBLKS**

This setting determines the number of blocks of memory allocated for storing memory variable, field, and procedure names when a program is running (the RTBLKSIZE setting establishes the size of one block). The default is 10, and you may specify any number between 1 and 150.

SAFETY = ON/off

SCOREBOARD = ON/off

SEPARATOR = <*separator character*>

SPACE = ON/off

SQL = on/OFF

* **SQLDATABASE = <*file name*>**

This setting identifies an SQL data base that dBASE IV opens automatically when you start up the program in SQL mode by adding the SQL = ON command to CONFIG.DB.

* **SQLHOME = <*path name*>**

This setting identifies the drive and subdirectory that store the SQL system files.

STATUS = on/OFF

STEP = on/OFF

TABS = <*tab settings list*>

TALK = ON/off

* **TEDIT = <*file name*>**

This option specifies an external text editor or word processing program that will substitute for the standard dBASE IV program editor. You must enter the file name exactly as you would type it at the MS-DOS prompt to invoke the editor (it must not include an extension).

TRAP = on/OFF

TYPEAHEAD = <*number*>

UNIQUE = on/OFF

VIEW = <*file name*>

* **WP = <*file name*>**

This option specifies an external text editor or word processing program that will substitute for the standard dBASE IV memo field editor. You must enter the file name exactly as you would type it at the MS-DOS prompt to invoke the editor (it must not include an extension).

APPENDIX G

Standard File Extensions

Extension	Type of File
$$$	Temporary output file that remains when dBASE IV cannot complete an operation that creates a file
APP	Application definition created by the applications generator
BAK	Backup copy of a text file modified using the dBASE IV text editor
BAR	Horizontal bar menu definition created by the applications generator
BCH	Batch process definition created by the applications generator
BIN	Binary file (assembly language program)
CAT	Catalog data base file
CHT	ChartMaster file
COD	Template language source program file

Extension	Type of File
CPT	Encrypted copy of a DBT (memo text) file created by the PROTECT command
CRP	Encrypted copy of a DBF (data base) file created by the PROTECT command
CVT	Backup copy of a DBF (data base) file modified by the CONVERT command to support multiuser record lock detection
DB2	dBASE II data base file exported by dBASE IV or renamed from the standard DBF extension in order to import the data
DBF	Data base file
DBK	Backup copy of a DBF file (data base file) that dBASE IV creates when you modify the structure
DBO	Compiled program file
DBT	Data base text (memo text) file
DEF	Template language selector definition file
DIF	Data Interchange Format file (used by VisiCalc for data exchange)
DOC	Application documentation text file created by the applications generator
FIL	Files list definition created by the applications generator
FMO	Compiled screen form (FMT) file
FMT	Format file (screen form file) generated by the screen layout editor based on specifications in the screen form (SCR) file
FR3	dBASE III report form file, renamed after conversion to a dBASE IV report form
FRG	Program generated by the report layout editor based on specifications in the report form (FRM) file
FRM	Report form file created by the report layout editor
FRO	Compiled report program (FRG) file

Extension	Type of File
FW2	Framework II data base frame file
GEN	Compiled template language program file used by the dBASE IV program generators
KEY	Macro library file
LB3	dBASE III label form file, renamed after conversion to a dBASE IV label form
LBG	Program generated by the label layout editor based on specifications in the label form (LBL) file
LBL	Label form file created by the label layout editor
LBO	Compiled label program (LBG) file
LOG	Transaction log file created by the BEGIN TRANSACTION ... END TRANSACTION program structure
MDX	Multiple index file
MEM	Memory variable file
NDX	Stand-alone index file
NPI	Report, label, or screen form file required when you use the template language program generator outside dBASE IV
POP	Pop-up menu definition created by the applications generator
PR2	Printer driver file
PR3	PostScript printer driver file
PRF	Print settings form file
PRG	Program or procedure file
PRS	SQL program or procedure file
PRT	Report, label, or LIST output file that includes printer codes
QBE	View query file created using Query-by-Example
QBO	Compiled view query (QBE) file
QRY	dBASE III PLUS query file (which stores a filter condition)

Extension	Type of File
RPD	RapidFile data base
SC3	dBASE III PLUS screen form file, renamed after conversion to a dBASE IV screen form file
SCR	Screen form file created by screen layout editor
STR	Structure list definition created by the applications generator
T44	Temporary output file that remains when dBASE IV cannot complete a sort or an indexing operation
TBK	Backup copy of a memo text file created when you modify the structure of a data base file
TXT	ASCII text file that contains only standard printable characters, created by commands such as REPORT, LABEL, LIST, and SET ALTERNATE or by copying data to SDF or delimited format (or by an external program)
UPD	Update query file created using Query-by-Example
UPO	Compiled update query (UPD) file
VAL	Values list definition created by the applications generator
VUE	dBASE III PLUS view file (which stores the dBASE III PLUS equivalent of a view query definition)
W44	Temporary output file that remains when dBASE IV cannot complete a sort or an indexing operation
WIN	Window definition file
WK1	Lotus 1-2-3 version 2 worksheet file
WKS	Lotus 1-2-3 version 1A worksheet file

INDEX

D

E

G

H

N

O

P

S

T

U

V

W

Y

Z